managing
human
resources

LEONARD R. SAYLES

Professor of Business Administration
Graduate School of Business
Columbia University

GEORGE STRAUSS

Professor, School of Business Administration and
Associate Director, Institute of Industrial Relations
University of California, Berkeley

PRENTICE-HALL, INC.   *Englewood Cliffs, New Jersey 07632*

managing human resources

SECOND EDITION

Library of Congress Cataloging in Publication Data

SAYLES, LEONARD R
    Managing human resources.

    Includes bibliographical references and indexes.
    1. Personnel management. I. Strauss, George,
joint author. II. Title.
HF5549.S183 1981   658.3   80–16838
ISBN 0–13–550418–X

Managing Human Resources, second edition
Leonard R. Sayles and George Strauss

10 9 8 7 6 5 4 3 2 1

This is a Special Projects book,
edited, designed, and supervised by
Maurine Lewis, director
Ray Keating, manufacturing buyer
Don Martinetti, cover designer

Prentice-Hall International, Inc., *London*
Prentice-Hall of Australia Pty. Limited, *Sydney*
Prentice-Hall of Canada, Ltd., *Toronto*
Prentice-Hall of India Private Limited, *New Delhi*
Prentice-Hall of Japan, Inc., *Tokyo*
Prentice-Hall of Southeast Asia Pte. Ltd., *Singapore*
Whitehall Books Limited, *Wellington, New Zealand*

for our children

Emilie
Emily
Liz
Robert

preface

There is no more exciting, challenging field than that dealing with human resources, and the field is becoming more extensive and more complex. Hiring and promoting women and minority group members, conforming to protective and legally required health and safety standards, manpower planning in a highly uncertain economy, choosing among a broadening range of employee benefit programs—to name but a few of the more dynamic areas within the personnel field—all impose challenging responsibilities upon the manager, the personnel practitioner, and those seeking a career in this field.

The human resource function is like a lightning rod, attracting tensions and pressures from the community, the controls of government, and the anxieties and evergrowing demands of the workforce for equity and expression. The president of a billion-dollar, multinational corporation once told us that 90 percent of his time was spent on personnel matters. His may be an exceptional situation, yet few chief executive officers do not spend some significant amount of their time on personnel-related matters.

For managers or students of management, *Managing Human Resources* is a practical book that avoids excessive concentration on technical formulas and codified techniques. Instead, it emphasizes actual organizational problems that occur in designing and implementing constructive personnel programs. It shows interrelationships among traditional topics such as compensation and training and selection. We stress the behavior required of the personnel specialist who seeks to gain acceptance of his or her professional expertise among managers already coping with more job requirements than they can meet. Although knowledge of traditional personnel techniques like testing and job evaluation is still essential, we place more emphasis on systems and coordination—how hiring impacts training, career paths, seniority, and even benefit plan administration, for example.

Since it is no longer possible to consider the personnel function in a vacuum, we stress the importance of the social, political, legal, and economic environments. Every manager must be more sophisticated in interpreting laws and government agency regulations, and this renewed legal emphasis must be applied in a systems context, with understanding of how people react, how organizations function, and how policies are translated into practice or dissipated by inept administration.

The same systems emphasis can be seen in our treatment of organization development and job design. Rather than emphasize techniques and definitions, we provide many real life examples to show how individual problems must be dealt with in a larger organizational context.

Our discussion deals with a variety of settings: large organizations and small; factories, hospitals, universities, manufacturing plants, banks, retail chains; small, family businesses. Each type of organization has unique problems.

Most important, we have tried to avoid listing requirements for "good" this or that, patronizing the reader with statements about the ideal, rational system for solving people problems. We hope you will come to share with us the recognition that neither excellent technique nor good intentions alone successfully solve complex, resistant employment problems. Skillful human resource management involves a challenging admixture of technical knowledge, behavioral sophistication, and sound judgment. Through a wide variety of examples, of quotations from actual people—workers and managers at every level, of both sexes and many races—we hope to communicate the feel for the problem and the way solutions should be approached.

A decade ago the personnel field was declining in status. Many felt that the main problems in the field were solved. People-sensitive managers had made great strides in the 1950s and '60s, and it appeared that human—in contrast to marketing or financial or technological—problems would require less management attention. Many organizations concluded that too much time and money had been spent "making people happy," with too little productive return.

The last few years have taught us the naiveté of such assumptions. As a consequence, recognition and organizational status of the personnel field have been rising. To be sure, there is still a vast disparity in nomenclature. There are departments of manpower planning, organizational and personnel development, employee relations, and human resource management. But whatever the formal title, almost all organizations recognize the field's critical importance, and every manager must have reasonable familiarity with its major concepts.

Thus, we have tried to write a textbook for present and future managers and personnel specialists, a book that will match up to the profound needs of this demanding, changing, crucial management field.

LEONARD SAYLES
GEORGE STRAUSS

contents

ix

part 2   personnel skills

part 3   employee development
and protection

part 4   management and organization development

21 *quality of work life*

part 7   conclusion

22 *personnel challenges and the future*

Leonard R. Sayles

LEONARD SAYLES and GEORGE STRAUSS have been major contributors to the behavioral science, management, and industrial relations fields for almost thirty years. Their texts, scholarly monographs, and articles are widely used throughout the world. Many are classics in their respective subjects, frequently cited and reprinted.

The genesis of their work and this text was a relatively new doctoral program at M.I.T. shortly after World War II. Both men had been attracted by scholars such as Douglas McGregor, Kurt Lewin, and Charles Myers, who were building an interdisciplinary program in industrial relations and the social sciences. By chance, Strauss's and Sayles's dissertations were on related topics, and they created their first prize-winning book, *The Local Union* (Harper & Row, 1953).

That book and their succeeding publications were stimulated by another coincidence. Both got their first postdoctoral jobs at Cornell, where they worked with William Foote Whyte. Whyte encouraged and strengthened their research capabilities; and shortly, Sayles had published *Behavior of Industrial Work Groups;* Strauss finished *Unions in the Building Trades.* Both contributed to Whyte's *Money and Motivation.*

After leaving Cornell (Strauss to Buffalo, then to Berkeley; Sayles to Michigan, then to Columbia) both taught personnel. At that time, many texts described practices or formal procedures, but had little discussion of underlying organizational forces or the burgeoning behavioral science research. To aid their own teaching, Strauss and Sayles began writing major texts for the personnel/human resources field in 1960.

In recent years, Strauss has published benchmark review articles that summarize critically and creatively our knowledge about such diverse subjects as organization development, MBO, job satisfaction, worker participation and union-management cooperation, and supervisory styles. He was co-founder of the Organizational Behavior Teaching Society and has served on the executive board of the Industrial Relations Research Association, as chairman of the city of Berkeley's Personnel Board, and as Associate Dean of the School of Business, University of California at Berkeley. He is currently Associate Director of their Institute of Industrial Relations and co-chairperson of the board of editors of the journal *Industrial Relations.*

George Strauss

Sayles is perhaps best known for his book-length studies of managerial behavior in complex organizations: *Managing Large Systems* (with M. Chandler); *Managerial Behavior, The Measure of Management* (with E. Chapple); and *Leadership: What Effective Managers Really Do and How They Do It.* He has also served on the executive board of the IRRA, as a director of Columbia's Graduate School of Business MBA program, and as a corporate director. He has been elected to the National Academy of Public Administration and frequently has served as a consultant on human resource problems for companies and for government.

Currently, Strauss is a professor at Berkeley; Sayles, at Columbia. Their cross-country collaboration is carried out by mail and telephone, through countless revisions. They criticize each other's drafts and do almost all their own research and writing. They have also co-authored two other Prentice-Hall texts: *Personnel: the Human Problems of Management* and *Human Behavior in Organizations.*

part 1

introduction: the personnel function

personnel management: past, present, and future

Ninety percent of the Americans living around 1800 worked in agriculture. More recently, manufacturing dominated the economy. But just 35 years ago, more than one-quarter of the male labor force was also still self-employed—not only as farmers, but as shopkeepers, repairmen, lawyers. Today less than 10 percent are self-employed, most work in organizations, and 64 out of every 100 employees are engaged in service activities, not manufacturing: education, insurance, social welfare, and myriad professional and technical functions.

Automated factories, in which products are untouched by human hands, were commonly forecast for the 1990s; but as this time approaches without the forecast being realized, human hands still proliferate. There is continued demand for office and factory workers, and especially for more professionals—chemists, systems engineers, account managers, and technical personnel. Employees continue to be a critical resource. Committed, satisfied employees work much more effectively than do those who are bored, dissatisfied, or actively antagonistic.

Thus, since most employees work in organizations, at jobs where typically there is no easy measure of personal output (as there was on the farm or in the early factories), effective methods of personnel management are indispensable. In what is increasingly called our post-industrial society, employees are more sensitive to the

quality of work and supervision, and management often has a heavy investment in their technical training.

Although most managers recognize the importance of the human dimension, they differ greatly in how they translate that recognition into action. A great deal of what is thought and practiced today—conceptions about people and the role of personnel—has been inherited from previous generations of managers. To understand the personnel field today, we need to know something about its antecedents.

The autocratic manager

Early managers felt little need for personnel administration. Workers were considered little more than machines; actually, they were considered less worthy of attention, because machines were more expensive to replace. Authority—power over other people—was the key managerial element, unencumbered by concerns about employee motivation or satisfaction. At their crudest, managers forced people to work by threatening to fire them if they didn't. They assumed, of course, people worked only to earn money and that people will work only if driven to it by fear of losing their jobs.

Autocratic managers assumed that since no one likes work, people will try to work as little as possible. To prevent them from doing so, there must be close supervision. Management must tell every worker exactly what to do and how to do it, giving the worker the narrowest possible discretion. Rules were often promulgated just "to show who's boss." Individuals were kept busy "to keep them out of trouble."

This thinking was inherent in some of the less sophisticated versions of scientific management: people are hired to work rather than to think, and the smallest possible amount of human ability should be used on the job. This has been called the *commodity* or *contractual theory of labor,* in that it holds that labor can be bought and sold as if it were material supplies—and can be treated in the same way. (For most jobs then the proverbial "strong back" substituted for the agile mind.)

Autocratic managers felt sure that employees were expendable and interchangeable. This approach paid off fairly well in the early days of the industrial revolution, when workers and their families were so close to starvation that their material needs for food, clothing, and shelter were paramount. Nevertheless, this managerial attitude sowed the seeds of its own destruction by producing a frustrated and aggressive work force that eventually sought protection and revenge through unionization. Autocratic managers were also doomed by technological changes that required better trained and more adaptive employees who were motivated more by opportunity than by fear.

The paternalistic manager

In many organizations, the stern, punishing manager was later replaced by a more benign authority figure who believed that organizations were just like families. The boss was the good father, and employees were dependent children who had to be taught obedience. The "good" children received special "parental" rewards, such as company housing, gifts at Christmas, a retirement fund, special allowances to cover illness or other family emergencies; the "bad" children were punished, often simply by discharge.

The impetus for this paternalistic approach came not only from a legitimate sense of employers' responsibility for the welfare of their workers, but also from stirrings of unionism after World War I. Under the banner of the "new industrial relations," management became interested in a wide variety of projects, from cafeterias and recreation programs for employees to cooking classes for their wives. Some of these programs were designed to change the employees' personal lives as well as their on-the-job performance. The sociology department program of the Ford Motor Company of an earlier day went further than most programs. Headed by a Protestant minister, this department was manned by thirty investigators.

In what amounted to a brief reign of benevolent paternalism, these gentlemen and their house-to-house canvassers imposed . . . a set of rules which blended good sense with Ford whims and Puritan virtues.

At worst . . . its agents became, to some extent, collectors of tales and suspicions. . . . Hearsay as well as fact found its way into a card catalogue where a record was kept of every worker's deviations. . . . Frittering away one's evenings "unwisely," taking in male boarders, sending funds to the "old country"—these things came to be regarded as earmarks of "unwholesome living." The use of liquor was forbidden . . . as was marital discord that resulted in a separation or divorce action.[1]

Although Ford's program was short-lived, similar patterns of paternalism were developed in other companies. There is little evidence that any of them were particularly successful in eliciting employees' gratitude, in motivating workers to do a better job, or even in staving off the development of unions. In fact, some of the companies with the best-known histories of paternalism later became scenes of bitter labor-management strife.

Paternalism resulted in resentment, rather than gratitude; employees were forced to play the role of dependent (and docile) children who had little or no control over what they received. Further, benefits that are given can be taken away. Troublemakers were summarily dismissed and those unwilling to cater to the boss were deprived of many benefits awarded to favorites. Even where benefits were distributed equitably, their value tended to wear thin over time, as employees took them for granted and felt appreciative only when they were increased.

Although paternalism has become less popular in industrialized countries like the United States, where workers want their benefits guaranteed by contract and the strength of their unions, it still holds sway in more agrarian cultures. For example, the uncertainties of life in Latin America often induce employees to welcome the protection of a powerful *patron*. They give their loyalty and support to their boss in exchange for his personal protection against arbitrary discharge, arrest, or other forms of hardship in the plant and the community. Paternalism flourishes in societies where individuals feel impotent in the face of powerful external forces.

---

[1] Keith Seward, *The Legend of Henry Ford* (New York: Holt, 1948), p. 59.

Japan probably provides the best example of paternalism still flourishing in a modern, highly industrialized society. The Japanese company often provides lifetime employment guarantees with benefits keyed to worker loyalty. Employees are likely to give up vacation time with enthusiasm and even request additional work assignments when the organization appears to need such contributions. In turn, long-service employees receive a wide range of extra payments and special privileges. For many, the company is almost as meaningful as the family, with neither employees nor management embarrassed by this close, paternalistic relationship.

The bureaucratic manager

In the early decades of the twentieth century, businesspeople came under the influence of engineers who sought to substitute rational, "scientific" management for the highly personal, idiosyncratic style of the owner-manager.[2]

Improving worker performance

Early industrial engineers maintained a rather simplistic, almost mechanical view of employees. They reasoned that employees were analogous to machines, whose output depends on the amount of power input and the frictional drag.

$$\text{Employee performance} = \frac{\text{Energy expended}}{\text{Friction}}$$

Engineers like Frederick Taylor saw employee initiative being stifled by traditional wage systems; they believed that the way to motivate workers was to pay them according to the amount they produced, rather than on the basis of hours worked. Thus began an impressive elaboration of so-called incentive or piecework systems. Complications arising from their administration made work for the Personnel record keepers, and the disputes they engendered created work for a newer generation of Personnel grievance specialists, but that's getting ahead of our story. This simple-minded view of employee motivation may be illustrated by the earlier phases of the now famous Western Electric Studies, or the Hawthorne Research, as it is sometimes called.[3] In some of these experiments, employees were provided with additional food during rest periods at work, almost as if these calories would stoke up the internal furnaces and cause employees to produce more effectively. Thus money and calories were used to increase the energy workers would expend.

Most of the effort to improve employee performance in this period (and much to this day) was devoted to reducing the frictional or "drag" elements of the job and work environment. Taylor and others were concerned with designing tools, work methods, and materials that would be more accommodating to the typical employee's physique and perceptual apparatus. This concern

[2] Among the best-known students of this movement was the engineer Frederick Taylor and the sociologist Max Weber. Others include management specialists Gulick, Urwick, and Fayol.

[3] Fritz Roethlisberger and William Dickson, *Management and the Worker* (Cambridge, Mass.: Harvard University Press, 1939).

with methods was one precursor of Personnel's concern today with training (see chap. 10).

(see chap. 10).

Better selection

While engineers were endeavoring to make work easier for typical or average employees, psychologists were helping management discover the not so typical employee. After all, management reasoned, if the average employee can produce 100 units an hour, an employee with better than average mental and physical abilities should produce 130 units, because the work will be easier for him. As a result of military experience classifying recruits during World War I, psychologists were brought into industry to help pick out the most able workers. They developed testing techniques for assessing individual differences, and Personnel began concentrating on selection methods.

The efforts of engineers and psychologists were linked together. Jobs were carefully described, and workers were picked because their specific abilities matched these descriptions. It was expected that the selection and matching process would conserve energy by providing well-squared pegs for well-squared holes, with additional energy to be produced by incentive plans.

Keeping records and codifying rules

Some of the earliest efforts at substituting rational procedures for intuition and family traditions simply involved better record keeping, for which purpose many personnel departments were first established. Personnel records included information such as the date the employee was hired, educational background, succession of jobs, and disciplinary penalties received. They provided a record of time and production for payrolls. These were relatively routine clerical tasks that relieved other members of the organization for more productive work. These Personnel functions are still important in view of the growing emphasis on pension and insurance programs, seniority benefits, and a wide variety of in-company social welfare.

From documenting the operations of the business, managers turned to explicit recording of company policies and procedures. Elements that we may now take for granted—such as equal pay for equal work, additional pay for promotion to a more difficult assignment, nondiscriminatory hiring—could be embodied in company policy statements that would minimize *ad hoc* or discriminatory decision making. For example, without written policies, a manager who needs Brown's skills may give her a raise when she threatens to quit; at the same time, the manager may give Jones additional work without a raise because he knows that Jones needs to work within walking distance of his home.

The defensive manager

The influence of Personnel expanded during the 1930s and 1940s. With their title changed to "industrial relations," many personnel departments began to take charge of hiring, firing, wage determination, handling union grievances, and determining who should be transferred or promoted. The personnel department suddenly gained so much power partly because of management's widespread recognition of the importance of the human element, but chiefly because of the threat of unionism. Unions were on the offensive throughout this period. They charged management with setting substandard wages, with encouraging foremen to act as petty tyrants, and with denying employees their human dignity. Faced with such charges, many companies felt the best way to keep unions out was to eliminate the grievances that made workers turn to them. Because management believed that inept supervisors were largely responsible for what observers conceded were still haphazard personnel policies, many companies gave the personnel department broad powers to establish and to police uniform payment, promotion, and seniority procedures.

Although unions were organized in many companies despite Personnel's efforts, they increased the department's status. Personnel now had the responsibility for negotiating the labor contract and handling grievances. Moreover, because unions constantly seek inconsistencies in management policies and try to establish precedents in one department that can be used elsewhere, the personnel department was given greater power throughout the organization.

In some ways, this period of defensive personnel work is being repeated today with the increased governmental pressure, particularly through fair employment legislation, and vigorous agitation from organized women, blacks, Chicanos, and other groups who feel subject to discriminatory practices. They demand that management avoid discrimination in selecting and promoting minority group members and even take affirmative action to make up for past misconduct. This development returns personnel record keeping to center stage, but with more sophisticated records and statistics. Extensive records are necessary to demonstrate nondiscrimination in recruitment, selection, job assignment, advancement, and layoff. Are male employees, for example, promoted more rapidly than comparably skilled and motivated women?

Government also contributed to the personnel field by earlier legislation. Since the early 1900s, a growing stream of protective labor laws, both state and federal, have provided social security and regulated wages, hours, and safety and hygienic conditions in the work environment.

In addition to proving management's case or finding ways to bolster its response to these governmental pressures, Personnel was also called upon to provide training—to teach supervisors to identify unsafe work practices or to handle grievances stemming from union demands for equitable workloads, pay scales, and disciplinary policies.

The professional manager

In time, the emphasis on specialization that Taylor and others helped introduce at the worker level began to permeate management itself. After all, management is a highly complex task, and few people can be expected to master all its facets. Organization charts blossomed, with finance, production, marketing, engineering, public relations, and—of course—personnel and industrial relations specialists. Each of these specializations had its own department staffs with university-trained professionals. Not unlike the "functional foreman" Taylor once prescribed (one for each key element in production), each speciali-

7

zation developed its own set of principles, techniques, and procedures by which it sought to influence the decisions of line management.

With the stimulus of research findings from graduate schools of administration, industrial sociologists, and social psychologists, specialists in industrial relations challenged the simple tenets of scientific management. Worker performance came to mean something more than getting the right person on a well-designed job and paying that person an equitable wage. Emphasis shifted from individual workers to the impact of the group in shaping attitudes, determining productivity, and restricting change. The interaction of personality differences and supervisory styles was explored.

Training programs were designed to communicate more effective methods of supervision that embodied what was known about the impact of leadership methods on employee aspirations. Each company's specialists compared its programs with what professional colleagues in other companies and the universities were doing and saying.[4] And similar developments were occurring in financial management and marketing management.

Some costs of professionalism

Line managers became increasingly restive with this proliferation of programs and specialties. What started as a trickle of additional instructions in the defensive management stage became a torrent of new bosses in the era of professional management. Managers had to gain approval for their actions not only from their line superiors but also from all these technically sophisticated staff specialists such as personnel, finance, and administration. At times, the specialists' demands were contradictory. For example, purchasing departments were able to show that profits would be increased by contracting out certain work now being done internally. Labor relations specialists argued that such contracting out could cause costly strikes by employees fearful of losing their jobs. Furthermore, there was little integration among techniques within a field. For example, personnel methods, like wage and salary administration, were developed to a fine art, but these techniques were not related to manpower planning.

Professional managers took pride in the technical virtuosity with which they approached their jobs and in their ability to base decisions on research and acceptable formulas rather than on intuition and experience. Managers, however, grew suspicious that specialists were more interested in the growth of their own fields than in the effectiveness of the total business. Line managers became convinced that the professionals in Personnel were more interested in employee happiness than in productivity, and Personnel was viewed increasingly as a very separate function, far removed from the main business of the organization: producing goods and services efficiently.

---

[4] These programs and techniques were quickly disseminated through professional meetings such as those sponsored by the Conference Board, the American Management Association, and comparable management groups organized by industry or government. The number of professional societies in the personnel field expanded: American Society for Personnel Administration, American Society for Training and Development, Public Personnel Association, and the American Compensation Association.

Today, managers are increasingly taking what might be called a systems view of the personnel function. Among the elements that comprise such a managerial style are the following:

1. *Policy integration.* Policies and procedures cannot be evaluated on their individual merit, but only in terms of how well they fit together and work toward an efficient and effective organization.

2. *Adaptation to unique organizational needs.* Organizations can be highly distinctive and heterogeneous. (A hospital is not like a factory; the personnel administration requirements of the maintenance staff, for example, are very different from those of the medical staff.)

3. *Recognition of amorphous boundaries.* Organizations are not insulated from the outside community. Race relations in the community, for example, are a part of the system with which the personnel manager must be concerned.

4. *Reconciliation of long-run and short-run goals.* Organizations need to maintain a balance between satisfying short-run pressures and providing for long-run organizational needs.

Now to look briefly at each of these aspects.

Policy integration

The personnel manager should be more than just a technician concentrating on personnel procedures. Not only must the manager be able to see the interdependencies among personnel programs and policies, but he or she must aid top management in perceiving these interdependencies. For example, changes in technology may require the substitution of electronic engineers for mechanical engineers. This will change recruitment patterns, probably create problems in salary differentials between these groups, change promotion patterns, and perhaps affect union relations. Because no single element in a system can be changed without its affecting all the other elements, the wise manager seeks to deal with these interdependencies simultaneously.

This example suggests that personnel policies must be integrated with other company policies. If an organization becomes more oriented to research and development, there will be an obvious impact on the personnel policies that affect the recruitment and retention of highly trained technical personnel.

Adaptation to unique organizational needs

Organizations are not all alike. Most industrial relations research and policy analysis assume a typical factory organization that consists primarily of blue-collar workers, with only a small managerial group. An increasing proportion of business, however, is white-collar, heavily clerical, or technical. There are more insurance salespeople than blue-collar steelworkers, and even manufacturing companies may have only a very small proportion of manual workers. White-collar employees may be even more demanding of promotional opportunities, fringe benefits, and salary improvements than are blue-collar workers, in part because of the former's greater educational investments.

In our advanced industrialized society, the service sector is growing much more rapidly than the manufacturing industry. In fact, employment in services has grown 116 percent in the last 20 years, while manufacturing employment has expanded by only 13 percent. Thus, schools, laboratories, government agencies, insurance companies, and hospitals now present a more realistic range of personnel settings than do the assembly line and machine shop.

Professional organizations. An increasing number of organizations— law firms, medical clinics, consulting firms—are built around highly trained professionals who are only partly dependent on the company. These professional groups are heavily represented in the nonprofit organizations: hospitals, universities, "think tanks." In such organizations, management is often perceived not as the "boss" but as a service group, and it is very difficult to exercise managerial control. When many specialties are represented, each group grows jealous of the other's prerogatives, and the organization becomes more like a squabbling, extended family than the rational bureaucracy Taylor and Max Weber admired. Many people who work in professional organizations do not consider themselves as employees subject to the usual managerial supervision. The physician, for example, uses the hospital for patients but is reluctant to be managed by the hospital administrators; and many professors consider their universities in the same light.

Government personnel. Today one out of six employees works for federal, state, or local government: teachers, social workers, engineers, accountants. Personnel policies are more likely to be determined by political forces, legislation, or union contract than by managers. Agencies like the Civil Service Commission also play a key role in establishing hiring and tenure standards. On the other side, government organizations are having to adapt to unionization, something traditional manufacturing business learned to do a long time ago.

Recognition of amorphous boundaries

Weber and Taylor believed that employees left their personal business at the entrance to their places of work. Family concerns and problems, however, do affect an individual on the job, just as community and political tensions affect the organization as a whole. Increasingly, management is recognizing this interdependence by encouraging employee participation in community, social, and political activities. More important, Personnel is often assigned the responsibility of relating the organization to community groups. This relationship will be explored in the following chapter.

Reconciliation of long-run and short-run goals

Managers should recognize that each day they must live with and successfully cope with pressures and demands that cannot be postponed. Thus they are tempted to settle union grievances at once, rather than respond to them in terms of the organization's long-run needs. For example, to keep a valuable employee from quitting, managers may create salary inequities that will trouble the organization for a long period. Personnel is often in the role of trading off today's requirements for tomorrow's responsibilities. It is no easy assignment!

Human resource accounting. Human resource accounting is a proposed method of long-run decision making. Many managers are interested in developing the leadership potential in employees whose present skills offer them little chance to exercise more responsibility. On the other hand, many managers are content to exploit their personnel for short-run results, without considering the other skills the employees might develop. Balance sheets do not account for the credit value of the company's human resources, although well-trained workers and motivated managers may be one of the most significant assets of the firm.[5]

Imaginative, farsighted companies are seeking ways to "account" for the increased value of their human resources contributed by their personnel programs. A modest start is the addition to an annual report to shareholders, which compares the current year with the previous one:

- [Numbers of] employees trained to assume greater responsibility
- [Numbers of] minority and women employees filling professional and managerial jobs
- [Numbers of] disabling injuries and illnesses (in relation to size of the work force)

Some accountants hope that in the future the balance sheet itself might reflect the increasing value of a motivated, trained, and well-supervised work force.

The future: escalating demands

In the past, personnel professionals tended to view techniques and programs as self-contained management goals. A systems orientation, however, encourages the development of programs that respond to ever-changing organizational requirements. Alert management perceives the dynamic quality of the work force itself.

Retired Personnel Director: "Sometimes when I think of the old days, I wonder why we never realized how easy our job was. Just fifty years ago, in fact, a majority of our employees had been born in Europe. They came to work here, almost when they got off the boat. And how glad they were to be here, and thankful for what they got. The company was their first home, not their second. They worked with friends who may have come from the same town in the old country and who certainly lived near them now in the same neighborhood. They believed in hard work; to them the boss was a god, and they never doubted their responsibilities to him and the company. There was no conflict in their loyalties to work and to their families. How could you be a good family man without being a good worker? Work, God, family, and friends were all wrapped up together.

"But now! Wow, what a change."

Employees no longer respond willingly and automatically to instructions or orders. This eroding respect for authority is also demonstrated by increased employee absenteeism and casual neglect of established rules and procedures. Thus, maintaining discipline becomes more problematic as employees are more willing, even anxious to challenge status and privilege. Although dissatisfactions are frequently channeled through the union grievance process, employees are being bolder about self-expression. Paradoxically, as employees become

[5] Clark Chastain, "Evolution of Human Resource Accounting," *Univ. of Michigan Business Review,* 31 (Jan. 1979), 16–23. See also the works of Eric Flamholtz.

more reluctant to identify with the organization, they are still increasing the demands they make upon it. Requests for day-care centers (to care for employees' children), for more paid leisure, for dental and psychiatric care, and other new benefits that are costly and complex to administer are some of these increased demands. And let's not forget the generation gap. Styles of dress and deportment of the younger generation do not stop at the office or plant door. American culture is probably more dynamic, more rapidly changing than at any time in history, and this movement inevitably creates a need for dynamic personnel practices.

Organizations find that a large proportion of new employees exhibit life styles that are in sharp contrast to those of their supervisors and older employees. Personnel departments therefore must recognize diversity in behavior and values. In the past, many implicit if not explicit personnel policies rewarded those who most resembled the ideal of an obedient and conformist white, middle-class, upwardly mobile male. Such policies today are subject to increasing legal challenges by government, minority groups, and women.

Coping with defensive or alienated employees requires a structuring of a whole series of personnel policies. The systems approach can be illustrated by noting what has happened in companies that have sought to hire more employees from minority groups. At first, personnel departments simply changed their hiring standards, making sure the procedures were nondiscriminatory. When this didn't work, they revised their recruiting and testing methods. Then Personnel began to recognize the need for new types of training programs for new employees as well as their supervisors. In addition, Personnel soon found that existing promotion patterns, seniority rules, and even relations with the union required examination. The conclusion is that there are no compartmentalized problems to which we can find simple answers. The organization is a sociotechnical system; changes ramify throughout the system, and we can't work on an isolated element and expect good results.

With a greater proportion of their employees being white-collar workers—most of whom surpass their predecessors in education and expectations—companies must create more fulfilling, responsible tasks, in contrast to the finely divided, easy-to-supervise jobs envisioned by the fathers of scientific management. Worth noting is the increasing educational attainments of blue-collar employees: the average operative has a high school education.

Earlier personnel theories assumed that there were just two kinds of workers—loyal family retainers and strong-backed "economic men"—who were motivated to hold their jobs and incomes at almost any personal cost. Now it is much more difficult to make assumptions concerning the motivation of employees. There is an ever-widening range of motivation extending from the worker who dislikes any on-the-job constraints and who finds work repellent, to the overmotivated professional whose drive and conscientiousness interfere with the work of others. For some employees, money is the most important factor on the job; for others, interesting, absorbing work is much more critical. The personnel specialist must expect to find more and more contradictions and apparently illogical demands. Employees still want more paternalism (such as company-sponsored childcare facilities, company-arranged automobile insurance, and vacation packages); at the same time they will resent any intrusion by the organization into their private lives (such as a request to work overtime or to change a scheduled vacation).

Similarly, even though we speak confidently about the "systems" approach to management, key elements of "defensive" management are likely to be retained by many organizations. Minority employees, as well as others, are becoming more adept at appealing to appropriate government agencies when they believe their rights have been violated. At the same time, government will play an increasingly large role in monitoring the hiring, advancement, layoff, and retirement policies of private organizations. Unambiguous policies, administrative watchfulness, and adequate records consistent with government-imposed standards will be required. In addition to government, a variety of citizen advocacy groups will be investigating and pressuring the organization to be aware of ecology, consumerism, local planning, and other areas that were all but ignored a few years ago.

As the range of organizational settings becomes broader, as expectations become more diverse and contradictory, and as we recognize that the work life of an individual requires the same freedom and self-affirmation that a person seeks in social and political spheres, the challenge of personnel work will increase. There is certainly nothing on the horizon to decrease its importance. Our society increasingly depends on human relationships; and by the same token, service-industry and managerial work, particularly, are almost entirely dependent on harmonious on-the-job relationships.

Conclusion

The field of personnel has evolved from a rather simplistic view of employees and their needs to a more sophisticated approach to a complex subject: managing the relationship of human beings to their work organizations. The accompanying table summarizes the major steps in this evolution.

Unfortunately, many personnel practitioners still insulate themselves from the organization by adopting the stance of the technical expert. They aspire to become proficient administrators of technical programs and meticulous procedures such as job evaluation, testing programs, and safety campaigns. Each procedure is supposed to give scientific answers to questions such as: How much should this job be paid? Which applicant should be hired? How can the number of accidents be reduced?

Present-day personnel managers, however, cannot depend upon some narrow methodology with easily quantified factors. In providing assistance to "clients" who have entrusted them with responsibility for aiding in the solution of profound and significant problems, they must be willing to consider all factors in both the problem and the solution. This means using unquantifiable skills, such as sensitivity, empathy, judgment, and wisdom, as well as formal evaluations of the goals and needs of the organization and its employees.

In recent years, the influence and prestige of the personnel function has expanded. Management no longer conceives of personnel work solely as a series of techniques to keep hourly workers placid or to meet governmental obligations. Management itself constitutes a growing work force with its own

Evolution of management's view of the personnel function	Managerial style	Underlying philosophy	Conceives of employees as
	Autocratic	Raw power; property rights	Interchangeable, easily replaced, and manipulable, like commodities
	Paternalistic	Traditional family with a strong, unchallenged father	Dependent children, the good ones meriting special favors, the bad ones to be punished
	Bureaucratic	Logic; rationality	Machines whose output can be increased by proper selection, monetary incentives, and "scientifically" determined working conditions
	Defensive	Legalistic	Potential litigants about whom meticulous records must be kept in order to minimize government or union interference
	Professional	Closed system and "scientific method"; compartmentalized knowledge	Participants in a wide range of special "human relations programs"
	Systems	Open system; many internal and external organization interdependencies	Inextricable from the total organizational context; management adapts programs and policies to develop its human resources and accepts many "contingencies"

problems of selection, remuneration, and promotion. Increasingly, large professional and specialist groups within organizations have high expectations and they—even more than the white-collar or blue-collar rank and file—pressure the organization for improvement in their relative positions.

In the chapters that follow, we shall examine the most typical personnel problems and challenges that face the modern organization. Both in the analysis of the problem and exploration of possible solutions, we shall endeavor to provide the context within which these problems arise and within which any solution must work. For the student as well as the personnel executive, our approach may appear to introduce too many complexities, too many qualifications and equivocations, but no experienced manager ever said that solving human problems was easy. After all, Personnel is the crossroads of the organization, the place where community and union pressures, government regulations, employee aspirations, and many organizational pressures and problems come into focus and intersect one another.

Although adequate financing, economic planning, and other management skills obviously are important, organizations require their human resources in order to function. Thus the major purpose of this text is to provide methods and frameworks of analysis that will enable the student to deal with today's personnel problems and to develop competent and effective solutions for tomorrow's.

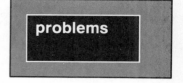

1 · *The Big Reward*

Computer Components had been in business only eighteen months, having been started by a systems engineer from a major "big frame" manufacturer who wished to go into business for himself. Alan Phipps was now making another of the kind of intuitive, quick decisions that had enabled him to attract half a dozen good managers and garner $15 million in sales the first year. His sales manager, Bill Cohen, had just brought back a $750,000 order for the major unit of peripheral equipment they manufactured. Delighted with this, Phipps planned to give Cohen an immediate $10,000 bonus.

When the financial v.p., Staats, heard of the decision, he rushed into Phipps's office and told him that this was a big mistake.

"Alan, you've got to remember you're running a business that's going to be in operation for years to come. Are you planning to do this every time a big sale is made? That's the precedent you're setting. And even if that were feasible, what's it going to do to relationships within our managerial group? How is Ella going to feel, who heads up Engineering, and Heller, who has to fill this order with what we laughingly call our 'manufacturing facility'? They work hard, too, you know."

Phipps quickly replied, "Your problem is that you believe in letting textbook theories and conservative bookkeeping run a business; and if I did that, we would all still be working for you-know-who. I want Bill to know how pleased I am and to be able to see my appreciation and to know he's really one of my boys. Sure, I may not be in a position to do it every time, but I know that Bill will knock himself out for Computer Components, and we won't have to worry about anybody stealing him away."

Staats thought for a moment, "Okay, if you want to reward him, fine. But let's do it in a businesslike way. In fact, we ought to set up some formula, so that the man making the sale gets something like one-half of one percent, spread over three years, of course, or something like that; or maybe we could have a sliding scale. But at least it would be something set down in writing and not Big Daddy deciding off the top of his head."

Phipps grumbled, "There you go, wanting to turn this into a stuffy, ultraconservative big company with hardening of the arteries. We'll never grow if I and you, too, can't make quick off-the-cuff decisions."

2 · *The President's Letter*

The following letter was sent to the Harvard Business Review by the president of a medium-sized insurance company. The president is explaining why his company has so few immediate personnel problems in its Home Office (which, we may assume, houses about 500 employees, most engaged in routine, clerical operations.) *

The reason lies not in the attitudes of workers but in the attitude of management. It is true that lavish offers of fringe benefits give no assurance of mollified workers. This company has gone far in the fringe area, but I have never felt that what we did accounted for the remarkable *esprit de corps* our people show. I feel it is how we do it.

* Vol. 32, No. 6 (November 1954), reproduced by permission of the author and publisher.

By that I mean that for eleven years since I came to head this company my first objective in dealings with our people has been to dignify them as individuals and to express a feeling of pride in them which quickly won their recognition. This is the pattern followed by my staff. Supervisory attitudes—management's real intent—are quickly observed and evaluated by employees. My company takes this seriously.

Alex Osborn of B.B.D.&O. is an old friend of mine. You may have seen his two recent books, one captioned "Your Creative Power," and the other more recent one entitled "Applied Imagination." These books have been widely circulated among our officers and supervisory people, and many things have come out of them. For example, we took a longer look at our suggestion plan and approached it on the basis that whatever the quantity or quality of suggestions, the Suggestion Committee must deal, not only with an open mind, but liberally, with suggestions in the first year. While we get many suggestions that cannot be given dollar awards, we make sure that occasionally a good suggestion gets a walloping return. We now invest a rather substantial sum in suggestion awards, and I submit we get a great deal of genuine interest and benefit. Our plan works well and it costs us about the same as one qualified clerical person.

I am interested in the local orchestra, and a few years ago it was brought to my attention that there were several unsold boxes. I hit upon a plan evolved from Osborn's thinking that pays off three ways, and it has been most successful. Our people are encouraged to bring flowers from their garden to decorate the lobby of our building. They are given a credit line for so doing and feel good about it; secondly, our lobby is as attractive as any you will find; and thirdly, those who add to its beauty are rewarded by pairs of tickets to the concerts. The orchestra benefits as do our people. The plan appealed to every bank and insurance company in this town, save two, and there are no unsold boxes. Parenthetically, I maintain a box adjacent to that purchased for the employees. I am usually there and find an opportunity to visit either before the concert or during intermission with my people and their husbands and wives and friends.

Perhaps the most significant thing we have done is one which has given dignity to every person in the building and it happens to be in the field of philanthropy. In 1947, I was General Chairman for the Community Chest Campaign, and the slogan adopted by the company's employees committee that year was "PAR FOR E.A.R." [E.A.R. is the president], and in that year there was 100% giving. The company became pleasantly notorious throughout the city for this 100% accomplishment;

and believe it or not, with a constantly changing personnel, the record of 100% giving—every officer, every employee, every cafeteria and building maintenance worker—has been maintained through the years since. Every year the drive is completed on the first day and a telegram sent to the general chairman. In the public meetings which follow, our people are photographed and feted. Every individual feels personally responsible for the result.

Our pay scales are measured by objective job analysis and careful performance rating. Our hours are the best, our working conditions as good as any, and there is a constant effort to be humane in all matters.

We have had interesting conversations with the group acting as the Board of Governors of the "Employees' Club" over the years, and we have met every reasonable request they have made. Biweekly pay was one of the requests which we adopted costing us about 8% more in salary, smoking in work areas which we permitted, music in work areas which we maintain. We are always willing to listen to our people. If they want something that will help them in their work and in their happiness here we will go far to supply it.

Ours is not a perfect shop, and I may be lulled into thinking it is happier than I suggest, but of one thing I am sure, while most of our officers have had collegiate experiences, there isn't one who came into the world with a gold spoon in his mouth, and that may account for their interest in people and their problems.

I have a great feeling of intimacy with our employees. I write dozens of longhand letters to those who do me and this company favors, and I write a specially dictated letter to each person on his reaching a fifth, tenth, etc., anniversary.

We make a good deal of a Christmas Party that is really a family affair. There is no drinking in connection with it, though we are not opposed to drinking as such. We bring in the families and children of all people who wish to come. It is a very successful affair.

Similarly we take an interest in our retired people and annually give them the finest dinner and entertainment in the best place available. We encourage them to visit the office and to attend the functions held by active employees.

If our people should become upset about anything I am prepared to say it would be my fault, because there is nothing reasonable they could urge that we could afford to do, that we aren't doing, or be willing to do. If we could not do it my experience with them has been that we could spell out the reasons convincingly and acceptably.

We take good care of our older people and

pay an extra service allowance for length of service which is quite considerable in the case of the older and in some cases, less productive people. We have meetings in which the dignity of the individuals is advanced with deliberate care.

Morale cannot be won in a day or purchased at any price. It takes a long time to develop good morale and it takes constant planning to preserve it. On the other hand, I could lose it all in one day's misbehavior. All I would need to do would be to walk through a work area and complain about

the posture of a couple of people and ask whether it was necessary to burn as many lights. It would help to turn on lights but it would never do to turn one off.

The important thing is that the work be congenial; and if that is not so, liberal rules and wage scales become of less importance. Care must be taken in the employment of people and more care in the treatment of them later. We try to take that care and that I think is why we apparently do so well in our company.

professional paternalistic

1. Evaluate the effectiveness of this company's program.
2. Which managerial philosophies are being utilized by the president?

3 • *The Japanese Way*

A Japanese executive visiting the United States to investigate problems that might be faced if his company established a U.S. facility, warned his top management:

"We must be very careful not to adopt the U.S. personnel philosophy. Most American companies treat their employees as interchangeable parts. And they encourage them to think almost solely of themselves. Thus they assume that the job can be learned in a few weeks or months, then the individual should show performance and correct decisions that his or her manager can appraise and reward. Employees are encouraged to compete with one another for results and rewards. This is in sharp contrast to a Japanese company, in which we assume that an employee may take years to learn the underlying spirit, values, and goals of the

organization. Further, we place much more emphasis on evolving a consensus in making decisions and sharing the responsibility for that decision over a broad group. Rather than pay for short-run performance, we provide earnings commensurate with the individual's personal circumstances and length of service; the loyalty that has been demonstrated is very important. Further, we expect to make a commitment for almost the total working life of the employee. . . .

"This Japanese philosophy provides us with employees who are highly committed to their company, who they may even believe is like their family. American personnel management is too impersonal; therefore, the employees lack the motivation to do their best for the company. . . ."

1. Do you like the Japanese approach to managing people? What are its advantages and disadvantages?
2. Would it really fit into American culture?*

* For a more complete statement of these differences see Yoshi Tsurumi, "Two Models of Corporation and International Transfer of Technology," *Columbia Journal of Work Business* (Summer 1979), pp. 43–50.

the personnel department: organization and function

Having reviewed management's often ambivalent and vacillating view of its personnel responsibilities, it is time to look more directly at the mechanism by which personnel philosophy is translated into action. True, as suggested by the oft-repeated phrase "management is people," Personnel is the job of every manager. Yet the personnel department has a special role to play in this field. And the fact that Personnel is the responsibility both of the entire organization and of one special department makes the relations between that department and the rest of the organization particularly difficult.

In this chapter we shall be concerned with the unique contribution of the personnel specialist and the personnel department. After a brief description of this department's scope and function, we shall examine the organizational implications of its work. As we shall see, Personnel makes its input in two ways: through its contribution to overall *policy* and through daily contacts with line managers. Both of these functions will be examined.

Scope of personnel administration

We can obtain a static but rather impressive view of the personnel field by looking at an organization chart showing the personnel department's functions in a typical large organization.

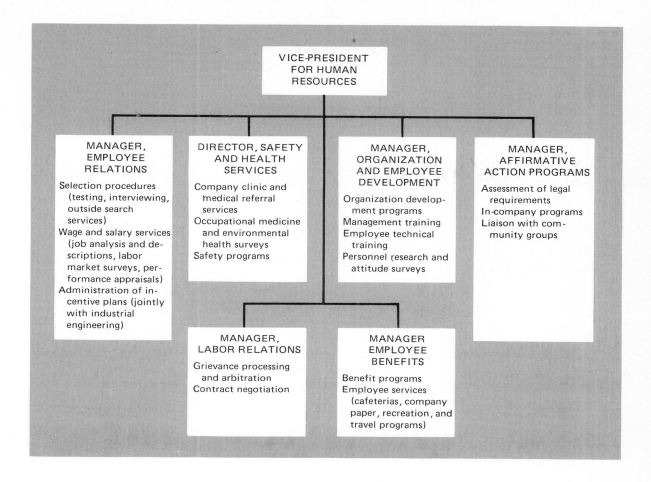

VICE-PRESIDENT FOR HUMAN RESOURCES

MANAGER, EMPLOYEE RELATIONS

Selection procedures (testing, interviewing, outside search services)
Wage and salary services (job analysis and descriptions, labor market surveys, performance appraisals)
Administration of incentive plans (jointly with industrial engineering)

DIRECTOR, SAFETY AND HEALTH SERVICES

Company clinic and medical referral services
Occupational medicine and environmental health surveys
Safety programs

MANAGER, ORGANIZATION AND EMPLOYEE DEVELOPMENT

Organization development programs
Management training
Employee technical training
Personnel research and attitude surveys

MANAGER, AFFIRMATIVE ACTION PROGRAMS

Assessment of legal requirements
In-company programs
Liaison with community groups

MANAGER, LABOR RELATIONS

Grievance processing and arbitration
Contract negotiation

MANAGER EMPLOYEE BENEFITS

Benefit programs
Employee services (cafeterias, company paper, recreation, and travel programs)

Personnel's policy-making role

Personnel is concerned with organizational policies for human resource management. Most large organizations have elaborate written personnel policies that take the place of *ad hoc* decision-making and contribute to greater organizationwide consistency. Although uniform standards can reduce flexibility, they also minimize the possibility that favoritism or shortsightedness will injure relationships.

"Things have changed a lot around here since we've been purchased by General Conglomerate. We old-timers liked being able to deal with the boss himself, and Mr. Henley did try to do what was right and fair. But there were suspicions that he played favorites, and we lost a number of good people when he insisted on paying bigger salaries to long-service employees than to newcomers who did the same work. Now with all these new rules, no one can complain of favoritism."

Company policies are designed to communicate to employees the basic ground rules under which the organization functions and thus avoid discrimination, inconsistency, and confusion over rights and obligations. Consistent policies mean that similar jobs receive the same pay and that an employee's request for an educational leave ˙in department X receives the same response as a similar request in department Y. Thus, when a company has a policy of "not discriminating in employment against husbands and wives of existing employees so long as there is no superior-subordinate relationship involved in their respective jobs," the corporate personnel department is able to relieve the anxiety of a division manager who wants to hire the spouse of one of the engineers. Obviously, centralized rule-making permits upper management to influence a wider range of decision making more efficiently than if it required every individual decision to be submitted for advance approval.

Types of policies

Personnel policies can really be anything from general statements of principle (We do *not* discriminate in employment) to narrow rules (No employee shall receive more than one salary increase in any 6-months' period). Many organizations preface their personnel rules with broad statements of policy, philosophy, and objectives to establish a context within which the rules fit. Many organizations take great pride, in fact, in stating basic principles that stress fairness, rewards commensurate to contributions, opportunity for individuals to develop capabilities, and other socially responsible values. Obviously, the more broadly these policies are stated, the easier they are to administer, but the fewer specific problems they solve.

Somewhat narrower in scope and therefore more operational are policies that suggest *approaches* to problem-solving without specifying answers. Thus Personnel may encourage the establishment of sound procedures in critical areas:

- All divisions of the company will post job announcements when vacancies occur. These notices will describe duties, salary, and the relevant qualifications and indicate the procedures by which interested employees may make application.
- Each division will appoint a safety officer who is responsible for a continuing audit of work practices and equipment and for making an annual report to the corporate safety committee analyzing lost-time accidents and proposing changes in procedures and physical facilities to minimize accidents.
- Supervisors will consult with a member of the industrial relations staff before responding to a written union grievance.

Of course, the narrowest, most explicit, and most confining are policies that prescribe specific rules to cover specific situations; these can be the source of the greatest controversy and discomfort because they allow the least leeway.

- No employee can receive an increase in salary greater than 10 percent of base salary at the time of promotion.
- No travel compensation can be authorized greater than $60 per day.

Policy-making dilemmas

Rules are never perfect. And personnel administrators, because they deal with so many sensitive and critical human issues, must be especially aware of the problems inherent in interpreting and administering policies—ambiguity, contradictions, and rigidity.

Ambiguity.   Few policies resolve all decision dilemmas unambiguously. If they did, there would be many fewer grievances, fewer lawyers, and fewer arguments. Even the policy given above concerning husbands and wives working in the same organization allows ample room for argument. Suppose engineers use the office staff to handle their correspondence and for other clerical support activities, so that the engineer is in a position of giving "instructions" to the office manager, and the office manager can play favorites in providing quick service. Will the appointment of an engineer's wife as office manager create problems?

Contradictions.   Sometimes ambiguity is increased by contradictions between policies.

The County Health Agency personnel policies stress its commitment to promotion from within the organization, in contrast to filling higher positions with outsiders. The agency also follows the policy of making layoffs according to job (as opposed to agency) seniority. In other words, if Ms. X wanted to accept a promotion from statistical clerk (in which she had worked 15 years) to "field investigator," she would automatically become the most junior field investigator. If there were cutbacks in that group, she would be the first to be laid off even though she had much longer agency service than her fellow investigators. Given this policy, few senior employees were willing to accept promotion. One policy cancelled the other.

Other strains result when personnel policies conflict with financial policies or other organizational goals. Equal employment policies can clash with the firm's intentions to minimize short-run costs, since minority employees may be expensive to train. Realistically, managers must recognize that organizations are not directed toward a single all-embracing goal such as efficiency or profitability. The wise, experienced executive accommodates to these contradictions. Long- and short-term objectives must be balanced against one another. There are no simple answers to the continuing dilemmas faced by supervisors who are being pressured for both immediate results *and* continuing progress toward long-term objectives. Or as some put it, efficiency and effectiveness cannot be achieved simultaneously.

Further, it is difficult, nay impossible, clearly to separate personnel decisions and policies from other managerial responsibilities. When the marketing division seeks to establish a separate "customer service" group to handle its institutional customers (rather than allowing the existing service department to do this work) is this a marketing or a personnel decision? Very obviously it is both.

Rigidity.   Policies are not intended to cover all eventualities. Although the rules regarding travel allowances may specify "air travel by coach," there may be times when excessive fatigue, illness, or even the need to conduct business while traveling necessitates first-class air travel. The good administrator is able to distinguish between legitimate and illegitimate exceptions. Nevertheless, it is easy for Personnel to be perceived by line managers as needlessly rigid in its administration of policies—and sometimes with justification.

Harold Stephens, a minority employee, has received three tardiness warnings this single month, and according to company discipline policy, should be discharged. Yet there are extenuating circumstances. Stephens comes from a broken home, has been a drug addict, and is working on his first regular job. He has done remarkably well in adjusting, although he is still having trouble with getting to work on time. His supervisor fears that discharge will destroy all the progress Stephens has made, but the supervisor's bosses are worried that an exception to the rule will set an undesirable precedent and thus weaken the organization's ability to enforce discipline in other less "worthy" cases.

On the other hand, clearly written policies can actually make managers more adaptive. Without policy guides, managers may be intimidated or tend to be ultraconservative for fear of incurring their boss's wrath. Also, the existence of a policy does *not* mean that there can be no exceptions. Rather, the policy simply highlights the exceptional case that, in turn, requires documentation and additional managerial attention.

Most supervisors found the company policy prohibiting more than one salary increase for any employee in a calendar year very useful. Everyone understood the limits, so to speak. For rare instances in which an employee deserved more than one increase, managers knew they would have to provide extraordinary justification. And so did the employee involved.

As the above examples indicate, good sense and the balancing of a variety of considerations are necessary ingredients for personnel decision making.

Keeping policies up-to-date

Industrialized, urban societies are characterized by rapidly changing community mores and technologies. Unlike tradition-bound agrarian cultures that tend to be static, methods and policies appropriate yesterday can be useless or even a handicap today. Like human beings, organizations tend to have momentum: procedures and ways of doing things, once established, tend to continue long after their usefulness ceases. As with all management functions, Personnel must find ways of keeping policies up-to-date and relevant. How can this be accomplished?

Sensitivity to internal environment. Good personnel executives appear to have a sixth sense which tells them that something is wrong. Since they are less involved in meeting production schedules and have contacts throughout the organization, they are able to tell the "forest from the trees." Personnel can often spot situations in which managers are devoting endless administrative time and energy to solving the same problem over and over again. This is a sure sign of policy obsolescence. For example:

Early in its history, the Foster Service established what at that time was a very enlightened policy, requiring that managers have experience in at least three of the five major functional divisions before being promoted into the ranks of top management. In recent years, the organization has been in a high-technology field, and many of the best engineering managers are reluctant to move into what they consider the "softer" finance and marketing departments. Further, there is little incentive to accept these moves because the top management team is reasonably young and stable. In the next few years, there will be several key openings, but there are no insiders with the background stipulated in the current policy. Personnel confronted the president with the need to review the promotion policy.

The Foremost Medical Laboratories, doing diagnostic tests for doctors, was located in a small community outside Boston. Its salary level was relatively low for an area that contained many well-paid jobs in technical organizations. Consequently, the labs had high and costly turnover, largely of women technicians, and much time was devoted to filling these vacancies. The personnel director noted that many well-educated wives lived in the area, but apparently few wanted full-time employment. Although the laboratories had insisted on hiring only full-time employees in the past, a work schedule that would allow women with children to see them off to school in the morning and be home in time to welcome them back might have substantial appeal. The director had a number of discussions with the president. These stressed the cost of the turnover, the difficulty of securing adequate replacements at the salary level the company was able to pay, and the work schedules that could be developed consistent with the needs of the various lab managers. Shortly after, the president agreed to this new policy.

Sensitivity to external environment. By training and interest, the personnel executive ought to be expert in sensing changes in the external environment that shortly will affect that organization. For example, not many years ago, organizations were very disapproving of men with beards and women wearing pants. Obviously, in the 1980s, such policies are obsolete. Just looking around the community would tell a personnel executive that the company's policies concerning employee appearance may need frequent changes.

Similarly, many universities had policies that forbade faculty appointment for professors' spouses. These so-called nepotism rules had their roots in the Depression, when many educational establishments responded to community pressures for sharing scarce jobs. With justification, women were outraged at policies implying that their professional careers are less important than those of their husbands.

Many companies have outdated policies that serve to accentuate the status distinctions between white-collar and blue-collar workers. The blue-collar people punch time clocks, cannot make or receive telephone calls or even leave their workplace without formal permission. In our more permissive age, when employees insist on being treated with dignity, such policies exacerbate employer-employee relationships.

Even good policies are no better than their administration, and it is to the administrative aspect of Personnel that we now turn.

Lateral relations: a behavioral view of personnel Personnel executives like to participate in making the big decisions that shape and control the actions of lower-level managers and workers. Participating in policy making is consistent with the professional point of view we described in the previous chapter. Just as marketing executives make marketing policy, personnel executives feel they should make personnel policy.

But there are crucial differences between the two kinds of executives. As we noted in Chapter 1, organizations distinguish between staff and line functions, and the line are assigned much of the real decision-making power. Even more to the point, policies are not self-enforcing. The easiest thing to do is to announce a new top-level decision. Getting it to work is quite another problem. Much day-to-day work is required to ensure that managers understand policy directives and are willing and able to implement them. Regardless of whether Personnel actually makes policy, its effectiveness in doing the backup work will help determine whether policies are anything more than pompous words enshrined in imposing manuals.

Chapter 1 advocated a "system view" of Personnel's role. A systems view simply means that we cannot compartmentalize functions and that most of what happens in a modern organization is the result of a number of specialists working together. If the international sales department wants to transfer a group of salespeople overseas, is this a marketing or a personnel decision? Obviously it is both.

Personnel's overall effectiveness depends largely on how well it handles its day-to-day non-policy-making job of working with line managers. Now let us look at how Personnel coordinates its work and capabilities with the operations of other departments. After all, that is the heart of personnel work.

What is staff?

Personnel is a staff department. Traditionally, the term *staff* has encompassed those subsidiary or technical functions and activities that support the primary *line* activities of the organization. Thus, engineering, accounting, and personnel are usually considered staff functions, while production or operations are line. Line is usually assumed to have more power and authority.

What does it mean to be a staff rather than a line manager? Answering this question involves taking a much closer look at the actual behavior and functions of Personnel, its role in the life of the organization, and particularly its interaction with line managers.

We have already listed many critical functions—safety, remuneration, manpower planning, selection, and the like. But the real question is, what do personnel specialists actually do in any of these areas? Do they, for example, *set* wages, *determine* manpower policies, *select* employees, and *take* responsibility for safe working conditions? The answer is often NO. Top management itself has to do some of these things; others are the result of lower-level management decisions, and most decisions involve a number of managers working together.

For any functional area, such as salary administration, there are a number of roles that Personnel can play in relation to the line organization—service, advisory, stabilization, audit, and liaison (definitions will follow). It may help us to become familiar with these roles if we look at the actual working day of a personnel executive. On a typical day, the personnel director of the First Fiduciary Insurance Company might participate in the following calls, all involving salary administration:

- In her "howdy rounds" through the organization, the personnel director had noted growing misunderstanding and distress over the pay differences between back-office clerical personnel and those who worked "on the carpet" in the public areas of the main office. In fact, job requirements were different; the jobs really weren't comparable, but there was a long history of suspicion between the two groups, in part engendered by the appearance of status and privilege enjoyed by those out front. The problem had come to a head recently when the vice-president for operations, who was in charge of back-office staff, explained decreasing productivity to the company's president by "our inability to pay the same wages that those who work up front get." The personnel director had been present at this meeting, and at many others at which these differentials had been argued. She decided to call a meeting of all supervisors in both areas and have her own staff make a presentation covering all clerical salaries in the office. She would then endeavor to focus a discussion on alternative approaches to reducing these rivalries. (Liaison relationship)

- The head of data processing calls to set up an appointment to discuss programing salary costs. He is considering contracting out some of their software efforts if it will save money, but he wants to try to predict the probable reactions of the present programing staff as well as that of the union. (Advisory relationship)

- A senior vice-president calls, asking her to check salary levels for receptionists at other banks and insurance companies in the metropolitan area. The vice-president is concerned that they are "falling behind" prevailing rates. (Service relationship)

- The back-office manager has created a new job in the check-sorting group and is complaining that the salary assigned to the group leader's job under the job evaluation plan is too low to get the person she wants to take the job. The manager wants to know if the job can be "reevaluated" and the salary rate increased. (Stabilization relationship)

- The personnel director calls the head of one of the suburban branches to remind him that for the past two quarters his payroll costs have exceeded the office's standard for its smaller branches. Personnel's analysis of this variance has disclosed that the high salary costs are attributable to the above-average number of merit increases the branch manager gave out at the end of the year. Prior to calling, the personnel director checked the files and noted that this particular branch manager had consistently taken the position that his superior employees deserved more favorable treatment than an "average" branch. (Audit relationship)

- While mentally planning the meeting, the director also reminded herself to call the president to recommend that top management reconsider its present policy concerning salary increments for supervisors and middle management. Based on the results of a recent study she had conducted, it was evident that superior executives were not receiving significant pay differentials over those "just getting by." She felt certain that eventually this would affect motivation and that management had to act. (Traditional relationship: subordinate recommends change to superior)

Let us now step back and identify the various staff-line roles Personnel can play. Of course it must be remembered that giving a title to someone, even describing a role, does not automatically mean those so labeled can perform the tasks. Therefore, after the brief descriptions, we will look at the behavioral problems associated with performing each role.

Some critical staff roles

Liaison or intermediary relationships. The modern organization is comprised of a number of specialized groups, each with its own way of viewing the world, its own biases and prejudices. Conflicts between departments and groups are therefore common. Because personnel executives have reason for wide contacts through the organization, they are often in a position to mediate these intergroup differences, much as an outside consultant might smooth troubled waters.[1]

Advisory relationships. Although the people problems of the organization are not the unique province of the personnel department, personnel specialists do have unique expertise to contribute. Top management assumes that line managers will call in Personnel to provide advice and counsel whenever vexing problems emerge. Providing help sounds like a simple role to play (after all, who does not want help?); but as we shall see, it is among the most difficult roles to handle effectively.

Service relationships. The major justification for centralizing certain tasks is to permit more efficient and technically sophisticated handling of activities than would be possible if each group or department did everything for itself. Thus, Personnel may handle recruitment and training activities on a centralized basis. The record keeping described in Chapter 1 is another service role.

Stabilization relationships. Few policies are self-enforcing, and top management is often concerned that department managers may make inconsistent decisions. For both these reasons, line managers may be required to check their decisions with staff groups before putting them into action. A manager may *decide* to increase the salary of an assistant, but Personnel has to approve that increase, presumably to ensure that his assistant isn't getting paid too much in comparison with some other assistant.

Audit relationships. Staff managers are also placed in the position of evaluating or appraising the work of line managers and reporting their findings to upper management. Personnel may audit how well line managers are keeping payroll costs in line or how well they are utilizing corporate training resources.

Problem solving and introducing change

Finally, in addition to the activities already mentioned, Personnel frequently becomes involved in less routine problem solving and helping to introduce organizational change. These tasks usually require a combination of the patterns we have already described. A typical sequence might be this one:

- Personnel *auditing* discloses excessive and costly turnover.
- As a *service* function, Personnel research conducts survey of employee opinion that discloses widespread employee dissatisfaction with promotional opportunities.
- Through its *advisory* relationships with key division heads, Personnel seeks to sensitize managers to the need for developing a fairer promotional policy.

[1] For an analysis of the mediation function, see Richard Walton, *Interpersonal Peacemaking: Confrontations and Third Party Consultation* (Reading, Mass.: Addison-Wesley, 1969). All of these roles are described in more detail in Leonard Sayles, *Leadership* (New York: McGraw-Hill, 1979), pp. 71–92.

- Establishment of new promotion policies requires a consensus among those executives whose departments would be affected; and by means of its *liaison* skills, Personnel endeavors to get these units to make the necessary kinds of changes.

With this brief introduction, let us look more closely at Personnel's liaison, advisory, and service relationships.

Liaison relationships

People who work in different departments or at different organizational levels usually develop very distinctive points of view. Marketing people find it hard to appreciate how production managers think; union leaders are likely to view problems differently from managers. First-line supervisors often feel their higher-level bosses misunderstand them and do things that hurt their positions. Thus, one of the most important contributions that personnel executives can make is to improve communications within the organization. Why is the personnel department the one to do this, and how can it be accomplished?

The "why" is easier. Given its staff role, Personnel is likely to move relatively freely between organizational groups and levels. Provided it de-emphasizes its own authority and status, it should have relatively easy entree and also the skills to facilitate communications among groups. But what are these skills? For the most part, they are interpreter or mediator skills, as the following commentary suggests:

"Henry Fisher is one of the best personnel men I know. He spends a great deal of time with union officials, just shooting the breeze or having a drink. By his deeds and work he has shown them that he can be trusted not to reveal confidences and that he levels with them. Because of this frequency of contact and his easy style, he is able to explain the reasons behind management decisions the union might have considered threatening or capricious. In turn, he finds out from the union which grievances they feel most strongly about, and this information helps sensitize management to the union's point of view."

Note what skills are emphasized:

- Wide-ranging contact patterns and ability to communicate easily with all groups and status levels.
- Absence of pretentions or efforts to assert status.
- Ability to gain the confidence of others by basic honesty, keeping one's word, and accurately reflecting sentiments that have been expressed to them.
- Ability to translate one group's point of view into terms that are meaningful to other groups.

Thus the liaison person demonstrates that he or she respects the values and understands the needs and positions of the different groups with which he interacts. He can talk to each group in its own language. He is especially sensitive to learning the basic feelings of a group, so that he can help other groups understand those feelings. As a trusted intermediary, he is often able to serve as a conduit between contending parties when direct contact might lead to emotional outbursts or a rigidifying of respective positions.

Personnel Manager: "You can just imagine how sore Product Engineering was when they learned that Marketing had offered Phillips that high-paying position. Phillips was PE's best engineer, and they figured that Marketing was just out to give them the *shiv* after that fracas over the new line of refrigerators. Well, I learned about all of this almost by accident while talking with one of the group leaders in PE on another matter. I made it my business to see the head of PE the next day. I could tell him how long and hard Marketing had worked to define this new job, how many people had been looked at, and why Phillips was really a natural."

Experienced personnel managers seek to make their contacts and activities do double duty. They hope to *learn* more from each such contact about how various individuals and segments of the organization view their problems and relationships. At the same time, they seek to *communicate* how the relevant others in the organization perceive the same situations. In doing so, they seek to tie the organization together more closely.

The skills gained in this manner become extremely valuable in the organization's relationships with community groups, such as minority groups and environmentalists. Conflict can be minimized by managers who are able to deal with all sides of social issues and who are quick to detect changes in the community and political climate. Such linkages to the outside world provide the organization with a critical sensory function that aids adaptiveness.

We can distinguish three different kinds of liaison or intermediary relationship:

Mediator.   Personnel acts to bring together two or more managers who have difficulty in communicating, who have divergent goals or perspectives, and who need an "outsider" to smooth over the frictions in their relationship.

Appeal channel.   For organized workers, the trade union (discussed in Chapter 4) is the primary mechanism for registering complaints over the boss's head. Unorganized, professional, and managerial employees often look to Personnel for this function. Its broad understanding of compensation, promotion policies, and practices, and its wide-ranging contacts ought to make it a good *ombudsman* (a currently popular term) to represent employees to key management people and to *verify,* investigate, and counsel.

The case of Philomena Hardy is typical. Having been passed over for promotion several times, she really wondered whether there was much future for her in the laboratory. Her boss was both reticent and vague about his evaluations. She asked the personnel director to bring her case to the lab director's attention.

Outside contact.   As part of their jobs, personnel people develop contacts with a variety of outside agencies that deal with industrial relations problems— governmental agencies, educational institutions, community organizations, and the like. By serving as a contact person, the personnel director saves individual departments a great deal of trouble. Take as an example an engineering department seeking to hire a new engineer. Without Personnel's assistance, it may have to obtain information from the following, among others:

- The Department of Labor—about community salary rates for engineers
- The Equal Employment Opportunity Commission—about affirmative action requirements
- A psychological consultant—about testing procedures
- Employment agencies and university placement officers—about available candidates for the job.

Obviously, the engineering department would much prefer Personnel to take over these time-consuming tasks and contacts. Similarly, outside organizations need a point of contact in dealing with the company.

Of course, as we have already observed, providing these linkages is also an excellent way of acquiring information about organizational health. Insight obtained in this manner, in turn, makes Personnel's advisory function more effective.

The advisory relationship

The traditional staff role is that of being an expert *adviser* to line management. As we shall see, it is easy to direct Personnel: be helpful, be an expert in human relations, give advice but don't give orders. But it is much more difficult to comprehend and master the actual day-to-day behavior required to support and maintain such a relationship. Much of the remainder of this chapter will be devoted to exploring *how* this can best be accomplished.

When providing information, the personnel manager simply furnishes the facts that will help the manager make a sound decision. For instance:

- The disciplinary clause of the union agreement reads thus and so.
- The "going rate" for engineers like Jones in our present labor market is $1950 per month.

Or the Personnel manager may play a more active role and furnish advice:

- You are likely to provoke a wildcat strike if you give Bill Williams a disciplinary layoff.
- On the basis of the record, Jones looks like a better bet for promotion, since the woman on the job will have to assume a good deal of initiative without close supervision.
- If you hire Smith at that salary, you are going to have some dissatisfied older employees in your department.

Finally, the Personnel manager can make decisions:

- Don't discharge Brown; give him a warning slip.
- Hire Green to replace the person who left.

Sometimes there is a very narrow line between providing facts, advice, and actual decision making. Thus, by selecting facts carefully, the personnel manager can actually sway the line manager's decision. Also, what is given as "advice" may be interpreted by the recipient as a decision.

The temptation to exceed the advisory role. Historically, management has tended to turn over more and more functions to well-trained experts who have specialized knowledge in a relatively narrow field. When experts were first used to supplement the skills of line supervisors, the distinctions among information, advice, and decision making were rarely made. Further, management showed a readiness to accept expert advice uncritically. Anxious to avoid trouble with the unions, for example, management allowed the industrial relations department to tell supervisors whom to hire, what to pay them, and how to answer their grievances. The result was often disastrous to the prestige and status of supervisors, as we saw in Chapter 1.

A number of factors made this passive role difficult. Merely sitting by until the line asks the staff person for help may make it difficult for the staff person to get her departmental budget approved. Experienced managers learn that budgets (meaning the people and activities you can support) depend upon showing results, which in Personnel's case often means showing programs that have been accepted. Thus Personnel is tempted to intervene directly when problems emerge rather than simply wait to be asked to provide help. Further, many managers are constitutionally unable to accept what appears to be a passive role; they are too impatient and eager to seek out problems and show their abilities. Finally, staff executives may also have some legitimate anxieties that if personnel problems worsen, they'll be blamed even though their counsel was never solicited. In other words, they feel responsible for the quality of human relations in the organization, since that is their specialty, although they lack authority to take direct action.

In practice it takes a strong-willed personnel manager to resist the temptation to become a decision maker. The customary role of adviser and counselor too easily leads to the next step: actually making decisions. Even when care is taken to avoid usurping the line supervisor's responsibility, the personnel manager's actions may still be misinterpreted. The following case illustrates this problem:

A grievance was filed against Gus Homes, a departmental supervisor, for failing to divide equally the opportunities for overtime work at extra pay. Homes argued that employees who failed to meet production standards on regular work should not be given overtime. The union contract said nothing about overtime, although general plant practice sanctioned equal division. The personnel director, anxious to avoid any union bargaining on the overtime issue, urged Homes to change his mind. Homes refused.

Some weeks later, Homes was transferred to a less desirable job. The plant grapevine reported that the manager had "given him the axe" on the recommendation of the personnel director. The truth of the matter was that the manager had believed for some time that Homes should be removed from his department. The overtime situation was just one of many reasons that seemed to justify the move.

From this point on, other supervisors thought twice before refusing the personnel director's "advice." His recommendations had become cloaked with line authority; he had become another boss.

When the manager wants more than advice. Line managers themselves may encourage staff experts to broaden their range of activities. The willingness of the personnel rep to help out on a difficult problem may provide the supervisor with welcome relief from burdensome responsibilities. In effect, the supervisor says to the personnel rep, "Good, you handle the personnel, and I'll take care of the technical problems." Then, if a decision backfires, the line supervisor can simply point out that Personnel's advice was followed. What a pleasant relief this excuse provides!

And so it is easy to understand the line supervisor's reluctance to question the expertise of the specialists top management has hired. The subordinate manager who challenges their ability runs the risk of making a bad decision for which he will have to bear all the responsibility. He may prefer to interpret "advice" as a decision, in order to avoid assuming responsibility and pass the buck to the expert. Paradoxically, a manager may resent an advisory group's power and at the same time grumble that it is failing to take responsibility for decisions. As one supervisor expressed it:

"We stay away from the industrial relations department as much as possible—they're always trying to sell us on some new program that makes more work. When we do go to them with a problem, we can't get a straight answer. They won't tell us how to handle it. They give us a lot of pros and cons and stuff that leaves us more confused than when we went in."

The tendency for advice to become orders. Both Personnel and line managers have a temptation to turn advice into an order. Let us enlarge on this. There can be some fear involved that it is a mistake to ignore the advice of a high-powered expert group even though, in theory, they are "just staff." Based on what many line managers have told us, we think the decision matrix illustrated here explains why it is the safest option for a line manager to treat staff advice as though it were an order.

If personnel manager's advice turns out to be	and the line manager has		Why line managers minimize danger by accepting staff "advice" uncritically
	accepted the advice	*rejected the advice*	
good	Tendency to accept staff advice is reinforced	Line manager is in serious trouble	
bad	Line can now blame staff for poor advice, and can pass the buck	Line can feel justified but may have made an organizational enemy	

If one looks at the matrix, it is clear that the line manager minimized danger by tending to accept the proffered advice. The more serious risks are assumed when line says NO. Behind this kind of calculation is the belief that staff groups such as Personnel may be more influential than they appear to be on the organization chart. They may find it easier to meet with, and influence, top management; and chains of command are usually shorter in staff groups.

Conflicting advice. Another reason advising is difficult is that the line manager may be receiving conflicting advice from diverse sources. We have simplified the case by implying that at one time and for one problem, only one adviser (the personnel officer) is involved. In fact, in the modern organization, expertise is distributed among many specialized groups. A given problem can call for knowledge of engineering, standards, methods, personnel, and finance. The boundary lines are never clear, and each group feels that it has the real answer to the difficulty. A manager may thus be deluged with helpers, many of whom are inclined to point out their associations with higher management in order to encourage the manager's adoption of a particular solution to the problem.

Strengthening the advisory relationship

Let us summarize the discussion to this point. The ideal adviser waits to be called, to provide help for the line manager when it is requested. Here, then, is a dilemma: the passive staff person may well be perceived as filling the advisory role but in the process may lose the department's budget and status. To make matters worse, if as a result of Personnel's not being called upon, managers make critical mistakes and perhaps cause a wildcat work stoppage, Personnel will share the blame with the same supervisors who did not ask for help and counsel. They can't escape by saying "My help wasn't asked."

Encouraging managers to seek help. A way out of this dilemma is to structure the situation so that managers want help. The existence of the control (i.e., audit) measures described in the next chapter can motivate managers to seek out Personnel for assistance in improving their performance.[2]

Personnel Manager: "Our knowledge of training was never used until top management asked for an annual report on what each department was doing to upgrade the skills of its employees. Within a week of learning that this report would be part of the annual performance review, we had eight requests from department heads to consult with them on training."

Building and maintaining a sound advisory relationship is not simply a matter of using control data to prove to line managers that they need help. Rather, this relationship requires carefully patterned give-and-take. Personnel staff must learn to work with managers in terms of their needs and problems. An example should make this requirement clear.

[2] Edward Gross, "Sources of Lateral Authority in Personnel Departments," *Industrial Relations*, 3, no. 3 (May 1964), 121–33.

The personnel department has noticed that turnover is very high in Chet Anthony's department. Chet's boss, the vice-president in charge of sales, urges the personnel director, Phillips, to do something to halt the loss of valuable personnel. What should the personnel director do? How should he approach Anthony?

What happens if he calls on Anthony to say that both he and the vice-president are worried about his high turnover rate? Chances are that Anthony will react this way:

"Here is someone representing the vice-president. Phillips carries the boss's authority. All right, what do they want me to do? If they're willing to put up the money for higher salaries or take the responsibility for putting in some new-fangled ideas, that's up to them; it's no skin off my teeth."

Clearly the battle is lost before it has begun, for Anthony has no intention of telling Phillips what his problems really are. From this point on, Anthony may cover up as much as possible and try to shift the blame for any future problems onto Personnel.

And if Phillips makes suggestions, Anthony may term them "too theoretical" or "impractical" or else accept them superficially (perhaps just to settle the issue), only to destroy them in practice through subtle sabotage. He may agree to introduce some technique of general supervision and even hold meetings with his subordinates and ask for their advice but continue to hold the threat of punishment over the head of anyone who does not immediately accept his point of view.

How, then, can the personnel director influence the department head without "pulling rank"? Primarily by persuading Anthony to regard him as a *source of help*. Anthony has certain objectives that he is trying to achieve. He may be anxious to establish a record that will earn him a promotion, or to win prestige in the eyes of his fellow managers, or to minimize the amount of administrative red tape. Phillips can exert influence by convincing Anthony that his skills and knowledge will help him reach his goals.

The staff expert must keep in mind that Anthony's way of handling his department has evolved over a long period of time in response to his own particular needs. For any real change to take place, Anthony must discover for himself that his behavior is inadequate to the situation, and he must be genuinely ready to accept help.

Phillips might start the discussion by commenting that he has noticed a rise in turnover in Anthony's department, and he thinks he should bring it to his attention. Then Anthony should be encouraged to speak freely about his reaction to the problem: its implications and possible causes. By not appearing to be a judge or critic, but by encouraging free expression, Phillips seeks to get Anthony to accept the existence of a supervisory problem needing solution.

Next, Phillips might encourage Anthony to consider the alternative solutions to the problem and the probable success of each. This is the most crucial point of all, for Anthony must work through for himself the ramifications of suggested changes. He must regard as his own any programs that are developed and must assume responsibility for implementing them. Anthony may have to make a presentation before his boss to get a new appropriation to assist in solving this problem. "Role-playing" (to be discussed in Chapter 16) could be used to try out various approaches to the boss. Such training, counseling, and try-outs should be designed not only to increase the line official's skill but also to bolster his confidence in himself. In effect, Phillips should try to use all his knowledge of individual needs and informal group behavior, of supervisory skills (such as interviewing and discipline), and of labor relations, to help the line supervisor make *his own* decision.

In this case, Anthony may decide that his own supervisors need a training program to improve their managerial skills. But he would prefer to have the whole program handled by the personnel department—after all, this is "out of his field" and personnel people are the experts. Phillips should be wary of such efforts to shift the responsibility to his department. Lacking responsibility for the program, Anthony would never be sure that it was exactly what he wanted; the supervisors participating in the program would not associate it with the "boss's" attitudes and desires.

Of course, Phillips must not be merely a passive listener. He must provide information and evaluations when asked—though only as a means to help Anthony make a realistic decision. He might reveal some of the dimensions of the problem by probing more deeply into the turnover statistics: Who is leaving—what age groups, from what occupational groups? How does turnover here compare with turnover in other departments? What are the possible causes: wages, supervision (including Anthony's), other factors in the work environment? Personnel, like any other specialist department, has analytical tools at its command—in this case, perhaps, a community salary survey or a review of department employment records.

Thus, a simple "yes" or "no" answer—a "do this" or "do that" response—by Personnel to line problems wastes an important opportunity. Research in learning suggests that training is more effective and individuals more highly motivated to learn when they have immediate problems they want to solve. The best time to help train a supervisor to make better decisions in the future is when there is an immediate problem.

In the process of working together on a variety of problems, Phillips can learn Anthony's attitudes toward his job and its problems. He also can present a picture of Personnel's role and position in the organization. He can make it clear that the goals of the personnel department are to help other groups and individuals help themselves to deal with their human-relations problems, and to provide specific skills and techniques when they are called for by the line managers.

Eventually with the passage of time, subsequent discussions with the personnel department should enable Anthony to handle his personnel problems by himself and to ask for help only when an especially difficult problem crops up. The end result should be a better-informed supervisor with considerable skill in applying to his day-to-day problems the knowledge developed by personnel experts.

Let us summarize the elements that seem to characterize a healthy advisory relationship:

1. The manager initiates the call to Personnel for help with problems, feeling free to discuss them with a sympathetic listener who is not in the line of authority.
2. The manager comes to understand the role and to utilize the skills embodied in the personnel group, and, in turn, the personnel staff grows familiar with the special interests and needs of the managerial group it services.
3. Personnel helps the manager to understand the dimensions and alternative solutions to problems and to develop skill in evaluating alternatives.
4. The manager learns how better to cope with human problems of the group and to regard those problems as means of developing new abilities and insights.
5. The personnel staff develops greater acceptance for its ideas and points of view not through putting pressure on the line manager to change "or else," but through developing confidence in the staff's "helping" role and through proving in practice that it can contribute to the supervisor's effectiveness.
6. The line organization receives credit for any improvements that result; staff helps implement line decisions.

You will have realized, of course, that we have been describing an ideal staff-line relationship, one that is difficult to achieve in practice. Good advisory staff work is, in fact, like education—it slowly takes effect after some critical mass of knowledge has been built up in the mind of the student. Thus, the adviser is concerned with the longer-run impact of "teaching."

It may appear unrealistic—politically and in terms of human nature—to conceive of managers being influential when they maintain a purely advisory or service role. Where does their power come from; where is their clout? The personnel specialist's skills and ideas are accepted when they clearly contribute to the line managers' attainment of objectives. The specialist's unique position is an avenue to good contacts throughout the organization—among various levels of management, with the union and other pressure groups—contacts that yield invaluable knowledge, and knowledge *is* power.

The modern personnel administrator seeks to influence the organization's policies, particularly as they relate to the treatment of its human resources. The ability to make such contributions requires that Personnel be alert to both external and internal changes that require new management responses. Thus, Personnel must be sensitive to line management and have wide-ranging relationship with it, in order to receive relevant information and maintain its acceptability.

Personnel is often listened to just because it does *not* exercise traditional authority, and the managers seeking aid with problems know they are not being ordered to do something. One highly effective adviser explained the difference most cogently:

"I've seen it happen many times. A manager is told to accept some new top management procedure or to work more closely with another manager, and the order gets sabotaged. There are a hundred ways you can 'prove' that what you're told to do is unworkable.

But just because I don't use threats or power, my ideas get a full hearing, and managers are often willing to try out new things I suggest because they know it's voluntary and they can stop any time they want."

Thus the personnel specialist becomes a trusted source of assistance and knowledge, someone with whom one can discuss problems openly—even admit errors and bad judgment—with the understanding that these problems and anxieties will not be used against anyone.

The typical line manager finds it exhilarating to work with a staff person who is there to help, not to indict or sell. Top managers are always asking "why" questions, which provoke defensiveness and withholding of information (e.g., "Why did you miss your target last month?"). The adviser asks "how" questions: How can turnover be reduced? What help do you need? Where do you think your most serious problems are? Such questions tap the knowledge and interests of the manager which, when combined with the staff person's insights and knowledge, often provide a number of attractive alternative courses of action.

Service relationships

Personnel departments also carry out service activities far removed from the day-to-day problems of other parts of the organization. Examples of this include the processing of claims and records relating to company welfare programs; the operation of company medical facilities, fire and plant-protection units, and reception desks; administering suggestion plans; and running cafeterias. Sometimes Personnel becomes almost a catchall for activities that don't fit elsewhere.

In performing a service activity, the staff department does something for the line department. Usually the relationship is quite amicable, for line departments have little interest or ability in these specialized areas and are glad to have staff relieve them of what they feel are headaches. The division manager may be glad to have Personnel handle the writing of job descriptions or recruiting, testing, and training programs.

Line asks for too many services.

Even a service relationship can generate frictions. At times, line management requests services that staff believes are unnecessary, ill-advised, or should be handled by the line. A line department may ask the personnel department to run a training program for first-line supervisors, even though the personnel department is convinced that such a program will be useless until higher management itself participates in it. A manager may pass the buck to the personnel department in the handling of a ticklish disciplinary problem. Or the general manager may ask the already overburdened personnel director to edit a new company newspaper.

Some of the services requested may appear wasteful. A training program is not always the answer to employee-relations problems.

The personnel manager at the Fillerton Mines was in a quandary concerning the division manager's request for a new safety program. The accident rate had climbed seriously, and the manager wanted Personnel to purchase an expensive bulletin-board poster series stressing safety, as well as a supervisory film series. Personnel, for its part, felt that the real problem stemmed from line management's having given safety too low a priority—as against production and labor cost considerations. Personnel believed that safety had to be accepted as a line management responsibility. To accomplish this required direct communication between top management and lower levels of line management and a conviction that managers would be evaluated in terms of their safety performance. Films and posters would just give the appearance of doing something without getting to the heart of the problem.

The amount of time required to provide services can be substantial and the administrative requirements demanding. Often skilled professionals are diverted from more important work. A typical frustrating example is company food services, always a fruitful source of complaint. There is some trend toward contracting out such functions on the grounds that a specialized outsider can do them more efficiently and with less drain on in-company administrative resources.

In every organization there is the danger that staff enthusiasms outrun practicalities. Many times these enthusiasms take the form of keeping up with the Joneses: seeing what other companies are doing in special personnel services and trying to duplicate or imitate these, regardless of whether there is any real need for these services.

A division personnel manager came to one of the authors asking for assistance in developing a sensitivity training program [see Chapter 16] for division management. Why? Because the organization's top executive had just attended such a program and felt it had been extremely useful. Counterparts from a number of well-known corporations described their growing use of this management development technique, convincing the top executive that the technique should be spread rapidly throughout the organization. The personnel manager had considerable doubts about the value of such training in this particular division at this particular time, but felt that under the circumstances there was no alternative.

Personnel staff should try to persuade line departments not to request unnecessary services. In the last analysis, however, staff may have to provide such services if the line authority insists—at least, if line is willing to pay for them out of its budget.

Conflicts over scarce services. When line's demand for services becomes too great, staff must ration its limited time and energies among rival claimants. Department A wants Personnel to devote more of its efforts to recruiting engineers; department B thinks Personnel should concentrate on finding better accountants. The staff department must show great tact in setting priorities; for every time it turns down one department's request for services, it hurts its advisory relationship with that department. Preferably, top management establishes standards for these priorities.

Line resists staff performance of services. In contrast to the previous example, some line departments, imbued with the do-it-yourself philosophy, object to having staff perform certain services. Thus, the engineering department may feel that it should recruit its own engineers, since "personnel usually doesn't know what makes a good engineer tick." Certainly when the line department has direct control over a service, it does not have to compete with other departments for scarce resources. Furthermore, line may feel that staff does not understand its special needs. Often, too, line supervisors are suspicious that Personnel wants to take over a service in order to increase its own importance and the size of its budget and its staff.

As in the case of stabilization activities, the line can be very critical of staff service activities that seem unduly complex, making work for its own sake—just red tape:

"Rather than preparing a page of useful information for the person in the job, Personnel sends up a job analyst who interviews everyone in sight, types up a dozen complicated forms, and then issues a formal job description that no one will ever look at, once it is filed away. Those people are following some textbook procedure to the letter: the whole activity accomplishes nothing."

Line's resistance is intensified if management charges the cost of the new service against the line department's budget [3] or if it requires line managers to spend time and energy on the new activity.

We once watched the difficulties encountered by the personnel department in one company when it attempted to introduce a new management-development program, which line officials tried to sabotage. In another company, however, an almost identical program was welcomed by line managers. Why the difference?

In the second company, the firm's president had indicated that one of the new *controls* he would begin watching was the number of promotable executives produced by each department. Line managers asked the personnel department to *help them* create management-development programs. In the first company, the initiative had come exclusively from Personnel.

In short, line managers welcome staff activities that promise to help them achieve their own goals and resist those that do not seem intimately related to their needs.

Personnel initiates programs. Personnel departments sometimes find themselves engaged in service activities that they feel should really be handled by line simply because line refuses to accept responsibility for them. At other times, staff throws its energies into service activities seemingly as a compensation for its failure to develop satisfactory advisory relationships with line. One personnel director told us:

"I handle grievances myself. I know you professors think this is wrong—it detracts from the supervisor's prestige and so forth. But I can't trust them to handle grievances properly—every time I let them try, I get into trouble. I've tried training programs, but I can't get them to change their ways. Someday our present supervisors will retire, and I'll let the new people handle the responsibility. But for the moment I can't risk ruining my union relations just to back up a theory."

---

[3] It is common accounting practice to prorate the cost of service programs to all line departments according to some criterion like number of employees or gross sales.

Staff often retreats into rendering service to line management, because their working relations need not be as close for service as for advice. A safety director may have tried in vain to get supervisors to attend a safety course or to induce them to discipline employees who engage in unsafe practices. In despair, the safety director resorts to a poster campaign—not because safety posters can compete with a supervisor's order in changing employee behavior, but because no one will object to posters and at least something will be achieved, and there will be something in the way of "activity" to show management.

Relations with line departments. Realistically, few functions can be divided up neatly between people or even departments, and overlap is inevitable. Thus, much of Personnel's service work has to be integrated closely with other on-going activities of line management. The success or usefulness of the service will depend upon how well the various groups who contribute are able to adapt their own requirements and procedures to the needs of other elements in the work flow.

The advent of computers has provided Personnel with a major new tool to conduct its service activities with more efficiency and the ability to consider a broader range of activities. Once employee records are computerized, many research tasks are facilitated in areas such as test validation and affirmative action. In addition to research, computers facilitate the making of selection decisions; it becomes simple to print out the names of those employees whose backgrounds indicate some special skills (e.g., foreign language facility or knowledge of biochemistry). A greater range of employee fringe benefit plans can be administered with computerized records than would be possible with traditional record-keeping methods. Alternative cost-benefit calculations for planning purposes are speeded, and the range of possibilities can be stretched.

Personnel research

Large companies, in particular, use research to supplement their personnel services. Research involves the conduct of studies and, in some cases, experiments to evaluate the usefulness and validity of existing or proposed company practices. The kind of research undertaken extends from rather simple descriptive studies to problem-solving assignments, to sophisticated planning and assessment programs.

Large organizations in recent years have shown increasing interest in studying employee motivation and evaluating the effectiveness of alternative personnel methods. AT&T has undertaken studies that explore the impact of job enrichment on employee motivation. General Electric has attempted to develop better employee appraisal and communications techniques that will not cause resentment but will encourage work improvements. Texas Instruments has researched the impact of differences of leadership style and training techniques on productivity.

Similar work has been done on the government level. The armed services and the United States Civil Service Commission have sponsored extensive research on personnel selection techniques. During the mid-1960s, both the City of Berkeley (California) and the New York Port Authority engaged in pioneering studies to assess whether testing discriminated against minority groups. Only very large organizations, of course, are likely to be in a position to afford qualified behavioral scientists such as social psychologists, human factor specialists, psychometricians, and sociologists, among other social scientists.[4] Designing surveys, experimental methodology, and field interviews all require extensive specialized training. Poorly conducted research can produce highly misleading or meaningless data.

It is thus not surprising that relatively few business organizations have behaviorally oriented personnel research staffs. Most of the studies have been conducted by a small number of well-known firms: AT&T, Sears, IBM, General Electric, Exxon, and Texas Instruments, for example, and the total quantity of research is quite small.[5] Even these firms sometimes find it difficult to win acceptance for the research function, which appears too academic and too removed from the company's immediate needs.[6] When immediate and unambiguous answers to problems are not forthcoming, the line is likely to accuse personnel research of doing things that are satisfying professionally but do not pay their way. The research function can also threaten other groups within the personnel department who fear that research may uncover their own inefficiencies.

Problem solving. Personnel research can also compare the effects of alternative programs. Careful research (involving a comparison of on-the-job performance and test scores) is needed to assess the validity of employee selection tests. Research can also identify who needs or will profit most from training. Similarly, management may note that departments differ in turnover or safety or grievances, and a study of these records may assist in uncovering some of the underlying causes.

Planning. Research may also be undertaken to help shape future policy. For example, a wide variety of fringe benefits is available—vacations, pensions, insurance, and the like—and all are costly. For any given expenditure level of fringe benefit monies, which particular package of benefits will best meet organization and employee needs? The answer to this question may vary considerably from organization to organization; and before an intelligent decision can be made, considerable research may be necessary—perhaps a survey of

---

[4] Human factor specialists are concerned with the design of instruments and the physical conditions of work to allow for maximum utilization of employee sensory functions. Psychometricians construct and evaluate testing procedures.

[5] A classic summary of the field of personnel research is provided by William Byham, *The Uses of Personnel Research*, AMA Research Study 91 (New York: American Management Association, 1968).

[6] Well-established internal research groups are also able to develop productive relationships with university-based research teams. However, behavioral scientists sometimes speak a special language; the company-based behavioral scientists will be in a better position to shape the focus of the study, understand its limitations, and communicate the findings to line management.

employee preferences as well as a careful analysis of the probable costs of alternative benefit packages.

There is little question that Personnel should be research-oriented. Few man-power problems have obvious answers; often the definition of the problem itself is unclear. Rather than responding with overquick answers, personnel administrators need to help the organization to comprehend the basic human and technical factors that shape human behavior. At a simple level, even descriptive studies help (i.e., what has happened or where are we?); larger organizations can afford more elaborate research.

Conclusion

Ideally, Personnel should be a lobbyist favoring managerial attention to human problems. Just as Finance emphasizes cost and margins and Marketing stresses the customer, Personnel is people-centered. Success here will depend on the degree to which it is perceived as making hardheaded, realistic contributions to the solution of management problems.

The nature of the personnel function, however, is often confusing and ambiguous. Personnel people engage in high- and low-status activities at the same time; they serve as expert advisers to the president, and they operate the cafeteria. Thus personnel work has had and continues to have status problems. Its historical association with social work and record keeping, its frequent responsibilities for a miscellaneous collection of peripheral activities, and the fact that shortsighted top managements often transfer less than successful executives to "safe" personnel positions—all tend to diminish its status. Further, Personnel deals with complex and recalcitrant materials. Figures and products are relatively manipulable; they "stay put," and there are reliable, workable theories that explain how they can be put to appropriate use. Despite much social research, the behavior of human beings is less predictable. Nevertheless, few companies fail to recognize that the effective management of human resources is a crucial factor in organizational success. Insofar as personnel managers prove themselves effective in contributing to this objective, their status and influence are assured.

Although personnel work is a separate specialty, it is also at the heart of every manager's job. Close coordination must exist between Personnel and other organizational functions, and a delicate balance must be kept between those aspects of Personnel that should be handled by the line manager and those that should be handled by the staff specialist. Successful personnel executives gain the confidence and respect of colleagues in other departments and persuade them that Personnel wants to help them with *their* problems and *their* objectives. Personnel's techniques are shown to be useful and valid; its objectives are not to embarrass or show up other departments. But Personnel is certain to run into trouble if it claims credit for constant victories or is too concerned with status.

Personnel people should be especially careful to avoid touting fads and cure-alls. They should stress that no single program or procedure will alone (or even in combination) solve all organizational problems. Indeed, personnel people, above all, should be constantly aware of the interrelatedness of all aspects of the overall *personnel system* and should educate line management to accept the concept that only an *integrated* series of activities is likely to lead to lasting improvement in organizational effectiveness.

Staff-line relationships become critical because policies are only as good as their administration. Further, most human problems that arise are not precisely answered by policy prescriptions. As a general once said, "Regrettably, the most important battles are always fought where the map is creased." We also need some way of distinguishing the different types of staff-line relationships, the ways in which Personnel relates to other members of the organization. Naive managers think they work only with their subordinates; in reality, the modern organization requires managers to work laterally (with their peers) as much as, or more than, up and down the chain of command. Personnel, particularly, is involved in a welter of lateral relationships. We have discussed two such relationships, advisory and service. The next chapter will explore still others.

problems

1 · *Encountering Enthusiasm*

Calvin Fressi has been transferred from corporate staff to the position of division personnel manager, reporting to Hank Wilson, division manager. Wilson is a tough, skeptical manager who resents his own boss, distrusts Personnel, and rules by fear and tantrum. He has vetoed nearly every suggestion that might improve the human relations climate of the division, and Fressi has despaired of any improvement.

Recently, Wilson attended a management seminar conducted by a nearby university where he saw a demonstration of a new training method that involved small group "encounter" sessions. He came back ecstatic and told Fressi he wanted his managers (but not himself) to be put through this as quickly as consultants and trainers could be hired. Fressi was dubious. First, the real problems involved Wilson's own behavior, and Wilson wasn't buying any changes there. The program would cost a good deal that could be invested in some things

with more immediate payoff, with even less cost. Wilson just wanted to get on the band wagon, perhaps to show top management he was doing something in the personnel area. Further, assuming there was no payoff, this experience (whether a failure or success) would also give Wilson some ammunition to complain more loudly (as he had in the past) about personnel staff charges to his payroll.

On the other hand, Wilson had asked him to do this, really the first thing he had been asked to do. He obviously really wanted it and had been impressed with what he had seen at the university. What if the program was wasteful or fruitless? Might it not improve their own relationship? But suppose it was successful and the meetings helped to build unity in what was now a loosely knit group of supervisors? Their new unit might express itself in strong anti-Wilson activities, and then what?

1. Is cost effectiveness analysis relevant here?
2. What should Fressi do?

2 · *A Case for Role-Playing: Dealing with a Supervisor Accused of Discrimination*

Role for Personnel Director. You are convinced that the supervisor of the hospital kitchen staff is discriminating among employees. There is now a union grievance on your desk charging that the supervisor has failed to equalize overtime in the department as required in the contract. Two women were passed over for Friday night work that involved an extra 4 hours (or pay for 6 hours), which amounts to about $20 in lost wages for each woman, Ms. Smith and Ms. Jenkins.

The supervisor claims to have asked the women on Friday whether they would like to work overtime and they said they wanted to get an early start for a weekend trip. The union claims that the supervisor purposely waited until late Friday before announcing the opportunity in order to discriminate against these particular women. In the past, the supervisor has indicated dissatisfaction with their work and attitudes.

In playing the role of personnel director, have clearly in mind the objectives you want to accomplish through your discussion with the supervisor.

Role for the Supervisor. You have been pressed to cut costs. Your department is a sort of graveyard to which women who have failed elsewhere are transferred. You don't like to admit this, however, because it lowers your prestige. (In fact, you yourself may have been put in this department for the same reason.) Where possible, you try to give the women who do accomplish something a little extra break, feeling that it is the only way to encourage them, since all jobs pay the same. The work is unpleasant, though relatively easy and not fatiguing. The two worst shirkers are Ms. Smith and Ms. Jenkins. They are always baiting you, and you are pretty sure they are telling other people in the department false things about you behind your back.

You did wait until late in the day, hoping that they would refuse. You don't see how you can face them if they win the grievance and get back pay. You feel that would destroy any chance of improving the morale and efficiency of your department.

1. Role-play the personnel director's interview with the supervisor.
2. Assuming that the personnel director has an unsuccessful interview with the supervisor, what should the director's next move be?

Personnel's control functions

The preceding chapter examined Personnel's problem-solving and service roles in helping other organizational units do their work more effectively. But as we noted, Personnel is not just a benevolent helper; like other staff groups, it is often assigned authority-laden control roles that line managers may view as restrictive.

This chapter will consider two control roles: *auditing* and *stabilization*. Auditing involves checking on performance *after* action is taken, as in compiling accident data for submission to top management. Stabilization involves the authority to require staff approval *before* taking action, as in requiring Personnel's authorization before granting salary increases. Auditing is part of the feedback loop that helps the organization evaluate its performance; stabilization is a technique to obtain better supervisory decisions that will properly reflect the various values and objectives sought by the organization.

Why are such functions assigned to staff departments like Personnel? Largely because every organization is trying to meet a number of potentially conflicting goals at once: a company may be trying (a) to reach a high output for a new product, (b) at low cost, (c) with a minimum of accidents, and (d) without instigating strikes. In theory, the line manager should take all these goals into account at once. Daily on-the-job pressures, however, demand attention to only one or two problems, usually maintaining

production or cutting costs. Other problems (union relations, for instance) may appear to be less critical at the moment and possible to ignore. Thus it is the staff department's function to keep watch over these seemingly secondary areas and to ensure that all the organization's goals are kept in appropriate balance, either through refusing advance approval (stabilization) or by reporting errors after the fact (auditing).

The auditing role

Auditing (or control or monitoring, as it can be called) fulfills several important management objectives:

1. It helps top management evaluate how well its policies as a whole are working.
2. It identifies trouble spots—specific areas that require special attention.
3. It keeps subordinates alert to what is expected of them; it stimulates them to pay particular attention to those areas assigned highest priority by top management.

It is easy to promulgate policies, difficult to ensure their execution. The promulgation of progressive policies—for example, nondiscriminatory hiring and promotion on the basis of merit—is not enough. Such policies are rarely self-enforcing, and some sort of auditing (checking up) is required to ensure that they are implemented on a uniform basis.

Asking questions on a regular basis

But why should Personnel be the department to do this? Isn't it top management's function to make such checkups? Yes, it is; but top management, often engrossed in handling immediate problems, rarely has the time to carry out this function unaided. As a consequence, standards gradually erode, resulting in serious long-run damage.

The Stockton Hospital was experiencing a nursing shortage, and nurses were being asked to work extensive overtime in violation of a policy limiting overtime usage. As the weeks passed, however, fatigue took its toll, and absenteeism and tardiness began to increase. Yet, when overtime was reduced in one ward, several nurses complained that their pay was being cut and asked to be transferred to another ward, where high overtime still prevailed.

Here, an expedient solution to a temporary problem created long-term difficulties. Sometimes the deterioration of standards is so gradual that it is difficult to observe without meticulous monitoring.

The Keller Company proudly stated that all promotions were to be based on capability, irrespective of length of service. But a vigorous union and the absence of consistent top-management support frequently encouraged supervisors to promote the most senior employee because "it was less trouble that way." This tendency increased, until a recent survey detected that 84 percent of all promotions went to the most senior employees. Clearly, merit and ability were no longer significant factors.

Line management often defers action until a serious crisis occurs (for example, the government threatens to cancel a critical contract because minorities are being promoted too slowly). Thus, a staff group like Personnel, which has the technical resources and the perspective to ask indelicate and potentially embarrassing questions on a *regular basis,* performs a very important function. Regular audits make it possible to detect significant trends *before* they become crises (when problem solving is much more difficult). In addition, regular audits make the whole control process less threatening. When management steps in during a real crisis, tempers are short, executives are under stress, and everyone is likely to be fearful and resentful.

Measuring organizational health

Increasingly, personnel departments are being called upon to audit or appraise the overall effectiveness of an organization's human resource utilization and to provide what have been called "social indicators" of organizational health—for example, turnover rates. We shall discuss some of these indicators below. But another concept of health is simply the commitment to self-renewal. That is, the healthy organization is one which is able to develop the latent capacities of all its employees and provide career and promotional opportunities to fulfill their ambitions for rewarding positions. Relevant here, as measures, would be the amount of manpower development, the percentage of employees who avail themselves of voluntary educational programs, and changes in the skill levels and kinds of skills in the employee's repertoire over time. (This concept of organizational health is closely related to the political scientist's view of democracy: a social system that enables people to develop and express themselves to the fullest extent possible.)

Performance standards

Managers expect to be held to standards of accountability, and most managers prefer to have these established unambiguously, so they know where to direct their energies.[1] In effect, the standard establishes a target, and at the end of the target period (week, month, or year) both manager and boss can compare the expected standard of performance with the actual level of achievement. Shortfalls, if any, are a signal for investigation and remedial action. In the manpower area, managers may have standards for objectives such as hiring minority employees, training, labor productivity, and overtime utilization.

Policy execution

Personnel also gets involved in auditing some of the less quantifiable aspects of the manager's job, particularly those aspects which have been the subject of top-management policy pronouncements. To meet management's objective of paying its employees the going rate, Personnel must regularly compare in-company pay scales with wages paid by other companies. Similarly, when top management decides that women are to receive equal consideration for promotions into management, implementation by skeptical managers will depend on continued surveilance of the career lines and frequency of promotion of women compared with men who have equivalent training and experience.

[1] Although performance standards are a traditional management tool, their extension to a greater number of areas under the control of the supervisor—beyond the typical cost accounting categories and with more subordinate participation—is often termed Management by Objectives. MBO is assessed in more detail in Chapter 15.

Universities often have a policy requiring professors who receive sabbatical leaves to use that period of time to do meaningful research, not simply to earn extra money. Otherwise, unmonitored sabbaticals may come to be used simply to take another teaching or consulting job. Company policy may encourage managers to provide employees reasonable time off with pay to participate in community service activities such as membership on a YMCA board or participation in a Community Chest drive. It is easy to understand why this policy needs to be monitored: everyday time and cost pressures may induce the busy manager to reject requests from subordinates for time off to work on community activities that interfere with the employee's immediate job.

Often management wants a more sophisticated audit of whether its policies are both sensible and effective. In this case, rather than simply asking whether policies are being followed, management asks whether the policies are really achieving results consistent with their costs.

Cost-benefit comparisons

Budgets provide a good example of why this is needed. Rarely are budgets developed from scratch on the basis of the actual need for various functions. Most budgets are incremental; i.e., the executives who draw them up assume that the coming year's allocations will likely be a percentage above (or infrequently a modest cut below) the previous year's figure. Increasingly, however, management is asking: How does unit performance compare with costs, and where can funds be shifted to obtain improved performance? The technique is called cost-benefit analysis.

Even the personnel department itself now must prove the value of its activities in economic terms. In the past, when every organization wanted to keep up with the newest techniques and programs being used by other organizations, it was adequate to say, "We need this because the All-American Company has installed the same program." Now continuous scrutiny is required to ascertain (1) whether the resources going into any given program are producing results of greater value than their costs, and (2) whether the resources used in one program could produce more for the organization if all or part of them were redirected to other programs.

Obviously, the more money spent on recruitment, the better the candidates the organization can consider. But the real question is whether an extra expediture on recruitment will be more productive than an equivalent sum used for training. Put more succinctly, Personnel must determine what *combination* of training and recruitment is likely to give the organization the highest return *per dollar spent.* Budgets must be regularly scrutinized to test whether possible reallocations of funds might produce greater returns to the organization.[2] As economists would say, the personnel manager must be alert to "marginal" and "opportunity cost" considerations. Thus the personnel manager must constantly ask questions such as these:

What would happen if 20 percent of what we now spend on new employee orientation was shifted to more on-the-job training? What would have to be cut out? What would we lose by these omissions? What would these funds buy us in the way of other benefits?

[2] Peter Pyhrr, *Zero-Base Budgeting* (New York: Wiley, 1972).

Ideally, no expenditure should be made unless it increases the value of human assets by at least an equal amount. The trend toward human resource accounting described in Chapter 1 is an effort to formalize and quantify these cost-benefit concerns.

Examples of cost-benefit analysis. When done effectively, cost-benefit analysis becomes a systems approach to personnel management, as the following example demonstrates.

The Phelps Company had long been proud of its "no layoff" policy, which simply meant that the company endeavored to guarantee that no employee who was performing adequately would lose his or her job because of lack of work. But recently the manufacturing vice-president has become quite concerned that labor costs soar during periods when demand for the company's product declines. In a recent executive committee meeting, she confronted the president with the demand that "We should be just like other companies: when there isn't enough work to go around, we lay off employees." After a vigorous debate on the usefulness of the policy, the president asked Personnel to evaluate how well the policy is working: "Is it worth what it costs us?"

A simple presystems approach to evaluation would be for Personnel to inquire what comparable companies were doing in this area. But clearly, the policies of other companies may be mistaken—or their situations may be different. Alternatively, Personnel might compare the costs of retaining employees who were not needed and the monetary value of the morale boost provided by job security. However, if Personnel is alert to the broader systems view of its responsibilities, it will investigate *all* the ramifications of the policy in question.

At the outset, of course, one benefit of not changing the policy is that the change itself could be traumatic; employees have grown used to the present system and might deeply resent *any* change. But other important benefit factors also need to be considered:

1. The organization must train its employees broadly, so that they can assume other duties when their particular jobs are surplus. (This is both a cost and a benefit.)

2. At present, employees willingly accept transfers, temporary assignments, changed jobs, and a changing mix of job duties, believing that such flexibility will not mean reduced job security. (Employees in other companies often resist such changes in the belief that this is management's way of reducing the total number of jobs and that layoffs will result eventually, if not immediately.)

3. Managers exert care in hiring, since they know they are making a long-term commitment to new employees.

4. The assurance of job security deters some good employees from quitting, even for higher wages.

5. Unemployment compensation payments are lower.

6. Reduced turnover greatly lessens the cost of the paperwork associated with administering layoffs and recalls and, of course, the more substantial costs of new hires.

On the cost side, however, management may find these negative elements:

1. There are substantial payroll costs associated with the periodic need to place surplus employees on make-work activities.

2. During such "surplus" periods, managers become accustomed to lower output levels and looser work standards, since the organization is out to save jobs, not increase efficiency. This general looseness may carry over to more normal periods.

3. Employees enjoy a form of tenure, which can mean that the organization will be burdened with a work force having skills and interests that cannot be applied to new products and new technologies. It may be more difficult to adjust the skill/training mix of the work force to new requirements.

Thus, the "no layoff" policy has ramifications for hiring, training, transfer, and even salary policies and practices. Obviously the organization cannot give precise quantitative assessments for each of these dimensions. Personnel, however, can perform the critical function of alerting top management to the broad range of human resource implications of the policy in question.

The example of a cost-benefit technique developed by the Xerox Corporation and reproduced on p. 50 illustrates the costs and benefits of a proposed job enrichment program for field service employees who install and maintain equipment in customer offices.

Types of personnel measures

It is tempting to assume that the manager can quite easily measure the cost or effectiveness of some new program. For example, if management is considering installing job enrichment, the decision could be based on comparing morale and productivity on "enriched" jobs with those in more traditionally designed jobs. Unfortunately, such direct measures may often not be available; and when they are, the data may not be comparable. Productivity is itself difficult to measure. The quantity of tooling, supervision, and materials may differ between the two groups.

Therefore, in attempting to assess various personnel policies and programs, management often settles for indirect measures. Such measures have one element in common: They are all substitutes for direct observation of how well things are going. Usually it is assumed that the state of human relations in the organization will be reflected in how employees respond to attitude surveys or that employee dissatisfaction will be indicated through grievances and turnover. These measures will also reflect the quality of supervision and training and the effectiveness of various personnel programs designed to increase identification with the firm and its management.

We shall describe four personnel measures. The first two—*absenteeism* and *turnover* data—are among the widely used yardsticks of organizational health and themselves are symptomatic of a variety of personnel problems. Personnel watches absenteeism and turnover data closely not only because both are expensive in themselves, but because they may be symptoms of deeper problems, particularly employee discontent. An employee who dislikes a job or a boss is far more likely to use a slight cold or a dentist's appointment as

Analysis of proposed job enrichment program	*Costs and benefits*	*Potential revenue impact*	*Probability of occurrence*	*Probable gross benefit (cost)*
	Identifiable benefits			
	Reduction in service force turnover of 1 point	$ 450,000	.2	$ 90,000
	Extension of 1.2 point reduction in absenteeism, as demonstrated in pilot project	2,132,500	.8	1,706,000
	Extension of 5% increase in service force productivity, as demonstrated in initial efforts	85,500,000	.1	8,550,000
	Total benefits	**$88,082,500**	**.12**	**$10,346,000**
	Tangible costs to Xerox of acting			
	Group personnel staff time to develop program, and line management time to implement program in all branches	(472,950)	.9	425,655
	Total costs	**($ 472,950)**	**.9**	**$ 425,655**
	Probable net benefits			**$ 9,920,345**

Intangible benefits

Increased morale in service force, with improved customer service and satisfaction.

"Contagious effect" of job enrichment to other groups; e.g., sales and clericals.

Improved service manager development with concurrent sharpening of their motivational skills. As an extreme example, one manager at Avon Hills increased his team's productivity 70%.

Economic risks

Continued escalation of service costs as a percent of revenue.

Assumptions and other considerations

Cost estimates assume 4.4 man years of group staff time, .26 man years of branch manager time, and 15.8 man years of service manager time to implement program in a population of 1,053 service managers.

Benefit estimates assume elimination of 3 days absenteeism per month for each of 1,053 service teams, favorable productivity, and that turnover experience in pilot branches can be cascaded to all branches.

Source: Logan M. Cheek, "Cost Effectiveness for Personnel," *Harvard Business Review,* 51, no. 3 (May–June 1973), 99.

an excuse for taking a day off. If the sense of alienation is great enough (and the unemployment rate in the community is not too high), the employee will quit altogether.

Two other personnel measures will also be discussed. Employee *attitude surveys* are conducted primarily for audit purposes. More *unobtrusive measures* of organizational health are provided by the routine operations of the organization itself. Examples of these include data such as scrap records, number and kind of accidents, and the like. We shall discuss these various indices in turn.

Absenteeism

Absenteeism reflects legitimately excused time off from work (illness and injury, for example) as well as disinterest and low morale—say the preference to go hunting rather than to go to work. Often it is difficult to evaluate excuses. Most personnel offices can make distinctions by observing the frequency of absence and whether it correlates with good weather, holiday seasons, and weekends. Mondays and Fridays are typically "bad" days.[3] Although most absenteeism data do not distinguish between voluntary (avoidable) and involuntary (unavoidable) absence from work, the Bureau of Labor Statistics compiles some survey data that make this distinction.[4]

There have been efforts to relate absenteeism to characteristics of employees or the economy. It has been assumed that workers are more likely to be absent during periods of high employment (less fear about losing the job) and that younger workers are more absence prone. The data do not support this. Absenteeism is predictably higher in industries where the workweek is long [5] and where work groups are large or amorphous.

Turnover

Turnover is a measure of change in the work force. This figure can be affected by new hiring, by layoffs, and by voluntary resignations. To a management concerned with auditing organizational health, voluntary resignations are obviously most critical.

Data is collected monthly by the U.S. Bureau of Labor Statistics on four elements of turnover: new hires and recalls (in combination called accessions) and quits and layoffs (called separations). Since the data is collected by industry, one can quickly observe the impact of the general level of wages on the highly sensitive quit rates, or voluntary departures.[6] In the table, note the marked differences in quit rates for the high-wage chemical, petroleum, and transportation equipment (heavily auto manufacturing) compared to low-paying wood and food processing.

We expect to find turnover increasing when the labor market is tight,

[3] Bureau of National Affairs, Personnel Policies Forum, *Absenteeism and Its Control*, Survey No. 90 (Washington, D.C.: June 1970).

[4] Early data are summarized in Janice Hedges, "Absence from Work—A Look at Some National Data," *Monthly Labor Review*, 96, no. 7 (July 1973), 24–30.

[5] Robert Flanagan, George Strauss, and Lloyd Ulman, "Work Discontent and Work Place Behavior," *Industrial Relations*, 13, no. 2 (May 1974), 101–23.

[6] Turnover rates are calculated by firm or industry for a given calendar period using the formula:

$$\frac{\text{Total number of quits (or layoffs or hires)}}{\text{Average number of employees on payroll}} \times 100$$

Labor turnover rates (quit rates) in selected manufacturing industry groups (August 1979)	Industry group	Quit rate
	Lumber and wood products	5.5
	Food and kindred products	5.6
	Chemical and allied products	1.9
	Petroleum and coal products	1.7
	Transportation equipment	1.7

when there are lots of jobs and relatively few unemployed. Employees' true feelings come to the surface when alternative opportunities are readily available.

One study suggests that turnover among nonmanagerial employees is likely to reflect outside influences such as health, family pressures, or transportation difficulties, whereas managerial and professional turnover may be more indicative of job and pay dissatisfactions. Turnover tends to be higher in organizations that are larger, have longer workweeks, utilize incentive plans, and have high absenteeism. Similarly, turnover tends to be lower when there is relatively high unemployment, when workers are more experienced, and when workers are older.[7]

One must be careful not to assume that turnover (meaning both voluntary quits and layoffs) is always a bad thing. Organizations have to adjust their work forces to changes in the demand for their products and services. Further, in most large, dynamic organizations, it is reasonable to assume that some employees or their bosses will discover that their talents and interests are not compatible with the job opportunities. Under such circumstances, the selecting-out process contributes to the long-run welfare of both the individual and the organization. Disgruntled employees can contaminate their work groups. On the other hand, turnover is expensive, and excessive turnover is very wasteful of hiring and training procedures. When an unskilled worker quits, it may cost the firm $1,500 (to cover what it has already invested in employment and training and what it will cost to acquire and train a replacement). Skilled employees and managers can each represent tens of thousands of dollars in training and replacement costs. Avoidance of turnover has been a major impetus to the development of so-called fringe benefits, which reward the long-service employee with longer vacations and the promise of a substantial pension, among other benefits (see Chapter 18).

How management reacts to turnover depends upon the business cycle. When business is booming and the labor market is tight, competent new employees are hard to recruit. Under these conditions, managers become reluctant to discharge marginal employees whose work barely gets by. This reluctance may disappear when economic conditions get worse and these marginal workers are no longer needed.

[7] See James Price, *The Study of Turnover* (Ames, Iowa: Iowa State Press, 1977).

Looking at turnover and absenteeism helps us understand why comparative data are generally more useful than simple totals. We know that turnover is influenced by factors other than the health of the organization. Large organizations may pay higher wages, and higher-paid employees probably have lower turnover. Often, organizations in urban areas suffer more turnover than do those in more rural settings, and periods of high employment and intense competition for labor understandably increase the frequency with which employees change jobs. Quit rates are relatively high in construction and low in government. They are higher among young workers than older ones. Thus if management simply knows the turnover rate for a given unit of the organization, this doesn't provide much real information for control purposes until the rate is evaluated in the light of whatever the relevant comparisons may be.

Attitude surveys

When most of us think about an attitude survey, we probably think of the pollster ringing the doorbell and asking us our opinion about the next election or our preference in brands of toothpaste. Related techniques are used to determine how employees feel about their jobs and organizations.

Attitude surveys can be conducted in a number of ways. Survey techniques are a profession in themselves and require specialized technical knowledge. Psychologists in universities, management consulting firms, and some company personnel research divisions have grown highly skilled in the preparation of questions, in methods of administration, and in evaluation of the results. Some companies purchase survey questionnaires developed by firms specializing in such services. One of the best known is the SRA Employee Inventory, distributed by Science Research Associates. The Survey Research Center of the University of Michigan and the Opinion Research Corporation have also achieved nationwide reputations for the development of attitude surveys.

Large multiunit organizations that use a common survey instrument can compare the "morale" scores of their various components. Somewhat the same type of comparison can be provided by national survey firms that analyze data by type of industry or size of organization. Some polling instruments make use of single-item questionnaires such as "On the whole, how do you feel about your job?" (very satisfied, satisfied, dissatisfied, very dissatisfied). For other purposes it may be better to ask a battery of questions that probe attitudes toward specific aspects of work.

The responses to a question such as "How satisfied are you with your pay?" may be more ambiguous than may first appear, and thus it takes substantial skill to interpret the data produced. If the respondent answers "satisfied," he or she may be thinking of the total earnings package including overtime and a profit-sharing bonus, or just the hourly wage rate. A "satisfied" answer may also mean that although the money is not very satisfactory in terms of what it will buy, the employee feels lucky to be earning more than the person across the aisle who seems to have a much dirtier, heavier job, yet earns less. Similarly, a "dissatisfied" answer might mean that the person just can't keep up with the rising cost of living, even though he or she feels the company is being fair. Negative responses also may refer to inequities in earnings between employees or just to the fact that earnings have not *increased* over the years the person has been with the company.

The simple total of the number of satisfied or dissatisfied workers thus tells the management very little, even about the relative seriousness of the problem they may have in the wage area. An employee's relations to the company will obviously be affected differently by dissatisfactions, depending on whether the source of the dissatisfaction is the outside community or a company practice.

Other forms of questions may invite employees to choose among various alternatives:

The following items describe different conditions that may be bothering you in your work. Check the ones that need to be improved:

Ventilation	( )	Unpleasant noise	( )
Lighting	( )	Faulty or unsafe equipment	( )
Temperature	( )	Dirty work station	( )
Air cleanliness	( )	Other _____	( )

Some surveys try to elicit more detailed (and perhaps deeper) answers through so-called open-ended questions, such as "What would you say are your most serious dissatisfactions with your present job?" A modification of this technique is the sentence-completion procedure, in which the respondent is requested to complete sentences like "The most serious complaint I have about my present job is _____." These and other more sophisticated forms of survey are far more expensive to score than the check-your-answer forms and are less frequently used.

Once the forms have been filled out, the results must be tabulated and analyzed. Simple, so-called straight runs (e.g., 70 percent of the employees like their jobs) are usually less informative than cross tabulations such as this:

	Job attitude	
Supervisory behavior	*Like their job*	*Dislike their job*
Supervisor speaks to them often	85%	15%
Supervisor speaks to them rarely	45	55

Many companies use attitude surveys like thermometers or fever charts. They reveal whether there is an illness in the organization but not the exact source or nature of the problem.[8] As we discuss below, the more difficult task is to determine what these surveys mean.

[8] Rensis Likert, *The Human Organization* (New York: McGraw-Hill, 1968), p. 132.

Within any organization there are vast quantities of statistical information being created almost daily. Even without the use of formal questionnaires and audits, the organization produces information that can be reassessed by staff experts in order to obtain measures of managerial and employee effectiveness. Here are some examples of what we mean:

- Unsolicited letters either praising or condemning the organization from employees, customers, community residents, shareholders
- Scrap records
- Earnings from piecework and commission
- Measures of management time spent at meetings
- Numbers of usable suggestions submitted by employees
- Amount of overtime worked
- Amount of absenteeism
- Time lost in illness and/or accidents
- Voluntary turnover rate
- Number of transfers requested
- Number of grievances, wildcat strikes
- Labor cost variances

Note that all these data have been produced for purposes other than personnel audit and are therefore both economical to obtain and less likely to be purposely biased.[9]

Designing the personnel information system

Identifying the data to be collected for purposes of a personnel audit is but one step in the larger process of designing an effective personnel information system. Unless all the steps are handled well, the controls utilized will not stimulate line managers to take appropriate remedial measures. Critical choices have to be made if the control system is going to be effective. Information neither collects itself nor speaks for itself; it must be interpreted with care. It can be used either to "catch" people and bludgeon them into submission or to alert them to, and help them solve, problems. Which of these occurs depends upon how the total system of information collection and evaluation is designed. The most important questions to be decided are these:

1. How will the data be collected?
2. What sorts of questions will be asked of the data?
3. Who evaluates and interprets the meaning of the data and who sees the results?

[9] For an excellent analysis of the use of these kinds of data, see the highly original study by Eugene J. Webb et al., *Unobtrusive Measures: Nonreactive Research in the Social Sciences* (Chicago: Rand McNally, 1966).

4. Who is responsible for taking action where problems are indicated?

5. What is done about the unmeasured areas of supervisory responsibility?

Let us consider these questions in turn.

Collecting data

If managers collect data on their own performances, they may well bias them in their own favor. Individual supervisors who report their own department accident records may be tempted to suppress or hide potentially embarrassing incidents. A manager's appraisal of an employee whom the manager herself has selected may not be good evidence of how well the selection system is operating. Similarly, scheduled inspection tours or investigating teams are almost sure to be met by specially arranged "spit and polish."

On the other hand, if a staff department has to play the role of spy or informer in collecting control data, it is likely to vitiate any goodwill it has accumulated, and this will make it impossible to carry out its other counseling and advisory relationships. These are some of the reasons why we have recommended the use of the unobtrusive measures described above—working with data that have already been collected for other purposes.

Sometimes outsiders—consultants, opinion pollsters, and university-based researchers—are employed to probe employee and supervisory opinion and accumulate data on supervisory practices. Such outsider data always appear more credible than insider reports, even though, in fact, these data may be less carefully assembled.

Asking questions of the data

What do the data mean? How can they be used to provide meaningful information about organizational effectiveness? Given the data that are produced almost automatically within the typical organization, questions like those below can then be posed:

- How does our number of lost-time accidents compare with other firms in our industry?
- Which departments have more than the company average of accidents, illness, or tardiness?
- Which departments produce a disproportionate share of promotable personnel? Which less?
- From what departments do most requests for transfer come?
- Which supervisors are more likely to have and recommend candidates for training programs or for promotion; which appear rarely to have suitable candidates?
- In which departments is absenteeism increasing over the last year?

Personnel managers in this age of quantification may be tempted to analyze the actual differences in performance between groups or departments. However, the absolute numbers may be misleading because of all the extraneous factors that can contribute to these differences. (Work areas with constantly changing, unpredictable production schedules will have a more difficult time staying within their labor cost budget than will departments with completely routinized operations.) Therefore, for most purposes, trend comparisons may be preferable. These simply compare departments that are getting *worse* with those that are getting better.

All data are not equally valid. It is Personnel's responsibility to assist management in determining what the data mean. Apparently objective data may in fact be subject to a variety of human biases. How, for example, are we to interpret a finding that 20 percent of a given year's crop of white executives are evaluated by their bosses as being "outstanding," whereas only 10 percent of the black executives receive a similar rating? Does this mean that the white executives are in fact superior or that the bosses are prejudiced?

Evaluating and disseminating the data

Even where the possibility of bias is less obvious, all data must be interpreted with care.

Mary Elk and Mike Arena sell in adjoining territories. Mary increases her sales twice as fast as Mike does. Does this mean that Mary is a better salesperson or that economic conditions are better in her territory?

A study shows that high production is associated with democratic supervision. Does this mean that workers produce more for democratic supervisors because they react well to this kind of supervision or that a supervisor who is assigned a work group which is already hard working can afford "democracy"?

It needs to be recognized that reliable data are difficult to obtain, and assessing their significance is even more complex. If supervisor A has more grievances than his counterpart B, it can mean that

- Supervisor B has as many problems but settles most of them informally, without the use of the formal union procedure.
- Supervisor B is weak and makes too many concessions; therefore, his employees never have to resort to a grievance.
- Supervisor A has a number of candidates for high union office in his department.
- Supervisor B's boss is more understanding and flexible in giving him room to maneuver in his department and in helping to establish a reasonable work environment.

Manager A has a much higher turnover in her department than Manager B. What does this mean? Below are some of the possibilities:

- A is a poor manager, and her people are more likely to quit.
- A's department has many more new employees, many of whom are young and unmarried, and these typically are more likely to leave voluntarily.
- The company has announced a cutback in the division in which A's department is located; many ambitious employees are leaving, fearing layoff.
- A's department is located in a "tight" labor market in which competitors are bidding for labor; B is located in an area of labor surplus.
- B is reluctant to appraise employees critically, whereas A has higher standards and encourages those who do not fit the job or who are not suited to the work to seek other employment.

Of course, the purpose of monitoring is not to accumulate data. Most organizations generate more than adequate quantities! The purpose is to stimulate remedial action. Often actions by more than one person or department

From figures to action

are required. In some cases the action may require consultation between a supervisor and higher management. On other occasions the staff person responsible for data collection might work with line managers, *jointly* arriving at an agreement regarding the implications of the data.

"When we in Personnel saw these absenteeism figures climbing, we were really aroused. We got together with the production managers to see what the data meant. One thing we learned (and we should have known this) was that the departments had hired a large number of housewives, and in September there is a lot of staying home to get the children ready for school. Also the departments had just finished a very trying, rush period. Employees were exhausted, and some supervisors had indicated that they wouldn't care if people took a little time off. This analysis led into a lengthy discussion of the impact of this kind of cyclical pattern—and the inevitable laxness it created. At the end, the managers were all agreeing that they had handled both the rush work and the ensuing slack period badly. We learned a good deal in Personnel, and I think they did too."

Without such participation, there can be serious misinterpretations and hard feelings:

"They hold those accident figures over us like a club. No recognition is given to the fact that we have the oldest machinery in the whole company, and until they spend some money on our department they can't expect anything better."

Having access to company, industry, and community data, staff experts in Personnel are often in an excellent position to help supervisors interpret the meaning of their own results:

Personnel specialist to supervisor: "Mary, as you can see by these charts, this is the third month in a row that absenteeism in your department has topped all our clerical groups; it is almost 50 percent higher than other department stores have been experiencing here in the Midwest. It looks to me as though a good deal of the problem is being produced by seven or eight people, nearly all of whom work in the second-floor annex. Let's look at their permanent employment records and see if we can both identify some common factors here. Then we can consider some of the things you might do to remedy this bad situation."

Based on such data, the ensuing discussion will probably weigh the potential contribution of the ages, backgrounds, and experience of the "offenders," previous supervisory actions, and the likely effect of various steps the supervisor can take. (The increased availability of computerized employment records can mean more sophisticated and rapid analysis.)

Dealing with unmeasured responsibilities

Experienced managers realize that merely reporting quantified measures of performance can distort supervisory efforts. The manager who knows that top management receives reports on how many subordinates take training programs will obviously increase efforts to get these subordinates signed up in such programs. Conversely, if success in developing promotable subordinates is not audited, there will be limited or no effort expended in this direction.

Why not, therefore, measure everything? Regrettably, many aspects of the managerial job are not easy to reduce to statistics, particularly the superior-subordinate relationship itself. Further, statistics are likely to encourage efforts to meet short-run goals rather than long-run goals. Employee development efforts may take years to bear fruit; an average employee who is encouraged by her manager may show excellent performance five years later. In the meantime, since most management consists of making choices among many things that could be done in the limited time available, the development-oriented manager may show up as less effective on some of the short-run measures, such as profits.

There is also the danger that overemphasis on quantitative measures may lead to a distortion of effort. If the number of grievances filed against a foreman are counted as a negative factor in measuring foreman efficiency, the foreman may avoid taking necessary actions that might lead to grievances, no matter how unjustified these grievances may be. One of the authors carried out research in a plant in which there was a major campaign to reduce so-called lost-time accidents. Supervisors in departments with the poorer records were chastised severely; some were discharged. As a result, managers would do almost anything to keep an injured employee at work. At times an employee who was unable to work had to be picked up and delivered to his home by the supervisor, since the worker was unable to transport himself because of his injury. Obviously, the lost-time statistics here could not be taken at face value.

Further cost/benefit considerations

Particularly with the advent of computers, enormous quantities of data can be generated to assist the staff personnel department and the line manager in assessing their organization's health. There are also dangers here, however. Generating data is costly, even with computers, and managers may find that they are deluged with more data than they can profitably use. The costs of data collection and analysis must be compared with the possible benefits:

Of what value are the data in helping us to appraise the effectiveness of our own personnel policies? (Do our data enable us to say whether the company's policy of educational leaves contributes tangible benefits to the organization?)

Of what value are the data in helping managers improve their day-to-day performance? (How are managers utilizing the information we provide them on the relative frequency of employee illness in their departments compared to other departments? Does it affect their employee counseling or interviewing, and are there any indications that the availability of such data leads to any reduction in lost working days?)

Stabilization relationships

Personnel frequently engages in a stabilization relationship. In many instances, line managers must clear with Personnel before they can go ahead with their plans. The purpose here, of course, is to ensure that the decisions of individual departments do not hurt larger organizational objectives. Personnel's approval may be required before pay increases are granted, union grievances answered, employees hired, or job offers made.

"We needed to hire a programmer; and after we described the job, Personnel told us we could offer only $270 a week. You can't hire a good programmer in this area for that salary, and when we told Personnel the rate had to be higher, they simply said that there was a companywide salary plan, and they couldn't allow a single job to distort the whole plan. I don't see why they should have the last word on this; after all, the salary comes out of our budget."

Impairment of responsibility. Line managers resent restrictions on their freedom when it emanates from groups such as Personnel, which appears to have excessive authority with no concomitant responsibility. Resentment may also arise if it is felt that Personnel is a lower-status group dictating to a higher-status group.

As another cause of trouble, see what happens when the manager is required to get the permission of the industrial relations department before discharging an employee. The manager now may be inclined to shrug off responsibility for the future performance of the man. "After all, I really wanted to get rid of him, but they made me keep him," reasons the manager. The manager has many difficult and risky decisions to make. This one may cause a work stoppage, that one may lose a valuable man. If management wants the manager to take responsibility for making difficult, unpleasant decisions, Personnel should not "second guess" these decisions.

Who is the boss? Another serious ramification of staff decision making is the potential erosion of the manager's leadership role. As employees begin to detect that the personnel department is determining their rate of pay, who is hired and who is fired, they find little reason for dealing with their direct supervisor as the "boss." The supervisor, in turn, will find it increasingly difficult to motivate or control the behavior of subordinates, since she no longer controls the rewards and penalties or determines the basic decisions in her department.

Alternatively, the personnel department can become the "good boss" when employees discover that they can obtain relief from their supervisor's decisions by taking them to Personnel. In other cases, the supervisor passes the buck to the personnel department; she tells a subordinate, "I'd be glad to give you that raise, but they (the personnel people) won't let me."

Seeing only part of the picture. Further, few supervisory problems lend themselves to unilateral decisions by staff departments, largely because a single staff expert, by virtue of job and training, sees only part of the picture. Often a seemingly trivial decision concerning something like the change of one person's work schedule may involve questions of cost, production balancing, safety, quality, work-group stability, and a host of special circumstances that can be known only to the immediate supervisor in the department where the question has arisen. The supervisor can call on one or more experts like the personnel specialist for advice on parts of the problem, but rarely can the expert solve the whole problem.

Passing the buck. On the other hand, we should not forget that many line supervisors *want* Personnel to make decisions in some of these difficult human problems of administration. The readiness with which line officials surrender responsibility for unpleasant personnel matters has been described by Mason Haire:

If we are assembling widgets we usually know just what to do. . . . However, at the next step up the hierarchy the job is very different. Now, although the superior is responsible for the number of widgets turned out, he can't assemble them himself. He must accomplish the production through a very uncertain medium that intervenes between him and the widgets themselves—the people on the production line. It is a medium that is changeable, unpredictable, and intractable. It is a little like trying to pick a cherry from the bottom of a tall glass with wobbly straws. It is easy to see what you are trying to do, but the instrument with which you are working is very hard to control. In many cases it seems likely that it is because of the difficulty of the medium through which production must be accomplished that managers turn away from the medium itself, in an unconscious effort to escape the problem, and say, "My job is production—I'll hire an expert staff man to worry about the people." [10]

However, many managers who wish that Personnel would step in and take over their human relations troubles still resent Personnel's interference when it stops them from transferring an employee or giving a raise.

Balancing relationships

Line management may look upon Personnel's audit and stabilization control activities as just another form of pressure designed to make life still more difficult. At the operating level, the manager has to cope with informal groups, adjust to demands—and this means often departing from the plans, procedures, and policies top management has established. Understandably, the manager regards Personnel's control activities as a threat to the established ways of doing things. Line managers are motivated to hide their methods of operation, to juggle figures, seek excuses, or shift responsibility in order to cover up deviations from standards. In the process, they develop an antipathy for the "checkers" who are "just showing off their technical virtuosity . . . they don't understand the problems we face on the firing line."

Perhaps the most serious problem stemming from Personnel's power in the organization is the potential damage to what is often presumed to be its major function in the organization: providing expert advice. Inevitably, line managers resent Personnel's power to measure performance and influence top management's appraisal of them. Is it reasonable to expect a line manager to reveal his or her problems and department's shortcomings when Personnel is also in the position of auditing his performance and sometimes denying requests for salary adjustments and the like? As auditors, personnel people should be conscious of the difficulties each manager faces in meeting the standards set for his unit by top management. By helping the manager think through difficulties and by providing new skills and techniques in coping with them, Personnel also can discharge its training responsibility.

Therefore, it is critical for Personnel to develop a relationship with line management that balances any constraining forces with timely participation and sharing. Below we describe the four elements that should be present in auditing and stabilization.

1. Successful personnel managers have learned that they are more effective in improving line performance if they discuss the results of their evaluations with the manager involved *before* they send them on to higher management. This gives managers a chance to improve performance before the boss learns they are doing a poor job. Instead of a pressure device, the staff report then becomes a device to help the manager remedy defects in operations and meet the standards established by top management. When the problems

[10] Mason Haire, *Psychology in Management* (New York: McGraw-Hill, 1956), pp. 49–56.

uncovered by staff investigations can be handled without recourse to higher levels of the organization, one usually finds that staff and line groups work together harmoniously.

2. Personnel is well advised to involve line managers in the data gathering and interpretation process from the very beginning. Line should be given a voice in deciding what data should be collected and how it should be disseminated. At times Personnel may distribute the data to the managers concerned without comment, letting the numbers speak for themselves. Alternatively, the data can be used as a springboard for organization development (see Chapter 16). Here the supervisors themselves are encouraged to give meaning to the data; and, of course, they are more likely to accept interpretations they themselves have made.

3. Line managers also will be more willing to accept a staff control report if they can see how its contents will help them achieve their objectives, and if it is timely. Personnel's chief job is to help line management learn to detect and solve its own problems; the line's motivation to learn is heightened when it acknowledges that it has a problem. One personnel director described her technique for dealing with the salary increase problem this way:

"If we wait until the manager gives out his increases, we are in trouble, because then all we can do is blow the whistle on those that have exceeded the percentage top management has established. Also we get into a dogfight over whether or not special circumstances justify a higher increase in a particular case. So we concentrate most of our efforts on working with managers and showing them how to get the most mileage out of their budgeted salary increases and how to prevent problem cases when they handle those whom they've got to disappoint."

4. The degree to which Personnel can develop impersonal, quantitative measures (in contrast, say, to subjective appraisals of supervisory leadership effectiveness) reduces the staff-line tension that is generally associated with auditing.

Personnel's role in decentralized organizations

The personnel function in large organizations is likely to be performed at several different levels. There is likely to be a small staff reporting directly to the chief executive officer, its status equal to that of other key staff departments such as Finance or Marketing. If the organization practices a policy of decentralization, this central-office department will be limited primarily to an advisory role (to the chief executive and his or her immediate subordinates), although it may also perform occasional auditing tasks to assure top management that its major industrial relations policies are effective. A small number of service programs may well be conducted on an organizationwide basis by this staff as well—e.g., labor relations and some aspects of organization development.

Staff departments in decentralized organizations face special difficulties. Their immediate supervisor is usually the line manager who heads the branch or divisional operation, but they also have a functional relationship to the central office staff group (see chart). Thus, a personnel specialist in the Akron, Ohio office of the Superior Insurance Company takes orders from the district

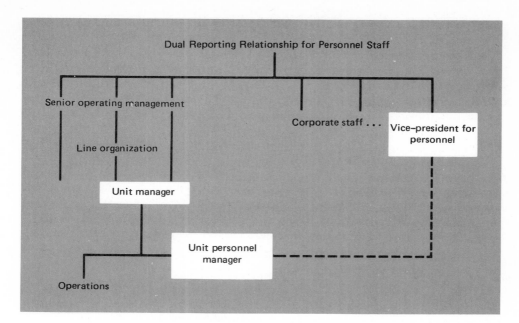

Dual Reporting Relationship for Personnel Staff

Senior operating management

Corporate staff . . .

Vice–president for personnel

Line organization

Unit manager

Unit personnel manager

Operations

manager in that office but advances only if the vice-president for Personnel in New York City authorizes promotion. Conflict often arises when the central staff tries to establish a new program—for example, an employee appraisal system—throughout the organization. The New York office urges local personnel to lobby for the new program, but the management in Akron is far from enthusiastic about having New York interfere with local employee relations. The local staff person is caught up in a role conflict, trying to satisfy the incompatible standards of two distinct groups.

What is the right mixture of staff patterns? In the field or out at operating locations, Personnel is more likely to handle advisory and service tasks. The personnel department may also be closely integrated into a managerial work group. In sharp contrast in centralized organizations' headquarters more emphasis is on evaluating and controlling line managers in the field: setting standards for them and requiring them to respond to functional controls. Isolated staff executives at headquarters find it difficult to develop a relaxed advisory-oriented, give-and-take relationship with line managers.

Personality and skill differences among staff personnel will also shape the mix that evolves. Advisers must be endowed with a certain temperament: they must wait patiently for others to bring them problems; they must counsel without pressure or the use of power. These criteria differ from the standards required for administering large service functions or negotiating acceptance of stabilization responsibilities.

The distribution of functions and responsibilities may also vary, depending on the level of management that interacts with the staff personnel executive. To the top managers of the organization, staff is likely to enjoy an advisory relationship; service functions may predominate at middle levels (divisional and plant management); audit and stabilization functions characterize the centralized staff's interaction with lower-level management.

Even within a given personnel activity, one can observe an intricate mixture of staff and line functions. The following list describes the staff and line contributions within a single *service* function: hiring new employees. Note particularly how closely line and staff must coordinate their activities.

Division of labor for the employment function*

Department supervision (line)	Personnel-employment specialist (staff)
1. Prepare requisition outlining specific qualifications of employees needed to fill specific positions. Help create reputation that will attract applicants. [First step.]	1. Develop sources of qualified applicants from local labor market. This requires carefully planned community relations, speeches, advertisements, and active high-school, college, and technical-school recruiting. [Second step.]
2. Interview and select from candidates screened by Personnel. Make specific job assignments that will utilize new employees' highest skills to promote maximum production. [Fifth step.]	2. Conduct skilled interviews, give scientific tests, and make thorough reference checks, etc., using requisition and job description as guides. Screening must meet company standards and conform with employment laws. [Third step.]
3. Indoctrinate employees with specific details regarding the sections and jobs where they are to be assigned—safety rules, pay, hours, "our customs." [Seventh step.]	3. Refer best candidates to supervisor, after physical examinations and qualifications for the positions available have been carefully evaluated. [Fourth step.]
4. Instruct and train on the job according to planned training program already worked out with Personnel. [Eighth step.]	4. Give new employees preliminary indoctrination about the company, benefit plans, general safety, first aid, shift hours, etc. [Sixth step.]
5. Follow up, develop, and rate employee job performance; decide on promotion, transfer, layoff, or discharge. [Ninth step.]	5. Keep complete record of current performance and future potential of each employee. [Tenth step.]
6. Hold separation interview when employees leave—determine causes. Make internal department adjustments to minimize turnover. [Eleventh step.]	6. Diagnose information given in separation interviews, determine causes, and take positive steps to correct. [Twelfth step.]

* Robert Saltonstall, "Who's Who in Personnel Administration," *Harvard Business Review,* Volume 33, No. 4 (July 1955), 75–83.

Conclusion

Because of these interrelated reasons, Personnel management is given responsibility for monitoring and stabilization:

1. To assure top management that its policies are being, and will continue to be, implemented down the line; that they will not be ignored, sabotaged, or distorted.

2. To assess whether personnel programs cost more than they are worth and to make them still fulfill desired and necessary functions.

3. To identify policies that need to be modified or changed in response to changing circumstances.

Reconciling various views. Personnel is responsible for directing higher management's attention to human-relations trouble spots and for helping to develop remedial actions. But it can do neither job unless it enjoys a good working relationship with the line officials who must report problems and institute changes. Unless this relationship exists, the staff can compare any number of lengthy reports and analyses, but most will automatically be filed away and never referred to again.

Although we have examined alternative philosophies and a variety of tasks performed by Personnel, the actual role of the personnel expert will depend upon how that person fits into the day-to-day functioning of the organization: who consults him or her, when, what activities and operations he is responsible for, what monitoring he performs, and what credence is given to his analyses and evaluations.

Looking to the future. One thing is clear: the problems of tomorrow will not be those of today. The organization encompasses a wide variety of human beings; it exists in a cultural milieu that embraces the life of a community. Thus, the mores of society and the values of diverse social groups—in fact, most of the pressures of daily life—will have their organizational counterparts. At times, these pressures may involve the jealousy or suspicions of various racial or religious groups. Economic instabilities, fear of unemployment, and the striving of women for equal opportunities all complicate the personnel field. Growing public concern with pollution, with land usage, and with corporate citizenship, similarly, will change the nature of personnel problems.

The field of Personnel resembles a lightning rod, attracting the tensions and human conflicts that abound in the organization and the community. If professionally handled, these challenges can be a constructive, not destructive, force in the life of the organization. Just as, on balance, the need to deal with unions and their demands probably strengthened the capability of American industry in the past, management's need to cope systematically with a new and unanticipated series of problems tomorrow can strengthen the firm.

Looking to the future of Personnel, it seems clear that a heavier proportion of time and effort will be devoted to planning and control functions. As companies have become much more planning conscious in other fields (marketing, finance, production), they have also sought to establish clearer policies on their requirements and use of human resources. Because manpower planning has become such a critical function, we shall devote Chapter 8 to this subject.

problems

1 · *Forced Ranking of Engineers*

As a result of a top management decision, the development division of Crowder Engineering has been required to implement an "anti-obsolescence" program. The policy, to be coordinated by the personnel department, requires each unit head to rank all his employees, thereby identifying each group's lowest 10 percent. The policy states that this low-ranked group will be considered for discharge, transfer, or early retirement, depending on further individual evaluations.

The corporate personnel manager supports the program strongly. The division personnel manager has been less than enthusiastic about it, on the grounds that the development division has a select group of employees; he also believes that dropping 10 percent of the employees across the board is a serious mistake. Further, in efforts to explain the program to unit heads within the divisions, he has encountered great resistance.

Under the corporate timetable, unit heads were to submit their rankings to their division managers by July 1. As of June 30, only 6 out of the 27 unit heads had submitted their forms. On that day the division manager received a call from the executive vice-president at corporate headquarters, reminding him that the rankings would be due the next day. The following dialogue took place after the manager excitedly called his personnel manager to his office:

Division manager: Mary, how come you let me down? Here we are just about overdue on those rankings, and you never alerted me that we were going to be in trouble on this. Your job is to keep me out of trouble with the head office on personnel matters. You are in contact with those unit heads, and if you spot that they are not doing something they are supposed to be doing, come to me with it, and come quick. Now what the blazes can we do this late?

Personnel manager: This is one of the most unpopular policies that has ever come out of headquarters. I've been trying to convince our people to go along with it, but frankly I find it hard to be convincing! And, Joe, if I run to you and "squeal" on your people who may be violating some policy or other, they'll never have any confidence in me. They won't tell me things about their real personnel difficulties, and I won't be able to provide the kind of assistance you want me to provide to them, to keep this operation functioning smoothly.

Division manager: But you put me out on a limb when you don't keep me informed. I want you to "squeal" if you find someone who isn't doing his job in the personnel area; that's as much a part of your job as helping those guys. You're my eyes out there in the labs.

1. How can the personnel manager reconcile the demands of advisory and audit responsibilities to the division manager?
2. The personnel manager also has a functional relationship to the corporate personnel department. Evaluate that relationship in this context.
3. What should the personnel manager do when asked to enforce an unpopular policy that he or she has doubts about?

2 · *Influential Personnel*

The finishing department in a large paper-manufacturing plant has been the source of many grievances. The personnel director of the plant has been collecting data showing that the superintendent of the department is partly at fault (attitude survey results and turnover data, etc.). The superintendent, a member of the "old school," assigns heavy disciplinary penalties for the slightest violation of shop rules. The most recent grievance, which almost resulted in a strike, concerned a two-week layoff he had given to a man for "loafing on the job." Caught smoking in the washroom, the man had insisted it was common practice for workers to leave their machines for brief intervals when setup people were changing rolls. The union won its grievance, and the employee received two weeks' back pay for the "unjustified" layoff.

This was just one of a series of such instances. To date, the finishing department has had two wildcat strikes and several slowdowns. It is common knowledge in the company that the personnel director has had several discussions with this superintendent about his handling of disciplinary problems and his dealings with the unions.

The plant manager is primarily concerned about maintaining output levels. Competition is severe and stoppages impair the company's ability to fill orders. For this reason, the plant manager has decided to transfer the superintendent of the finishing department to a considerably less important job. In doing this, he pointed out to the superintendent that the transfer is a direct result of his failure to follow good personnel practices and that he has had ample opportunity to "mend his ways" with the help of the personnel director. Word quickly spreads through the organization that the "word of the personnel director is law" and that supervisors violate her "suggestions" at the risk of transfer or discharge.

1. How can the personnel director, under these circumstances, retain her staff status and avoid "undermining" the authority of line supervisors?
2. Are there any steps she can take to avoid being perceived as another boss?

3 · *Conflicts over Personnel's Role*

The Foremost Company hired a management consultant to assess its management structure. The consultant noted a good deal of controversy surrounding the role of the personnel department. This department had grown substantially in size but its specialists were rarely consulted or given much credibility by key managers. The consultant summarized the existing attitudes as follows:

Attitude of Personnel Staff toward Divisional Management

1. We are experts, we are well trained in behavioral science methods, we keep up with our field and know the latest techniques other companies are utilizing, but we are ignored. Often when we make recommendations for changes in management practices or write extensive reports evaluating current organizational problems, our work is simply ignored.
2. Divisional managers are old-fashioned and narrow-minded, they are never willing to take the time or spend the money required for new programs that will have major long-run payoffs. They are very short sighted.

3. They laugh at us and call us "college kids."

Attitudes of Divisional Management toward Personnel

1. They are highly unrealistic people who don't have to worry about costs or efficiency, and they are more interested in criticizing and making work for us than in making us more efficient.
2. They have little responsibility for profitability but lots of opportunity to cross us up. They slow down requests for salary increases and they are totally unresponsive to our requests for better personnel screening.
3. When you bring them a problem where action is required, they are more likely to propose some hare-brained research project or a major new (and costly) program—with Personnel getting another activity to list in its annual budget request—than they are to give us a clear no-nonsense answer. In fact, when you ask them a question, you are more likely to get a very highly qualified statement—lots of "ifs," "buts," and "maybes"—than a fixed answer (for which they would be held responsible!).

1. Take each of the above arguments and prepare a counterargument (view of the other side).
2. Then go the next step and prepare a personnel role that will tend to minimize these conflicts.
3. Role-play the conflicting points of view in which the personnel director, the head of manufacturing, and their common boss—i.e., the company president—seek to resolve their differences. See Chapter 14, under the heading "Simulation," for a description of role-playing.

4 · *Short Illnesses or Long Weekends?*

Carla Anders is the first personnel director in the Dorchester Medical Laboratory, which handles a variety of medical tests for doctors in the greater Boston area. During her first few months on the job, Ms. Anders notes that one of the longer-service lab technicians, Pfister, is frequently absent Mondays and several days after major holidays. His boss tells Carla that Hank is otherwise a fine employee, but his lost days represent a serious problem for the company, since they are unscheduled, and work backs up. Further, Hank usually says they are due to one or another minor illnesses, and the

company pays for 25 days of illness. While Hank occasionally produces a doctor's note indicating that he had a "severe cold" or "generalized body aches," the supervisor is rather sure that, given the sickness and the minor problems represented, much of this is simply extra vacation.

Carla wonders why the supervisor has let this continue over the years. She also remembers some of the tension that occurred when she joined a predominately male organization.

What steps should she take with respect to both the supervisor and Hank?

the impact of the union

More than 20 million Americans belong to unions. This simple fact has profound implications for management. Although we cannot treat union-management relations in depth in this chapter, we will consider why employees join or do not join unions, how unions function within the organization, and their impact on management. First, however, let us note that labor relations do *not* represent as distinct a problem in relationships for the organization as we might first assume.

Why union problems are not unique

Occupational associations are common. Typically, we find that when employees work together and share common experiences they tend to develop into a group and to acquire goals of their own, which may differ sharply from the goals of the total enterprise. These groups are usually informal (with informal leaders and unwritten objectives). Sometimes, however, where there is a great deal of common occupational identification, employees form occupational associations. There are such associations for purchasing agents, nurses, industrial engineers, and the like. These groups may begin largely for social reasons, then move on to aid members to advance themselves and the status of the occupation. Eventually, some begin to consider bargaining directly with the employer for im-

proved salaries and working conditions. The American Nurses Association (for example) took on aspects of a bona fide union when it decided to engage in collective bargaining.

Bargaining. It is easy to believe that without unions everyone would work together in harmony for common organizational objectives. Actually, bargaining is a way of life in nearly all organizations, even where there are no unions. Supervisors often exchange favors or make "deals" as a means of gaining cooperation from their subordinates. Large organizations include many different specialized groups even within management itself, and these groups negotiate with one another, trading off one advantage for another. The Purchasing department bargains with engineering almost as much as labor bargains with management.

Outsiders. The union, interested primarily in its own survival and growth, appears to management as an outside force with goals different from those of the firm. But companies have become accustomed to dealing with many "outsiders": government officials who insist upon special accounting or quality control procedures, outside contractors who work inside firms, and countless others who penetrate an organization's boundaries.

Differing perceptions. Management often argues that there are no real conflicts of interest between workers and the company. Both stand to gain if profits and productivity improve. This is often true, but the significant point is that employees believe that there is a conflict of interest, say, between profits and wages. Although their overall interests may not always be in conflict, workers and management tend to see problems from different vantage points. To the manager, a new machine may represent a cost saving device that will strengthen the company, but to the employee it will appear as a job threat.

It is now a well-established uniformity of organizational behavior that wherever groups of people occupy widely differing positions in a hierarchy (vertically arranged organization structure) and carry out different activities, they are bound to see their interests as being different.[1]

Conflict. At one time it was believed that a harmonious consensus within an organization was normal and that only unions introduced intergroup conflict. Yet given the inevitable differences among groups within an organization (between production and sales, for example), conflict and differing objectives permeate modern organizations. Of course, these internal conflicts do not result in the actual breaks in relationship that occur in strikes, but they are similarly obstructive to organizational effectiveness. (Under many circumstances, conflict can be healthy, too, as we shall see.)

[1] William F. Whyte, "Models for Building and Changing Organizations," *Human Organization*, Vol. 26 (Spring 1967), p. 25.

Appeals. Many supervisors fear that with the advent of the union all their time will be consumed handling grievances and that their power will be slowly whittled away. Yet many nonunion companies have established regular procedures that permit subordinates to appeal to a higher level when they feel that their boss is treating them unfairly. In fact, some progressive companies pride themselves on their "open door" policies, which formalize the right of an employee to carry problems over the boss's head.

The course of union development

Scattered efforts to form trade unions were made early in the nineteenth century; by the close of the century, the American Federation of Labor was well established in a number of skilled crafts. Yet until the 1930s union membership outside these crafts was highly unstable. Though unskilled workers sometimes joined unions in times of prosperity, they abandoned them when hard times returned. This pattern began to change drastically during the Great Depression of the 1930s, when a relatively large, permanent trade-union membership emerged not only in the traditional crafts where workers had found it easier to organize, but also in mass-production industry.

Certain changes in the American economic and political environment coincided with this development.

1. The Depression cost American business a great deal in prestige and employee confidence. Unions, on the other hand, gained prestige. Many observers regarded them as a healthy check on business power (a check that might help to moderate the business cycle). Gradually, unions began to escape the stigma of being somehow un-American.

2. Government at the state and federal levels, which had traditionally handicapped union organization (for example, by unfavorable court decisions and the use of injunctions), became more favorably disposed to labor. Legislation like the Wagner Act (1935) actively encouraged union organization.

3. A substantial segment of the working population began to accept as permanent the role of wage earner, realizing that it was not just a temporary stop on the road to owning one's own business. The American dream of moving constantly along to better jobs had lost its luster for some and was replaced by a desire to protect one's present situation. With this acceptance came an interest in improving one's lot as an employee through union membership.

4. The decline in immigration and the rise in educational standards tended to make our population more homogeneous. Relatively high standards of education raised the level of employee aspirations. No longer satisfied with just having a job, they demanded more and more from their jobs. And they regarded the union as a valuable ally in getting what they wanted.

5. Communities more readily accepted unions, and their participation in civic and governmental affairs increased union prestige. Membership became even more attractive as unions were given credit for the dramatic rise in wages that occurred during and after World War II.

Slowdown in growth: 1950–1964

After World War II, union growth began to slow down. As indicated by the next graph, membership (in both absolute and relative terms) reached its peak in the mid-1950s, and then began to decline. A number of factors explain this phenomenon.

By 1950, most easily organized employees had already been unionized.

Sources: 1900–1953, National Bureau of Economic Research; 1952–1978, Bureau of Labor Statistics. Note: data from these two sources disagree to some extent.

Union membership in the United States since 1900.

Union strength was concentrated in manufacturing, mining, transportation, and public utilities. In these industries, most of the blue-collar workers were already organized. The bulk of the unorganized factory workers were in difficult-to-organize areas such as small towns or the South, or they were employed by either small companies or companies such as Eastman Kodak or IBM, which had the reputation for providing employees with liberal salaries, fringe benefits, and extraordinary job security.

Equally significant, as the table of manpower statistics reveals, the proportion of workers in easy-to-organize industries began to decline. From 1953 to the early 1960s, the economy slowed down while technological change occurred at a rapid rate. Manufacturing employment as a whole declined. Although white-collar (nonproduction) employment within manufacturing increased quite sharply, blue-collar employment declined even more rapidly. Similar declines occurred in mining, transportation, and utility employment, leaving construction as the only expanding, highly unionized industry.

The greatest growth in employment in recent years has been in industries with a predominance of white-collar work: trade, finance, insurance, services, government, and others; but for several reasons, white-collar workers are difficult to organize. Since union membership is associated with blue-collar work, many white-collar workers fear that joining a union would lower their social status. Many white-collar employees work in close proximity to management

71

Total labor force	66.6	73.0	102.5	35.9
Military	3.5	2.6	2.1	−1.4
Agriculture	6.2	5.2	3.3	2.9
Unemployed	1.8	4.7	6.0	4.2
Nonagriculture employees	50.2	54.0	85.8	35.6
Manufacturing	17.5	16.3	20.3	2.8
Production workers *	(14.0)	(12.1)	(14.6)	(.6)
Nonproduction workers	(3.5)	(4.2)	(5.7)	(2.2)
Mining *	.9	.7	.8	−.1
Transportation and utilities *	4.3	3.9	4.9	.6
Construction *	2.6	2.8	4.2	1.6
Wholesale and retail trade	10.2	11.3	19.4	9.2
Finance, insurance, and real estate	2.1	2.7	4.7	2.6
Services	5.9	7.7	16.0	10.1
Government	6.6	8.6	15.5	8.9

* Largely unionized sectors.

Source: Bureau of Labor Statistics. Household data for labor force. Establishment data for employees.

and hope to move into management positions themselves. The fact that white-collar workers are separated into small, uncohesive groups makes it difficult for them to develop the kind of consensus needed for union organization.[2] Professional and technical employees tend to believe that they can get along on their own and that their individual chances for advancement should not be tied to the status of the whole group.

The slowdown in union growth (particularly in the late 1950s) can be attributed also to the exposure of corruption in a small number of unions. As a result of such disclosures, unions lost some of their reputation as crusaders for improvements in the lot of the common man. On the other hand, management had done much to eliminate the tyrannical supervision that often contributed to unionization in the 1930s.

Another barrier to union growth was the passage of two laws, the Taft-Hartley Act in 1947 and the Landrum-Griffin Act in 1959. Though neither had the disastrous effect on unions that some had feared, both made unions' organizing campaigns more difficult, especially by restricting the use of the secondary boycott, a traditional organizing weapon.

New growth: 1965–1974

In 1965, union membership began to turn up again, at least in absolute terms. Here, too, a number of factors seemed to be at play.

1. Growing prosperity meant increased employment in the easily organized industries, especially manufacturing.

[2] It is interesting that engineers sometimes join unions when they work closely together in large undifferentiated groups, as in some huge aircraft and electronics plants.

2. There were some slight breakthroughs in two generally unorganized sectors. The Farm Workers won some notable organizing victories in California agriculture. And great strides were made in organizing hospitals, especially after the National Labor Relations Act was amended to place employees of nonprofit hospitals under its protection. Though the number of white-collar union members increased, the percentage of white-collar workers organized in private business was no higher in 1980 than it was in the mid-1950s.

3. The big change was in the government sector. From 1956 to 1976 membership in government employee unions increased fourfold. And this does not include independent associations (such as the million-member National Educational Association) which in recent years have gone on strike, negotiated contracts, and differed from real unions only in name.

In fact, with close to 50 percent of the government civilian work force organized, government employees became more heavily unionized than the nonfarm private work force (about 25 percent). The growth of government unions was due to a number of interrelated factors: the rapid increase in government employment generally; a series of executive orders by Presidents Kennedy and Nixon, which made organizing and bargaining easier at the federal level; another series of similar laws in most major states; a number of successful strikes (particularly in New York City) that won unionized government employees substantial salary increases; and the civil rights movement, which introduced black workers into government unions, especially in the South (it was during an organizing drive that Martin Luther King was murdered).

Slowdown again: 1975–?

Total union membership reached a new peak in 1974, dropped off and then rose slightly. Several factors appear responsible. The recession of 1974 was unusually sharp. Taxpayer revolts and budget cuts increased employer resistance in the government sector, and the public employee unions lost a number of important strikes. Faced by foreign competition and declining profit margins, nonunion private firms increased their resistance to being unionized, and unionized firms adopted tough stands against demands for further wage increases. Union-won wage increases barely kept up with the cost of living in many sectors. On the other hand, construction unions, which had won large wage increases during the early 1970s, may have partly priced themselves out of the market; anyway "open shop," non-union firms grew rapidly in a sector that had once been strongly organized. Unions in "automated" industries, such as telephones, public utilities, and chemicals, found it hard to win strikes, since a small group of managers could keep production going. Finally, many unions argued that legal loopholes made it possible for many large companies to get away with blatant violations of the provisions of the National Labor Relations Act protecting the right to organize.

New problems

In addition to these problems, unions were facing a period of transition as they entered the 1980s. The mass production unions were organized during the 1930s by a generation of charismatic, energetic leaders, most of them quite young at the time. By 1980, this generation had been succeeded by a considerably younger set of officers, some of whom had been active in the student riots of the 1960s. What changes this new, untried generation would bring was still uncertain.

In addition, it was questionable whether traditional union bargaining demands and techniques would continue to be appropriate. In the past, unions have focused on satisfying economic and security needs. But Maslow predicts that as these become satisfied, social and especially egoistic needs will become more important. Unions in the past have been suspicious of job redesign and "quality of worklife" programs. Perhaps the new generation of leaders and members will take a different position regarding these issues.

Finally, government has shown increasing concern with the impact of collective bargaining: the government has sought to restrain inflationary pressures and to ensure that collective bargaining agreements adhere to the new legal requirements regarding equal employment, pensions, and occupational health and safety. These developments have increased the government's role in bargaining, making it a third party to unions and management.

Why workers join unions

Why do workers join unions? Many managers have two oversimplified explanations. The first is that the company has been foolish or selfish or both. By providing unsatisfactory working conditions and wages, by permitting supervisors to play favorites, management has actually encouraged its employees to seek out a union. Such conditions undoubtedly stimulate the growth of unions. But what about the many well-managed organizations that have been unionized? What has motivated the workers of these companies to join unions?

Here is where the second explanation comes into play. Unionization, it says, must be the result of outside agitators and radicals, whose lies and deceit stir up an otherwise satisfied work force. This reason also is an oversimplification. To be sure, professional organizers from the outside have a great deal to do with bringing workers into the union fold. And they often make use of strategically located insiders who are willing to take on the task of agitating for the new union. But this is only a small part of the total explanation, as we discuss below.

Desire for better economic and working conditions

Most people want to increase their income—even those who work in top-paying companies. Few individuals believe their jobs are perfect. In the United States, the greatest growth period of unions coincided with a rapidly rising income level for workers. Whether the unions have really obtained higher wages and better pension, insurance, and other benefits for their members, or whether these would have come anyway through normal economic and social processes, is not the point. The point is that an impressive number of employees *believe* that unions are responsible for improving their economic lot. Certainly they realize that the bargaining power of the individual employee is not very great. He or she can accept the wage or salary the company offers, or he can look for a job elsewhere. With other employees in a union, however, his economic clout is considerably greater.

In our society, many employees are unhappy when they are completely dependent on someone else for the satisfaction of their needs. Even when that "someone else" is very good (as many managements have been) and provides good wages, steady employment, and desirable working conditions, workers tend to be uneasy when they have no power to control the benefits received. In fact, management makes matters worse by emphasizing how much it has "given" its employees (that is, benefits provided at the discretion of the company, not offered because they *had* to be). *Desire for control over benefits*

Even in organizations where employees have always been treated with complete fairness and justice, stories circulate that John Jones over in Department 16 has been severely penalized for something he didn't do because a supervisor "had it in for him." In any situation where we lack the power to control what happens to us, we are more than ready to believe these "atrocity" stories and think, "Next time that could happen to us." The truth or falsity of the rumor may be unimportant.

In small companies, management is often able to maintain close relations with its employees; the president may even know each person by name. But as organizations grow bigger, such communications tend to break down. In a large company the individual's sense of dependency and lack of control over what happens to him can be very great.

Many an employee feels that, as far as his company is concerned, he is nothing more than a time-clock number. Though many would not want the responsibility of management, they would like greater opportunity to express themselves. In part, this is just the desire to complain when hurt. But more important, as individuals we all have a need to express our point of view— not just to "get more" for ourselves, but to enjoy the feeling of being a whole person instead of a pair of hired hands. *Desire to be heard*

Despite the existence of an appeals procedure, most employees feel that without a union they have no means of safely going over the head of their boss with a problem. After all, they must rely on the boss to do many things for them. There are a hundred and one ways in which a supervisor can make their working life unpleasant and unrewarding. Discretion is frequently the better part of valor; when the supervisor says "No," most employees accept it as final.

This feeling of helplessness is particularly acute when the immediate supervisor is unsympathetic to their demands, either because he has no decision-making authority of his own, or because he has a natural unwillingness to reverse his own decisions. If only they can gain access to higher levels in the organization, employees reason, they may find someone with the authority to satisfy their requests.

The union promises workers an opportunity to protest inequities, to believe that if something goes wrong they will be heard. The union offers a direct road to participation, for its leaders have access to the top decision-making levels of the organization.

Many employees, of course, do not have a choice about joining a union. Approximately nine-tenths of unionized blue-collar workers labor under a union shop agreement; that is, they are required to maintain their union membership as a condition of employment.

Legal framework

In the United States the basic labor law is the National Labor Relations Act, which covers most large companies (specifically those engaged in interstate commerce). The NLRA is based on the Wagner Act (passed in 1935), but it has been modified by the Taft-Hartley Act (1947) and the Landrum-Griffin Act (1959). Most provisions of this act are administered by the National Labor Relations Board (NLRB).

The NLRB has two main functions. One function is to administer the procedure by which unions become certified as *collective bargaining agents.* How does this procedure work? Suppose a union seeks to unionize a nonunion plant. Once it begins to get some support from the workers, it asks them to sign cards that authorize the union to represent them in negotiations with the employer. As soon as 30 percent of the employees sign these cards, the union is free to petition the NLRB to hold a *representation election.* The NLRB must then determine whether the group of employees the union wishes to represent is "appropriate" to form a bargaining unit. After this is determined, the board holds a secret-ballot election in which employees can choose one of three alternatives: to be represented by the union that filed the petition, to be represented by an "intervening" union that has the support of 10 percent of the employees, or to reject union representation entirely. If a union wins this election, it is certified as the collective bargaining agent and has the legal right to bargain with the employer.

The NLRB's second major function is to curb *unfair labor practices* by either labor or management. For example, the act prohibits management from refusing to bargain with certified unions, from discriminating against employees because of union activity, or from establishing company-dominated unions. Similar provisions pertain to unions. Perhaps the most important of these outlaws the secondary boycott (a strike called against one employer to force it to cease doing business with another).

The act also provides for the Federal Mediation and Conciliation Service, a neutral middleman to help labor and management resolve their disputes (acting in much the same way as a marriage counselor trying to settle family disputes). Finally, the act permits the President to obtain a court injunction requiring an 80-day "cooling-off" period before a strike that would affect national health and safety.

It should be emphasized that the law only sets the ground rules for bargaining. The terms of the contract that arises from bargaining are completely up to the parties. If the parties cannot agree, the union is free to go on strike, or the employer may engage in a lockout (that is, it can shut its doors and refuse to provide employment).

*Internal
organization
of the union*

Now let us look at the rather complex structure of the unions themselves. Some employees are organized on the basis of the company or plant in which they work—for example, all the blue-collar employees of the Porter Chemical Company's Atlanta plant are eligible to join a local industrial union in which membership is restricted to Porter's employees. Frequently the white-collar clerical employees of such a company or its most highly skilled maintenance employees may belong to separate local unions. Industries that employ clearly defined trades are not usually organized by unions on a plant or company basis. Rather, all employees in a specific geographic area, usually a community, who have the qualifications to practice the trade are eligible for membership in a local craft union—for example, all unionized bricklayers in Rochester, New York, belong to the same local, regardless of which employer they work for. Community-wide locals are also found where the employer unit is relatively small (for example, all the dry-cleaning plant employees in town might belong to a single local of the Teamsters), or where employees are likely to shift from one employer to another (for example, in the needle trades).

*The local
union*

Why do we emphasize this difference between unions that are organized on the basis of an employer unit and unions that are organized on the basis of a geographic area? Because the governments of these two types of local union are quite different. If the membership is derived from many different companies in a clearly defined geographical area, the union is likely to vest a great deal of authority in an elected business agent who works full time on the negotiation of contracts, grievance problems, and the protection of the union's job jurisdiction.[3] Since these agents service many widely dispersed members who work for a variety of employers, they are very powerful, and management must be willing to deal with them regularly. Unfortunately, most of the corruption mentioned above has arisen from this type of union, and because of the growth of so-called service industries in the United States, these unions are expanding at the expense of unions organized by employer units.

By contrast, in unions organized on a company or plant basis, authority is usually dispersed among a number of leaders, many of whom continue to work at their regular jobs and handle union business on a released-time basis.

The local union has two types of officers. *Executive-board members* handle the union's internal business—finances, administration of election procedures, appointment of committee members, social functions, and so forth.[4] *Grievance officials* handle relationships with management—the union's collective-bargaining business. Grievance officials have a variety of titles, depending on

*The local
leadership*

[3] Communitywide unions often run *hiring halls* and make arrangements so only union members will be hired. This is the *closed shop*. (In the closed shop, workers must join the union before they get a job; by contrast, with a *union shop* they must join only after they are hired.)
[4] In some unions, the executive board is involved at some stage of the grievance procedure as well.

the union and their rank: business agent, committeeperson, steward, grievanceperson, chief steward, and so forth. Most of these officials continue to work for the company in their regular jobs while they are serving in their union capacity, and the company often pays for the time they spend handling employee grievances. Larger and wealthier locals, however, may engage full-time elected officials to handle their grievances and negotiations.

The membership

The most active union members—the elected officers—are employees who have more energy and ambition than they can expend on their jobs. Essentially discontented and anxious to get ahead, they often turn to the union when their drives are frustrated elsewhere.[5] Many of these people may also be excellent workers, and management frequently finds that leadership in the union may provide a clue to supervisory ability.

This active group, together with members who do not hold office but who attend union meetings and participate in the local's political life, is likely to include no more than 5 percent of the membership, and frequently a good bit less. Most of the members prefer to "let George do it" when it comes to taking an active role. They pay their dues as they would pay premiums on an insurance policy, and they have little to do with the organization except when a grievance arises or when a strike takes place. On the other hand, when major issues arise, such as the ratification of a controversial new labor-management agreement, attendance at union meetings may increase considerably.

Few members feel that union membership conflicts with their obligation to the company that provides their jobs and wages. Indeed, many workers have dual loyalty to company and union; for them, the union is a way of making the company better. Of course, unions also attract members with deep-seated hostilities toward management. Such persons are likely to be most active when the union is originally organized; over time, they either become more conservative or are replaced by individuals with greater skills as administrators.

The international union

Most local unions are affiliated with an international union that provides them with certain services.[6] You are probably familiar with the names of many of these organizations: The Autoworkers, the Teamsters,[7] and the State County and Municipal Workers (each has over a million members). Primarily, the internationals deal with problems that are out of reach of the local, such as companywide bargaining, government relations, and organizing the unorganized.

The international union usually hires *international representatives* to help the local union get established. These officials often participate in the later stages of the grievance procedure (which is described in the next section). Usually their most important job, however, is handling contract negotiations.

[5] Leonard Sayles and George Strauss, *The Local Union* (New York: Harcourt, 1967) pp. 56–70.
[6] Often a national organization is referred to as an "international" union in recognition of the fact that it may have members in Canada.
[7] These are not the formal names of these international unions, but the unions are commonly referred to in this fashion.

The decision-making body for the international union is the convention, which is held once every year or two, or even more infrequently.

A large number of American international unions have joined together in the AFL-CIO.[8] The AFL-CIO has almost no direct power over collective-bargaining matters, for most of its activities concern problems of the labor movement and relationships with government. There are other units in the union movement, such as city councils and state federations, which are organized to represent union interests in dealing with various levels of local and state government.[9] The international union, however, is by far the strongest unit.

The union as a political body

If management is to deal with a union successfully, it must recognize that the union is a *political* body. Most union officials are elected, and many union decisions—particularly at the local level—are made by direct vote of the membership. Therefore, decisions do not necessarily flow from top down as they do in management; officers cannot guarantee that the members will do as they are told, particularly in democratic unions, and members can always engage in wildcat strikes. Consequently, in order to win elections, officers must always win something in their negotiations with management. For this reason, they sometimes go through the motions of pressing grievances in which they do not believe.

Still, there is widespread apathy among union members. The local union meeting, which is the major decision-making forum for the local, is usually poorly attended. And yet, in spite of this apathy, management must recognize that union leaders must try to satisfy their members' needs. Failure to recognize this fact may lead to a serious miscalculation of the behavior of union leaders. Whereas a top-management official in a negotiation may be able to make firm decisions on his own, a union negotiator may have to get membership approval before he can make a binding commitment. Unions are certainly not models of pure democracy, but in most unions an aroused membership can turn out its leadership in favor of another group. Indeed a continuing problem in recent years has been the tendency of rank-and-file union members to vote not to ratify contracts that had been negotiated by their leadership.

Intergroup conflicts

An important component of the political life of the union is struggle *between* groups within the rank and file: each wants improved benefits for itself and each wants to protect itself from the encroachments of other groups. Among the issues which could lead to internal disagreement are the following:

Younger workers want higher wages; older ones prefer higher pensions.

[8] However, several important international unions are not included in the AFL-CIO. As of 1979, this group included the West Coast Longshoremen, the Teamsters, and the Auto Workers. The Canadian equivalent of the AFL-CIO is the Canadian Congress of Labor. The CLC includes both international unions with U.S.-Canadian membership and purely Canadian Unions.

[9] In sharp contrast to unions in most other countries—where unions are frequently highly active in politics and even dominate political parties—unions in the United States and Canada have only a mild interest in politics and seek to obtain their objectives primarily through economic means.

Higher-paid employees want percentage wage increases, while lower-paid employees want the same hourly increases (for example, 30¢) to go to everyone.

Younger members are interested in the 4-day, 10-hour-a-day week; married women members want flex-time; older men are suspicious of both.

Management adds a new finishing process. Workers in Department 35 claim jurisdiction over this work while the employees in Final Assembly insist that the new work ought to become part of their department.

Such conflicts are not surprising when we remember that most job satisfactions or dissatisfactions are felt in relative, not absolute terms. Thus, the leadership must balance off the claims of one group against those of another in the light of their relative political strength as well as the real equities. Some groups, if they don't get their way, will be able to defeat the officers at the next election or even to mount an illegal wildcat strike that will embarrass the officials in their dealings with management. Other groups put up no resistance if they lose their demands.

Varieties of work-group pressure

Work groups seem to react to problems in different ways, depending on the kinds of job they do. At least four varieties of groups may be identified:

Apathetic Groups are least likely to pressure the union into fighting for them. They are often made up of workers with low-status, relatively unskilled jobs who lack internal cohesion and leadership.

Erratic Groups at times exhibit very bellicose behavior, even walking off the job. Other times, with just as important problems facing them, they seem to be uninterested in any union actions on their behalf. These groups often include assembly line and crew workers, where there is a great deal of interdependence in work operations.

Strategic Groups are the most calculating and self-conscious groups within the rank and file and frequently exert pressure for more benefits for themselves. They are never satisfied, always feel "relative deprivation," and know how to exert effective political pressure on the union leadership. The most typical workers in such groups are individual machine operators who work independently, not in crews. They also hold jobs near the top (but not at the top) of the plant's status ladder.

Conservative Groups are seemingly content with their high-status position. These groups only occasionally feel the need to pressure the union to do battle for them. When they are dissatisfied, they are restrained and very rational in their approach. Often, maintenance workers and other skilled craftsmen demonstrate this pattern.

Union-management relations

The two main aspects of union-management relations are bargaining for contracts and handling grievances. The contract, the basic document that regulates relations between the parties, generally runs for at least a year; in recent years, two- or three-year contracts have become common. Some contracts cover only a single plant or even a small group of workers in that plant. Others may cover a multiplant company, such as General Motors (when this happens, supplemental agreements are often negotiated on a plant-by-plant basis to deal with special local problems). Where craft unions prevail, as in the construction industry, the contract typically covers all the workers within a particular craft who live in a specific geographical area (such as all the electri-

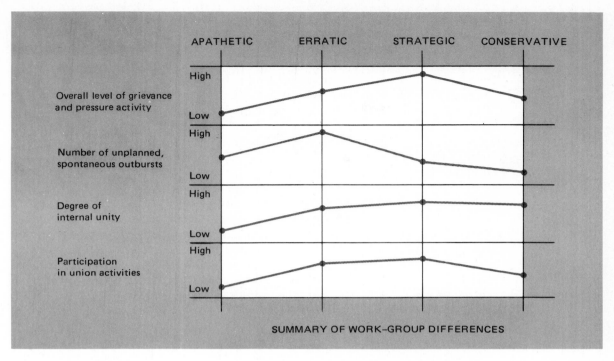

APATHETIC   ERRATIC   STRATEGIC   CONSERVATIVE

Overall level of grievance
and pressure activity

Number of unplanned,
spontaneous outbursts

Degree of
internal unity

Participation
in union activities

SUMMARY OF WORK–GROUP DIFFERENCES

cians in Hinsdale County). In a few instances essentially a single contract covers the industry throughout the country. This is true in the case of coal miners and railroad workers.

The tendency has been to broaden the area of bargaining. Small employers have banded together in employers' associations to form a united front against their common union or to provide "strike insurance," as the airlines did, to protect a company that may be singled out for union pressure. Because one company may deal with a number of unions as General Electric does, "coalition bargaining" has become common; that is, the various unions cooperate closely with each other during the bargaining period.

Regardless of how it is reached, the contract is usually a lengthy document (particularly when it includes special agreements in areas such as fringe benefits). The contract deals not only with wages, hours, and fringe benefits, but also with promotions, layoffs, discipline, and transfers.

It should be emphasized that even with a union, management continues to make the most of the personnel decisions: who shall be hired, disciplined, promoted, given a pay increase, have their working conditions improved, and so forth. Very few decisions are made jointly. But *after* a manager takes action, the union can challenge the decision and file a grievance claiming that management is acting in violation of the contract or of past practice (which becomes the equivalent of a contract). Thus the grievance procedure is, in effect, a judicial process that determines the rights of the parties.

The typical grievance procedure moves in steps; at each the problem is discussed by union and management people on their respective levels. The first step may involve the foreman and the steward; the second, the superintendent and the chief steward, and so on. Most contracts provide that if no agreement is reached at these lower steps, the matter will be referred to an impartial third-party arbitrator (often a lawyer or a professor) who is selected jointly by the parties. After the arbitrator holds a hearing in which both sides present their case, he or she writes a decision based on his interpretation of the contract. Normally, his decision is final.[10]

Mary Jones has a grievance

Let us examine a hypothetical case to illustrate the ramifications of what may appear to be a simple grievance. Notice especially the number of people involved and their diverse points of view.[11]

The employee's problem. Mary Jones works as a laboratory assistant in the animal experimental station of a large drug company. Her work involves feeding and weighing animals, building and occasionally cleaning cages. Recently, Jones has noticed that she is required to spend much more time cleaning cages than are the other assistants. Since this is an unpleasant chore and has the lowest status of all her tasks, she thinks it is unfair that she should have to do so much of it. Further, she thinks she is being discriminated against since she is the only black in the group.

The supervisor's reaction. When Jones discusses her problem with the supervisor, Brown, she is told that job assignments are arranged in order to use the work force most efficiently. All assistants are hired with the understanding that they will be doing one or all of the tasks noted above. Brown feels that some of the other employees are more skilled in handling the animals and doing minor construction work. So it seems a better use of personnel to have Jones spend her time cleaning cages.

Enter the union. Unsatisfied by Brown's answer, Jones considers calling in the union for help.[12] She hesitates to do anything for a while, fearing that filing a grievance may antagonize her supervisor. Then Jones decides that, after all, help is what she pays dues for, so she talks to the union steward. After discussing the problem with Brown, the steward reports back:

"Brown refuses to do anything. He says it's his right to make decisions like this one, and he is not discriminating against you. I'm not satisfied with his answer. I'll see the chief steward tonight at the union meeting and see what she says."

[10] In one year General Motors and the United Automobile Workers processed a total of 256,000 grievances, 2,500 of which were appealed to arbitration. The General Motors situation may be more prone to grievances than most, however.

[11] This case does not describe the exact procedure for handling every complaint. The number of steps and the union and management personnel who become involved at each step vary greatly from one labor contract to another. But this case is typical. Many "grievances," however, are not written down and processed through a formal procedure; they are handled informally in the regular, day-to-day contacts of union and management officials.

[12] She might also have filed a discrimination charge with the Equal Employment Opportunities Commission. She might also have consulted her union "black caucus."

Note what has happened: the steward has tried unsuccessfully to represent the worker and has now turned the case over to a higher level in the union, which can reach higher management.

The union's reaction. The steward goes to the chief steward and describes the case. Here is the chief steward's reaction:

"This is not a simple case; we have to be careful. In the first place we have to consider the reaction of the other people in the department. Jones is the newest employee; they may get pretty sore if more of this cleaning work is thrown at them. The whole thing may backfire. Our present contract is weak on this point. There is actually nothing to prevent the company from changing people's work. If they start giving her a lot of the dirty jobs and they want to be mean about it, they might be able to justify paying her less money since her work may now be less skilled than before. Our only chance to win would be if we could show that the supervisor was doing this to Jones because of racial discrimination. That would be covered by Article 14 of the contract. Discuss it with Jones, and if she has some evidence on this, get her to sign a grievance."

Note the implication behind this reaction: the union does not merely represent the individual worker. The union must consider its total membership. Actually, as you have already learned, many grievances and worker demands are directed against other employees, not against management. The union depends on the support of its total membership; dissatisfied members may succeed in ejecting officers or in overthrowing the union itself. Clearly, the union must consider the overall implications of each grievance and demand. (Consider also that the chief steward may be motivated by racial prejudice.)

Moreover, the union must consider its strategic position vis-à-vis management. The union has certain institutional objectives. For example, it is seeking to strengthen its own position in the company somewhat independently of particular employee or group needs. Creating a fuss about Jones' complaint might lead management to insist on its contractual right to change jobs as it sees fit. Of course, the members might be aroused to seek a stronger contract at the next negotiations.

The middle steps of the grievance procedure. Jones agrees to sign the formal grievance papers charging Brown with discrimination. She notes that her assignment to excessive cleaning duties followed an argument with Brown over new coveralls. "When I complained that my coveralls (supplied by the company) were torn, Brown said I was always complaining and ought to have something important to complain about for a change." The grievance is also signed by the steward; the supervisor himself signs it, but only after adding this note: "Grievance refused—employee has not been discriminated against." Then the chief steward sends the grievance to the laboratory manager, asking for an appointment to talk over the matter.

Management's reaction. After the manager receives the grievance, he calls in the supervisor, Brown, to get his version of the case; he also checks with the personnel director to see whether similar cases have established precedents that would affect the settlement.

The manager is at first concerned that this might be a case of racial discrimination. The company has a firm policy here. Having satisfied himself that discrimination was not involved, the manager feels that he cannot grant the grievance. To do so would be to open the door to a stream of union challenges of work assignments. The manager tells the chief steward that even though an employee may feel he is getting more than his share of the unpleasant jobs, it is up to the supervisor to make such decisions in accordance with work requirements and available manpower. So while he will caution Brown to make sure such assignments are dictated by work needs and not by personal feelings toward particular employees, the grievance will have to be refused. The manager's answer to the grievance is, "No contract violation; supervisor was acting within normal management prerogatives."

Higher levels of the grievance procedure. The next move is clearly up to the union. The chief steward and the steward explain to Jones that she has a weak case. No one has heard the supervisor threaten Jones, and even if the supervisor admitted using threats, that would not prove he was discriminating. Well, yes, there are some other steps that might be taken. The union's business agent could take the case up with the division manager of the drug company. If the company still refused to agree to divide the work more equitably, the case could then be taken to arbitration, or Jones could take her case to the EEOC.

Jones is told that the chances of winning, however, are not good. The chief steward advises her to be alert for other evidence of discrimination that would enable the union to reopen the case. She promises that the union will also try to obtain a contract clause next year to prohibit, without specific union approval, changes in work assignments that are equivalent to job transfers.

Even though the chances of success were slight, the chief steward might have decided to push the case anyway. Grievances provide interesting, challenging work and relieve monotony. And yet most union leaders are not anxious to build up a reputation for pressing weak cases too vigorously. They want their opposite numbers in management to believe that they are sensible, if tough.

Impact of the union on management

What overall effect does the existence of a union have on the organization as a whole and on the management of personnel? The following discussion, which goes beyond the specific grievance problems we have described, will also suggest some of the reasons why many companies have resisted unionization.

Challenges to management decisions. The existence of a union means that all personnel decisions are subject to close scrutiny and, perhaps, active challenge. In a nonunion situation, employees may grow dissatisfied and harbor a sense of injustice or injury, but they are not necessarily willing to express their attitudes. The union gives them a means of taking action, not only by approaching the immediate supervisor, but also by reaching higher in the management structure with their demands. For the manager who relishes unchecked authority, this is an unpleasant experience. Almost any manager would prefer to have his orders and decisions go unchallenged.

Personal differences and competition for loyalty. The union competes with management for employee loyalty. It takes credit for any benefit won, even when management is willing to give this benefit voluntarily. Furthermore, it dramatizes and sometimes magnifies issues. In a sense it looks for trouble. Particularly during the organization stage, when the union is trying to establish itself, it may caricature management and management's desire to "sweat labor." Such charges of dishonesty and highhanded tyranny come as a rude shock to executives, particularly those who think of themselves as fair and considerate. Thus personal conflict sometimes makes differences harder to settle than they would be in a less adversary relationship.

Review of personnel policies. Management will exercise care in shaping personnel policies when it is aware that the union can challenge its actions. Mistakes can be costly, not only in terms of the time and goodwill lost through processing grievances, but also in terms of the new contractual demands that are likely to spring from employee dissatisfaction.

In one company, the supervisor gave overtime work (at time-and-a-half extra pay) only to workers he felt had done a better-than-average job. The union claimed that this was favoritism and demanded that overtime be distributed with absolute equality among all employees. To avoid such an ironclad rule, the company quietly passed down the word to its supervisors that overtime should be distributed at least roughly equally and that monthly reports on how this is done should be submitted to the personnel department.

Overall, the growth of unions has been an impetus to the development of better personnel policies.

Rigidify rules. Unions demand that personnel policies relating to pay, promotion, transfers from job to job, discipline, vacations, fringe benefits, and the like be written into the contract. Although this ensures equal treatment for all employees, it greatly reduces management's discretion. On the other hand, many nonunion plants have standard rules covering such matters, to preserve some uniformity in policy and to prevent obvious inequities from developing. (Further, in some unionized plants where foreman-steward relations are good, the inflexibility of rules may be reduced by informal agreements to waive contractual provisions. A rule preventing foremen from working may be ignored in a production crisis if the foreman does not strictly enforce discipline.)

Threats to efficiency. Management fears that the union may want to introduce barriers to efficient work methods, reduce work loads, and generally inhibit productivity. The union usually wants to introduce rules that prevent workers from working outside their "job classification," that is, from doing work other than that listed in the description of their job. If a manager is prevented from assigning work in a way that will take advantage of the employees' aptitudes and experience, management reasons that labor costs are bound to go up.

Some observers argue that the increased costs resulting from union pressures "shock" management into finding more efficient work methods.

Centralization of decision-making. A manager who fails to understand the contract may inadvertently prompt an embarrassing grievance. It may set a costly precedent and strengthen the union's argument that the company is "unfair." In our hypothetical Jones case, the laboratory manager was anxious to avoid establishing the precedent that work assignments were not a management prerogative. Fearing such contingencies, many companies no longer allow lower-level supervisors the authority to make certain personnel decisions. This authority has been delegated to higher levels of management and, in many cases, to staff departments with specialists trained in labor relations.

Introduction of "outsiders" in labor relations. As we have seen, an international union usually embraces members from a number of different firms.[13] Not only does the union have institutional goals distinct from those of the company (it wants to grow and prosper and its officers want to be re-elected), but it is also concerned with more than one employer. The union seeks wage increases in one company to set a precedent that will make it easier to negotiate a favorable contract elsewhere. Frequently, arbitration decisions set precedents affecting labor relations in many companies. As a result, many company officials feel that the problems that union officers force them to consider are not restricted to the interests of the particular organization and its employees.

Business agents and international representatives are not employees of the firms with which they negotiate. Although in principle many managers resent the fact that the union brings "outsiders" onto the scene, in practice they often find that the outsiders are more dispassionate and better able to understand the company's viewpoint than their own employees would be.

Evolution of sound union-management relations

There is little question that the introduction of a union may prove a traumatic experience for management. At the outset, the union may try to dramatize every company mistake, and the early days may be spent in destructive warfare. In some cases this period may drag on for years in a kind of armed truce, with both sides trying to capitalize on the other's mistakes. While grudgingly accepting the existence of the union, managers may seek to limit its influence and they may compete actively with the union for the loyalty of the membership. Yet many companies and their managements develop a more harmonious relationship and admit

[13] Many independent unions, however, which are not affiliated with international unions, have no organizational relationships beyond the company in which they are organized.

that the union can have a beneficial effect on the organization if dealt with properly.

The most important factor contributing to sound labor relations is the recognition by management that its own actions and policies have a major impact on union behavior. To some extent "a management gets the kind of union it deserves."

Opportunities for improved human relations

To the management that is willing to explore new techniques, the introduction of a union into the organization need not be a catastrophe. The union can actually help management improve employee relations.

Labor relations involve a problem that every company must face, whether or not its workers are unionized: this is the problem of adjusting the needs of the individual to the needs of the organization. Without a union, employees may find other means of protesting what they think is unfair: slowdowns, sabotage, or quitting. The union provides a peaceful means of resolving such disputes or differences in a way that will maintain productivity and preserve the work force intact.

Supervisors who are sensitive to human relations prefer to obtain group agreement before initiating changes in work procedure. Rather than deal with a large number of individuals with diverse points of view, they realize that it is far more efficient to sit down with a responsible union leader. He is the single spokesman who presumably represents the unified opinion of the entire work group and can subsequently sell his analysis to the group. In a sense, strong local unions are a guarantee that agreements will be honored.

Unions are sometimes described as "managers of discontent." As such they often bring to the surface vaguely felt dissatisfactions and even magnify them. (Managers sometimes say "unions create trouble." Mostly, they merely identify and dramatize trouble that is already present.) Yet, as managers of discontent, unions also help to keep discontent in bounds and to channel it, so it can be dealt with in an orderly fashion.

Management learns that it can introduce changes in working conditions with much less friction if it consults the union beforehand. Rather than sit back and wait for the union to raise problems, the company can make the first move to involve union officials in clearing up potential trouble areas.

"We knew we were going to have a lot of squawks over new job assignments when we brought automation into the department. This could have meant a hundred grievances and months of wasteful talk. Instead we went to the union and told them what our plans were. We got them to work with us in deciding who was going to stay in the department and how transfers would be arranged. We also negotiated the rates on the new jobs."

Consulting with the union prior to the development of grievances often produces a valuable byproduct. As we have seen, union officials are typically active people who want to keep busy. If they can be involved in handling constructive questions, they are less likely to seek out problems and grievances.

The chances of converting hostility-ridden, destructive labor relations into a constructive pattern depend largely on the manager's ability to adapt

The manager's role

Management representatives quickly learn to differentiate between the grievances on which the union leaders face strong political pressures and those which they are merely "going through motions" of pressing. . . . A shrewd management learns not to embarrass union officials before a close election. . . .

We have observed many episodes such as the following telephone call by a union leader to a personnel director:

"Look, Bill, we'll admit that Charlie Jones was drunk last week. Frankly we don't have a leg to stand on. If you'll take it easy on him—after all this is his first offense—we'll waive the formal hearing. And that'll save you a lot of time and money. . . ."

These are not collusive dealings but rather part of the flexible process by which both sides adjust to new problem situations which could not have been foreseen when the contract was written.

to the existence of the union. When a union is first established, the manager may have difficulty dealing with subordinates who can speak to him as equals. At the outset, he needs to distinguish between the outspoken rabble-rouser and the genuine informal leader. The free-wheeling organizer may be motivated by deep-seated personality problems or personal grievances. Often he or she does not have the confidence of the group as a whole.

The manager should recognize that most employees experience no serious conflict between loyalty to the union (which they see as a sort of insurance program to protect them against future contingencies) and loyalty to management (which they see as a source of jobs and economic well-being). The manager who rejects or becomes suspicious of everyone voicing pro-union sentiments can alienate a number of very capable employees who, if they are accorded responsibility and trust, might identify themselves strongly with the company.

The manager also should be alert to the special problems affecting the union leader's behavior: He may be under conflicting pressures, one group wanting him to do one thing, another group insisting on something else. The manager should recognize the political position of union leaders and learn how to cope with them intelligently, rather than bemoan the fact that unions are political institutions.[14]

Thus, as time passes, the union abandons its role as a *competitor* for the loyalty of the worker. It takes on the role of a *policeman* who calls "halt" when a company representative makes a mistake, but who also keeps the member-employee within the bounds of legal decisions and practices. In some companies, this evolutionary process advances to the point where the union becomes a genuine *collaborator*, sharing with management the problems of improving efficiency and productivity.

[14] Some management observers believe that it is easier to negotiate with an undemocratic union than with a democratic one, since the leaders of the undemocratic unions are less subject to membership pressures. Indeed, it has been argued that the Landrum-Griffin Act, which was supposed to ensure union democracy, has actually contributed to labor-management strife.

Conclusion   The problems of labor relations are not distinct
from other human-relations problems. The exis-
tence of a union reflects employee needs and dissatisfactions. Although the
union cannot eliminate management's responsibility for the conduct of personnel administration, it can become an integral part of the employment relationship. Some human-relations problems, particularly in larger organizations, may
be almost beyond the ability of management to solve, and the manager need
not feel that the establishment of a union is evidence of his own failure. Thus,
it is unrealistic to think of personnel administration as an *alternative* to unionization, although companies like IBM, Eastman Kodak, and duPont are largely
unorganized, in part because their personnel standards (pay, fair treatment,
promotional opportunities, job security) were so high, higher than those in
unionized plants.

Union-management relations provide another challenge for the personnel
function. The necessity of working through these problems is just as much a
part of the managerial job as developing budgets and work schedules and
issuing orders. While negotiation and consultation are time-consuming, frequently frustrating, and certainly threatening, they require some of the same
personnel skills and persistence that are necessary to carry out other organizational functions. These responsibilities cannot be avoided if the organization
is to be healthy.

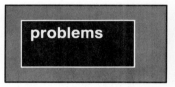

problems

1 • *What Is Negotiable?*

The following item appeared in the *Daily
California,* the student newspaper of the University of California, Berkeley.

In response to demands by black athletes that
certain of their numbers be moved to the first-
string Cal team, Coach Willsey replied, "I believe
there are certain prerogatives that belong solely
to the head of the team, and these include determining the relative abilities of various members
of the team and placement of athletes in the various
positions: simply the determination of who will play
and where. I do not believe these prerogatives are
negotiable. I cannot ignore these responsibilities
and violate the ethics of my profession."

1. How justified is the coach? Would your answer be very different were he president of General Motors
   and replying to a newly organized union of executives? Why?
2. From the point of view of the team's playing efficiency, what would be the advantages and disadvantages
   of a system in which college football players were organized into a union that would negotiate with the
   coach regarding the terms and conditions of their playing? Is your answer affected by the fact that big-
   league college football is no longer purely amateur?
3. Should students as a group negotiate with their professors? About what?

2 • *A Change in Schedule*

The company guards at the Elmwood Company were among the last groups to join a union,
but they had always expressed a great deal of dissatisfaction over their work schedules. For many years
there had been charges of favoritism in the assignment of work hours. Guard work had to be carried
on around the clock, and employees who were assigned to the less desirable shifts or to week-end

duty complained that they should have better working hours.

The issue of "fair working schedules" was plugged hard by the new union in signing up new members, and it was one of the first questions raised by the union leaders when they met with management to negotiate their first labor contract. In fact, this issue took up the first two weeks of negotiation.

When the issue was finally settled, management discovered that the agreement with the new guard union specified a work schedule that was almost identical with the one that had existed prior to unionization. Nevertheless, the union and the membership seemed satisfied with the agreement, and there was no longer the heavy stream of complaints about work assignments.

1. How do you explain this strange development? Were the employees dissatisfied before? If so, why did they appear satisfied after the agreement was made?
2. What scheduling difficulties may the union leaders have become aware of during their two-week discussion with company representatives?

3 • *Wildcat Strike*

During the 20 years Terry Keller has worked for the Ridge Lee Company, she has risen to the top of her promotion ladder: one of the highest-paid nonsupervisory employees in the company. About five years ago, the workers in the company were organized by a union, but Keller played no active part in the organizing campaign. About a year ago, Keller developed an illness that was difficult to diagnose; although she lost strength and energy, she was able to continue at work. Because of her good record and long service, the company found a number of special assignments for her and maintained her wages until she regained her health.

Recently, the employees in the shop where Keller works staged a wildcat one-day walkout that did not have the formal authorization of the local union. Employees in other departments were not involved. Keller's department claimed that their wages had declined in relation to wages in many other departments because they had had no opportunity to work more than 40 hours a week. Many of the other departments were working 45 hours and 50 hours a week.

Much to the surprise and disappointment of Keller's supervisor, she not only participated in this protest demonstration, but actually appeared to be one of the leaders.

1. Does Keller's action seem reasonable in light of the consideration management accorded her during her illness?
2. What should the supervisor do with Keller now?
3. How typical do you think this case is?
4. What is your reaction to the department's complaint?

part 2

personnel skills

communications: the information transmission process

Much of what is said about management and personnel relations simply assumes that human beings will understand what they say to one another as they interact at work. In fact, we have given most of our emphasis to *what* should be said—correct tactics and strategies to improve personnel relationships—and rather little attention to *how* it should be said. But people are constantly misunderstanding one another in their day-to-day organizational relations.

"I thought you wanted me to start that new job *after* I finished what I was doing."

"How did I know he was *serious* about quitting?"

"I *discount* almost everything I hear from those jokers in Corporate Communications!"

"But I was sure you meant London, *Ontario.*"

In this chapter, we shall explore the source of these misunderstandings and the methods to improve interpersonal communications.[1]

[1] This chapter seeks to provide a somewhat simplified overview of the subject of communication theory, which has received substantial attention from social psychologists. For good summaries of the research literature see Richard Farace, Peter Monge, and Hamish Russell, *Communicating and Organizing* (Reading, Mass.: Addison Wesley, 1977); Nan Lin, *The Study of Human Communication* (Indianapolis, Ind.: Bobbs Merrill, 1971).

On the surface, face-to-face communications appear simple. Have you ever listened to two old friends talking together? Rarely do they use complete sentences; often a single word, a grunt or a groan or a raised eyebrow communicates as much meaning as lengthy speeches would convey between casual acquaintances. A few syllables go a long way.

But successful communication does not necessarily take place automatically whenever two people get together. Let's examine a situation more typical of business life. The shop-clerk tells his boss with pride, "This is the heaviest day we've ever had." But the boss thinks the clerk is lazy and looking for an excuse not to unload new stock. So he answers angrily, and the subordinate concludes that the boss is overbearing and ungrateful.

The communication process; the sender's world

Most of us have a simple, straightforward view of communication:

Sender's thought or idea	$\longrightarrow$ Converted to words and speech	$\longrightarrow$ Receiver's hearing	$\longrightarrow$ Receiver's understanding

Were the process that straightforward, life would be much simpler. Let's look at reality, then: first, the sender's world.

Intention. The sender, whether colleague or boss or subordinate, has something to communicate to the other person: information, instructions, a point of view, some data.

What is transmitted

Impression management. The presumably logical, objective content of communication is complicated by other motives. Often, the sender "stage manages" the communication to convey an overall impression of personal prestige, helpfulness, or power.[2] We are all familiar with acquaintances who use each contact to communicate a total image of themselves. Listen to this manager, instructing a subordinate:

"I could tell—when the VP called me into her office to give me this assignment—that she really relied on my extensive knowledge of food chains. Then I asked for you to work with me, because this is going to be so big and important that I hoped you could get a part of the glory. Now here is what I want you to do first on this supermarket project of mine."

It's pretty obvious what's being communicated: self-importance and "I want you to think of me as your powerful protector."

Emotional state. The sender unintentionally is also saying things about his or her own emotional state. Some of this reflects the immediately preceding circumstances. Pushed? Panicky? Under stress? Relaxed? The sense of agitation or calm will be transmitted along with the actual words the sender is using.

[2] Much of the work on impression management is the product of Erving Goffman. See *Relations in Public* (New York: Basic Books), 1971.

Covert feelings.   The sender also has hidden feelings (some may be even unconscious) toward himself (or herself) and toward the recipient of the communication. Imagine the difference in the tone of the interchange if the sender is feeling guilty and inadequate, rather than self-confident.

The receiver may be distrusted or disliked or, contrariwise, a close and dear friend who can always be relied upon to do the right thing. These inner, private feelings surface in a variety of ways in actual communication. And added to these are the emotions generated by the apparent attitude of the intended receiver. Does he or she appear interested in, and receptive to, what is being said, or resistant, even hostile? This feedback, in turn, shapes the message that goes out.

Modes of communication

Intended and unintended meanings are transmitted to the other person by more than simple words; there are many dimensions to the mode of communication.

Argot and jargon.   Occupational and professional groups evolve their own specialized language that sociologists call argot. Some argot reflects the need to invent precise but simple ways of saying things that have to be used repeatedly. Generations of managers learn to scrawl ASAP on notes, to indicate that something is important, wanted as soon as possible. It is easy to forget that a newcomer may not be familiar with all these specialized terms, although at times they may be used simply to symbolize group solidarity or to exclude outsiders.

Differences in how groups use everyday terms can cause trouble. This example is from NASA's bio-satellite program:

The investigators (bioscientists) thought they were being specific when they asked for a sterile system [one free of all bacteria] to conduct monkey urine. But the engineers (designing the satellite) didn't understand the meaning of "sterile.". . . The engineers took *sterile* simply to mean "clean—void of all obvious dirt and contamination." As a result, invisible bacteria could live in the system, which would infect and kill the orbiting monkeys.[3]

We have become sensitive to the complex language forms, the long cumbersome sentences and erudite language associated with government documents and social science monographs. Their authors believe that this jargon is important to signify the importance of what they are saying.

Symbols.   Many words have strong emotional meanings that go far beyond their dictionary definitions. When a manager says she isn't sure the union shop is "desirable" (presumably because it forces workers to join a union), she is communicating to the union that she doesn't like, trust, or accept unions and probably hopes to weaken them. In much the same vein, when a new employee is told he can't have a parking place in the lot near the executive offices, he hears this as meaning: "You haven't arrived yet; you're really not one of the important bosses."

[3] Leonard Sayles and Margaret Chandler, *Managing Large Systems* (New York: Harper, 1971), pp. 233–34.

Of course, semantically speaking, all words are symbols; they serve to represent reality, but they are not reality. There is thus ample room for misunderstanding, as the quotations at the beginning of the chapter suggest. Each of us uses words slightly differently, with different intended meanings and connotations. When a prospective employee is called "aggressive," is that term communicating virtue: energy, initiative, and perseverance? Or does it mean irritatingly pushy, even belligerent? Speech gives great leeway for nuance, connotation, and hidden meanings.

There are nonverbal symbols, too. An Afro haircut, a flag in one's lapel, a white coat (in the lab or hospital)—all are saying things about the status and beliefs of the wearer, and they can trigger rather strong reactions in the other person.

Interaction styles. One communicates by the patterning of one's interaction as well as by words. Some people speak in long monologues; others use short bursts followed by long silences. Some are good at synchronizing their talking and silence periods with the interaction patterns of other people; they are flexible. Still others are rigid and cannot adjust.[4] Speaker and listener like each other and listen better when they have a comfortable interaction pattern, when their speaking and silent periods are synchronized.

Nonverbal cues. Almost everyone has now heard of body language and how much is communicated by posture and facial expression. A scowling speaker's words sound threatening; many people are suspicious of those who don't look them squarely in the eyes. The position of one's hands can suggest fear or openness, and there are countless other cues given by bodily actions and positions.[5]

Even the distance between the speaker and the listener connotes something about how friendly they are and their relationship.[6]

Spatial relations. Communication is also affected by the surrounding physical environment, the ease or difficulty with which people can converse. As generations of students and teachers have discovered, chairs arranged in a circle, where people face one another, stimulate easy give-and-take more than the typical, rowed lecture hall does. Even height differences have their impact: the listener who is lower than the speaker often feels repressed or demeaned. Open offices are designed to encourage spontaneous exchanges

---

[4] For a more complete description of how interaction patterns affect communication, see Eliot Chapple, *Culture and Biological Man* (New York: Holt, 1970), pp. 245–67.

[5] A summary of the best work in this field is presented in Ray L. Birdwhistell, *Kinesics and Context* (New York: Ballantine, 1972).

[6] Edward Hall has developed what he calls the science of "proxemics," and he believes that there are cross-cultural differences in terms of what one considers an appropriate and comfortable distance separating two people engaged in discourse. In the U.S., we become oppressed and discomforted when the speaker comes too close; but in Latin America, getting close to your listener is viewed as friendship. Hall's work and that of others are summarized in John Short, E. Williams and B. Christie, *The Social Psychology of Telecommunications* (London: Wiley, 1976), pp. 46–49.

of information; closed-in offices can intimidate people and reduce communication.[7] Too much grandeur can be overwhelming.

"I found it hard to really listen to what he was saying. He was behind that huge mahogany desk and sitting in an oversized executive chair, while I was perched on a small armless one. It wasn't until he came around from behind that barrier and said, 'Let's sit around the coffee table' that I could begin to feel easy enough to hear the subtleties of what he wanted me to do on this new job."

Of course, there can be too much of a good thing. People also need privacy, some sense of personal space that is violated only at their request. Many open-office plans are discomforting for that reason; they also inhibit frank interpersonal discussions.

Tone. Communication also has an overall quality or tone that influences the hearer. If the speaker appears to be supportive, the message that comes through is very different from the message of a speaker who appears to be antagonistic. In recent years, much emphasis has been placed on "transaction analysis," which, in part, emphasizes these differences in tone. TA asserts that all communication represents one of these three levels:

Parent   Child   Adult

With the *parent* tone, the sender is emphasizing that the receiver is somewhat childlike, and words like *should* and *ought* are dominant. The speaker is evaluating and judging the other person.

A supervisor dispairingly whines at a subordinate, "Haven't you learned to keep this work area neat yet and those files orderly? It's about time you started acting responsibly."

Such a parental judgmental tone typically evokes a childlike response: "Aw, can't you see I'm busy; I do the best I can." And, of course, that seemingly irresponsible reply will stimulate an even more critical rejoinder.

To avoid this spiral of parental criticism and childlike, irresponsible reply, the tone should be more *adult*—less judging, complaining, or self-justifying. Each party deals with issues as problems they will explore together.[8]

The world of the receiver

But receivers of communication are not passive receptacles, either. They also seek to make certain impressions. They have emotional states that may impede understanding, and they have feelings about the senders.

When we are insecure, worried, or fearful, what we hear and see seems more threatening than when we are secure and at peace with the world. Rumors of all sorts spring up when management makes a change of any kind

---

[7] A growing field, sometimes called environmental or ecological psychology, deals with the impact of physical arrangements on human interaction. See Robert Sommer, *Personal Space: The Behavioral Basis of Design* (Englewood Cliffs, N.J.: Prentice-Hall, 1969).

[8] For a good overview of transaction analysis, see Thomas Harris, *I'm OK—You're OK* (New York: Avon Books, 1973).

without adequate explanation, even a change as simple as moving desks around the office. This is particularly true during an economic recession. Then, statements and actions that under less trying circumstances would have passed unnoticed become grounds for fear. "Yes, Joe might be right. They are going to double the workload." "I saw the foreman looking at the seniority list. I guess the rumors are right; a lot of men will be laid off because of the new equipment." By the same token, when we are angry or depressed, we tend to reject out of hand what might otherwise seem like reasonable requests or good ideas.

Listeners usually hear what they expect to hear, rather than what is actually being said. On ceremonious occasions such as the opening of a new building, in a context emphasizing good will and good cheer, no one will interpret the speaker's remarks as bad news. But if a summons to the head office is associated with criticism, it is difficult not to interpret the big boss's comments as censure, regardless of what is said there.

The receiver's expectations

If the sender is perceived as trustworthy or even friendly and supportive, what is said is likely to be accepted and believed. Conversely, a disliked or distrusted person will find it difficult to communicate anything but the most banal facts. This is an aspect of stereotyping. We tend to hear good and true things from those we like; those we dislike speak untruths.

In labor management relations, where there has been overt conflict, it is difficult for management to have credibility in statements to the leaders or members of the union. Everything is suspect. "They're just saying that to frighten or deceive us."

Stereotyping. People expect to hear comments reflecting the speaker's associations. Outsiders are often perceived as threatening or upsetting to the group norms and routines; therefore, almost any request made by the outsider may be interpreted as inappropriate or pressureful. The same request for service from an insider would be heard as appropriate.

Many years ago, an experimenter clipped an item from a well-known union publication titled, *The Four Goals of Labor.* He then pasted it up with a caption: "from the National Association of Manufacturers." Not surprisingly, when the material was shown to union members they were overwhelmingly critical of it as an unfair, biased representation of labor's goals.

Clearly, the group with which we identify ourselves—the reference group, as psychologists call it—creates some of this bias. Advertisers discovered long ago that as individuals, we rarely change our minds by ourselves. Our attitudes toward politics, music, recreation, work pace, and all other activities and interests are largely colored by the group with which we identify.

Influence of reference group

This being the case, the manager may be wasting time trying to convince an individual employee to work harder when there is a strong group standard to the contrary. The employee would be risking ostracism in going along with the manager's request. Similarly, management often uses slogans and posters to indoctrinate workers with the importance of promoting safety, cutting scrap losses, making suggestions, or engaging in good housekeeping. They even send personal letters to employees' homes. The trouble with these efforts is that they are directed to the *individual,* whereas the basic attitudes and convictions are determined by the *group.* Thus, if fellow workers see the supervisor as harsh and unfair, chances are that the employee will feel the same way.

In a large organization, the difficulties of perception are compounded. An announcement may go to dozens of groups with different occupational and status interests. What each group "hears" depends on its own interests. An announcement that the company has purchased the patent for a product that will be manufactured in a new plant on the West Coast may be heard in these different ways.

Design engineer: "This may be an indication that the company prefers to go outside the organization for new ideas, and that is bound to hurt our status."
Production engineer: "This new product will mean more work for us. Some of us may have a chance to move out West."
Worker: "The new products aren't going to be manufactured in the home plant. That means if business should get slack, we're likely to be laid off. A bad trend."

Ignoring information that conflicts with what we already "know"

Most of us resist change. We tend to reject new ideas, particularly if they conflict with what we already believe. In some ways our communications receiving apparatus (sense organs and brain) works like an efficient filter. When we read a newspaper or listen to a political speech, we tend to note only those things that confirm our present beliefs. On the other hand, we tend to ignore anything that conflicts with our beliefs. Sometimes our filters work so efficiently that we do not hear new information at all. Even when we do hear it, we either reject it as a fallacious notion or find some way of twisting and shaping its meaning to fit our preconceptions. Because we hear and see what we *expect* to hear and see, we are rarely disappointed.

Communications sometimes fail to have the desired effect because they run counter to other information that the receiver possesses. Statements that hard work leads to promotion are ignored in a company where promotions often are made on the basis of seniority or favoritism. A guarantee that "the company never cuts an incentive rate because employees are earning too much" is disregarded if rates have, in fact, been cut as a result of minor engineering changes.

Cognitive dissonance. In recent years, a great deal of psychological research has been conducted on the mechanisms by which human beings cope with what they perceive to be irreconcilable communication inputs, or *cognitive dissonance.*[9] This research suggests that one can predict very strong differences between the reaction to information that is consistent with what the receiver already believes, and the reaction to new information that is inconsistent with those beliefs. These differences are summarized below.

[9] For a fuller discussion, see Elliot Aronson, *The Social Animal* (San Francisco: Freeman, 1976), pp. 85–139.

Communication is consistent with existing beliefs	*Communication is inconsistent with existing beliefs*
Seeks additional exposure, more information	Avoids exposure
Accepts information as valid	Rejects validity
Remembers what is heard	Easily forgets
Memory is accurate	Memory distorts information

This sort of bias is one of the reasons why company newspapers (so-called house organs) find it difficult to gain worker acceptance. Once employees become convinced that the paper is just a management mouthpiece, many will believe nothing it prints, no matter how objective or verifiable. So, too, with pamphlets and other give-aways. If these are tagged as propaganda, all the information they contain becomes suspect, even useful information about health and household safety.

During February, 1971, the National Emergency Warning Center (an arm of the U.S. Office of Civil Defense) transmitted a coded message to all civilian radio stations, warning of an impending nuclear attack. Although the message was sent in error, its form and content were precisely correct, and nearly all civilian stations were supposed to go off the air after announcing that "the President has directed an emergency action notification." Even though every station knew the correct procedure, and each had been drilled in its response, all but a small number ignored the message. Apparently most station managers found the coded alert inconsistent with what they believed to be reality.

It is difficult for a manager to shed a reputation for being hardboiled or unfair. He may go through a training program and emerge with every intention of turning over a new leaf, but subordinates will be suspicious of his motives and assume that his new approach is just a trick. They will distort and misconstrue every move he makes. He is now unpredictable.

Defensive avoidance. By a somewhat similar mental process, we ignore or distort much that is threatening, unnerving, or requiring upsetting changes in our routines, beliefs, and actions.

Social psychologists reassessing why Pearl Harbor was unprepared for a Japanese attack even though a number of warnings were issued from Washington believed that the warnings were never "heard." Our military high command deceived themselves into thinking that each announcement simply confirmed their pre-existing belief that the Japanese either were not going to war or were likely to move toward other targets.[10]

Noise. Related to these concepts is the one of noise. The sender's communication often must compete with a number of irrelevant stimuli: not only

[10] Irving Janis and Leon Mann, *Decision-Making* (New York: Free Press, 1977), pp. 120–29.

literal noise, which muffles and distorts sound, but other people speaking, visual and aural sensations emanating from a wide variety of sources. Air traffic controllers, trying to hear the pilot of an incoming plane, can be deluged with a variety of other sights and sounds, so a critical word is lost or confused with another term. In one mid-air collision, the controller thought the pilot knew where the other plane was because he missed hearing the pilot use the word. *think*. The controller heard the pilot say only, "It has passed us," so the controller stopped worrying about how close the two planes were to each other.

Living in a world of words and being deluged by sounds all the time, we learn to tune out many things. While a mother usually hears her child crying, the father often sleeps through, although he would hear his wife call. Many things a manager says are ignored, actually never heard, because they sound so much alike: "Work efficiently. . . . This order is very important. . . . Save materials. . . . The company is depending on you." To themselves, they say, "So what else is new?" Thus, before we can hear a message, we must learn to discriminate between background noise (timeworn clichés) and significant, relevant, new information, worthy of attention.

Unfortunately, in critical situations—safety emergencies, work crises—it is likely that general confusion will cause critical words to be missed or misinterpreted.

Thus it is not only easy, it is almost inevitable for substantial error to creep into communication because of this thicket of distorting obstacles:

SENDER'S INTENTION
↓
Impression management
↓
Emotional state
↓
Covert feelings
↓
Multiple modes of communication
↓
Tone
↓
RECEIVER'S WORLD
↓
Emotional state
↓
Stereotyping
↓
Reference group beliefs
↓
Cognitive dissonance
↓
Defensive avoidance
↓
Noise
↓
RECEIVER'S UNDERSTANDING

*Improving
communication*

Among other things, good communication requires solving simultaneously two quite different
problems. Managers must learn to improve *trans-
mission*—what words, ideas and feelings are actually sent to the other person.
At the same time they must cope with their own *reception*—what they perceive
the other persons' reactions and statements to be. We shall devote the rest
of this chapter to a discussion of several methods by which a manager can
maximize success in communicating. At first glance, these techniques may
appear mechanical substitutes for mutual trust and understanding. However,
a wide variety of research confirms the efficacy of considering communications
as both a psychological and technical problem.

*Adjusting to
the world of
the receiver*

In communicating, the temptation is to adjust to *yourself*. You have the
need to say something and to say it in a particular way. In fact, often you
communicate when your emotional needs to speak are strongest and the odds
of being understood the lowest.

"I was just boiling with rage. He had done it wrong again, so I explained why we needed
to keep this particular customer: how much they had purchased in the past, who else
would be impressed with their being a steady customer, their tie-in with the consolidated
buying syndicate, and all the rest. But I could tell the production scheduler wasn't understanding!"

Of course he wasn't! The manager was gaining satisfaction by venting
his feelings; he was not trying to get through to the other person.

How does the speaker adjust to the *receiver?* Several passive techniques
are available, as well as more dynamic ones. The passive techniques involve
thinking ahead and endeavoring to be aware of the listener's needs, possible
symbolic interpretations, and the right time to communicate. Dynamic techniques revolve around *feedback* and reinforcement, to be discussed later.

*The receiver's
expectations*

It is extremely difficult to get through to a listener whose expectations
and predilections are contradicted by what you are trying to communicate.
If your typist has been in the habit of preparing only a single carbon, you
must *stress* a request for two carbons. If being sent to the front office is regarded
by employees as a sign of impending discipline, you must take pains to communicate that this is not the reason if, in fact, it is not.

In short, you must be sensitive to the private world of the receiver, try
to predict the impact of what you say and do on the other person's feelings
and attitudes, and tailor your messages to fit your receiver's vocabulary, interests, and values. Managers who work with a variety of groups in the organization must learn techniques of "simultaneous translation" to avoid misunderstandings. The greater the gap between your background and experience and
that of the receiver, the greater the effort you must make to find some common
ground of understanding.

*Awareness of
symbolic meaning*

As we have seen, symbols play a vital role in the private world of the
listener. Here is a case in which effective communication was blocked until
symbolic meanings were taken into account.

101

To help in the preparation of market analyses, the district sales manager asked the salespeople to compute correlation coefficients from their records. These coefficients could be calculated quite simply and painlessly by use of a simple formula. But the sales representatives refused to do what they were asked. One excuse followed another: the computations were too complicated, it was clerk's work and not part of their job description, the coefficients were really useless, and so on. There seemed to be no way to convince them to perform this simple task.

Why was this modest request greeted with such stubborn resistance? The very degree of the salespeople's reaction was the key to the problem. Investigation revealed that coefficient correlations had been tried three years earlier, when the department was headed by an inept supervisor who was universally disliked. Among other things, he had tried to revamp all the departmental procedures and in the process had introduced this statistical technique. Ever since, the sales representatives had associated the term "coefficient correlation" with autocratic supervision. To them, it had become a symbol of oppressive management. Once the company had plumbed this seemingly irrational attitude, it was a simple matter to develop a different terminology for the operation, to conduct training in how the computations should be carried out, and to gain ready acceptance for the whole activity.

The moral of this story is clear: if there is extraordinary, unexpected resistance to a proposal, try to find out whether some symbolic meaning is associated with it.

Often, those who wish to communicate must prepare the way for effective listening by taking the time to prove that they share certain symbolic values that they presume to be of importance to the others.

A supervisor describing some new work procedures to her department: Here is the way we are going to handle Eastern Division Receivables. The procedure grows out of that hassle we had with the comptroller's office and the computer people. We're always the forgotten ones in these new procedures, and the computer people get their way. This time we took "first place" in the final agreement on procedures, and we aren't going to have to handle those silly blue forms anymore either, the ones that took us all so much time. Now, here is how we'll have to handle the. . . .

The speaker is showing solidarity with the group and with some previous issues that have riled people: the status of the computer, the blue forms, the position of the comptroller's office. These have nothing directly to do with the new procedure she wants to communicate, but if her listeners feel that she shares their values and needs, they are more likely to listen with alertness and sympathetic understanding and accept her as a credible source of new information.

Where these common symbols do not exist, the sender may have to build up systematically some shared experiences and, thus, shared symbols, before communicating more difficult, more controversial subjects.

Critical timing

Messages can come too early and too late; theoretically, there is an ideal time when the odds are greater that the message will get through.

Communications come too early when they presume to deal with problems or subjects that the listener has not experienced: "I didn't understand a word they were saying about human relations problems because I had never worked and certainly had never been a supervisor." On the other hand, an employee who is frustrated by a problem may be highly receptive to new ideas.

Similarly, when people are away from their regular work environment or work group (and not frightened), they may be more receptive to materials that conflict with their prejudices, predispositions, and "conventional wisdom." An engineer described his experiences as part of a company task force:

I've never learned so much so quickly. Part of it was being thrown in with finance and marketing people from other parts of the corporation and working as a team overseas. Everything was new to me; I had never done this sort of work before, and there was nobody there to tell me what I expected to hear.[11]

Thus, it may be useful to wait until there is time available to get people to another location (e.g., taking executives to a resort "retreat" to rethink corporate policy) or away from their normal associations.

A manager can also make the mistake of asking a subordinate to communicate results or findings prematurely. At least, when the manager wants the subordinate to continue to be open-minded and alert to new possibilities (say in R & D) too-early communications may rigidify expectations. Don't get people to take a stand too early, in other words, until you are sure they have as much information and data as they need to draw sensible conclusions.

Communications come too late when opinions have already hardened or the subject has become a battleground between groups or individuals. One way of limiting the amount of noise or distortion is to communicate your message before those other beliefs or attitudes come into play. Then the communication will meet less resistance and your chances of getting it accepted will be greatly increased.

Management announced that Foreman Green would retire in a few months and would be replaced by a man named Williams from another department. One of the men felt that Williams had done him an injustice years ago and spread the word among his fellow employees that Williams was a tyrant who played favorites.

Long before Williams set foot in the new department, a petition was sent to top management requesting that a different foreman be assigned. And once Williams showed up, everything he said and did was fitted into the picture the employees had already established. Every job assignment he made was scrutinized for favoritism. Even harmless statements were often interpreted as threats.

[11] A harsh, devious form of this principle is involved in brainwashing, which involves separating the individual from all familiar supports (friends, home, etc.) so he will be more receptive to the constant haranguing of his captors. Less devious is the value of foreign travel in stimulating learning.

A situation like this is an ideal breeding-ground for misunderstanding and unrest. Yet management could have minimized the problem by taking positive action before the picture of the new supervisor was established, perhaps by having the employees meet him as soon as the announcement was made.

It is a waste of time to try to communicate during an argument or bitter debate, when the person has to defend his preconceptions. During such acrimonious discussion, to concede (or even to "hear" accurately) would mean admitting that you are less worthy than the other person.

When issues have become polarized in an organization, informal groups pressure their members to hold only orthodox views and not to concede anything to outsiders.

"There was no use talking with the Shipping people about anything after that battle over losing the Krystar business. Anything you said to them about procedures, they interpreted as being just a continuation of the arguments. And no one from Shipping would dare agree with anything we said in Production or even listen to us—he would be massacred by his colleagues for heresy."

Feedback

Perhaps the single most important method of improving communications is *feedback*. This term, adopted from electrical engineering, refers to the ability of certain complex machines (technically, systems) to check on their own performance and to correct it if necessary—often called cybernetics.

We all use this principle of feedback in our human communications—perhaps without realizing it. Even in casual conversations we are constantly on the alert for cues to whether we are being understood (such as attentive nods from the other person). A good teacher is always interested in audience reaction among students. If they seem confused or drowsy, the lecture isn't getting across. Good managers are equally conscious of the need to determine subordinates' reactions to what they are trying to communicate.

An interesting study illustrates the importance of feedback.

Two students were placed in different rooms, and one was asked to communicate to the other the position of an interconnected series of dominoes placed on a grid. Both had identical grids in front of them. The sender was permitted to explain to the receiver, in any way, the relative positions of the dominoes. Yet it was impossible to complete the task successfully when the receiver was forbidden to respond—that is, when communications were entirely one-way. No matter how painstakingly the sender explained the pattern, the receiver never understood all of it.

Apparently, some opportunity to ask for further information, at least to answer "yes" or "no" to the questions of the sender (e.g., "Did you understand what I said?") is essential if complex information is to be communicated. Without feedback, false perceptions creep in, and even a small error that goes uncorrected may become magnified into a major distortion.

This experiment also revealed that communications gain in speed and efficiency as more and more feedback is permitted. Limiting receivers to "yes" or "no" responses is less effective than allowing them to expand their comments to whatever they deem appropriate.[12]

Face-to-face communications are superior, under most circumstances, to written orders, printed announcements, or business letters. The sender must experience direct feedback from the receiver to know what the receiver is hearing or failing to hear. How else can the sender become aware of the hidden meaning—the symbolic significance—the receiver is ascribing to the words? What better way to bring out into the open contradictory information already in the receiver's mind that may cause the communication to be rejected or ignored?

Face-to-face communications

Another reason for the greater effectiveness of personal confrontation is that most of us communicate more easily, completely, and frequently by voice. Probably the greatest advantage of such communications is that they provide immediate feedback. Merely by looking at the audience, skillful speakers can judge how it is reacting to what they are saying. If necessary, they can modify their approach or vary the intensity of voice. (The human voice can provide a wider variety of emphasis and pace than any printed page, regardless of the number of type fonts used.)

Even better feedback is possible if the recipients of the message are allowed to comment or ask questions. This gives supervisors an opportunity to explain their meaning or to consider unexpected problems. (Printed material can provide explanations, but few writers can anticipate all the questions that might be asked.)

It is almost impossible to criticize someone's performance in writing without giving serious offense. The cold type or words always sound more harsh and condemnatory than they may have been intended, and such written criticisms often provoke strong emotional counterreactions. The result is that the recipient tends to reject the entire message as having come from a hostile source. The same criticism discussed in a face-to-face exchange can be made much more acceptable and thus will be heard.

Furthermore, we usually ascribe more credibility to what we hear spoken than to words attributed to someone in print. Employees conditioned to the "slick" releases of public relations offices tend to discount many of the printed announcements they read. Actually hearing the boss say that the company is in serious trouble, however, may carry a great deal more weight than would a statement in the house organ, particularly if employees have an opportunity to ask the boss direct questions.

U.S. Secretaries of State like Kissinger and Vance have had to travel a great deal to develop mutual understandings and to convey subtle elements of our country's foreign policy. No memoranda or letters can substitute for face-to-face discussion. With direct contact each can check what the other is hearing and thinking:

"Tell me now, in your words, what you think this assignment is all about."

[12] For a fuller description of this experiment by the original researcher, see Harold Leavitt, *Managerial Psychology*, 4th ed. (Chicago: Univ. of Chicago Press, 1978), pp. 119–20.

"I think I hear you telling me that the first part is clear, but the second half of that assignment seems ambiguous. Is that correct?"

Written communications

Written communications still have an important place; they may be indispensable in some circumstances. Lengthy, detailed procedures should be put in writing, so that the person to whom they are addressed can have a chance to study them at leisure. The spoken word exists only for an instant, then vanishes. The written message provides a permanent record to which receivers can refer to make sure they understand what has been said, and to which senders can refer as evidence that they have in fact said it. Frequently, too, the relative formality of written communications gives the message greater weight than it would have if it were delivered orally.

For very important messages, both the spoken and written word may be used in combination. If a new procedure is to be introduced, the supervisor might call a meeting of subordinates to give them a rough outline of the change and to: (1) explain why the change is necessary, (2) answer their questions, and (3) perhaps make adjustments to meet objections. Once general agreement has been reached, the new procedure can be reduced to writing for future reference.

Assessing nonverbal cues

How do we know if the person to whom we are communicating understands, agrees, or sympathizes with us, or is indifferent, unconvinced, or confused? In a face-to-face situation, we can observe other people and judge their responses by their total behavioral set. We can watch for nonverbal cues—the expressions of puzzlement, anger, or comprehension that flicker across the face of the listener, or the subtle body motions that reveal impatience, animosity, or agreement. These cues give eloquent expression to attitudes that the receiver may be reluctant or unable to express in words.

Indeed, by their posture and facial expression, the set of their lips, the movement of an eyebrow, people often tell us more than they do in hours of talk or scores of written memoranda. A subordinate is seldom eager to challenge the orders of a superior. But in the course of informal, face-to-face discussion, an alert supervisor can detect the subordinate's lack of enthusiasm by tone of voice and general physical behavior.

Few of us appreciate just how much valuable information these nonverbal cues transmit. As many have observed, when communication is at peak efficiency, words are often superfluous. Good examples of this are the hospital operating room, the jazz band, and some small interdependent work teams in industry. The close coordination necessary for these groups to achieve their goal is attained largely through small bodily movements and expression changes.

Reinforcing words with action

Words by themselves are suspect. Employees are more likely to accept new propositions when they observe an actual change in behavior or participate themselves in the process of change. Supervisors in one company were told that they would have the final say in granting individual pay increases, a radical departure from past practice. Most supervisors were skeptical about whether management really meant what it said. But this feeling disappeared when they began filling out recommendation forms themselves and sending them to the personnel department (a minor clerical job that in the past had been done in the superintendent's office). The consistent reinforcement of verbal announcements by action increases the likelihood that the communication will be accepted.

Employees learn that their supervisors, not the personnel department, control pay increases when they see them taking this action and hear directly from them that they are to receive the increase. Where Personnel does the notifying, employees perceive otherwise.

Management must be careful not to allow supersalesmanship techniques to dominate its thinking in communicating to employees. One cannot advertise one type of personnel program and deliver another. In the same vein, low-pressure statements are probably more effective than high-pressure pronouncements. Instead of telling workers how generous their pension benefits are, it may be more effective to give them comparative data on pension plans for the industry or community and let them draw their own conclusion.

Once management has acquired a reputation for accuracy and credibility, it can do a more effective job of communicating information on new problems.

Early in World War II, when the radio stations of most countries were widely suspected of distorting the war news, the British broadcasting system adopted a policy of frankly reporting Allied setbacks. This gave the British an advantage in morale and tactics over their enemies when the tide turned in favor of the Allies, for Europeans of all nationalities were ready to believe the news of the German rout—simply because it came from a source that had proved itself trustworthy.

Written communications should be as readable as possible. Every manager must ensure that statements are couched in simple, direct language. Government agencies have been the favorite butt of jokes about gobbledegook, but many private organizations also are guilty of torturing simple statements into complicated puzzles and using specialized and complex jargon. Low readability is undoubtedly a factor in the breakdown of communications. (And since most people talk more simply than they write, that is another reason for using face-to-face communications whenever possible.) High readability, however, is not an answer in itself to the fundamental barriers to communication that we have discussed.

Using direct simple language

Emotionally charged rhetoric should be left to debating teams. Strong adjectives and expletives, innuendoes and exaggerations cause most listeners to turn off, not on, and raise questions concerning the credibility and balance of the speaker. Crowds, particularly in political gatherings, can be aroused by demagoguery, but most reasonably intelligent listeners, alone or in small groups, reject the inflated statements of the silver-tongued politician.

Communications engineers have developed techniques for measuring the amount of redundancy in a message—roughly the amount of repetition it contains. The supervisor who wants to give a direct order or transmit technical information should make sure that the message includes substantial redun-

Introducing a helpful amount of redundancy

dancy. Then, if any word or phrase is misunderstood, there are other elements in the communication that will carry the point. To give a very simple example:

A firm manufacturing several thousand varieties of chemical compounds used a numerical coding system to refer to each of the products. Increasingly, management found that mistakes were creeping into the ordering system. When a supervisor requested a shipment of compound #28394, a clerical error would occasionally result in a wasted shipment of #23894. Each digit was crucial, and the slightest mistake was costly. Eventually, the firm adopted individual names for each compound, and these words had a great deal of built-in redundancy, as do nearly all words. If a clerk ordered "calitin" instead of "calithin," the shipping department knew what he meant.

If each word is crucially important, it pays to say the same thing in several ways. In giving complicated directions, it is wise to repeat them several times, perhaps in different ways, to guarantee successful transmission.

At times, however, a manager may want to avoid redundancy and concentrate instead on introducing novelty or originality into communications. We tend to ignore many of the messages we receive, simply because they sound so familiar. Most of us repeat our favorite clichés so often that people no longer listen to what we say; it is all so predictable. ("I know what the boss is going to say the minute he starts on that line about us all being one big happy team.")

There is some need for surprise, in modest doses to be sure, if we are to gain the attention of those with whom we wish to communicate. This is particularly true when our message contains something that contradicts expectations. To repeat our previous example: if your typist has been in the habit of preparing only one carbon, you must stress your request for two.

Conclusion

The swiftest, most effective communication takes place among people with common points of view. Managers who enjoy good relationships with their subordinates have much less difficulty in explaining why air-conditioning equipment cannot be installed for another year than do the managers who are not trusted. When people feel secure, they can talk to one another easily. Where discontent is rife, so is misunderstanding, misinterpretation, rumor, and distortion. In this sense, communication is a dependent variable. Where there is mutual trust and human relations are good, it is easy; where there is distrust, it is almost impossible. Therefore, the communications area is *not* the place to start improving supervisor-subordinate relationships.

Nevertheless, the problem of communicating accurately and effectively in each contact makes managers' jobs more difficult. They must guard against the natural inclination in our highly verbal society to assume that simply *telling somebody* is enough to ensure successful communication. Fortunately, as we have seen, the manager can resort to a number of techniques to facilitate the transmission of understanding between people in their day-to-day activities.

Sensitivity to receiver

Awareness of symbolic meanings

Careful timing

Feedback

EFFORTS
TO
COMMUNICATE

Face-to-face communication

CLEAR
MESSAGE

Nonverbal cues

Reinforcing words with action

Simple language

Redundancy

Techniques for improved communication.

One must be careful not to draw the conclusion that "the more communication the better" is always true. There are limits to how much an individual can absorb and be responsive to. Needless information can overwhelm important data. Also, there may be private fears, hopes, and hostilities within an organization that ought not to be communicated because they would only engender adverse reactions.

Many managers regrettably conceive of communications as a selling job, persuading the wary and the unconvinced by an overwhelming array of facts and arguments. They conceive of feedback in terms of having an answer for every objection, and they believe that as long as their words are comprehensible to subordinates, they will go along with what is said. This is a highly naive view of the problem of communications that can only lead to further misunderstanding. Communications is a matter of both transmitting and receiving.

This chapter has emphasized transmitting. In Chapter 6 we will consider one of the most useful techniques for receiving information: interviewing.

1 · *Sending the Same Message with Different Meanings*

Two students are to take the role of a supervisor and subordinate, while the class observes. After each pair's performance, the members of the class are to report what they observe happening and how they would have felt in the situation, paying particular attention to various verbal and nonverbal cues, tones of address, and the actual give-and-take. The class should ask itself how effective was the communication and why?

The situation. Supervisor wants to send an assistant to Chicago to expedite delivery of supplies that are now late and critically needed. Here are four different scripts.

1. Top management has just berated the supervisor. Supervisor, while still angry, calls in subordinate. Subordinate is not trusted very much but is only person available. Supervisor wants to make sure the job is done right but is fearful it won't be.

2. Supervisor is anxious to impress subordinate with the fact that he or she has discretionary funds and authority to send people on trips. Select favored subordinate (partially as a reward) to send on this Chicago trip.

3. Supervisor is very worried that subordinate is too inexperienced to put adequate pressure on vendor. Subordinate believes that supervisor is too bossy, probably knows less than he or she does, and distrusts supervisor.

4. Supervisor takes *parent* role (in TA terms) and subordinate assumes *child* role.

2 · *Disappearing Merchandise*

Carlin Mailaway specializes in reproduction of traditional New England china and pewter and sells them by means of a nationally distributed catalog. The company has won a dominant position in the market it serves.

Recently, Carlin instituted a more formal inventory system. The results were appalling to the General Manager, Jean Coffin. According to the second quarterly inventory, at least $2,000 worth of merchandise had disappeared "mysteriously" during the preceding three months. Almost simultaneously, the warehouse supervisor found several pieces of merchandise wrapped as trash in a refuse barrel, as though they had been placed there by someone who intended to retrieve them later.

As soon as the figures were confirmed by a sample rechecking, Coffin dictated a letter to the warehouse supervisor and sent copies out to every one of the 28 employees working in the warehouse.

The letter read as follows:

Our auditing procedures have just disclosed a shocking loss of goods in our warehouse. In the future, no unauthorized personnel are to be allowed into the warehouse section of our building, and all employees working in the area will be expected to refrain from carrying packages in or out of the department and to permit close scrutiny of their persons as they leave work.

In no sense should any of our loyal, faithful employees interpret this as a slur against their characters. We know that they would want these stern provisions to be introduced to eliminate any possibility that they might be implicated.

We will appreciate your cooperation, and we thank you for your help in the past.

1. As a long-service employee in this department, how would you interpret this letter? Would others interpret it differently, do you think? Which ones and why?
2. What would you think the general manager's motives were in writing this letter?
3. What alternative procedures might have been considered? What would their shortcomings and advantages be?
4. How might the manager's letter have been better conceived and written?

communications: the problem-solving process

6

"My boss doesn't give a hoot about me. As far as he is concerned I am another piece of machinery."

"I'll say this about my boss: no matter what your problem, she'll hear you through."

Effective communication requires effort both by the sender of the message and the receiver. The previous chapter was concerned with the sending of the message. In this chapter we shall deal with the specifics of the receiving or listening process. Listening is one of the most important of all management tools. Yet, though people learn to listen before they learn to talk, relatively few listen well.

Listening is sometimes viewed as interviewing, and in this chapter we use the two terms, listening and interviewing, interchangeably. This may cause some confusion, since most people think of interviewing in the sense of formal interviews connected with getting a job. By *interviewing* we mean much more than this: we mean deliberate, active listening whose purpose is to draw other people out, to discover what they really want to say, to give them a chance to express themselves fully, and to assist in the solution of mutual problems.

The following interchange illustrates dangers that arise when managers fail to listen.

Jane: Bill, I think the time has come for us to investigate new office copying equipment.

Bill: No, our budget won't stand it. We invested too much when we decided to buy rather than rent Brand X equipment three years ago.

Jane: But we can rent this time, and we'll have equipment available when we need it. The cost won't be much more than our present repair bills, and we'll save on clerical time. Furthermore. . . .

Bill (interrupting): No, this isn't the year. We don't have the budget. You'll have to do a better job with what you've got.

Jane: If you only knew how badly off we are now. . . .

Bill: No.

Of course, Bill may be right, but he hasn't listened to Jane. He has cut her down, injured her self-esteem, and cast doubt as to her ability to handle her job. The next stage may be escalation:

Jane: You're just being pig-headed because it wasn't your idea.

Whether Jane says this or not, she feels it. What could have been an objective discussion leading to cost-benefit analysis has degenerated into a personal flareup. Note how differently the scenario might have been:

Jane: Bill, I think the time has come for us to investigate new office copying equipment.

Bill: Tell me more what you have in mind Jane.

Bill doesn't have to agree with Jane after the discussion is over, but her feelings about him and the job will be very different if he hears her out.

Management first became aware of the value of listening in industrial relations during the 1930s as a consequence of studies conducted at the Hawthorne plant of the Western Electric Company. These studies were primarily concerned with the determinants of morale and productivity. Attempting to uncover basic feelings, however, the researchers found that questioning subjects about specific aspects of their jobs resulted in superficial, lifeless answers. Even worse—or so it seemed at the time—instead of giving straightforward responses, interviewees tended to talk about what interested them most at the moment.

Following this clue, the interviewers tried a radically new experiment, they sat back and let the interviewees direct the interviews. Now they discovered that people began to express their *feelings*. Employees launched into long tirades (to which the interviewers patiently listened) revealing attitudes that might otherwise have been kept carefully guarded. In fact, some employees expressed attitudes that they had not been consciously aware of themselves. As a consequence, the interviewers discovered surprising relationships about which they would never have learned by asking direct questions.

More important: the employees benefited greatly. Just by talking freely in the presence of a sympathetic listener, they got their problems off their chests and felt better. They experienced what psychologists call *catharsis* (from the Greek: to make pure). In addition, merely by talking things over, the employees began to gain insights into the nature of their own problems. Once they had relieved their feelings by speaking openly in a receptive environment, they were able to look at their problems more objectively. And their clearer understandings, supplemented by further discussion, often enabled them to work out solutions (at least to those problems that they were in a position to solve themselves).

Impressed by the value of the Hawthorne experience, Western Electric instituted a program of formal counseling. Specially chosen counselors were trained in the use of *nondirective* interviews. (By *nondirective interviews* we mean—as we shall explain later—a type of interview in which the interviewer encourages the interviewee to express his own thoughts with considerable freedom—as contrasted to directive interviewing, in which the interviewer asks direct questions and tries to keep the discussion within predetermined limits.)

These "free-floating" counselors were given no regular supervisory duties. Their function was merely to listen to employees' problems without giving advice. Other companies rapidly followed Western Electric's example. Particularly during World War II counseling was very popular, especially to help women workers.

The counselors faced a tough ethical problem of what to do with the information they received. If they repeated to management what they had been told, the workers would no longer trust them. On the other hand, if they could use their information in a discreet manner, they might be able to eliminate the causes of trouble. Often the counselors compromised by giving management general reports without revealing details that might identify individuals.

In recent years the use of such counselors as a personnel tool has declined. It was discovered that this technique has many drawbacks, including the following:

- Although counseling might help an individual make a better adjustment to a poor environment (say to an inept supervisor), it did not improve the environment itself. Employees often began to feel that they were wasting their time talking to a counselor who could do little for them, and they ended up almost as frustrated as before.

- Counseling is directed almost entirely toward changing *individual* attitudes and behavior, in spite of evidence that group attitudes are often more important than individual attitudes.

- The counseling system gave subordinates a chance to bypass and tattle on their supervisors. Naturally, the supervisors objected.

- The counselors discovered that they were spending most of their time with a few disturbed individuals who really needed deep psychotherapy.

The basic trouble with "free-floating" counseling was its separation from line management. Line management emphasized downward communication; counseling provided upward communication. But the two forms of communication went along different channels.

Management began to learn that effective communications must go both ways. Upward communication and downward communication, listening and order-giving, are both more effective if done by the *same* person. Furthermore, if they are merged into the same process, something new and better emerges. Thus, there has come the realization that interviewing or active listening is not a special technique for use by personnel experts only, but a vital aspect of good management generally.

Listening as a management tool

To enumerate the uses of listening would be almost to itemize the functions of management itself. Listening is useful for bosses dealing with subordinates, for subordinates dealing with their bosses, for staff people dealing with line people (and vice versa) and for colleagues at the same level dealing with one another. Listening is obviously well suited to formal interviews, such as those used for hiring, exit, and requests for transfer. But it is also appropriate for other purposes, such as the following:

Low morale: finding out the cause of employee dissatisfaction, turnover, or absenteeism.

Discipline: discovering why employees are performing unsatisfactorily and helping them to evolve means of correcting themselves.

Order-giving: getting reaction to and acceptance of orders, to see that the person who receives the order really understands it.

Resistance to change: gaining acceptance of new techniques, tools, procedures.

Merit rating and evaluation: helping an employee correct his weaknesses.

Grievance-handling: finding out the real causes of a union grievance and getting the union officers to agree to a constructive solution.

Settling disputes: finding out the causes of the disputes between employees and getting them to agree to settlement.

The listening approach is not something to be applied only when dealing with specific problems. It is a general attitude which the manager can apply day in and day out in dealings with fellow supervisors, subordinates, and the boss. In a nutshell, it is a matter of always being ready to listen to the other person's point of view and trying to take it into account before taking action oneself.

Establishing confidence

Managers must take the initiative in encouraging subordinates to come to them with their problems. They must show that they are willing to hear them out. Otherwise minor irritations may grow to tremendous proportions, even before the manager has become aware of the danger.

If the initial discussion is a pleasant experience, the subordinate will come back more freely and more regularly when new problems arise. If it has been an unpleasant experience and if he feels he has been "put on the spot," he will be reluctant to reveal what is on his mind in the future.

The manager should be aware that some of the people who report to him will be easier to get to know than others. Some will talk quite freely and easily. Others will hold back because of fear or natural timidity. Managers must be careful not to spend all their time with those to whom it is easy to talk.

To avoid the charge of favoritism, and to insure that he is able to deal with the problems of all his employees, the manager must go out of his way to make contact with employees who are reluctant to come to him. The manager must recognize that there is an invisible barrier which separates him from his subordinates. For some, this status difference is of little importance, but for many it makes effective upward communication much harder.

Finally, listening takes time. The manager should make time available for his subordinates to talk to him. But if he doesn't have time at the moment, it is far better to postpone the discussion to some specific hour than to rush through a discussion in an abrupt, distracted manner.

Nondirective listening is useful not just when someone initiates action for you (as Jane tried to do with Bill in the case that begins this chapter), but also when you try to initiate action yourself, that is, when you try to get your boss, your subordinate, or someone at your own level to accept your ideas. *Initiating action*

Suppose you are the division manager, and you want to introduce a new system of quality control. Although you have not yet consulted the production supervisor, you have heard through the grapevine that she has strong objections to the new system. Yet her cooperation is essential if the system is to succeed.

You feel fairly certain that your plan is good and that the production supervisor's objections are not well grounded. You are the boss, of course, and you could give her a direct order to put the plan into effect. (Question: How would the supervisor react to this order? How loyally would she carry it out?)

Instead, you decide to listen to her point of view. In spite of the grapevine, you can't be sure you know what her objections are until she has spoken to you, personally. (Question: What would happen if you had already made up your mind and just went through the formalities of listening?)

So you call her into your office, explain to her that you would like her reactions to the proposed plan, and briefly explain what is involved (assuming she is not aware of this already). You emphasize that you still have an open mind as to whether to adopt the plan at all and that within limits (which you are careful to explain) the details of the plan are subject to modification.

You then ask for her comments. You listen carefully and encourage her to express herself more fully. As she speaks, she relaxes and explains her point of view with more restraint than she would if she felt she were on the defensive. Instead of trying to answer her arguments, you encourage her to tell you everything she thinks and feels about the change. When she finishes, you briefly summarize what she has said, to make sure you understand—and also to indicate to her that *you* understand.

After speaking her piece, she feels free to listen to your point of view, which may have changed since you heard her comments. You fill in some of the areas where you feel she was misinformed and indicate the points on which you have changed your own thinking. You agree that many of the problems she raises are real ones and ask for her suggestions in dealing with them. You make concessions yourself. Eventually, you work out a detailed program which includes as much of her input as seems feasible (subject, of course, to similar consultation with other affected managers).

At the end, even if the supervisor is not fully convinced of the wisdom of the modified plan, she agrees to carry it out and probably feels pleased that you consulted her.

The above example illustrates the flexibility of the listening technique as a means of initiating action (though we must emphasize that the results are frequently not as good as we have pictured).[1] Note the steps you went through in the above example.

1. Stating the nature of your proposal, indicating that it was tentative.
2. Listening carefully to the supervisor's reactions.
3. Summarizing these to indicate that you understood them.
4. Seeking her cooperation in working out a solution, careully indicating the framework within which the solution must be made.
5. Modifying your original proposal in the light of her suggestions.
6. Making a joint commitment to carry out the agreed upon action.

Off-the-job problems

Managers sometimes use listening techniques to help employees solve personal off-the-job problems. Normally stable individuals have unexpected trouble and try to use their boss as a wailing wall. However, the bosses should be careful not to run their subordinates' personal lives.

The manager should be particularly cautious when sensitive areas are reached in the course of a discussion. What most people want is a sympathetic, understanding listener rather than an adviser. They may ask for advice, but actually they want only a chance to talk. Even when advice-giving is successful, there is the danger that the employee may become over-dependent on his boss and run to him whenever he has a minor problem.

The manager should be still more careful when deepseated personality problems are involved. In such a case it is wise to refer the person to a professionally trained specialist rather than to play amateur psychologist. The average manager is not equipped to do counseling, nor is this part of his job. The patient-psychiatrist or client-counselor relationship is just not consistent with that of subordinate and boss. And the nondirective technique may trick subordinates into blurting out confidences they will later regret.

The use of the nondirective approach

In understanding how the nondirective approach should be used, it is helpful to think of the interview as running through three stages: feelings, facts, solutions.

1. Feelings. The interviewee is encouraged to release his feelings; the interviewer is concerned with helping the interviewee express himself. This stage is the most purely nondirective, for the interviewer still has little idea where the discussion will go.

2. Facts. Having blown off steam, the interviewee is now ready to look at the facts rationally. In this stage the interviewer can be more directive and may even use "probes" (to be discussed later) to bring out information

[1] For an illustration of how these same techniques may be used by a personnel director in dealing with a line manager, see the Anthony case on p. 33.

that the interviewee has not already volunteered. In fact, the interviewer may contribute additional information on his own.

3. Solutions. Once the facts have been assembled, the interviewee is in a position to weigh alternate solutions and pick the best one. As we have mentioned frequently, it is preferable to help the interviewee work out his own solution; however, the supervisor may have to be rather strongly directive to make sure that the solution is consistent with the needs of the organization.

These, then, are the three major stages of the listening process, although it may switch back and forth from one stage to another as different problems are considered. Still on a given problem the interviewer should stick to the order indicated: feelings, facts, solutions. Certainly one should avoid the common human tendency to jump to a solution before getting all the facts.

Equally important, he should not waste his time trying to isolate the facts before the interviewee has had a chance to express his feelings, to blow off steam. Why? Because feelings color facts, and as long as someone is emotionally excited he is unlikely to approach problems rationally. Furthermore—and the point is subtle—the feelings of the people concerned in the situation are themselves facts that must be considered. For instance, the office manager has been having trouble getting Bill to do a full day's work. The most important fact in this solution may be the manager's intense dislike of Bill as a person. Until the manager's feeling is recognized as a complicating element, "facts" he presents will be distorted by his antagonism toward Bill.

Does this mean that the interviewer should never express himself—that he should never try to correct the other person if he is wrong nor try to change his opinion? Of course not. It may be enough for the psychiatrist or the professional counselor merely to listen. The manager must also take action. But in most cases, before he takes action he should wait until he has heard the employee's whole story.

The nondirective approach is not a magic solution to all human-relations problems, of course. There are times when a supervisor may have to be quite firm and directive in the solution stage of the discussion to make sure that the solution is consistent with the needs of the organization. For instance, the supervisor may listen patiently to the subordinate's objections to a new system; the subordinate may persist in his resistance; and the supervisor may still have to overrule him, explaining why, and insist that the system be used. However, the subordinate will have had the satisfaction of being consulted, of knowing that he had his day in court to present his side of the story.

Listening techniques

Skillful listening is an art, and like all arts it requires training and experience. It can be learned better by practice than by reading a book, especially when the practice is supervised by an experienced instructor. Fortunately, one can gain unsupervised practice every day of the year.

Each manager must develop a system that is comfortable for him and that fits his personality, but he should avoid using the same technique with all people and for all purposes. An interview held for disciplinary reasons will naturally be different from an interview held for the purpose of order-giving.

Regardless of the form of the interview, here are a few hints that may prove useful.

Encouraging the other person to talk

Your primary objective is to get the other person to talk freely, *not to talk yourself.* The best way to find out what the other person wants to say is to listen, and the best interview is usually the one in which the interviewer talks least.

But listening is not easy, for our natural impulse is to talk. This is particularly true when we feel threatened by what is being said to us—for instance, when we are being criticized. Under these circumstances our normal impulse is to defend ourselves rather than to listen.

Listening is more than just not talking, however. It requires an active effort to convey that you understand and are interested in what the other person is saying—almost that you are helping him say it. A friendly facial expression and an attentive but relaxed attitude are important. A good listener also makes use of door-opening comments such as "uh-huh," "I understand," "That explains it," "Could you tell me more?" or "I'd be interested in your point of view."

Even silence can be used to keep a person talking. When he pauses in his discourse, he is either being polite and giving you a chance to talk, or else he wants you to comment, to evaluate what he is saying. Merely by not taking his challenge, perhaps by a nod, by waiting through his pause, you indicate that you have nothing to say at the moment, that you want him to continue talking.

Reflective summary

One of the most effective ways to encourage the other person to talk is the *reflective summary,* in which you try to sum up the feelings the other person has expressed, disregarding the factual details and incidents. For example: "The reason I want to quit is that the so-and-so boss keeps pestering me. He won't give me a chance!" Then he (or she) stops, wondering whether he has gotten himself into trouble by saying too much. Your response, "He won't give you a chance?" encourages him to tell the rest of his story, but it does not commit you in any sense. Such a summary serves a number of purposes:

1. It shows the other person that you are giving his ideas careful consideration and that you understand him—in other words, that you are being fair.
2. It gives him a chance to restate and elaborate his attitudes if he feels that you haven't quite grasped his point.
3. It serves to highlight what he has really been saying. Often people are surprised to learn what their words have meant to someone else, and are rewarded with deeper insight into their own attitudes.

The reflective summary is particularly effective if you reflect not only what the other person has actually said, but can somehow put into words what he has tried, unsuccessfully, to express. Be careful, however, not to hear more in his words than he intends to put into them. For if he finds you reading things into his words that he did not mean to be there, he will be doubly careful to watch what he says.

Your summary should indicate neither approval nor disapproval of what the interviewee is saying. It should simply indicate that you are listening attentively. For instance, he says, "It's got to the point where I may lose my temper and take a poke at the boss." If you were to say, "Well, that's quite understandable," you would almost be inviting him to carry out his threat! A more satisfactory response would be "You are sore at him because. . . ."

There are limits, however, to the extent to which reflective summaries are appropriate. It sounds patronizing and manipulative to parrot the interviewee's phrases without any indication that you are responding to their meaning. For example:

Employee: "So I want to find out exactly what I'm expected to do. How many units am I expected to do a day? It seems I'm getting a run around."

Boss: "You want to know exactly what you're expected to do. You want to know how many units a day you're supposed to do? You feel you are getting a run around."

The boss has heard the employee's words but has failed either to hear the fact-related question or to respond to the employee's feelings. Possibly the boss might have responded as follows:

Boss: "Perhaps we can do something to make your work assignment clearer, but I'm concerned about your feeling that you've been getting a run around."

Active listening requires that you put yourself in the other person's shoes. Only if you can understand the message sender's own frame of reference and his world of reality, can you really grasp the real meaning of his or her message.[2] Though few of us can qualify as psychiatrists, we can learn to listen with a "third ear" by asking ourselves such questions as: "What did Joe really mean when he told me he was 'fed up'? Was it his assignment? His family? His chances for promotion? Me, as his boss? Why did he remain silent when I asked him for details?"

Listening empathetically

There is a hidden content in many communications that can only be inferred by the listener. (This underlying element is frequently referred to as the *latent* content as distinct from the *manifest* content.) Although the listener should keep his imagination in check, he should try to go beyond the logical verbal meaning where there is some evidence that emotional feeling is involved. Most communications are, in fact, a combination of fact and feeling.

A good example of this hidden content is provided by the word *communications* itself. An office manager complains to the personnel director that all

[2] Empathetic listening does not necessarily mean that you *agree* with the other person's message, only that you are trying to *understand* it. Some authorities argue that the interviewer should *accept* the interviewee's feelings. We disagree. Perhaps acceptance is required for psychotherapy. But if an employee says, "I think Race X is inferior, and I'll be damned if I work with one of them," the boss may perhaps try to understand this feeling but has no obligation to accept it.

her human-relations problems stem from "poor communications." If the personnel director wants to be of assistance, he will try to get behind the manager's use of the word *communications*. The manager might mean that there are divisive cliques that tend to distort her orders or that she, the boss, never hears the "real truth" about what is going on in the office. She might be using the word *communications* to mean that cooperative teamwork is lacking, or to mean many other things. The point is that the words used by a speaker may not be very informative until we have an opportunity to question him on what he really means in terms of actual observable behavior. The listener must try to get back to the *referents* of the speaker and to avoid the easy assumption that both people are attaching the same meaning to abstract terms like *poor communication.*

Empathetic interviewing means also that you respond to the other person's comments as a person, yourself, not as a machine. To the best of your ability, you show sincere concern (insincere concern is easily discerned and is worse than nothing). There is nothing wrong in demonstrating emotion yourself; on the other hand, there is no need to match the other person's display, emotion by emotion. But it helps to be spontaneous, *yourself,* which means that none of the suggestions made in this chapter should be made mechanically. Unless you are straightforward and honest, you are unlikely to receive honesty in return.[3]

Probes

The "free-floating" counselor is interested primarily in getting at underlying feelings. And as a manager you, too, are interested in the feelings of your subordinates. But if you know that you must *act* on the basis of what you learn in the discussion, you will also want to get all the facts, the whole story.[4] This means that after the feeling stage has passed, you should to some extent direct the interview. Tactfully and calmly, you should steer the conversation, but without forcing the interviewee into an area he does not want to enter, and with no hint that you have already made up your mind.

One way to direct the interview is to build on what the interviewee has already said. By repeating certain words selected from what he has said, you can indicate that you would like him to talk more about this particular area. This device is called a "probe." For example, in explaining how a fight started between himself and another employee, Bill says, "Joe was always riding me. When he picked up my lunch bucket, that was the last straw." Now if the supervisor wants to find out more about what Joe has done to arouse Bill, he has a good chance to insert a probe: "You say Joe was always riding you?" Then he stops and waits for the Bill to go on. Notice that the interviewer does not say: "What did Joe do to make you so sore?" Rather, he simply repeats the employee's own words.

Weighing alternatives

Sometimes it is enough if the interview helps you find out how the other person feels about the situation and what the essential facts are as *he or she*

---

[3] For a good discussion, see Jack Gibb, "Defensive Communication," in Harold Leavitt and Louis Pondy, *Readings in Management Psychology,* 2nd ed. (Chicago: Univ. of Chicago Press, 1973).

[4] In other words, your interviewing is "organization centered," not "client centered."

sees them. In other instances, however, you may wish to help him devise a solution. How can you do this without seeming to impose your own ideas on him? The following approach may be useful.

Let us assume one of your managers wishes to discipline severely an employee who has been a troublemaker. The manager's first suggestion may be to fire the troublemaker immediately. If you keep aking for additional suggestions, she may suggest lesser penalties. Finally, she may even come around to suggesting certain changes in her own behavior.

Now, after the manager has offered all these suggestions, you would attempt to get her to examine each one:

What would its probable effect be?

How would the other employees react?

How would it help her solve her problem?

By helping the interviewee think through her problem, you may succeed in having her come to a conclusion that is hers, not yours. And if it is hers, she will be much more likely to act on it with enthusiasm.

Things to avoid

Too much warm-up

Many people feel that before getting down to the subject of an interview, particularly if it is an unpleasant one, they should try to place the interviewee at ease by discussing some irrelevant topic—baseball, traffic jams, the weather. This approach may relieve the supervisor's anxiety, but it intensifies that of the worker, particularly if he has some idea of why he has been called in. While he is on the "hot seat," he may be thinking, "Why doesn't this character get down to business? Why does he have to play cat-and-mouse? What's this building up to?" Such "warming-up" is useful at times; however, the interviewer should be careful to use it only when it actually reduces anxiety.

Premature judgment

The listener should avoid giving any indication of pleasure or displeasure at what the subordinate says. Judgment must be suspended until all the facts are in. This restraint is extremely important, because subordinates look for verbal or facial cues that will tip them off to what the superior wants or does not want to hear. (Of course, unconsciously, we are always forming impressions, even on the most meager facts. However, supervisors should be aware of their predispositions and try to keep them from warping their judgment or communication.)

Criticizing or moralizing puts the other person on the defensive. Even if he does not argue back, he will begin to edit what he says in order to win the interviewer's approval. He will concentrate on proving that he is right rather than on giving an honest explanation. Certainly, putting some one on the defensive makes it harder to find out what that person really thinks.

Even praise or sympathy should be avoided until the end of the discussion, for it makes the interviewee think his present approach is correct and encourages him to avoid the hard work of thinking the problem through.

Direct questions   One of the most frequent errors made by inexperienced interviewers is transforming the interview into a game of "twenty questions." Bill has fallen into the habit of coming to work late and his supervisor is anxious to straighten him out before discipline becomes necessary. Having had some training in human relations, the manager suspects that a home problem is involved. His end of the conversation may run something like this:

"Do you have trouble starting your car?"

"Is there any trouble at home?"

"Does your alarm clock go off on time?"

"Did you have a drink too many last night?"

To each question Bill replies, "No, it isn't that." And to himself he says, "That's none of his business." And then another question is shot at him.

Here the manager, not Bill, is directing the interview. Note that every one of these questions is phrased in such a manner as to put Bill immediately on the defensive and make him overcautious in what he says. Some of the questions, such as, "Did you have a drink too many last night?" are downright insulting.

The listener rarely knows the right questions to ask; if he did, he would probably know the answers as well. The other person's problem is usually more complex than it seems at first glance, and direct questions tend to narrow it down too quickly.

To complicate matters, most subordinates try to say what they think will please their supervisor. Direct questions often imply the kind of answer the supervisor wants, or at least give the subordinate an "out." For instance, the question "Did you have trouble starting your car?" provides a ready excuse for a tardy worker.

If the supervisor wants to find out what the subordinate really has on his mind, he should leave the situation as free as possible to permit the subordinate to emphasize the things that are important to *him*.

If possible, the interviewer should avoid questions that can be answered with a simple yes or no. "Well, do you like your job?" "Do you think the tools are in bad shape?" Questions of this sort shut off discussion because they can be answered by a relatively meaningless "Oh, I guess so," "I suppose you might say that."

Arguing   Little is gained from argument, particularly in the early stage of the interview. Yet everyone has a strong human tendency to correct the other person when he says something that is obviously wrong. Especially, if the interviewer himself is attacked personally, he must exercise tremendous restraint not to answer back.

For example, an employee says he is having trouble doing the work because the stock has been changed. "The company must be buying cheaper material these days." Now if you know that there has been no change whatsoever in the materials, you will be strongly tempted to "set the employee straight" on this point, although his complaint may be a symptom of something much more basic. If you give way to this temptation, you may simply transform the interview into a fruitless argument.

Hard as it may be, you should avoid being defensive, even when criticized. This is difficult, because often even your unconscious feelings are revealed through facial expressions.

When you finally get the complete picture as the employee sees it, you may be able to provide advice or information that has not previously been available. But again it is often better to help him work through his own problems. In any event, you should hold off giving advice until *after* the interviewee has told his entire story—until you have all the facts.

Advice-giving

Nondirective listening is not the solution to every problem. When someone is legitimately asking for information, for a helping hand, or for some resource you can provide him, he may have no need to talk things out. Sometimes managers abuse the nondirective technique by shifting the discussion from the technical aspects of the question at hand to the subordinate's motives in dealing with it. Such abuse occurs most commonly when the manager has a psychology or social work background. For example, a subordinate may have a sound practical objection to something the boss may want to do. Instead of listening to the objections themselves, the excessively psychologically oriented boss may look upon the subordinate's attitude as an example of hostility and may seek its emotional basis. Such an approach often adds to the hostility it is designed to alleviate.

*Active listening
at the wrong time*

Many people go through the motions of the nondirective interview but violate its spirit. They hope, by asking shrewd questions, to manipulate the interviewee into believing that he is thinking through his problem by himself, though the way questions are worded inevitably forces the interviewee to arrive at the interviewer's own predetermined conclusion.

Masterminding

Masterminding is used with various degrees of sophistication. One of the less subtle forms makes constant use of the leading question, the "don't you feel. . .?" approach: "Don't you feel it would be better for the company and your own future if you came to work on time?"

Questions like this usually permit only one answer. They are thinly veiled forms of advice, judgment, or just plain bawling out. They are even more directive than an overt, straightforward statement. The interviewee is often free to reject outright advice, and even if it is clear that he must accept it (in other words, when the advice is really an order) he may be unhappy about it, but willing to be a good soldier. Masterminding, however, not only requires the interviewee to do what the interviewer wants, but also to say that he likes it. The interviewee is treated like a child and the alleged interview degenerates into a form of brainwashing.

There are subtler forms of brainwashing in which interviewees may actually feel convinced of something at the time of the interview, only to realize that they have been duped after they have had a chance to think things over. Conversion at a forced rate seldom lasts. As the poet Robert Burns once said:

He who is convinced against his will,
Is of the same opinion still.

People change their attitudes slowly, and only when they are ready to do so.

Conclusion

Listening is a form of communications, and like other forms of communications it is most effective when it is two-way. A good interview is more than a oneway process in which the interviewee tells his story to the interviewer; the interviewer must in turn be constantly communicating his interest in the interviewee as a person and in what he has to say.

It is not enough for the manager to understand his employees; he must also give them the feeling that he is sincerely trying to help them. The manager must not only listen, but must also communicate the feeling to his employees that they are being listened to.

The basic purpose of nondirective listening is to enable the listener to find out how the individual sees the problem or situation at issue, and then to help him think and, above all, *feel* his way through to a solution. The goal of this whole philosophy is for the supervisor to be perceived as a source of help—as a person who can assist the subordinate to develop and do a better job.

It has been argued that the listening approach would be fine if a manager had nothing else to do all day except serve as a wailing wall, but that in practice he just doesn't have time to do much listening. Realistically, pressure and other demands may make him abrupt and unsympathetic in his dealings with subordinates. And yet the manager who makes time to listen may find not only that his human relations are better, but that in the long run he will save time by having fewer personnel crises to deal with.

Nondirective listening is not a cure-all for every situation. Effective listening requires considerable skill, and even a good listener discovers that many people find it difficult to discuss their problems. Moreover, many problems involve several people and require group discussion. Finally, certain problems cannot be decided at the manager-subordinate level. Still, in spite of these reservations the listening technique is a general-purpose tool for every manager.

problem

Listening Drill

In each of the following cases, which of the responses suggested would be more likely to lead to a constructive solution of the problem? Remember that these represent the opening of the interview.

1. You have come home from a hard day and your spouse greets you with:

    "What a day I've had. The baby was crying all morning. The washing machine broke down and I had to do the things by hand. Then I went downtown to buy a hat and had to wait twenty minutes for a bus. I couldn't find a thing I liked and everybody was so pushy and the store was so crowded. When I got back the baby-sitter had let the stew burn—and I'd worked on it so hard. I'm so mad I could cry. And I've got to go downtown tomorrow again to look for shoes."

a) "You must have had an awfully hard day."
b) "Your old shoes look pretty good to me."
c) "I'm tired too. You should hear what happened to me. First. . . ."
d) "Don't say another word. Put on your glad rags and we'll go out for dinner and don't mention it."
e) "You know, maybe we ought to get another baby-sitter."

2. A worker has been late three times in the last two weeks. You ask her why and she replies:

"I just can't seem to get up in the morning. Frankly, I've lost my enthusiasm for the job. It doesn't interest me any more. So when I do get up I've got to rush like mad to get here."

a) "Don't you think you are letting the company down?"
b) "Do you have an alarm clock?"
c) "You've got to lick this problem or I've got to lay you off and give you some time to think it over."
d) "The job doesn't interest you any more?"

e) "Are you having any trouble at home?"
f) "Have you thought of going to bed earlier?"

3. A worker who has been making little progress tells his boss:

"I just can't seem to get the hang of things. I try to find out what I'm supposed to do, but no one tells me. The other guys don't pay any attention to me and I can't figure it out by watching. Maybe I ought to quit."

a) "Why don't you give the job a chance? Most people take a while to learn it."
b) "Why don't you try harder? You can't get ahead without hard work."
c) "If I were you I would ask the other people to help you."
d) "Do you have any ideas why the other people don't help you?"
e) "I'll assign one of them to instruct you."
f) "You feel that the other fellows don't pay any attention to you?"
g) "Let me show you how to do it."

4. A toolmaker tells her foreman:

"I've had ten years' experience and no one ever told me I did a bum job. Sure I make a few mistakes, but why do I get all the blame?"

a) "All I want you to do is be a little more careful in your work."
b) "You feel the standards are too high?"
c) "I'm not saying it is your fault. I am just asking you to please do the piece over."
d) "You feel you are unfairly blamed?"

Role-play examples 2, 3, and 4, moving the dialogue from problem identification to a mutually acceptable solution.

using discipline for effective performance

Discipline suggests the harsher side of management. Usually it is required only after other approaches to employee problems have failed. Suppose you have clearly communicated to an employee the nature of his or her duties, have listened to his problems, have indicated your dissatisfaction with his performance—yet he or she still fails to meet the organization's standards. Then what? Then reluctantly, you are forced to resort to discipline.

But can discipline be made consistent with what we have said about general supervision? We think it can.

In the first place, the best discipline is self-discipline, the normal human tendency to do one's share and to live up to the rules of the game. Once people understand what is required of them, they can *usually* be counted on to do their jobs effectively and with good cheer. Yet some people (perhaps most of us) find that the possibility of discipline lurking in the background helps our better selves win out over our lazier selves. As one worker put it:

"If you can get away with one thing you always try to get away with something bigger. It's human nature. If you can sneak out of the plant with nails one day, the next day it may be a hammer, and the day after a buzz saw. But if you know they are going to check your lunch box, then you don't get into the habit of taking things in the first place."

Ordinarily, if employees feel that the rules by which they are governed are reasonable, they will observe them without question. That is to say, they will respect the rules not because they fear punishment, but because they believe in doing things the *right* way. Coming to work on time; following the supervisor's instructions; avoiding fighting, drinking, and stealing at work; punching the time clock—all these are accepted by a majority of employees as reasonable rules, as necessary conditions of work.

Standards accepted by the group are frequently enforced by the group. Still, it is useful for management to back up the group when it is seeking the same objectives as management. The following quotation from a worker on an automobile assembly line illustrates a common feeling:

"Who needs a guy who doesn't do his share? Or someone who is late and makes the rest of us work harder to keep up? We ignore guys who are too lazy to do a good day's work; the foreman should give them hell! But if he's just trying to irritate a pain-in-the-neck foreman, more power to him!"

Most employees are tolerant when a co-worker has an occasional off day, provided he does his part the rest of the time. But they resent seeing someone else "get away with murder" while they are doing a full day's work. In fact, unless the culprit is disciplined the rest of the group may adjust to his low level of performance.

Thus, consistent proof that all rules are being enforced serves to strengthen the informal group's efforts at correction. Clearly, good managerial practices will vastly reduce the need for discipline. But if employees realize that infractions of rules will be disciplined, good management will become even better.

Avoiding discipline

Of course, discipline is to be avoided if possible. Too often management views it as the first, rather than the last, step. How can the need for discipline be minimized?

1. Management should avoid introducing too many rules, especially rules that seem unrelated to the job at hand.

2. Management should make every effort to convince employees that the rules it introduces are reasonable. The United States' disastrous experience with Prohibition shows the futility of trying to enforce a law that seems unreasonable to the majority.

3. In many instances, failure on the job is due to poor assignment. The employee's skills and interests do not match the job. If that is the problem, it may be corrected by better training or a transfer.

4. At times, too, the problem arises from the failure of management to explain what the job requires or to be sufficiently alert to employee progress. Here, of course, better communications are required. Many apparent discipline problems are merely misunderstandings that can easily be settled in face-to-face conversation.

Steps such as this may help establish "positive discipline," an atmosphere in which subordinates willingly abide by rules that they consider fair. In such an atmosphere, unnecessary causes for discipline are removed, and the group may exert social pressures on wrongdoers.

Types of discipline

Assuming discipline is required, we must determine the severity of the penalty. Many companies now provide what is called progressive or corrective discipline, which calls for increasingly severe penalties each time a person is disciplined. Except for very serious wrongdoings, an employee is rarely discharged for a first offense. This is particularly true if the firm is unionized, since arbitrators insist that the offender be given a second chance unless the offense is particularly bad. Frequently they will insist that the employee receive a warning about the nature of the punishment for future violations. Before sustaining discharge, some arbitrators insist that evidence be provided to show that the supervisor made an effort to rehabilitate the rule violator. Progressive discipline implies that some effort be made at rehabilitation.

Ordinarily, the sequence of penalties under progressive discipline is as follows: (1) oral warnings; (2) written warnings; (3) disciplinary layoffs; (4) discharges.

Oral warnings represent an informal approach to correction. When an individual fails to maintain standards, or breaks a rule, a clear oral warning that repetition may eventually call for discipline is in order. The supervisor should, of course, concentrate on helping the subordinate figure out ways to prevent these troubles from recurring.

Written warnings are the first formal stage of progressive discipline. Psychologically, perhaps, they are not different from oral warnings, but they are made part of the employee's record—and they can be presented as evidence if more serious penalties follow or if the case is taken to arbitration.

Disciplinary layoffs (to be distinguished from layoffs due to lack of work) are next in severity. Usually they are for several days or weeks; layoffs in excess of a month are uncommon. Some companies skip this stage of discipline altogether, particularly when it is hard to find a trained replacement, on the grounds that it is too cumbersome to replace an employee for just a few weeks. Moreover, the disciplined employee may return from his layoff in an even nastier mood than when he left. On the other hand, there are some employees who pay little attention to oral warnings but to whom actual punishment, such as loss of income, is convincing proof that the company means business. A layoff may shock them back to their sense of responsibility.

Discharge remains the ultimate penalty, but one that is being used less commonly. The expense of training a new employee makes the loss of an experienced one very costly to the company, and the hardships that face an individual who has been discharged make arbitrators and unions reluctant to permit its use. Many arbitrators, indeed, refer to discharge as "industrial capital punishment"—and for good reason.

Consider the impact of a discharge on a man of say 55, with 30 years' seniority. In the first place, he may lose pension rights which would eventually be worth $60,000 or more, plus substantial vacation benefits. Few high-paying employers would be willing to hire a man of his age, especially after they check his references and discover his discharge. Certainly he can expect less pay than he was getting from the job to which his 30 years' service had carried him. Further, as a low-seniority man, he is now fully susceptible to all the winds of economic misfortune. Assuming he loses $6.00 an hour for the rest of his life, his financial loss may be as high as $150,000.

No wonder one arbitrator told us: "I am very reluctant to let someone be fired unless I feel the company's grounds are justified, both morally and legally. I think the employee should have every chance to mend his ways." Faced with this attitude among arbitrators, companies are forced to place greater emphasis on their selection and training programs. Workers who are discharged today are often individuals who simply don't care for their jobs, younger employees with no family responsibilities, or persons with severe behavior problems.

Demotion is seldom used as a disciplinary measure; it is ordinarily reserved for situations in which an employee has been mistakenly promoted or is no longer able to perform his job. As a disciplinary measure, demotion has a number of disadvantages. Losing pay over a period of time is a long, slow form of constant humiliation, as compared with the sharp slap of a layoff. Also, if a company is going to retain a trained employee in any capacity, it makes more sense to use his highest skill.

Managers whose performance is substandard are rarely laid off or formally demoted. Instead, they are often quietly transferred without cut in pay from responsible jobs with substantial promotional opportunities to dead-end jobs with little or no opportunity for salary increase or promotion. Or, in some companies, they are requested to "resign."

Most firms find that it is best not to treat either managerial or hourly paid employees so harshly that they give up hope or lose motivation.

The red-hot-stove rule

Inflicting discipline puts the manager in a dilemma. How can he or she expect his subordinates to continue to regard him as a source of help, when discipline is by nature painful? Can he impose discipline without generating resentment? We think so—through what Douglas McGregor called the "red-hot-stove rule." This rule draws an analogy between touching a hot stove and undergoing discipline. When you touch a red-hot stove, your discipline is *immediate*, with *warning*, *consistent*, and *impersonal*.

Apply these four characteristics to discipline. When you burn your hand, you are angry with yourself. Sometimes you are angry with the stove too, but not for long. You learn your lesson quickly, because:

1. The burn is *immediate*. There is no question of cause and effect.
2. You had *warning*. Since the stove was red-hot, you knew what would happen if you touched it.
3. The discipline is *consistent*. Everyone who touches the stove is burned.
4. The discipline is *impersonal*. A person is burned for touching the stove not because of who he or she is.

In short, the act and the discipline seem almost one. You are disciplined not because you are bad, but because you have committed a particular act. The discipline is directed against the act, not against the person. There will still be resentment against the source of the discipline, but as the discipline becomes automatic, the resentment is reduced. As one worker put it: "I really had it coming to me. I was looking for trouble. I can't blame the forelady. Her job was to enforce the rules. That's what she is paid for."

Let us see how the red-hot-stove rule works out in practice.

Immediate discipline

The manager should begin the disciplinary process as soon as possible after he notices a violation of the rules. (Of course, if he has lost his temper he should wait until he has cooled down.) Note what happens if he delays action:

Jane Jones has a bad tardiness record. She comes in a half-hour late, but thinks the manager hasn't noticed it. By noon, Jane decides she has nothing to worry about.

The manager *has* noticed it, but she is busy with another problem and she figures it might be a good idea to let Jane stew awhile. Late in the afternoon, just before closing time, she calls Jane into the office to give her a two-day layoff.

Naturally, Jane feels she has been treated unfairly and resents both the discipline and the manager. She assumes the manager has been harboring a grudge instead of being honest and open. In the future, she will never feel secure with the manager and will always wonder, "What's she going to pull on me next? Why does she have to play this cat-and-mouse game with me?"

If the discipline quickly follows the offense, it is more likely that the offending person will associate the discipline with the offense rather than with the person imposing the discipline—that is, the discipline will seem more automatic.

Of course, immediate discipline does not mean that an individual should be judged without full investigation. But it does mean that the manager should take notice of the offense as soon as possible and push the investigation with all due speed.

For instance, a man comes in to work after two days' absence. According to your records, he never called in to report sick: therefore, he is subject to discipline. "Immediate discipline" requires that you call him into your office for an explanation as soon as he gets to work. If he claims he was unconscious under a doctor's care during this period, you obviously are not going to discipline him until you have a chance to investigate. Even here you should push your investigation as rapidly as possible.

When the facts of a case are not clear, and yet immediate action is necessary, many companies provide for suspension. The employee is told that he is "suspended" without pay and that he will be informed later about what discipline will be imposed. This technique may be used when tempers are so high that calm appraisal is impossible, or when the guilt is obvious but the amount of penalty can be determined only after further investigation. Suspension also makes possible a consultation among various levels of management before the final penalty is determined. Since suspension is a form of layoff, however, it should not be used unless the offense calls for at least a layoff. If the suspension is longer than is justified by the offense—or if no suspension was justified at all—arbitrators will usually order back-pay.[1]

Advance warning

If discipline is to be accepted without resentment, both the individual who is being disciplined and his fellow workers must regard it as fair. And *unexpected* discipline is almost universally considered unfair. This means that (1) there must be clear warning that a given offense will lead to discipline, and (2) there must be clear warning of the amount of discipline that will be imposed for a given offense.

Assume that a rule has been posted for several months but that the manager has never disciplined anyone who violated it. Clearly, no one expects the rule to be enforced in the future either. Now the manager grabs one employee and makes an example of him. The victim might well cry, "Why me?" Discipline without warning violates the workers' expectations of fair supervision. Further, if the case were taken to arbitration, the company could lose.

Does this mean that once an order is laxly enforced, the company can never again enforce it? Perhaps, in a unionized situation, for an arbitrator could rule that a *precedent* of no enforcement has been established. If, however, there has been at least some enforcement of the rule (that is, if the company has not given clear evidence of its acquiescence to nonenforcement), the company can begin strict enforcement once it has issued clear warning of the change in policy.

We have already discussed the need for effective communications. Once more, let us emphasize management's responsibility to make sure that employees really know what the rules are and how they are to be enforced. Failure to communicate such information deprives employees of clear warning. Among other things, a communications program might include the following:

- The immediate supervisor, perhaps with the help of the personnel department, explains the rules to all new employees when they are inducted
- Bulletin-board notices are posted and handbooks are distributed to employees
- In some cases, lists of penalties are included in the union contract
- When rules are changed, the immediate supervisor calls a group meeting or notifies individuals informally
- When a rule is about to be violated or actually is violated (provided it is a minor, first offense) the supervisor issues an informal warning

[1] Traditionally, when a worker is discharged, he is expected to leave the plant immediately, even if he has an appeal in process. Several unions have proposed that, except for the most serious and obvious rule violations, the individual be allowed to continue to work until his or her case is finally resolved. This is the practice in a number of government agencies as well as in portions of Swedish industry. It is also the position of the American Association of University Professors with regard to the discipline of faculty members. This is increasingly the case in the government sector since courts have ruled that in some cases government employees have the right to have a formal hearing before they are discharged and to receive full pay—whether they work or not—until a final decision emerges from the hearing.

Many arbitrators interpreting the legal meaning of the contract might say that posting a notice on a bulletin board constitutes clear warning. But in terms of human relations, this is not enough. Written communications should be supplemented by oral communications. The better job management does of explaining a new rule and why it is necessary, the easier it will be to enforce it—simply because workers will be more likely to accept it as reasonable. Regardless of the legal requirements of arbitration, management is clearly to blame if employees unwittingly violate rules because they don't know what is expected of them. Good communications pay off by significantly reducing the amount of discipline that must be imposed.

Consistency

If two individuals commit the same offense and one is more severely disciplined than the other, naturally there will be cries of favoritism. One of the quickest ways for a manager to lose the respect of his subordinates and to lower the morale of the work group is to impose discipline in a whimsical, inconsistent way.

Consistent discipline helps to set limits (that is, to inform employees what they can and cannot do); inconsistent discipline inevitably leads to confusion and uncertainty. When some rules are permitted to go unenforced, employees may either (1) decide to ignore all rules, or (2) become confused about what is really required of them.

For instance, one day the boss lets Mary, his secretary, get by with handing in a report that is full of erasures. The next day he bawls her out for a sloppy report that is actually less sloppy than the previous day's. Under the circumstances, it is hard for Mary to know what standards are expected of her. She may well decide that the discipline has nothing to do with her act and "learn" only that the boss has a personal grudge against her. Not only won't she learn the rules, but she will be resentful as well.

Everybody wants to know the limits of permissible behavior. One way to establish these limits clearly and dramatically is to punish those who exceed them. We all tend to be unhappy and insecure in a situation where we are not sure what is expected of us. Child psychologists, for instance, have learned that children are not necessarily happier when they are given absolute freedom. One reason they get into so much mischief is that they are trying to find out how much they can get away with, at what point Daddy will spank.

The rules of fair warning and consistency require discipline to be neither greater nor less than expected. If the degree of discipline comes as a surprise, the organization may have failed to give adequate warning; if the punishment is less than expected, it will be difficult for the employees to accept a more serious penalty in the future. When there is uncertainty and misunderstanding as to whether the offense is to be punished and the degree of punishment, then the policy is inconsistent. If the rule-breaker sees the supervisor making arbitrary decisions, then he or she might blame the supervisor rather than the improper action for the discipline.

Consistency is hard to maintain. Some people we like; others we do not. Sometimes we see a rule violation as a personal insult, a direct challenge to our authority. Other times, prompted by our natural instinct to be understanding and kindhearted, we are tempted to give the rule-breaker another chance.

One source of inconsistency is management's tendency to be stricter in slack times and to ignore rule violations when manpower is short.

Crawford had a terrible absenteeism record. He missed work for two days without a legitimate excuse. Normally, given his record, his offense would justify an immediate two-week layoff. However, Crawford's services were badly needed on a rush job. No one else could take his place. So the supervisor added the incident to Crawford's personnel record and warned him that a further violation would lead to discharge.

Keeping Crawford on solved the immediate problem of maintaining production. But the long-term effects might have been more serious. What did Crawford and the other workers learn from this incident? One of several things: (1) The absentee rule was not to be enforced strictly, (2) the supervisor was playing favorites, or (3) strict discipline in time of slack work was merely a dodge to get around the seniority provisions of the union contract. In any case, the employees' respect for their supervisor probably took a nose dive.

Often a supervisor finds it easier to transfer a problem employee to another department than to face the hard task of disciplining him. In one case an employee who had consistently failed to live up to company rules had been transferred 11 times without any record of disciplinary action appearing in his personnel folder. This employee could hardly be blamed for not knowing what standards of behavior were expected of him. No one had taken the trouble either to help salvage him or to rid the company of a constant expense.

Consistency in enforcing discipline may be expensive in terms of lost production, but inconsistency may be even more so. Although the evidence is incomplete, it appears that the automobile plants that are most hesitant about enforcing rules against wildcat strikes (work stoppages not officially authorized by the union) have had the worst record of such strikes. Yet if a whole department goes on strike, it may be very costly to discipline everyone. Not only will the company lose the production of that department, but workers in other departments may walk out in sympathy.

Wildcat strikes are set off by a variety of causes (frustration with the work or slow handling of grievances, for instance). Obviously it is better to eliminate the causes than to punish the symptoms.[2] Still, if no discipline is imposed, workers "learn" that they can engage in such strikes with impunity. Companies that have been willing to sustain the short-run costs have found that wildcat strikes have decreased. Further, when management takes a firm stand, the union finds it easier to discourage its members from taking matters into their own hands. Many union leaders have told us candidly that they find it hard to observe the no-strike provisions of their contracts when management doesn't take the initiative in disciplining violators. "We can't be more against strikes than management."

Consider another problem involving consistency of discipline. We have heard foremen say, "I can only catch a small proportion of the rule violators,

[2] Indeed, if workers are prevented from wildcatting, they may release their aggressions in other ways—through slowdowns and absenteeism, for example.

but those I catch I punish severely." Is this fair? Many workers consider it a form of Russian roulette. Adventurous souls may try to see how much they can get away with, making a game of this procedure. Furthermore, scattered instances of discipline hardly constitute a clear warning.

If the rule is on the books, the manager should make an effort to enforce it, and enforce it uniformly. If that is impossible, the rule may have to be revised or dropped altogether. Sloppy enforcement of one rule encourages employees to disregard other rules.[3]

In some cases, 100 percent consistency is impossible. For instance, unless every employee is searched before leaving the workplace, it may be impossible to eliminate stealing. Unfortunately, since searches are expensive and deeply resented, the company must often rely on stern punishment of anyone who is accidentally caught stealing. Since workers generally accept antistealing rules as reasonable, there is usually little resentment of this policy, inconsistent though it seems.

Does consistency require that the penalty be determined by the offense, regardless of the personal history and background of the person who committed it? Of course not. We have already said it is common industrial practice to be more lenient on first offenses. Arbitrators are reluctant to let "industrial capital punishment" be imposed on an employee unless a reasonable effort has been made to rehabilitate him or her. Certainly each case should be considered on its own merits. Among the factors commonly considered are length of service, records of past performance and discipline, organizational practice in similar cases, and the extent to which the employee should have known the practice in question was prohibited.

Three employees are caught gambling, for example. One has been disciplined for the same offense before; the other two have not. The first employee is discharged; the other two are given written warnings. This, we would argue is a more consistent punishment than it may first appear to be. Although each case should be considered on its own merits, the overall disciplinary program must be kept consistent. Certainly if two individuals with the same personal histories commit the same offense, they should be treated equally.

How long should a rule violation be held against an employee? Current management practice tends toward disregarding offenses committed more than a year or two ago. Thus, an employee with a poor absenteeism record would start afresh if he maintained a good attendance record for a year.

There has been considerable discussion in industrial-relations circles about whether or not good personnel policy requires the posting of all rules and the setting of standard penalties for violations. For example: "Rough-house: First offense, warning. Second offense, one-day layoff. Third offense, one-week layoff. Fourth offense, discharge."

Those who favor such lists argue that they provide effective warning and greater consistency. Those who oppose them feel that they make it harder

---

[3] Often it is more effective to reward the good than to punish the bad. This is a good way to deal with rules that are difficult to enforce. Rather than penalize absenteeism, the employer may provide attractive prizes or extra holidays for employees with perfect attendance records. One problem here is that denying an employee a prize may itself be viewed as discipline.

for management to distinguish between various degrees of guilt. Mandatory discharge for stealing would mean that the employee who is seen taking a box of safety clips would receive the same penalty as one who was caught robbing the safe. One company with a rigid series of penalties was obliged to impose only a one-week layoff on an employee who had altered his output records—this was the standard penalty for inaccurately reporting production figures. Actually, the employee had been doctoring his records for years and had received hundreds of dollars in unearned incentive payments as a result. Had the company not set up a specific penalty in the rule book, it could have imposed a far more severe penalty.

Impersonality

Good supervisors encourage subordinates to express themselves freely and try to play down differences in status. They try to build the feeling that they and the worker are on the same team. Doesn't the imposition of discipline seriously endanger this relationship? It may. In fact, the disciplined worker might easily murmur, "That so-and-so. I thought she was my friend. I'd rather have a boss who wasn't such a hypocrite and then I'd know where I stood."

It is not easy to impose discipline without causing the person disciplined to feel resentful and aggressive. But the manager can minimize the danger to the relationship by imposing discipline as impersonally as possible. Discipline has the least negative effect if the individual feels that his behavior at the particular moment is the only thing being criticized, not his total personality.

In its opening stages, the disciplinary interview is not much different from most other forms of interview. First, state the problem as you see it; then ask for the subordinate's point of view, and listen. Ask *how* it happened, not *why*. Offer every chance for explanation. Try to avoid this sort of exchange:

Supervisor: Late again, I see. Didn't I tell you yesterday, if you were late once more this month, I'd give you a layoff. . . .
Employee: But . . .
Supervisor: (ignoring him) Well, you've had your last chance. You better go home.
Employee: But I did get here on time—only the superintendent called me in to her office to discuss the Savings Bond drive.

Instead, do your best to draw the employee out and try to discover the real story. Don't ask for his excuse, but concentrate on the *basic* reasons for the rule violation. Has he been poorly instructed on the job? Has he lost his motivation? Is he having trouble at home? Why? (Of course, you should have asked yourself some of these questions long before the employee's misconduct led to discipline.)

Sometimes your interview will give you all the facts you need. In other cases you may need to investigate further, perhaps by checking with other members of management. Avoid making a decision until you have the whole story, but reach your decision as soon as possible.

Once you have decided what discipline is appropriate, impose it quietly and impersonally. Suppose in a lateness case that the employee shows general irresponsibility, and that his only excuse for his latest tardiness was that he forgot to set his alarm clock.

> *Supervisor:* Well, I can see how it happened. But from the company's point of view, not setting your alarm clock is not an adequate excuse, particularly since this has happened three times this month.
> (Pause—to listen to objections.)
> You have already received two written warnings this month, and the rules now require that you receive a day's layoff.
> (Pause—again for objections.)
> Jim, you've got to figure out a way to get here on time. You do a fine job when you are here, but the rule (and I think it is a fair one) is that if this occurs again within 30 days you will receive a week's layoff; and if it occurs again you will lose your job. I don't want this to happen. Now what can be done about it?
> (Then discuss positive means of avoiding trouble in the future. Try to get him to suggest a workable plan—or suggest one yourself. Even if this doesn't work, end with):
> Jim, will you try harder to get here on time in the future?
> (The answer is likely to be "yes" and you have, for what it is worth, a positive end to the interview and a positive commitment to do something.)

Note that the discipline here has been imposed impersonally and the employee has been given every chance to express his objections. After imposing discipline the supervisor reverts to his role of *helping*. The interview ends on a positive note.

After disciplining a subordinate, you may understandably tend to avoid him or alter your attitude toward him in subtle, hardly noticeable ways. But these shifts in attitude are particularly dangerous, for they generate corresponding alterations in the subordinate's attitude. Eventually, the whole relationship may be destroyed. By contrast, if you treat the employee as you always have, you indicate that by-gones are by-gones, that it was the act that was punished, not the person.

Simple as this advice may seem, it is hard to carry out in practice. Both parties are upset by what has happened. It is easy to understand why the person who has been disciplined is resentful, but the act of imposing discipline is also emotionally distasteful to the person who imposes it. Most of us feel guilty when we hurt other people—even when such a feeling is not justified. To protect ourselves from guilt feelings, we have to build up a feeling of anger. But, since we fear the anger of the person we have disciplined, we become unapproachable and cold after we have imposed the penalty. As a result, we seem to be disciplining the other person *as a person,* rather than as the violator of a specific rule. Naturally his response is, "The boss is out to get me."

It requires a great deal of maturity to approach discipline without a sense of guilt or hostility, particularly if you feel that a subordinate's disregard of the rules is a reflection on your own managerial abilities.

Supervisors too frequently have the tendency to avoid taking corrective measures until drastic action is needed. Confronting people with their inadequacies is often personally painful. In any case, it is too easy to assume that the other person is aware of his limitations. Besides, keeping records is time-consuming. Evaluations are frequently subjective and often difficult to defend. Criticism leads to counter-criticism. And so to keep good relations on the job, the supervisor often keeps his opinions of his subordinates to himself until the situation becomes intolerable, at which time the supervisor imposes a disciplinary action without warning—thus turning suddenly, in the eyes of the subordinate, from a permissive, namby-pamby boss to an unfair, autocratic ogre.

Consider the case of Alton Scotia, who filed a grievance after being hired in January, as technical writer for a research project, and then was fired in December for "failure to learn his job." As Ruth Van Duzen, his former boss, describes it:

Our project is working under heavy pressure, and we have no room for people who can't pull their weight and certainly no room for people who still must be trained. Al's record looked good, and so we hired him as a full-fledged professional. That was our mistake and it didn't work out. I gave him several different kinds of assignments and each time his reports were so poor that I had to have someone else do them over. I don't think he understood what we were doing here; he even said so himself. I gave him the simplest work I could find and here he made mistakes.

I sat down with him twice to go over his work in detail. He doesn't take criticism well and we got into a nonproductive fight over his writing style, which frankly I think is simply awful (I've kept copies of his work to prove it). I could have kept a complete log of everything he did wrong, but this would have been too time-consuming; and, in any case, he didn't learn from the little I told him. It was clear he wasn't going to straighten out. Certainly my two meetings with him should have made it clear that he was in trouble. I hoped that he'd have sense enough to recognize the situation and quit by himself; but when he didn't, I had to let him go. Why should he hang around on a job where he doesn't fit?

Naturally, Al saw the situation somewhat differently.

The trouble is all Ruth's. She's a lousy supervisor. She would never explain what she wanted (I told her I didn't understand her assignments), but I did the best I could. She kept switching me around from job to job, so I could never learn. But she had criticisms of my work only twice—and these were very petty. She and I have different ideas as to style. Since she never said anything again, either good or bad, I assumed I was doing OK. I never had any idea my job was in jeopardy. According to laboratory regulations I'm supposed to get a written evaluation every six months and a formal warning before discharge. I received none of these. Not only am I out of a job, but my professional reputation has been besmirched. I am really going to fight this injustice!

The role of the union

As yet we have said little about the role of the union in matters of discipline. Unions rarely object strongly to discipline provided it is applied consistently and the rules are clearly publicized and generally considered reasonable. Of course, union officers may go through the motions of filing a grievance at the request of a disciplined member, much as a lawyer defends a guilty client, but they often feel as this union officer did:

"I've got to go to this grievance meeting and fight for that so-and-so. He had it coming to him and got what he deserved. How can he think he is so much better than anyone else that he doesn't have to follow the rules?"

Management should not expect the union to discipline members who violate the contract.[4] When the union does impose discipline, it is abandoning its traditional role as the worker's defender, and management is failing to assume its responsibilities.

Management must also be realistic about the union leader's political position. Often union leaders feel obliged to defend members whom they themselves think are guilty; to do otherwise would be to risk defeat at the next election. Once management recognizes that union leaders must often perform what is for them an unpleasant job, life becomes a good bit easier for both management and the union.

Management may be able to reduce the number of grievances prompted by disciplinary action by bringing the union into the earlier stages of the disciplinary procedure.

Bill Jones has been absent frequently. According to accepted plant practice, after five no-excuse absences, he can be laid off for a month. Jones' foreman informs the department steward that he intends to enforce the rule against absenteeism and that the steward might try to "straighten Jones out" before he gets into real trouble. Where the foreman-steward relationship is a good one, the steward will often warn the employee informally that continued violations may lead to a penalty that the union will find difficult to reduce.

In this way the union is given an opportunity to play a constructive role without being burdened with the responsibility for applying discipline.

Quasi-legal procedures

The presence of a union need not impair management's efforts to maintain a satisfactory disciplinary policy. But it may force management to adopt what might be called a "quasi-legal" procedure.

Most union contracts require (1) that the company may discipline employees only for "just cause," and (2) that any employee who feels unjustly disciplined may appeal to higher management through the grievance procedure and, if management's answer is unsatisfactory, to arbitration. The arbitrator makes the final decision on whether the discipline was for just cause. He may sustain the company's action completely, or reduce the penalty, or decide the penalty was entirely unwarranted and eliminate it altogether.

The grievance procedure provides a valuable protection to the individual worker, awkward though it may be for management. Management has the right—one might even say the *duty*—to establish the rules under which the organization shall operate. But a channel of appeal must be kept open from management decisions on whether or not these rules have been violated. Thus, the grievance procedure operates as a means of enforcing consistency.

In our Anglo-Saxon tradition, the accused is assumed innocent until proved guilty, and in establishing guilt the burden of proof is almost entirely on management. For instance, to prove that a worker has been loafing on the job, more than the supervisor's unsubstantiated word is required. Management must be able to produce objective, factual data which show that other

---

[4] There are a few exceptions in the building and clothing trades, where powerful unions may discipline members who violate the contract.

employees on comparable jobs consistently produce more than the alleged offender. And it must show that the worker's low production was not due to poor material or faulty equipment. Similarly, the union may challenge any rule that has not been clearly communicated to the employees or consistently enforced.

As a consequence, disciplinary matters must sometimes be handled in a legalistic, courtroom manner, particularly when they reach the arbitration stage. Unfortunately, both union and management may find themselves devoting more energy to legal intricacies than to dealing with the human problems involved. Each side tries to build up an air-tight case and to poke loopholes in the case of the opposition. The billowing clouds of legal technicalities often serve as a smoke screen that obscures the underlying human problems. Fortunately, the company that maintains a generally fair disciplinary policy as part of its standard procedure is less likely to become involved in the legalisms of arbitration.

The existence of the grievance procedure means that the supervisor's disciplinary penalty may be reduced or eliminated, either by higher management or by an arbitrator. It is even possible that an employee who the supervisor is sure has flagrantly violated the rules may be totally exonerated. Under these circumstances the supervisor naturally may feel frustrated when his or her decision is not backed up. However, such possible miscarriages of justice are the price that must be paid for development of a judicial system that permits every accused employee to have his "day in court." A basic tenet of our society is that it is better for the guilty to go free than for the innocent to be convicted.

The reason why "guilty" employees are acquitted at higher stages of the grievance procedure is usually that the supervisor has failed to gather evidence, to be consistent in his application of discipline, or to communicate the requirements of the job to employees. Hence it is important for higher management to train and advise supervisors on the requirements of a sound disciplinary policy. Even with training, managers find discipline difficult. They must prove incompetence before discharging an allegedly incompetent employee, and this requires them to keep "a little black book" listing the employee's inadequacies—hardly the way to develop trust or to build a cooperative relationship. If a discharged employee successfully appeals his or her case through the grievance procedure, the manager must resign himself to work with this employee, despite the fact that their relationship may be permanently poisoned. No wonder many managers will put up with incompetence—hoping perhaps that some day the employee will quit or retire—rather than spend the time, energy, and emotion required to begin a disciplinary process which may have an uncertain chance for success.

Government imposed standards

Until recently only unionized firms had to worry about discipline procedures being challenged. The nonunion employer was legally free to discipline or discharge employees for any reason at all. Recent legal developments, the full implications of which have not been fully worked out, tend to restrict the previously unfettered rights of nonunion employers in this area. Three trends are involved.

Protection against discrimination.   Various legislation protects employees against discrimination on the basis of race, ethnic background, sex, or age (if between 40 and 70). Women, members of ethnic and racial minorities, and older workers all have recourse to a variety of government agencies if they feel their discipline is really a form of discrimination. The easiest way for the employer to protect itself against such charges is to show that discipline occurred for "just cause." But, as in arbitration, the employer is required to demonstrate that the employee received adequate note ("advance warning") as to company rules and the requirements of the job, that the discipline was imposed in a consistent manner, and that the extent of discipline was not disproportionate to the nature of the offense committed. When older workers are discharged, not because of wrong doing, but because they can no longer do the job, it becomes particularly important to prove that discharge was due to the workers' demonstrated inability to meet the minimum requirements of the job, not because of advanced age. Often, this is difficult to prove.

Government employees.   There are even stricter standards regarding government employees. Apart from protections under various civil service laws and regulations, the Supreme Court has ruled that long-term government employees may acquire a "property interest" in their jobs. In turn, this can entitle them to a hearing and other procedural protections against discharge or layoff.

Free speech and free private lives.   Other court decisions have given employees at least some rights to free speech, even when they call attention to their employers' misdeeds. In contrast to the earlier legal principle that employees owe absolute loyalty to their employer, the new doctrine suggests that employees have the right to "blow the whistle" against their employers when, for example, the employers try to hide the fact that they have been polluting the environment.[5] A California engineer won legal damages from an employer that had discharged him for "disloyalty" (he had reported that the company's new computer console violated the state safety code). Five states have laws forbidding employers from infringing on their employees' political freedom. Some courts have extended free speech to include life styles and have held that employers may not impose "unreasonable" restrictions on clothing, hair style, and so forth. The predominant view, however, is that an organization may require its employees to adhere to common standards of dress and grooming, providing these standards tend to enhance the organization's public image. The Supreme Court, for example, has held that policemen may be required to keep their hair reasonably short.

There are other decisions which restrict employers' rights to interfere

---

[5] For a discussion of the circumstances under which courts seem likely to intervene in cases of whistle blowing, see Kenneth Walters, "Employee Freedom of Speech," *Industrial Relations,* Vol. 15, No. 1 (February 1976), pp. 26–43.

with their employees' private lives (such as their extramarital affairs) unless it can be proven that this off-the-job behavior has a direct impact on the company's welfare.

Taken as a whole, these trends suggest that arbitrary disciplinary procedures will be increasingly subject to governmental regulations. An indication of the future: The Oregon Supreme Court has held it illegal to use "a socially undesirable motive" to discharge an employee; for example, an employee may not be discharged just for agreeing to serve on a jury. Frequently heard, also, is a proposal to include non-union employees and most managers in laws now protecting only union members from arbitrary discipline. Final decision on the fairness of discipline would be made by impartial arbitrators jointly selected by the parties. Employees in many European countries now enjoy such rights.

Conclusion

Basically, discipline is a form of training. When discipline problems arise, it may be as much management's fault as the workers'. Many disciplinary problems grow out of management's failure to inform employees of what is expected of them.

On the other hand, effective discipline depends on more than one-way communication in which the supervisor tells employees what to do and punishes them if they don't. Employees may be aware of a rule, yet refuse to accept it. For instance, if many employees take extended lunch hours or use sick leave as a vacation, the remedy is not to punish the guilty but to win group acceptance of a new standard. Once this has been accomplished, discipline will be needed for only the small minority of recalcitrants.

For discipline to be accepted, the rules must be effectively communicated, and the penalties inflicted must be consistent. Discipline helps employees learn the requirements of their job; and if discipline is applied impersonally, without personal animus, it may increase subordinates' respect for their superior.

On the other hand, although fear of punishment may motivate many people to obey the rules, actual punishment almost always breeds resentment and reduced motivation in the person disciplined.[6] Thus the most effective disciplinary system is one in which rules (and their punishments) are so well accepted that discipline is almost never used.

problems

1 • *Discussing Mistakes*

Suppose an employee has been making a series of small mistakes. Is it better for the supervisor to (1) discuss each mistake with him as it occurs, or (2) discuss his *overall* record with him from time to time?

---

[6] Hoyt Wheeler, "Punishment Theory and Industrial Discipline," *Industrial Relations*, Vol. 15, No. 2 (May 1976), pp. 235–43.

2 • *The Scotia-Van Dusen Case*

1. How could Ruth Van Dusen have avoided the blow-up discussed on p. 137? What did she do wrong?

2. Suppose that Alton Scotia was covered by a union contract and his grievance was appealed to you as an arbitrator. What would be your ruling?

3. Assuming you are the personnel director and the company is ordered to reinstate Scotia to his old job, what advice would you give Van Dusen?

3 • *Fight*

The foreman catches two employees fighting. Smith had been kidding Jones about his hillbilly background. Jones took a poke at Smith. Smith hit back. Both have a good work record.

Although some organizations try to determine who really started the fight, others feel they will get nowhere trying to settle personal feuds between workers, and they should exercise discipline only when one party resorts to violence to settle a difference. What do you think? Should both men receive equal punishment? Should Jones be punished more severely for starting the fight—or Smith for provoking it?

4 • *No Gambling*

A supervisor says, "We have rules posted against gambling. Of course, we don't enforce them against small bets: we have an end-of-the-month pool based on paycheck numbers, and there is some card-playing for money in the washroom at lunch break. However, we have the rules posted as a standby measure if things get out of hand."

Do you agree with this approach?

5 • *The Bookies*

A company has posted a rule against gambling. Six months ago two men were given written notices about shooting dice. One day the local police arrest two other men on plant property for bookmaking. There is evidence that they have been collecting bets on horses in the plant. The men plead guilty before a local judge who imposes a light fine. When they return to the plant they are discharged. To date, both men's records have been perfect.

If this case were brought before you as an arbitrator, what would you decide? Would your answer be different if the crime were selling cocaine on plant property? Marijuana?

6 • *The Drunkard*

Jane Thatcher comes to work drunk. The supervisor sends her home with another worker, intending to speak to her when she is sober. As soon as Jane comes in the door the next morning, she drunkenly picks up a high-pressure fire hose and squirts the supervisor in the face. The company discharges her for insubordination, assault with a deadly weapon, intoxication, and violation of company rules. There are no posted rules or penalties.

The union doesn't deny that Jane was pretty high. However, it alleges that (1) she has been having trouble with her husband, (2) her record otherwise has been excellent for 15 years, (3) she was sent home but not given any warning on the first day, and (4) in other cases of drunkenness that occurred this year, the employees were referred to Alcoholics Anonymous.

The company responds: (1) the husband trouble is irrelevant, (2) Jane's work has not been good, even though she has not received previous formal discipline, (3) she was in no condition to appreciate a warning on the first day, and (4) the employees referred to Alcoholics Anonymous were quiet drinkers who hadn't committed major violations of company safety rules. It adds that Alcoholics Anonymous is for alcoholics; and aside from the two-day spree, there is no evidence that Jane is an alcoholic.

1. Was the company's position correct?
2. What sort of penalty should be imposed?

7 · *Hair and Dress*

Crosby Bus Line has a rule: "All drivers shall report to work neatly shaven and in a clean, neatly pressed uniform." The company is proud of its employees' appearance and believes that it improves customer relations.

Capen Buses, a competitor, goes somewhat further. Its rule covers all employees, including those in the garage:

No goatees, beards, or sideburns extending below the ear lobes; no Afro haircuts. Mustaches must be neatly trimmed and must not extend beyond the corner of the mouth. Hair must be trimmed so it does not cover the collar. Shirttails must be tucked in trousers. Female employees shall wear dresses. Men in the office shall wear coats, ties, and shoes with laces.

Capen justifies its rules on the grounds of public relations and safety. Bus drivers and office employees have much public contact. Garage employees wear uniforms with the company's name and are frequently on the streets and in restaurants. Long hair is a hazard, particularly for welders or those working under buses.

1. Comment on the two sets of rules. Is there justification for treating garage mechanics differently from office employees and bus drivers? Is it legitimate to let men but not women wear pants?
2. Norton Foster, a Crosby bus driver, returns from vacation with a well-trimmed beard. His boss asks him to remove it. Foster refuses. The boss suspends him until he shaves. Is this action justified?
3. What sort of dress rule, if any, might be reasonable in this situation? What factors are relevant in making a decision here?

8 · *Criminal Record*

The hospital employment application reads "Falsification of this form will be grounds for immediate discharge." Among its questions is: "Have you ever been convicted of a crime?" Alice Bowman was employed 3 years ago as a cashier and has had a perfect record. Suddenly the hospital found that 15 years ago, when she was 17, she was convicted of stealing an automobile and given a suspended sentence. Ten years ago she was given another suspended sentence for participation in a sit-down strike against a nuclear project. Five years ago she was fined $20 after a conviction for possessing marijuana. She had not mentioned any of these facts on her application.

1. Should Alice be disciplined?
2. Suppose the hospital had discovered her misstatement only 3 weeks (rather than 3 years) after she was hired. How long should it hold this rule violation against her?
3. Suppose Alice had told the truth when she filled out her application. What weight should have been given to these convictions in deciding whether to hire her?
4. Is it legitimate for the company to ask any questions at all about an employee's conviction record?

part 3

employee
development
and protection

manpower planning

To survive and prosper, an organization needs well-qualified, motivated employees available at the right time. Putting them there involves careful advance planning—manpower planning—integrating the many diverse parts of the organization's overall manpower system.[1]

THE MANPOWER SYSTEM

Projection of needs
Job analysis
Recruitment
Selection
Training and development

Career ladders
Transfers
Layoffs
Retirements

In this chapter's overall picture of the manpower planning process, we concentrate on four key elements: the projection of future needs; job description and specification (job analysis); career (promotional) ladders; and transfer, layoff, and retirement policies. Succeeding chapters deal with recruitment, selection, training, adaption of manpower programs to the needs of women and minority groups, and the special problems of managerial career planning.

[1] To some, the term *manpower* may connote sex discrimination; but regrettably, no other term has gained acceptance. We might have preferred a term like *personnel planning*.

Without an overall manpower plan, destructive problems are bound to occur. One company spent a great deal of effort recruiting highly qualified technical specialists, but had limited promotional opportunities for them, so the most energetic and ambitious ones resigned within two years.

Changes in one element of a manpower system will ramify to other elements. And these interrelationships, in turn, will be important determinants of employee satisfaction and performance. If large numbers of well-qualified candidates are recruited, the selection process will be easier. If the organization develops an extensive promotional ladder, it will have to select employees with potential for growth. This, in turn, will mean that more effort must be given to training.

The determination of manpower policy is not management's prerogative alone. Unions have a major interest, and individual employees (particularly those with managerial or professional training) are insisting on a voice; after all, their future is at stake. Government, too, is exerting a growing influence on manpower decisions, especially those affecting fair employment practices.

**Alternate
manpower
philosophies**

Organizations differ markedly in their approach to manpower planning. Differences in overall philosophy rarely appear in policy statements but can be inferred from the specific decisions their managements make. At least three different manpower "styles" can be discerned.

Selection. Some organizations, particularly those with limited promotional opportunities, emphasize selection. They seek fully trained employees capable of starting to work at once. Many professional organizations (social agencies, laboratories, schools, law and consulting firms) fit into this category, as do construction firms, the performing arts, and other organizations with short-run jobs.

Development. Emphasizing developmental activities such as training courses, on-the-job coaching, and job rotation allows employees to develop their own capabilities. In this way, organizations try to stabilize employment, offer substantial job security, avoid layoffs, and retrain people with obsolete skills. These firms even restructure their organization (e.g., through job enrichment) to provide greater opportunities for individual growth. Since the developmental approach requires substantial investments in personal growth, prosperous and growing firms (such as successful oil or computer companies) are more likely to adopt such policies than are firms that are exploiting short-run opportunities or fighting for their survival. On the other hand, these long-run commitments to employees may help successful firms to be even more profitable.

Sink or swim. Still other organizations invest little effort in selection or development. Their disregard results from either conscious policy or lack of resources. These organizations hire more people than they need. Those who prove themselves keep their jobs; others are quickly dropped. When jobs open up at higher level, outsiders are as likely to be hired as insiders.

The employee is treated as a variable cost or a disposable commodity, to be quickly removed when no longer needed. Morale here is predictably low.

Manpower forecasting

Successful planning requires forecasting the number of job vacancies that will occur and foreseeing how to fill them. To do this, it is helpful to focus on *manpower flows;* that is, on the stream of people who enter the organization, move up through it at various rates, and eventually leave it through various exit doors.

Here is a relatively simple approach to preparing such a personnel flow analysis. The table portrays the rates of movement of broad categories of management over a one-year period.

Personnel flows

Management personnel flow analysis

	Year 1		Year 2				Year 2
Management level	Number in group	Don't move	Promote to next level	Demote to next level	Separate from co.	Hired	Number in group
Lower	300	165 (55%)	60 (20%)	30 (10%)	45 (15%)	140 (47%)	315
Middle	200	140 (70%)	20 (10%)	10 (5%)	30 (15%)	20 (10%)	220
Upper	100	75 (75%)	0	5 (5%)	20 (20%)	5 (5%)	100
Total	**600**						**635**

Source: Adapted from Neil Churchill, "Analyzing and Modeling Human Resource Flows," *Monitoring the Human Resource System,* ed. Ruth Shaeffer (New York: The Conference Board, 1976), pp. 19–29.

Note that in this example 140 lower-level managers must be hired in Year 2 to allow for growth of only 15 in this category over the year. Even with only moderate changes at higher levels, the company must still recruit almost 40 percent of its managerial workforce each year, should these patterns continue.

Personnel flow analysis may help answer questions such as the following.

- How many and what kinds of employees will we need to hire over each of the next five years?
- What kinds of training programs will we need each year?
- Given our present personnel policies, how likely are we to meet our Affirmative Action goals?

Here is an example of how flow analysis helps answer the last question.

Assume that all managers are hired as junior executives: ⅔ are male; ⅓ are female; 20 percent are promoted to middle management each year. If females now comprise 15 percent of middle management, and management shifts to a policy of hiring women for half of its junior executive positions, it will take about 30 years before half of middle management is female!

Without flow analysis it would be easy to overestimate the impact of changes in hiring policy. It obviously takes a long time for changes to work their way through the system when the base line is a biased distribution, even with a relatively high promotion rate.

Good forecasting, combined with flow models, can provide management with early warnings of upcoming personnel problems; for example, possible personnel shortages and surpluses. (A surplus can arise because large numbers were hired at the same time with comparable skills to meet a sudden expansion. The bulge will somehow have to be digested by appropriate transfers, training, promotion, or even severance.) With appropriate warning, management can respond before major problems arise. Below is an example of the kind of problem that might be avoided by early warning.

The Delevan Company expanded rapidly during the 1960s, and few new managers have been hired until quite recently. Thus, its managers are drawn from a relatively compact age group, and most of them are in their 50s and late 40s. There is little between them and the next group of managers, now in their late 20s and early 30s. Further, since the older managers "ran the show" by themselves for all these years, they have not developed the habit of delegating authority. As a consequence, to meet the needs of the 1980s and 1990s, and to provide middle management in the interim, the company must (1) provide rapid development experience for the younger managers; (2) "pirate" qualified managers in their late 30s from other companies to fill middle-management slots; or (3) use a combination of these.

Manpower inventories and computers.   Computer technology permits management to make more effective use of employee records. In addition to personal biographical information such as age, work experience, previous education, and training, data-bank records contain employees' job histories. When the records are computerized, they make it possible to answer quickly questions like the following: How many employees, in what jobs, will be retiring in each future year? How many employees with appropriate education and experience will be available for promotion to engineering management next year? Who in our present workforce is qualified today to be considered for an opening as a commercial underwriter? Such inventories are helpful both in analysing long-range policy issues and in finding specific individuals qualified to fill immediate vacancies.

Dynamic factors

As the Delevan case illustrates, personnel flow analysis reflects the delayed impact of past personnel actions. Past trends often do not continue, and new factors that emerge substantially modify manpower flows. Thus, the personnel flow analysis must be supplemented with additional information on expected future changes, especially those affecting supply and demand.

Changes in demand.   Effective forecasting requires predicting the organization's future level of activities. What, for example, are the likely changes in demand for the organization's products and services? How will these changes affect the need for various kinds of employees? As existing products decline in importance, as new services are added, and as technology is changed, the organizations will have to make compensating changes in manpower. Here is one example.

The Claridge Company is phasing out its old product line and developing more sophisticated products. Manufacturing methods for the new products allow the use of semi-skilled assemblers, in contrast to skilled machinists who worked on older products. To avoid making these machinists obsolete, personnel proposes to use job enrichment methods to design new jobs with earnings comparable to those of the present machinists. If most machinists accept a retraining program and transfer, one-third of the new assembly jobs will have to be filled through new hires. The new products can be sold only by engineering-trained salespeople. Personnel, as yet, has not been able to identify any jobs that will be acceptable to existing sales representatives, who may have to take early retirement or layoff.

Even if production demands are known, predictions of manpower requirements are difficult to make. If management proposes to double its production rate of widgets by May 1 and triple it by October 1, how many widget makers will be needed by May 1? The answer is almost certainly not double the present number. If there are substantial economies of scale, perhaps only a few more widget makers will be required. On the other hand, increases in personnel usually have to precede increases in production. Inexperienced workers have learning curves; that is, at first they produce less output per manhour than do experienced workers. Even organizations have learning curves, as they gradually eliminate the "bugs" that rapid increases in production are likely to generate.

Labor supply. Although effective recruiting can increase the supply of qualified candidates, the organization's labor supply is heavily influenced by factors outside its control. Its ability to hire entry-level engineers this year, for example, is partly determined by the number of children born 22 years ago and the proportion of these who have gone on to engineering school. Immigration patterns (for example, Cubans to Florida) can similarly affect manpower demographics.

From recorded births and mortality rates, demographers can predict the number of people of working age a decade ahead. These gross predictions may be modified rather substantially, however, when cultural factors change. The postwar influx of working women came as a surprise, vastly increasing the labor supply, and now there are signs of another new trend—early retirement.[2] This is especially ironic in the light of recent U.S. legislation banning involuntary retirement for most employees up to age 70. Although conflicting forces make exact labor market predictions very difficult, demographers can now tell us that in the coming decade, the supply of 18- to 24-year-olds will decline about 15 percent, while the supply of 25- to 44-year olds will increase about 25 percent.

[2] "At General Motors, the average retirement age is 59 . . . [and at] Mobil Oil three-quarters of the workforce now retire before they reach 65." *Fortune,* May 8, 1978, p. 107.

Job analysis

Perhaps the most basic data in any manpower program is knowledge about existing jobs in the organization. While this may seem simple and obvious, it is not. Few organizations that have not undertaken systematic job analysis comprehend the nature of the work their employees perform, other than knowing that they have, for example, 323 typists, 219 skilled operators, and 29 technical specialists. What these people *actually* do is often far from clear.

Detailed and explicit knowledge about every job is necessary:

- to know how to recruit and whom to hire
- to know how much to pay employees on one job, relative to those on another (that is, for job evaluation)
- to design promotional ladders
- to set sensible workloads
- to evaluate the effectiveness of selection and training programs
- to meet governmental fair employment requirements

Job analysis includes two elements: *job descriptions* and *job specifications.* Description concerns itself with the content of the job: tasks, working conditions, and responsibilities. Specification emphasizes the experience, education, and skills the incumbent must bring to the job.

Components of job analysis

The following major components of a complete job analysis emphasize the position of the job in both a promotional and a workflow system.[3]

- Job title, work location, salary range.
- Skill, experience, training, and education requirements.
- Length of additional training required after employee is hired.
- Previous jobs within the organization likely to qualify employees for this job.
- Jobs for which successful completion of this job qualifies employee.
- Analytic, technical, and behavioral requirements: the kinds of equipment to be operated (e.g., mag typewriter); interpersonal skills required (e.g., interviewing); technical knowledge required (e.g., of linear programming); technical skills required (e.g., blueprint reading); physical skills required (e.g., to lift 50 lbs 30 times an hour).
- Working conditions, such as cleanliness, noise, stress, travel, safety risks.
- Performance standards: for every type of skill and ability, it is important to specify both the frequency this skill will be used and the level of expertise required. A research chemist may use a mass spectrometer once a year and thus need a less developed capability than someone who runs samples daily. But the research chemist should have the advanced knowledge to perform much more original experiments than does the quality control chemist.
- Role relations: Who evaluates employee? Who sends employee directives that employee must obey? To whom does employee turn for supplies or information?

[3] See U.S. Training and Employment Service, *Handbook for Analyzing Jobs* (Washington, D.C.: U.S. Govt. Printing Office), 1972; also, the U.S. Department of Labor's *Dictionary of Occupational Titles,* a guide to 22,000 job descriptions, periodically revised.

Who depends on employee for information? To whom does employee send completed parts or reports?

- Time span of decision making and magnitude of discretion. A lower-level employee's work may be reviewed each day, whereas a manager's decisions may not be judged for a year or more. Some employees make decisions involving only a few dollars; others commit millions.

The diagram summarizes the various elements and flows contributing to job analysis.

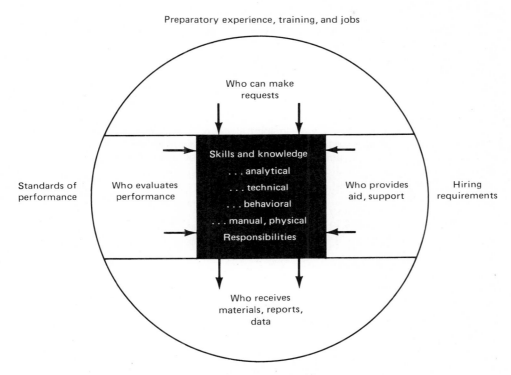

Preparatory experience, training, and jobs

Who can make requests

Standards of performance

Who evaluates performance

Skills and knowledge
. . . analytical
. . . technical
. . . behavioral
. . . manual, physical
Responsibilities

Who provides aid, support

Hiring requirements

Who receives materials, reports, data

Promotional opportunities

Methods of job analysis

Job analysis is usually conducted by the personnel department; ideally by utilizing questionnaires, by interviewing a sample of those doing the job and those supervising, and by actual observation.

There is enormous opportunity for misinformation in this process. Jobs have changed over time; employees like to inflate the significance of their jobs (both for ego satisfaction and to justify higher pay), and supervisors may be misinformed.

Had the job analyst interviewed only supervisors, he would have concluded that excellent vision was critical for the performance of a light assembly task. However, actual observation of successful employees disclosed that they worked by touch alone and hardly ever looked at what they were doing. The job specification might have required a vision test, which would have unnecessarily discriminated against those with poor eyesight.

Job analysis should go beyond simply recording existing job practices; it should also question whether these practices are appropriate. The following issues are among those that should be confronted.

Person vs. job. In the past, a job may have been stretched or shrunk unnecessarily to justify higher pay or to meet individual needs.

Displaying extraordinary energy, Marta Higgins had transformed a voucher approval clerk's job into that of assistant auditor. Rather than just match orders and invoices, she checked them against budget authorization and often negotiated with vendors over excess transportation costs. Much of this duplicated work carried out elsewhere in accounting, but Marta's boss had allowed her to expand her duties to satisfy her needs and also to justify a salary that would hold this outstanding employee.

Particularly in managerial jobs, employees with the same job titles but different personalities may handle their jobs in vastly different ways.

Though formally classified as a Manager of Training, Mae Ferdi's high energy level made it difficult for her to concentrate on designing training programs. Her boss liked delegating broad responsibility and disliked dealing with complaining line managers. As a result Ferdi's job evolved into a broader staff role concerned with troublesome employees with poor work records. She spent most of her time negotiating with managers, workers, and union representatives.

Breadth of job. The organization may have created too many routine jobs that fail to motivate employees. Contrariwise, if the labor market makes it hard to hire well trained employees, it may be necessary to break an existing job into several more specialized tasks. Jobs can be made so specialized, however, that serious coordination problems can arise. In one organization, the repair of a door required coordinating the schedules of three specialists: a lock and handle specialist, a door and jam specialist, and a hinge and closer specialist. One person would not handle the whole door.

Should management emphasize the differences or the common features among jobs? Broad categories enable employees to transfer freely among activities assumed to be at the same level of difficulty. Thus, if Machinist A is permitted to work in any of six departments, it will be much easier to balance workloads. But if the machinery varies greatly among departments, transfers may be unfair and unproductive.

Excessively high job standards. Job requirements may be inflated. During periods of labor surplus, management may require college diplomas for jobs on which they are not necessary. A stenographer's job specification may call for the ability to take high-speed dictation, even though so-called stenographers spend most of their time typing forms, filing, and taking phone messages.

Inclusiveness of descriptions. Particularly in unionized organizations, employees are unwilling to do work not specifically listed in their formal job description. Sometimes sensitive and negotiable issues are involved. Must a machinist (a high status job) demean himself by cleaning floors? Does one employee have to lift 60 pounds, or will two employees do it? As professionals become unionized, their job descriptions also become more explicit: that of a unionized college professor may specify the precise number of office hours to be held. While greater inclusiveness helps answer challenges about whether some task is required, it can also increase rigidity. In dynamic organizations, it may be useful to keep job descriptions more general and flexible.

Craft consciousness. Craft consciousness, the feeling that no one should work outside narrowly defined job duties, is common when promotional ladders are short. The concept is strongly entrenched in the construction trades. Carpenters will refuse to do any work but carpentry, and they will refuse to let other employees do carpentry work, even if this means that other employees must stand idle.

Unions, in general, encourage craft consciousness because they look upon it as a means of restricting management's power to make transfers. Further, workers feel that if they can prevent others from doing their work, they will be able to make their own jobs more secure.

Management itself, by carrying the division of labor to extremes, may be responsible for proliferating an unwieldy number of narrowly defined jobs. Employees, taking their cue from management, then proceed to erect artificial barriers that inhibit flexible transfers, although the transfers might expedite the flow of work and correct workflow inequities.

"I'm the only person in the office who can run this offset machine. It's not easy, let me tell you. Its old and it has lots of tricks. I don't want the other people using it. This way I know they really need me around here. When they occasionally run out of work on the machine, I don't think it is fair for me to have to do odd jobs. After all, running the machine is what I'm paid for."

How can management deal with excessive craft consciousness? One way is to develop broad job descriptions covering a variety of activities. Another is to define jobs in terms of the work that needs to be done rather than in terms of abstract job skills. A third is to provide promotional opportunities so that workers are not dead-ended permanently in one task.

Career paths

Every organization must decide how employees should normally progress from one job to another. Should they be promoted within relatively narrow specialized career paths, or should they be given broad exposure to a variety of jobs? How frequently should promotion take place? Under what circumstances should the organization bring in outsiders rather than promote insiders?

These questions focus on the design of career paths or promotional ladders. Organizations utilize these as a means of on-the-job training to prepare employees to fill more difficult and responsible positions.

"Our stores have a distinctive philosophy about how we handle customers and cater to the tastes of middle America. We like to bring in new salespeople and then rotate them into the backroom operations so they can get the feel of the problems involved in receiving, ticketing, and displaying merchandise. Then we are ready to move them to an assistant buyer's job, next buyer, and eventually to divisional manager. By this time they will have first-hand familiarity with all our operations and ways of doing business."

As the above illustrates, a well-designed career path has many advantages for an organization.

- It creates increasing challenge, employee growth, and on-the-job learning. It offers the individual an opportunity to grow to his or her full potential.
- It constantly replenishes the organization's qualified employees.
- An important source of employee motivation, promotion is one of the most highly visible rewards for fine performance.
- It allows the organization to appraise people on the basis of their actual performance rather than their potential, judged by some selection instrument. As we shall see in Chapter 9, predictions are difficult to make on the basis of interviewing and testing alone.
- Promotion through a career ladder is often cheaper than hiring fully qualified candidates from outside the organization.
- Promotional programs provide the best means for most organizations to meet affirmative action goals.

Characteristics of promotion ladders

Rarely does one find a simple promotion ladder extending from unskilled entry-level jobs to the presidency. Institutions develop very distinctive career paths as these examples suggest:

In police departments: everyone is expected to start at the bottom, as a rookie, and move up, even though there has been some recent discussion of bringing in college graduates at the higher status of "police agents."

The military traditionally has a two-career ladder system: enlisted personnel start as privates and advance as high as warrant officers; officers start as second lieutenants or ensigns and may end their careers as generals or admirals. But there have been increasing opportunities in recent years for some enlistees to become officers.

The hospital has an even more rigid caste system: nurses aides rarely become nurses (unless they quit their jobs and go to nursing school); nurses may aspire to be head nurses or even superintendents of nurses, but never doctors.

Typical manufacturing firms have at least four distinct ladders:

- Manual workers are hired into unskilled or labor pool jobs and are promoted on the basis of seniority up to higher paying or easier assembly and machine-tending positions.
- Skilled tradesmen often start as apprentices or helpers and move up to craft classifications.
- Clerical employees move from stenographer to receptionist to secretary and perhaps to executive assistant.
- Managers often start as trainees or as assistant supervisors and can, of course, move to top management (although most will not). Often there are separate ladders for sales, finance, or engineering, which converge for the last few steps in upper management. There may also be separate "professional ladders" in fields like accounting, law, and personnel.

Length of ladder.   Longer usually appears better. Minorities and women have complained for years that they have been hired for "dead-end jobs"; no matter how well they performed, the jobs didn't lead anywhere. Employees without degrees often find that they have less promotional opportunity.

Where the career ladder leads up to jobs that are much different from, or much more responsible than, those required at the *port of entry* (the bottom job), special care needs to be taken to be sure that hiring standards reflect this. There can be morale problems associated with new employees being *overqualified* for their *port of entry* job, marking time until they can be promoted to positions that call for more of their abilities. Petroleum refineries traditionally promote personnel from the labor gang up through many steps to a crew chief responsible for millions of dollars of technical equipment.

Some companies rely so heavily on promotion from within that they cannot afford to keep people who are not desirous of moving ahead. Universities typically follow the practice of "up or out," which simply means that assistant professors must either earn a promotion or seek employment elsewhere.

Breadth of ladder.   Breadth of job or career paths vary substantially. In more craft- and professionally-oriented work, the paths tend to be "narrow," and the experience obtained is all in a similar function. Many modern managements, on the other hand, pride themselves in providing very diverse exposures to rising executives.

Broader career paths increase the likelihood that there will be few or no dead-end jobs, because a wide variety of promotional opportunities are made available. Also, a more broadly and less parochially trained workforce with wider perspective can result. In organizations where people stay in one division, there is more likely to be a stronger intergroup hostility for most or all of their careers.[4] Career progressions shape attitudes and values; and as two experts concluded, it may be more effective to shape motivation by career experiences than by rules or supervisory styles.[5]

Technology shapes career ladders.   The breadth and length of career ladders can be related to the technology of the industry; it is not simply a managerial judgment. The automobile, steel, and aerospace industries offer examples of quite different patterns.

In automobiles, movement is on a broad basis because production jobs are all quite related in terms of training requirements, skills, and processes. . . . Consequently, there is broad movement in the industry, even arrangements for inter-plant transfers. . . .

[4] Multinational organizations sometimes design promotion ladders so that managers will come to identify with the total institution and not with any of its major operating divisions. Anders Edstrom and Jay Galbraith, "Management Transfer as a Coordination and Control Strategy," *Administrative Science Quarterly,* Vol. 22 (1978), 248–63.

[5] John Van Maanen and Edgar Schein, "Career Development," in J. Richard Hackman and J. Lloyd Suttle, eds., *Improving Life at Work* (Santa Monica, Calif.: Goodyear, 1977). They note that in some public schools, the way to make teachers emphasize tight discipline is to promote them to administrative positions only if they have a reputation for running a tight ship.

The steel progression is quite different. It features long, narrow seniority lines, with slow upward movement. Competence learned in one department—for example, blast furnaces—does not necessarily equip a person to work in another—for example, rolling mills. Once a worker starts up one roster, he has generally determined his type of work in the industry. This is especially important for blacks, for they have been traditionally placed in some departments (blast furnaces) and excluded from others (rolling mills). Given such a practice within a structure like that of steel, great difficulty is encountered in altering the pattern, because an employee in the blast furnace department who desires to transfer must start at the bottom of the rolling mill hierarchy, and this involves loss of pay and seniority. . . .

In the aerospace industry, training is all-important for upgrading because, by the very nature of the business, new techniques, methods, materials, and processes must be learned in order to handle new jobs. Promotion depends more on competence and work mastery after special training than on automatic job progression with on-the-job training.[6]

Technological change. Carefully drawn promotional ladders can be upset by unforeseen technological changes; therefore, management needs to build flexibility into career ladders, so that innovations can be absorbed without excessive shocks. For example, new minicomputers and distributed data processing has substantially reduced the need for centralized computer activities. Since line departments are increasingly able to handle their own data processing, management must find new promotional opportunities for computer personnel.

Permeability of the ladder. Promotion from within has its drawbacks. The long socialization process may have made insiders excessively rigid and homogeneous. To preserve flexibility, it is occasionally desirable to bring in outsiders with fresh viewpoints and skills for higher-level appointments. When this is done with some frequency, insiders will feel less betrayed. It should be noted that the more permeable the career ladder, the more emphasis on selection in contrast to on-the-job training.

Predictability and clarity. Some career ladders are sharply defined: head tellers are always selected from senior tellers, who, in turn, have moved up from trainee to teller. Others are less predictable: in X Company, the most common route to the presidency has always been through sales; but the most recent top executive has a financial background, and currently there are rumors that the board will bring in someone from outside the company.

One obvious advantage of undefined career paths is that they allow organizations to transfer, without appearing to demote, ineffective employees. Promotions then become available for others. Particularly in large organizations, it is possible to create ambiguities as to whether a person is going up, sideways, or down.

Some promotional paths are so predictable that employees can know as long as ten years ahead who will get what positions. This degree of predictability can injure motivation; the rewards are all predetermined. Equally unsatisfactory is total lack of predictability, where standards keep changing and

---

[6] Herbert Northrup and others, *Negro Employment in Basic Industries* (Philadelphia: Wharton School, University of Pennsylvania, 1970), pp. 729–30.

individual decisions appear capricious. In a more desirable situation, contenders have a reasonably clear idea of what is required to get ahead, and there are still a number of candidates for each new opening. At times, if no one is qualified or a new viewpoint is required, an outsider is brought in.

Keeping promotional ladders open. Where the organization relies heavily on promotion from within to fill higher-level jobs, critical rungs on the promotional ladder should not be filled by people who are uninterested in promotion. That would prevent more ambitious employees having the opportunity to obtain needed experience.

Very achievement-oriented employees may be reluctant to spend long periods of time on routine jobs, even though the experience may be useful later on. To reduce problems of this sort, management should constantly ask: Is the experience being provided by these lower-level jobs still necessary for effective performance at higher levels? Is the average duration of employment at each rung of the ladder reasonable, given the learning and challenge the particular job provides?

Number of promotions. The number of promotions possible is not inherent in the technology; management makes the choice. Take a clerical department with 20 employees doing various telephoning, typing, filing, and copying tasks. By deemphasizing the differences in job duties, the organization could place all jobs in the same salary grade. Conversely, by meticulously evaluating differences among jobs, the company could pay each employee a slightly different salary. There could be a 20-step promotional ladder.

What is the optimum number? Too few promotional steps may injure morale by reducing opportunities for personal progress and accomplishment. Too many promotional steps may mean that an excessive amount of time and effort must be spent in selecting candidates, gaining acceptance for the choices, and shifting employees. The result may be chaos.

There can be a good deal of ambiguity about promotion in professional jobs, for job definitions are often quite elastic. An engineer may be required to work on a more difficult assignment for several months before the change is officially recognized by what we would call a promotion, a job title with more prestige and salary.

In some industries, job rank may have little to do with work content. In universities, junior and senior faculty do roughly the same kind of work, although the latter may serve on more committees. Rank distinctions are provided to recognize the excellence of past performance and to justify salary differentials.

Dual ladders. What management regards as a substantial promotion may not seem as a promotion at all to the employee involved. Nurses and salespersons may not want to be administrators. Professional personnel especially may be reluctant to give up their professional work in order to become managers. The additional responsibilities of managerial jobs may more than outweigh the benefits associated with the new salary and title.

Many outstanding engineers and scientists are poor administrators. Some organizations get around this problem through use of *dual ladders* of promotion. In addition to the purely managerial ladder, a second ladder rewards technically competent individuals with titles such as engineering consultant and senior engineering consultant. Professionals on technical ladders earn salaries equivalent to those of their administrative counterparts. (Thus, a senior engineering consultant may earn as much as a laboratory manager.) Also, they are given greater freedom to choose their research projects, and they receive status privileges, such as private offices or labs and foreign trips. But dual ladders are rarely viewed as an ideal solution, if for no other reason than the fact that positions on the technical ladder are seen as consolation prizes for those who fail to make the more prestigious administrative ladder.[7]

Employee aspirations and the career ladder

In designing and administering promotional systems, management should concern itself with employees needs and aspirations. It would be naive to assume that all employees want the same thing or that their aspirations remain constant over a career. Some achievement-oriented employees endeavor to prove themselves through assuming constantly increasing responsibilities. Others put job security and easier work first.

Managers should not presume to know their employees' desires. The meaning of "getting ahead" differs among people. Where the work is dreary or demanding, a lower-paid but easier job may be perceived as a promotion. A factory worker may prefer a transfer to a more lucrative job on piecework. For a manager, the additional travel and responsibility of a new position may detract from its better salary and status. And as we have just discussed many professional workers are loath to move into administration.

Career changes. Management should recognize that employee career aspirations change because of external and internal causes. When employees discover that the chances of progressing within a given career line have diminished, the more ambitious get out and try a new career. Career changes of this sort have always been common; but now, an increasing number of seemingly successful employees are looking for new careers because of changed interests or, after many years on the same job, they feel burned out.

Job location. Job location is becoming more significant in career planning. In part, this reflects increasing interest in the quality of life (some people prefer San Francisco to New York; others make the opposite choice). It also indicates many two-career families. If the wife is offered a good job in Peoria, the husband may ask for a transfer to the company's office there. Or one spouse may refuse a promotion to a distant city because the other could not continue in the current job. Nevertheless, as we discuss in Chapter 12, the

[7] Herbert G. Kaufman, *Obsolesence and Professional Career Development* (New York: Amacom, 1974).

number of commuter marriages—in which husband and wife work in widely separated locations—is growing.

Open systems. To deal with this increasing demand for control over one's own promotional opportunities, a number of organizations have begun to experiment with what has been called *open systems* of manpower management. As we discuss at greater length in Chapter 14, a key characteristic of open systems is that they permit employees considerable freedom in making career choices. Job vacancies are posted, so that employees from a variety of departments can bid on them.

Another characteristic of an open system is freedom to fail. An employee may not be sure what it will be like to have new and perhaps greater responsibility or whether his capabilities match the promotion's requirements. Employees need the security of knowing that the penalties for failure will be modest; otherwise, many will be unwilling to assume the risk of accepting the difficult promotions.

"We promote our project managers directly out of the programming group. These PM's have a very tough managerial job to push through new developments. To encourage our best programmers, who to us seem qualified, we announce all appointments as temporary. If the programmers can't handle the managerial pressures, they go back into a technical role with no stigma; nobody knows they failed, and we don't hold it against them."

Some organizations assist this process by introducing some ambiguity into job titles and job change announcements. Employee A may have done badly on job A and is therefore being shifted to job B; but if the title sounds good, colleagues will never know it's a demotion. In one large computer company, employees who were unlikely to be promoted were shifted to jobs that were called "professional"; for example, professional sales rep.[8]

Handling candidates for promotion. Managers often fail to give accurate and timely feedback to employees who are not realistic candidates for promotion. Thus, when they are passed over, they are shocked and resentful. Alternatively, some managers actively discourage employees who have passed up promotion in favor of staying on their present jobs. The employee who knows the limits of his ability or interests still can make a major contribution. The armed services have discovered the value of long-service sergeants who stay with their units, providing stability, while commissioned officers come and go.

Newly-appointed supervisors are under great strain; they often encounter fear and resistance. Their manager needs to provide extra aid and understanding during this stressful period immediately after promotion.

[8] Fred Goldner and Richard Ritti, "Professionalization as Career Immobility," *American Journal of Sociology,* Vol. 72 (1967), 489–502.

Selecting who is to be promoted

Even with carefully designed promotional ladders and open systems, careful judgment is still required to choose which candidates will be promoted. This requires establishing criteria for choice. The most relevant are *merit* (current performance), *ability* (potential, future performance) and *seniority* (experience).

Merit. If promotion is to provide an incentive for good performance, the best-performing employees should be advanced. Since differences in merit may not be easily measured, however, the person who was not promoted may feel that favoritism was involved. Further, performance on some jobs reflects the impact of many different people and chance factors, so individual merit can be hard to measure.

Ability. There is also the question of potential performance on *other* jobs. Jones may be doing fine on his current assignment, but he lacks the ability to take on more responsibility. Smith, on the other hand, may be doing poorly at present because she is supervised inadequately or doing unchallenging work. Put her on different work, and she may blossom.

Long-term factors are also relevant. The individual best suited for an immediate promotion may not have the greatest long-term potential. The best candidate in the short-run may be a senior employee who has the ability to move only one more step up the promotional ladder. Under the circumstances, it may be better to promote a younger person who will eventually advance into higher management.

Seniority. The use of subjective criteria such as merit and ability leads many employees to feel that promotions are not made fairly. Unions object that as long as managers have the power to select their own candidates for promotion, it is simple for them to discourage employees from speaking out, even when they have grievances.

The charges of favoritism and bias that greet many promotions presumably based on merit can induce managers to favor an automatic decision criteria that avoids morale problems. An obvious criteria is length of service. Even when company policy or the union contract sets up merit and ability as the prime determinant, many an organization succumbs in time to this presumably more objective criterion. Supervisors in general believe that relations with their subordinates will be easier if they promote the senior employee, and almost all companies give some weight to seniority in practice, although firms that are unionized give it greater weight than do those that are not.

Insofar as the job requires an extended learning period, length of service ought to be correlated with ability. Certainly, over time, the employee learns more about the organization and its special requirements. Since employees, once selected, will move forward on the basis of seniority, management has a strong incentive to ensure that the initial selection decision is made properly (universities anguish over tenure decisions) and that the individual receives adequate training. Further, in most societies—ours perhaps less than more traditional cultures—there is *age grading;* that is, older people are assumed to deserve more privileges, promotion included.[9] Also, rewarding seniority encourages loyalty and commitment.

Nobody would deny that loyal service deserves reward. But the question is how many loyal employees become discouraged about their future when they realize that they can be promoted only as fast as length of service permits? Also, over an extended period of time, some long-service employees develop such a ritualistic devotion to detail and avoidance of mistakes that they lose their ability to adjust to new challenges.

While the seniors may be set in their ways, the juniors may be highly ambitious. If good people are not promoted relatively rapidly, they will leave.

CONTRASTING ARGUMENTS

For merit and ability	*For seniority*
• Rewards performance and attracts ambitious job applicants	• Rewards loyalty
• Permits management to select the most qualified, thus increasing productivity	• More objective, avoids favoritism
• Permits infusion of newer ideas and people	• Encourages effective selection and training

Some organizations seek to balance these arguments by selecting for promotion:

1. The senior among those who are considered the more able.
2. The senior, unless there is an outstanding candidate with less seniority.

Transfers

Not all movement is upward; employees may shift sideways. Some transfers may involve greater salary and responsibility, but people sometimes accept new assignments just to broaden their experience or to get around some blockage in their career ladder. Transfers are also used by management when employees have trouble with their work or develop personal friction with their boss or fellow employees. Remedial transfers, however, are often used to gloss over serious problems. When the manager is arbitrary, when employees receive inadequate training, or minority group members are discriminated against, it is usually better to resolve the problem directly, rather than to postpone it through transfer. The replacement for the person being transferred may face the same problems again.

When technological change is introduced or customers' demands change, the manpower needs of some departments can decline while those of other departments expand. To safeguard the jobs of long-service employees and to avoid losing the skills of trained personnel, most organizations try to transfer

[9] Interestingly, Japan has tried to combine the two approaches. Salary is largely a function of length of service, but job responsibilities are based primarily on merit. Thus, a young engineer may be paid less than a long-service skilled worker.

employees to other jobs. Moreover, an organization has less difficulty introducing change if it follows a liberal transfer policy and provides retraining for employees who move to new jobs.

Maintaining stable employment

Stable employment is good evidence of intelligent manpower planning. Erratic ups and downs in employment levels, expedient hiring, substantial overtime during some periods, and layoffs and short workweeks in others suggest poor planning. Well-managed companies try to avoid hiring in surges. They plan cutbacks far enough in advance so that *attrition* (normal quits and retirements) will bring employment down to an efficient level.

Many organizations take great pride in their policy of resisting layoffs. They claim that this policy pays off in a more loyal, secure workforce that is less likely to resist change. Obviously, a utility or a company fortunate enough to create a stable (or better, expanding) market for its goods finds such a committment easier to make than a company facing cyclical markets.

Numerous incentives encourage management to provide stable employment. State unemployment insurance laws as well as company sponsored supplementary benefit plans penalize the employer with a record of unstable employment. Layoffs and rehires are expensive to administer, and valuable employees may be lost to other employers. Changes in employment levels involve expensive shifts of workers within and between departments. Just the fear of layoff may encourage employees to restrict production as they wait to see who will be affected next.

All these problems stimulate employers to regulate employment through techniques such as the following:

- Trying to develop a more flexible workforce through careful selection and training, supplemented by contract provisions that permit free transfers among jobs (though craft consciousness can make this difficult).
- Using temporary employees and overtime in peak volume periods.
- Taking on additional products or service lines for which the demand will complement the existing products' demand (e.g., products with different sales cycles).
- Warehousing goods during slack demand and offering incentives for customers to stockpile during slow periods.
- Contracting short-term work or work that requires fluctuating numbers of employees; for example, maintenance and construction work.

None of these alternatives is ideal, of course. Temporary personnel agencies typically charge high rates; direct hiring is less costly. Long periods of overtime reduce output per hour, require expensive premium payments, and cause resentment when this overtime is discontinued. Inside workers resent outside contractors. Internal transfers cause many problems.

Reducing employment

Even with careful manpower planning, most organizations at some time must make the painful decision to reduce employment. When this occurs, management should provide an orderly pathway downward, to minimize the personal and organizational disruption that employment cuts inevitably cause.

Worksharing or layoffs?

If the cutback is a small one, the least painful method is attrition, allowing normal quits and retirement to reduce the work force. When attrition is not enough, the next choice is often between shorter workweeks for everyone or layoffs for some employees, usually the newer ones. Sharing work in effect divides unemployment; layoffs concentrate it.

What factors are relevant here? Often the choice is specified in the union contract, making discretion impossible. The nature of the industry may also dictate the response: a hospital may need a minimum crew at work at all times. Long-service employees naturally prefer layoffs, since they won't be the ones to suffer. The availability and magnitude of unemployment insurance benefits may also influence the choice. At some point, employees would rather accept these benefits and avoid the travel expense, taxes, and effort associated with reporting to work for relatively brief periods.

Seniority vs. merit in layoffs

Once the decision to make layoffs is accepted, management is tempted to dismiss marginal producers first. Many employees object that this is unfair.

"James gave 25 years of his life to the company. Sure he's slowed down, but the company got lots of work out of him in his prime. At age 50 he'll find it hard to get a job if this layoff lasts long."

Almost every industrial union (craft unions are often an exception) makes sure that its contract includes a clause requiring that employees be laid off in reverse order of their hiring: last hired, first to be dropped.

Calculating seniority

Even with the acceptance of seniority as a principle, there is a question of how seniority is to be determined. There are three major alternatives.

1. *Companywide seniority:* the length of time an employee has worked for the company.
2. *Departmental seniority:* the length of time an employee has worked in a particular department.
3. *Job seniority:* the length of time an employee has held a specific job in a particular department.

The method used determines which employee is laid off.

The employee with least seniority under formula 1 might be a recently hired file clerk in the engineering department. Then the newest stenographer in Accounts Receivable would be transferred to Engineering to take the job of this file clerk, who would be laid off.

The employee with least seniority under formula 2 might be a typist who has been with the organization for several years, but who recently transferred into the department when an opening occurred. (He will probably regret having shifted jobs!)

Under formula 3, the person laid off will be the one who has least seniority as a stenographer in the department.

Bumping. Let us introduce another complication: *bumping.* The application of seniority may mean that a whole series of moves is generated when a single employee is laid off.

In terms of our earlier example, with departmental seniority, the following would be a typical sequence. Accounts Receivable has too many stenographers. The stenographer with least service in that position would lose his job but have the privilege of taking any other job in the department held by someone with less departmental service. He must, of course, be capable of performing the job. Thus, this stenographer might bump a lower-seniority tabulating clerk. In turn, the tabulating clerk may bump a file clerk with even less seniority. And the process continues as long as displaced employees can find lower-seniority workers occupying jobs that they are able to perform. The process is even more complex when companywide seniority prevails. Large companies find that layoffs may generate thousands of job shifts, which, in turn, create massive recordkeeping and personnel problems.

Selecting among alternative systems

What seniority system is best from the point of view of the firm? The following factors are relevant.

Reducing frequency of movement. Job seniority (alternative 3) reduces the frequency of job-shifting. Shifts create grievances, ill feeling and confusion. Also, they reduce efficiency.

Although management may require that an employee be able to perform the job attained through bumping, it is hard to determine this ability without giving the employee a long trial period. Under the pressure of events, job shifts inevitably result in workers being switched from jobs they do efficiently to jobs on which their performance is marginal.

Retaining valuable employees. Narrow seniority units have costs of their own. Assume the need for machinists has declined temporarily. Using job seniority, the company might be required to lay off highly trained machinists while retaining untrained machinists' helpers. Then, if the machinists accepted jobs elsewhere, expensive recruiting and training would be required to replace them when business picked up.

Encourage mobility. Narrow seniority units discourage employees from accepting transfers, for they lose their seniority when they move from one unit to another. Wider seniority makes a more flexible workforce.

Employees' desires. In theory, unions and employees favor broad seniority. They argue that it is unfair to lay off an employee with 15 years seniority in one department when an employee with only 6 months seniority in another department is retained. Unions have sometimes sought corporationwide agreements to enable an employee who is terminated in one company location to move to another; on occasion they have demanded that moving expenses be provided.

In practice, employees frequently favor narrow units. The turbulence of frequent job shifting disturbs them as much as it does management. Further, many employees consider their job their own "property" and have no desire to leave it.

Termination

Management has the responsibility to inform employees when a layoff is likely to be permanent. Union contracts and company policies often specify that employees' recall rights, with priority to be determined by seniority, will not continue beyond one or two years. If the layoff persists this long, employees lose rights to other benefits associated with accrued service. If later rehired, they come back as new employees. Many companies pay a *severance* or *termination* allowance when employees lose their jobs through no fault of their own.

For the older employee, early retirement is an alternative to dismissal. This option is being increasingly used by companies after comparing the cost of: (1) allowing an employee to do make-work jobs at full salary until normal retirement or (2) bearing the additional cost of early retirement and a generous pension.

Outplacement

Large organizations are offering terminating employees more help in finding jobs. Consulting firms specialize in these so-called outplacement services, on a contract basis, for organizations undergoing manpower shifts. When an entire facility closes down, placement aid may be given to all employees; more typically, it is restricted to managerial and professional employees.

Outplacement services may have a salutary effect on a range of personnel practices. There is little question that managers are generally reluctant to discharge long-service marginal workers. They may even countenance overstaffing, to protect the economic welfare of well-liked, loyal employees. Their attitudes may change when supervisors know that employees will be helped to find new jobs.

A systems approach to manpower training

During recent years, the terms *human resources management, manpower systems,* and *manpower planning* have come to the fore. Their usage reflects a growing awareness that the organization's parts are so interdependent that a change cannot be introduced in one place without affecting that total system.

Despite this talk about systems planning, there is still a tendency to classify personnel problems into watertight categories. For example:

"We have a shortage of people qualified to be sales managers. This is a *recruitment* problem."

"Too many engineers are requesting transfer out of the power division. This is a *transfer* problem."

"Many of our best craftsmen are quitting. This is a *turnover* problem."

In fact, each of the above designations may be incorrect. What appears to be purely a recruitment problem may turn out, in fact, to involve training. Excessive transfers may reflect inadequate pay.

Let us put this another way. Traditional management thinking often involved a search for simple cause-and-effect relationships. In practice, it is rare to find such simple causality. Human behavior in organizations results from a complex interaction among a number of personnel processes, including supervision, remuneration, career paths, performance appraisal, and others. The challenge is to identify the interrelationships among these various processes.

Manpower planning requires management to look at organizational policies and assess their total impact on manpower utilization. Decisions made by individual departments ramify throughout the organization.

A company may have a nondiscrimination policy; but unless it is backed by suitable training of supervisors and effective monitoring, the policy may be ineffective.

A manager may be reluctant to fill a middle-level position with anyone who does not have a unique, narrowly defined experience. Yet, the job is a critical stepping stone to general management positions. The department's insistence on fully qualified personnel may have to be modified in the light of larger organizational needs.

In an effort to identify the underlying manpower system that shapes the flows of personnel through the organization, personnel research analysts ask questions such as the following:

Do engineers who quit during the first three years of employment graduate near the top, middle, or bottom of their class?

Do we lose more young managers who begin their careers with us in our trainee program or more who go directly to a first, nontraining assignment?

How do the internal company careers of staff people who advance rapidly differ from those who are promoted more slowly?

Long-run vs. short-run costs and benefits

A manpower planning approach to personnel problems should also counter the tendency of all managers to neglect long-run considerations. An investment in training may not pay off for many years—not until the employee has moved up to other jobs. A manager can be reluctant to invest in the future when his incentives encourage thinking about only the present. The organization requires some process by which these longer-run considerations can be factored into today's decisions. As in all planning, that is the contribution of manpower planning: to make sure that choices made today will assist the organization in moving to the objectives it has set for tomorrow.

Conclusion

Manpower planning is an integrated view of the personnel systems of the organization. It allows managers to make improved day-to-day decisions that will be consistent with the *total organization's longer-run needs*. Its successful operation requires:

1. An understanding of the existing interdependencies among personnel systems and personnel flows.

2. The establishment of guidelines and policies based on this understanding, within which managers will make their personnel decisions.

3. Some mechanism to detect when these policies either need changing or are being violated.

If this is done successfully, the organization will be in a better position to decide questions such as:

- Where should we begin hiring people?

- Where should we reduce hiring and allow attrition (i.e., quits, retirements, etc.) to decrease the size of the group?

- Where should promotion rates be accelerated, slowed down; similarly, where is more training required, less?

Ideally, the organization predicts the numbers of each kind of skill it will require and hires people who will grow into those positions. In the best of all manpower systems, the frequency and number of promotions just matches the ambition of the personnel and their ability to learn new tasks after mastering their previous jobs. Perhaps there should be one modification of that ideal balance: a certain number of outsiders should be introduced at various levels of the system, to provide some diversity of point of view and to avoid excessive in-breeding.

Designing that kind of manpower system requires the organization both to predict its future needs (forecasting) and to develop systematic job analyses that allow the development of learning ladders (jobs sequenced so that each is good preparation for the next higher rung).

Job analysis is also necessary to develop adequate selection and compensation systems: who is needed and what should they be paid (job evaluation). Job analysis, however needs to go beyond describing the current state of affairs. The content of each job is a critical element in determining the level of personnel that will be required, the satisfactions they will derive, and the kind of coordination and work-flow problems that will persist. Thus, management needs to review the design of jobs, to be sure that organizational objectives are being met.

Career paths or promotion ladders differ in length, breadth, and permeability. Although the technology of the organization restricts choices, management can shape promotion policy in terms of its broader personnel philosophy. Far-sighted companies place greater stress on self-selection, giving more options to the individual, and designing safeguards so that competent and ambitious employees will not be thwarted by dead-end jobs or long service in unchallenging jobs.

Both promotion and retention during periods of retrenchment require management to consider ability *and* seniority factors. These decisions are further complicated by alternative methods of calculating length of service.

Sensible, longer-run manpower planning also emphasizes employment stability. Employee motivation is decreased and labor costs are increased when employment is unstable.

1 · *Informal Promotion*

Myers was a mechanical engineer before being promoted to supervise a department of engineers. While Myers believed in delegation, he couldn't resist getting involved in the technical problems of the work. This took time from the many personnel and scheduling problems that came to him. Therefore, when Myers found that one of his subordinates, a young engineer by the name of Thompson, was eager to take on new responsibilities and handled them well, he began assigning certain administrative detail work to him. Thompson was, in effect, assistant supervisor, though his title appeared nowhere on the department's organization chart, and he handled many of the work-assignment decisions and relationships with other departments.

After four months, in which this informal arrangement had worked well, Myers requested a formal promotion for Thompson to a managerial job classification. While Myers's superiors were willing to add an additional manager to the division, they turned down Thompson as being too inexperienced and lacking a college degree.

Myers was left with a difficult problem. Should he take away the additional duties, although Thompson did not request him to do so, or should he encourage Thompson to seek a job in a division that would recognize his managerial capacities and not discriminate against him for his lack of a college degree?

1. What should Myers's decision be?
2. Did Myers handle the informal upgrading of Thompson appropriately? (Remember that Thompson liked his administrative work, wanted additional responsibility, and was, in fact, receiving good training.)
3. Are there circumstances that justify a "promotion" without a commensurate increase in income and status?

2 · *The Skilled and the Unskilled*

The Frank Home Oil Service has had a long-standing tradition of promotion from within, largely on the basis of length of service. Recruits were hired as laborers and moved up through promotional ladders to higher paying positions, including maintenance work. Older workers typically "bid" on the mechanics' jobs when there were openings, because this work was easier than delivery and pumping jobs. As new and more complicated equipment was purchased, the company found itself without adequate maintenance personnel.

It was finally able to negotiate an agreement with the union, permitting it to use aptitude tests in selecting new mechanics. The steady stream of older workers bidding on these jobs was now halted. To fill openings as they occurred, the company, for the first time, could go outside the organization and hire young trade-school graduates who quickly learned the requisite skills.

The immediate problem is that declining business is forcing a cutback in the maintenance department. Normally, departmental seniority is used to determine who will be laid off. The result in this case will be that nearly all of the relatively new and more able younger mechanics must go. The company fears that its maintenance work will be crippled and that a good share of the mechanics will leave the company permanently.

1. How would you analyze the company's problem? What mistakes have been made that other organizations can profit from?
2. What are the alternative solutions, and how would you go about trying to put any of them into effect?

selection techniques

Logically, the organization's first and perhaps most critical personnel activity is to acquire employees. The supply of qualified people limits organizational success just as sharply as does the supply of money, materials, or markets.

The process begins, of course, with recruitment— and the decision about where and how to look for job applicants. Next, decision makers must evaluate how applicants' abilities fit organizational needs. Several evaluation instruments are available: testing, interviews, application blanks, and the like. All these can serve (some better than others) as means of predicting behavior on the job. These instruments' ability to predict (technically known as *validity*) can be increased by careful research and design. But this is expensive. Therefore, the personnel decision maker is forced to choose how sophisticated the selection process will be, always taking into account the facts that selection techniques are costly and (in the United States) must meet equal employment regulations.

Recruitment

Nature of the labor market

In recruiting new employees, management must consider the nature of the labor market: what sorts of potential employees are available, and how do they look for work? Economists have studied these questions for years.

Labor market boundaries. Knowing the boundaries of the labor market helps management estimate the available supply of qualified personnel. A labor market consists of a geographical area in which the forces of supply (people looking for work) and demand (employers looking for people to hire) interact and thus affect the price of labor (wages and salaries). The labor market for certain unusual skills may be the entire United States. Top quality hotel chefs often move from Maine to Florida when appropriate openings occur. At the other extreme, clerical workers may be unwilling to take jobs that are not within a few miles of their homes. Availability of mass transit and good highways helps determine the labor market.[1]

Available skills. Few companies hire undifferentiated "labor"; rather, they hire workers with specific skills. Many large offices that move out of cities to suburban areas find a readily available supply of executives but a severe shortage of personnel with clerical skills. If a firm requires fully trained workers, it may have no choice but to locate near competitors. Companies that want to hire large numbers of highly skilled tool and die makers must locate in areas where these craftpersons live. Auto stylists are most likely to be found in Detroit, television technical staff in New York and Los Angeles.

Organizations that require relatively large numbers of employees with a particular skill often have a severe recruitment problem. If a firm needs only a single bookkeeper, it usually has little trouble finding one—even if it pays less than competitors and has a poor reputation in the community. But for an insurance company that must hire hundreds of stenographers every year, relative wages and working conditions are critical.

The organization's attractiveness and visibility. When Volkswagen announced it was going to build a new plant in rural Pennsylvania, it received thousands of applications. Publicity, the visibility of the VW name, and the knowledge that the auto industry pays high wages all contributed. Similar large, well-known organizations with a reputation for supplying "hygiene" satisfactions (fringe benefits, good working conditions, considerate supervision, and other amenities) may never have to recruit. Their personnel files bulge with applications. Small organizations and those with poorer reputations, particularly in times of relatively full employment, have to engage in vigorous recruiting.

Economic conditions. Economic conditions in the labor market itself affect recruitment. A new plant located in a depressed labor market may be swamped by unemployed workers. On the other hand, a firm trying to establish itself or to expand in an area with few qualified but unemployed workers has quite a different recruiting problem.

[1] Minority workers feel aggrieved when corporate facilities are located in suburban areas with no mass transit connections to the central city.

The next question is: what sorts of employees are available, and how do they seek employment? [2] We describe five types in the following paragraphs.

The new employee taking a first job. An inexperienced employee has a sketchy idea about job possibilities. He or she is likely to take several jobs during the first five or six years of employment (the "trial period," as it is called). Finally settling down is likely to be as much a result of growing family responsibilities and more realistic expectations as of finding genuine job satisfaction. The jobs held by one's parents, the ambitions encouraged within the family, and educational level all influence what jobs an employee regards as acceptable.

The unemployed worker. Many job seekers have been laid off because of slack times, poor performance, or the permanent closing of an employer's business. A company may hesitate to hire workers who have been laid off in slack times: they may return to their original employers as soon as possible because of accumulated seniority benefits. Of course, firms are suspicious of those who have been discharged from another job because of poor performance.

The already employed but dissatisfied employee. Firms that require special skills often recruit employed workers who are looking for a better job. Every job has disadvantages; according to economic theory, even slight differences in pay should motivate dissatisfied employees to shift jobs. Thus, we might expect that most employees would constantly be on the lookout for a better job. The fact is, however, that at any given time only a small percentage of employees are actually seeking other work.

Seniority and fringe benefits that are tied to length of service also reduce the motivation to look elsewhere. Family and friendship ties deter workers from searching for opportunities outside their immediate neighborhoods. Furthermore, early job-hunting experiences convince many that good jobs are scarce and that whatever its disadvantages, a job in hand is worth innumerable possibilities in the bush. Yet even employees who quit voluntarily rarely have a specific alternative in mind.

New employees, of course, don't have this commitment. Long-service employees have usually adjusted to their jobs; newly hired employees have made no such adjustment. They must accommodate themselves to fellow workers, to supervision, to the requirements of a specific job, and to the organizational "climate." Voluntary quits are highest by far during the first year or two of a new job. (It is for this reason, we might add, that turnover is particularly costly. To replace one long-service employee who quits, the company may have to hire two or three or even four new employees.)

There is modest evidence that both executives and staff and technical specialists are becoming more profession-oriented. Identifying with their field more than with their employer, they are likely to "job hop" if their present

[2] Chapter 11 will give special consideration to the problems of recruiting racial minorities.

post does not provide adequate psychological and financial returns. Executives who feel that promotional opportunities are blocked or that their rate of advancement is slowing with their present employer are most susceptible to alternatives promising substantially increased "greater long-term career responsibility." [3] Although this situation may increase the supply of trained manpower available for an expanding firm with exciting promotional opportunities, it increases the costs of turnover for other employers.

During periods of "over-full employment," when organizations actively compete for labor and when jobs are easy to get, many employees may begin to consider alternatives. Stories spread about how well Jim Izak did when he walked across the street to an employment office, and other employees begin to follow the same route.

Normally, however, most employees don't actively seek work until they are unemployed. If they are dissatisfied with their present job, they may be receptive to openings or offers that are brought to their attention.

The uncommitted. A small percentage of the labor force consists of perpetual malcontents. For one psychological reason or another, they are never satisfied and move endlessly from one job to another. In a sense, these workers fit the economist's model: they try to maximize the net advantages they receive in return for their labor. Personnel directors, however, find such employees poor prospects and prefer not to hire them.

There is also a so-called secondary labor market comprised of workers who drift from job to job and into unemployment with high frequency. Never having had a good job (and having low self-esteem), they presume that no employer will ever offer them anything but temporary work. When they get a permanent job, they may quit or fail to apply themselves, thus confirming their own predictions.

Raiding. Hiring employees from other companies is sometimes called "raiding." The term itself suggests that many employers consider this practice unethical. Some scrupulously refrain from recruiting employees from other firms in their community or industry. They may even require clearance from a potential recruit's present employer before they will accept his application. In actuality, however, so-called "no raiding agreements" are honored more in theory than in practice. To avoid the stigma of raiding, employers sometimes contact potential employees through such intermediaries as executive recruiting and consulting firms. (Significant legal liabilities, however, can be incurred if a company lures a key employee from a competitor to learn trade secrets or technical know-how.) Often a key executive's colleagues and subordinates will follow him or her to the new employer.

Methods of recruitment

Although a firm with an outstanding reputation attracts applicants even when no jobs are available, it still has to recruit for special skills. Most organizations find that they must devote substantial efforts to seeking good personnel.

[3] Roger Riclefs, "Getting Ahead," *The Wall Street Journal,* Sept. 18, 1978, p. 22.

Government regulations require that the search be conducted in such a manner that a fair proportion of women and minority group members are included in the pool of talent to be evaluated.

Informal methods. Two-thirds of newly hired employees learn about their new jobs through informal recruitment (recommendations of a friend and a spontaneous visit to the employment office). Organizations can make use of this pattern by encouraging employees to invite their friends to apply for available openings. Sometimes bonuses are offered for successful suggestions. There are obvious disadvantages to such an approach, however: most employees have friends only among similar social, class, and racial groups.

Government employment services. State employment services are located in almost every major city. They charge neither the employer nor the prospective employee for their services, for they have a public responsibility to service both. Further, they have access to a nationwide network of job opportunity information sources and can provide their clients with a wide variety of testing and counseling services. Unfortunately, many employers, believing that well-qualified employees find work through other channels, look to the government employment service for lesser skilled labor only. Thus a vicious cycle can evolve: because the best jobs may not be listed with the government service, better grade employees don't bother looking there. A reputation for having poor quality applicants brings the government service fewer good job listings. State employment services are closely connected with unemployment insurance benefits. At times, people who are getting benefits pretend to be interested in a job so their insurance payments will continue; such applicants too often disappoint the personnel departments to which they are sent.

Private employment agencies. These tend to specialize in specific occupations and professions—clerical, craft, or publishing, for example. Sometimes the employer pays the fee, sometimes the employee; in either case, the fee may be substantial (up to 25 to 35 percent of the first year's salary). Specialized executive recruiting ("head hunting") companies and management consulting firms find new managerial talent. They may scour the country for someone with highly specialized experience (such as directing a marketing program for household detergents) and prescribed personality attributes. Executive recruiters are even used to recruit corporate presidents.

Recruiting for high-level positions requires delicate negotiations. Most executives sought by these "head hunters" are employed but have indicated confidentially a willingness "to consider the matter." [4] Potential recruits do not want their present employers to know about these contacts. They may not want a potential employer to believe that they are in the market for a new job unless the terms are just right. Conceivably, the new employer may

[4] Indeed, an unemployed executive may have difficulty being considered by such firms. For a description of the process see Richard Conarroe, *Executive Search* (New York: Van Nostrand, 1976).

not want existing employees to know that outsiders are being considered. The recruiting firm can help maintain the secrecy of the negotiations.[5]

Advertisements. Advertisements in daily newspapers, over local radio stations, in trade journals, and in the magazines of professional associations usually attract applicants in great numbers but of highly variable quality. A more homogeneous group will respond to an advertisement in the *Journal of the American Chemical Society,* for example, than to one in the community's local newspaper. Similarly, papers catering to a minority readership will be useful in recruiting members of that group.

School recruiting. Many companies send representatives to interview seniors in high schools and colleges. This technique enables the company to paint an attractive picture of its employment opportunities and to screen candidates in advance. The better candidates are then invited to visit the company for further consideration. School placement officials can also help channel suitable candidates to the organization.

Union hiring halls. In some industries, both employers and employees accept the union hiring hall as an employment agency. This is particularly true in the construction and maritime industries and to a lesser extent in the unionized segments of the restaurant, printing, and entertainment industries. Note that in all these industries, employment is unstable. The worker feels a stronger attachment to the industry as a whole than to an individual firm.

Clearly it is to management's advantage to be able to tap a ready supply of skilled, experienced workers merely by lifting the phone and calling the union. This saves management the expense of recruiting and screening, and it also means that management will be less hesitant to lay off an unneeded or incompetent worker. The union's stock in trade becomes its ability to maintain a full complement of readily available skilled employees.

Professional contacts. As a work force becomes more professionalized, firms recruit through networks of personal relationships and small, specialized labor markets. Even in a country as large as the United States, many individuals sharing similar training and work experience get to know one another. Through trade association meetings, professional conventions, executive development sessions sponsored by universities and management groups, and day-to-day business dealings, managers and technical specialists develop wide circles of friends. Although the stated purpose of professional societies is to exchange learned papers, much time is devoted to exchanging job information. When an opening occurs, a manager can telephone an acquaintance who might be interested in the job or who can recommend another personal friend. Thus, personal circles of acquaintanceship overlap to such an extent that a well-

[5] Executive recruiters also assist in facilitating the new relationship and in "out placing" managers who are terminated.

placed executive might be able to locate the two dozen people who know the most about video disks in a matter of a few days. (Of course, such "old boy networks" can be highly discriminatory, violating both the letter and the spirit of fair employment legislation.)

Alternative selection philosophies

Attracting qualified job applicants is just the first step in the process of acquiring new employees. The firm must develop techniques for selecting, among these applicants, those to be accepted for employment. Management wishes to avoid hiring the employee who will either quit or turn out to be unqualified. Hiring and training costs are usually substantial. It often costs several hundred dollars to place a relatively unskilled employee on the payroll; many thousand dollars or more in the case of a professional or manager. Further, union and affirmative action standards and the expectations of employees and the community make it difficult to discharge those who fall below performance standards. This is especially a problem in many foreign countries.

Most organizations use a probationary period as a check on their selection system. Newly hired workers do not become regular employees until they have successfully completed a one-to-three month or even a one-year trial. Organizations can also avoid permanent commitments by using temporary workers supplied by agencies specializing in "renting" manpower.

Maintaining organizational image

Service organizations seek to please their clientele. Investment banks and elite law firms sometimes select Ivy League college graduates with impeccable social backgrounds; welfare agencies are expected to have staff drawn from groups similar to the population they serve. Both are restrictive criteria.

At times personality factors are emphasized, and recruiters seek those who will "fit in." Besides being legally indefensible, such practices make for static, excessively homogeneous organizations. Many organizations have legitimate reasons to favor what they feel are clearly superior candidates. Their organizations pay high wages and benefits (they promote from within), and they want well-trained employees who will be able to assume additional responsibilities.

Such inducements lead inevitably to hiring candidates who are overqualified for their starting jobs. The situation is made worse, however, when organizations arbitrarily insist on excessive formal credentials on the assumption that the more previous training the better.[6] Actually, employees who are underqualified may work harder to prove themselves.[7]

For both legal and economic reasons, organizations should broaden the pool of acceptable employees as much as possible. Customary and often capricious definitions of who "doesn't fit in" are a needless handicap. Under the pressure of fair employment demands to hire those who can meet minimum

[6] The cost of overqualification in terms of turnover and performance is assessed in Ivar Berg, *Education and Jobs: The Great Training Robbery* (New York: Praeger, 1970).

[7] This would be an example of what is called "cognitive dissonance": higher levels of performance helps new employees reduce the tension associated with their perception of themselves as having *lower* qualifications than the job would normally require.

entry-level requirements, many organizations discover that their selection criteria have been too rigid.

Fitting jobs to people

At the other extreme, management can adjust the jobs to the people who are available to fill them. During World War II, many male jobs were, with slight modifications, made suitable for women. Great progress has been made in recent years in modifying or redesigning jobs for those who are blind, infirm, or otherwise handicapped. Experiments in adjusting working hours to employ housewives on split shifts have proved successful. Skilled craftsmen's jobs have been broken into components that could be learned by relatively untrained novices.

Traditionally, industrial engineering has stressed fitting people to the time and motion requirements of machinery and production schedules. Now, psychologists specializing in "human engineering" encourage designing equipment that is better adapted to typical human characteristics. Recently, organizations have sought to broaden and enrich jobs so that production work will be more challenging to achievement-oriented employees (see Chapter 21).

Fitting people to jobs

Most selection efforts focus on fitting applicants to particular *jobs,* not simply screening out those thought to be inappropriate for organizations. Generally, emphasis is on individual evaluation techniques, which we will describe in the remainder of the chapter.

An important element in this approach to selection involves allowing the individual applicant to evaluate the job. A technique called "realistic job previews" (RJP) provides applicants with a precise preview of the work that they will be doing, including the difficult, unglamorous parts and the potentially frustrating components.[8] This can avoid the problem of employees having unrealistic expectations and quitting when their expectations are unfulfilled. RJP also introduces an important principle: self-selection. Individuals often know their own interests and capabilities better than an outsider might.

An employer may be liable for damages for inducing an employee to be recruited by inaccurate or unrealistic job promises:

A former employee of Control Data alleged that it had wooed him away from IBM by promising him a top position in a new division and then gave him a lower-level position in an existing division. A court awarded him $4.2 million as damages.[9]

Finding the right fit between people and jobs has two components. *Selection* deals with finding the best people for a given job; *placement* seeks the best job for a given individual. Larger organizations try to do both. By effective recruitment they hope to attract a large number of qualified applicants and then distribute them among various jobs according to their abilities. Most organizations continue to make placement decisions throughout an employee's career.

[8] J. P. Wanous, "Effects of a Realistic Job Preview on Job Acceptance, Job Attitudes and Job Survival," *Journal of Applied Psychology,* 58 (1973), pp. 327–32.
[9] The *Wall Street Journal,* Oct. 23, 1978, p. 37.

Selection instruments   Essentially, the selection process is one of prediction—making an informed estimate about which applicants have the highest odds for job success. There are at least five major selection instruments: application blanks (or, in their more carefully designed form, biographical inventories), interviews, physical examinations, formal tests, and assessment centers. Each of these instruments has advantages and disadvantages, and their degrees of scientific precision vary.

As we shall see, even the best measures are poor; nothing close to 100 percent prediction is likely. Under these circumstances the main reasons for using selection techniques at all are that they add useful information to the decision process (although this is not always the case) and that decisions made on the basis of selection techniques are at least slightly better than chance.

Application blanks (biographical inventories)

The application blank is the traditional device for recording such biographical information as age, previous education (subjects, degrees, and grades), and training; previous work experience, including nature of duties, salary, length of time on the job, and reasons for leaving; and such personal items as association memberships, police records, outstanding debts, home ownership, leisure time activities, and health histories.[10] Although applicants may lie about this information, most of it can be checked by independent means. In addition to purely objective items, questions may be asked about applicants' goals and interests, thus converting the application blank into something like a personality or interest test.

Application blanks may be used for a number of purposes. They test the candidates' abilities to write, to organize their thoughts, and to present facts clearly and succinctly. (Thus, they serve as a simple literacy or intelligence test.) They give the interviewer a point of departure for the formal job interview, and they provide the company with data for its permanent employee record. The application indicates, further, whether the applicant has consistently progressed to better jobs and whether his education and occupational experience have been logically patterned.

The biographical material on the application blanks may be used as if they were items on a test. A statistical analysis can be made of the relationship between each item and actual job success. For example, a study in a given situation might find that the following characteristics correlate with success in certain management jobs: graduation from college with good grades, participation in at least one competitive sport, and election to at least three collegiate offices. On the other hand, the study might find that for certain sales jobs, high grades are merely a predictor of high turnover, and the most successful sales reps are those with average grades. Once studies such as these are completed, scores ("weights") can be assigned to various items on what is now

[10] Under federal guidelines, it is illegal to require applicants to state, among other things, religion, ancestry, marital status, age (except whether applicant is between eighteen and sixty-five), birthplace of applicant or parents, and club memberships (which could indicate ethnic or religious background). Even the applicant's sex should not be asked!

often called a biographical inventory; these scores can then be used to predict success on the job.[11]

Often candidates are asked to list references on the application, though these may be of limited value because most people named will provide favorable references. There is a very low correlation between ratings given by references and observed job performance. Furthermore, when former employers are interviewed about candidates, there is little relationship between their verbal, face-to-face assessment and what they put on a short reference form.

Nevertheless, it is worthwhile to contact references. Perhaps some probing questions can be explored:

Describe the work problems that seemed most difficult for Ms. *X* to perform. What were her failures?

Compared to others in similar jobs, what were Ms. *X*'s most obvious strengths? Describe her most significant contributions.

The emphasis should be on getting the informant to describe actual on-the-job behavior.

Interviews

The interview is an almost universal selection device. The interview enables the person responsible for hiring to appraise the candidate and his behavior directly. The effective interview involves two-way communication. It permits the interviewer to learn more about the job applicant's background, interests, and values, and it provides an opportunity for the applicant to ask questions about the organization and the job.

Ideally, the interview provides a valid sample of applicants' behavior, motivation, and interpersonal skills. Even though the applicant is "on guard," carefully presenting the best possible picture, a skilled interviewer can draw him out far more successfully than can an application blank. Using the information recorded on the application blank as a springboard, the interviewer can guide the applicant into explaining why certain jobs appeal to him and others do not and into speaking freely about the influence of family and educational experiences. Here are some typical questions and probes:

"Tell me about the work experience you have had."

(For each position) "What did you like most about that job? What was most difficult? How did you happen to leave?" (Probe what was stressful, done easily, energy level commitment to work.)

"How did you find your next job? What were you looking for?" "What do you like to do in your spare time?" (Probe for evidence of social initiative, assumption of responsibility, leadership skills.)

Even trained interviewers differ in approach. In one sense the interview is a battle of wits. The applicant who wants to put his best foot forward engages in "impression management," seeking both to cover up deficiencies and to

---

[11] George England, *Development and Use of Weighted Application Blanks* (Minneapolis, Minn.: University of Minnesota Industrial Relations Center, 1971).

provide answers that will please the interviewer. The latter tries to penetrate these defenses and catch a glimpse of the "real person" underneath.

Particularly in the military and civil service, it is common for the interview to be conducted by a panel of interviewers who pool their final judgments. It is always possible to introduce stressful elements into the interview to assess the interviewee's reaction to frustration and pressure, for example, by interruptions and contradictions.

The interview is a flexible tool; it can be used for many different types of jobs and people. It can emphasize the applicant's formal qualifications or seek to plumb the depths of his personality. Because of this flexibility, there is sometimes a division of labor in interviewing—personnel seeks to assess personality, and the line manager interviews for technical ability and experience.

Even at its best, the interview is not a precise technique, and skillful interviewing is difficult to conduct. Candidates react very differently to different interviewers. Since there are no fixed criteria for success or failure, prejudiced interviewers can easily evaluate interviewees' performance in accordance with their own stereotypes. (If applicants are interviewed by several people, it may be possible to cross-check observations.) Unfortunately, there are still people who believe that they can assess other people on the basis of their tone of voice or whether they "look you straight in the eye."[12]

Too many interviewers look primarily for "negative information" (slipups, which show that the applicant is not the "right type") rather than for positive evidence of job potential. They also tend to rate interviewees who are like themselves higher than those who are different. One study suggests that the more the interviewer talks during the interview, the higher he rates the interviewee.[13]

Given these limitations, how well do interviews shape up against tests as a means of accurately predicting employee behavior? The evidence suggests that decisions made on the basis of interviews "are generally no more (and frequently less) accurate than those based on tests alone."[14] As we shall see, the predictive value of tests is also fairly low. By and large, interviews are more valid when they are structured than when they are unstructured. The interviewer should look for specific elements from the applicant's past history rather than try to assess the interviewee's psychodynamics.

Formal tests

To many people, tests are synonymous with selection methods, although many companies do not use tests at all. Tests have been developed in an effort to find more objective means of measuring the qualifications of job applicants. They are also used

[12] N. Schmitt, "Social and Situational Determinants of Interview Decisions," *Personnel Psychology* 29, 1976, pp. 79–101. For a popular treatment of selection interviewing, see R. Fear, *The Evaluation Interview* (New York: McGraw-Hill, 1978).

[13] D. Sydiaha, "Bales Interaction Process Analysis of Personnel Selection Interviews," *Journal of Applied Psychology,* 45 (1961), 399–401.

[14] Robert Carlson, Paul Thayer, Eugene Mayfield, and Donald Paterson, "Improvements in the Selection Interview," *Personnel Journal* 50, (April 1971), pp. 268–75.

with employees who are candidates for transfer or promotion. One of their major advantages is that they may uncover qualifications and talent that would not be detected by interviews or by listings of education and job experience. Firms use tests to eliminate the possibility that the prejudice of interviewer or supervisor, instead of potential ability, will govern selection decisions. Because of such tests' importance, we shall look closely at their design and their limitations, as well as at some of the policy problems involved in applying them to personnel selection and placement.[15]

Types of tests

Performance tests. The simplest and perhaps most obvious type of testing procedure is the work sample or performance test in which the applicant is asked to demonstrate ability to do the job. Prospective typists may be asked to type several pages, or a prospective machinist may be asked to interpret a blueprint and make certain adjustments on the equipment he or she will be expected to operate.

But how about jobs like sales representative or plant manager? Here the characteristics that make for success are less obvious, the requisite skills not so easy to test (although assessment centers, as we shall see, may provide the equivalent of a work sample). Nor are performance tests useful in selecting inexperienced workers.

Intelligence tests. On the assumption that alert, bright people can learn almost any job more quickly than those who are less intelligent, many companies use modified intelligence tests. On the other hand, for some simple, repetitious jobs management wishes to assure itself that intelligence is not *above* a certain level. Very bright employees are soon dissatisfied with such jobs.

Psychologists are not unanimous in recommending the use of intelligence tests, nor is there general agreement on the concept of "intelligence" itself—that is, on what is being measured by the test. Most argue that intelligence tests do not measure a single factor but a combination of such factors as verbal comprehension, mathematical aptitude, inductive reasoning, and straight memory. Obviously, the relative importance of these various factors varies from job to job. The typical test gives greater emphasis to "convergent thinking—organizing content in such a way as to produce a single correct solution to a problem" than to "divergent thinking—utilizing content to produce a wide range or variety of possible solutions to a problem." [16] Further, psychologists argue that intelligence tests are "culturally biased" in favor of those who have had extensive education and have come from middle-class backgrounds.

Aptitude tests. In a sense, an intelligence test is a kind of aptitude test that measures the candidate's overall learning ability. Psychologists have also

---

[15] Two valuable testing texts are Marvin Dunnette, *Personnel Selection and Testing* (Belmont, Calif.: Wadsworth, 1966) and Robert Guion, *Personnel Testing* (New York: McGraw-Hill, 1965). The most comprehensive, authoritative sourcebook for test users is Oscar K. Buros, ed., *The Eighth Mental Measurements Yearbook* (Highland Park, N.J.: Gryphon Press, 1979), 2 vols.

[16] Dunnette, p. 50.

developed specialized aptitude tests, which predict the likelihood that an applicant, given adequate training, will be able to learn a specific job.

Individuals differ in their ability to learn various types of technical jobs (such as programming) and also in their ability to master certain psychomotor skills (such as handling remote control devices that manipulate radioactive materials). Some people have the ability to conceptualize what a physical object that is turned inside out will look like, but they lack the muscular coordination and control to operate a complex machine tool. Most students are familiar with the aptitude tests designed to predict success in business, law, and medical schools.[17]

Personality tests. Ability suggests potential to learn; more important is willingness to learn and then to maintain a consistently high level of performance. For many positions, personality appears to be a critical factor in job performance. Personality tests seek to measure motivation to work, to identify potentially disqualifying "defects" in temperament (for example, inability to cope with day-to-day stress), and to discover other personality characteristics that may affect job behavior. Typical tests claim to assess the strength of such traits as ambition, self-confidence, decisiveness, optimism, patience, and willingness to assume responsibility.[18]

At times, personality affects job performance in unexpected ways.

During World War II, when great numbers of trained technicians were in demand, it was assumed that those who had mechanical aptitude would make good airplane mechanics. A careful analysis of this assumption proved otherwise. It turned out that a good shoe clerk in civilian life would become a better mechanic for military purposes than someone who had fixed cars most of his life and learned on a Model-T Ford. The critical trait was not mechanical aptitude but the ability of the trainee to follow instructions. The army then worked out its instruction manuals so meticulously that the best recruit turned out to be a mildly obsessional person who could read and follow directions. The last thing they wanted was someone with his own ideas on how to fix equipment.[19]

The most popular personality tests are the pencil-and-paper variety. A typical question might be: "true or false: 'I work hardest when I believe I will be praised for my work by my supervisor.'" Most of these paper-and-pencil tests claim to give a well-rounded picture of the applicant's personality, but many observers argue that they are superficial, easily faked, and misleading. Clinical psychologists favor depth interviews and projective tests (such as the Rorschach "Ink Blot Test" or the Thematic Aperception Test, which require many hours to administer and must be interpreted individually by trained

[17] More specifically, there are tests to measure such aptitudes as *numerical facility,* which might be relevant to those who must make change and do clerical tasks, *perceptual speed* for future inspectors, and *spatial visualization* for future draftsmen.

[18] Obviously, managerial work has a large personality component. For one approach to testing for what are presumed to be managerial personality characteristics, see John Miner and Mary Miner, *Motivation to Manage* (Atlanta, Ga.: Organizational Measurement Systems Press, 1977). They are interested in assessing competitiveness, acceptance of responsibility, drive for power, etc.

[19] Edward Hall, *The Silent Language* (Garden City, N.Y.: Doubleday, 1959), p. 94.

experts). Originally, many of these tests were developed to analyze the abnormal or deviant personality.

Testing has been controversial for years, but fair employment legislation has converted widespread assertions that testing was misleading or inaccurate into requirements that management be able to prove that tests accomplish what they purport to do or not be used.[20]

Regrettably, although it is obviously tempting for a personnel manager to hear that a test will measure potential employees' feelings of responsibility, most personality tests are not well validated for selection purposes. In fact, in 1965 the American Psychological Association went on record as considering it unethical to use such standard clinical tests as the Minnesota Multiphasic Personality Inventory as part of a selection procedure.

Test development and evaluation

No manager should use tests without some understanding of how they are developed and what their inherent limitations are. Although it is very tempting to have a selection device that *appears* to say objectively and unambiguously that applicant *A* will succeed while *B* will not, tests can't do that. Numerical scores can be very deceptive. Further, government regulations under EEOC now restrict the use of tests for selection decisions unless they have been proven to be valid. We shall explore the meaning of validity and the problem of test design in this section.

To understand the use and limitation of tests, we will look at the major assumptions behind testing procedures and then consider the problems they pose.

Underlying assumptions of testing procedures

Testing procedures assume that

1. there are significant differences in the extent to which individuals possess certain characteristics: intelligence, finger dexterity, knowledge of blueprint reading, motivation.

2. there is a direct and important relationship between the possession of one or more of these characteristics and the individual's ability to do certain jobs. This relationship should enable the manager to predict the candidate's eventual job performance.

3. the organization can measure these selected characteristics accurately and evaluate the relationship between test results and job performance.

These are highly demanding requirements. In some instances the degree of individual differences does not justify a testing program. As one psychologist points out, it would be wasteful to try to test differences in color discrimination

---

[20] Personality tests have long been controversial in part because of the privacy issue: employers had no right to question applicants about their private lives and sexual fantasies. More recently the criticism has focused on their lack of validity; it is argued that since there is no compelling evidence that they predict job performance, they ought not to be used. Even if the test does measure something that sounds like a disqualification ("inferiority feelings" or "hypersensitivity"), management should not jump to the conclusion that candidates with these characteristics will be incompetent or ineffective.

among female applicants for inspection jobs, because "color blindness in women is about as rare . . . as appearances of Halley's Comet." [21]

Similarly, a self-selection process, by which people themselves decide whether or not to apply for a specific job in a particular company, may minimize differences among applicants to the point where it is hardly worth the expense of testing.

The fact that some jobs can be handled successfully by more than one type of person throws doubt on the assumption that there is a close relationship between certain employee characteristics and job performance. For example, older workers, who are slower and less agile than some younger workers, may compensate by displaying greater attention, persistence, and energy.

Below, we summarize the extensive procedures required to develop useful tests.

1. A careful job analysis should be prepared (see Chapter 8), and it should not ignore less obvious requirements. On the basis of this analysis, the test designer identifies the critical elements of work behavior that are required of the job holder.

Ideal test development procedure

For example, a quality control room technician has to place product samples in a small furnace and assess their chemical components by a complex read-out process. The critical skills appear to be:

- Dexterously and quickly handling large numbers of small, fragile, easily destroyed samples that must be removed from larger batches and weighed on a delicate balance.
- Depending on these initial readings, a proper formula must be selected and data then fed into a desk calculator.
- Errors in procedure and equipment functioning need to be detected and repeat samples processed.
- When "out-of-limit" readings occur, plant production supervisor must be alerted.

The essential job components require fine muscle control, visual acuity, and simple arithmetic skill combined with certain reasoning capabilities and social initiative.

2. Given the analysis, an initial battery of tests ("predictors") is devised. Depending on the sophistication of the personnel department, either existing ("published") tests are purchased or original tests are developed. In either case, the responsibility for proving their validity in *this* setting rests with the employer; regardless of how logically they appear to be related to the job analyses, they must be validated.

3. The test or combination of tests is then administered to new job applicants, but the results are not used for hiring decisions. (They should not even be revealed to those doing the selecting.) Rather, employees are hired on a somewhat random basis from the existing applicant pool.[22] Otherwise, "crite-

[21] Mason Haire, "Use of Tests in Employee Selection," *Harvard Business Review* 28, No. 1 (Jan.–Feb. 1950), p. 44.

[22] Insofar as the applicant pool is not a good random sample of the labor market population, other problems result. These will be discussed shortly. At times, employers may collaborate on validation procedures to produce broader samples.

rion contamination" can occur—supervisors may perceive people with higher scores as being superior performers. (Alternatively, existing employees are given the proposed test.)

4. Next, one must develop reasonably objective measures of performance. Before the EEOC imposed restrictions, many employers took questionable short cuts. Test scores were often simply compared with highly subjective supervisory evaluations (which were sometimes influenced by the original test results) or even with scores on other tests. Good procedure requires that management identify critical work behavior and outcomes as criteria measures: production and error rates, regularity of attendance, number of promotions.

5. After some period of time (say, 18 months), employees' scores are compared with their performance on these criteria measures. Test items that correlate significantly with the relevant criteria are added to the new test battery; the others are discarded.[23]

6. Appropriate "cutoff scores" for the test battery must be determined. Those above that level get hired; those below are refused. At this stage, some organizations are tempted to assume that they will always obtain better performers if they limit the selection to the most highly ranked. (Civil service procedures often force managers in government to hire those candidates who score highest on the test.)

In fact, such a ranking procedure may be discriminatory and invalid. The statistical procedures used to validate test items do not tell the employer that future performance will be proportional to test scores. To know that, one would have to validate the tests separately for different clusters of scores.

Assume management discovers that successful equipment sales personnel have good vocabularies, and the company starts using a vocabulary test. Those with the very best vocabularies, however, may not be superior to those with simply good ones. In fact, they may be worse. They may use language that customers find pretentious at best, incomprehensible at worst.

7. Periodically step 5 is repeated to be sure the test continues to produce superior job performers. Over time it is likely that both the job and the applicant pool will change. In technology-based companies, for example, jobs that once required sales ability may require technical skills instead.

Just as important, the applicant pool may change. The test results are *meaningful only for applicants that are like the original sample used to validate the test.*

Validation

As the previous section discloses, validation is a highly technical and critical procedure. In the past, many tests were used simply because they looked relevant, claimed to measure something that managers believed (correctly or incorrectly) to be important, and provided numerical scores that

---

[23] Current government regulations and sensible test procedure suggest that the correlation must be statistically significant at the 0.05 level (there is a probability of no more than one in twenty that the correlation occurred by chance). But even with a significant correlation, the organization would not want to use items that did not have a reasonably high correlation. Otherwise, one could not expect worthwhile improvements in performance by using the test.

eased the tension of deciding who to select. Because of government-required fair employment practices, the tests themselves now must be tested and proven valid. But the concept of validation is itself complex and cumbersome. There are three types of validation that are acceptable to the government: criterion-related, content, and construct validity.

Criterion validity. One of the best methods of assessing validity requires painstakingly hiring a reasonable sample of the normal recruit population, employing them for some period of time, and comparing their test results with objective measures of job performance.

Content validity. Sometimes one does not have to go through the laborious, costly and lengthy procedure of criterion validation. A careful job analysis will reveal that the job has some clearly definable work products or behaviors that can be sampled in the testing setting. If a job requires some behavioral skill like typing or operating a certain type of machine tool, one can develop a procedure closely approximating the actual work. If one can show that the procedure is a reasonably representative sample or simulation of the real job, one fulfills the requirement for content validity. (Most personality and aptitude tests do *not* qualify for this type of validation, since it is not self-evident that the measured traits are essential for job success.)

In some cases, it may be acceptable for content validity to require the job applicant to have certain explicit training or experience. For example, the courts recently ruled that it was not discriminatory to require that newly hired teachers have completed certain specified preparatory college programs. The court felt that the instructional content of these courses obviously prepared their graduates to engage in school teaching. Similarly, a requirement that an applicant have two years experience as a freight train engineer could be said to have content validity for that specific job.

Construct validity. This is the most difficult and perhaps controversial type of test validation. Its use presumes that one can identify the psychological "constructs" underlying job performance. For example, one might assert that tolerance for ambiguity is a critical capability which underlies almost everything that a certain professional must do. One would also have to show that this "construct" (tolerance for ambiguity) is, in fact, a reasonably well established, understood and operationalized concept in the psychological literature. Then to claim construct validity one would need:

1. a carefully performed job analysis demonstrating that tolerance for ambiguity is a basic element in the critical work behavior for that job or job family
2. proof that the selection procedure being utilized actually measures this construct

In contrast to criterion validity, the organization doesn't have to show that people who do well on the test in question also do well on the specific job.

Success in training vs. success on the job

Many organizations actually have sought to predict success in training rather than success on the job. The data comes more quickly; examinations often are built into the training. But, of course, it is job success that really counts; and increasingly, government requirements stress the latter.

Concurrent vs. predictive validity

Is a test valid if it predicts performance shortly after the test has been taken, or must it predict job success in the future, perhaps several years later? If the test is validated by giving it to current employees and comparing their test results with objective measures of their performance, it is called *concurrent validity*.

But this can be misleading. The current crop of high performers may have looked (in terms of test performance) rather different when they were first hired. Perhaps their job experiences have changed them, and their current test scores result as much from what they've learned on the job as from any inherent qualities they may have.

Management often wants tests that will predict which applicants will eventually be able to assume some highly responsible task or role. Here management is interested in *predictive validity*, identifying characteristics that will, when combined with additional experience, produce job success. Under these circumstances, it would be important not to validate the test by working with current employees; one would have to go through the more laborious procedure of testing and then waiting some months or years to determine that test's predictive value.

What tests do: right and wrong predictions

The ideal (but nonexistent) test with a correlation coefficient of 1 would perfectly predict job performance from the test score. More realistically, if management uses test scores for selection, it will reject some people who would have been successful on the job and also accept some who will fail on the job. The figure shows the numbers selected correctly and incorrectly are dependent on three factors:

1. Correlation coefficient itself (test validity)
2. Job performance criterion score utilized
3. Test cutoff score for acceptable candidates

The poorer the validity, the more scattered the individual plots of best result versus job performance; the better the validity, the more the plots will fall along a straight line.

If the cutoff test score is lowered (to Y'), there may be a smaller number falsely rejected and a greater number correctly accepted. However, the price to be paid for this is an increase in the number accepted who should have been rejected. Raising the cutoff score, of course, may decrease the numbers falsely accepted—but at a potentially severe price of rejecting many who would have proven to be satisfactory performers, some of whom may just be poor at test taking.[24]

[24] Note that these consequences of raising and lowering cutoff scores *apply only* in those instances in which the relation between the test score and performance is linear (a straight line). In our previous example of vocabulary and sales performance, the relation was *not* linear.

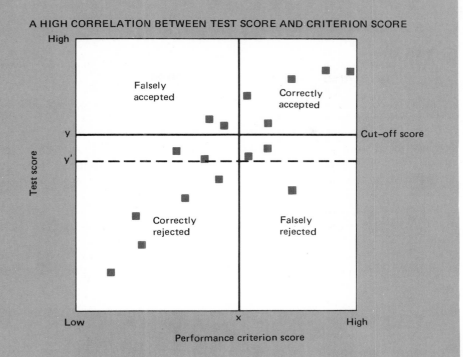

A HIGH CORRELATION BETWEEN TEST SCORE AND CRITERION SCORE

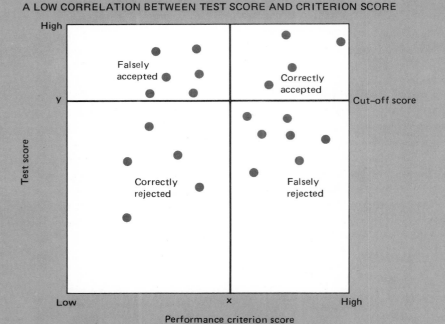

A LOW CORRELATION BETWEEN TEST SCORE AND CRITERION SCORE

Since testing is expensive and requires a large applicant pool, management should utilize tests only when it can be shown that they produce significant improvements in future work performance.[25]

Low validities. Even with the most careful development, tests predict imperfectly. Back in 1928, the famous psychologist Clark Hull noted that the best tests of the day had a maximum validity of 0.50. In technical terms this meant that at the most, these tests could predict only 25 percent of the differences among people's performances. Over 40 years later this ceiling still stands. Indeed, a comprehensive review of testing studies showed that the average validity of tests for most occupations was below 0.40, with tests doing a better job of predicting performance in training than in performance on the job.[26] Such statistics offer little support for *anyone* claiming to do much better than chance.

These disappointing results have led many psychologists to become disillusioned with testing generally. Some urge that greater emphasis be given to training. However, the major effort of those doing original research in this field has not been to raise the traditional overall validity measure but to get around it. They do this by improving the prediction of specific aspects of job performance for specific subgroups of people.

Recent research has emphasized that in practice, many tests are not equally effective with high scores and low scores (jaw-breaking name for this phenomenon: heteroscedasitic). Thus a test that may be useful in discriminating between "outstanding" candidates and those who are merely "very good" may be totally useless in discriminating between "average" and "poor." Consequently, test batteries that are useful when there is an abundance of highly qualified applicants may have little value when the labor market becomes tight.

Moderator variables. Tests do not necessarily predict equally well with all classes of applicants. Research on *moderator variables* has been concerned with the classes of jobs and job applicants for which tests have stronger or weaker predictive power. For example, certain tests are more useful in predicting the college success of women than of men, and of anxious students than of those who are not anxious. Within industry, aptitude tests seem to be more highly correlated with job performance for those who are highly motivated than for those who are not.

The object of this research, then, is to determine which tests work best with which class of applicants. For example, the results on one test may correlate better with performance on the criterion for whites than for blacks, and on another the results may be the opposite. Or the performance of one group may be predicted fairly well by tests but that of another better by interviews or biographical inventories.[27]

[25] Statistical formulas are available to measure how much tests contribute to the selection process. One method uses what is called a Taylor-Russell table.

[26] Edwin Ghiselli, *The Validity of Occupational Aptitude Tests* (New York: Wiley, 1966).

[27] For a review of some of the difficult statistical problems concerning moderator variables, see Sheldon Zedeck, "Problems with the use of 'Moderator' Variables," *Psychological Bulletin* 76, No. 4 (April 1971), pp. 295–310.

It is management's responsibility to prove that a test it gives is valid for all applicants who take it, even though they may differ in sex, race, and age.

Issues in testing

Organizations using tests must understand some of the problems in their use, particularly reliability, causality, and how test results are used in personnel decision making.

Reliability and trait stability.

The usefulness of a test depends upon the stability of the test data.

Test results may depend, in part, on how instructions are worded (does the proctor appear encouraging or discouraging?), the temperature of the room, and whether or not the test taker is bored or nervous. When various versions of the test give differing results or when the same test taken on different days by the same applicant gives different results, the test is considered unreliable. The precise differences can be computed to give a coefficient of reliability.

One of the techniques used to ensure test stability is checking to see if slightly different versions of a test given to the same person at different times (or the same test given to matched samples of people) give approximately the same results. Frequently, the test results obtained by scoring only the odd-numbered questions are checked against the scores derived from only the even-numbered questions. In addition, items may be introduced that word the same question differently; if different answers are given to these questions, one has good reason to doubt the test results as a whole.

Also, some individual characteristics may be in flux. This might be expected of personality characteristics. At times people feel more confident, more achievement-oriented, perhaps, than at other times. It is important to identify traits that are stable; otherwise, one can obtain erroneous measures.

Statistical rather than individual predictions.

Test scores can never firmly predict what will happen if a specific individual, Jones, is hired. They can't say absolutely that one applicant is better than another; all they can do is give the odds. At best, test scores simply tell management that a greater proportion of the people who score above a certain point will be successful than those who score below that point. The testers tell management that in general, people whose test results look like Jones's are successful or are not successful.

Other limitations of tests

Correlations, not causes.

One must remember that a test does not explain why someone succeeds or fails. Even if testing discloses that job success is associated with a particular personality characteristic, that trait does not necessarily contribute to performance. Individuals with that trait may simply have some other unmeasured and unknown characteristic that helps them on the job. Of course, this is the limitation of all correlations; they are not meant to indicate causality.

One famous test for mental health asked whether the test taker took baths or showers. A test for financial responsibility (based on a biographical inventory) had these illogical results: for living at present address less than one year, 5 points; one to two years, 0 points; two to three years, 5 points; three to five years, 0 points. (The more points, the presumed greater financial reliability.) Obviously, these simply represent factors that appear to vary in the same direction as an applicant's desirability. But it would be most embarrassing to try to justify rejection by showing the applicant that he had answered such questions "wrongly."

Decision making

Our discussion so far has dealt with the process by which personnel decision makers gather evidence for making hiring decisions. But how is this evidence pulled together? And how much evidence is required?

Clinical vs. mechanical decision making. How is the final decision made? Typically, the line manager or the personnel specialist (or the two together) look over the application blanks, test results, and interview summaries and make their decision on the basis of their subjective weighting of these imperfect indices and any other facts they have at hand. Though this process can be called a *clinical approach,* often it is more hunch and intuition. Some experienced personnel managers feel that only in this way can the various important but unmeasurable intangibles be given proper consideration. If such subjective means produce a labor force that is biased against proportional representation for women or minorities, management is vulnerable to charges of discrimination and a variety of penalties (see Chapter 11). Increasingly, therefore, at least for larger companies, there is an incentive to develop more objectively proceduralized methods.

This has been called the *mechanical approach.* The data gathered through interviews and application blanks are quantified and, along with test scores, subjected to elaborate computer analysis. The computer determines the highest possible correlation between predictors and the criterion measure of performance. At the end, weights are given to each of the predictor items. In other words, all the selection measures (tests, interviews, and the like) are treated as if they were part of a single test. The studies to date suggest that the mechanical approach may have greater validity than the clinical—that computers can make better decisions than people.[28] But the mechanical approach is expensive to develop. It can easily get out of date as job requirements change. Further, the approach is feasible only for jobs for which a substantial number of people are going to be hired.

Costs. The selection process is expensive. Since almost endless sums can be expended in increasingly high-powered selection techniques, at some point the organization must ask whether the added expense is worth the results. As indicated earlier, a typical test may only correlate 0.30 with job performance. This means that only about 10 percent of the variability in future employee performance can be reduced by using the test. In many cases, too

---

[28] J. Sawyer, "Measurement and Prediction, Clinical and Statistical," *Psychological Bulletin* 66 (1966), pp. 178–200.

little may cost too much. The higher the company's standards, the more costly the program becomes. If only the top 20 percent of those who apply are hired, five applicants must be recruited, tested, and interviewed for every one employed. During periods of relatively full employment (as is often the case for certain skills), the company is forced either to increase its recruiting efforts or to lower its standards.

The company's degree of selectivity, in turn, depends on the costs of making a wrong decision. Obviously, more care will be given to the selection of an executive than an unskilled worker, or to hiring a permanent employee as opposed to a temporary worker. Standards will be looser if it is easy to discharge an employee once it becomes obvious that he was a poor choice, tighter if the new recruit is protected against discharge by a union contract—especially if (as occurs in some industries) the new employee can progress almost automatically, by seniority, to a highly responsible position.

Selection of executives

Executive selection involves some special problems of its own. Most blue-collar and white-collar workers are selected for specific jobs (though there are exceptions). Executives, for the most part, are selected not for specific jobs but for a career. This means that the job requirements and the criteria for success are much more nebulous than for other jobs. Blue-collar and some white-collar workers require manual skills, or at least skills that are relatively easily tested. Executive skills, to the extent they can be defined, are generally in the areas of decision making and human relations.

In part because the requirements for being an executive are vague, there is little agreement about how to pick one. Some companies rely almost entirely on interviews. Others also make use of personality tests. Still others have experimented with assessment centers.

Personality tests

Because few—if any—personality tests can be used for the positive purpose of identifying leaders or innovators, they are most commonly used to weed out misfits. Since executive positions require people who can work closely with other people, personnel selectors look for adaptable, conformist personalities who fit the overall organizational "climate." But by trying to make everybody alike, management runs the risk of excluding creative, imaginative talent—the type of people who can become strong managers.

Personality tests . . . are loaded with debatable assumptions and questions of value. The result . . . is a set of yardsticks that reward the conformist, the pedestrian, the unimaginative—at the expense of the exceptional individual whom management most needs to attract.[29]

Low validities. Personality tests generally show discouragingly low predictive powers. One reason for this defect may be that many of the tests have been designed to assist in the diagnosis of mentally ill people. They were not intended to predict on-the-job behavior. In any case, given the wide

[29] William H. Whyte, Jr., "The Fallacies of Personality Testing," *Fortune* (Sept. 1954), p. 118.

variety of situations within which executives work, it is reasonable to assume that no two jobs require the same mixture of traits.

There seems to be general agreement among the experts that unless personality tests are carefully validated in the particular situation in which they are to be used, their predictive validity is little better than chance (and frequently they are less valuable than weighted application blanks or interest tests). On the other hand,

in *some* situations, for *some* purposes, *some* personality measures can offer useful predictions. . . . [However], a homemade personality or interest measure, carefully and competently developed for a specific situation is a better bet for prediction than is a standard personality measure with a standard system of scoring.[30]

On balance, if personality tests are used at all they should be only one of a number of factors entering into the final selection decision.[31]

Assessment centers

In part because of the limitations of interviews and personality tests, many companies have begun using assessment centers. Here potential executives are submitted to a variety of assessment techniques. Those participating may be graduating seniors or MBAs being considered for employment (as at Sears), blue- or white-collar workers being considered for promotion into management (as in the Bell system), or young managers in the twenty-five to thirty year age bracket being considered for promotion to higher levels (as at General Electric).

Assessment centers typically process candidates in groups of ten to fifteen, putting them through up to four days of exercises. These may include such standard instruments as depth interviews; personality, interest, and intelligence tests; and biographical inventories. But the unique aspects of the assessment center approach is that candidates are given a series of typical management problems to work on as a group.[32] For example, a group of five may be set up as a "simulated company" to make toys, a problem that involves aspects of purchasing, sales, design, manufacturing, finance, and inventory control (real toys are made with real parts). No formal leaders are appointed.

While the five wrestle with their problem, they are observed by experienced managers who have been trained to observe behavior and patterns of interpersonal relations.[33] At the end of each period, the observers gather to

[30] Robert M. Guion and Richard F. Gottier, "Validity of Personality Measures in Personnel Selection," *Personnel Psychology* (Summer 1965), p. 159. We would add that one of the most difficult aspects of developing validity measures of tests purporting to measure managerial ability is the lack of good criterion measures. It is difficult to obtain unambiguous, objective data on who is a good manager and who is not.

[31] Exxon, for example, has found high correlation (as high as 0.70) between managerial success and a battery of job-potential measures, including a biographical inventory, two measures of intelligence, a specially scored personality test, and a test of "managerial judgment." No one of the instruments alone has proved as effective in predicting performance as has the battery as a whole (Exxon's Early Identification of Management Potential program).

[32] These problems may include cases, in-basket exercises, and management games, all of which are also useful in training (see Chapter 16).

[33] The experience of observing is itself a valuable form of training. To spread this opportunity and to avoid anyone's becoming stale, observers are normally rotated.

make an overall evaluation of each candidate's performance in the light of all available evidence. These judgments are passed on to management. Most organizations also provide each candidate with a verbal appraisal of relative strengths and weaknesses, along with some counseling.

Assessment centers bring greater realism to the selection process. They measure behavior rather than just personality or aptitude. Both candidates and observers have confidence in the results.

The observers can actually see emerging leadership (who takes control or receives deference from peers), reactions to stress and time pressures, communication skills, alertness, and the kinds of priorities candidates will give to a wide range of typical management problems. By simulating higher-level jobs, management hopes to get a better view of how a manager will handle such positions than performance on the current job may provide.[34]

It should be pointed out that assessment centers, although attractive in concept, are subject to many of the same abuses we have already described, plus some additional ones. They rely on the skills of managers who must be trained to do the observing. Inevitably, subjective factors enter into the process. There is a strong temptation to contaminate any validation of the technique by telling future bosses who scored well. High scorers then tend to get promoted because of the test. This makes it appear that the test was a good predictor.[35] Assessment centers combine many testing procedures, some of which are flawed, on the assumption that combinations work better than individual selection methods.

Their strength is that managers try to view realistically the whole person in a simulation of key elements of the future job: interpersonal and time pressures, difficult judgments involving trade-offs, and the need to build a consensus from conflicting elements.

Role of the manager

We have spoken before about the relative authority of staff and line executives. Since selection procedures contribute significantly to a manager's effectiveness, ultimate responsibility for decision making must reside with the line. Personnel specialists can help the manager select subordinates by recruiting and screening appropriately qualified candidates. But the final decision on hiring for a specific job must rest with the manager.

The danger is that managers tend to ascribe more validity to test scores than test specialists do. When a test claims to measure "impulsiveness" or "self-sufficiency," the manager may forget that these are just *labels* and that a given applicant who scores high in these characteristics may or may not

[34] Douglas Bray, Richard Campbell, and Donald Grant, *Formative Years in Business: A Long Term AT&T Study of Managerial Lives* (New York: Wiley, 1974). AT&T claims that eight years after assessment center ratings were given (but not disclosed), those with high rankings outnumbered those with lower rankings 2 to 1 in promotions to middle management.

[35] For a general critique of assessment centers, see Ann Howard, "An Assessment of Assessment Centers," *Academy of Management Journal* 17, (1974), pp. 115–34. For a positive view, see Allen Kraut, "A Hard Look at Management Assessment Centers and Their Future," *Personnel Journal* 51 (May 1972), 317–26.

demonstrate them on the job. Specialists readily admit that test results do not guarantee success or failure; they know that test scores are simply another set of data to be added to information about the applicant's previous experience, training, work evaluations, interview information, and the impressions of those who know him.

Tests for present employees

Managers confront harsh challenges from some of their present employees when tests are used for promotion. Employees are afraid that their future is being determined by mystical forces over which they have no control. As one said, "It doesn't make any difference how well you perform on the job; it's what you do on the test that counts." Unions object strongly when test results are used to deny promotions to senior employees.

There may be some legitimate justifications for testing existing employees even though management already has information about them. Tests may uncover hidden talents. Unsupportive supervisors may have held back able employees, and test and assessment center results may bypass these supervisors and go directly to upper management. Management can make it clear that test results are never the *sine qua non* for advancement but only one type of information. If well used, tests may help the employee find jobs and career lines that will be both satisfying and rewarding.

Conclusion

To survive, every organization must attract an adequate supply of employees and then assign them to the jobs for which they are best suited. In administering its recruitment program, the company must devise specific programs tailored to the numbers and skills it needs and to prevailing conditions in the labor market. Moreover, it must systematically evaluate alternative selection techniques' relative advantages and costs.

There is a vast difference between selecting people for jobs that require predictable and controlled behavior (a draftsman or machinist) and selecting people who will be creative or innovative. For many of these more complex jobs, we are not even sure that certain abilities or behavior patterns will lead to success. Nor are jobs themselves easy to classify, particularly complex managerial positions. Different people will handle the same job in strikingly different ways. The requirements of a job may change radically when a new supervisor takes over, and there is no way of predicting organizational changes of this sort.

When psychologists first began to explore individual differences, many people thought that applying their research to selection would introduce a new era in employee relations. Previously, employee failures had been attributed to laziness or recalcitrance; now it could be argued that the real fault lay in trying to force square pegs into round holes. Testing enthusiasts claimed that careful appraisal of individual capabilities would solve most personnel problems. Proper placement would assure a high level of performance and eliminate employee discontent.

These predictions have proved somewhat extravagant. The individual human being has shown himself to be more difficult to appraise and categorize than was anticipated. Frequently an employee with the requisite skills and learning potential fails for lack of motivation or other personality deficiencies. In recent years, greater emphasis has been given to biographical inventories and assessment centers as possible measures of motivation.

The manager needs to understand the complexities of test validation and the likelihood that most tests have more limited applicability than their titles suggest. Many job elements are untouched by the test, although they may be critical to performance. Even the very best tests can claim to explain only a quarter to a third of the variability in employee performance.

Historically, only large companies and the federal government sought to validate tests. Most firms simply purchased well-advertised test packages promising scientific accuracy and the elimination of spurious subjective selection methods. Slipshod and discriminatory practices resulted; tests were used for jobs to which they didn't apply and for applicant populations for which they weren't valid. Now federal regulations require proof of validation for the specific jobs and applicant pool for which they are being used.

Although costly and often cumbersome, the correction is healthy. Many companies both deceived themselves and needlessly discriminated. Just as important, required procedures encourage the development of more accurate job analyses and better criteria for job success.

Selection and training are, in part, alternative means of obtaining qualified employees; the more emphasis on finding a currently qualified candidate, the less need there may be for training. When the selection philosophy emphasizes finding people with future potential, training plays a greater role. With this in mind, in the next chapter we shall examine training.

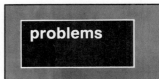

problems

1 • *How Do You Spot a Good Copywriter?*

Springfield, Zoar, and Gowanda is a large, successful advertising agency. One of the reasons for its success has been its ability to produce fresh, creative, eye-catching copy. The company employs about 60 copywriters working in 15 different departments.

The department heads, who are responsible for hiring, have different ideas about what makes a good copywriter. Their predilections are based pretty much on chance experience and ingrained stereotypes. One supervisor will tell you: "I can tell a good copywriter right away—all you have to do is to give an applicant 15 minutes to come up with an original advertisement for something like condensed milk and see what happens." Others use this criterion: "I ask to see all the ads the applicant has ever written, with the 10 best and 10 worst selected by the copywriter. Then I spend the next evening reading them over and comparing my judgment with the applicant's."

The results of this haphazard approach to selection have not been good. At present the company needs 5 new copywriters, and one-third of the present staff has not worked out well. The agency's personnel department would like to use a more systematic procedure for evaluating applicants, including some technique for testing writing skill. The new program would be costly, however, and there would be little point in setting it up if the department heads ignored its findings.

1. If you were head of the agency, how would you set up an improved selection procedure that would not detract from the department heads' responsibility for turning out high-quality copy?
2. What information would you need before deciding on such a new policy?
3. How would you introduce and gain acceptance for the new approach?

2 · *Applicant*

The Ripley Paint Company trains the salespeople it hires to sell its product line to retail stores. The company seeks personable employees who have the energy and initiative to make the requisite calls on customers and the ability to speak enthusiastically and intelligently about the company's products. Flexibility, patience, and accuracy in transferring orders to order forms are also important requirements.

Ann Henry has applied for a sales job. The interviewer who is going to talk with her has noted the following entries on her application blank:

Ann is 25 years old.

She has completed one year of college at a small teachers' college in the Midwest.

She has held two jobs since leaving school; no work experience prior to that time. The jobs were: laboratory assistant, Memorial Hospital (2 years), New York, and credit manager for collection agency (2 years), Buffalo.

No job is listed for one year. Ann notes on her application that she was recovering from an illness during that period.

1. If you were the interviewer, what objectives would you set for your interview with Ann?
2. How would you phrase your questions?

3 · *Wanted: Custom Tailors*

You are the executive vice president of a large "high-style" women's dress manufacturing organization. Your firm finds it increasingly difficult to find candidates for custom-tailoring positions.

These craftspeople, in the past, at least, have been apprentice-trained in Europe, and most of the better American tailors have been immigrants.

1. What proposals would you make to your company for ways of increasing the supply of custom-tailors available to your organization? (You employ about a hundred of them, many of whom are nearing retirement.)
2. In your proposal, consider the sources of information and the channels of communication you would explore in developing a proposal with reasonable chances of success. Remember that costs are a significant factor.

4 · *A Personnel Point of View*

" 'Personnel should provide advice and service; line should make the final hiring decisions.' That's a lot of nonsense. In my company line doesn't want to be bothered. They hire us to be the experts. If the wrong hiring decisions are made, we are held responsible in any case. So we have to use the techniques that our professional experience tells us are best. Research tells us that the so-called 'mechanical' approach to decision making

in this area is superior to the 'clinical' approach, and so we have completely automated our selection process. Our tests are scored by IBM machines. Interviews and application blanks are coded, and the whole shooting match is fed into the computer. It makes the final decisions, certainly not the line manager."

Comment on this point of view.

5 · *A Management Dilemma*

You have just learned that one of your key managers has been approached by an executive recruiting "head-hunting" firm, and he is considering an attractive offer with a rapidly growing semiconductor manufacturer. This manager has been in charge of a critical operation for you and has

helped maintain its profitability. However, he does not know that this operation will probably be dismembered in a couple of years. He is under the impression that top management intends to make major new investments in the area, but the real plans are confidential and you have been sworn to secrecy. If you had to replace him, the chances are good that the operation would show poor performance for at least a year, and your own record would be blemished.

You assume he will come to you for advice; you've been his mentor for several years, and you are torn between your responsibilities to the company and to your assistant.

How would you decide this dilemma?

6 · *Return Engagement*

John Woczek had quit several years ago and worked for a competitor, another department store chain headquartered on the West Coast. Although he had given six weeks' notice, he had quit at a critical time, just as a new computer system was being installed and debugged. There were great pressures on, and need for, his managerial talent.

At the time, he had been head of the housewares division.

Apparently, things did not go well for him in a comparable job at the larger corporation, and he is now (three years later) applying for his old job, which happens to be open. An executive recruiter suggested his name.

1. How important is loyalty, and can Woczek be "loyal"?
2. What else would you want to know in deciding whether or not to rehire him?

learning, training, and behavior modification

The efficiency of any organization depends directly on how well its members are trained. Newly hired employees usually need some training before they take up their work; older employees require training to keep alert to demands of their present jobs and to prepare for transfers and promotions.

Training also motivates employees to work harder. Employees who understand their jobs are likely to have higher morale. They are able to see a closer relationship between their effort and performance. Further, the very fact that management is confident enough of their abilities to invest in training provides an assurance that they are valued employees. Such programs are particularly important in dynamic companies undergoing technological changes. Workers often resist changes such as automation for fear that they will be incapable of handling the newly created jobs.

Effective managers recognize training as an ongoing, continuous process, not a one-shot activity. New problems, new procedures and equipment, new knowledge, and new jobs are constantly creating the need for employee instruction. Next to schools and colleges and the military, industry is the third largest educational institution in the United States. Each year, companies spend millions of dollars on training, and the total annual budget of all firms probably runs into the billions.[1]

[1] Seymour Lusterman, *Education in Industry* (New York: Conference Board, 1977).

This chapter begins with a discussion of the role and objectives of organizational training programs, then considers the discoveries psychologists have made about learning patterns and behavior modification, and concludes with specific examples of training programs and technologies. (Training programs for managers are assessed in Chapter 16.)

The nature of training

At one extreme, training consists of a few hours (or only a few minutes) of induction by the supervisor, who gives the new employee a skeleton outline of company policies, the location of the cafeteria, and a summary of work rules. At the other extreme, training consists of several years of formal courses designed to develop qualified specialists. Between these extremes are countless programs designed to fit the needs of particular organizations: short courses discussing local safety hazards (one of the most common training areas; this is often handled by a safety specialist) or the customers' use of company products and services; instruction in writing sales slips; courses in sales techniques or internal auditing.

But it is misleading to think of job training purely in terms of formal courses and programs. Almost everything that happens to employees after they join a company serves as a training experience. Actions that are rewarded and provide satisfaction tend to be repeated; those that are punished tend to be abandoned.

In addition to those who are formally assigned to train employees, there are many people within the organization who provide these rewards and punishments. Supervisors may train subordinates without even being aware of it. If employees note which actions provoke discipline and which do not, they begin to understand what is required and what can be done with impunity. Good housekeeping practices that are praised and slovenly workmanship that goes uncriticized constitute learning experiences. Similarly, the methods, short cuts, and routines practiced by fellow employees are assimilated by the novice learning the way in a new job situation. The informal work group, with its clearly defined codes of behavior, has a powerful effect on its members; formal groups like the union also exert a strong influence.

The training derived from these varied sources may sharply conflict with the prescribed method of operation. Management must be careful to see that the impact of casual, day-to-day experiences does not overshadow the practices stressed in more formal training sessions.

Who should train?

In many companies training is minimal and very informal. It consists of assigning new employees as helpers to old employees or telling an old employee to "show this fellow what he should do." At times the results are excellent, but often the old-timer fails to train new employees adequately. Sometimes the failure reflects the old-timer's indifference or even hostility to breaking in a new employee, a job he feels he is not being paid to do; the old-timer may even fear that he is creating a competitor for his own position. More often, the old-timer fails because he is unable to communicate and lacks systematic knowledge of learning principles. The generation gap accentuates this problem. Even differences in background—for example, between white and black workers—could make a learning situation difficult. When supervisors cannot speak the language used by subordinates, training may be nonexistent. The abilities of those who work and train simultaneously are obviously critical in the following example:

A study in a General Motors factory suggests that employees assigned to "above average" operators for training were less likely to be absent in future periods than those assigned to work with less effective employees. Also, where their supervisors were "charged" (against their departmental budget) for a new employee's first day of work, these supervisors were inclined to minimize training in favor of a more immediately productive work assignment.[2]

All managements do not follow the same approach to training. Some hold line management directly responsible; others assign at least part of the responsibility to people who specialize in training. Sometimes these training specialists report directly to line management; more frequently, a special training section is established in the personnel department.

As a staff expert, of course, the training specialist faces the problems of staff everywhere. Line management may resent the trainer's efforts as interference; the specialist may try to teach employees methods that conflict with those their boss wants them to use (either because standard company procedures are not being followed, or because the trainer has not kept pace with developments "out on the floor"). Conflicts often arise when the training specialist insists on telling employees already under the direction of a line supervisor how they should do their job. Equally unfortunate, once a training specialist has been appointed, the line supervisor may decide to abandon all responsibility for training. Some companies have tried to create an amicable division of responsibilities by having the staff trainer conduct classes off the work floor and by holding the line supervisor responsible for all training in production areas. (In turn, the staff person trains the line to be better trainers in the future.)

Types of training

Induction training for new employees

Progressive companies have long recognized the need for properly introducing new employees to their jobs. Not only do companies familiarize new people with the tasks they will be expected to perform, but they also provide information about company rules and personnel policies, introduce fellow workers, and give them an idea of how their jobs fit into the total operation. A carefully planned orientation-induction program helps the new employees to identify with the organization and its procedures and gives them some feeling for the significance of the work they will be doing. This helps to overcome fears and anxieties that are bound to arise on a new job. It also makes new members feel a part of the group. Progressive companies show employees how their jobs relate to others in the work flow and to the final product, believing that this fuller view of

[2] Howard Carlson, "Organizational Research and Organizational Change: GM's Approach," *Personnel*, Vol. 54, No. 4 (July 1977), 15.

the total process produces more positive work attitudes and improved productivity. Haste and lack of sensitivity at this early stage, however, will spawn unnecessary personnel problems later. An employee may refuse to do a task, claiming that it's not part of the job (because the duties had never been completely explained).

For the young employee who has never had a job before, the world of work may be a completely new way of life. Just as travel to a new country or changing to a new residence can mean culture shock, so the student fresh from school discovers that many preconceptions about industry do not fit. On the other hand, the very newness of the situation is also an advantage. The new employee experiences *unfreezing,* since the previous social supports and situational cues have been removed. This can be the very best time to train; the new employee should be highly receptive to new procedures and techniques.

Proper induction training should make it unnecessary for the employee to learn improper methods and procedures, then be obliged to forget them. "Unlearning" is both difficult and time consuming; however, no supervisor can expect to communicate everything about a new job at the outset. Some of the initial information is bound to seem meaningless and confusing to the inexperienced subordinate, who simply has not had enough experience to appreciate the significance of the explanation.

Cashier trainees in department stores report that they found much of their induction training meaningless because, never having been on the job, they knew nothing of the situations to which the information would apply. Once they had gone out on the job, however, and started receiving mutilated, faulty sales slips, they felt a need for the training they had considered worthless.

Learning new techniques and concepts

In our dynamic society, most jobs are constantly changing. Even trained professionals such as doctors and physicists find that they must periodically take new courses to examine the relevant changes in their fields. New equipment and products require employees and salespeople to update their skills and guard against stagnation. Even gradual change eventually makes many skills obsolete. Highly technological companies have discovered that university courses may lag behind the creation of new knowledge. They must therefore develop and offer their own courses.

Thus, continuous monitoring of the actual jobs performed, skills required, and equipment utilized will reveal changes that call for new training. A major policy question is how much should the organization do to keep employee knowledge and skills updated, and how much should the individual do for himself?

A typical problem is related in the box at the top of the next page. Determine whether management made the right decision.

To implement such a policy the company might provide tuition rebates, paid time off to employees who wish to attend courses, and generous leaves of absence to employees who wish to obtain advanced degrees. Also, course attendance could be a factor considered in performance evaluation.

Carters was the chief engineer on the Pluto project. For more than 3 years she worked at least 50 hours each week to deal with a never-ending series of technical and managerial problems. It was an exhausting pace. Two years later, Carters was bypassed for promotion because she did not have up-to-date knowledge in the laser field, the current major thrust of the division. In conjunction with a nearby university, the company regularly sponsored a variety of relevant courses, but Carters never enrolled.

Such problems involve difficult questions of motivation and responsibility. A study committee made up of engineers, educators, and administrators in a major corporation made the following recommendation:

The professional must have the means to keep up with the field: the time and the facilities. If the company will establish a carefully planned program of continuing voluntary education, conscientious professionals will supply their own motivation. Management, however, must recognize the ensuing basic conflicts between immediate job demands and continuing professional growth.

Remedial training
　　　　A narrow line separates remedial training from learning new techniques (and the line is especially narrow in the case of professionals). Where skills and knowledge have become rusty (or were poorly learned in the first place) a vicious cycle such as the one illustrated may result. Thus, training is not a one-step process; it is a continuing managerial responsibility.

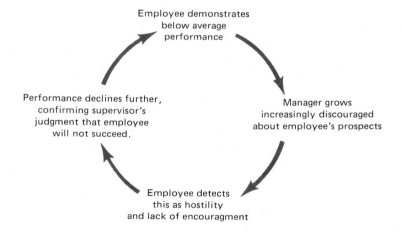

Training older employees may be more difficult than giving new employees induction training. Old-timers may resent being told that they cannot do their job, or they may suspect that the training is an attempt to "show them up," perhaps for disciplinary reasons, or to step up output—all at their expense.

As an alternative to remedial training for specific individuals, some companies teach regular refresher courses in areas such as safety, job methods, and housekeeping. This practice avoids spotlighting the poor performers and may head off the workers' tendency to slip into shortcuts. Periodic training also permits systematic introduction of new methods and techniques. New accounting practices, new company products or government regulations, and new equipment require explanation. Recurrent presentation of explanations substantially reduces the possibility that important changes will be overlooked.

*Aiding displaced
employees*

Farsighted management takes the view that if employees are displaced by new technology, management has a responsibility to retrain them, so that they will be able to maintain their earnings and status. Guarantees also serve to decrease worker and union resistance to change.

Among the special problems faced in such programs are the age and previous education of the displaced employees. Particularly in companies where automated equipment is replacing unskilled labor, the employee may be handicapped by inadequate training in arithmetic, English, and so on. Thus, pretraining preparation may be necessary.

In addition, older employees may lack confidence in their own flexibility and be upset by threatened elimination of long-established work procedures, social groups, and job skills. Matching this may be management's doubts concerning older workers' ability to develop new skills. There is evidence, however, that if properly handled, the employee over forty is capable of substantial retraining.

The following is one example of such a retraining program:

A computer company found that many of its manufacturing line assemblers were no longer needed, because a major share of the components consisted of semiconductor circuitry embedded on chips and wafers. These dexterous and mechanically inclined employees were retrained to work as field repair personnel for the company's line of electric typewriters.

Injured employees may not be able to return to their original jobs because of some physical handicap. If they can be retrained for a new job, the company's insurance liability may be reduced. More importantly, the employee can be rehabilitated to assume a responsible position and can attain the satisfaction that comes from being self-supporting.[3]

*Training for
advancement*

Effective training may help people climb promotional ladders to more responsible and better jobs. Sequential ordering of jobs also permits them to learn, primarily through observation, some of the skills of higher-ranked positions while doing their present job. Taking over the duties of higher-ranked colleagues during their vacations or absences is another opportunity for informal training.

Many companies have developed internal schools, offering a range of courses relevant to self-development (from speed reading to programming). Other organizations make use of nearby educational facilities. Thus, typists

[3] See M. Fedo, "Rehabilitation Is Good Business," *The New York Times,* August 6, 1978, D-4. Fedo notes that California, Georgia, and Hawaii now require companies to provide retraining for injured workers.

can learn to be administrative assistants; technicians can become full-fledged engineers.

The main function of such programs is to give highly motivated people a chance to attain more responsible, higher-paying positions. Although the organization may supply facilities or even tuition money, employees must have the energy, the dedication, and the willingness to assume burdens beyond their immediate jobs. Such self-selection procedures are sensible components of a good personnel program.

But should those who successfully complete a training program always be promoted before those who do not? If so, all employees should be aware of the policy and the implications of ignoring a "voluntary" off-hours course. Few employees will be motivated to undertake training unless they perceive this as leading to greater future rewards. And if their training leads nowhere they may be more frustrated than if they had never taken the training in the first place.

Apprenticeship

Organizations that employ skilled tradesmen like machinists, construction workers, or printers may conduct formal apprenticeship programs. Here, on-the-job training directed by skilled journeymen is supplemented by classroom instruction. Smaller companies that cannot afford programs of their own often join together to sponsor communitywide training programs, usually in collaboration with unions and the public school system.

Trade unions that represent skilled craftsmen have a strong interest in these programs. At times, the unions want to keep down the number of people trained, so that excessive competition for job opportunities can be avoided. In fact, many agreements specify a definite ratio between the number of journeymen and apprentices, thus limiting the number of trainees.[4]

Typically, an apprentice becomes a journeyman in two to five years. The school portion of a typical program for an electrician might include, among other subjects, shop math, blueprint reading, basic physical science, and local building codes. This material is studied while the apprentice engages in more practical on-the-job training. The best programs provide for rotation among jobs and even among employers, so that the apprentice learns all aspects of the trade.

These programs are more common in Europe, where a much wider variety of jobs (such as hotel and office work) have formal apprenticeships, and one young person out of five participates. Apprentice-like programs extend to other jobs in this country as well. The distributive trades (retailing) are often taught in cooperative training programs involving technical institutes and department stores.

Traditionally, would-be accountants and lawyers were apprenticed to fully qualified professionals who taught them the "trade." After supervised practice for a set number of years, they were allowed to take an examination to qualify for *certification.* It is possible that as more occupational groups seek

---

[4] Government sponsored outreach programs have served to increase the number of minority apprentices in many U.S. cities.

to professionalize and require supervised experience and a qualifying exam for their members, the apprenticeship or internship form of training will become more widespread.

Companies have an important role to play in helping the disadvantaged to develop useful, well paid labor market skills. Although discrimination against the handicapped is illegal, employers have a responsibility to go further. The government provides financial incentives for firms to undertake on-the-job training for disadvantaged workers who lack experience and skill. The objective of this aid is to help qualify the disadvantaged for that important first job and, in some cases, to qualify them for continued employment in the organization that trains them. The following is an excellent example of an industry program supported by federal funding under the Comprehensive Employment and Training Act (CETA).

Training the disadvantaged

TAT—Training and Technology—is an outstanding industry/education/government collaboration to train unskilled and disadvantaged people in technical trades such as machining, welding, physical and mechanical operations. Union Carbide provides the instructor-foremen and the industrial setting, the government-owned nuclear plant it operates at Oak Ridge, Tennessee. Oak Ridge Associated Universities handles administration, research, and community relations (including placement). The federal government funds the program through CETA. Trainees enter the plant gates at the same time (and with the same badges) as other workers. They spend 40 hours a week working with advanced production equipment, and studying math, science, and blueprint reading. Standards are high. Graduates (3,000 so far) acquire good "work habits" as well as marketable skills. Placement has been 96 percent at an average (1975–76) of $5.59 per hour. Union Carbide has hired one-third of the graduates, and sixty other employers have hired the rest. Considering the average wage earned by TAT graduates ($7,509 for the '72–'73 class) and their employment rate (90%), the rate of return to the individuals is 200 percent; to the federal government, 21 to 26 percent (considering costs and taxes paid).[5]

Using learning theory

Whatever type of training the organization provides, it is worthwhile to know and to be aware of the psychological principles of learning.

Motivation. Indifferent, reluctant students will learn little, even from a brilliant instructor. To benefit from training, employees must be anxious to improve their abilities and job performance. That attitude will enhance their opportunities for advancement. Clearly, the return the company receives from its investment in training will depend upon the level of morale in the organization.

On the other hand, overly intense motivation may inhibit learning. If an indidividual becomes too tense (too fearful) or if he sets goals that are greater than his ability to attain them, the results may be acute disappointment and loss of motivation.

[5] Committee for Economic Development, *Jobs for the Hard-to-Employ: New Directions for a Public-Private Partnership.* Review and Discussion Guide. New York, p. 10. Distributed in 1978.

Reinforcement. Related to motivation is the need for *reinforcement.* For learning to take place, the individual must receive some encouragement or reward. The reward need not be tangible. Usually there is a balance between intrinsic rewards (sense of personal progress and accomplishment) and extrinsic rewards (encouragement and praise provided by an outsider such as teacher or supervisor). The upcoming section on behavior modification will consider this subject in depth.

Feedback. To improve performance effectively, reinforcement must include feedback, or *knowledge of results.* Imagine how difficult it would be to improve one's marksmanship without being able to see the target. The relationship between behavior and the impact or result of behavior must be clear to the trainee if self-correction is to take place.

Learning by doing. Workers learn more when they are actively involved than when they are passively listening to a description of what ought to be done. Motor activity directly stimulates the higher mental processes. As the number of senses involved increases, learning becomes more effective. To learn a poem quickly and accurately, it is much more efficient to recite it aloud than to read and reread it silently. Doing, rather than just seeing or hearing, we are more likely to devote more of ourselves to the task. We become more *involved* in the learning process.

This principle has obvious implications for the supervisor's role in training. Instead of relying exclusively on lectures or on training films and manuals, the supervisor should encourage the employee to try out new jobs, to ask questions, and to go through all the requisite motions. Of course, mistakes are caught and corrected, the correction being reinforced by having the trainee repeat the activity properly. Apprenticeship programs, in which the trainee learns by repetition, are an excellent example of this approach. Newly-acquired techniques that are not utilized are quickly forgotten.

Spaced repetition. Training need not be continous, however. Many experiments have shown that *spaced repetition*—that is, learning periods distributed throughout the program—are more efficient than attempts to teach trainees everything at once. Trainees are less likely to forget actions they have repeated several times.

Parts vs. whole. Learning is expedited when the total process or skill to be mastered is divided into small, digestible segments. Thus, the trainee can obtain satisfaction from reaching subgoals one by one. Whether training emphasizes the whole or parts depends in part on what is to be learned. An electrician can learn simple wiring and the corresponding calculations first, then gradually move in logical steps to more complex circuitry; but this progression is hampered when jobs cannot be divided into segments. Anyone who has learned to swim knows how difficult it is to combine leg movements with arm movements. If a job is broken into fragments that must be mastered individually, learning to integrate them into one smooth, continuous process

could create a problem. Learning is also inhibited if the segments to be mastered are too small or meaningless.

But how small is *too small* for an individual segment? Wherever possible, the learner should try to master as a single unit all activities that must be performed in an unbroken sequence. In this way, each part becomes an internalized cue that stimulates the next part of the sequence. The supervisor may have to encourage the learner to try out what seems at the outset to be an impossibly large segment; but it is more efficient in the long run for the trainee to make many mistakes trying to master a logically constituted unit than to concentrate on learning the parts as if each were to be performed separately.[6]

Since it is difficult to state precisely when it is more efficient to practice a whole task rather than its components, the merits of part vs. whole learning are frequently debated, particularly among psychologists.

Providing theory. How much *theory* or background does the trainee need? Obviously, the electrician has no need to go back to quantum mechanics. However, the effectiveness with which he learns repair or maintenance methods will be materially enhanced if he has some knowledge of electrical theory. The theory itself may not be essential to the specific tasks he will be performing, but it will help him to transfer his knowledge to new jobs, equipment, and processes. If the employee is to develop insight into new problems that arise during the course of his work, he must achieve more basic understanding of his activities than that provided by the "this-is-how-you-do-it" type of training. Logical training is always more effective than rote training—at least, for jobs that call for any degree of sophisticated performance. Managers should explain *why* when they give direction, to ensure that the employee will be able to handle the unanticipated situations.

Interference. Relearning can be more difficult than learning. Interference (sometimes called *protective inhibition*) represents the mental confusion caused by the interaction of past and present learning. Many accounting professors prefer to teach their introductory course to students who have no background in accounting. They claim that with a background of poor methods and explanations, it will be harder for students to absorb newer, more sophisticated ideas. In the sales areas of many companies, supervisors prefer to "train from scratch." They fear that poor behavior and attitudes might be ingrained in those with previous experience.

Skills are learned in distinct patterns, often called *learning curves.* When employees begin to learn a new skill, they are likely to be unusually clumsy. This can be very discouraging, particularly to employees who pride themselves on agility and ability; and so, during this early stage, the learner needs the supervisor's encouragement. (This, of course, is one justification for conducting

Typical learning patterns

[6] Wayne Cascio, *Applied Psychology in Personnel Management* (Reston, Va.: Reston, 1978), p. 289.

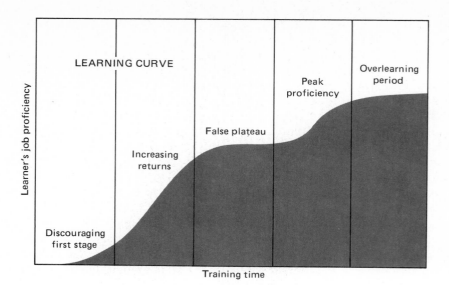

LEARNING CURVE

Learner's job proficiency

Discouraging
first stage

Increasing
returns

False plateau

Peak
proficiency

Overlearning
period

Training time

certain kinds of training off-the-job.) The duration of this stage is a function of the complexity and newness of the skill being learned—it may be only a few minutes or it could last a few weeks.

After this period, the typical learning rate is rapid. This is the stage of increasing returns, in which small amounts of practice by the trainee produce substantial increases in job proficiency. During this second period, the employee's confidence and satisfaction rise.

After more training has elapsed, a *plateau* develops. Now, additional training time does not result in significant increases in proficiency, and both the supervisor and the learner may be deceived, thinking that maximum proficiency has been attained.

These plateaus seem to be the result of two factors: (1) a loss of motivation—satisfaction from early surges of progress is dissipated, and further progress is more difficult; (2) the trainee's need for substantial blocks of time to develop new and improved skills. Initially the employee may be forced to learn a new job in segments, thinking consciously about each part of the job. Intensive practice is required before a real break-through takes place, permitting the separate parts to merge and the motions to join into a single, coordinated sequence of actions.

Through practice, certain phases of the action patterns are automatized, superfluous activities are dropped out, precision of movement and smoothness of coordination are effected, excess tension is eliminated, the energy requirements of the total performance are greatly reduced, and the trainee develops self-assurance and confidence in his performance.[7]

The supervisor should not assume that training is complete because a peak has been reached. Continued repetition needs to be encouraged so that

[7] E. E. Ghiselli and C. W. Brown, *Personnel and Industrial Psychology*, 2nd ed. (New York: McGraw-Hill, 1955), p. 384.

overlearning will take place. Experienced automobile drivers, even if they have not driven for years, will retain the skill, largely as a result of overlearning. Apparently, the reflex sequences that link muscular responses and sensory stimuli become more deeply ingrained when we continue to practice after we have reached top performance.

One note of caution: the learning curve for every employee is different. There are profound variations in each person's inherent ability to synchronize muscular movements, to effect eye–hand coordinations, and to sense subtle differences in tactile and muscular responses. These physical differences, in addition to variations in motivation and morale, result in wide disparities in learning rates. This is why trainees must be allowed to progress at their own rates.

These differences pose serious problems for the supervisor. Who should be rewarded, the highly motivated but less able employee or the more able but unmotivated employee, if both achieve the same performance level? Would your answer be the same if you knew that the more gifted employee was not exerting any effort and was performing below his or her level? Professors face this question every day.

Use of behavior modification techniques

Although the techniques of behavior mod, as it is called, are not new, there has been fast growing interest in applying behavioral theory to the training field.[8] This type of training concentrates on the learning principle of reinforcement; however, advocates of behavior mod believe that almost all learning takes place solely as a result of immediate rewards and punishments for certain actions. The trainer or supervisor, by stage-managing these reinforcements, can make learning more efficient and long lasting.

The technique of behavior mod can be learned easily by any supervisor. In fact, these techniques are a useful part of every manager's job in helping employees improve everyday job performance. The following represent the major techniques of behavior mod:

Techniques of behavior modification

- Convert objectives into required behavior.
- Break behavioral job description into discrete measurable elements.
- Obtain reliable numerical data on current performance.
- Reinforce desirable behavior.
- Determine appropriate reinforcement schedule.
- Use "shaping."
- Create behavioral "chains."
- Use "modeling."

[8] Much of this behaviorism grows out of the work on operant conditioning by B. F. Skinner, who began his studies in the 1930s by training animals. See B. F. Skinner, *Science and Human Behavior* (New York: Free Press, 1953) and *Contingencies of Reinforcement* (Englewood Cliffs, N.J.: Prentice-Hall, 1972).

Convert objectives into required behavior.   Managers often have vague objectives for training, such as "better quality," "work more safely," "increased output." But how to reach these goals should be set forth in explicit, behavioral terms that describe exactly what is expected of the employee. It is important that these observable actions (not inner thoughts or intentions) be described. Here are two examples.

A stewardess should be able to serve 50 passengers refreshments of their choice within 30 minutes, including making change and answering passenger questions.

A loader working at the warehouse dock should be able to load and pack a van so that individual pieces are stacked and protected against movement or rubbing. Pieces must be arranged for sequential unloading along a predetermined customer route, but space must not be wasted.

Break behavioral job description into discrete, measurable elements. Next, the job should be broken into units small enough to be comfortably taught, observed, and measured. In the preceding example of the stewardess, serving refreshments consists of a number of discrete activities:

- Taking and remembering the proper number of orders before going back to the serving cart, including offering the appropriate choices and knowing what options are available to the customer.
- Locating ordered drinks on serving cart or obtaining them from galley (including making tea, pouring coffee).
- Serving passengers their ordered drink in proper fashion (including proper handling of ice, napkins, cream and sugar; placing drinks on passenger's tray).
- Responding to requests for changes, mistakes, and reorders; handling financial transactions.

Included, also, is job behavior that produces negative results. The stewardess might overfill coffee cups or obtain the wrong brand of whiskey; a machinist may break a tool and be compelled to seek a replacement.

Obtain reliable numerical data on current performance.   Behavior modification assumes a knowledge of current, pre-training performance in precise, quantitative terms. This means that the trainer or manager must not only observe how the job is being done, but exactly how often step A is omitted, step B is performed correctly, and what errors are occurring. This information provides a base line to detect progress and to encourage further improvement. For purposes of measurement, the manager can use a simple form to record job elements and frequencies.

Reinforce desirable behavior.   The next step is designed to increase the frequency of desired behavior and to decrease the frequency of undesirable behavior. Behavior immediately rewarded (or "reinforced," in the language of behavior mod) establishes itself in the repertoire of the learner. In fact, the behavior will be elicited more frequently as the rewards continue. Unrewarded behavior tends to disappear or is displayed infrequently.

TALLY SHEET FOR PRE-TRAINING FREQUENCY COUNT

	Time 8-10	10-12	1-3	3-5	Daily total	Other observations
Job element A Arranges incoming orders in proper sequence						
Job element B Identifies priority items and calls correct staff						
Job element C Miscalculates discretionary items						

ALTERNATIVE REINFORCEMENTS. Managers have several options: (1) positive reinforcement, (2) negative reinforcement, (3) punishment.

Behavior modification places strong emphasis on reward. When someone is learning a difficult new skill, failure is threatening, and anxiety is high. Since the same atmosphere prevails when the employee is confronted with the need to change, it is easy to see why learning is inhibited. There are few rewards and many punishments. The new task is harder because it is strange and unfamiliar. The results are often poorer than either the employee or the supervisor expects. The worker's ego is bruised, and fellow workers may ridicule. A vicious circle is established: anxiety→poor performance→greater anxiety→likely failure.

The opposite approach should be followed under the principles of behavior modification. Every slight improvement is rewarded, and continuing improvement will follow because of this reinforcement. The learning task, as we shall see, is carefully subdivided to encourage success experiences. This, in turn, strengthens the response.

The manager can design the work situation so that the employee will be *positively rewarded* immediately for correct performance. The nature of the reward depends on a number of factors. In part, the reward depends on the employee and his needs. It could be an admiring look from a respected older colleague, a word of reassurance from the supervisor, a token (sums of these tokens can be used to purchase company products or sporting tickets), or it could be break time or more leisure.

One company, Emery Air Freight, enumerated 150 kinds of supervisory reinforcement ". . . ranging from a smile and a nod of encouragement, to 'Let me buy you a coffee,' to detailed praise for a job well done." [9] For the stewardess, here are some verbal reinforcements that might be used:

"That's real improvement. On the last flight, you became a little flustered when passengers asked for the more unusual beverages: warmed milk or a cold drink with a hot drink. This time you took those special orders in stride and still were able to serve 30 passengers in a half an hour. Soon, you should find it easy to get closer to the 50 standard."

But the manager must remember that the same type of reward does not satisfy everyone. Highly motivated employees find praise and the knowledge that they are improving (positive feedback) amply rewarding. In other settings and for other kinds of tasks, small privileges or tokens that can be turned in for money, company products, or additional leisure may be used. But whatever form it takes, the reward must be given immediately after successful performance.

The observant manager can detect positive reinforcements that have created undesirable work patterns and seek to stop these.

An employee coming into work late is rewarded by approving glances from fellow workers who are impressed with the late arrival's courage.

Inflated expense account expenditures are rarely, if ever, challenged.

Alternatively, the manager may want to use *negative reinforcement,* the reinforcement we get when we no longer are subjected to an unpleasant experience. The following passage is an example of this:

Inspectors were ignoring certain minor defects in parts because when they informed operators of the problems, the operators would berate them for being too petty. When retraining the inspectors, the supervisor showed them how to draw chalk lines around the defects and leave the parts on the work-in-process bench, eliminating any actual exchange with the operator.

The new behavior is learned because it eliminates what constituted a form of punishment. Reducing discomfort is a form of motivation similar to increasing comfort through rewards. Learning is facilitated, since the desirable new behavior eliminates an unpleasant aspect of the job. The manager must analyze each job to find these relationships, of course.

The third reinforcement alternative is perhaps the most obvious, and also the least effective. Punishment means providing an unpleasant consequence for an unacceptable action. Although this discourages repetition of the action, it can also have a plethora of side effects (see Chapter 7, "Discipline"). The anxiety and anger produced can nullify the corrective action; thus the effect of punishment on the employee is often difficult to control.

The theory of behavior modification predicts that behavior producing

---

[9] William Dowling, "At Emery Air Freight: Positive Reinforcement Boosts Performance," *Organizational Dynamics* (Winter 1973), p. 45.

no consequence will be extinguished over time. For example, if a manager asks for written suggestions to improve operations but never responds to such proposals, the behavior will soon be dropped from the employees' repertoire. In contrast, management should deduce that repeated (but undesirable) behavior must be providing the employee with some reward, not necessarily an intended one.

Supervisor to employee: "Jack, I wish you would go out and unload that new shipment; we'll need the parts soon."

Employee (irate and heated): "How can I get anything done if you keep shifting my work? That's not part of my regular job anyhow."

Supervisor (surprised and distressed): "All right, finish what you're doing and I'll get someone else this time, but next time. . . ."

The employee has "learned" that anger can be a useful tool. Even the employee who is punished may become a hero to fellow workers and may enjoy a few days off. The manager must be sure he is not inadvertently rewarding undesirable behavior.

Determine appropriate reinforcement schedule. Obviously, the manager or trainer cannot go on interminably providing immediate reinforcement. Ideally, one uses high frequency or *continuous reinforcement* to establish the desired level of skill and performance, that is, for quickest learning. The employee is expected to maintain that level through lower frequency or *intermittent reinforcement.* In fact, Skinner and his co-workers have found that an employee is more likely to maintain a certain level of performance if the supervisor uses intermittent rather than continuous reinforcement. The latter is often provided on what is called a *variable ratio schedule.* Rather than reinforcing every hour or every sixth or sixteenth successful completion, the reward is randomly scheduled. (This is understandable. Behavior continuously reinforced would become extinguished quickly when reinforcement is eliminated; this is not so with a random reward schedule.)

The power of intermittent reinforcement can be observed in everyday life experiences. Gambling is one of the more obvious examples. Winning once motivates people to keep playing, hoping for that next lucky break. Knowing that the boss may suddenly drop by encourages reasonable discipline in a physically isolated group.

Managers also use *fixed schedule* reinforcement. Incentives (as discussed in Chapter 19) are a good example: every 50 pieces produce an increment in earnings. Employees who have not missed a day for 6 months are rewarded with extra shift pay.

"Shaping." The manager can use behavior mod principles outside the training area. After observing on-the-job behavior, the manager is able to identify desirable elements in current employee behavior. Often an employee will show unusual initiative or skill in some aspect of the job, but the behavior will eventually disappear if it is not reinforced. *Shaping* consists of drawing out and improving special skill.

The disadvantaged employee may be unused to punctuality. Rather than looking for failures, the manager waits for something close to the desired goal and provides immediate praise and recognition. "Continuous reinforcement is initially used with weak responses . . . As the work responses grow stronger . . . the reinforcement is shifted to a variable ratio basis in order to facilitate stable performance." [10]

The supervisor must carefully relate all positive reinforcements to the desired behavior and not to other activities occurring simultaneously. A supervisor praised an employee who spent 20 minutes after work straightening up the work area. The supervisor, who was seeking to shape the employee's conscientiousness, was unaware that the worker pilfered company property during this extra time. The supervisor unwittingly reinforced the deception.

Creating behavioral chains. Of course, the total job consists of a conglomeration of elements. These elements must connect to form a smooth chain of cause and effect. The following is one possible chain for a small part of the flight attendant's job.

A passenger presses the call button, and the flight attendant on galley duty observes the light, walks to the passenger, and asks, "May I help you?"

Passenger asks if infant's milk bottle can be warmed. Flight attendant courteously takes the bottle, walks to galley, places bottle in warming device, waits a few minutes, removes bottle, and tests temperature by touching to arm. If satisfactory, attendant returns it to the passenger with extra napkins.

Each step becomes a cue for the inception of the next step. Ideally, the response to each cue stimulus will become automatic. Each learned behavioral element (for example, responding to the call button with a pleasant greeting and request to be of assistance) becomes the stimulus for the next response in the chain. Each link in the behavioral chain is first positively reinforced; then, the successful performance of an additional link must be achieved for additional reinforcement.[11]

The manager may want to study the work setting and sequencing of job elements to be sure that the overall work arrangement will encourage smooth, semiautomatic chains of stimulus and response, cue and behavior.

Bill was supposed to turn on the drain pump as soon as the red light flashed. However, since he also had to prepare a new batch of material in a nearby mixing vat, he often missed seeing the light, resulting in drainage problems and even wastage. The use of a horn, instead of a light, provided a surer cue.

In addition to having the trainee link elements together in a chain, the manager or trainer may also manipulate cues.

The manager notes that every mail delivery initiates a flirtatious work break. The timing of the mail delivery or its location might be shifted.

[10] Fred Luthans and Robert Kreitner, *Organizational Behavior Modification,* (Glenview, Illinois: Scott, Foresman, 1975), p. 74.

[11] Luthans and Kreitner, *Organizational Behavior Modification,* p. 136.

Accounts Payable calls Operating whenever a voucher appears with an unrecorded charge number. In the operating department, an analyst must check files or seek information from supervisor. Instead of checking each number individually, the supervisor should initiate a procedure in which all missing account numbers are sought once a day or even twice a week to allow for a smoother work flow.

Now, we are incorporating industrial engineering (work lay-out) and human engineering (designing instruments and work settings to fit human characteristics). The observations associated with behavior modification will identify poorly designed work chains that must be improved, since the most efficient learning depends upon each job element becoming a cue for the next element in the sequence.

Use of "modeling." Another technique of behavior mod, modeling, has three sub-types: [12]

- *Imitation.* Either in person or by means of a TV cassette, the trainee watches a skilled employee doing the job, then imitates that demonstration. The performance can be repeated many times and stopped to allow trainees to enact certain parts.
- *Seeing consequences.* Employees learn by seeing fellow employees rewarded (or punished) for what they do. If a high level of performance in others will lead to promotion, then newer employees with the same goals will follow the same path. This is another form of modeling.
- *Cueing.* The employees may know the right thing to do, yet they may be inhibited or reluctant to do this until someone they respect performs the task. (When the group's informal leader takes a turn reticketing merchandise, the other clerks start doing it.)

Management can use the modeling technique to transfer technology from one location to another: when a research and development lab develops a new process to be used by manufacturing. The most effective way to transfer skills is to have those employees who learned the technique initially move with the work to the new location. While temporarily stationed there, they become models for the workers who must learn the new process. Workers will learn their new job more quickly and effectively by following a model than they would by following written instructions.

The training principles just discussed can be applied to the problem of ineffective employees.

Application of behavior modification

Prime Bank purchased a number of small computers. After eight months of operation, the machines did not effect the predicted cost savings. Investigation disclosed half the operators were ineffective; that is, their equipment broke down more frequently and their machines processed significantly less data. Their supervisors attributed the trouble to poor work attitudes, even to occasional sabotage. Fortunately, management called in the training director to undertake

[12] See Albert Bandura, ed., *Psychological Modelling, Conflicting Models* (Chicago: Aldine, 1971). Also, A. Bandura, *Principles of Behavior Modification,* (New York: Holt, 1969).

a small-scale job study before initiating disciplinary action. The training director's data suggested that employees actually differed in their ability to detect symptoms of malfunctioning that precedes costly breakdowns. The work group attributed this to a "feel" for the vagaries of the machines. Some operators had this sensitivity, some didn't. Rather than assuming these to be trait or personality differences, the training director sought a behavioral foundation for the sensitivity of the better operators. Systematic observation and interviewing disclosed that the best operators had added the following four work steps to their method of operation:

1. They periodically monitored the machine's performance to detect early signs of malfunction, such as slightly torn paper, changes in machine sound, evenness of printing.

2. They had learned several alternative minor adjustments to help eliminate malfunctioning, and they observed whether operation improved after the adjustment.

3. When minor adjustments failed, they immediately called Maintenance.

4. When Maintenance arrived, the operators waited near the machine to provide specific information concerning the exact malfunction. This helped to hasten the repair work.

This information was given to the supervisor along with actual operator output data, which showed that most differences in performance were due to the different lengths of time that the equipment was out of service. The additional job procedures were reviewed, and the supervisor was urged to instruct all operators and to provide continuous positive reinforcement until the operators improved their work habits.

Within six weeks, significant improvements were noted. Intuition had been translated into explicit behavioral skills.

Critique of behavior modification

Like other techniques, it has advocates who often claim too much. By themselves, these reinforcements will not transform a work force and eliminate morale problems. The job analysis we have described presumes that there is only one best way to do every job and that personality differences and social needs can be ignored by the manager. Some employees may resent both the absence of their participation in developing these programs and the emphasis on what they can perceive as subtle manipulation. In summary, behavior modification may overstress the degree to which employee action is determined by simple stimulus-response chains.[13] Understanding the principles, however— as long as they don't become the sole management principles—can aid every manager to improve performance. Company trainees who enter programs sponsored by external organizations may benefit by comparing experiences and ideas with outsiders. Contact with others from diverse environments helps to reduce *provincialism*.

Classroom training

Training technology

Larger companies can afford to set up classes, the most conventional kind of training. Sometimes classes meet immediately before or after regular working hours, and the trainees are uncompensated. Usually, if management deems the material sufficiently important, employees are paid their regular salaries while attending class.

Employees can engage in off-the-job classroom training by taking advantage of correspondence courses, nearby schools—perhaps a school could be

[13] This has been a long-standing criticism of behaviorism in psychology; its ignoring personality dynamics, group memberships and the like, and its somewhat mechanistic approach.

persuaded to offer a special course tailored to company needs—or professional societies and training institutes. In recent years, an increasing number of private companies have gone into the business of teaching courses for industry.

When an organization trains employees in a simulation of the actual work-place, the program is called *vestibule training,* to distinguish it from classroom programs. There is one great advantage to on-the-job training. It enables the new employee to experience the work, the setting, and the total situation as it will be in the company. Off-the-job settings can be unrealistically quiet and pressure-free, and the equipment and materials will probably be in better condition than they will be in actual practice.

Vestibule training

For demanding jobs, where a mistake can be very costly, it makes sense to begin training in a protected environment.

> NASA obviously could not provide on-the-job training for astronauts who would land on the moon. Instead, they provided a simulated moonscape environment and a replica of the control panel of a lunar module, all within a Houston laboratory.
>
> Oil companies have designed simulated tankers and tanker controls to teach future captains to maneuver very large crude oil carriers. A mistake in maneuvering could cause a destructive spill, and waste enormous quantities of oil. Power plants invest up to $5 million for analog computer simulators to train future operators.
>
> Vendors of technical equipment often maintain special schools to instruct their customers' employees in the operation of newly purchased machinery.

These programs have the advantage of allowing trainees to work slowly and to make mistakes without impairing schedules or threatening life or property. The learner is shielded from the impatience of the supervisor and the pressures of the real work setting.

The critical limitation of vestibule training relates to what psychologists call *transfer,* the ability of the trainee to apply to the job the methods and principles learned in training.[14] Many skills simply cannot be learned in slow motion. In effect, doing a task slowly—particularly a difficult muscular-sensory coordination job—may transform it into an entirely different process. Also, learning to cope with the noise and other distractions of the real working area are as important as mastering specific body motions and intellectual responses. Another disadvantage is that employees are being taught by instructors who will not work with them or evaluate their performance once they move to the actual job. Finally, vestibule training is expensive.

Apprenticeships.　Apprenticeships involve carefully designed work experiences that are sequenced and graded. This allows the employee to move

[14] For a summary of what is known about transfer and other psychological aspects of training, see E. McCormick and J. Tiffin, *Industrial Psychology,* 6th ed. (Englewood Cliffs, N.J.: Prentice-Hall, 1974).

from simple tasks to the more complex. The theory taught in the classroom corresponds to practice on the job. Ideally, such training, by providing almost immediate opportunities to try out theory, should increase the employee's motivation to learn.

Newer training technologies

Computers, projectors, closed circuit TV, video cassettes and other technical aids are changing company training and education in general. When learning a complicated new assembly operation, each employee is placed in a booth where visual and auditory stimuli are presented in a carefully designed sequence. Questions or challenges are posed, enabling the trainee to assess whether or not progress is being made (and to receive regular reinforcement). If the trainee makes mistakes, material is repeated, or remedial branches of the program are displayed. Each employee learns at his own pace with little need for external instruction. Since the student actively participates and responds to questions, learning is facilitated.

Programmed text materials have been developed to supplement these teaching laboratories. Unlike a traditional textbook, a programmed text utilizes the principles of reinforcement, feedback, involvement, and repetition. After each element of new information, a question tests comprehension. If the correct answer is given, the next step is taken, requiring another response. Each new step helps learners to consolidate all previously learned material and to assess their capacity to absorb new knowledge. When a mistake is made, the trainee is made aware of the error immediately (feedback) and is referred to a branch program that either repeats earlier information or provides another approach. Although the steps may at first appear elementary, and some of the answers almost self-evident, the process builds confidence and increases motivation.

There is no question that programmed learning facilitates self-study, but some of the more unrestrained enthusiasm and claims for its efficacy have diminished because of more sober evaluation during the past several years. One of its motivational appeals—its novelty—pales after extended use. The employee could easily be bored by the monotonous frames that consist of short statements and short questions to be answered. This system is useful primarily for factual material; it is not conducive to training employees in various skills or helping them change their attitudes. The programs themselves are relatively expensive to develop and practical only when large numbers use each program.

There have also been changes in classroom technology. The use of closed circuit TV and playback equipment is on the increase, enabling groups to experiment with a variety of supervisory, sales, and negotiating techniques, then observe themselves in action. These methods have been used for years by members of football teams who, while viewing a tape of the previous game, criticize their own performance. Such equipment also allows organizations to tie together geographically dispersed units.

Video cassettes and video-disks have substantial advantages for off-the-job training. Newer equipment can be stopped at any point, portions can be rerun, and even the speed and magnification can be adjusted. These machines are especially useful in the modeling technique we described above. The machine as model is much more adaptable than its human counterpart, and it never gets fatigued.

How much training?

As we noted in Chapter 8, to determine how much to spend on training, management must consider a number of manpower questions; particularly, hiring and compensation policies. Can a company afford to spend money to develop employees who could leave at any time, thus permitting another firm to take advantage of the company's training program? Some companies have no choice: their needs are so acute and the supply of trained personnel so meager that training programs are an absolute necessity. These firms must ensure that their wage and salary levels, the quality of their supervision, and their promotional opportunities are sufficiently attractive to hold personnel once they are trained. Companies cannot assume that their employees' gratitude for training will outbalance genuine disadvantages or reduce the gap between newly created expectations and reality.

To answer these questions, Personnel must determine whether the training program increases employee productivity. On routine jobs, productivity before and after can be calculated. It is more difficult to measure improved performance in other types of jobs, since it is common for a number of people to work toward one final product. Management must also realize that as training proceeds, other factors are constantly changing. Thus, it is difficult to prove that helping an engineer obtain a master's degree will improve his or her work. In this, as in other personnel programs, management needs evidence of cost effectiveness.[15]

The organization faces agonizing problems when existing skills and hard-earned knowledge become obsolete, and the company must institute massive retraining of current employees. Responsible firms invest money for retraining, although it may seem cheaper to hire new people. Management feels that in the long run, employees who recognize that the company is investing in their future will increase their commitment to the organization.

Conclusion

Training means changing behavior patterns—always a difficult task. In doing a job, the skills employed, the energy applied, the checking, and coordination with other people—all partly reflect the personality of the worker. The manager must assume that old patterns of behavior brought certain satisfactions, otherwise, the employee would have abandoned them. Since changes in work methods threaten these satisfactions, the employee might resist new training. This resistance may be bolstered by a desire for approbation of the work group and by psychological needs for security and a sense of accomplishment. Efforts to increase productivity through teaching better work habits may run counter to group-enforced output norms.

[15] In technical subjects, like engineering, management may measure training effectiveness by the ability of trainees to answer specially designed examination questions after training, compared to their understanding of these subjects before the course.

When developing a course of study, the supervisor and the trainer ought to be familiar with the human learning process and the role of motivation and reinforcement. They must determine the structure of the material to be learned and balance theory with practice. The supervisor must identify natural sequences that facilitate learning by providing internal cues; trainees should move from the simpler processes to the more complex.

The success of any training program is directly related to the success of other aspects of the personnel program. If employees are already highly motivated and they identify with organizational goals, well-conceived training programs will lead to better performance. On the contrary, if morale is low and employees are suspicious of management, training will be ineffective. In one company, a course devoted to simplifying work procedures was seriously handicapped because workers associated it with the widely disliked time-study department. If the trainees fail to see how they will benefit by adopting the techniques taught to them, no amount of good teaching will change their behavior.

Nevertheless, if employees are to derive satisfaction from their work experience, they must know the correct procedures and when to follow them. Employees who lack confidence in their ability to perform successfully will never be efficient, no matter how vigorously management pursues the other aspects of its personnel program. Training can also influence attitudes toward the personnel program. Employees are more favorably inclined toward an employer who invests in their development. Education and training are integral to American life.

The most important lesson of this chapter is that managers really have no choice. They are training employees with every action. The effective supervisor must be sensitive to the need for training and to the ways in which people learn. As students know, learning a new task is not easy; yet, life and work constitute a continuous learning process.

problems

1 • *What Reward for Diligence?*

John Adams has been with the Draper Equipment Company for 10 years. He was eager to take courses for self-improvement and to obtain an advanced degree. As a purchasing invoice clerk, he was never an outstanding employee. After obtaining a night school degree in business, he began to take graduate courses when the company adopted a tuition rebate plan. He also participated in several of the company's voluntary, after-hours training programs and computer courses taught by faculty members from a nearby college. After seven years, he qualified for a master's degree in business at the City University. When he recently discussed promotional opportunities with his supervisor, he was told that his work record was only slightly above average and that there were no openings in his field.

1. Does the company owe Adams something for his diligent pursuit of an advanced degree?
2. How should this kind of problem be dealt with to avoid the disappointment and frustration associated with being overqualified for a job?

2 • *Handling Unsatisfactory Performance*

Wilma Granger works in the accounts receivable section of a large department store billing department. In a random check of her accounts, her supervisor found a number of mistakes. In addition, Wilma's overall output is low.

1. How should the supervisor determine whether this poor work is due to inadequate training or other causes?
2. If the investigation discloses inadequate training, how should remedial training be introduced?
3. What type of training program should be instituted?

3 • *The Need to Learn a New Skill in a Social Work Agency*

For years, the Community Aide Agency had used a specially trained telephone appointments clerk to handle requests from prospective clients. His job was to obtain general information about the caller's problem (financial, legal, psychological) and then to make an appointment for a formal intake interview with one of the trained social workers. When a new agency manager reviewed this procedure, she changed the social workers' jobs and created a need for retraining.

The new manager was alerted to the problem by two caseworkers she brought with her from another agency. Both of them had handled telephone crises calls and noted that, at times, callers would have serious, even life-threatening problems; but they would still be given the next available intake appointment, which could be several weeks away. Previous experience had taught the caseworkers that it was efficient to combine the first telephone call with the intake interview. The caller was often able and more willing to reveal intimate and important aspects of the problem over the phone than at some later, more guarded time.

The manager decided that each social worker should take a turn answering new clients' calls. They were told to use their judgment concerning the length of the phone call, whether extended intake information should be obtained, and whether the caller should have an immediate emergency appointment or be scheduled into the normal listings. In addition, training in the new procedure would be provided by the two new caseworkers who had come with the manager to the agency and had prior experience with telephone counseling.

The rest of the staff rebelled. They refused to be coached by the new workers, claiming:

"We're trained social workers with degrees; they're not, and I assure you there isn't anything they know that we need to know."

"The manager is simply trying to increase the status of her favorites who worked with her in that other agency."

"If we do this telephone work, we're going to have to cut back on the number of cases we handle in our regular client contacts."

The manager was deeply distressed by these rumblings. The caseworkers who were to do the telephone training had excellent experience in this kind of work; the regular social workers had not. They were now handling only a few cases per day and had plenty of time to put in an hour or two each day on telephone counseling.

1. Assess the various kinds of informal group, professional, and supervisory problems that are impacting this training problem.
2. What can the manager do to introduce these new procedures effectively?

minority employment and affirmative action programs

Minority employment is perhaps the most urgent and perplexing personnel problem faced by management in the second half of the twentieth century. Persistent poverty in the midst of plenty, demands for civil rights, riots in our major cities, and new laws and court decisions have combined to force our society to face up to its discriminatory employment practices. Forty years ago organizations were free to hire whomever they liked. Today it is national policy to eliminate discrimination in employment on the basis of race, color, creed, sex, and physical handicap. Discrimination against older people is also banned, and employment barriers based on homosexuality or noncitizenship are being called into question.

All this has led to an organizational revolution that is still far from finished. It is requiring substantial changes in recruitment, selection, promotion, and transfer policies. It has forced organizations to think through and make more explicit their hiring policies. And it is requiring some profound changes in interpersonal behavior patterns. None of this is yet complete; indeed, some of the implications of these changes are only now being felt. Even with the best will in the world (and this frequently is not present), eliminating discrimination in employment is a difficult task.

Concern with discrimination began with blacks, but inequality is not confined to one group. Mexican Ameri-

cans and Puerto Ricans, particularly those who speak English poorly, are little better off. Indians are clearly the most disadvantaged group in our society, their unemployment rates ranging around 40 percent and their average life expectancy two-thirds that of whites. Discrimination against women, older people, and the handicapped has somewhat different effects than does discrimination against racial minorities, but it also results in maldistribution of income and in talents being inadequately utilized.

For the most part this chapter will deal with discrimination against blacks, though much of what we have to say has relevance for other groups. We will look first at the causes of inequality, next at governmental measures designed to foster equal employment, and then at the impact of these measures on organizational personnel policies. The last part of the chapter will be concerned especially with older people, the handicapped, homosexuals, and noncitizens. Discrimination against women is such a broad field that a separate chapter will be devoted to the topic.

The nature of the problem

Ever since the mid-1950s, nonwhite unemployment has been roughly twice that of whites. Despite substantial efforts to redress this imbalance, it has persisted through periods of prosperity and recession and holds equally true for men, women, and teenagers. Continuing nonwhite teenage unemployment of 20 percent or higher (and higher yet in the ghettos, barrios, and reservations) contributes greatly to unrest, crime, and drug use. Further, the high unemployment rates exclude a substantial number of "discouraged" minority workers, who would like to work but have given up seeking it.

Not only do nonwhites suffer from higher rates of unemployment than does the population as a whole, but those who are working are concentrated in relatively low-status, low-paying occupations. These jobs are particularly susceptible to unemployment cycles, and the number of such jobs is growing relatively less fast than higher-skilled jobs. When nonwhites have found employment in better-paying industries, traditionally they have been hired for the heaviest, least desirable jobs. They have been the last hired and the first fired.

Nevertheless, much progress has been made in recent years. During the eighteen-year period from 1962 to 1980, nonwhite employment more than doubled in manufacturing, sales, and crafts classifications, and it more than tripled among professionals and clericals. Still, these gains have been made from very low bases. Nonwhites are still concentrated in lower-status, lower-paying occupations.

Causes of inequality

There are two reasons for inequality in employment. First, employers tend to hire proportionally fewer blacks than whites, especially for the better paid jobs, and second, for a variety of reasons, blacks, on the average, tend to be less qualified than whites. Particularly in the past, even if blacks were as well qualified as whites, they found it harder to get equivalent work. But the very fact that blacks were convinced that they would suffer discrimination reduced their motivation to become qualified. Let us examine these two explanations.

Outright discrimination. There is a long history of racial bias in this country, some of which was once enshrined by law. Even companies which have believed themselves socially responsible have engaged in discrimination. Managers want to be considered good citizens, but for many, being a good citizen may mean adjusting to community values rather than trying to change them. In engaging in discrimination, management merely followed what it felt the community wanted (and in many cases this corresponded with the managers' own prejudices). Nor were managers the only ones to discriminate. Some unions discriminated too.

Nonperception of discrimination. Despite their willingness to follow community patterns, few managers today consider themselves discriminatory or nonobjective in their selection policies. Certainly few northern businessmen have justified a refusal to hire *qualified* minorities. The problem was that of defining qualification. At least unconsciously, many managers felt that certain jobs were not suited for minorities, just as some jobs were not suited for women or old men. Often management just did not see the black applicant as a potential skilled tradesman, salesclerk, or executive. Stereotypes such as these were easy to maintain because there were in fact few qualified minorities, and those who were qualified realized there would be very little point in applying for jobs not available to them.

Poor communications. In some cases, discrimination has occurred by default: a sincerely felt, top-management policy not to discriminate has not been implemented at operating levels. In large organizations, such policies are not self-enforcing. In most cases they represent sharp contrasts with past practice, and many employees tend to resist them. Since there is such a sharp conflict between creed and deed in this area and pious platitudes are so frequently uttered, it is understandable that many employees are uncertain whether new nondiscriminatory policies are to be taken seriously.

"Others may object." At times managers have justified discriminatory policies along these lines: "Personally, I would like to increase the number of minorities we hire, but my employees might object (remember I hire a lot of women) and so would a lot of my customers." Of course, there is some validity to this point of view: many employees and many customers are, in fact, prejudiced. But once management takes a firm position that it is going to integrate a department, most employees go along. Customers, too, adjust eventually. (Black waiters are well accepted in the South; only in the North do they find it hard to get jobs.)

Hiring practices. Hiring practices are often stacked against minority job applicants. Many companies do their hiring chiefly on the basis of word of mouth or give preference to those recommended by friends. Their recruiters most frequently visit predominantly white high schools or colleges, and their want ads are rarely placed in minority papers.

Hiring standards are often unnecessarily rigid: high school graduation may be required for unskilled jobs, thus eliminating the minority dropout, and tests may be "culturally biased"—but all of this will be discussed later.

Technological change and plant location. Other developments have tended to reduce further the number of jobs traditionally open to blacks. Black employment opportunities were best in hard, dirty jobs that no one else wanted, jobs that are being eliminated by technological change.[1] The few skilled trades that have employed significant numbers of blacks—carpentry, bricklaying, plastering, and painting—all offer declining or unstable employment. Until recently blacks were largely unrepresented in the expanding trades related to electricity, plumbing, and sheetmetal work.

To make matters worse, older manufacturing plants in central cities have shut down, while new plants have been built in locations difficult to reach by public transportation from urban ghettos. The kinds of jobs that are growing in the central city—managerial, professional, and clerical—require at least a high school diploma and conformity to middle-class standards of clothing, speech, and behavior.

Inadequate background

Until recently, substantial numbers of qualified blacks were working at skills well below their competence (college graduates, for example, working as mail carriers), and blacks found it harder to get work than did equally qualified whites. This situation has not been eliminated. Nevertheless, for many jobs and in many communities, the reverse is true; the demand for black engineers or well-trained secretaries, for example, is far greater than the supply. In some cities, a high percentage of minorities who are easily trainable have already been hired. The hardest group to employ consists of "hard core" minority members who lack not just job skills but also the attitudes necessary to hold steady jobs. These deficiencies in skill and attitude derive in large part from inadequate education and from growing up in what has been called "the culture of poverty."

The culture of poverty. A significant number of minority members have grown up in a *culture of poverty* that has conditioned their attitudes toward work, given them a sense of defeatism, and failed to equip them with the skills necessary to find and hold a steady job. (Lest this discussion itself propagate some very unrealistic stereotypes we should stress two important points. First, the culture of poverty is far from a minority group monopoly; there are more poor whites living in a culture of poverty than there are minority group members; and second, most minority group members hold steady jobs, those in the culture of poverty constituting a minority of a minority.)

[1] Technological changes may also make some jobs more desirable, thus encouraging the redefinition of former "colored" jobs into "white" jobs. At the time when locomotive firemen had to shovel coal, there were large numbers of black firemen in the South. Once automatic stokers were introduced, the job became less unpleasant and black firemen were displaced by whites. Today, diesels have eliminated even white firemen.

White middle-class children have learned from their parents that getting ahead means hard work and that having a job means getting up every morning, working fixed hours, and taking vacations and holidays only as scheduled. But if one grows up in the ghettos or barrios of such communities as New York, Chicago, and Los Angeles, one learns not the Protestant ethic but some very different lessons indeed.[2] Young people living in such communities grow up amid a bewildering set of economic, social, and psychological barriers to adequate preparation for work. Poverty, disorganized family life, and the effects of past and present discrimination permeate their lives.

Physical isolation in the ghetto plus black youth's needs for self-expression, racial pride, and uniqueness create a distinctive style of dress, manner, and speech. These, in turn, make finding a job more difficult. Furthermore, there are relatively few role models in the youth's circle of friends and families who provide examples of success through education and mastery of nonmenial occupations. Although Willie Mays, Martin Luther King, Jr., Cicely Tyson, Mayor Bradley of Los Angeles, and Muhammed Ali are sources of racial pride, they are no substitute for knowing what it means to be a successful architect, electrician, or executive. Nor do black kids have the advantages of many white kids whose parents and friends can help them find jobs.

Although an affluent society surrounds blacks and appears daily on TV to demonstrate what "whitey" has accomplished through education, hard-core blacks have little proof that education and hard work pay off. This is especially true for the large number of black families who come from agricultural regions in the South, where the economic value of education to blacks is low and the quality of education is inferior.

Experience has taught hard-core members that they have little chance to get ahead, that there is no point in even trying. Just holding on to what they have is hard enough. Thus, they have what psychologists call a short-term time perspective. From their point of view, luck is a more important determinant of success than hard work.

Only when one knows where his next week's or next month's shelter will come from can he and his children afford to go in for long-term education and training, the endless search for opportunities, and the tedious apple-polishing that attainment of higher skills and occupational status requires.[3]

Such workers are little motivated to work hard on the job.

Often defeatist attitude affects their job-hunting approach. Having learned that certain companies and certain jobs are closed to minorities, they confine their job-seeking efforts to the low-status occupations in which minorities were traditionally employed. They tend to be apprehensive in entering employment offices where they feel they are not wanted. They have been

---

[2] Among the best descriptions of the culture of poverty are Claude Brown, *Manchild in the Promised Land,* and the *Autobiography of Malcolm X.* See also Oscar Lewis, *La Vida.*

[3] Allison Davis, "The Motivation of Underprivileged Workers," in William F. Whyte, ed., *Industry and Society* (New York: McGraw-Hill, 1946), p. 89.

discriminated against so long that they don't trust advertisements that say "Equal Opportunity Employer."

Even their limited job experiences sometimes teach them the wrong lessons. Having short-term jobs, they have learned that the slower they work, the longer the job lasts. Prejudiced employers, justifying low wages on the ground that minorities are "lazy and dishonest," sometimes tolerate slipshod workmanship, petty thievery, and casual attendance practices.[4] Above all, members of the hard core learn not to trust the "Man" (the white boss), to be suspicious of his motives, and to expect little from the job.

Each man comes to the job with a long job history characterized by his not being able to support himself and his family. Each man carries this knowledge, born of experience, with him. He comes to the job flat and stale, wearied by the sameness of it all, convinced of his own incompetence, terrifed of responsibility—of being tested still again and found wanting.[5]

As a result of this experience, many members of the hard core begin to value independence above all. This attitudinal barrier helps explain why turnover has been so high among members of the hard core who have obtained regular jobs. For this group, a well-paid job is not enough. They need assistance in adjusting to a new life-style and culture. Among other things, they need a new sense of self-worth.

Government programs Government efforts to break the cycle are of two sorts: first, there are training efforts designed to raise minority qualifications; second, there are regulations to eliminate discrimination and to foster "affirmative action" to increase minority employment. (We will not discuss governmental programs designed to promote minority-owned business or to reduce discrimination in areas other than employment.)

Training programs

The federal government has instituted a wide variety of training programs designed to improve the skills and job-holding capabilities of the disadvantaged. These programs are essentially of two types: *institutional,* conducted in the classroom, and *on-the-job* (OJT), conducted at the workplace.

In institutional programs, training for specific jobs is often preceded by remedial training in such basic skills as reading and writing. Often it is accompanied by counseling, testing, and placement services. But for many high school dropouts, institutional training seems just another form of school with all its negative consequences; they object to book work and have doubts whether training will ever lead to a serious job.

On-the-job training avoids some of these problems. Trainees work on real jobs which, in most instances, they keep upon graduation. The training is obviously practical, even though some auxiliary instruction may be provided each week. Individuals are hired who cannot meet normal company standards

[4] Furthermore, many of these jobs pay little more than one can get on relief or from "hustling" (illegal activity). Hustling, in fact, may be less demeaning than many of the jobs blacks can obtain.
[5] Elliott Liebow, *Tally's Corner* (Boston: Little, Brown, 1966), pp. 53–54.

(for example, those with prison records). Training—including where needed classroom training in reading, writing, and arithmetic—is provided by the company. For companies willing to sign a specific contract, the government grants a subsidy to offset additional costs.

OJT programs have been reasonably successful. Thousands of jobs have been provided, though somewhat fewer than originally planned. Numerous imaginative approaches to training the hard core have been developed. On the other hand, there is some question whether many people were hired who might not have been hired anyway, without the program.

Equal employment activities

Training programs provide only a very partial answer to the problems of discrimination. Beginning during World War II, an increasingly stringent series of governmental regulations has been designed to eliminate discrimination and to foster greater balance in employment at all occupational levels. Two sorts of regulations are involved: *contract compliance procedures*, which are directed at governmental contractors, and *equal employment legislation*, which applies to all employers.

Contract compliance procedures. Each year the federal government spends billions of dollars on supplies, equipment, and roads. Major government contracts now require contractors to provide equal employment opportunity. Over the years these requirements have spread to educational and local governmental agencies that receive federal subsidies (a category including most police and health departments, schools, and universities) and to subcontractors of prime governmental contractors. Enforcement of these rules has become tougher and tougher. No longer is it enough not to discriminate. The contractor must develop an *affirmative action* plan to ensure equal employment. Each company is required periodically to report the racial composition of its work force on a job-by-job basis. If there is an insufficient number of minority members in any job category, the company is required to state the steps it will take to eliminate the imbalance and to specify *goals* and *timetables* indicating the speed at which it intends to reach equal employment. The contract compliance requirements for any given firm are administered by the Office of Federal Contract Compliance Programs (OFCCP) in the Department of Labor.

Equal employment legislation. The first legislation outlawing discrimination in employment was passed by key northern states (New York and Massachusetts, among others). Title VII of the Civil Rights Act of 1964 made such discrimination a federal offense. At first, enforcement of Title VII was encumbered by procedural restrictions, but in 1972 Congress considerably strengthened the powers of the Equal Employment Opportunity Commission (EEOC), the principal agency in this area.

Today legal action against alleged discrimination may be initiated by the EEOC, by the Department of Justice, by any aggrieved individual, or on behalf of any aggrieved class of individuals (the latter being called a class action suit). Frequently, two or more of these groups act separately or together. Employers are also liable to charges before state and local fair employment practice commissions, before the National Labor Relations Board, to suits under Section 301 of the Taft-Hartley Act, to grievance charges under collective bargaining agreements, and of course to actions under contract compliance procedures—all for the same alleged act of discrimination.

At first the courts required strict proofs of discrimination, more than the fact that there were no minority workers on the payroll. It had to be shown that a qualified minority worker actually applied for a job and that a less qualified white was hired in his place. Proof of this sort was difficult to obtain. Today, however, the courts are looking to results rather than the methods by which they are achieved. If a company located in a community with a substantial minority population has only a token number of minority employees, the courts now routinely inquire into the company's recruitment and selection techniques and may order it to take remedial action to ensure that inequality be reduced (and the same approach has been applied to situations where it is found that women are underemployed). Recent court decisions go well beyond eliminating discrimination in hiring for lower-level jobs; the focus has shifted to obtaining a more proportional representation of minorities *and* women at all levels of the organization, including management. Finally, the remedies ordered have become tougher. Such remedies may include the following:

1. The offending firm will normally be required to pay back pay to compensate workers for wages they lost because of discrimination, even if there is no showing of "bad faith" on the part of the employer.

In one major case, nine leading steel companies and the Steel Workers union agreed to pay an estimated $31 million of such back pay to 45,000 minority and female workers who suffered loss of income because company-union promotional policies restricted them to lower paying jobs. Back pay per indivdual ranged from $250 to $1000.

2. A specific series of remedial actions may be required to rectify past discrimination (even though the organization may not be currently discriminating). These may include what has sometimes been called "reverse discrimination." Suppose blacks constitute only 5 percent of a given job classification yet the court finds that without discrimination 10 percent would have been employed. The company may be ordered to hire at least one black for every two whites hired until black employment reached the 10 percent level.

In the steel case mentioned above the companies agreed that at least in the first year, job vacancies would be reserved for various groups as follows: production and maintenance jobs: at least 20 percent women; trade and craft jobs: at least 50 percent women and minorities; clerical and technical jobs: at least 15 percent minorities; supervisory jobs and management training: at least 25 percent minorities and women. The agreement also provided that seniority for job bidding in steel mills would be on a plant-wide basis rather than on the basis of departments or job progressions.

Similarly, in several cases involving police and fire departments the courts have ordered that one minority applicant be hired for every one or two nonminority hired until the proportions of minorities in the police or fire department approximate the proportion in the general population.

3. When a successful suit is undertaken on behalf of a private individual or class of individuals, the courts have also awarded substantial attorney's fees to the winning plaintiffs. The possibility of winning such fees, of course, provides an incentive to the "public interest" law firms that have arisen to represent clients who do not have the resources to file suits on their own.

Taken as a whole, these remedies can be very expensive. AT&T agreed to pay back payments of well over $75 million to settle two cases, and other companies are faced with costs of proportional magnitude. No wonder equal employment has become an urgent priority in many companies and no longer a matter of philanthropy or social obligation. "Let's face it," one top executive put it, "Our company is not in compliance with Title VII and the other antidiscrimination laws. Neither is any other company I know of. All we can do is move just as rapidly as possible—and hope we don't get hit with too many class-action suits in the meantime."

Alternative management policies

What can management do when faced with these pressures? Technically, management's choices include the following. It can:

- Discriminate against minorities, even though this policy can now be quite costly.
- Be neutral and "color and sex blind," not changing its recruitment or selection policies but insisting that decisions be made strictly on ability without regard to color or sex.
- Change its recruitment policies to attract a larger number of minority applicants and modify its tests and other selection techniques to ensure that they fairly measure minority members' *real* abilities. In other words, it can maintain its personnel standards intact but make an effort to hire minority people who meet these standards, and it can develop better methods of determining ability.
- Pick minority members for job vacancies, even though they are not the *best* qualified candidates (just as long as they meet minimum standards) and reduce excessively strict standards (such as a high school diploma or a prison-free record for assembly-line work).
- Provide special training for those who do not meet minimum standards but eventually might be qualified, the *qualifiable*.
- Try to adjust the job to the candidate and rearrange job responsibilities to create jobs within the capabilities of hard-core members.

Major alternatives   Since the late 1960s, management's choices have focused on two alternatives. Some believed that it was enough to be colorblind and scrupulously impartial. Others felt their organizations should take affirmative action to recruit and develop minorities.

Colorblindness.   Many of those who believed in color (and sex) blindness, or neutrality, felt that reverse discrimination in favor of minorities (or women) was just as unfair as discrimination against them. Further, they doubted whether management had a moral responsibility to solve social problems, and they objected to demands that they lower their standards. Two psychologists stated this position:

It is clearly the obligation of the employer not to discriminate among persons on the grounds of race, religion, or national origin, but it is clearly not the obligation of the employer to hire or to promote the less qualified in an attempt to compensate for some injustice of society in general.[6]

Affirmative action. Affirmative action is demanded because colorblindness rarely results in integration. "You can post an equal-employment sign for a hundred years," the director of an employers' association remarked, "and a hundred years from now there will be no change in the work force." Furthermore, as the previous section emphasized, government contractors are now required to develop affirmative action plans, and firms that are not contractors fail to develop such plans at their peril.

Does affirmative action mean reverse discrimination? Those who are committed to the principle of integration normally use the euphemism "affirmative action" in public but in private admit that this involves reverse discrimination—at least in the sense that opportunities that are not available to whites are granted to blacks and that when two candidates are roughly equally qualified, the black will get the job.

The state of the law

The law in this area is complex, changing, and even contradictory. The sections that follow provide a quite simplified version of the main requirements.

Underutilization

The Civil Rights Act makes it illegal to discriminate against any employee or applicant for employment on the basis of race, religion, or sex. Acts of discrimination are outlawed against any group (Catholics, Jews, Italians, Poles, and French-Canadians, for example, have all been subject to discrimination on various occasions). Additional protections have been extended to certain specific *protected groups:* blacks, Asians (including Pacific Islanders), American Indians (including Alaskan natives), Hispanics (including Mexicans, Puerto Ricans, Cubans, Central or South Americans, and others of Spanish origin or culture regardless of race), and women. With regard to these groups, the EEOC states the employer's legal position this way:

If a statistical survey shows that minorities and females are not participating in your work force at all levels in reasonable relation to their presence in the population and the labor force, the burden of proof is on you to show that this is not the result of discrimination, however inadvertent.

Employers are required to keep records of the numbers of workers in each job category by sex and minority-group status. If the percentage of women or minorities in *any* job classification is less than "would be reasonably expected

[6] J. E. Doppelt and G. K. Bennett, "Testing Job Applicants from Disadvantaged Groups." *Test Service Bulletin,* No. 57, The Psychological Corporation, May 1967.

The Timken Company has traditionally hired its employees from people living in a 15-mile radius of its Bucyrus, Ohio, plant. Of the people who live in this area, fewer than 1 percent are minorities. Mansfield, a city of 55,000 located 25 miles from the plant (35–45 minutes driving time on a two-lane highway), has a population that is 15 percent minority. In the past there has been very little commuting between Bucyrus and Mansfield. Should Mansfield be considered as part of Timkin's "relevant labor market," thus increasing the number of blacks it must employ to maintain a "reasonable relation"? The government argued that it should be, but the courts ruled otherwise.

The community in which another company is located is 20 percent black, but blacks constitute almost 50 percent of its applicants for truck driver. On the other hand, there are almost no black applicants for engineering jobs, and the company has traditionally required an engineering degree for most of its managerial positions. Only 2 percent of the graduates of the engineering program in the local college are black, a figure not much out of line with national experience. What is the "relevant labor force" for drivers? for engineers? (The answer to the second question depends in part on the company's ability to upgrade engineering technicians and on whether it can abandon its engineering degree requirement for managers.)

by their presence in the *relevant labor market,"* these workers are viewed as being *underutilized.* If this occurs the organization (1) must be able to demonstrate that its selection and promotion procedures are *job related,* and (2) if it is a government contractor, it must also set *goals* and *timetables* designed to bring participation up to acceptable levels in the "minimum feasible time."

Relevant labor market

What is meant by "relevant labor market" depends largely on the circumstances, and many critical questions remain to be decided. Among the factors that should be considered are the percentage of women and minority-group members in the population and the work force, the availability of women and minorities with the required skills, the extent of unemployment in various groups, and opportunities for training and upgrading.

For unskilled workers, the labor force clearly means all individuals working or looking for work within an area "in which it is reasonable to expect persons to commute." Thus if blacks constitute 30 percent of a community's labor force but only 5 percent of the unskilled employees of a given firm within the community, then it is reasonably clear that blacks are being "underutilized." The relevant labor market may be different for men than for women, and it may differ greatly among occupations. If a university has traditionally insisted that its professors have Ph.D.'s, its "labor force" would probably consist of the nationwide pool of Ph.D.'s in the field in question. If only 5 percent of the Ph.D.'s were female (as is true in many fields of business and engineering), then 5 percent would presumably constitute the "reasonable relation." Other cases are more difficult, as the illustrations above indicate.

In practice, such issues are settled on a case-by-case basis, frequently through bargaining. Employers complain that the grounds for decisions are rarely made clear and that the number of minority people they are expected to hire increases each year. Enforcement agents reply that without ever tighter standards, there would be no progress in minority hiring.

The Supreme Court has held that Title VII "requires that all employers remove all artificial, arbitrary, and unnecessary barriers to employment when the barriers operate invidiously to discriminate on the basis of racial or other impermissible grounds. . . . The Act proscribes not only overt discrimination but also practices that are fair in form, but discriminatory in operation. The touchstone is business necessity. If an employment practice operates to exclude Negroes and cannot be shown to be related to job performance, the practice is prohibited." Or to be more specific, if an employment practice leads to an adverse effect, then the company must prove that the practice is job related and predict actual performance on the job. Validation, the process by which job relatedness is demonstrated, was discussed on pages 184–88. *Job-related procedures*

Though a number of proofs of "adverse effect" have been accepted, the most common relates to the effect of a practice on the rejection rate of job applicants. The rule of thumb is that there is an adverse effect when a specific personnel selection technique leads to an acceptance rate for a "protected" sex or minority group that is less than 80 percent of the acceptance rate for applicants from the most successful group. For example, adverse effect occurs if 40 percent of the white applicants and 30 percent of the black applicants are accepted, since the black acceptance rate in this case is only 75 percent of the white rate. (An exception to this rule might be made, however, if the employer had made a special recruitment drive that resulted in an exceptional number of poorly qualified black applicants.) *Adverse effect*

Governmental contractors whose employment of women and minorities fails to bear the "reasonable relation" we mentioned are expected to set goals and timetables that will steadily reduce underutilization. Timetables are allowed because the government requires immediate elimination of underutilization only in exceptional circumstances. Instead, the process is expected to occur only as vacancies arise. "Goals" are required rather than "quotas" because they are only projections rather than rigid requirements; the employer is permitted to miss its goal provided it made a "good faith effort" to meet it; the burden of proof, however, is on the employer. (Employers often argue that the difference between goals and quotas is only a matter of semantics— in fact, they are allowed little leeway.) *Goals and timetables*

The development of goals requires careful consideration of the kinds of manpower flows described in Chapter 8. Goals can be reached more quickly for jobs with a high turnover or for jobs with large numbers of available qualified women and minority candidates. The chart portrays the affirmative active goals through 1979 of one major company, the Chase Manhattan Bank, for managers and professionals in its U.S. locations.

Overall goals are not enough, however. Organizations must establish specific goals for every job and department in which women and minorities are underutilized. It is not enough for a company to have equal representation

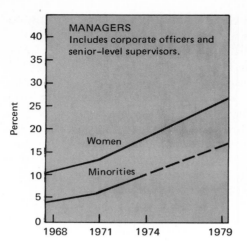

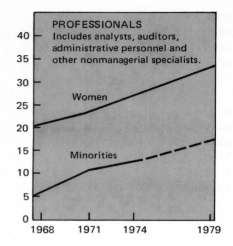

overall, as long as there are islands of underutilization. Thus an organization cannot point to the large number of women in its clerical pool as a defense for having no women in its sales force.

Obviously, some goals are more difficult to meet than others. Given the length of time needed to train a top manager, it may be unrealistic to expect the imbalance at the top management level to be eliminated in five, ten, or even fifteen years. But it is realistic to expect that imbalances at lower, hiring levels will be eliminated quickly and that substantial percentages of minorities will be promoted.

Quotas. We have seen that in order to remedy past discrimination, courts may order that a certain set percentage, say 40 percent, of an employer's new hires be minority members, regardless of the qualifications of nonminority members. May an employer voluntarily set such quotas to reduce underutilization, even when the employer is not guilty of specific past discrimination? This was the issue which faced the Supreme Court in the celebrated *Bakke* case in 1978. To increase the number of its minority students, the University of California Medical School at Davis established a "special admissions" procedure which in practice reserved a set number of places for minorities. Bakke, a white, applied for admission and was turned down even though he scored higher on the normal admission criteria than did many "special admit" students. Bakke sued the university, charging that he was a victim of unconstitutional discrimination.

Faced with this issue, the Court split sharply. Four justices agreed with Bakke. Four others felt that racial preference was justified or even desirable in this case. The ninth justice, Powell, found against quotas as such, since they provide absolute preference for one race without giving any weight to the relative merits of other candidates. On the other hand, he said, race could be considered *one* of the relevant factors in admission decisions.

The Court's ruling left many questions open, especially *how much* weight could be given to race. Further, it seemed to put employers in an anomalous position: courts may order quotas to eliminate racial imbalances (particularly where there has been past discrimination), and governmental agencies may raise questions if "goals" are not met. But if employers introduce quotas voluntarily, could they be sued by unsuccessful white job applicants?

Affirmative Action

In 1979 the Supreme Court partially answered this question in the case of *Kaiser Aluminum and Chemical v. Weber.* It held that the Civil Rights Act of 1964 permits the voluntary implementation of affirmative action programs granting preferences to black workers, at least as long as such a program "is a temporary measure . . . not intended to maintain racial balance, but simply to eliminate a manifest racial imbalance." The EEOC urges organizations developing such an affirmative action plan to consider the following:

Some organizations feel that they have conducted a serious goal-setting process and made "good-faith" efforts to achieve goals, but that negative *external* factors—such as "unavailability of 'qualified' candidates"—are responsible for lack of significant improvement.

EEOC experience indicates that it is far more likely that negative *internal* factors are responsible—i.e., *continuing discriminatory barriers in the employment system.*

Therefore, *to achieve long-range goals and intermediate yearly targets, you must first identify where such barriers may be operating,* and then take necessary steps to eliminate them, and to equalize opportunities for those suffering effects of past discrimination.

For example: your analysis may reveal underutilization of certain groups in certain jobs. Until you review your entire employment process, step by step, it will be difficult to pinpoint the *cause* of underutilization. How much is due to inadequate recruiting efforts? How much to failure of applicants to survive standards and steps in your selection and promotion process? How *valid* is each of these standards in predicting which candidates can perform particular jobs successfully?

The rest of this chapter will consider the kinds of adjustments required if organizations intend to meet their legal obligations and to engage in affirmative action. Perhaps in no other personnel area is it as important to view the organization as an integrated system and to consider the interrelationships, for instance, among recruitment, job requirements, training, and discipline.

Recruitment

Effective affirmative action frequently requires radical redesign of the organization's recruitment efforts. Traditional recruitment has too often been directed toward whites only. Many blacks have never learned how to look for jobs. Further, they are convinced that they are unlikely to be hired for previously "white" jobs, regardless of equal opportunity laws. As a consequence, special recruitment efforts must be directed toward blacks to convince them that jobs *actually* are open to them. As a first step, employers should advertise job openings in minority newspapers and over minority radio stations. In addition, they should send recruiters to minority high schools and colleges and cooperate closely with such agencies as the Urban League, which specializes in working in the ghetto, and with leaders of the minority community. Companies should make greater use of the public employment service; in some cases, employers are required to list their vacancies with it.

The EEOC urges employers to "avoid recruitment primarily by 'word of mouth' or 'walk in.' This tends to perpetuate the present composition of your work force in various job categories. Where minorities and females are not well represented at all levels, reliance on such recruitment has been ruled by the courts to be a 'discriminatory practice.'" The EEOC also requires that each employer maintain an "Applicant Flow Record," which indicates, for each job applicant, "name, race, national origin, sex, referral source, date of application, and position applied for," as well as specific records for minority group members and women not hired, with an indication of who made the decision not to hire and the reason for the decision.

Selection

The selection process is critical to successful integration. Even apparently trivial incidentals make a difference. Minority applicants can be easily scared off by unsympathetic receptionists. Long waits, complicated application blanks, or an official-looking employment office make applicants ill at ease.

Interviewing involves subjective judgments. The prejudiced interviewer finds it easy to give a negative rating to almost every minority applicant. Even the middle-class interviewer who tries conscientiously to be unprejudiced finds it hard to establish communications with the hard-core applicant. The words they use and the values they hold may be so different that each finds it difficult to understand the other. Interviewers must understand "street talk," and it helps if some are minority members themselves (yet, for a black interviewer, being black may not be enough—hard-core youths are often suspicious of middle-class Uncle Toms).

For these reasons it was once argued that selection should be made on the basis of objective criteria, such as years of experience or test results. Unfortunately, the use of presumably objective criteria has not helped advance the cause of racial equality. The heart of the minority problem is insufficient opportunity to acquire experience on the most desirable jobs. And very significantly, there is evidence that blacks tend to do better in interviews than they do on tests. Indeed, tests constitute a major barrier to black employment.[7]

Testing

It is argued that all tests are unfair because they fail to make allowances for the inadequacies of minority education. This argument goes too far. If tests do relate to the job, and if minorities do not score highly because of the inadequacy of minority schools, then the schools are at fault, not the tests. On the other hand, if tests do not measure some abilities related to the job, then their exclusive use could lead to bias.

Even if we can dismiss the argument that *all* tests are unfair, still there is considerable evidence that tests are frequently used in a discriminatory fashion.

[7] Orientals, on the other hand, often have greater trouble with interviews.

Unfair administration. Recent studies show that tests are frequently administered in a slipshod manner with confusing instructions and little privacy. In most instances, minorities and whites are equally subjected to this treatment, but blacks are harmed by it more. By and large, hard-core blacks have had relatively little experience taking tests, and this limited experience has often been associated with failure. As a consequence, they tend to feel more tense in a test situation. On the other hand, studies show that blacks do better in tests administered by black examiners or when the applicants feel a sense of approval on the part of the examiner.

Improper validation. As we have seen, only a small minority of companies follow standard psychological procedures to validate tests for *specific* jobs. Most companies either buy standard tests or develop tests of their own. The homemade test may seem to do the job; but unless it is properly validated, it may be unintentionally discriminatory.

Cultural bias. Both kinds of tests, standard tests and those developed for use in a particular organization, normally are validated, if at all, in terms of white norms only. Thus, one may question whether they can adequately predict the abilities of hard-core blacks. Many so-called intelligence tests measure information that is more common in a white community than in a black one. The vocabulary section of a typical intelligence test may ask for the meaning of words such as *jumble, obstinate,* or *ameliorate* rather than words used in the ghetto.[8]

A vocabulary test may reveal only cultural background, but measures of cultural background may be appropriate for certain purposes. A "ghetto vocabulary test" may be useful for selecting supervisors (both black and white) who will be expected to work with ghetto workers. On the other hand, secretaries of all races should be able to pass a "middle-class" vocabulary test if they are to work for middle-class bosses or with middle-class customers.

The real question is the relationship between test results and job performance. If blacks do less well than whites on a test, but equally well on the job, obviously the test is biased. How extensively such bias exists is hard to tell. Until recently, tests were almost never separately validated for blacks and whites. Since blacks were excluded from many jobs, most validation has been in terms of an exclusively white population.

Only in the last few years has there been much research on the extent of cultural bias in testing. The results so far suggest that testing practice in general is unsatisfactory. Some tests are nondiscriminatory only in the sense that their predictive power is equally low with blacks and whites. Other tests predict white success but not black—or vice versa. Taken as a whole, however, the research suggests that race is less of a moderator variable than had been initially suspected. Relatively little bias has been shown, and where it occurs it is more likely to benefit minorities than whites.

[8] Race may make a difference not only in tests but also in the interpretation of job application blanks. An arrest record or failure to complete high school may have different meaning in terms of predicting job success for whites than blacks.

The Civil Rights Act of 1964, which prohibits discrimination in employment on the basis of race, creed, or sex, also contains the Tower Amendment, which provides that

It shall not be an unlawful practice for an employer . . . to give and act upon the results of any professionally developed ability test provided that such test, its administration, or action upon the results is not designed, intended, or used to discriminate because of race, color, religion, sex, or national origin.

What does "professionally developed" mean? Is any test developed by a professional psychologist a professionally developed test? Is it enough that it be validated for some general use, or must it be validated in terms of a particular job? *Griggs* v. *Duke Power Company,* one of the first cases to deal with such problems, considered the legality of requiring black laborers to pass the Wonderlic intelligence and the Bennett aptitude tests before they could be promoted. Both tests have been developed by professionals and were widely used in industry; neither had been validated in terms of the jobs in the Duke Power Company.

Among the questions asked in the Wonderlic are the following:

Two of the following proverbs have similar meanings. Which ones are they?

1. Perfect valor is to do without witnesses what one would do before the world.

2. Valor and boastfulness never buckle on the same sword.

3. The better part of valor is discretion.

4. True valor lies in the middle between cowardice and rashness.

5. There is a time to wink as well as to see.[9]

The District Court ruled in favor of the company, finding that "Nowhere does the Act require that employers may utilize only those tests which accurately measure the ability and skills required of a particular job or jobs. . . ." Obviously, this was a controversial ruling. The opposite position was expressed in one of the briefs filed on appeal on behalf of the black employees. It argued that the questions presented in the Wonderlic "*perhaps* have utility in a law school aptitude exam. As a measure of ability to fill jobs in an industrial plant they are ludicrous. And as a barrier to Negro advancement they are vicious— the more so because employers are growing increasingly enamoured of these kinds of tests and Wonderlic is one of the most popular."

In a strong opinion, the Supreme Court ruled for the black employees, saying in effect that a test could not be used where (a) in fact it operated to exclude blacks from jobs, and (b) it did not "bear a demonstrable relationship

[9] *Daily Labor Report,* June 29, 1970, p. A-13. For a discussion, see Sheldon Zedeck and Mary Tenopyr, "Issues in Selection, Testing, and the Law," in Leonard Hausman and others, eds., *Equal Rights and Industrial Relations* (Madison, Wisconsin: Industrial Relations Research Association, 1977). This paper also summarizes the extensive technical problems in measuring whether tests are discriminatory.

to successful performance of the jobs for which it was used." The opinion continued:

Nothing in the Act precludes the use of testing or measuring procedures: obviously they are useful. What Congress has forbidden is giving these devices and mechanisms controlling force unless they are demonstrably a reasonable measure of job performance. . . . What Congress has commanded is that any tests used must measure the person for the job and not the person in the abstract.

The *Griggs* decision set the tone for governmental regulation of testing. Once tests eliminate more minorities than whites (once they show adverse effect), they must be shown as job related. That is, they must be validated. The validation procedures required are technical and complex (and before going further the reader should review pp. 182–90. Essentially the regulations merely require that the employers follow the best practice—but doing so can be difficult and expensive. "Validation is a very specific, technical and complex process," warns the EEOC, and "validation requires use of trained industrial psychologists."

What the law requires

Job analysis. Every job must receive a careful, professional job analysis (see pp. 150–53). The purpose is to determine the critical skills actually required by the job. As the Supreme Court put it, "The touchstone is business necessity." The employer may prefer employees with great physical stamina, but if none of the job operations require such stamina, it is improper to require it (provided, of course, that such a requirement has an "adverse effect").

"Business necessity" has been interpreted strictly when a job requirement tends to exclude an entire race or sex. In defending its refusal to hire male flight attendants, Pan American produced evidence showing that "females were superior in performing the nonmechanical aspects of the job such as reassuring anxious passengers and providing personalized service." Nevertheless, the Court ruled that "discrimination based on sex is valid only when the *essence* of the business would be undermined by not hiring members of one sex exclusively" and that the "primary function of an airline is to transport passengers safely from one point to another," not to "cater to the psychological needs of passengers."

On the other hand, Greyhound was upheld in its refusal to hire bus drivers over forty years of age on safety grounds, because safety related to the essence of Greyhound's operations.[10]

Validity. The 1978 *Uniform Guidelines on Employee Selection Procedures* permit all three main forms of validity (criterion-based, content, and construct), although they warn that construct validity is difficult.

---

[10] Greyhound presented elaborate evidence showing that safety decreased with age but increased with seniority. Newly hired bus drivers over age 40 would never gain enough seniority to counteract their advancing age.

1. Only objective criteria may be used in criterion-related validity. Test results must predict actual behavior on the job, not just a supervisor's subjective judgment that Employee X does better than Employee Y, particularly when the supervisor is given only vague standards by which to judge performance.

2. If several selection procedures are available, the employer should use the procedure with the least adverse impact.

3. Tests that have a substantial adverse impact will be scrutinized more closely than those that do not.

4. Finally, if an organization's "bottom line" shows no adverse impact—that is, if its *overall* selection process does not eliminate a proportionally larger number of minorities and women than white males—then the Guidelines provide the employers will normally not be required to validate each individual step of the selection process. Understandably, this bottom line concept has been criticized for putting numbers over fairness, and for permitting individual job applicants (either minority or nonminority) to suffer discrimination, as long as the organization is hiring the right number of minorities overall.

*Testing
in Practice*

Although validation is required only when there is an adverse effect, the chances of adverse effect against some group is so great that in practice most tests must be validated. Critics argue that this is enormously difficult, that even the record keeping required by current regulations is tremendously expensive, that the regulations are overly complex and almost incomprehensible, and that some of the procedures required are technically impossible. In defense of the regulating agencies, it must be conceded that strenuous (though not always successful) efforts have been made to make regulations easy to understand. Nevertheless, when these new regulations were introduced, few personnel departments had the technical capability to meet them; consequently, they had to hire many new people trained in testing and statistical procedures, and they had to use many technical consultants. The cost of hiring new employees, already substantial, considerably increased.[11]

The difficulties of validating every test for every job plus the fear of governmental inspections and litigation have caused companies to deemphasize their use of tests, but this hardly solves the problem. It is not enough to substitute interviews for written tests. The regulations now require that *all* selection techniques and requirements showing adverse effect must be validated.[12] If more blacks than whites are screened out by interviews, the organization must prove that applicants who do well in interviews in fact do better on the job than those who do poorly on interviews. Similarly, if the requirement of a college degree for a given job screens out more of one race or another, it must be demonstrated that employees with college degrees do better on the job than do those without such degrees.

[11] As of 1979, AT&T had some 750 people in its equal employment department. (Carol J. Loomis, "AT&T in the Throes of 'Equal Employment'," *Fortune*, 99, January 15, 1979, p. 56.)

[12] Some companies returned to tests, on the grounds that interviews were even more difficult to validate.

One of the effects of government regulation is to force companies to be highly explicit about every step in their hiring and promotional processes and to put into writing the grounds for every decision. Each time a female or minority job applicant or employee gets turned down or is denied a promotion, the organization must be prepared to explain the exact reasons for its decision. It is rarely enough to say, "I didn't think he looked very promising" or "Somehow she didn't give the right vibes"; it is much easier to defend a decision when specific, preferably measurable, characteristics of the individual can be cited. As a consequence, there is considerable pressure to abandon the "clinical" approach to personnel decision-making—which permits the decision-maker to make an overall determination, based not only on quantitative evidence but also on impressions, intuition, and judgment—in favor of the "mechanistic" approach, which relies almost entirely on objective, quantifiable data that can be combined in a standardized fashion. Similarly the regulations encourage the use of structured rather than non-directive interviews, if for no other reason than to avoid the use of improper questions, such as asking a married woman if she plans children.

By the late 1970s, the heat was on supervisory and managerial jobs where the connection between qualifications and performance is particularly difficult to measure. Management representatives insisted that in these key jobs it was critically important to reward merit, even if merit is difficult to document; on the other hand, as one lawyer commented, "If you don't know the qualifications for a particular job, perhaps the government is correct in saying 'You've got to have a significant number of women and minority managers, regardless of their apparent qualifications.'"

One personnel man expressed a common complaint:

"The government regulations ignore the fact that selection and testing is still only an art, it hasn't progressed far enough to be called a science. Human beings and industrial jobs are both too complex—and too little understood—to be measured with the exactness that science requires. Common sense requires the use of judgment, but judgment is a subjective factor inconsistent with the law's requirement of scientific objectivity."

One final point. Many personnel people claim that all this emphasis on validating selection procedures is just a sham. As one put it,

"A validated test is a test which gets you the percentage of minorities your affirmative action program requires. No matter how technically sophisticated your selection procedure may be, those government agents are interested not in procedures but in results; and they will harass you until they get the results they want—the increased hiring of women and minorities.

"The new guidelines reinforce this with their bottom-line concept. They make it terribly expensive to validate a test, but then say you can avoid the expense—in fact you can discriminate against individuals as much as you want—as long as your bottom line is a racially balanced work force. We get the hint."

Off the record, some governmental agents agree that this is exactly what is intended. One commented, tongue in cheek, "Our purpose is to make sure the best qualified man is hired, provided she is a woman or a minority."

Our discussion touched on technical questions of psychology and law. More important is organizational philosophy. If organizations look upon the selection process as a means of *selecting out* candidates who either are not the best they can possibly find or who fail to meet their preconceived notion of a good employee, then they adopt statistically more and more high-powered testing procedures, thus living by the letter of the law.

Being truly colorblind is difficult with all the unconscious factors influencing choice. But if a company wholeheartedly wants to be more than "colorblind" and seeks to increase the number of its minority and women employees, it will be less concerned with the niceties of validation. Its approach will be to *select in,* and it will abandon its normal selection standards if these bar the employment of seemingly attractive women or minority candidates. This is a risky approach, since a number of those hired may not turn out well. It may not yield the best qualified of all candidates, and it raises some serious moral questions about the rejection of better qualified white males just because of their color and sex. But it does help meet affirmative action goals. And given the primitive state of the art of selection, perhaps it is impossible to judge exactly who is the best person anyway.

How far any organization goes in this policy of *selecting in* may well depend on its sense of social responsibility and the degree to which it is subject to governmental pressure. The general tenor of government regulations is to force companies to hire not the best person, regardless of race and sex, but as many minority and women candidates as they can, provided these candidates can be trained to meet the minimum standards required by the job.

Changing job specifications

Sometimes these "minimum standards required by the job" can be lowered without serious harm. Job entry standards tend to rise during times of unemployment and to fall when manpower is scarce. During the recession of the late 1950s, when many high school graduates were looking for work, companies began to require a high school diploma for even the simplest jobs. Other requirements—age, weight, ability to speak English, and the like—have been adopted because qualified candidates were available. When companies carefully reexamine qualifications, they find that many can be lowered. Some organizations that refused to hire anyone who had ever been arrested (though perhaps acquitted), even for laborers' jobs, now hire released convicts. Credit checks and other techniques designed to determine employee stability are coming under increasing question, especially if they lead to the rejection of one ethnic group more than another. The courts have disallowed company rules prohibiting the hiring of convicted felons or providing for the discharge of employees whose wages have been garnisheed (attached for debt collection purposes) where (a) these rules screen out proportionally more blacks than whites, (b) the rules are not related to valid business necessity, or (c) other selection procedures are available that accomplish the same goals with less racial impact.

The key issue is the relationship between the job requirement and the ability to do a good job. Height requirements tend to screen out disproportionate numbers of orientals and Hispanics, and the courts have permitted their use only in the few cases where they have a "rational relationship" to job performance. By contrast, one court ruled in favor of a hotel that required front office personnel to speak English well, even though this had an adverse impact on the promotion of Hispanic employees, since effective communications with guests was a "business necessity" for a hotel.

Particularly for jobs in the governmental sector, "credentialism" requirements have been under question. Must one have a master's degree in librarianship to be the supervisor of a small branch library—or can one work one's way up from a library clerk's position? (And to raise a sensitive question, must professors have Ph.D.'s?) Many organizations are now permitting job applicants to substitute experience for educational requirements. The common requirement of a college degree for managerial positions is being attacked (except where it can be validated). This move away from credentialism may also change career paths and make it more likely that higher-level employees will be promoted from within rather than recruited from without.

On occasion, it is enough to relax job requirements slightly while the new worker develops qualifications.

A large company sought to introduce at least one black into its accounting department. Not finding anyone who met the normal requirement—a bachelor's degree in accounting—they hired a junior college graduate who had majored in bookkeeping. He was fully trained for most aspects of the work normally handled by new hires, and while he learned the job he worked for his accounting degree at night.

Job standards may be set high with promotions in mind (see p. 157). Particularly when the collective bargaining contract includes a strict seniority clause, companies set their hiring standards in terms of the top jobs that employees are likely to reach. Governmental agencies may pressure companies to lower these standards to the requirements of the job being filled. Arguably, skills necessary for promotion can be developed on the job—but companies are worried about the people who fail to develop.

There may be charges of discrimination if those who do not develop are not promoted, particularly if promotions have previously been almost automatic. The only solution—expensive and not always successful—is to give underqualified employees continual training, perhaps far more than had previously been given "majority" workers.

Jobs have even been simplified to fit the abilities of those available to fill them—a fairly common procedure during World War II—but this fosters specialization and routine, the opposite of job enrichment. Understandably, blacks often resent being placed on the "Mickey Mouse," "second-class" jobs thus devised.

Training

As governmental pressures force organizations to place less reliance on selection procedures, organizations give greater emphasis to training, both for new employees and for advancement.

Training for new employees

Training is critically important when companies hire employees from among the hard-core disadvantaged. Intensification of the regular skills training program is often enough. However, instruction in reading, writing, and what might be called industrial survival skills has been added by companies that hire the hard core. The better programs include considerable individual counseling and informal group discussion. The subjects may include family problems, managing money, and handling debt. Program length varies. In some, after a week or so of orientation, trainees are placed on regular jobs. Alternatively, trainees may spend several hours each day in class and the remainder at work, often in vestibule training (p. 217), which shelters them from the social and physical pressures of full-scale production.

For the hard core, the evidence suggests that specific training to fill specific jobs has a greater payoff than does training that seeks to change attitudes or develop social skills—although all have a place in an integrated program. Presumably, job skill training is seen as leading to more direct, immediate rewards. Skill training is also more effective if trainees are given a pay increase when they complete training and if they see training as leading to further promotions.[13]

Training for advancement

Training for advancement is also important, since minorities have traditionally been concentrated in unskilled, bottom-level jobs. A number of companies offer remedial education—including reading and writing—to prepare their older minority employees for promotion.

In the building trades, blacks have been excluded from apprenticeship, a major "port of entry," by the requirement of a high school diploma and fairly rigid examinations. Under great government pressure, the building trades have increased minority representation by eliminating discrimination, lowering entry standards, and preparing minority youths through special preapprenticeship classes to pass admission examinations. As a consequence, minority representation in such programs has substantially increased. Some manufacturing plants have made similar efforts, and the EEOC guidelines provide that when minorities move over into apprenticeship, they do not suffer a loss of pay.

Promotions

Affirmative action covers promotions as well as employment. The company that permits its supervisors to make promotional decisions purely on the basis of the subjective judgment that X is better than Y risks finding itself in court if Y is a woman or a minority member.

The regulations tend to view promotional decisions as a form of test. The employer must provide an "objective job description" for each promotional position. The standards required for promotion must be stated in writing and validated. If performance evaluation instruments are used, these too must be validated. And at the very least, the employer must document the reasons

---

[13] Paul Salipante and Paul Goodman, "Training, Counseling, and Retention of the Hard-Core Unemployed," *Journal of Applied Psychology*, Vol. 61 (February 1976), 1–11.

for every promotion made. Further, employees should be notified of job opportunities and qualifications required for promotion.

If carefully validated standards for promotion (free of subjective elements) are not developed (or, as frequently happens, cannot be developed), governmental agencies have often required employers to give women and minority group members a fair chance to try for the higher-rated jobs (even though a white male may be better qualified by traditional criteria). Thus the burden shifts to the employer to show that the woman or minority group member does not meet *minimum* qualification standards. The question is no longer which person is *best* qualified. To show that the employee is not qualified, the employer must carefully document both the nature of the job assignment and the fact that the employee failed to complete it satisfactorily. Some employers object that all this documentation requires the supervisor to keep a "black book" on each employee—to engage in the kind of close, nonsupportive supervision most personnel policy frowns on today.

Career ladders and seniority

Promotion is blocked not only by lack of training but also by career ladders that relegate women and minority members to dead-end jobs. The EEOC guidelines recommend that employers look for pockets in which women and minorities are concentrated—and then develop new career ladders by which employees in these pockets can obtain opportunities (including training) to move to better jobs elsewhere. Some governmental agencies, for example, have established special training courses or positions as management interns designed to train secretaries for executive jobs; nurses have received special instruction to be nurse-practitioners so as to relieve physicians of routine cases; minority members with construction experience have been upgraded to "building-inspector learnees" and eventually to building inspectors in situations where formerly the inspector job required a college degree.

Company efforts to meet affirmative action goals are sometimes stymied by collective bargaining seniority rules, which stipulate that job openings go to individuals with the longest service (who often happen to be white males). The AT&T consent decree provided a form of superseniority called an "affirmative action override," which gives minorities and women a preference for promotion over white males with equal seniority.

The forms seniority takes may also have a discriminatory effect. It was common in the South, for instance, to have two seniority rosters, one black and one white. Blacks could not bid for white jobs, and vice versa; however, the white jobs were always the better ones. Such blatant discrimination is clearly illegal today, but equivalent results can be obtained through departmental seniority, which is the rule in many industries. In the steel industry, for example, blacks were hired primarily for work in blast furnaces, coke ovens, and labor gangs, while rolling mills were staffed almost entirely by whites. A high-seniority man could obtain a promotion in his own department, but he could not bump into another department except under very restricted conditions, and even then his seniority would date from the time he switched departments, rather than from the date of original hire. Since primarily white departments tended to have long career ladders culminating in high-paying jobs, while career ladders in black departments were short, the effect was to reserve the best jobs for whites. One of the provisions of the steel industry settlement was the elimination of departmental seniority and the payment of back pay to minority group members for losses they incurred because of the operation of departmental seniority.

In dealing with seniority the courts have been faced with Section 703(h) of the Civil Rights Act of 1964 which states that it shall not be unlawful

for an employer to apply . . . different terms, conditions, or privileges of employment pursuant to a bona fide seniority or merit system . . . provided such differences are not the result of an intention to discriminate.

Given this section the courts have ruled that seniority lists do not need to be revamped to eliminate the effects of past discrimination. (However, individuals who had *personally* been discriminatorily denied jobs in the past should have their seniority recalculated to the date when they should have been hired).

Unions

The racial issue presents problems to unions, just as it does to management. The union movement has traditionally been the champion of the underdog, and its gains have helped blacks perhaps more than any other group. Unions have consistently fought hard for civil rights legislation. Many international unions have insisted that strong anti-discrimination clauses be included in collective bargaining contracts.

On the whole, however, international unions have been more active in fighting discrimination than have unions at the local level. Local unions in manufacturing, on occasion, have stubbornly supported discriminatory seniority systems, even against the combined pressure of their international union, the government, and the company. Some local union leaders were in the forefront of the "hard-hat" anti-black backlash of the early 1970s. And union opposition in the building trades made it almost impossible until the mid-1960s for blacks to become union electricians, plumbers, sheetmetal workers, and operating engineers in most major cities. Such prejudiced attitudes are understandable. White workers who are only slightly higher than blacks in the socioeconomic pecking order are afraid that minority advances threaten their hard-won security and that society is appeasing minority demands at their expense.

Recent legal activities have affected unions as well as management. Unions have become the defendants in court cases; when they have participated in discriminatory personnel practices, they have been ordered to pay punitive damages and to contribute to back-pay settlements. Faced with these pressures, unions have become more active in pressing grievances against discrimination and in modifying contracts to eliminate practices (including seniority rules) that might be discriminatory. Blacks, for their part, have sought to protect their interests through black caucuses within unions, and blacks have been increasingly elected to union leadership positions.

Supervisors and managers

Progress in integrating the supervisory and managerial levels has been somewhat slower than at lower levels. At first most minority managers were concentrated in two categories: either they were supervisors of largely black departments, or they were placed in such departments as personnel, public relations, or urban affairs (the department handling relations with blacks).

One reason why there are so few black managers is that until recently minorities were not considered management material at all. Furthermore, relatively few black college graduates had the engineering or business administration degrees commonly expected for such jobs. When blacks did move into management, turnover was often high. Black managers complained that they were given meaningless token jobs and that they were treated like little more than errand runners. Many felt not only rejected by their fellow managers but isolated from their black brothers and sisters in the mainstream of the black movement.

As might be expected, relations between new minority managers and white subordinates are often strained at first. Even minorities may resent having minority bosses.[14] The subordinates expect their minority bosses to be easier on them; the new bosses, for their part, feel they have to be extra tough to avoid charges of favoritism.

For the most part these are transitional problems, and they will lessen as minorities and whites learn to work together. Substantial progress has been made in a number of large organizations, no doubt spurred on by governmental pressures. Many companies established "fast track" promotional ladders (see Chapter 14) for women and minorities. Others started special training and career counseling programs that were so successful that these have been made available to all managers.

General Motors, AT&T, Chase Manhattan Bank, and Alcoa more than doubled the proportion of their minority managers over a 5- or 6-year period. At Sears, the number of black managers increased twenty-eight-fold from 1966 to 1978 (although in 1978 they constituted but 7.2 percent of the managerial work force, and many of the new managers were in lower-level positions). Nevertheless, assuming continued government pressures, it seems reasonable to expect that black managers will move to higher positions through normal progression.

Introducing minority employees

Equal employment requires that the policy be accepted by line supervisors and the employees on the job. Subordinate line managers may resist change in the composition of their work force not just because of prejudice but because they fear that integration will reduce production and disrupt interpersonal relations on the job. All reports indicate that the first step toward eliminating opposition of this sort is for top management to communicate a firm no-nonsense position that it intends to enforce its equal employment

---

[14] Theodore V. Purcell and Gerald V. Cavanagh, *Blacks in the Industrial World* (New York: Free Press, 1972), p. 168.

policy. But sometimes actions as well as words are required to get the message across.[15] Variants of the following story are told in a number of companies that have successfully introduced integration:

During a meeting that a company called to announce a new equal employment policy, one supervisor stated that he would submit his resignation as soon as the first black was placed in his department. The top executive countered quickly, "If your resignation is submitted on that ground, it will be accepted immediately." This stilled all opposition.

Often it is desirable to familiarize line managers with the gist of recent court decisions and to make each manager accountable for affirmative-action results, rewarding those who do well and refusing promotions or salary increases to those who do not.

But more than a firm policy is required. Steps can be taken to reduce as well as overcome resistance to change. Some of the more successful company programs include discussion sessions in which supervisors, their bosses, and outside consultants deal frankly with problems that the introduction of minority workers might create.[16] Attempts have been made to equip supervisors with insights and skills necessary to understand and deal with the background and motivation of workers whose cultural values are very different from those of middle-class whites. These programs may include role-playing, in which individual supervisors take on the role of a confused minority worker dealing with an unsympathetic supervisor.

Programs of this sort help supervisors understand company policy and prepare them for the problems they may face on the job. In addition, they help them avoid inadvertent mistakes. All too often weeks of supervisory effort to win the confidence of hard-core employees can be destroyed in minutes by a simple mistake, such as calling a grown man "boy."

Changes in the managerial reward and control systems may be necessary to make equal employment work. The supervisor who agrees to train a group of minority workers may have less time for other duties; in the short run, too, his or her costs may rise and his departmental productivity fall. If promotions and bonuses are based entirely on meeting production and budget goals, he will hardly be sympathetic to accepting added responsibilities for which he will not be rewarded. General Electric now takes equal employment into account in its "annual management audit," which is used in allocating bonuses, and it asks each of its 26,000 managers to set annual and five-year equal employment goals.

[15] Equal employment policies have required some companies to centralize some personnel decisions. Subordinate managers have less freedom to select new hires, and often top officials are appointed to monitor the program. "A historic problem at General Motors was the reluctance of some decentralized managers to give effect to equal employment opportunity. The corporation then adopted a strong policy that reduced local managerial discretion in this regard and then brought it under even stricter central office control." Herbert R. Northrup and others, *Negro Employment in Basic Industry* (Philadelphia: University of Pennsylvania Press, 1970), p. 98.

[16] On the other hand, there is the danger that excessive emphasis on racial differences may merely perpetuate stereotypes. It is just as dangerous for supervisors to treat minority-culture workers as being very different from the majority whites as it is to treat them as being exactly alike.

Tardiness, absence, turnover, wearing unconventional clothing and hair-dos, poor quality and low quantity of work, resistance to rules—these are some of the complaints heard from supervisors of minority employees recently recruited from the hard core. Some complaints may be exaggerated. Others represent a generation gap; what might be considered weird and unconventional in an office or plant may be quite normal on campus.

In any case, hard-core employees who have never before held regular jobs often find it difficult to adjust to the stern demands of industrial discipline. As a means of bridging the gap between white workers and blacks, some companies have assigned each new minority worker an older "big brother" or "big sister" to provide advice and assistance. Other companies have hired special minority counselors who presumably are conversant with the mores of both ghetto and business (just as counselors were used during World War II with great success to help women to adjust to factory jobs).

But how tough should the supervisor be in dealing with the minority employee on his first full-time regular job? If he or she enforces the rules on attendance, production standards, and like, hard-core employees may quit (thus making it more difficult for the organization to reach its equal employment goals); or they may even file charges of discrimination with appropriate government agencies. But if he allows minority employees to "get away with murder," other employees will want equal rights. A frustrated (and perhaps prejudiced) supervisor expressed her dilemma as follows:

"I have a minority employee who is a real goof-off. Every time I try to correct her, she accuses me of racism. With great effort I could document her inefficiency, but I'm sure she would file a Title VII suit. It would cost $30,000 to defend it—so our legal department tells me—and the total charge would be borne by our departmental budget, whether we win or not. So, I've given up trying, but it's hard on the morale of other employees who resent doing more work than she does."

One possible solution to this problem is to allow minority trainees considerable leeway during their first few weeks of work, but to tighten up gradually, so that by the time they gain the status of regular employees they are subject to generally the same standards as other employees are.[17] As one minority leader put it, "To hold blacks to lower standards just because they are blacks represents the worst form of racism."

"Discipline shows that you care," argues a book that cites the following advice, given by a black supervisor to his white colleagues, on how to handle black subordinates:

I would like to see supervision . . . working a little closer to these people. . . . I would like to see more on-the-spot corrections. Don't be afraid of being slugged in the jaw. Forget about what you see on TV. . . . [Be] brave enough to stand up to a kid and

[17] There have been a number of ingenious attempts to encourage the development of stable work patterns on the part of high-school dropouts and others who seem to have had trouble adjusting to the demands of steady jobs. These include giving "positive reinforcements" whenever the employee meets standards. For example, instead of threatening the employee with discharge for excessive absenteeism, a small cash reward (or at least words of praise) is provided *immediately* whenever the worker comes to work on time (or finishes a job according to specifications).

say, "Now look, you've got to get here on time. And when I tell you this, I intend for you to do it."[18]

From the supervisor's point of view, it was important for the supervisor to show the new minority employee that he cared for him as an individual; reducing standards would tell this employee, "We don't care whether you ever adjust to the routine of plant life."

White morale problems

New England Telephone and Telegraph's top executives recently got a long letter from a young white male in middle management who complained that his future looked pretty dim because of the company's push to advance women and members of racial minorities into management slots. Are guys like him going to have "to pay for [this company's] discriminatory practices during the last century?" he asked. The top brass sent him a long-winded reply that boiled down to: Yes.[19]

Affirmative action can create morale problems for white males who believe that the entire program is operated at their expense. One personnel director explained his approach to the "white backlash" problem as follows:

We have agreed with the government that for the next five years two-fifths of those promoted to middle management will be women or minorities. Since we have only recently begun to hire significant numbers of either group for lower management, it is obvious that the women and the minorities who get promoted will be a lot younger and less experienced than white men who were promoted in the past. It is also obvious that promotions for white males will be much slower than they had expected. Further, there will be a lot of cases where men will find that women who were once their subordinates will be promoted over them to become their superiors.

All this will lead to a good deal of unhappiness and the most we can do is be completely honest. I've tried to level with everybody as to their prospects and point out that we are paying the costs of hundreds of years of discrimination. Some fine young fellows will be hurt while we play "catch up," but after that is over we can begin again with everyone on an equal basis. In any case, a recession would hurt the promotional chances for white males more than our affirmative action program will. There are enough challenging opportunities in this company for everyone.

White males naturally believe themselves discriminated against, particularly when they perceive that certain jobs are reserved for women and minority groups. They are not prepared to sacrifice their careers just because an earlier generation practiced discrimination. Understandably there have been a number of reverse discrimination cases filed by whites who feel themselves unfairly treated.

Protection for other groups

In recent years, legal protection has been extended to other disadvantaged groups. Laws and court decisions have begun to outlaw discrimination against women, the handicapped, homosexuals, aliens, older workers, and those who follow certain religious practices. We discuss women in a separate

[18] Purcell and Cavanagh, *op. cit.,* pp. 265–266.
[19] Liz Gallese, "White Males Complain They Are Now Victims of Job Discrimination," *The Wall Street Journal,* February 28, 1974. p. 1.

chapter; here we consider the developing policies with regard to these other groups.

The handicapped

The Rehabilitation Act of 1973 requires governmental contractors to undertake an affirmative action program to hire the handicapped and prohibits discrimination on the part of the contractors against the handicapped as long as they are qualified to do the work. Since there are over 11 million handicapped persons of working age in the United States, the law has considerable impact.

The act covers both physical and mental handicaps (including drug addiction and alcoholism). As a result of this law some companies have eliminated weight limits for employment. Others have hired blind typists. In one case an employer was ordered to hire a stutterer who had been turned down for a delivery truck route on the grounds that the job required much public contact. Under an analogous state law, a taxicab company was required to employ a one-armed driver on the grounds that "nothing has been presented to show that this *individual person . . .* was a less capable driver than any other." Further, it is doubtful whether employers can continue the common practice of denying employment to cancer victims or others whose employment might increase the costs of the employers' health benefit program.

Yet there are many unresolved issues. Under what circumstances may an employer refuse to hire an epileptic who may have a seizure near dangerous machinery? Or under what circumstances can people with bad backs be denied jobs that require some lifting? Obviously, affirmative action and safety considerations can easily conflict.

More than hiring is involved. Federal contractors are required to "make reasonable accommodation" to the handicapped employee or job applicants' limitations unless the contractor can demonstrate that such accommodation would impose upon it "an undue hardship." How much a hardship constitutes "undue" hardship is unclear, but the cost of accommodation is one factor that may be taken into account. Under some circumstances, employers may have to translate written examinations into braille or give them orally, make part-time work (or even work at home) available for those who can't work a full day, modify equipment so that one-armed employees can handle it, or permit Seeing Eye dogs on the job. Regulations require employers to reduce architectural barriers, especially by providing ramps and special restroom facilities for the wheelchair bound. Eliminating architectural barriers may be fairly easy when new facilities are built, but alterations on old buildings can be very expensive. Some companies claim to have spent as much as $30,000 to accommodate a single employee.

Among the many unsettled issues are those relating to collective bargaining. Suppose that the union contract provides for desirable jobs to be assigned on the basis of seniority. An employee suffers a disability, and the only job she can now handle is held by an employee with greater seniority than hers. May she displace the senior employee? (In some companies, employees must wait 20 years before they become eligible for "sit down" jobs.)

Some of the barriers to the employment of the handicapped reflect merely prejudice or an overly conservative approach to taking risks. The handicapped have frequently proved to be just as good employees as anyone else. However, as our examples illustrate, eliminating other barriers may be both expensive and difficult.

Homosexuals

Until recently, many organizations denied jobs to people they suspected to be homosexuals. Numerous reasons were given for this besides the belief that homosexuality is morally repulsive. Homosexual activities were illegal in many states; further, many assumed that homosexuals were subject to blackmail and that customers and other employees would feel uncomfortable in their presence.

Laws and social attitudes regarding homosexuality have changed considerably. There is increasing tolerance for unconventional activities of all sorts. Many gays—both men and women—have "come out of the closet." Gay activist groups have flourished. In some states, laws against homosexual activity have been repealed; in others, they have become dead letters. A number of cities have passed ordinances granting homosexuals equal opportunities in housing, employment, and public accommodation; in other communities, however, such ordinances have been rejected by the voters.

The courts have held that homosexual federal employees cannot be discharged for homosexuality alone. However, the discharge of a federal employee was upheld because he had "publically flaunted and broadcast his homosexual activities" so that it might lead to "possible embarrassment to, and lost public confidence" in his employer. Other courts have refused to intervene when *private* employers allegedly discriminated against homosexuals or gay men with feminine appearance.

A number of companies have quietly begun to hire known homosexuals, especially if they behave conventionally at work. AT&T put it, "An individual's sexual preference isn't a criterion for becoming an employee or remaining an employee." The company added, however, that an employee whose "overt actions on the job prove to be a disruptive influence on the work force" could be disciplined. Despite these changes, barriers to employment of homosexuals may still be among the last to fall.

Veterans

The Veterans Assistance Act of 1974 required federal contractors to take affirmative action to hire Viet Nam veterans. This requirement lapsed in 1979. However, all veterans (except those entering the service after October 1976) continue to receive five points credit on competitive examinations for federal civil service jobs and promotions (10 points if they are disabled). In seeking to limit this preference, President Carter and various women's groups point out that it has resulted in half the federal civilian jobs being held by veterans, and thus it discriminates against women. Nevertheless, the Supreme Court has held that similar preferences for state employment are not invalid.

Aliens

It has been the practice of most governmental agencies as well as some private companies not to hire aliens, on the grounds that jobs should be reserved for citizens. Several courts have ruled against such discrimination when practiced either by the government or by private employers.

Older workers

The Age Discrimination in Employment Act of 1967 made it illegal to discriminate against people 40 to 65 years old because of their age. A 1978 Act increased this protection to age 70 and also banned mandatory retirement before that age. The two exceptions are executives whose retirement income would exceed $27,000 annually and college professors (this latter exception expires in 1982). Some states now prohibit mandatory retirement at any age.

The federal law especially prohibits help wanted advertisements containing words and phrases implying that older workers will not be considered for job vacancies. Among the offending phrases are those asking for "an ambitious young man," a "junior executive," and a "recent college graduate." To avoid possible discrimination charges, some employers have eliminated questions relating to age from their employment application blanks.

These laws have been enforced with increasing rigor. Standard Oil of California agreed to pay $2 million to 160 older employees who had been dismissed, allegedly because of their age, when the company engaged in widespread layoffs. The government claimed that these employees were laid off without proper documentation that their job performances were below those of younger employees who were retained. A $27,000 award was granted a 62-year-old recently discharged clothes designer on the grounds that his former employer had failed to prove that a younger designer would necessarily come up with younger looking, more profitable fashions.

Another case involved a paper company that hired fewer than 6 percent of its employees from the over-40 age group, even though 22 percent of its job applicants were from this group. Strict enforcement of this law may call into question the practice of many companies of recruiting management trainees primarily from college graduating classes. The "fast track" method of management development (see Chapter 14) has been challenged in suits filed by over-40 executives who allege that they were demoted or denied promotion to make way for younger "whiz kids." There have been similar charges that federally funded research laboratories take advantage of budgetary crises to get rid of old scientists; once funds are restored "new" jobs are created which are filled by newly minted Ph.D.'s. (Off the record, this practice is sometimes justified as the only way to get rid of deadwood.)

The net effect of all these developments has been to force management to rethink its treatment of older workers. In the past, humanitarian employers were willing to turn a blind eye to loyal long-service employees whose work had deteriorated only a few years before the normal retirement age of 65; but with the retirement age raised to 70, this solution has become more expensive. Less humanitarian management exercised its unrestricted right to demote, discharge, or involuntarily retire older managers whose efficiency had fallen off, or even who merely blocked the way for younger people—and to do so without the necessity of offering any justification whatsoever. Today, if an older employee is treated less well than a younger one, the organization must be prepared to justify its reasons for doing so. This requires careful and continuous performance appraisal and elaborate record keeping. Employers are accustomed to having unions challenge promotional and transfer actions with regard to blue-collar workers. Now they must also be prepared for courtroom challenges to their managerial and professional promotional decisions.

Nevertheless, it would be a great mistake to adopt a purely legalistic approach to this problem. Preretirement counseling, changed job assignments, and partial retirement schemes (see Chapter 8) are all means by which the organization can adjust to its employees' reduced work capacities.

**Religious
practices**

Discrimination in employment on the grounds of religion is, of course, forbidden (with the obvious exception of employment by a religious institution). But what about religious practices? Among the rulings to date, it has been found illegal to fire an atheist who refuses to attend staff meetings that begin and end with religious services. Amish people and Sikhs have been exempted from the requirements under the Occupational Safety and Health Act that hard hats be worn on construction jobs.

Can a company discharge an employee for refusing to work on a religious holiday in violation of the tenets of his religion—for example, can a Seventh Day Adventist be forced to work on his sabbath? The answer is that the employer must make a reasonable effort to accommodate such practices and must permit time off for them unless this causes "undue hardship in the conduct of the employer's business." In most cases such accommodations are made informally.

A 1977 case involved an airlines cargo handler whose religion forbad Saturday work. According to the union contract, his seniority was too low for him to bid for a work schedule not involving Saturday. Yet the company needed *someone* for Saturday work, and it was unable to arrange a voluntary trade with another employee. Should the company ignore the union contract and force a more senior employee to switch shifts? Or must it permit the employee to work only four days a week and pay another employee higher overtime rates to work this employee's Saturday shift? Neither is necessary, said a sharply divided Supreme Court majority, for either course would "involve unequal treatment of employees on the basis of their religion."

**Conflicting
preferences**

As perhaps might be expected, employer representatives have greeted these expanded requirements with dismay. "They're playing with affirmative action like a toy. By seeking to cover every sector, they're going to end up not protecting anyone," one personnel executive told the *Wall Street Journal*. And another added, "How do you decide what's the pecking order?"

Controversial issues

Programs of the magnitude of those discussed above obviously give rise to many controversies. Among the issues are the following.

**Discrimination
against whites**

Critics argue that affirmative action programs discriminate against white males, who are being made to suffer for the sins of previous generations. Although the law was designed to provide equal *opportunities* (an equal chance for every person to be considered on his or her merits, regardless of race or sex), in practice the whole administration of the law—its emphasis on counting people by race, its establishment of goals and timetables, and its stress on the "bottom line" concept—has been to require equal *results*. Therefore, according to critics, companies may no longer hire the best qualified candidate and are forced to discriminate against white males so as to meet their goals. In the press for instant equality among *groups*, it is argued, the rights of *individuals* have been trampled.[20]

Supporters of the program have a number of answers. First, they insist that despite thirty years of equal employment effort, discrimination against women and minorities is still far greater than any possible problems suffered by whites. Second, they argue that any possible impact on white males will be trivial.[21] "If 40 percent of the jobs are reserved for women and minorities, the white males still have their 60 percent." Finally, they suggest that the art of selection is so poorly developed that it is impossible to show any discrimination against whites now; what is easy to demonstrate is that selection systems worked tremendous hardships against women and minorities in the past. And some have even stronger opinions: "I see it as a tantrum, for heaven's sake—like saying that if the game isn't stacked I won't play," one female consultant commented on the male objections. "They're in shock to think they'll have to compete with three-fourths of the rest of the world as well, that they won't get brownie points for being white and male. Isn't a boy's final putdown the fact that he got beaten by a girl?" [22]

All parties agree with the rhetoric that "qualifications should replace skin color as basis for employment decisions." Personnel people argue that the impact of recent regulations has been to make skin color the all-important criterion. Minority representatives insist that just the opposite is true: The regulations to date have received only token enforcement, widespread discrimination still exists, and much tighter controls are essential if freedom of opportunity is to become a reality.

How Equal Employment?

The second major question relates to objectives. Critics suggest that the goal of our present national policy is for the racial and sexual composition of *every* job in *every* organization to mirror the racial and sexual composition of the population as a whole. If the labor force in a community is 10 percent black, 5 percent Spanish-American, 85 percent white, 40 percent female, and 60 percent male, and if the company has 20 vice-presidents, present national policy requires the organization to set a long-run goal for 2 of the vice-presidents to be black, 1 Spanish-American, and 17 white; similarly, 12 should be males and 8 females.

---

[20] Critics cite the Civil Rights Act, which states: "Nothing contained [in the Act] shall be interpreted to require . . . any employer . . . to grant preferential treatment to any individual . . . because of race, color, religion, sex . . . on account of an imbalance which may exist with respect to the total number or percentage of persons of any race, color, religion, sex. . . ."

[21] Black leader Bayard Rustin, himself an opponent of quotas, argues that white complaints "border on the absurd. The problems of white working people, as serious as they are, do not approach the grim consequences of racial poverty."

[22] Gallese, "White Males Complain They Are Now Victims of Job Discrimination."

Once this balance is reached, what happens when a vice-president of one sex and ethnic group retires? Presumably, the goal would be to replace that individual with someone from the same sex and ethnic group; otherwise the balance is upset. To be sure, exceptions can be made if they are justified, but it is always administratively simpler to avoid trying to make justifications and to replace a black woman with another black woman. Thus, once a balance has been reached, there would be a considerable tendency to treat each job as if it were earmarked for a person of a given ethnic group and sex. In this way, an individual's chance for promotion would depend largely on whether vacancies occurred in jobs held by his or her own ethnic-sex group.

Critics argue that this policy carries things too far. Besides artificially restricting promotional opportunities and reducing flexibility in the use of personnel, it is based on the unrealistic assumption that abilities and preferences are evenly divided among races and sexes—that, for instance, the same proportion of men and women, blacks and whites want to be lawyers as want to be doctors, cooks, mathematicians, or jazz musicians. Yet organizations are required to make this their goal and to keep elaborate records indicating how close they come to reaching it.

Supporters of the program reply that all this wildly exaggerates the problem. Goals are required to give a sense of direction, and clearly we need to reduce the present imbalance. Certainly the wide distribution of races and sexes over all jobs is indeed a desirable national goal. Statistical measures are required to ensure progress; indeed, history shows that without some sort of measurement no progress is made.

Confusion, imbalance, and governmental interference

The third question relates to employer complaints that government regulations are confusing, their enforcement imbalanced, and their net effect excessive central governmental interference with decisions that can best be made on a local basis.

Confusion. Employers protest that they are subject to regulation by a large number of courts and agencies, which issue proliferating, confusing, and constantly more stringent rulings. Keeping up with these rules is difficult enough for major corporations; it may be virtually impossible for the small firm. Further, because of overlapping jurisdictions, it is hard to find final interpretations of the law. "In case of doubt," one employer put it, "the only way to avoid a suit is to give the job to the minority person over the white. But what do you do if one claimant is a minority and the other a woman? It will take a year to get an answer." Few observers will deny that confusion exists; however, some strenuous efforts have been made to reduce it. Supporters concede that the program is complex—but so, they contend, is the problem.

Legal imbalance. Employers object to the fact that claimants have what labor relations people call "a number of bites on the apples." An employer may pass a compliance review by the OFCCP and sign a consent agreement with the EEOC to remedy certain objectionable practices and still be subject to suit under a variety of laws. If the claimant loses a suit in one court on the basis of one law, he or she can go to another court to sue under another law, all with regard to the same act of alleged discrimination. Thus the employer has to win *every* case; if it loses only one, it faces large damages. Similarly, if the employer wins its case, both sides pay for their attorneys. But if the claimant wins only *part* of his, the employer typically must pay the attorneys on both sides. Finally, the long delays in the courts and administrative agencies are also alleged to place an unfair burden on the employer. If the company finally loses a case, it must pay for the same work twice—once to the person who actually did the work and once, in the form of back pay, to the person to whom it is finally decided the job should have been given in the first place. Finally, the whole thrust of the law has been to shift the burden of the employer to prove that it did not discriminate, a violation of the Anglo-Saxon concept that people are presumed innocent until proven guilty.

Civil rights groups argue that this seeming unfairness is required to redress the previous imbalance. Awards to claimants' lawyers, for example, are justified on the grounds that otherwise individual minority group members would be unable to challenge giant corporations. Employers are required to defend their selection practices only when there is prima facie evidence that minorities are not being hired.

Conflicting demands. The recent spate of reverse discrimination suits brought by whites is especially resented by employers who feel they have made an all-out effort to meet governmental and societal demands. As one employer put it:

We're really between the rock and the hard place. We've spent millions on training. We've suffered the long training time before ghetto employees become proficient to do a full day's work. We've endured white employees' loss of morale. We've absorbed the inefficiency of hiring marginal and handicapped workers who will never pay their way. We've learned to live with these restraints. We know them. But with these reverse discrimination suits we don't know where we stand. We are sued whatever we do. We can't take a step without consulting a dozen lawyers, and usually they guess wrong.

Governmental interference. According to critics, the government is dictating the details of personnel policy; in the final analysis, decisions as to who will be hired or promoted are being made by the courts, with companies subject to heavy penalties if their initial decisions are found to be wrong. Rules, paperwork, and litigation are proliferating, contributing to America's reputation as the most legalistic country in the world. How can business be done, it is asked, when elaborate documentation is required for every personnel decision? Rigid rules, developed on a national basis, prevent flexibility or consideration of individual situations. For example, employers now wonder whether it is still legal to adjust their employment standards as the labor market gets more or less tight.

Critics also argue that neither courts nor government enforcement personnel have much understanding of the realities of industrial relations; both seek to impose uniform procedures on *all* industries, treating higher education, for example, just like trucking. Thus, personnel activity must be conducted with one eye on Washington, and organizations engage in "defensive personnel work" (somewhat equivalent to the "defensive medicine" practiced by doctors threatened by malpractice suits). Personnel directors claim that they feel forced to base their selection techniques not on what they feel is professionally best but on what they think they can get approved. As a consequence, innovative techniques to accomplish affirmative action or other valid personnel objectives tend to be laid aside as too risky.

Finally, critics argue that the high cost of affirmative action must be added to the cost of such other government-mandated programs as ERISA (Chap. 18) and OSHA (Chap. 13) as well as the cost of environmental protection and energy conservation regulations. "We can't absorb these costs plus union wage demands," an anguished employer cried. "No wonder we have inflation and lose business to foreigners."

Once more, supporters of present policies insist that the arguments are exaggerated. The rules are reasonable. To be sure, they restrict company freedom in the personnel area, but no more than do union contracts, for instance. And through requiring that personnel policies be defendable and just, they merely force the company to do what it should be doing anyway. The rules encourage innovation rather than the reverse. Costs may go up in the short run, but in the long run everyone will gain by unleashing of the unused talents of people previously kept in menial jobs. And social justice is valuable in itself—beyond dollars and cents considerations.

Finally, civil rights advocates claim that since the early 1970s, there has been a slackening in public and governmental support for affirmative action objectives. They point to a variety of indicators, above all the Supreme Court's changed composition. These changes have led to a loss of morale among certain groups of enforcement personnel and fears that the goal of a nondiscriminatory society will once again be postponed.

Conclusion

The searching questions asked by racial minority and women's groups have revealed that few personnel policies are unbiased. Recruitment, selection, training, promotion, and compensation policies have all been found to discriminate. Stereotypes as to the capabilities of women and minority groups preserve irrational personnel policies.

But it is no longer enough to eliminate overt discrimination. Social and governmental pressures are forcing companies beyond colorblindness to "affirmative action." For the most part, management has accepted the responsibility of reducing racial discrimination, even at the cost of lower profits. Still, as the last section emphasizes, our national policy is costly, and it is in danger of becoming too rigid. It is making personnel practice far more legalistic and less responsive to individual creativity. Finally, in the interest of correcting a longer and much more serious injustice to minority groups it inflicts numerous injustices to individual white males.

As the next chapter demonstrates, equal employment for women involves most of the problems discussed already, plus some special problems of its own.

1 · *Arcade Chemical Company*

The Arcade Chemical Company is located in Franklinville, a small town of about 10,000 with about 500 blacks. Most of the adult blacks grew up in the South and have come to Franklinville to work on the surrounding farms. Few of the older generation have gone to high school at all, and even among the younger generation the dropout rate is high.

At present the company has only two black employees (both janitors), and there is strong government pressure to expand this number.

The plant is highly automated, and most jobs, except for janitor and laborer, require considerable technical skill. Most new employees are hired as laborers. From this job they normally are promoted, on the basis of seniority, to successively more responsible jobs till finally they become chief operators, in charge of $5 million worth of equipment. The union contract provides that promotions will be on the basis of seniority, where merit and ability are equal. In practice, however, this has been interpreted as meaning that the senior employee gets the job unless the company can prove that he or she is not qualified to handle it. The company has an intensive training program for all its employees.

Because of these technical demands, the company has, since 1952, required all new employees to be high school graduates. In recent years a majority of those hired have been graduates of the local community college.

In addition to requiring a high school diploma, the company insists that all new hires pass a technical aptitude test, which has been validated (concurrent validation) in terms of the present chief operators.

Last year the company had ten black applicants, none of whom were hired. Six were rejected because they lacked a high school diploma, and the other four scored quite low on the entrance test (and two had arrest records).

1. What steps can the company take to reduce its racial imbalance?
2. What problems are involved in each and how can these problems be resolved?

2 · *Police Appointments*

For selecting police officers, the city uses the following techniques: (1) The Strong Vocational Interest Inventory; (2) a paper-and-pencil personality inventory, which, among other things, probes into sexual interests; (3) a verbal comprehension test; (4) a physical examination; and (5) interviews by the city's personnel director and the chief of police.

A rejected black applicant appeals to the city council and alleges that these techniques are biased and unfair. He argues: (1) None of the tests have been validated in terms of applicants (especially black applicants) for jobs with this city's police department. (2) The verbal comprehension test reveals knowledge of middle-class words, not the language of the ghetto. Anyway, police officers don't have to be scholars. (3) Personality and sex interests are personal matters that the government has no right to probe. (4) The personnel director and the chief of police are both white and prejudiced, as shown by the fact that though the city's population is 10 percent black, only 3 percent of the police force is black.

The personnel director answers: (1) Verbal comprehension is important for a police officer, who must understand laws and instructions couched in middle-class language. (2) The verbal comprehension test has been validated (concurrent validation) in terms of performance of present police officers (as rated by their superiors). Correlation between test scores and rated performance is low (.10), but this is expected, since verbal comprehension is obviously only one of a number of factors relevant to police performance. The test does contribute useful additional information to the selection decision. (3) The personality test is used solely to weed out psychopaths and sexual deviants. Surely, these are not wanted on the force. (4) The Strong Inventory has been validated in terms of the population as a whole: it does predict who will be happy as police officers. Obviously, unhappy police are not likely to be good police. (5) The city has been making a determined effort to find quali-fied black applicants. Of the fifteen new police officers appointed in the last two years, three have been blacks (two of whom, unfortunately, have recently resigned to accept much better-paying jobs in private industry).

Evaluate these arguments. What do you propose?

3 · *Eliminating the Effects of Past Discrimination*

The Swormsville Company has a job career ladder which starts at job class 1, the lowest paid, and ends at job class 24, the highest. Normally one moves up the ladder, from job class to job class, with the man who has had the job longest in any one job class being given preference whenever there is a vacancy in the next higher job class. In the past, however, there was one major exception: no black could be promoted above job class 5.

Assuming this discriminatory provision is eliminated, what should the rights be of Mr. X, a black with 24 years departmental seniority, who is still in job class 5 while whites with equal seniority are now in job class 15? Three possibilities have been suggested:

1. Mr. X moves immediately to job 15, even though this means displacing someone currently on the job and even though he does not have the training and experience to handle the job.
2. Mr. X will be given special training and he will be moved upward from job to job as fast as his abilities permit him, in each case having first priority for any vacancy, but not displacing anyone from a job.
3. As the longest-service man in job class 5, Mr. X can move to job class 6 when there is a vacancy, but he can't move to job class 7 until all those presently in job class 6 are promoted.

Which of these alternatives seem fairest? Can you devise a fairer one? Would the nature of the jobs make any difference to your answer?

women
and
management

12

Although women are not a minority (they comprise 51 percent of the U.S. population), in the world of work they have faced many of the handicaps described in the preceding chapter. Women are not newcomers to the working world, as some may believe, but their role is changing, as are social values. We shall look at some of the limitations that have inhibited their participation and how these limitations are changing. We shall also explore the contributions of implicit and explicit management policies in reducing discrimination.

Working women: past and present

Most women have always worked. The exceptions were women born to very high status who spent their time in leisure, while the vast majority of women were required to help the family obtain adequate food, clothing, and shelter. In our society of the nineteenth and twentieth centuries, however, the ideal of the nonworking "lady" appeared—someone too fragile or unworldly for business or the professions. A successful husband or father was supposed to desire and encourage this protected existence for his daughter or wife, and it became a mark of status to have a wife who did not have to work. What had been the privilege of the elite was held up as an ideal for all women. In recent years an increasing number of women have rejected the ideal of the "lady" in favor of active, responsible occupational roles.

Of course, this ideal of protected lady and homemaker was not realized by many women. With neither protector nor secure home, mill girls, secretaries, and store clerks had to accept low-paid jobs with no career opportunities. Regrettably, many managers still think of women as temporary employees who are working to put away a little extra money or working before marriage or as "an experience." They ignore the economic facts of life.

- Most young women in school today both want and expect to have a career.
- Nearly 40 percent of the current work force is female. Over half of all adult women are in the labor force.
- A great majority of women work because of necessity. They are either the sole support of themselves (and other family members) or a major source of support, their husbands' earnings being modest.
- It is predicted that 40 percent of marriages will end in divorce.
- Smaller families and society's acceptance of working mothers means that women intending to have children can still have almost the same working life as their male counterparts. Currently, in 41 percent of married couples, both spouses work.

But there is another side to this picture: many women work only part time because of family commitments. Careers are interrupted by child bearing. In the mid-1970s, the average working female spent only 25 years in the labor force, compared to 45 for her male counterpart. But the gap is rapidly diminishing.

Regrettably, the remarkably strong trend toward women working has not been matched by income equality. Studies show a very significant difference between the earnings of men and women. Although the pay differentials are now illegal, women are paid less than men for comparable jobs. Some of the inequities have been due to outright discrimination, but women are also more likely to end up in lower paying jobs and industries. They become clericals instead of machinists or work in the arts instead of business. Since they have shorter careers, they are not promoted as far; and since they are not expected to stay on the job for a long time, the employer feels little incentive to invest in their training. For a long time, higher paying craft and managerial jobs were off limits to all but a few women.

Changing laws and mores

Federal law prohibits sex discrimination. With the strong backing of a vigorous women's movement, the government has sought to persuade companies to open up to women a full range of jobs and career ladders. Highly visible companies, in particular, have been heavily penalized for past discrimination and required to establish goals and timetables for increased female employment in formerly restricted managerial, professional, and even craft jobs.[1]

[1] As mentioned in the previous chapter, AT&T paid $75 million in back pay to settle two cases of discrimination.

The results of both government action and changing societal mores have often been quite striking. Here are just a few examples:

In the period 1972–1976, the number of women in higher level AT&T managerial jobs (paying over $30,000) more than doubled to 888), while female clericals were decreasing in number. By 1974 Bell had 14,000 women employed in craft jobs; almost one-third of inside craft jobs were filled by women. By 1978 10.9 percent of Bell's clerical jobs were filled by males, while 7.5 percent of its operators were male, up from much lower figures earlier. Celanese increased the number of women managers from .7 percent of the total in the mid-60s to 5.6 percent a decade later. At Sears, the number of women managers jumped from 20 percent to 36 percent of the total from 1966 to 1978.

In addition, women have become sensitized to their rights and opportunities. With the encouragement of organizations such as NOW (National Organization for Women), women have begun to press grievances and law suits to open up jobs previously denied them. In the past, women were often perceived and even saw themselves as inferior or dependent, an appendage to a husband. In contrast, many now feel fiercely independent. Society once pitied the working woman because her family could not care for her properly (or perhaps she lacked adequate femininity); now it accepts the fact that women want satisfying jobs and careers as much as men do. Business, law, and medical schools are deluged with female applicants; women apply for (and get) employment as ship and locomotive engineers, coal miners, and telephone road crew members.

The new woman and changing life-styles

There have been corresponding changes within the family. Dutiful women were expected to think of family first and job second; with men it was the reverse. Increasingly, when a shift in location is required, the wife's career as well as the husband's is factored into the decision. There are increasing numbers of "commuter marriages," in which husband and wife accept jobs in different communities and see each other on weekends.[2]

These newer life-styles can also mean that housework is shared, and even child rearing becomes a joint responsibility. But, women are more likely to be burdened with double responsibilities: homemaking *and* a job. One working wife's lament:

"When my husband brings work home, the children and I know he has to be left alone and given every assistance. I amuse the children, make and clean up the dinner and the house. . . . but when my job makes extra demands, he doesn't understand at all. He still expects me to do all those 'wifely' tasks, so I end up putting in a 14-hour day." [3]

Attitudes toward women at work have not changed as much as these examples suggest. In many organizations, women still find it difficult to obtain equal treatment. There are overt or covert barriers to obtaining what are considered male jobs, and managers still think of women as both unsuited to certain occupations and uncommitted to career and work. Much of this is

Sources of continuing inequality

[2] For more information on two-career families and their attitudes, see M. P. Fogarty, R. Rapaport, and R. N. Rapaport, *Sex, Career, and Family* (Beverly Hills: Sage, 1971); L. L. Holstrom, *The Two-Career Family* (Cambridge: Schenkman, 1973).

[3] In 1977, 58 percent of women with children 6–17 years old were in the labor force and 40 percent of those with children under 6 years old considered themselves in the labor force!

the result of simple prejudice: the belief that women cannot or will not do certain jobs.

The role of prejudice and tradition in determining what are perceived as appropriate jobs for women becomes apparent when one examines the question historically and cross-culturally. Originally, both teaching and secretarial work were *male* occupations, and women were not accepted as bank tellers until World War II. Dentistry is largely a female occupation in some European countries, and three-quarters of all Russian doctors are women. This suggests that the problem of gaining acceptance for women across the spectrum of jobs in industry is one of attitude—of both men and women—not physique or biology.

Obviously, physical differences between men and women can modify their aptitudes for particular jobs, but are there other differences that affect a woman's approach to getting a job or holding on to one?

Societal expectations, self-perceptions of women. As the women's movement has helped us realize, women have grown up in a culture that presumed boys and girls had different needs and capabilities.[4] Boys are often told that aggressiveness (quest for power, money, and career achievement) is not only permissible but desirable—the way to be truly masculine. Girls, on the other hand, may learn to be submissive and even to hide their capabilities in order to please boyfriends and conform to the traditional feminine ideal of "sweet passivity."

Some studies suggest that women concentrate on the job at hand and are greater perfectionists than men are. This tendency can lead to their ignoring organizational politics and cues to the kind of informal group behavior that is best for rapid promotion. They may also injure their own chances for success by accepting less credit for success than is due them and more self-blame for failure than would their male counterparts. Thus, to some employers, a male job candidate can appear to have a temperament more suited to a fast-paced, authoritarian, and competitive organizational environment.[5]

For most managerial careers and many professions, the early years after college are critical. Often in the decade between ages 25 and 35, reputations are made. Energetic, competitive young people seek to accomplish as much as possible and to gain the attention of superiors who will mark them for promotion. Unfortunately, these can be the years in which women are most likely to be involved with child-rearing responsibilities. Hence, they can lose the important early momentum by not being assigned to the "fast track."

Believing themselves to have poor opportunities for advancement and challenging work, women often shied away from adequate career preparation,

[4] In fact, recent research suggests there are almost no significant personality predisposition differences resulting from biological differences between boys and girls. Eleanor Maccoby and Carol Jacklin, *Psychology of Sex Differences* (Palo Alto, Calif.: Stanford University Press, 1975).

[5] It is not difficult to fathom the source of this prejudice. Even young boys perceive males as more powerful, aggressive, dominant, and intelligent than females are. And young girls share these beliefs! Richard Friedman and Ralph Richart, eds., *Sex Differences in Behavior* (New York, Wiley, 1975), p. 181.

particularly in business and engineering. Inferring that management usually preferred to promote men, they did not fight as hard as their male counterparts to prove their capabilities. Thus, companies often assumed that women really did not want to be engineering managers or comptrollers, since there were so few suitable female candidates for such jobs. Seeing few role models to emulate (that is, women who have really been successful in traditionally male occupations), women became discouraged. Expectations do govern behavior. Many women performed below their capacities because they became embittered by observing less-qualified men receiving earlier and more frequent promotions. This then became a self-confirming prophecy.

Eliminating discriminatory practices

Thus organizations were tempted to discriminate against women in a wide variety of ways that are now both illegal and surely inappropriate.

Recruitment and selection

In making employment decisions, it is illegal to inquire about, or utilize, information concerning marital status or children unless similar questions are asked of men. In the past, employers would assume that single women would be more loyal and children would cause lots of absenteeism or even quitting. (Many supervisors may even be unaware that they make these presumptions.) Now, managers are conscious of legal prohibitions involved in hiring. Moreover, they are often motivated to hire and promote women because they know that their effectiveness in affirmative action may be taken into account when they, themselves, are considered for promotion.

Often, if female employees are hired to work in close cooperation with male employees—going on overnight business trips, sharing a police car, or waiting in a firehouse—the spouses of the employees will put pressure on the organization to modify the situation.[6] Pressures are also generated by prejudiced customers:

"I own an independent recording studio and my best customer (a rock musician) insists that female control room personnel don't do as good a job for him as their male counterparts. I don't want to lose him as a customer; what do I do?"

Job requirements

Before fair-employment laws were passed, few personnel managers concerned themselves with whether job requirements predetermined which sex would be eligible for a job. Now, however, under the Civil Rights Act, it is illegal to insist that a certain job is "men's work" or "women's work," except where sex is a "bona fide occupational qualification" (BFOQ). Of course, creating that phrase does not determine what is or is not a BFOQ.

In addition to banning sex categories, the law has been interpreted to forbid other discriminatory job requirements. It would be discriminatory to set appearance requirements that did not apply to both sexes; for example, to insist that stewardesses (but not stewards) not wear glasses or weigh more than 130 pounds, unless some unambiguous safety or technical factor imposed

---

[6] Obviously, women can argue logically that the pressure should not be directed toward them just because men were on these jobs first. Further, such fears are often exaggerated.

this requirement. The Supreme Court has ruled that weight-height requirements for prison guards are illegal, since they tended to reject more women applicants than men.[7] But women can be excluded from guard jobs in all male prisons with open dormitories. There, women in contact positions could pose a security problem.

Many personnel officers have assumed that women could not handle most managerial jobs because of the inside pressure and outside activities. Yet there is little scientific evidence to show that women cope less well with pressure. As we have noted, women may learn at an earlier age some of the skills of appearing to be agreeable, even deferential, in order to smooth social discourse; but we know of no research that shows women to be more vulnerable to stress or coercion. In the past, women have been handicapped by being excluded from certain all-male social clubs, bars, and fraternities where a certain amount of business was transacted (for instance, the Rotary or Kiwanis Clubs in small cities or towns), but the life of the all-male club is probably limited and its business value exaggerated.

Pay equality

The federal Equal Pay Act of 1963 requires companies to provide men and women with equivalent salaries for "substantially equal" jobs. Although most organizations have paid the same for jobs with the same title, there was frequent discrimination against women when different titles were used for *approximately* the same job. Thus maids and janitors may do similar work, but in many instances male janitors are paid much more than maids. A man might be called an "assistant to" the division chief, while a woman doing comparable work would be called "secretary" or even "executive secretary." In universities, men executives are called deans or assistant deans more frequently than are women, who must often settle for the title "administrative assistant" and half the pay.

The EEOC has also criticized formal job evaluation techniques for helping to maintain discriminatory pay practices:

- Clerical (often largely female) jobs are evaluated separately from production jobs, which may preserve a differential favoring male production workers.
- Weights given to the various factors that are presumed to determine equitable pay are assigned arbitrarily, often favoring male dominated jobs (e.g., moving heavy objects).
- The actual assessment of jobs (assignment of points for a given factor for a given job) is also arbitrary and frequently performed by managers who have a built-in bias that men's jobs deserve higher pay than jobs largely held by women.

Additional discrimination may arise when jobs change over a period of time; for example, when secretaries gradually assume the functions of an administrative assistant. But all of these factors, which may have biased pay practices, are coming under review by organizations responsive to existing legislation and court rulings.

---

[7] The case involved Alabama prisons. By implication, strength might be used as a selection criteria if it could be shown that this was necessary for job performance.

Even when there are no discriminatory rules, there may be many more or less subtle cues indicating that women are not wanted.

"After I turned in a great report, my boss turned to me and said, 'Gosh, and you've got great legs, too!' "

"When I speak up at a meeting, the next speaker never refers to my remarks but mentions the last male who spoke."

"Nobody showed up for the conference. Then I learned that the date had been shifted when 'the boys' got together in the washroom last week."

"When I answer the phone, the caller assumes it is a secretary and asks, 'Is your boss in?' "

Organizations are now altering job titles and descriptive terms to remove their sexual connotations. Salesmen become salespeople; stewardesses become cabin attendants. The conscious or unconscious use of an improper phrase turns a conversation, letter, or memorandum into a discouraging, demeaning put-down for women. Below are a few typical labels that women employees resent. Appropriate alternatives are listed.

Put-down	*Alternatives*
Girls	Women; young women
Lady lawyer, authoress	Lawyer; author
Mrs. Kent and Elmer Graff	Jean Kent and Elmer Graff
Another hysterical woman	Another problem employee

In other words, women employees resent being singled out as unique. They do not want to be patronized, considered as sex objects, or stereotyped (with implications that they are consistently flighty, emotional, dependent). Their marital status or physical attractiveness should not affect how they are received as individuals. Certainly, the following clichés should be avoided:

Well, that's a woman for you. . . . He's the best man for the job. . . . Just one of the boys. . . . Don't you think it would be a good idea if Jane [never John] went out and got coffee? . . . I'll have my girl look up that data.

Stereotypes establish a vicious circle. Motivated, energetic women get the message: "This organization has little respect for women; it views them in stereotypical terms." Then one or both of the following occur. The more dominant women express their resentment by challenging the male "culture" or by quitting. This can further ingrain prejudice that women are difficult to work with and that loyalty is rare. Then men repeat clichés: "No way to please them; they are hurt if you don't think they're attractive, and call you sexist when you do. . . . It's unfair; women get pushed ahead of capable men. . . . Women are afraid of success, anyhow."

Employers who have not traditionally hired women (for example, in mines and aboard freighters) have often complained that it would be unduly expensive to provide separate washrooms and dressing facilities. But the courts have ruled that such traditions and costs are no excuse for failing to offer equal opportunities.

In Chapter 13, we shall discuss a new problem in the placement of women. Because some chemicals can adversely affect unborn children, departments producing these chemicals are reluctant to employ women who may become pregnant. Women claim this is discrimination, but the issue is a complex one.

Styles of dress

One aspect of the women's movement and the new culture of the 1960s and 1970s was the change in attitudes toward dress and appearance. Here men and women are not competitive. In fact, men have probably gained greater freedom as a result of women's pressures for less stringent restrictions. The battle in the late 1960s was over skirt length and whether women could wear pants. Victories here have been followed by men shirking the traditional white shirt and dark suit in favor of sportier clothes, unisex styles, and longer hair. (Even the military has relaxed its hair standards.)

The more difficult problems involve management's sensitivity to its public image: "What will our customers (or clients or any outsider) think about our trustworthiness if our employees appear slovenly, suggestive, or leisure-oriented in their dress?" There is no simple answer to the conflict between executives who are sensitive to public relations and employees who like to do their own thing. Managers need to know that personal freedom and the rights of the individual are substantial issues.[8]

Male belief systems

Management must recognize and cope with the fact that some men are uncomfortable about their relations with women, and this feeling will show itself in selection decisions as well as uneasiness when women appear in formerly all-male environments. Some of this attitude reflects competitiveness and fear that a woman will appear more capable. Some men have unresolved sensitivities about their personal relationship with the opposite sex. Others are angry about any management move that they consider to be reverse discrimination. They may also be concerned when, as part of a new nonsexist placement program, they are assigned to what was formerly considered women's work. Some of these beliefs may be dealt with through "consciousness-raising" group methods that bring these deep-seated attitudes to the surface, where they can be confronted.[9]

Supervisors also need aid in coping with subordinates who display stronger insecurities. Some men could perceive equality of pay and of job opportunities to constitute a demotion in status. Thus, supervisors must be prepared to explain, negotiate, and stand firm. Workers are quick to sense when their supervisors are unenthusiastic about policies or when the word is not expected to reflect the deed.

[8] One U.S. court of appeals has ruled that it is not discriminatory for Giant Foods to insist that male employees wear their hair above the earlobes, even though women are allowed to wear long hair if it is secured (to protect exposed food).

[9] As noted in Chapter 16, however, required attendance at programs inquiring into personal beliefs may violate an employee's constitutional rights.

Women, too, need training in how to confront their bosses with their capabilities and expectations for career advancement. The woman employee often has to take the initiative in reviewing with her ambivalent boss the skills and capabilities she has demonstrated and her desire for additional responsibilities.

"John, I would like an appointment to review with you at some length the various projects I've worked on, what I think I've learned, and the organizing skills that I think I've demonstrated. When we've gone over my record, I would like to tell you something about my ambitions for the future and get your reaction to my record and what you think I can do to improve my chances of moving into middle management here."

Given the very recent past, with organizations discriminating against women, it is not surprising that there may be the need to encourage greater assertiveness among women. At least some may have been caught in that older conflict: to be insistent and ambitious may cause one to appear unfeminine, while not taking initiative may assure stagnation.[10]

Strong feelings are usually held on the subject of women supervisors. It is often asserted that not only men but also women find it difficult to work for a woman. Some women even complain that women supervisors are particularly strict with other women and lax with men. (Similar comments are often made about black supervisors and black subordinates.) Here again, prejudice and a self-confirming prophecy are often involved, and the greater problems occur at times of transition, when organizations are altering earlier discriminatory practices.

As we have seen, family responsibility is one deterrent to a fuller utilization of women over the whole range of jobs and careers. Even with changes in marriage styles and relations between the sexes, women do bear children and often must be more intimately involved than their father is with the child's early rearing. Thus, management's increased attention to, and experience with, more flexible job hours is of special significance to women, though it is also relevant to male employees. Both flex-time and part-time work can be very attractive to employees with other responsibilities. They can expand the organization's labor market and attract excellent personnel who might otherwise be excluded from consideration.

Women in management

One of the most serious forms of discrimination has involved excluding women from the more important, managerial, high-paying career lines and segregating women workers in lower-paying, dead-end jobs. As a result, women may perform effectively as secretaries, switchboard operators, or receptionists, but the jobs do not lead anywhere. In like manner, women executive trainees

[10] Rosabeth Kantor, *Men and Women of the Corporation* (New York: Basic Books, 1977) is a compelling account of the problems and roles of women in a large corporation. Suggestions for how women can improve their promotional opportunities are contained in Margaret Henning and Anne Jardim, *The Managerial Woman* (Garden City: Doubleday, Anchor Press, 1977).

were often funneled into departments that provided smaller numbers of promotional opportunities.

The First Trust Bank has an executive training program for business school graduates; however, women who completed the program were usually directed into staff jobs, while men became junior loan officers. Although the positions paid the same, loan officers were on the fast track for promotion into top management.

In reviewing job-placement practices, management has to reconsider its assumptions about women's interests. Many managers assume that the typical female employee would not want an executive position involving frequent out-of-town travel, relocation every few years, much pressure, and even after-hours work.[11] This is "man's work," they would say. Thus, even obviously eligible women might be passed over when an executive position opened up. Good managers learn to ask the most eligible employee (who may well be female):

"The job in marketing research is one I think you're qualified for, and it would be a real promotion in terms of salary and responsibility. However, you should know that there are long hours involved, often weekend work, and at least one or two trips a month out of town. Do you think you're interested?"

The manager should not make assumptions:

"I'm not even going to mention this opening to her. She's an attractive woman with lots of other interests; why would she want this much pressure and unpredictable travel?"

Why should any manager presume to know or to speak for an employee's ambitions or interests?

Tokenism. Women resent employment policies that result in a small or "token" number of women being placed in highly visible positions: a single corporate secretary, directorship, or vice-president for an unimportant staff service. Some women refer to themselves as "mascots" when their positions are not on a significant promotion ladder, and they do not have significant work responsibilities.

Certainly the legal requirements and the legitimate expectations of women employees cannot be satisfied by tokenism. Even more demoralizing is the practice of having women (or members of any minority group) fill jobs with prestigious titles carrying little real authority or responsibility.

Sponsors. Young executives frequently move ahead fast when they have a "sponsor," a senior employee who shows them "the ropes" and pushes them when promotions become available. In the past, sponsors have been necessary especially for women; in fact, many of the older generations of female executives admit that without a sponsor they would still be secretaries. In the future,

---

[11] As we discuss in Chapter 14, companies are now discovering that many men also dislike being moved from community to community.

affirmative-action requirements may force the organization to consider *all* candidates more thoroughly on a systematic basis, so sponsors may be less needed.

Women sometimes complain that female executives are rarely willing to act as sponsors for younger women:

Whatever the reason, men seem to take greater pride than women in the promotion of their protégés, even when recommending a younger, less experienced hand may involve a measure of risk. Perhaps for women today the concept of any reflected glory, even professionally, is still too much like motherhood—their traditional monopoly from which they are trying so hard to escape.[12]

Regardless of the validity of this commentary, some women believe it to be accurate and so they shy away from being supervised by other women. Eventually, however, an "old girls" network may complement that of the "old boys."

Nepotism rules.   Since it was not unusual for organizations to prohibit the employment of close relatives, women could not get work where their husbands were employed. This was a particular hardship for academic families living in a community in which there was only one college. In recent years, such rules have been relaxed substantially; but where direct supervisory-subordinate relationships are involved, rules forbidding nepotism are still likely to apply.

Benefit programs

During the 1970s the women's movement charged that benefit programs were discriminatory and their concerns with pension and pregnancy benefits have now been satisfied by the courts. Previously, management had often paid smaller pensions to women or required higher contributions since, on the average, women live longer than men. Now, contributions and benefit levels must be equal. Similarly, many companies wanted to exclude pregnancy from their paid sick leave plans (on the grounds that childbearing was not an "illness" and was voluntary). Months of absence were expensive, and often women did not return after childbirth. Congressional legislation, however, specified pregnancy as one of the conditions that must be covered if a company has a sickness or disability plan under which employees receive paid sick leave.[13]

Disagreements also arose over when a pregnant woman should cease working. Under a 1978 federal law, employers are prohibited from placing a pregnant woman on involuntary leave unless there is clear evidence that pregnancy significantly interferes with work or that the job may endanger the unborn child.[14] This legislation also prohibits employers from refusing to hire or promote women because of pregnancy and childbirth.

[12] Grace Hechinger, "Catty Claws on the Lib Ladder," *The Wall Street Journal,* April 24, 1973, p. 10.

[13] Abortions, unless performed for medical reasons, may be excluded.

[14] The courts have allowed the airlines to require cabin attendants to take medical leave as soon as the attendant knows she is pregnant.

Traditionally, companies have been fearful that pregnancy and childbirth would terminate the career of promising young women or at least cause an extended hiatus. They were thus reluctant to invest heavily in training and development that might be wasted if the employee decided to raise a family instead of working. Today, however, more women are working even though they have young children, and many return expeditiously after childbirth.

Prudential Insurance provides its women employees with a six-months' maternity leave. In addition, it is experimenting with providing special project "homework" for executives during such a leave, so that they keep their careers "on track" and maintain their ties with the company.[15]

Women's rights advocates have also argued that men should be given the opportunity to take care of children and that men should thus be given paternity benefits, as is the practice in Sweden. The city of Berkeley, California, permits fathers (whether married or not) to receive 10 days' paid paternity benefit (counted as sick leave) and up to a year without pay after the birth or adoption of a child.

Privileges and perquisites

Claiming that many mothers cannot work because of the lack of economical, trust-worthy child-care facilities, some women have been active advocates of company subsidized day-care centers. A few very progressive organizations have provided such centers. Women may also request more extensive lounge facilities and additional protective measures; for example, taxi service to their homes because of dangers associated with being on the streets at night.

The courts and EEOC, however, have ruled that additional benefits may not result in discrimination between the sexes; therefore, men may claim the same privileges. The ruling holds for state legislation designed to protect women from adverse working hours or from strenuous jobs. It cannot discriminate in favor of, or against, one sex.

Conclusion

Rapid changes in our culture and our values make it difficult to evaluate personnel policy alternatives affecting women at work. A changing culture affects the working world and attitudes toward the role of women—both at work and in the home.

The key question concerns sex roles. Historically and cross-culturally, relations between the sexes have varied greatly. In many cultures, women do most of the physical work, while the men engage in more social and political pursuits. Still other cultures banish women to the deep recesses of the home, hardly ever to be seen by strangers and forbidden to partake of meals with male household members.

There is little doubt that men and women in the United States and in many other Western countries are moving toward much greater equality and sharing of major life tasks. But does this mean that all division of labor by gender will disappear? Conservatives argue that you cannot repeal biology. On the average, men do have stronger physiques (bigger muscles), and only

[15] *The Wall Street Journal,* September 13, 1978.

women can bear and nurse their children. Liberals counter that physically demanding jobs are on the decline and fathers can boil bottles as easily as mothers can. Further, as the life span lengthens and average family size decreases, the proportion of a woman's time spent in child rearing also diminishes. For many mothers, the child-rearing function is sharply reduced by age 30 and is over by age 40—and they have half their lifetimes ahead.

We suspect that in the future, the extent of differentiation will decline, but some will persist. More women than men will still engage in child rearing and taking care of the home and more men than women will still devote full time to careers. In a growing number of families, however, the husband will stay home and take care of the children, or the burdens will be equally divided. Nevertheless, we expect that this will occur only in exceptional cases. More typically, women will probably devote full time to their jobs until they have their first child; then they will take on part-time or flex-time work and, after several years, return to a full-time career.

Foreseeing the temporary interruption, some women are more likely to select jobs that permit such intermissions (they may range from secretary to physician). On other job paths—such as management, where career interruption may be more costly—successful women may be chiefly those who have decided not to raise families or who have persuaded their husbands, close relatives, or housekeepers to accept responsibility in this area. The years between age 25 to 35 are critical for aspiring executives, yet this is the period when many women are devoting much of their energy to their families. In many companies, a majority of executives have already reached their peak in middle-management positions by age 45; only an already selected few are likely to move to top-management positions. This is a difficult time for an aspiring female executive to begin her second career.

There is also the possibility of a backlash, a growing friction between men and women over jobs and promotions. Affirmative-action hiring goals are likely to be much higher for females than for blacks or Hispanics. (For example, 35 percent in one case; 15 percent in the other!) Many men are easily threatened by women in the best of cases (the culture has taught them to be wary); and when the work situation is no longer a refuge from the war between the sexes but a prime battleground, sparks can fly.

Suppose a woman is promoted more rapidly than her husband. Will the male ego be bruised? Does he take pride and pleasure in *her* success and accomplishment, as she would probably take in his? Over time, as women occupy a broader range of jobs and as male attitudes toward their presumed superiority changes, such sexual rivalries should diminish markedly. Husbands will find relief from the solitary burdens of total financial responsibility for the family's welfare and may be freer to do the things they really want to do—such as risking a change of job or career. ("After all, if it turns out to be a disaster or more costly than I thought, we can manage on my wife's salary for a while.") A second breadwinner means more of life's luxuries in good times and more security in bad.

The last few years have witnessed a virtual revolution in the movement of women into the full range of jobs in our labor market. Their relative numbers in many managerial posts and some professions are still small, but there is substantial momentum behind the changing role of women. Since attitudes and prejudices change less rapidly than organizations, however, Personnel will have substantial work: training, counseling, and evaluating management in this critical area.

Women have their own problems of adjustment. Some are still concerned about what happens to their femininity and attractiveness to men when they play more dominant, competitive roles at work. Fortunately, the culture is changing rapidly, so that our views of what is a "feminine" role and what is a "masculine" role are losing their former rigidity. Men can be helpful by offering encouragement and a positive attitude toward competent, ambitious, assertive women.

problems

1 · A Major Bank Training Program

The United Chicago Bank is a large multinational company. Several years ago, a group of women charged the bank with reluctance to promote women to the position of bank officer. The bank settled their class action suit by promising to set up several training programs that would prepare women for executive posts. Women who had worked for the bank for 5 years prior to the suit, had a high school diploma, and were at least in the highest grade clerical positions would be eligible. To induce eligible women to apply, the bank also offered an incentive payment of $3,500 to any woman who successfully completed the program.

The year-long program consisted of relatively difficult college level courses in accounting, finance, and personnel and a sequence of temporary on-the-job training posts. Most of the women discovered they had to work nights and weekends to keep up.

The international program, designed to fill positions in the international division of the bank, ran into an unexpected problem. By the time the second group of trainees had completed the program, international headquarters had shifted to Europe, with the understanding that most of its positions would be filled by Europeans. (A few jobs had already been filled by graduates of the first class.)

Management could not decide what to do with these women. Largely as a result of these programs, there was now a surplus of qualified women throughout the bank. Of the 65 who started, only 25 had finished the international program, and they felt they had worked very hard to gain their promised promotions. Most of them, ranging in age from 24 to 50, had been clerical employees, and this was to be a big step up.

1. Since the reorganization plan for the international division had not been developed at the time the program began, what can management do to rectify its new manpower planning problem?
2. Were the inducements to enter training too attractive?
3. How would you weigh the relative advantages and disadvantages of having more demanding eligibility requirements for entrance to the training program (e.g., a college degree)?

2 · Two Short Cases

Female employees who work late at night are given free cab rides home, as a security measure. Male employees claim that they should be given the same free rides when they work eve-nings, although they do not claim that they are afraid of being out late. What should be the company's response?

Jane Anzio was promoted to a claims supervisor, only to discover that none of the women in her group take her seriously. They do not violate her orders, nor are they insubordinate, but they come as close as they can to ignoring her and her new status. They never come to her with questions; instead, they pretend that Jack Hubbard (the most senior claims person) is their boss. How should Jane handle this?

3 • *The University Maids*

The Old State University had little experience with personnel administration. The faculty took care of itself, student wives held most of the secretarial posts, and there were few full-time employees in the traditional sense of the term. Therefore, the president was very distressed when federal funds for research were withheld because a group of dormitory maids claimed they had been discriminated against by being laid off.

To reduce the cost of dormitory operation, the university was cutting the staff of maids from 60 to 45 (with the understanding that students would do more of their own housework). The fifteen maids charged that they should have been eligible (on the basis of performance and seniority) to do other jobs in the university. More specifically, they asked to be assigned to positions of guard and watchman. To date, these jobs had always been filled by men, and there had been no transfers between these positions.

The president was loathe to approve this on several counts. He felt that it was dangerous for women to be guards, and he knew that guards had to be able to work night as well as day shifts. Intruders or prowlers would be less likely to be intimidated by a woman, particularly since some of the women were very slight of build. Also, he felt that these were not jobs suitable for the older women (although some of those dropped were quite young).

The male guards also objected to this request, on the grounds that it was unfair to have employees from another work group interfering with their seniority lines. In truth, the more recently hired guards were somewhat concerned that they might be displaced by women having longer service with the university.

1. How would you evaluate the several claims here?
2. Would your evaluation be affected if you knew that all of the younger guards were black and newly hired?
3. What criteria should be used to select maids for guard positions? Should future maids be selected on the presumption that they might also seek such transfers?

employee health and safety

Until recent years, managers generally considered employee health and safety relatively minor concerns. The dark, dirty, dangerous workshops of the early days of the industrial revolution were history. Tools and factories had been redesigned, safety equipment had been introduced, and workers were bombarded with warnings to work safely. The modern workplace was considered a good place to work. Now, this complacency has been shattered by rising accident statistics and the discovery that many materials and processes used in manufacturing pose long-term threats to health, even threatening to life itself. In 1972, Congress passed legislation requiring new initiatives on the part of management to cope with a whole spectrum of safety problems. Employee health and safety today is thus a complex, multidimensional problem. Here we shall deal with three elements of this multifaceted problem: accidents occurring on the job, illnesses arising out of work, and the underlying legislation.

Scope of the problem

In the early 1960s, there was considerable optimism about a "cure" for industry's safety problems. Between 1926 and 1956, the accident frequency rate in manufacturing had declined by about 50 percent. But by 1970, accidents were occurring 27 percent more frequently than in the

preceding decade.[1] Further, we have recently learned that black lung, cancer, asbestosis, and other diseases are associated with industrial and mining processes.[2] The scope of this growing challenge to management can be inferred from these annual statistics for the United States:

- 5 million workers are injured in private industry.
- 2 million workers are disabled.
- 14,000 deaths occur in work accidents.
- 100,000 deaths occur from occupationally caused illnesses.
- 400,000 new cases of disabling illness occur.
- $9 billion are spent on these illnesses and injuries, including perhaps as many as 240 million man-days lost.

Shocking as these figures are, they understate the true costs of industry's health and safety problems. Fearing accidents and resenting uncorrected hazards, workers produce less. Companies pay high insurance premiums to cover their liabilities for accidents. Injuries further reduce productivity and possibly necessitate training costs for substitute employees. Some authorities have estimated that for serious accidents there may be $4 of indirect costs associated with every dollar of direct costs.

We shall see that safety problems can be caused by obvious as well as not-so-obvious factors. Sometimes our common assumptions may be just plain wrong.

Why do health and safety problems occur?

Type of industry. Some occupations are more hazardous than others. Depending on the size of a firm, an employee's chances of injury are 5 to 10 times greater in construction than in insurance. Mining, on the average is 5 times more dangerous than financial services. But these data can be misleading. In the coal industry, for example, some companies operate mines 4 times as hazardous as those managed by other companies. The chemical industry has a low accident rate, but occupational illness is a problem.

Management attitudes. Management's policies and efforts also make a difference. Historically, Du Pont's accident rate has been much lower than that of the chemical industry as a whole. In 1974, it had one-twentieth the average number of accidents. The ordnance industry (munitions) has a far better record than food products manufacturing. It is likely that the obvious danger associated with manufacturing munitions spurs both workers and management to be extra careful. Closer examination of government accident statis-

[1] Accidents are on the increase, but it is not clear how much of this is due to better reporting or to changes in occupations and the age-sex-race composition of the work force. For example, the work force has become younger on the average, and the accident rate for young people is consistently higher in the factory, as it is on the highway. One could surmise that in an age of greater stress—culture change, divorce, increased mobility—human tensions would show themselves in greater propensity to have accidents. In fact, during the 1960s, off-the-job accidents were increasing more rapidly than work accidents.

[2] One of the more gruesome accounts of unsolved safety problems in industry is provided by Rachel Scott, *Muscle and Blood* (New York: Dutton, 1974).

Selected examples of occupational injury and illness incidence rates, by industry, U.S., 1975	Industry	Incidence rates per 100 full-time workers	
		Total cases	Lost workday cases
	Entire private sector	8.8	3.2
	Mining	10.9	5.6
	Contract construction	15.7	5.4
	Manufacturing	12.5	4.3
	Transportation and public utilities	9.2	4.6
	Wholesale and retail trade	7.2	2.6

tics discloses that on the average, very large companies within the same industry have better safety records than smaller companies. In fact, some of the differences between industries' safety performance may reflect these differences in size and management policies.

Technology. One obvious culprit appears to be modern technology. Industry uses more high-speed equipment, more lasers and radiation, and a whole variety of organic chemicals and plastics, but we are just beginning to explore the effects of modern technology on the human body.

Employee attitudes. No matter how safe the job, reckless employee behavior can create accidents. In fact, it is often difficult to separate human from technological causes. Some employees may consciously or unconsciously use accidents as a means of escaping disagreeable jobs; certainly low morale can produce carelessness. Although many employers feel that employees are more accident-prone today than they were a decade or two ago, there is no clear evidence supporting this view.

Improving safety

Students and practitioners in the field of safety have approached the problem from a number of points of view. The extremes have been the *engineering* approach and the *selection* approach. In the engineering approach, it is assumed that accidents can be avoided by the construction of a "safe" plant, free from potential hazards. In the selection approach, it is assumed that accidents can be avoided if the company refuses to hire workers whose personality characteristics or physical makeup suggests they are accident-prone. Although both approaches have some modest validity, there has been a growing realization that they both involve oversimplifications and that a major cause of accidents is the relationship between the individual and his environment—or to put it in simpler terms, poor work habits.

To eliminate poor habits, management first tried to develop a safety department that would make and police regulations, analyze accident causes, and conduct education programs. The limitations of this approach, however, have caused companies to regard safety as a *line* responsibility that should be handled by each supervisor. A staff safety department aids the supervisor by motivating people to accept more responsibility and to seek additional training. There are, then, 4 main approaches to safety: (1) engineering, (2) selection, (3) staff, and (4) line. Let us examine each.

The engineering approach, which concentrates on reducing technological hazards by redesigning machinery, equipment, and working procedures, has been extremely productive. Indeed, much of the credit for the substantial reduction in accidents over the last fifty years must go to safety engineers for introducing devices ranging from rounded corners on desks, mirrors placed at sharp turns, improvements in lighting, ventilation, and heating, and props in mines, to Geiger counters and sophisticated monitoring controls.

The engineering approach

Resistance to safety engineering. Certain human relations problems arise in trying to gain employees' acceptance of safer work methods. Even if the new way is no harder than the old, *it is different:* it breaks established ways of doing things. Where piecework is involved, learning the new way may result in loss of income. All the well-known problems of resistance to change are involved, as indicated by the following examples:

One company installed a device consisting of a steel-cored cable to pull workers' hands out of the way when they got too close to the press. No notice of the change was given either to the union or the workers. When the president of the union heard of the new device, he objected strongly to workers being "chained" to their machines. The men refused to work with it.

The workers may have felt that this device, though safer, was just one step along the road to transforming them into machines. Had they been consulted in advance about whether or not they were willing to try the device, probably there would have been much less resistance.

In another plant, the safety man had great difficulty persuading young women to wear safety nets on their heads. "They're too ugly," the women complained. When he provided more stylishly designed caps and gave each woman her choice of color, the problem disappeared. The same thing happened with safety shoes, once the men were allowed to choose from among different models.

Workers will avoid new work methods if they can make more money by skipping time-consuming safety measures. Many injuries are caused when workers position material under a press and forget to remove their fingers in time. Some companies have installed controls that require the worker to push two separated buttons, one with each hand some distance away from the press, before it will operate. Since this takes time and effort and results in loss of incentive earnings, workers have devised ways of pushing both buttons at the same time with a stick.

Even when workers show no particular resistance to safety devices, they sometimes forget to use them. For some employees, such risk-taking may be a form of Russian roulette, a demonstration of *machismo*. Workers in one plant told gleefully of the heroic figure who had deceived management for years by wearing safety goggles with the glass taken out. In other instances, no bravado is involved; it is simply adaptation or forgetfulness. Because of these factors, engineers endeavor to design equipment that cannot be operated if safety measures are ignored. Ideally, one does not merely add attachments to the machine to make it safer, but redesigns the equipment entirely.

Human factor research. Often human factor specialists or human engineers are useful in such design work. For example, human engineers are aware that dials are difficult to read because the person reading them must notice precisely where the pointer is on some continuous scale. But if a light flashes or a bell rings when a dangerous operating level is reached, the worker will recognize the condition more quickly.

The human factor is not always simple to analyze. Safety measures that reduce part of a hazard may actually increase the number of accidents by encouraging workers to become complacent and work less carefully. In electrical installation work, a number of accidents occurred when inspectors pressed high-tension bars with fiber-barreled flashlights that were not conductors of low voltage, but did conduct high voltage. The men had not adjusted to the limited degree of safety. Metal-barreled flashlights solved the problem. Since the metal flashlights obviously were conductors, the men adjusted properly and avoided contact with the bars altogether. This particular incident illustrates one reason for the relatively impressive safety record of the ordnance industry. Obvious danger makes people careful.

Safety engineers recognize that exclusive emphasis on the engineering approach—improving mechanical and safety equipment—can reach a point of diminishing returns and that human error can be a more important factor. Unfortunately, it is difficult to separate the two. Machinery may be safe as long as human operators are perfectly attentive and infallible, but these requirements are unrealistic.

Management's motives may also be misconstrued. An American minerals company operating in Africa sought to reduce the incidence of illness caused by drinking polluted water from a nearby stream. Warning notices were posted, and employees were instructed to drink only from company-installed pipes. The situation coincided with a good deal of employer-employee bitterness associated with maternity-leave policies. Soon there was a widely accepted rumor that the company was placing birth control chemicals in the water so that there would be less time lost during maternity leaves.

The selection approach

We have concentrated on unsafe *conditions*. To balance the picture, we must also look at unsafe *actions*, the employees' contribution to the safety problem. When we study a group of workers who are doing the same job and are subject to the same physical environment, we usually discover that a few people have substantially more accidents than the rest. There is a tendency for those who have more than the average number of accidents in one period to have more during a later period. We all know people who are always stumbling and dropping things. Regardless of whether they are driving a car, pouring milk, or counting change, they make mistakes. Evidence of this sort has led some researchers to try to identify the physical and psychological characteristics that make a person accident-prone. (Other researchers, however, claim that true accident-proneness can be exaggerated. They point out that just by the laws of chance we would expect accidents to be unevenly distributed among the work force.)

Just as many illnesses (such as ulcers and high blood pressure) are partially due to psychological troubles, so high accident rates seem related to psychological disturbances. People may be so concerned about their problems that they forget proper safeguards, or they may subconsciously want to be injured in order to punish themselves or to avoid a difficult situation. Workers who are unusually impulsive or who work off aggression on the job may have the most accidents. Many accidents occur on no-attention jobs when something unexpected interrupts the worker's usual rhythm. Instead of smoothly adapting to the interruption, accident-prone people are momentarily terrified. Their defense mechanism does not react in an orderly fashion. But authorities disagree on whether it is possible to screen out people who are likely to have accidents.

At present, experts are becoming more convinced that accident-proneness is not an innate personality characteristic. Instead, susceptibility to accidents may vary over time, depending in part on the conditions under which a person works. Accidents are more frequent among younger workers, those who are just learning their jobs, and in general among those who are making difficult adjustments. Many people who seem to be accident-prone may suddenly stop having accidents.

Accident-proneness and working conditions are only two of the many determinants of accidents. Individuals, group attitudes, improper supervision, and technology are also at fault. Management has begun to realize that neither industrial engineering departments nor employment departments can, alone or in conjunction, stop accidents completely. The emphasis has now shifted toward involving all levels of management and the work force.

The staff approach: the safety department

The safety director is a staff person who usually reports to the personnel director or the industrial engineer, although in some organizations he or she is directly responsible to the division or plant manager. The director's functions normally include the general promotion of safety education (through such devices as posters and safety campaigns), analyzing the causes of accidents, preparing accident statistics and records, and purchasing safety equipment. But these activities are only incidental to the safety director's main responsibility for devising and administering a plantwide safety program. The director is usually given a grant of power that reads somewhat like this: "To inspect the plant for unsafe conditions, to promote sound safety practices, to make safety rules, and to report, when necessary, violations to the plant manager." Powers as broad as these may well lead to conflict with line supervisors.

The safety director sees a grinder working without the required goggles. Should he speak to the grinder, the foreman, or the plant manager? Whatever he does will make someone feel bypassed.

The safety director decides that the drop-hammer mechanism is unsafe. She feels that the worker should be required to push a button every time he wants the hammer to operate. This would be safer but would cut production. To whom should she speak first? How should she handle the expected opposition?

These problems are almost inevitable once a staff person assumes responsibility for making and enforcing rules. How are the line supervisors likely to respond to such an extension of staff activities?

1. If the safety director preempts too much authority, the supervisors may decide that safety can be forgotten; it's somebody else's responsibility.
2. The supervisors may sabotage or ignore regulations they have had no part in making. Often they feel (sometimes with justice) that a rule should not apply to their particular situation.
3. The supervisors and the safety director may just pass the buck back and forth. Whenever an accident occurs, each may put the blame on the other. If production costs rise too high, supervisors can always say that Safety is at fault (this is particularly true where Safety has the authority to order new equipment).
4. In most cases, accidents are caused by a worker doing a job in a dangerous fashion. Yet, if the safety director instructs a worker on how to do the job, that would be usurping one of the supervisor's primary responsibilities. Sometimes the supervisor tells the worker what he *should* do, and the safety director tells him what he *should not* do. This, too, can often lead to conflict.
5. The supervisors and workers may both begin to resent the safety specialist's efforts to implement a program. One safety expert complained: "I feel like a cop. Everybody suspects me. When I come around, everybody covers up. All I am trying to do is help them. Yet I never get cooperation from anyone. I have to fight every inch of the way."

No wonder safety directors often retreat from their efforts to enforce safety rules and try to achieve the same results through "educational" activities. As long as safety directors stick to posters, propaganda, and contests, they are unlikely to annoy anyone.

Special programs. Publicity devices such as posters, slogans, and contests form the backbone of many safety programs. Most posters and jingles are punchy and amusing, but how much can these devices be expected to accomplish? To answer this question, we must turn to psychologists who have studied how attitudes and behavior can be changed. In general, experts agree that posters and jingles can help to make consumers think of a particular brand when they are buying. But they seem to be less effective in changing basic attitudes. Gory displays arousing fear of dismemberment or even death may be repressed by the viewer, serving no purpose whatsoever.

Many organizations insist that employees attend periodic safety meetings, often run by the safety department. These meetings are quite valuable if they stimulate group discussion of actual problems. Ordinarily, however, the participants simply sit and listen to canned programs couched in unsophisticated terms. A head nurse told of the experience in her hospital:

We are supposed to attend a safety meeting once a month. You can always predict what will happen: one month they show you how to use a fire extinguisher, another month they tell you not to leave mops where people can trip over them and to make sure that the floors aren't waxed too heavily. Every six months they show a movie—the same one—I know it by heart. I have better things to do; I have patients to take care of.

Hoping that group pressure and competitive spirit will dramatically reduce the accident rate, many safety directors sponsor contests between departments. They post elaborate charts to mark the contestants' standings and present small prizes to winning departments.

Records, statistics, and analysis. Normally, whenever an accident occurs, the supervisor is required (both by law and by management) to fill out a form including information such as the time, place, and cause of the accident; the extent of the injury; and a statement of what can be done to prevent such accidents in the future. (Some of these forms are so complicated that supervisors often feel they have been designed as punishment for permitting an accident to occur.) Records of this sort serve several purposes: (1) they are useful if litigation arises; (2) they serve a control function, indicating areas of supervisory ineffectiveness to higher management; and (3) they help management diagnose the causes of accidents, providing a springboard for corrective measures.

It is the responsibility of the safety department to review, classify, and tabulate these reports. In fact, the safety program sometimes degenerates into a "whodunit" as the safety director tries to assign each accident to its proper category. At times, responsibility is extremely difficult to fix. Suppose the maintenance department has failed to keep a machine in proper order, oil drips out on the floor; the janitor fails to sweep it up; a worker from another department runs through the department, slips, and is injured. Which department should be assigned the blame? The maintenance department, the department in which the fall occurred, or the department whose member was hurt?

In the safety field, as in other areas, statistics can be useful or misleading, depending upon how they are used. Statistics emphasize the past. Alert management is aware that there are always new problems to solve, using statistical information. Medical research is constantly discovering new substances that can induce illness. Similarly, changes in layout, new equipment, or even manpower can create new hazards. How quickly, for example, does a company change its warning signs as it begins to hire non-English-speaking employees?

The staff role: an evaluation

A young woman was appointed as the first personnel director of a small company that had a particularly bad safety record. One of her first official acts was to cancel the company's contract with an agency that supplied safety posters. Why did she take such an unorthodox step? Her answer was very revealing: "I wanted everyone to know that just because we had safety posters didn't mean that we had a safety campaign."

It is regrettable that the tendency in the safety field, as in other areas of personnel administration, is to rely on gadgets to provide easy solutions to hard problems. The process is a familiar one. Management recognizes that accidents are a serious expense. Line management is too busy, so an expert who can handle the problem for them is hired. This done, line management breathes a sigh of relief: "That problem is solved."

The safety expert does have vital roles: adviser and counselor, expert on both human relations and engineering, a person who helps but does not supplant the foreman. If the safety expert observes workers operating unsafely, he or she should neither instruct them (except in emergency) nor report them to top management, but discuss the matter with the foreman. Together they should try to figure out why the workers are taking risks and how they can be motivated to work safely. Even more important, the safety expert should help coordinate line management's safety activities—activities that invite the participation of the union as well as the individual worker.

**The line
approach**

Safety, like productivity and morale, is a line management problem that involves working with groups, developing employee motivation, and enforcing standards.

Group factors. Although certain individuals may be prone to accidents, safety is, to a considerable extent, a function of group attitudes and norms. In a gang of teenagers, it may be smart to take risks; in a group of mature businesspeople, irresponsibility is frowned on. To miners as a group, safety is of tremendous importance. (In one gypsum plant the "prop" man, who installed wooden props to hold up the roof, was found to enjoy high social status even though his job required little skill.) [3] United States corporations operating plants in certain Latin American countries have found that accident rates are difficult to reduce there because of the widespread feeling that using a safety device is inconsistent with masculinity.

Clearly, the establishment of proper group attitudes is one of the most important requirements of an effective safety program. This is particularly true when the safety rules make the workers' jobs harder or more unpleasant or are regarded as an unjustified restriction of freedom. If management can get the group to participate, safe work habits may become accepted as a norm that will be enforced by the group just as rigorously as any production bogey. The group itself may punish the worker who takes chances or fails to use proper equipment. In many plants, non-smoking rules are consistently ignored in spite of constant attempts to enforce them. This is not the case in oil refineries, where the legitimacy of the rule is well accepted. One employee reported that "regardless of who you are in the plant, if you see someone smoking you can stop him. I know. The first day I was there I absentmindedly reached

[3] Alvin Gouldner, *Patterns of Industrial Bureaucracy* (New York: Free Press, 1954), p. 12.

for a cigarette and was practically lynched. The boys have special fun catching visitors, especially big shots." This is an example of a group-enforced pattern of behavior.

Group meetings provide a unique opportunity for the supervisor or safety department to ferret out possible accident hazards and to elicit suggestions from the workers. After all, employees know more about their jobs than anyone else. Furthermore, most safety rules are much easier to enforce if those who must obey them also have a voice in determining them.

Supervision. In many cases, the attitude of the rank-and-file workers toward safety is a reflection of the attitude of their immediate supervisor. A worker in a railway freight yard once told the following story:

"There's a company rule that you aren't supposed to cut between cars. If the safety man sees you, he will give you three days off. But the supervisor doesn't care. In fact, when you have to get the numbers of some cars, that's the only way to get them. If you don't get the numbers, he'll give you time off. And he is more likely to catch you than the safety man."

In safety, as in other areas of supervision, attitudes of lower levels of the hierarchy reflect the attitudes of top management. To the supervisor operating under the pressure typical of modern industry, maximum production and maximum safety are simply incompatible. If top management really wants "Safety First," it must clearly indicate that it is willing to pay the possible price in terms of lower production. It must get tough with supervisors who permit the continuation of unsafe practices. Safety records must be consulted in deciding who should get promoted. If management speaks righteously about safety but permits a dangerous condition to persist for "just another few days" so that no production will be lost, it must expect only lip service from everyone down the line. As with affirmative action, policies must be enforced by the reward system.

Companies that have the best safety records customarily use accident reports as one of the control statistics to judge supervisory efficiency. Overemphasizing these records, however, may induce supervisors to concentrate their efforts on *looking* good. They may fall into the habit of buck-passing and may even try to persuade injured workers to report to work in order to avoid being charged with a "lost-time accident."

What, specifically, can supervisors do to promote safety?

1. Train new employees. Do more than exhort new employees to work safely: point out possible causes of accidents and help develop work habits and motions that will keep them out of danger.
2. Make it clear that although high production is a goal, workers will never be required to work so fast that they run risks.
3. Listen to and consult employees. Some of the best safety ideas come from listening and being clearly interested in suggestions.
4. Engage in constructive discipline. Tactfully point out to employees when they are working unsafely, and firmly impose punishment when lesser measures fail.
5. Make a daily routine of checking on unsafe conditions and unsafe behavior.

In one company each foreman is expected to speak about safety to at least two of his employees each day.

Training and motivation. NASA and the Apollo program provide us with other insights into line management's contribution to safety. In the NASA effort, a great deal of time and energy was devoted to teaching people what to do in case of an emergency, and these "contingency plans" were practiced until they became almost automatic. Such planning and practice circumvent the problems that typically arise when established routines are interrupted in an emergency.

New York City's subway system had a serious fire. When the fire department telephoned transit management and asked them to turn off the electric power to allow firefighters to enter the tunnels, the request was ignored. There were apparently two reasons. It was not clear who was authorized to make that decision, and the transit people felt that they needed power in the tunnels to facilitate evacuation of passengers. Regardless of who was right, this conflict over who should defer to whom nearly resulted in tragedy.

In 1979, allegedly minor technical problems with valves nearly escalated to a nuclear power plant disaster because control room technicians had not practiced quick responses to a variety of ambiguous monitor-gauge readings. (The readings suggested problems with the core cooling system.) Further, the technicians were not able to contact high-level, experienced nuclear engineers in Washington. After the emergency, a special "hot line" was established for all commercial nuclear power plants.

Thus, fire drills usually provide for various monitors and floor leaders who will assume command and for a new management pattern that will help them to cope with the crisis conditions.

Discipline and safety. As we noted in Chapter 7, discipline should not precede training and education. Utilizing safety features on equipment may make the job more difficult, and wearing safety clothing can be uncomfortable and unsightly. Thus some employees, knowing the dangers involved, persist in violating safety rules.

In such cases, management must exercise the same progressive discipline used for any other rule infraction. It is just as important to protect the employee from himself as to protect the organization.[4] On the other hand, some managers are concerned that employees will become "Philadelphia lawyers" on safety matters and use unsafe conditions as an excuse to avoid work or annoy a supervisor. Some employees may use safety as a ruse, but there is usually some problem requiring attention.

Many arbitrators hold that if there is "imminent danger," an employee may refuse to do the task, not waiting for the complaint to work its way through the grievance process. But what is "imminent danger," and who decides—on what basis?

---

[4] It is interesting that under federal law (OSHA) an employer is held responsible for violations of established safety standards even though employees are failing to follow management work instructions.

Kurtz, a laboratory worker, complains to his supervisor, Ellen Rosten, that he shouldn't have to do a particular testing procedure because the sample could spatter and injure his eyes. Rosten tells him (truthfully) that the lab safety inspector designed the plastic guard that surrounds the sample while it is being heated. Kurtz insists that the guard isn't large enough to prevent an occasional spatter from hitting his eye; and when the two can't agree, Rosten suggests that the employee write to the lab union-management safety committee or file a grievance. He refuses, saying that procedures always take too long, and he isn't going to risk his eyesight. The supervisor must now decide whether or not to discipline the employee for failing to follow instructions and refusing to do a required, normal part of his job.

No safety rule or standard will answer questions like this one. Rather, the personnel department needs to help supervisors learn to discuss with employers their fears and discontents, so that minor problems do not become insurmountable disagreements. Further, Personnel needs to develop organizational procedures, so that others (union representatives and company safety experts) get involved when the supervisor is unsuccessful in resolving the matter in an atmosphere of problem-solving rather than win/lose.[5]

Occupational diseases

Even more serious health problems may develop from working conditions that have a slow but deleterious effect on employee well-being. The view that the modern plant and mine are healthy places to work has been challenged, if not destroyed, by a series of studies showing the number of long-term illnesses that can be contracted at work.

The beginning of this growing concern with health hazards in the workplace may be traced to the pioneering work of Dr. Albert Selikoff. Interested in pulmonary diseases, he opened a clinic in Paterson, New Jersey, in the early 1950s. Among his first patients were 17 men who had worked in a recently closed plant that had fabricated asbestos. Within 7 years, 6 of these had died and now only two survive. Most died of cancer. This stimulated his research interest in examining the relationship between cancer and asbestos, and he was soon able to show that former employees' lung cancer rate was 700 percent higher than the general population's. Further research of his disclosed that as many as 30 percent of a work force exposed to any significant amount of asbestos dust is likely to get cancer of the lung, stomach, or colon.[6]

The distressing side to this story was the general indifference of both industry and the government, although the dangers of asbestos handling have been known for 60 years, and conclusive proof of the relationship between occupational exposure to asbestos and lung cancer had been established a decade before Dr. Selikoff began his research. Now almost each day brings word of some new industrial source of illness.

[5] For nonunionized employees, the situation is ambiguous. The courts have not ruled definitively whether it would be a violation of federal law to discipline an employee for refusing to work on a job he or she believes to be unsafe.

[6] Robert Sherrill, "Asbestos, the Saver of Lives, Has a Deadly Side," *The New York Times Magazine*, January 21, 1973, pp. 12ff.

Most occupational diseases stem from exposure to, or contact with, various organic chemicals (e.g., vinyl chloride, which produces liver cancer); fumes (e.g., lead used in metal plants, which produces lead poisoning); airborne fibrous materials (e.g., asbestos or coal dust, which produces chronic respiratory disease and cancer); radiation (which produces cataracts and cancer); or high noise levels (which produce deafness). Though far less dramatic than accidents in terms of immediate impact, these hidden dangers to health can produce equally serious and permanent disabilities.

Several problems associated with occupationally derived diseases are therefore distinctive and separate from the accident question. One problem is that—unlike the obvious danger of whirring machinery, molten metal, overhead cranes carrying heavy weights, or flimsy scaffolding—debilitating illnesses stem from factors that are often not even easily observable. The airborne particles that can be so injurious to lungs are microscopic in size; many of the most dangerous chemicals neither burn nor appear to injure the skin or eyes. Radiation (infrared, X-ray) can neither be seen nor felt. So there can be a false sense of security that management is providing safe working conditions, when, in fact, employees are being exposed to substantial threats to health and even to life.

The multiplication of potential hazards. Modern industry is multiplying the potential sources of health problems. Each year, hundreds of new chemical compounds are introduced. More and more companies are making use of laser beams, X-ray technology, nuclear isotopes, and other high-energy electronic equipment, as well as complex organic compounds. For many of these, there is no simple test to establish safe exposure levels. In some factories, employees work with more than 5,000 different chemicals, only 10 percent of which have federal safety standards. At least 8,000 substances used in the world of work may be toxic.

Many modern chemicals that are suspected of being potential sources of illness if ingested are utilized in hundreds of different factories and perhaps dozens of industries. Six hundred million pounds of trichloroethylene, which causes cancer in laboratory animals and can cause respiratory failure and cardiac arrest when ingested, are produced annually in the United States. This chemical is used in the clothing industry to dissolve plastic basting thread. It is also used as an anesthetic for minor operations, as a degreasing agent in the metal industry, and as a means of removing caffeine from coffee. In addition to 280,000 workers, a number of hospital patients and consumers of decaffeinated coffee are constantly exposed to trichloroethylene. It is sobering to note that 1.5 million employees have some contact with inorganic arsenic. Even hospitals are dangerous. Technicians working with blood can contract hepatitis, nurses exposed to anesthetic gases can suffer miscarriages.

Too much heat or sound. Human health can be endangered by prolonged exposure to high temperatures, particularly when combined with high humidities, placing a great strain on the heart.[7] Similarly, loud noise (over 80 decibels) creates stress, and there is great debate between management and unions over maximum permissible sound levels. Physicians are just beginning to observe the long-run effects of exposure to high levels of sound and vibration. It has been estimated that as many as 10 million workers in the United States may have poor hearing resulting from excessive occupational noise. Research suggests that continuous excessive noise causes increased heartbeat and respiration—stress responses—that can eventually damage the body.

The time-lag before symptoms appear.   Some effects of exposure do not manifest themselves as illness until many years later. This *latency period* complicates management's efforts to be responsive to work hazards. The classic case involved employees of factories producing luminous dials for watches and clocks. Before the dangers of radioactivity were well known, employees used brushes to paint radioactive materials on dials. To keep a sharp point on the brushes, they often licked them. Many years later, they found that they had serious symptoms of cancer. Like lung and blood diseases, some cancers develop slowly.

As the years go by, it is difficult to trace illnesses back to specific job-related exposures. The employee has held several jobs, perhaps even retired, and it is difficult to pinpoint any single cause of ill health. Further, not every employee gets the same exposure, nor does everyone react the same way, so that dangerous elements of jobs may be disguised, somewhat like time bombs, and go off years later in the bodies of an unlucky percentage of the work force.

The difficulty of isolating the problem.   Unlike an unsafe machine, which can be guarded or modified, chemical hazards often spread almost beyond control. Asbestos dust can permeate clothing, food dispensing areas, cars, hair, or anything within or near the confines of the plant in which it is processed. To eliminate a chemical or material that has been proved dangerous may require that machinery, walls, floors, and related furnishings be scrubbed down or even burned or buried to eliminate contamination. Such efforts can be extraordinarily costly, as firms that operate "clean rooms" to fabricate ultrasensitive electronics have discovered. Once an area has been contaminated, the company may have to control the substance through careful regulation of air currents and temperatures and use of special masks, clothing, and glasses. Often a harmless material becomes dangerous when it is heated or comes in contact with a hot surface, or when it combines with some other chemical or is released into the air. Thus it is not enough to know which substances

---

[7] In one of his first industrial jobs, one of the authors was required to work in a test room that was kept at 120°F and 90 percent relative humidity. Management was very careful to limit exposure to these conditions to 15-minute intervals, permit only light work, and require that another employee be nearby (outside the intense heat area) in case of emergency.

are dangerous in themselves; chemicals must be traced and tracked throughout the industrial process.[8]

Employee reluctance and employer negligence. Employees may show some signs of illness, such as chronic bronchial problems, but they may be either careless about seeking remedial action or fearful that efforts to obtain some compensation may cost them their jobs. Perhaps they are unsophisticated about the relationship between job pollutants or hazards and their own physical condition. Also, there is the concern that if the company doctor finds employees too sick to work, they will lose their jobs or be transferred to less taxing, lower-paying positions.[9]

Many employers have not been conscientious about seeking to identify "slow" illnesses. The unscrupulous ones wish to avoid paying for injuries that cannot be easily verified as the company's responsibility. Others suspect that malingerers will seek compensation for problems that are not the company's responsibility. Because medical knowledge is imperfect and all the cause-effect relationships have not been worked out, employers fear that they will be saddled with liabilities that are not rightfully theirs. In some cases, the potential may appear astronomical, a virtual Pandora's box. Imagine a situation in which hundreds of thousands of former employees have to be traced and examined to determine whether their health has been permanently impaired.[10]

Employee behavior needs to be changed, too—not an easy task. Smoking may make smoker and nonsmoker more susceptible to atmospheric irritants. Employers have always had difficulty restraining smoking, even in dangerous areas. Truck drivers would be less subject to accidents if they broke up their long trips with periodic exercises (instead of coffee), but imagine how difficult it would be to institute that change. Further, the dangers inherent in trucking would be diminished if employees did less driving at high speeds. This would require changing the typical reward system, however, which is based on mileage covered, not time, and the drivers would object strongly.

The Occupational Safety and Health Act

Passage of the Occupational Safety and Health Act of 1970 (OSHA) resulted from a growing national concern with unsolved problems of safety at the workplace, wide differences among states in the vigor of their regulatory practices, and a belief that companies had not been forceful enough in seeking to eliminate hazards.

---

[8] We may actually be oversimplifying the problem. It is often difficult to assess whether a suspicious material is dangerous in its pure form, dangerous only when it is mixed with other substances, or dangerous only when some impurity creeps in because of careless manufacture or handling. Interaction of cancer-causing substances can accentuate the problem. Asbestos workers who smoke are 8 times more likely to get cancer than are smokers in the general population. The risk is 92 times greater than that of nonsmokers in general.

[9] Recently, unions have demanded that when workers shift out of occupations endangering their health, their new jobs will pay them at the same rate and give them the same seniority protection they had on their previous "unsafe" jobs.

[10] It has been estimated that benefits to mine workers stricken with black lung disease (from exposure to coal dust) will cost $5 billion in the 1975–1985 decade.

The law imposes on employers a general duty to provide employees with a safe and healthy work environment and to live up to explicit standards defining "safe" and "healthy." These standards are formulated by an agency established by OSHA: the National Institute for Occupational Safety and Health. On the basis of research and hearings (at which researchers, management, and union representatives appear), working condition standards are established. The following is an example of this:

One standard required management to provide a work environment in which the noise level did not exceed 90 decibels on what is called the A scale, with the exception that up to 115 decibels would be allowed for durations shorter than 15 minutes during an 8-hour day. Unions and their medical advisers argued that 80 decibels should be the standard since some people will experience gradual hearing deterioration at higher levels. Industry representatives argued that this was unduly restrictive, that the costs of maintaining such a low level would be prohibitive, and that few employees would be injured by the higher standard. Further, earmuffs would provide inexpensive hearing protection.

What is a safe standard? Even after there is evidence that some chemical or dust may be the source of health problems, there can be considerable dispute involving management, unions, and government over what is suitable protection for workers exposed to the substance. Here is one example of how the problem manifests itself.

After a number of studies had shown vinyl chloride gas was likely to cause cancer, the U.S. Department of Labor issued a temporary standard of an allowable 50 parts vinyl chloride per million parts of air. A number of physicians and the affected unions felt that the standard should be no detectable level of vinyl chloride in the workplace. Management, in turn, felt that the original standard was severe enough. It argued that stricter standards would be very costly and could eliminate many jobs, and the evidence supporting zero concentrations was not clear.

Here were some of the possible solutions:
1. Retain the "no detectable level" standard.
2. Set the standard somewhere between zero and the old 50 ppm level.
3. Require employees to wear face masks and perhaps air-supplied work suits (these are uncomfortable and need to be monitored for leaks).
4. Ban the production of vinyl chloride (now a very widely used chemical).
5. Develop a substitute plastic to take its place.

As it turned out, the industry was too pessimistic. After about eighteen months, most manufacturers had reduced air concentrations to 2 parts per million, although the total industry costs were around $300 million.

At some point, a standard has to be established to guide management and to provide adequate controls for both management and government monitoring. These standards are often called threshold limit values.

Threshold limit values (TLVs). In debates over establishing standards, the term *threshold limit value* is often used. This is the level of a particular substance or condition that will not produce disease in the majority of workers exposed. Thus, if a standard is set on the basis of a TLV allowing for a maximum percentage of some chemical in the air inhaled by employees, it is assumed that most workers will find this a safe place to work.

There are, however, some limitations to the effectiveness of such standards. Conceivably, heavy smokers, older people, or pregnant women might be more susceptible. In the case of a TLV for noise, which has sometimes been proposed at the level of 90 decibels, 15 percent of those exposed are likely to experience some hearing loss after 20 years. Most workers, however, will not become deaf. The appropriate degree of safety is often ambiguous, especially because TLVs are often set for prime age males. Also, there is often no way to be sure of the nature of the additive effects when several toxic substances are in the work environment at the same time or when there is both inhalation and skin absorption.

Vulnerability is a related issue. Although a healthy employee may not be injured by working with noxious substances, someone who already has certain propensities or is not perfectly healthy may be more vulnerable. Should the workplace be safe for everyone or for 95 percent of people or 75 percent? Surely no employer has the right to risk another human being's life or health, and everything possible should be done to reduce illness-causing conditions. But that statement does not answer the question, "What does *everything possible* mean in practice?"

Not only does everyone face risks in the home and on the road, but there is no way to make the workplace absolutely safe without enormous costs and in some cases the sacrifice of other benefits. As the standard becomes more severe, the cost of living up to the standard can go up enormously. Getting rid of the last 5 percent of a problem may cost a hundred times more than eliminating the first 95 percent.

Problems created for employers

Placement dilemmas. Federal and state statutes require that employers grant equal job opportunities to existing or prospective employees with physical, medical, or mental disabilities. Employers are often reluctant to hire a physically handicapped person who is more likely to have an accident because of some problem that inhibits quick reaction and mobility. They also fear that their medical insurance and workmen's compensation costs may increase. There are many instances in which firms have failed to hire those who have had heart problems or cancer, on the assumption that the illness is likely to recur and either be associated with the job or cause a great deal of lost time.

Quite aside from its legality, such discrimination can be grossly unfair to handicapped employees. Many of the handicapped have developed compensatory skills and reactions that enable them to overcome their problems, and many are more effective, productive employees than those who have not had to develop alternative methods of coping with day-to-day existence.

The more difficult problems occur when the company's medical staff actually fears that some precondition may be worsened by job exposure.[11]

[11] According to an interpretation of the relevant New York State law, an employee cannot be rejected for a job even though his *future* condition may involve a future payroll risk because he would draw excessively on fringe benefits, because co-workers or customers would prefer he not be employed, or because the job *may turn out to be* injurious to his health. Section 503 of the Rehabilitation Act of 1973 prohibits recipients of federal contracts from discriminating against handicapped people who are otherwise eligible for a given job.

Pregnant women, their unborn children, and heavy smokers may be much more vulnerable to certain chemicals than are other employees. Obviously, many other health problems can be worsened by the job. Profound problems may result:

An American Cyanamid plant utilized lead in one process, and lead dust can endanger the fetus of a pregnant woman. Five female employees felt seriously aggrieved. "The women said they had had themselves sterilized because the company led them to fear that they might otherwise lose their jobs. . . . Company officials said they had tried to discourage the operations, and that women employees were told they could no longer work in the pigment department but could transfer to other jobs without a decrease in pay for 90 days." [12] The company hoped to find permanent jobs for them after that but the women apparently were fearful.

Workmen's Compensation (to be discussed later in the chapter) and most conceptions of management responsibility assume that a neat line divides work-related illness and off-the-job illness. In theory, each worker comes to the job as a whole, healthy person; and if injury or illness occurs, it must be due to a totally work-related circumstance or to something that is not at all work related. Of course, many compensation awards do not follow this simple dichotomy.

In a sense, management is being pulled in opposite directions. Compensation awards and insurance costs tell the employer not to hire the handicapped or the potentially ill or disturbed. Fair employment commissions say just the opposite.

A has a heart condition and B does not. They both perform the same kind of strenuous work. A's heart fails, but B's does not. Should A's family recover workmen's compensation benefits? The social pressure to provide such benefits is strong, and many commissions and courts yield. But does it make economic sense to place financial burdens upon enterprises because they happen to employ cardiac cases? The desirability of providing employment to those with circulatory or any other deficiencies seems quite clear. [13]

But how far should that argument be carried? Should an employer be encouraged to place employees on jobs that are likely to injure them?

The New York Times reported (February 3, 1980) that leading petrochemical companies were quietly developing *genetic screening* tests to exclude "hypersusceptible" employees from certain jobs. There is evidence—still inconclusive—that employees with broken chromosomes are more vulnerable to the cancer-causing properties of some chemicals.

Fetuses are particularly vulnerable to lead oxide emissions in the manufacture of batteries, to various other chemicals, and to radiation. Should pregnant women be excluded from all jobs where fetal damage is a possibility? Should this be extended to all women who *might* become pregnant (since sometimes the danger is greatest during the first two weeks of pregnancy, before the woman knows she is pregnant)?

[12] *The New York Times,* January 7, 1979, p. E9.

[13] Merton Bernstein, "The Need for Reconsidering the Role of Workmen's Compensation," *University of Pennsylvania Law Review,* Vol. 119, No. 6 (May 1971), 997.

Heavy smokers are more likely to get lung diseases and therefore could be more adversely affected by jobs where there are noxious fumes. How can an employer discriminate between smokers and nonsmokers in filling these jobs, and how do you decide who is a heavy smoker?

Inspections and citations. OSHA also provides for periodic government inspection of workplaces, and more significantly, it enables workers and their union representatives to participate in "walk around" evaluations of the premises. Obviously, this will allow and encourage employees to identify hazardous conditions that management may have purposely or unknowingly neglected, and it adds an additional bite to the law. Employees also have the right to appeal directly to the Department of Labor if they feel they are being required to work under unsafe conditions. Companies found in violation of OSHA standards or not correcting conditions cited during inspections can be charged substantial fines. Under some circumstances, the process or the plant can be shut down.

To make sure that state industrial safety agencies are vigorous enforcers of these standards, OSHA provides that the federal government will supply a major share of the funding for state programs, *if* they meet federal standards. Some states, such as New York, are simply turning over these functions to the federal government, and the unions hope that others will follow.

Excessive costs and record-keeping burdens. Voluminous record keeping and reporting are also required for illnesses and accidents. Many companies, particularly smaller ones, have complained that the total cost of safety and health programs under this new legislation imposes an unbearable economic hardship.[14] They argue further that standards are constantly changing and that they are subject to the Environmental Protection Agency, to state organizations, and to OSHA standards, any one of which may conflict with others. The smaller-business people, particularly, have problems with the volatility and complexity of the regulations. They typically do not read the *Federal Register,* where regulations will be published, but they are liable to substantial penalties for ignoring these regulations. To be sure, there is some possibility that the pendulum may have swung too far—perhaps there is too much regulation—but this is the cost of many years of neglect and indifference.

The OSHA is one of the most resented pieces of regulatory legislation. It is a cumbersome and complex piece of legislation, and its directives are costly and often contradictory.[15] The following statement suggests the intensity of debate over the economic consequences of OSHA regulations:

[14] Employers argue that OSHA rarely considers costs. Continental Can contested OSHA's insistence that it install various engineering improvements costing $33 million (plus $175,000 in annual maintenance costs). The courts ruled that Continental Can could buy earmuffs (totalling $100,000) instead, to protect the hearing of its employees.

[15] By the end of 1978, OSHA admitted some of these problems by reducing the number of its rules. Almost 1,000 were eliminated.

Businessmen see OSHA as a conglomerate of impractical bureaucrats harassing business-men with inane but costly rules about such things as the need for coat hooks on the doors of toilet stalls. Labor unions say the agency is too timid to challenge business for failing to curb serious health hazards.[16]

There is also the continuing controversy over engineering versus supervisory approaches to safety. Businesspeople believe most accidents are caused by careless employees committing unsafe acts that will never be spotted by roaming OSHA inspectors. Changes in work habits, therefore, would be less costly and more sensible than reengineering an entire plant. In 1978, the government decided that before OSHA orders further health and safety regulations, it must weigh their costs against their benefits.

The medical department and personnel problems

In the records required by law, as well as in codes of safe working conditions, it is presumed that the company has access to medical facilities. Small companies may simply have a nurse or an agreement with a local doctor, but most larger organizations have a medical department. Its functions usually include the following responsibilities:

1. Preemployment physical examinations
2. First aid for injured employees or those who become ill at work
3. Examination of employees after serious illness to ascertain readiness for work
4. Evaluation of whether specific disabilities disqualify employees from certain jobs
5. Referral of employees with more serious illnesses to appropriate community medical facilities
6. Monitoring of employees exposed to hazardous conditions (urinalysis, blood tests)

Although these seem routine and obvious functions, controversial aspects of the relationship between the medical office and the employee sometimes pose serious dilemmas for the personnel administrator. The traditional responsibility of the doctor to the patient is clearly defined: the doctor owes a patient complete privacy and the best possible treatment. The doctor serves the patient's interest. But in industry, the doctor is employed by the firm, not by the patient; because of this, conflicts in interest may develop.

An executive with a sore throat visits the company doctor and reveals that he hates his present job, feels that the work is silly, and often sabotages his assignments. "I am even tempted to tip off some of our competitors about this new product line we're developing." *Query:* Can the doctor ethically do anything about this information? What possible response can he make to the executive?

Jane Rizzo is sent for a physical examination prior to assuming an important overseas post with the organization. The doctor discovers a physical problem that could incapacitate her,

[16] *The Wall Street Journal,* May 19, 1977, p. 38.

should her situation worsen, and particularly if she is under any stress. He discusses it with her, but her response is, "I want that promotion; it's what I've always wanted to do, and it's my big chance to move with this organization. I'm willing to risk my health; after all, it's my decision." The doctor also knows that it costs about $20,000 to relocate an executive overseas and that the company is anxious to keep people in these assignments after they gain the requisite experience with the new culture. *Query:* Assuming Ms. Rizzo is well enough now to assume the job, can the doctor inform the organization of the long-term risk without violating his responsibility to the patient?

During routine examinations, a company doctor discovers several examples of a minor illness that may be related to certain working conditions. The employees are unaware of any symptoms. They could also be due to a variety of off-the-job exposures. If the doctor treats these symptoms and/or discusses their possible relationship to working conditions, employees may initiate legal action against the company. *Query:* Where does the doctor's primary obligation lie?

Alcohol and drugs

Up to now we have been concerned with working conditions that create health hazards for workers, but there are also worker "abuse" problems that create hazards for the workplace.

Excessive drinking and the use of narcotics (and certain other stimulating and pacifying drugs) can be health problems especially difficult to treat. They can also be safety problems. Workers under the influence of drugs or alcohol are very likely to be hazards to fellow employees as well as to themselves. Both judgment and coordination are likely to be impaired. Further, there can be legal implications, for a company can be held responsible for violating criminal statutes if drugs are distributed and consumed on the premises.

Aside from health, safety, and legal problems, addicts obviously make poor workers. They are subject to increased absenteeism, accidents, and sickness. It is estimated that in one way or another, alcoholics cost their employers at least an extra 25 percent of their salaries and that 6 percent of American workers are alcoholics.

Managers are often fooled by employees who have developed an impressive array of deceptions to hide their addictive problem. They fabricate elaborate excuses for absences and always have explanations for their bleary eyes, shaking hands, mood changes. Employees suspected of addiction may resist examination and, in fact, there may be serious legal consequences associated with accusing someone of drug addiction and requiring a urine test.

Such problems are best overcome in the context of seeking to rehabilitate rather than to discipline; if detection does not mean discharge, there may be more cooperation. Rehabilitation programs are often called "constructive coercion" because an employee learns that it is necessary to enter a treatment program or be fired for poor performance and attendance problems. Management finds it can get union aid and support for such coercion because the union accepts the seriousness of the problem, as long as there is no great distinction between how executives and workers are treated. Apparently, two out of three employees consenting to enter such programs are successful in ridding themselves of the addiction.[17] Interestingly, they are more likely to

[17] *Nation's Business* (May 1974), p. 67.

"take the cure" when there is job pressure than when they are simply urged by friends and family.

Many companies are stressing health maintenance in addition to the control of health-threatening conditions. To date, the emphasis has been placed on executives: encouraging stress reduction by gymnasium workouts, weight control programs, and even bio-feedback and meditation techniques. High pressures accompany many jobs, and highly motivated managers further exaggerate deadlines and quotas. It is hoped that the health of these employees will be protected as they follow the proper physical regimens.

Workmen's compensation

Prior to the passage of workmen's compensation laws, anybody injured at work could sue the company for damages, but this was not an easy recourse. One had to hire a lawyer and sue through the courts, an expensive, time-consuming, and perhaps unsuccessful process, because the company had a number of ways to avoid liability. Now, instead of going to court, all a worker must do is file a claim with the compensation board. Although the board's proceedings are often time-consuming and technical, they are far less lengthy than the usual legal proceedings. A lawyer is not necessary. More important, management is directly responsible for all accidents *arising out of, and in the course of,* a worker's employment. Most employers take out insurance to meet these risks, either through a state insurance fund or through private companies, although some states permit large firms to be self-insured. In any case, the company's insurance costs depend on its safety record.

Several examples may suggest the breadth of meaning of the phrase *out of, and in the course of, a worker's employment.*[18]

Two workers engage in roughhouse in the company cafeteria at lunch hour, and one knocks out another's tooth.

After work is over, an employee carelessly sprains an ankle in the company parking lot.

A painter with a heart condition gets a heart attack and falls off a ladder.

A salesman away from home is injured in an auto accident while driving to a movie at 10 P.M., after his sales calls.

Recently, psychological "injury" and mental distress have also become compensable. One of the more striking cases of an employee becoming ill because of the stress and strain of day-to-day working conditions and thus entitled to workmen's compensation is described below:

In 1970 a Chrysler employee reacted to being discharged by killing three plant supervisors and was remanded to a state mental hospital after being declared legally insane. The Michigan Bureau of Workmen's Compensation ruled Chrysler liable because working conditions in the plant aggravated a preexisting tendency toward schizophrenia and paranoia.

[18] The laws vary considerably from state to state. Under the circumstances listed, however, the company would be liable in many states.

According to the hearing officer, the plant was a hotbed of racial tension, the employee had been referred to in derogatory antiblack terms by his supervisor, denied advancement opportunities, and finally fired after refusing to do a job he considered to be dangerous. (It was after the last that the killings took place.) [19]

More recently, in New York State an employee was awarded disability benefits to compensate for the emotional stress incurred when she viewed the suicide of her boss. The court ruled that if a job exposes an employee to the misfortunes of others, it may trigger symptoms of mental illness, particularly in those who may already be somewhat emotionally unstable.[20] As we have already noted, however, it would be inappropriate for an organization to endeavor to exclude from the work force or from stressful jobs those who might be inclined toward such instability.

In most states, employees who are "injured" under circumstances such as those above receive their medical expenses plus a proportion of the income lost for all the weeks out of work. While recuperating, workers receive weekly compensation benefits that are often far below their prior earnings. In fact, disabled employees can find themselves with a very low income, and there has been a great deal of pressure recently from unions and others to increase the benefit level, perhaps to two-thirds of actual previous earnings.

Union-management relations

In contrast to wage determination and discipline, safety is an area in which the interests of labor and of management perhaps could be harmonious. Everyone gains by keeping accidents at a minimum, and no safety program can be conducted effectively without joint effort. Ironically, however, unions and management often use the question of safety as a pawn in the struggle for power.[21]

Many unions have been actively seeking to get OSHA to set safety and health standards at higher levels than management feels are justified by the costs involved. They encourage more government surveillance. As we have already seen, some people may suffer hearing loss when sound levels go over 80 decibels, but some industrial equipment can be modified to keep below this level only at enormous cost. Unions are fearful that without constant pressure, management will seek the least expensive standard. Therefore, in addition to lobbying, they hire independent health consultants and fund research determining the relationship between working conditions and employee health. They send local officers to training programs to prepare them to evaluate and monitor working conditions. In some cases, contracts are written so that union-management disagreements can be pursued through the grievance procedure to arbitration. One conflict between unions and management is over

---

[19] *The Wall Street Journal*, March 13, 1973, p. 16.

[20] Reported in *The Wall Street Journal*, May 7, 1975, p. 15.

[21] Actually, union-management cooperation in safety may serve as a starting point for cooperation in other fields. As Herbert Hoover put it years ago, "Good-will and cooperation with respect to safety—which is a noncontroversial subject as between employer and employee—lead to good-will and cooperation in other more delicate problems of shop management, such as hours of work and wages."

the engineering versus work habits issue. Unions want the companies to stop using hazardous chemicals; they do not feel that workers should be forced to wear uncomfortable and potentially defective respirators. Unions also feel that workers transferred to a less hazardous job for health reasons should not suffer a reduction in pay.

In the past, many managements resisted cooperative health and safety programs. They feared that unions would use safety as a lever to force workload and other concessions, and that employees were ill-equipped to make constructive suggestions. Management now recognizes that employees can be alert observers of health and safety hazards and that joint committees can make constructive contributions. For these committees to be genuinely successful, the rank-and-file members must feel they are playing a real part in the safety program.

Technology seems to be inadvertently creating more problems daily, and modern medicine uncovers older hazards that we did not know existed; but positive attitudes energetically applied could, as Herbert Hoover long ago predicted, become a starting point for increased cooperation.

Conclusion

Safety and health cost money, but money alone will not buy them. Clearly, organizations that consistently have fewer accidents are willing to pay the substantial costs of constant educational programs, surveillance, equipment modifications, and research. They avoid the easy management view that, after all, a certain number of accidents are inevitable, particularly in hazardous work.

If this is true of accidents, it is even more true of illness associated with certain tasks and working conditions. Unfortunately, illness due to poor working conditions does not show itself immediately, and it is easy to confuse the symptoms with normal sicknesses. To create the best possible working conditions, industry has a major responsibility both to undertake investigations on its own and to respond quickly to new information disclosed by government and university investigations. In almost every instance, these studies suggest rather expensive modifications of materials and equipment.

No amount of research, however, can simulate all the combinations of conditions that equipment and raw materials will undergo in actual use. New problems will keep emerging.

When working hazards have been identified, management usually has a variety of technological options that have different costs associated with them. Regrettably, those with the lowest costs usually provide the lesser degrees of protection. There may be some economic limits to how much total elimination of risk is feasible.

- *Modest cost:* Instituting management and employee education on how to avoid excessive exposure.
- *Medium cost:* Changing worker behavior by requiring protective clothing.
- *Higher cost:* Changing the design of the job (e.g., machine guards).
- *Highest cost:* Radically altering the technology.

Yet, there is enormous human benefit to be gained if the dismal record described in the beginning of the chapter can be improved. Illness and accidents also cost industry heavily in lost time, in insurance premiums, and in reduced productivity that stems from fear of accidents and disrespect for a management that provides poor working conditions.

There is no one, sure-fire approach to safety. Thus safety and health demand the support of every level of management. Workers as well as supervisors must participate, for workers often spot danger areas and devise effective solutions. But when they fail to perceive safety as something vital to their welfare, they will resist the most carefully devised safety program. Health and safety must be considered the responsibility of the whole organization; any attempt to departmentalize it inevitably leads to confusion and inefficiency.

Personnel covers a broad area and has a significant contribution to make to this field. Safety and health are not isolated problems; they are part of the larger organizational and environmental system that includes technology, personality, and supervisory and management styles. Further, both organizations and society have choices (trade-offs) to make. As the work environment becomes increasingly hazard-free, the costs of products and services rises. How much are we all willing to pay? Obviously there are no easy or final answers to such value questions.

problems

1 • *Case of the Alcoholic Executive: Cause or Effect?*

Bill Cazione, now 49 years old, had worked for 19 years with the Campo County Welfare Agency. He had started as a social worker and eventually became manager of one of the divisions. About two years ago, a new agency head was appointed. Margaret Fielding had a number of innovative ideas for revamping procedures and programs. She and Cazione clashed frequently in meetings and in private discussions. Ms. Fielding asserted that Cazione was highly resistant to new ideas, rigid in his thinking, and resentful of a female boss. Cazione told his friends that Fielding was always "riding him" and that she was full of textbook theories that were inapplicable to the agency.

During this period Cazione became depressed and developed a drinking problem. He sought help from a local clinic and was able to keep the problem under control for the most part, but there were days when he did not work well. After a year of this, Ms. Fielding proposed to the county personnel director that Cazione's employment be terminated. On learning of this, Cazione hired a lawyer, who told the personnel director that they were prepared to bring suit charging that the severe stress of the job, particularly the constant "badgering" by the new supervisor, had caused the illness. In addition to demanding that Cazione be retained in his present job, the lawyer threatened suit for damages for alcoholism that was solely the result of job pressures.

1. Given the limited facts you now have, what would your own views of the situation be—assuming that both parties were telling pretty much the truth? That is, assume that Cazione is rigid and resentful and that his boss is aggressive and derisive.
2. As personnel director, what additional questions would you want answered in advising Fielding?
3. What are the implications for management's ability to discharge here?

2 • *How Heavy Is Heavy?*

The union at Double Knit Textile claimed that employees in the machine shop were required to push around equipment that weighed at least 100 pounds, and the union wanted to establish a rule that no employee would have to do any pushing or moving. Management called the claim exaggerated. Rarely, perhaps once a week in the course of work, an employee would have to shove aside one object—a few feet at most—but never lift it, and usually the object weighed under 50 pounds. Further, to enforce a rule against machinists doing any moving would require the costly and unnecessary addition of extra personnel and equipment in the machine room. Additional hiring was, management felt, the real purpose of the grievance. Also, the rule could slow down work and require difficult coordination.

The union's rebuttal was that even if the moving occurred only once a year, it exposed the worker to the possibility of a serious physical strain. Since it was unrealistic to weigh everything and separate the "under 50 pounds" from the "over 50 pounds," all shoving and lifting should be prohibited except by specially trained and equipped laborers.

1. What would your counsel be as personnel director of this company?
2. What research, if any, would you do, or what advice would you seek?

3 • *Responsibility for Safety*

Personnel Director: "We've got to watch our production people constantly [on safety]. Our safety rep must go over all orders for tools. A lot of our departments have high explosion dangers, and we've got to use spark-proof hammers. But a spark-proof hammer costs three times as much and only lasts a third as long as a regular hammer, so the foremen are always trying to get steel ones."

Question: "If the safety expert objects to what the foremen want to buy, who has the final say?"

Personnel Director: "The safety specialist all the time. We want to build up a good record."

1. Discuss the impact of this point of view on line-staff relations.
2. What would be a better approach?

4 • *The Company Physician*

How would you answer questions on pp. 295–96 relating to the relative responsibility of the company physician to the organization and to the individual patient/employee?

part 4

management and organization development

managerial career planning

14

An effective management team may be as important to the survival of an organization as any tangible item on the balance sheet. Yet management development is among the most difficult of personnel tasks. Good managers don't always show up as they're needed; neither can they be produced in some routine, completely predictable fashion. After all, managers are people, and people have interests of their own. They are less and less willing to have others plan their careers for them. Thus, a meaningful development program must balance organizational and human needs.

Management development is the subject of our next three chapters. This chapter will be concerned with providing experiences that will enable managers to develop their full potential. The next two chapters will handle specific areas: performance appraisal (Chapter 15) and organization development and management training (Chapter 16).

The changing nature of management career planning

At one time, management development seemed relatively simple. True, the number of managerial jobs increasing much faster than the size of the work generally. Nevertheless, once organizations accept idea that management was a profession for *which one could be trained, it* was believed that management development was *just a matter of training.* Provided there were sufficient advance lead tim an *sufficiently sophisticated* training programs, managers could be trained o dei *d.*

Recent developments have made management *d.* more difficult. Perhaps the most important of these ha *er planning much* the "baby bulge," the bumper crop of babies born after Wor *the impact of* from 1947 to 1957. During the 1980s managers born durin *II, especially* be in their late twenties and early thirties—critical ages for *period will* MBA explosion means that as a group they are better educa *ers. The* their predecessors. Unfortunately, their very numbers may me *were* advance up the organizational ladder will be frustratingly slow. *eir*

Adding to the strain, the postwar cohort is the first group equal employment rules have been reasonably effective: the large of white males in this cohort must compete against minorities and w many of whom benefit from affirmative action goals.

Life style changes complicate matters further. Managers are less do than they once were. Some are suspicious of the "system," and many deman the freedom to plan their own careers. They feel less loyalty to their employers and they center less exclusively on their jobs. For many, cultural, recreation, and family activities are more important than the fur-lined trap of financial success, and they question whether selling a sugar-laden breakfast food represents a meaningful way of life. Faced with these dilemmas, they are more willing than their predecessors to change jobs or even to try a second career in a completely new occupation. Further, they are less likely to accept transfers to other parts of the country, especially if this interferes with the careers of their working spouses or if they are already in a desirable location like San Francisco.

In short, these managers are less willing to sit passively by while key career decisions are made for them; they are more likely to make demands as to assignments and pay. As one observer put it:

"These young people are coolly outspoken. They'll tell you how much they think they should be paid, how good or bad they think their bosses are, what's wrong with the work they do, and so on." [1]

Not only is there growing resistance to company paternalism but more development must be crammed into a shorter time. Since World War II, the average age of top executives has dropped. The typical newly appointed vice-president or general manager today is in his or her middle or late forties. The median age at which chief executive officers of major U.S. companies egin their assignments is now 50.[2] On the other hand, higher educational ndards have deferred the age of entry into employment. Thus, the period

is Banks, "Here Come the Individualists," *Harvard Magazine*, September 1977, p. 24.
m G. Browne and Kurt Motamedi, "Transition at the Top," *California Management Review*, 2 (Winter 1977), p. 70.

managerial career planning

14

An effective management team may be as important to the survival of an organization as any tangible item on the balance sheet. Yet management development is among the most difficult of personnel tasks. Good managers don't always show up as they're needed; neither can they be produced in some routine, completely predictable fashion. After all, managers are people, and people have interests of their own. They are less and less willing to have others plan their careers for them. Thus, a meaningful development program must balance organizational and human needs.

Management development is the subject of our next three chapters. This chapter will be concerned with providing experiences that will enable managers to develop their full potential. The next two chapters will handle specific areas: performance appraisal (Chapter 15) and organization development and management training (Chapter 16).

The changing nature of management career planning

At one time, management development seemed relatively simple. True, the number of managerial jobs was increasing much faster than the size of the work force generally. Nevertheless, once organizations accepted the idea that management was a profession for which one could be trained, it was believed that management development was just a matter of training. Provided there were sufficient advance lead time and sufficiently sophisticated training programs, managers could be trained on demand.

Recent developments have made management career planning much more difficult. Perhaps the most important of these has been the impact of the "baby bulge," the bumper crop of babies born after World War II, especially from 1947 to 1957. During the 1980s managers born during this period will be in their late twenties and early thirties—critical ages for managers. The MBA explosion means that as a group they are better educated than were their predecessors. Unfortunately, their very numbers may mean that their advance up the organizational ladder will be frustratingly slow.

Adding to the strain, the postwar cohort is the first group for whom equal employment rules have been reasonably effective: the large number of white males in this cohort must compete against minorities and women, many of whom benefit from affirmative action goals.

Life style changes complicate matters further. Managers are less docile than they once were. Some are suspicious of the "system," and many demand the freedom to plan their own careers. They feel less loyalty to their employers, and they center less exclusively on their jobs. For many, cultural, recreation, and family activities are more important than the fur-lined trap of financial success, and they question whether selling a sugar-laden breakfast food represents a meaningful way of life. Faced with these dilemmas, they are more willing than their predecessors to change jobs or even to try a second career in a completely new occupation. Further, they are less likely to accept transfers to other parts of the country, especially if this interferes with the careers of their working spouses or if they are already in a desirable location like San Francisco.

In short, these managers are less willing to sit passively by while key career decisions are made for them; they are more likely to make demands as to assignments and pay. As one observer put it:

"These young people are coolly outspoken. They'll tell you how much they think they should be paid, how good or bad they think their bosses are, what's wrong with the work they do, and so on." [1]

Not only is there growing resistance to company paternalism but more development must be crammed into a shorter time. Since World War II, the average age of top executives has dropped. The typical newly appointed vice-president or general manager today is in his or her middle or late forties. The median age at which chief executive officers of major U.S. companies begin their assignments is now 50.[2] On the other hand, higher educational standards have deferred the age of entry into employment. Thus, the period

[1] Louis Banks, "Here Come the Individualists," *Harvard Magazine*, September 1977, p. 24.
[2] William G. Browne and Kurt Motamedi, "Transition at the Top," *California Management Review*, 20, No. 2 (Winter 1977), p. 70.

between first entry into employment and attainment of a top management position has been reduced to 20–25 years.

The object of a managerial career planning program is to make each of these years count and to provide each manager with a rich learning experience so that he or she has a productive *and* satisfying career. Managerial career planning has other objectives as well. It should permit each manager's performance to be carefully observed (see Chapter 15) so that in this highly competitive race only the very best get to the top. But it must also provide continuing opportunities for personal growth for the vast majority who are destined to go no further than the middle and lower management. Increasingly, too, it should permit individual managers to participate in decisions affecting their own careers with the goal of improving the match between individual desires and organizational opportunities.

Some basic issues

Before we look at the details of management development, it may be useful to introduce some basic controversial questions that will underlie our discussion in the next three chapters.

Change people or change the organization?

The first controversy relates to the effectiveness of such special development programs as planned rotation, performance evaluation, and training classes. On one side are those who argue that such programs develop proper skills and attitudes. But those on the other side claim that attitudes and skills (at least in the management area) can't be changed directly; the most that can be done is to create a challenging and permissive environment in which people can develop themselves. In a sense this is a question of strategy: Should our first emphasis be on changing the people or changing the organization? If we change people first, perhaps the organization will work better. But if we change the organization first (by changing organization structure, workflow, or reward systems), perhaps this changed environment may produce, if not better people, at least a situation to which people can adapt more successfully.

To take a specific example (to which we shall return in Chapter 16), training programs accomplish little if the new behavior is disapproved by the trainee's boss; after all, a manager is more likely to be concerned with what his boss thinks than what he learns in class. This suggests that it is best to have each manager train his or her own subordinates. But the boss's behavior may be far from exemplary. Even were it exemplary, he or she may not have the time or ability to teach effectively. Further, the boss is likely to teach only his *own* way of handling his *own* job; what the organization may need are new ways of handling not just one job but management generally.

Conformity or diversity?

Should the purpose of development be to instill certain common values in managers, or should it be to encourage a person's own style of behavior, one that seems best to fit one's own personality and the requirements of one's special job?

Many development programs are, in effect, forms of indoctrination. By providing a uniform way of thinking and a standardized approach to programs, indoctrination facilitates communication, makes behavior more predictable, and permits a substantial amount of innovative behavior within a common frame of reference without close supervision.[3] Yet some observers are concerned that developmental procedures might create too many "organization man" conformists who are concerned chiefly with pleasing the boss. Indoctrination has been attacked as stultifying innovative thinking and as a form of brainwashing inconsistent with individual dignity.

Generalists or specialists?

Should organizations develop all-purpose *generalists* with broad points of view or more narrow *specialists* who think in terms of their own particular functions? With the development of specialists, conformity to organizational values is reduced, but perhaps a new conformity to the specific viewpoint of the given specialty is encouraged. Someone trained as a computer programmer, for instance, is likely to think in terms of problems which can be expressed in computer language. There is a dilemma here. Each boss wants to hire specialists and reward specialization at the lower level, yet each organization wants generalists at higher levels. Where are the generalists to come from?

Decision making or human relations?

Assuming the organization decides to develop general management rather than specialized skills, should these be human relations or decision-making skills? What is the main job of the manager: to make decisions or to deal with people? As we shall see, two frequently used forms of training, the T-group and the business game, involve these two radically different views of the manager's job.

The T-group technique (see Chapter 16) assumes that the manager's main function is to deal with people. The T-group is designed to help executives develop greater sensitivity to their own behavior. By contrast, business games, particularly those involving computers, generally require analytic ability and little human-relations skill. Once a decision is made there is little problem of implementation. All the participants need do is write the answer; the computer obeys without question. Naturally, contrasts in approach can be overstated. We need better decisions and better means of implementing them.

Fast trackers or all employees?

Who should be developed—just those with special promise or everyone? Because of the critical shortage of manpower after World War II, the early emphasis was on crash programs to discover individuals capable of moving quickly to top management. In the effort to ferret out such exceptional individuals, there arose the widespread use of tests and evaluation forms designed to identify traits that might point to future ability rather than present performance. The "fast trackers" (also called "crown princes" or "water walkers") thus singled out were given special training (often at universities) and marked for rapid promotion.

As might be expected, this program led to resentment among those who had not been selected and to a feeling that it was unfair to base promotions on vague character traits instead of on proven performance. Also, the process seemed to favor safe conformists and thus weed out original thinkers. Further,

[3] Rosabeth Kanter, *Men and Women of the Corporation* (New York: Basic Books, 1977); William H. Whyte, *The Organization Man* (New York: Simon and Schuster, 1956).

by favoring those who began their career with a quick burst of speed, the program placed late bloomers at a disadvantage.

Even aside from fast tracking, many companies stress the competitive aspect of their development program. Excess competition among managers often harms essential teamwork. Further, by emphasizing the few who make it to the top, competitive programs slight the vast majority who will advance to middle management at best. Ignoring such people can be disastrous to organizational morale. The average manager needs developmental assistance as much—or more—than does the star.

*Open or
closed systems?*

How much freedom should individuals have to pick their own career paths? Many organizations have "closed systems," in which managers are given little choice as to the kinds of jobs they do or the kinds of training or developmental opportunities they receive. Their careers are likely to be determined for them, often by the personnel department. If they are caught in unrewarding, seemingly dead-end jobs, they are not allowed to apply for positions elsewhere in the organization.

As we discussed earlier, however, managers are demanding increased control over their own destinies. In response to this demand, many companies have instituted "open systems," which permit greater individual self-determination. These organizations believe it inconsistent to expect managers to take responsibility for important organizational decisions but not give them responsibility for decisions affecting their own careers.

Recent trends

The recent emphasis has been to provide a diversity of programs designed to help *all* managers (not just fast trackers) perform more adequately on their present jobs, as well as to provide special training for those who show promise of moving higher up. Organizations are not trying so hard to mold managers into a single form. Instead they are helping managers design their own custom-made developmental programs, thus creating a more open system.

There have been other changes as well. Personality traits (which cannot be easily changed) are receiving less emphasis than performance (which can); evaluation forms are being used to help subordinates improve their performance rather than simply as a means of determining who will be promoted; and greater emphasis is being given to changing the organization as a whole rather than training individual managers.

Getting ahead in large firms

It may help us to understand the management development process if we look briefly at research dealing with successful, rapidly promoted managers.[4] According to this research, successful managers in large firms have the following characteristics:

[4] For example, Douglas Bray, *et al., Formative Years in Business* (New York: Wiley, 1974); Douglas Hall, *Careers in Organizations* (Pacific Palisades, Calif.: Goodyear, 1976); William R. Dill, Thomas L. Hilton, and Walter Reitman, *The New Managers* (Englewood Cliffs, N.J.: Prentice-Hall, 1962); Fred Goldner, "Success v. Failure: Prior Managerial Perspectives," *Industrial Relations,* Vol. 9, No. 4 (September, 1970), pp. 453–67; Cyril Sofer, *Men in Midcareer* (London: Cambridge University Press, 1970); Jeffrey Pfeffer, "Toward an Examination of Stratification in Organizations," *Administrative Science Quarterly,* 22, No. 4 (December 1977), pp. 553–67.

- They move rapidly from job to job, both within a single company and from company to company.
- They earn their spurs handling critical assignments; these seem to be more important than doing well on routine work.
- They are flexible, realistic, and sensitive to the complexities of their work environment. Because they recognize that not all career paths provide equal opportunity for moving up, they turn down seemingly attractive dead-end jobs. They are adept in "being at the right place at the right time," particularly in finding positions of high visibility that permit them to demonstrate their ability to higher management.
- They constantly seek new challenges and are quick to respond to new ideas in both their personal and organizational lives. They distance themselves from parental values and accept community responsibilities early.
- Compared with less successful managers, they are both challenged by and comfortable in situations filled with high risk and ambiguity. Similarly, they are comfortable using power.
- They engage in "anticipatory socialization"; at each step they copy the values of those a step above them.
- Depending on the situation, they may be either conformists or nonconformists. In terms of social behavior and attitudes, they conform; but in their own area of job competence they take the initiative *at the proper time*. Perhaps a sense of timing is among the critical requirements of a good executive.
- They are helped by sponsors or "mentors," higher managers who are impressed by their abilities, find them useful to have around, look after their interests, and perhaps give them tips on how to get along. Best of all, they have sponsors who are moving up rapidly themselves.

To summarize, it is necessary for rising young executives to persuade their superiors that they have the human relations abilities to be good "team" members. But getting along with people may be a less significant criterion for advancement than having the analytical ability to diagnose problems, evaluate information, and make sound recommendations. Nevertheless, the all important requirement is to be on the constant lookout for opportunities to demonstrate one's abilities rather than to wait idly by for fate to bring its own rewards.

Situational factors. Beyond this, a series of situational factors may affect executive success. Research so far is fragmentary, but it suggests the following:

- The manager's first assignment is critical. If it is tough and demanding—and he or she does well on it—and particularly if he has a boss who brings out his best qualities—he performs better on succeeding jobs and moves ahead faster.
- Beyond this, to make rapid progress it is important to be assigned to a series of increasingly more challenging and visible jobs. Not only does doing well on such jobs permit young managers to demonstrate their abilities, it also helps develop their skill and self-confidence.
- Functional specialities differ in their promotional opportunities. In some companies marketing may be the high road to top management, in others it is finance. However, the favored field may change over time. When selling is the critical organizational problem, marketing specialists tend to progress more rapidly. When cost-cutting becomes all important, the advantage may shift to finance.

- Organizational structure also makes a difference. Departments organized on a product basis tend to provide their managers broader training than do departments organized on a functional basis. In many organizations line managers progress more rapidly than do staff managers. Finally flat organization provides the individual greater visibility and challenge than does tall organization.

- Rapidity of promotion is also affected by the socio-economic class of one's parents and the college one attends. Having rich parents helps you get ahead. But the relationship is particularly strong in career lines where individual performance is difficult to measure (for example, on staff jobs and in service organizations, such as banks, as opposed to manufacturing).

Politically sensitive aspiring young managers may be aware of these factors and so do their best to be assigned to the appropriate situation. But choices such as this are always hazardous (how can one accurately predict whether finance or marketing will be more critical ten years from now?). Further, the managers may have no control over their assignments, and being in the right place at the right time is largely still a matter of luck.

Strategies available to the individual manager are imperfect. But the organization faces a similar problem. How can it maximize its flow of well trained managers? The first step involves planning.

The career planning process

Until recently, managerial planning was considered as purely an organizational prerogative. Individual managers hoped that if they did a good job they would be recognized and promoted. Although politically adept managers knew how to influence the process of job assignments and training opportunities, there was no formal mechanism by which the manager's own opinion was sought. This is still the case in many, if not most organizations. Nevertheless opportunities are being increasingly provided for employees to participate in planning their own careers. We shall examine first the traditional process of organization-oriented career planning and then look at modifications that permit greater individual participation.

Traditional planned career progression

Many organizations keep track of the progress of each of their managers and tentatively schedule their future movements from job to job, to ensure that they will get optimum training and experience. The organization attempts to mesh individual careers with company needs and to balance supply and demand. The cost to the organization of having too few trained managers is obvious; less obvious but equally severe is the cost in terms of frustration and disillusionment of having too many well trained managers, many of whom will quit unless their abilities are used.

Frequently, policy is this area is the responsibility of a top-level management committee, while the administrative work is handled by the personnel department or a special coordinator of management development.

In one typical mid-sized company (15,000 employees) this committee is comprised of all department heads, vice-presidents, and the president. Their main purpose is to oversee movements amongst managerial level employees but in so doing they annually review the strengths and weaknesses of each manager. A five year career plan is then developed in consultation with the individual manager, and the committee oversees the individual's development in terms of this plan. This information is also used in the selection of new replacements.[5]

Usually the equal employment officer will also be involved to insure that the organization meets its obligations with regard to the promotion of women and minorities. Indeed, affirmative action plans frequently require the development of such long-range plans.

Two key career planning tools are *executive inventories* and *replacement charts.* An executive inventory consists of a file card or folder for each executive with key information such as age, length of service, education, and previous job history. The inventory card often also includes a summary of past performance evaluations as well as a statement about the type of experience and training the manager still needs and an estimate as to how far he or she might go in the future.[6] Replacement charts are useful in developing long-range plans. The chart on the opposite page is typical, although it somewhat exaggerates the range of possibilities among six managers.

From executive inventories and replacement charts, it is technically possible to plan many years in advance. For instance,

Ms. A.
    Jan. 1982 Superintendent
    Jan. 1984 Retires (to be replaced by Mr. B)
Mr. B.
    Jan. 1982 General foreman
    June 1983 Executive Development Program at X University
    Jan. 1984 Superintendent
Mr. C.
    Jan. 1982 General foreman
    June 1982 Assistant personnel director
    Jan. 1983 Chief inspector
    June 1983 Assistant plant manager (position to be created)
    Jan. 1984 Plant manager
Ms. E.
    Jan. 1982 Foreman
    June 1982 Assistant chief, production scheduling
    Jan. 1983 Assistant personnel director
    Jan. 1984 Assistant director, industrial engineering
    Jan. 1985 Marketing department, African division
    Jan. 1986 Marketing department, corporate headquarters

Note that Mr. B is to receive special training to prepare him for Ms. A's job. Mr. C is to move in three different jobs to gain experience. He will jump the superintendent's position altogether and after six months' experience

---

[5] Marilyn Morgan, Douglas Hall, and Alison Martier, "Career Development Strategies in Industry," *Personnel,* 56 (March 1979), 15.

[6] Frequently these data are computerized. When a job comes up, all management need to is set the standards for the type of individual best qualified. The computer does the rest. There are those who claim that once the standards are set, a minimum of human judgment is required. Obviously, it is more complicated than this.

REPLACEMENT CHART

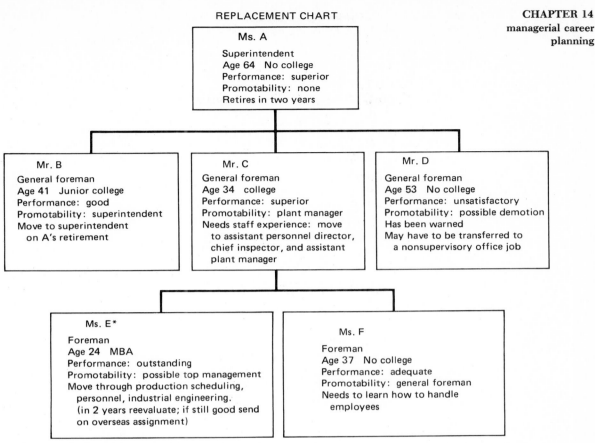

Ms. A

Superintendent
Age 64   No college
Performance: superior
Promotability: none
Retires in two years

Mr. B

General foreman
Age 41   Junior college
Performance: good
Promotability: superintendent
Move to superintendent
   on A's retirement

Mr. C

General foreman
Age 34   college
Performance: superior
Promotability: plant manager
Needs staff experience: move
   to assistant personnel director,
   chief inspector, and assistant
   plant manager

Mr. D

General foreman
Age 53   No college
Performance: unsatisfactory
Promotability: possible demotion
Has been warned
May have to be transferred to
   a nonsupervisory office job

Ms. E*

Foreman
Age 24   MBA
Performance: outstanding
Promotability: possible top management
Move through production scheduling,
   personnel, industrial engineering.
   (in 2 years reevaluate; if still good send
   on overseas assignment)

Ms. F

Foreman
Age 37   No college
Performance: adequate
Promotability: general foreman
Needs to learn how to handle
   employees

*Affirmative action trainee.

as an understudy, succeed to the position of plant manager. Ms. E is slated for a still more brilliant future. After short tours in three local staff departments and an overseas assignment, she will move to corporate headquarters. (She is lucky to stay in her present location so long; in many companies, promising young executives move more frequently than once in three years.)

Note that all these plans must be extremely tentative. If Ms. E fails to develop as anticipated, the schedule must be changed. Yet the very existence of such forecasts may lead to what some observers call a "self-fulfilling prophecy." The very fact that Ms. E is tagged as a "comer" means that she receives special opportunities; she is likely to become a good manager because everyone expects her to. Those who are less favored get less attention and so tend to lose hope. Furthermore, the system we are illustrating is "closed": typically the managers involved are told little about their future prospects and given little choice about the moves they are to make.

Indeed, replacement schedules frequently look better on paper than in practice. People quit or die; business recessions dictate cutbacks in operations; products fail to develop as expected; individuals turn "sour." As a consequence, some experts argue that there are too many variables to make planning for very far in the future much more reliable than crystal gazing.

Managers are becoming increasingly resistant to having their careers planned for them. Organizations are responding to these pressures in a number of ways, all of which provide individuals greater freedom to decide for themselves the kinds of careers they want.

Open systems. As mentioned earlier, it is becoming common for organizations to post job openings and to allow individuals who are interested to bid on them. This gives a wider range of options to both the boss, who has the job to fill, and the subordinate who can choose among jobs to bid on. Often this results in people applying who might not otherwise be considered. It makes it less likely that individuals are assigned to jobs they really don't want. And since it provides new opportunities for people who feel trapped on their present jobs, it also reduces the amount of "hoarding" which occurs when a given department holds on to more highly qualified managers than it really needs. Further, it makes the individual less dependent on a single boss.

Open systems principles permit individual managers to decide for themselves whether they are willing to be transferred to another community or line of work. (In the past, for example, it was often assumed that married women managers would never be interested in assignments that required them to move.) Under an open system, managers can also pick the type of training programs they will attend and determine for themselves whether they want to try out risky assignments with a high possibility of failure.

More information. For wise career planning both the manager and the organization need accurate information. We have already seen how "realistic job previews" help reduce disillusionment and turnover which so often occurs when people accept jobs on the basis of smooth salesmanship, which paints a glowing picture of the job's advantages without mentioning its disadvantages. Realistic descriptions of transfer opportunities are also useful. Furthermore, before being asked to move, a manager should have a chance to visit the new community and the job. More important, the potential transferee should have a frank discussion with his potential new boss so that both parties can openly state their expectations. If the subordinate is interested only in a position that provides good opportunities for promotion in two years, he should candidly say so. Honesty of this sort is difficult to develop, but once developed it greatly reduces the dissatisfaction that occurs when the parties misunderstand each other's expectations.

The manager also needs to know more about his own abilities. Assessment centers play an important role in self-directed careers. Although some organizations use such centers chiefly to evaluate new job applicants, many others use them to help managers who have been on the job for several years. Of course, a major purpose of such centers is to provide data for the organization to use in making hiring and promotional decisions. Increasingly, however,

Self-directed careers

312

evaluations developed through the assessment process are also being fed back to the managers who were evaluated. Frequently the evaluations lead managers to make major changes in their career aspirations. Faced with evidence, for example, that he or she is very hesitant in giving orders, a manager may decide to pursue a career as a staff analyst rather than a line manager.

Career counseling programs. To help perplexed managers think through the ramifications of alternative job choices, a number of organizations have developed career counseling programs. These vary considerably in scope. Some merely provide information about job opportunities. Others offer testing and counseling, particularly for employees who are having difficulty on their present jobs.[7] More elaborate programs include one or two day workshops in which a large part of the managerial work force participate. Traveler's Insurance Company, for example, runs "Career Planning Conferences" organized by outside consultants. These Conferences are designed to help employees

take a new look at their careers and where they are going. . . . In class sessions, participants are encouraged to talk about what they feel about the company and how to deal with the realities and imperfections of everyday organizational life. Program sessions cover such issues as . . . how to cope with your boss. . . . Private counseling sessions reveal considerable concern with family issues. . . . Each participant develops a six months' development plan. Then there is a follow-up contact six months later asking, "Where are you?" and "What were the problems in following through?" [8]

Often spouses take part in such programs, since their interests are also critically involved.

Care should be taken to insure that counseling programs do not lead to unrealistic aspirations. Counselors may encourage managers to set personal goals they are unlikely to attain. To avoid this problem, it may be useful to schedule career counseling programs just after assessment centers. The assessment center provides information about the manager's promotional potential; the career planning program helps them evaluate the meaning of this information for their lives.

Broadening the range of options. Open career systems allow managers to make major changes in their career directions. This may involve a change of occupation, a change of employer, or both. A secretary may move into management, or a manager may change companies. Education, of course, increases options, and many companies now reimburse employees for at least part of the tuition costs for courses taken after work. (About 100,000 students are now enrolled in evening MBA courses; many of these students already hold junior management positions.) Furthermore, it is becoming increasingly common for employees to be given unpaid (and even partly paid) leaves of

---

[7] The counselors may be either members of the organization's personnel department or outside consultants.

[8] Hall, *Careers in Organizations,* p. 168.

absence to do public service work for the community, to study full-time, or even to sample a new occupation.

Why should a company subsidize programs that may encourage its managers to go to work for another organization? Presumably, most managers won't change jobs. Either they return to their present position with new skills and broadened horizons (or simply with just more realistic views about their prospects), or they find a new line of work with their present employer. But even if they change employers altogether, it may be better for the company for such managers to quit early than to remain indefinitely on jobs for which they are not suited and on which the are likely to become unhappy and unproductive.

Overseas assignments. The equivalent of realistic job preview and career counseling is especially important for managers (and their spouses) who are considering overseas assignments. Sending a manager overseas is always expensive for the organization; it also involves a major commitment for the manager. But managers frequently adjust poorly to foreign assignments, and many insist on returning home early. Too often managers and their families are shipped overseas with limited knowledge about the living conditions and the psychological demands they will face in the country to which they are sent. Often, too, managers ask for overseas assignments for the wrong reasons. Perhaps they are poorly adjusted at home, or perhaps they have unrealistic expectations as to the promotional opportunities overseas assignments provide. Careful career planning is especially important here, and overseas counseling programs (which may include introducing managers to families who have just returned from the proposed overseas post) are being adopted by many large companies.

Managerial career stages

Regardless of whether there is self-directed or traditional career planning, most managers go through three career stages: an initiation period, a period of upward mobility, and a period of peaking and plateauing. Each of these periods presents problems for the individual manager and for the organization as a whole. In the sections that follow, we shall look at these problems and at developmental programs designed to deal with them.

Initiation period

As we have mentioned, the manager's first year is critical for his ensuing career. Experiences at this stage will shape his future attitudes and behavior.

Discontent and turnover. Large organizations make strenuous efforts to hire new college graduates, believing (correctly in our opinion) that a continual inflow of talented manpower is essential for organizational success. Typically, however, 50 percent of these graduates leave their jobs in the first five years, and those who leave are, on the average, every bit as good as those who stay. In part, high turnover results from a clash between what new graduates expect and what jobs actually offer them. The typical graduate expects his first job to be challenging and meaningful. (Often these unrealistic expectations are encouraged by company recruiters' lavish promises.) People who hold MBAs especially want to use the skills they developed in class. The organization, however, may assign tasks to a new employee

that are so trivial as to carry the clear message that the new man is not worthy of doing anything important, or in contrast, assignments require such specific and specialized knowledge that failure is inevitable, proving to the new man that "he really isn't so smart after all." Both strategies seem purposely designed to threaten the self-esteem of the newly hired college graduate.[9]

Why do organizations make such an all-out effort to hire talented new graduates, and then put them through such a disillusioning experience? In part, this is a normal clash between generations. Older managers understandably feel threatened by brash youngsters who are better educated than they. Such unfamiliar phrases as "stochastic variables," which younger managers once used to impress their professors, may win only antagonism on the job. Further, young people have different values, life styles, and modes of dress. From the point of view of their elders, they are insufficiently subservient. Instead, they may seek to introduce the advanced techniques they learned in school and even ask that the organization subscribe to their own values (about environmental ethics, for example).

Misuse of recent graduates is in part a result of poor planning. The number of challenging jobs that neophyte managers can handle is limited, and many organizations hire more young managers than they have meaningful jobs for, because they expect (quite rightly) that a high percent will quit. In some cases, stockpiling of managers, especially of young MBAs, is a matter of prestige—some organizations believe that hiring many MBAs is itself a sign of progressive management.

But more than a generation clash and poor planning is involved. In many organizations, the beginning of a new manager's career serves much the same purpose as a fraternity or sorority initiation or boot camp. In a sense, the initiation process "unfreezes" the manager (see p. 345). Those who survive the painful process of *organizational socialization* become indoctrinated with organizational values, just as those who survive Marine boot training identify more closely with the Marines.

But the trouble is that a high percentage of young managers fail to survive. When the turnover rate passes 50 percent, it is obvious that the initiation is not working effectively. This is especially true because the net result may be to create conformist "organization types" among those who stay and to lose the more innovative independents.

Executive training programs. Most organizations know that newly hired graduates need a smooth introduction into management, and a number of companies have established special training programs. The programs, which may last from six weeks to more than a year, provide a general orientation

[9] Marvin Dunnette, Richard Avery, and Paul Banas, "Why Do They Leave?" *Personnel*, 50, No. 3 (May 1973), p. 32.

to the company and its policies. They also allow present management to observe and evaluate trainees.

Typically, trainees are rotated from one department to another every few weeks or months. Often, on-the-job training is interspersed with classes. Every month or two, the trainees are evaluated by their supervisor of the moment and by the overall program coordinator. At the end of the formal training period, each trainee is assigned to the department to which he or she seems best suited.

Such programs are designed to provide recent college graduates with an easy transition from the campus to the very different atmosphere of business. Further, they give them a breadth of experience and insight that they would never obtain were they to stay in a single department. Indeed, the whole process is designed to help the trainee and the company pick the job for which the trainee is best qualified.

In practice, however, these programs have serious limitations. Trainees are never evaluated under natural conditions; everyone knows that they are special individuals and treats them accordingly. The "experience" of the trainee in any one department often consists of little more than superficial observation. Their trivial assignments make little use of their college training. Sometimes young managers are put to work on the production floor. Of course, many higher level managers believe that everyone who is to act as a supervisor of rank-and-file workers should have some experience in production. On the other hand, as we have seen, young college graduates find this kind of "Mickey Mouse" work frustrating.

Because of these problems, personnel people are becoming increasingly convinced that at the beginning of a young executive's career a challenging job is more important than breadth of experience. Such companies as AT&T, Procter and Gamble, and Ford have experimented with giving prospective managers challenging assignments at the very outset—problems that will test their ingenuity, but presumably not be beyond their capacity to solve. Typically, such assignments concern operating activities and, after a year or so, require leading a work team. These assignments are difficult enough for a significant proportion of trainees to fail (sometimes as many as one in five are terminated in the first year). Early evidence suggests that for those who succeed, however, the experience is well worthwhile.

On the other hand, challenging assignments for inexperienced managers may be hard to develop. Much depends upon the boss to whom the trainee is assigned, particularly on whether he or she is aware of the problems new managers face and sympathetic to the trainee's life style and aspirations (rather than fearful of a potential rival). In some companies, managers who work with such trainees are specially selected and trained and no manager allowed to supervise more than one trainee.

Upward movement   Once past the initiation period, how are lower-level managers trained for higher positions? A number of programs offer "guided" experience that helps prepare the maturing manager for promotion. We shall discuss three of these: understudies, rotation, and special broadening assignments.

Understudies.   In some organizations before an executive can be moved to a higher position, he or she is required to train a replacement. The understudy program is the least ambitious management development and requires the least centralized control. Modest as it is, however, it raises many questions. Should the selection be made by the boss or by some central management development committee? Should there be one understudy or several? If there is only one, those who have not been chosen may give up hope. If there are several, they may become rivals.

Understudy programs provide a strong incentive for the boss to train successors. On the other hand, if the successor is merely a carbon copy of the boss, there is little chance that he will introduce innovative ideas. Further, with an understudy program no one can move up until the boss dies, retires, quits, or is promoted; consequently, in departments with many good subordinate managers, some talent is bound to be wasted.

Systematic rotation.   As we have suggested, one striking characteristic of successful managers is their rapid mobility. They move frequently from job to job and city to city. Some of these movements involve promotions; others, lateral transfers at the same level. In any case, "zigzag mobility," not straight upward progression, seems to be the typical path to success.

Many organizations have planned rotation programs that make extensive use of replacement charts. Who is to be moved, where, and when, is decided on a coordinated, organizationwide basis. In other organizations, rotation is unplanned, but movement is regarded as a sign of progress; to stay frozen on one job for too long signifies failure. Rarely is anyone *forced* to move; but those who decline the opportunity for transfer know that their chances for future advancement are severely limited.

Planned or unplanned, rotation is expensive. Besides the organization's out-of-pocket expenses for administering the program and defaying the costs of moving managers from one location to another (often exceeding $25,000 per move), there is a substantial loss in executive time when a manager gives up an old job and sets about learning a new one. Why, then, are so many organizations willing to undergo this expense?

1. A systematic rotation program develops not specialists but generalists—managers who can take a broad, companywide point of view, managers whose chief abilities are handling people and making decisions.

2. Rotation helps indoctrinate employees with common perspectives. As one manager said, "There is a company way of doing things, and by moving people around we make sure that even people in the boondocks know it. By shaking people up we get more homogeneous in our viewpoint. We understand each other better, and in emergencies we can predict how people in other divisions react." [10]

[10] Multinational firms in particular view intercountry transfers as a means for passing technological and administrative skills through the organization.

3. Rotation provides variety and challenge. The manager who is transferred faces a whole new set of problems and is less likely to get stale.

4. The outsider often brings new ideas and fresh points of view. Having no vested interest in the old ways of doing things, he or she can make changes quickly. In contrast, a manager who has been in the department for many years has personal ties and must always be careful not to step on friends' toes.

5. Because rotation makes it possible to compare one person against another, it tends to give everyone an equal chance. Rotation provides visibility and gives a manager a chance to make a good showing in the line of work for which he is suited best. Also it protects him from being frozen in a job merely because his department is expanding less rapidly than others. Further, it reduces the chance that his advancement will be stymied because of personality differences with his boss.

6. Rotation fosters organizational flexibility. If one line of work suddenly expands, there always will be a number of people around who have had some experience with it.

Problems with rotation. In spite of the obvious advantages of rotation as a program of management development, it does give rise to certain problems.

1. Rotation often means that the manager must pull up stakes and move to a new location. Beyond the time and emotional strain involved in packing, unpacking, and finding a new house, constant movement makes it difficult for managers to develop roots, and it disrupts their ties with relatives and friends. This is particularly hard on children. Sooner or later, of course, most people who are obliged to move around a good bit learn to adjust. They learn not to make friendships and not to become closely involved in community affairs. By ruthlessly rooting out other ties, rotation may develop the Organization Man or Woman who identifies only with the company for which he or she works—hardly a well-balanced individual.

When rotation involves moving from one community to another, it greatly strains marriages in which both spouses work. Unless they can arrange to be transferred to the same community at the same time, one spouse must leave his or her job or do a great deal of commuting.

Many outstanding managers have refused to continue in the "rat race." Fully aware that refusing a transfer may kill all chance of further advancement, they insist on staying put (this is particularly the case when a transfer may involve a move from a relatively desirable community to one that is less desirable). Clearly, managerial abilities are misused when top managers are picked on the basis of their willingness to rotate rather than their capability.

2. Just as moving around discourages the executive from undertaking long-range projects at home, so it makes him reluctant to take a long-range approach to his job. The manager who knows that he will be transferred in a year's time will concentrate on short-range projects with quick payoff—immediate cost reduction, perhaps, rather than personnel development. He knows that he will have none of the satisfaction of completing long-range projects and that when they are completed, the credit will go to his successor. Understandably, he is tempted to make changes which *look* good, since there is rarely time to test how they work out in practice.

3. Rotation means that managers spend a large part of their time learning the job. Since one purpose of rotation is training, new managers are assigned to the job not because they are the best person for it (the best person may be an underling with years of experience in the department), but because the job provides training. But it may take the new manager months or years to learn the technological and social geography of his department. Often, just after the department and the manager become accustomed to each other's idiosyncracies the manager is transferred, someone new comes in, and there is confusion once more.

4. Rotation sometimes leads to subtle class distinctions. Individuals who are not rotated tend to develop defensive reactions and identify with their own department against "carpetbaggers" from without. This cleavage leads to misunderstanding and poor communications; top management exerts pressure to get the local "stick-in-the-muds" to accept change, and local people unite to resist every effort. "Bosses come and go," a long-service clerk put it. "Each one has his pet peeves. We pretend to go along; but to tell the truth we run things our own way." Thus, changing managers rapidly may in fact inhibit change!

5. Although rotation provides managers a broader range of experiences, it does so at the cost of reducing their chances of being an expert in any one field.

6. The rotation system may easily become overcentralized, inflexible, and "closed." The division manager, for instance, may have little to say about who is moved into his division and may be forced to accept as an assistant someone he or she has never seen before. A manager who is promoted under these circumstances is less likely to show loyalty to his boss than he would if the boss had been personally responsible for the promotion.

Clearly, rotation has both advantages and disadvantages. Some managers find it challenging and exciting. Others find it frustrating for both themselves and their families. Some departments benefit from being shaken up by outsiders; others suffer in morale and efficiency in the hands of an outside manager unfamiliar with the special technical and human problems of the situation. Given increasing resistance on the part of managers (and their spouses) to being moved, rotation, especially between communities, is declining as a form of management development.

Special broadening assignments. Although rotation gives trainees broad experience, this experience is at a relatively low level. Yet different kinds of skills are required at various organizational levels. At the lower levels perhaps technical ability, a willingness to obey orders, and skill in dealing with people are the chief requirements. At higher levels the ability to innovate and to make bold, long-range decisions becomes more important. Managers who do outstanding jobs at lower or middle levels may be totally ineffective at the top; on the other hand, the brilliant innovator might seem very inadequate in a subordinate post.

Since, at the lower levels, getting ahead depends on the recommendations of one's immediate boss, some managers get no chance to advance because the boss is too unimaginative to appreciate their abilities (or even feels threatened by them). Under these circumstances the easy-going conformist may be favored over the sometimes abrasive idea-generator. In addition, outstanding managers sometimes lose their spark as they slowly work their way upward.

To distinguish individuals who are outstandingly qualified for high positions, some organizations give their promising junior executives special assignments that permit them to sample top-level responsibilities. The nature of the assignments in this form of vestibule training varies greatly. Normally assignments are devised on a temporary or part-time basis (in "open systems" the manager is consulted about his choice of experiences). Some organizations have "junior boards of directors" to which the senior board of directors may refer special problems. More frequently, trainees are assigned to capital budgeting, product development, or long-range planning committees where they work in the company of more senior executives. At times a trainee may be assigned to study a problem, prepare recommendations, and present and defend them in person before a top-management committee. Or he may be assigned to work as a personal assistant to a member of top management.

For special assignments to be successful as development tools, they must meet several requirements:

- The problems assigned must be genuinely broadening; that is, they must cut across departmental lines and involve long-range planning.
- The trainee must operate under the direct observation of top executives who are personally responsible for evaluating the trainee's performance.
- The problems must be *tough*, challenging ones—tough enough for the really outstanding solution to be distinguished from the merely adequate one.

Special assignments permit junior managers to be observed and evaluated by a group of top executives, thus reducing their dependence on a single boss. Juniors are judged on their ability to handle a top-level job, not just skill in coping with lower-level jobs. Further, the program may bring a wealth of useful suggestions to top management, as well as provide the junior manager with invaluable experience.

Each of the three forms of career development has its special merits. An understudy program is well designed to provide a successor for a particular manager. Rotation, despite its drawbacks, does develop well-rounded, organizationally oriented managers. Special broadening assignments seem best adopted to fast-track executives on their way to the executive suite.

Eventually everyone reaches one's peak, even the chairman of the board. For a high proportion of managers, this occurs by age 45. For a high proportion, too, the peak occurs at relatively low levels of management. In some circumstances, peaking out means merely that managers stay on their present level indefinitely; they "plateau." In other circumstances, they move laterally from positions typically reserved for those still upward bound, or they are demoted or fired.

Movement is so accepted in many organizations that managers may be transferred from one job to another without knowing they have reached their peak or actually been demoted. The fact that a manager has peaked is cloaked with an ambiguity which helps save face, cushion shock, avoid nasty scenes, and preserve the manager's remaining productivity. One means to camouflage a manager's demotion is to "kick him upstairs" (give him a title like "special assistant to the division manager" or to place him on a "long-range planning assignment"). Alternatively, the responsibilities of his job may be discretely cut back, or he or she may be passed up for a raise when salaries are increasing generally.

The fact that a manager has plateaued need not mean that he is performing unsatisfactorily on his *present* job. Quite the contrary. The job and the manager may be nicely matched, and many plateaued managers have little desire for added responsibility. Nevertheless, there is always the danger that after years on the same job the manager's motivation and performance will begin to decline, and he will suffer from obsolescence. To counteract these tendencies, broadening assignments and training programs may be useful. Often a manager who has become stale in one line of work may perk up when transferred to something completely new and thus, in effect, enjoy a second career in the same organization.

One of the dangers of long-range planning is that it may separate fast-track from slow-track employees too soon, with the result that a person who is stigmatized as slow-track may never have a second chance. Someone labeled as "slow track" may be merely a slow starter or he may have received job assignments that prevent him from showing his true strength. Here too a change in job assignments may help revive a faltering career.

There is much that an organization can do to reduce the feeling that a manager is a failure merely because he or she has stopped advancing. A regular program of appraisal interviews (see our next chapter) may help him achieve a realistic attitude toward his prospects and give him a clearer indication of where he stands. Such interviews tend to counteract overoptimism and help the manager accept adverse decisions and still maintain normal self-respect. If salary schedules make allowance for years of service, the manager who has been bypassed can still look forward to increased earnings.

Aside from managers who are likely to stay at the same level, there are others who have been promoted into jobs with responsibilities beyond their level of competence or who have declined in ability because of age. In such cases, demotion or discharge may be desirable. In organizations where there is a heavy stress on rapid advancement, it is something of a disgrace to be passed up for promotion and a much harder blow to be demoted. In such organizations elaborate camouflages may be necessary. In other organizations, however, downward movement carries no overtone of failure. Academic department heads, for example, typically serve a fixed term and then are delighted to return to full-time teaching. In industry, demotion can be less damaging if it is not accompanied by a pay cut. With open system personnel policies, managers sometimes voluntarily transfer to lower pressure jobs, which permit more hours at home.

Occasionally an organization may decide that discharge or involuntary retirement is the only answer. This is never an easy solution, and the passage of the Age Discrimination in Employment Act has made it more difficult. The employer now has to bear the burden of showing that the grounds for termination were incompetence rather than age. Here, too, performance appraisal will help prepare the subordinate for the eventual decision and also strengthen management's case if the matter gets to court.[11]

In short, career planning is generally concerned with the initiation and upward movement periods of a manager's career. Yet the plateau may involve more years of the manager's life, and it requires just as much sensitive attention as do earlier periods.

Development as a management responsibility

The emphasis in this chapter has been on formal programs that expose managers to a variety of problems. These programs differ in the level at which exposure occurs and the degree of challenge each exposure provides. But exposure alone does not guarantee learning.

As we have seen, having a sympathetic superior or sponsor, especially in the first year on the job, can be critical for a young manager's future career. True, superiors can't develop subordinates; they must develop themselves. Nevertheless, superiors can provide the atmosphere in which subordinates can experiment or grow, or they can stifle any attempt to self-development. For a development program to be effective, every manager must assume personal responsibility (1) for providing immediate subordinates with challenging responsibilities and effective counseling and (2) for insisting that these subordinates in turn contribute to the development of those under them.

Thus we may ask: What importance does management place on development? Are managers ever rewarded for doing an outstanding job of training subordinates? Or do the chief rewards also go to the manager who keeps immediate costs low and gets production out? Often managers learn that their only reward for training a subordinate is to have him leave and be replaced by someone with less experience. Knowing that a good subordinate is hard to find, the manager is tempted to recommend poorer subordinates for special training programs to get rid of them. Too often, units that do a good job of training find themselves raided by other units.

What should be the role of the personnel department? It should act as a staff agency to which both boss and subordinate can turn for assistance in career development activities. It can monitor formal programs. It can train

[11] Outplacement services (Chap. 8) help ease the pain which accompanies termination.

superiors to be better counselors and coaches, and it can help subordinates think through their career alternatives.

Conclusion

Management career planning programs are rapidly changing. The emphasis in the past was on the fast-track executive, whose sole motivation was to move to the top as fast as possible. Assuming that all managers would (or should) put their company's interests first, few organizations exerted much effort to determine their managers' preferences.

Today career planning is viewed as a joint responsibility, involving not just the manager and the employing organization, but also the manager's family. Instead of just one career ladder—going straight up, with perhaps a minor zigzag—consideration is being given to a variety of alternative career patterns. It is increasingly recognized that managers need not become stale or obsolete just because their progress upwards has slowed. Lateral or even downwards movement can stimulate ailing careers. More and more, individuals may have two or more careers throughout their lives, and these careers may occur in one or several organizations. Regardless of whether we consider the bright young manager just out of school or the older manager who has been years on the same job, the emphasis is on challenge and change to facilitate growth.

Organizations themselves are changing. Aside from recessions and secular declines, both of which reduce promotional opportunities, there are long-run changes in the types of managers needed (today, for example, there is a big demand for environmental specialists). These changes make it much harder (but also more important) to predict future demands for managerial manpower. All this suggests that development programs must be flexible. Clearly, it is desirable to have an orderly system that gives everyone an equal opportunity (dependent on real ability) for training, experience, and consideration for promotion. But an over-orderly or rigid rotation or promotional system can put the organization in a straightjacket and almost eliminate individual choice.

Indeed, as time goes by, organizational career planning may become harder. As people demand more freedom it will be more difficult to integrate individual demands with organizational needs. More than formal programs will be required. Instead, we will need a creative atmosphere in which individual managers are encouraged to contribute suggestions, to make decisions on their own, and to take risks. In a collaborate environment, rigid status differences are deemphasized, and being promoted becomes less important.

Both boss-subordinate relations and the overall organizational climate are crucial for individual development. The aspiring manager needs feedback about his or her growth, and the organization as a whole needs to deal with barriers that inhibit managerial creativity. We consider these problems in our next two chapters, which deal with performance appraisal and organization development.

1 • *Bemus Company*

The Bemus Company was founded in the basement of its president, Andrew Bemus, about ten years ago. Mr. Bemus had developed a highly sensitive instrument, which immediately found use in defense and civilian production fields. As a consequence, the firm grew very rapidly. It had 7 employees 9 years ago, 200 employees 5 years ago, and over 1,000 today.

As of today, most of the company's top management consists of Mr. Bemus' earliest associates, many of whom are under the age of 45. They are a highly self-confident group who have worked together closely over the years.

And yet trouble seems to lie ahead. Sharp competition from other companies has developed for the first time, and profit margins have fallen. Labor costs are obviously too high, and there is much confusion and divided responsibility in management. Most decisions are made by the top-management group and there is little delegation of authority. Many of the more recently hired engineers complain that their ideas are given very little consideration by the inner clique and that there is little or no chance for promotion, since all the top jobs are handled by younger men. As a consequence, three of the more brilliant recent hires have resigned after spending only a short time with the company.

1. What sort of management development program does this company need?
2. Assuming that you were recently hired from the outside as personnel director, what steps would you take to win acceptance for this program?

2 • *Which Responsibility Is More Important?*

Cato has known Cohen ever since she came to work 10 years ago. Her promotion progress has been excellent, and she now heads a large department. She has just been asked to assume the divisional presidency for graphic arts. Cato, as part of senior management, knows that the corporation is worried about that division and intends to sell it unless its profitability is restored within a year— a very short time. If Cohen stays in her present promotion line, she would not get a crack at a divisional presidency for several more years. However, if graphic arts goes under, her career chances will be injured both because she will no longer be in the division that knows and likes her work and because, inevitability, those heading a failing operation get some of the blame.

The president of the corporation has told Cato of his plans in confidence. He is reluctant to publicize this information, for fear good people in that division will leave, and no promising manager may be willing to assume the divisional presidency with such a "short fuse."

1. Advise Cato what to do to fulfill his responsibilities.

3 • *A Quick Change*

Trout has been groomed for his presidency for the past eight years, taking on every tough assignment. It was his job, and he knew it; but just as it became available, the board of directors had a change of heart. The company was now so committed to expanding its international operations that it needed someone with lots of experience in that phase. Trout had none! An executive search firm was retained, and in 3 months an outsider had the job.

1. Do you think there is any way to save Trout for this company?
2. Explain how you would try, on the assumption that he is an outstanding executive and much needed.

performance appraisal and management by objectives

In the typical large organization, every manager is subject to a periodic performance appraisal. As is true of other aspects of management development, the primary purpose of these appraisals has shifted in recent years. Originally a device to provide guidance to management in selecting managers for promotion or salary increases, appraisals are now also used for coaching managers to improve their performance.

An effective performance-appraisal program provides management with a rational basis for determining who should be promoted or receive salary increases. It permits each manager to be considered on the same basis as everyone else. Thus, hopefully, fewer charges of favoritism are made and better managers are selected for promotion. Long-range personnel planning (and the use of replacement charts) are also facilitated, since management can determine who should be promoted now, who should be ready after further experience and training, and who, although satisfactory on the present job, is not a likely prospect for a more difficult one. Further, management can tailor transfers to meet individual needs, and it can identify managers who need special training. Finally, as we saw in Chapter 9, performance appraisal is often needed to provide criteria for validating selection procedures or to defend against charges of discrimination.

Performance appraisal can also be used as a springboard for coaching managers and for helping them set goals for their own development. Unfortunately, the procedures that are most useful for selection purposes are less useful for self-development. As a consequence, many organizations have abandoned their *traditional* procedures, in which employees' traits were rated by their bosses, for newer less biased methods. Some organizations have abandoned ratings as such in favor of Management By Objectives (MBO) which typically involves the setting of goals by superiors and subordinates working together. Although MBO is also an important planning tool (and should not be mistakenly viewed as merely another form of performance evaluation), traditional performance evaluation and MBO are sufficiently linked together for us to consider them in the same chapter.

We shall look first at traditional performance appraisal and then at MBO. Before doing this, let us point out that performance appraisal is often conducted at the hourly-paid (especially among clerical workers) as well as the management level; for hourly-paid workers it is often called "merit rating" (see pp. 387–90). Further, performance appraisal is common for professional and technical employees.

Traditional performance rating

Stripped to its essentials, traditional performance rating is a matter of filling out a form (see illustration, p. 327). Normally the form is filled out by the manager's immediate supervisor and then checked by the supervisor's boss. Sometimes the rating is done by a committee:

RCA tries to minimize subjectivity by having each RCA manager rated by a group of fellow workers, generally including his immediate superior, two or three higher level managers, two or three peers, and one or two workers in lower positions.[1]

Occasionally the rating committee may also include "customers" of the individual being rated. (A maintenance manager might be rated by the production managers he or she serves.) Committee ratings have two great advantages. First, since each rater sees the person being rated from a different vantage point, the overall appraisal may be more balanced. Second, since a number of people participate, there may be greater feeling that the rating process is fair.[2]

Rating scales

A conventional rating form of the check-the-box type is sometimes called a "graphic rating" or a "rating scale." The important part here is the overall summary rating or score, which makes it possible to compare large numbers of managers. The ratings on specific factors do serve a purpose, however, in helping to pinpoint areas in which a subordinate needs further development.

In one variety of rating scale, the overall score is determined by adding up the scores given to specific factors (note the score is 35 in the form illustrated). In spite of its deceptive simplicity, this approach has severe limita-

[1] *The Wall Street Journal,* May 23, 1978.

[2] Some evidence suggests that in making ratings, the factors that peers emphasize are different from those their bosses do, and peers tend to be more lenient.

Name *Wilson Olcott* Position *Asst. Director, Mktg. Research* Date rated *6/25/19--*

Date hired *April 12, 19--* On position since *August 8, 19--*

	Unsatisfactory	Fair	Good	Very good	Exceptional	
Job knowledge: Extent of theoretical knowledge and practical know how as related to present job.	1	2	3	4	⑤	*5*
Judgment: Ability to obtain and analyze facts and apply sound judgment.	1	2	3	④	5	*4*
Organizing ability: Effectiveness in planning own work and that of subordinates.	1	2	③	4	5	*3*
Attitude: Enthusiasm shown for job; loyalty to company and superiors; ability to accept criticism and changes in company policy.	1	2	③	4	5	*3*
Dependability: Reliability in carrying out assignments conscientiously and with effectiveness.	1	2	3	④	5	*4*
Creativity: Ability to apply imagination to job, to develop new plans, cut costs, etc.	1	2	3	4	⑤	*5*
Dealing with people: Ability to get along with others; tact, diplomacy; ability to command and influence people.	1	②	3	4	5	*2*
Delegation: Ability to assign work to others and coordinate others though distribution of workload and responsibility.	1	2	③	4	5	*3*
Leadership: Ability to stimulate subordinates to perform their jobs effectively.	1	②	3	4	5	*2*
Personal efficiency: Speed and effectiveness in carrying out duties not assigned to subordinates.	1	2	3	④	5	*4*

Total points *35*

Evaluated by *Burt Neufane*

Title *Director Mktg. Research*

Approved by *Gerry Falconner*

Title *Mktg. Manager*

Unsatisfactory: 10–15
Fair: 16–25 points
Good: 26-35 points
Very good: 36-45 points
Excellent: 46-50 points

tions. Consider some of the basic assumptions lying behind it: one is that each of the factors (creativity, judgment, and so forth) is of *equal* importance and that this holds true on all jobs. Yet clearly, on some jobs creativity is more important than effectiveness in dealing with people, and on others just the reverse is true. Another assumption is that these qualities are "additive"— for instance, strength in job knowledge will offset lack of leadership.

Unwilling to accept these assumptions, some companies permit their managers to give their subordinates an overall rating directly, without adding up separate factor scores. This summary rating of overall ability may be given either in numerical terms, from one to 100, or in descriptive terms, from "unsatisfactory" to "outstanding."

Both forms of ratings are often supplemented by open-ended, essay-type questions. At times the essay portion of the evaluation form takes considerably more space than does the quantitative portion. These subjective, qualitative evaluations tend to give a fuller picture than is presented by numerical ratings alone. They are also more useful for coaching, but they are of little help in comparing large numbers of people for purposes of pay increases or promotion.

Both forms of numerical ratings are subject to certain human evaluative errors. (Incidentally, these same errors distort merit rating and job evaluation, to which we will return in Chapter 17.)

Ambiguity.   Factors need to be described clearly, so that all raters have the same sort of behavior in mind. Further, unless all raters agree on what such terms as "good" and "excellent" mean, their final ratings simply cannot be compared.

Insufficient evidence.   The boss frequently gets a limited and often a distorted view of the subordinate's performance. Particularly in jobs for which actual results are difficult to measure, the subordinate's ability to get along with the boss may have a greater impact on his or her rating than does actual performance on the job. The less contact the rater has with the ratee or the less knowledge the rater has of the ratee's job, the less useful the rating. Rating committees naturally help reduce this problem.

Differing perceptions.   People differ in their standards of judgment. Even when they have no conscious prejudice, raters tend to rate subordinates similar to themselves in background, values, and style of behavior higher than they rate subordinates with dissimilar life styles (the "similar-to-me" effect). More than such obvious factors as racial discrimination are involved here. The manager who is accustomed to making quick decisions may be antagonized by the person who moves ponderously and deliberately, and vice versa. Sometimes executives who are poor managers themselves evaluate the competence of better qualified subordinates. (There is evidence that better managers also make better raters.)

Excessive leniency or strictness.   As every student knows, there is a big difference between hard and easy graders. In industry, some raters rate everybody high, others are very strict, and still others play it safe by sticking to the middle. Ratings tend to be higher if the manager knows they will be revealed to subordinates. Managers often hesitate to give low ratings for fear of antagonizing their subordinates and making them less cooperative. Furthermore, supervisors fear that low ratings will reflect on their own abilities. There is always the chance that their boss will say, "If your subordinate is as bad as all this, why didn't you do something about it?" Some executives regularly rate new employees very low, then gradually raise them—thus making the employee feel good and displaying to their superiors their skill as trainers.

In many organizations there is a tendency for ratings to rise over time. During World War II nearly every soldier got the highest rating. To get the next-to-highest rating was evidence of downright incompetence.

These problems become less serious when top management stresses the importance of a wide rating spread and raises questions whenever ratings cluster at one level.

The halo effect.   There is a natural tendency for raters to be influenced in rating one factor by the ratings they give on another. If a manager has a general impression that a subordinate is good, he will rate him high on all factors—and vice versa. Or his rating on the first factor listed or on the factor he thinks most important may contaminate his ratings on all others. (One way to reduce the halo effect is to rate all the subordinates on a single item before going on to the next, rather than rating one subordinate at a time.)

Influence of the job.   Performance rating is designed to evaluate how well an individual does on a particular job. Although in theory performance rating is vastly different from job evaluation (which rates the job, not the manager) in practice it is common to give managers on higher-paid jobs higher ratings just because of their position.

Recency.   Finally, raters tend to give recent events greater weight than those occurring at the beginning of the rating period.

All these human errors in rating can be at least partially counteracted by ensuring that the managers who do the rating are properly trained.

Traits or performance?

A more fundamental criticism of the traditional rating scale is that it places excessive emphasis on personality traits as opposed to measurable objective performance. Management development was originally introduced into many companies as a crash program designed to reveal executives who were promotable to top positions. Actual performance on the job was often considered secondary, in part because the emphasis was all on *potential* for development.

In any event, many organizations ask raters to evaluate subordinates on such factors as optimism, drive, and ability to learn. The armed services, for example, have asked for ratings of such qualities as "initiative," "force," "moral courage," and "loyalty."

What has proved wrong with this emphasis on traits? In the first place, the ratings are of little use in helping employees do a better job. It is hard for people to make real changes in their "personality," though they may put up a false front and pretend to be, in the words of one form, "radiant, confident, cheerful, courteous."

In trait rating, standards are often unclear. Exactly what is "loyalty," and how does one differentiate among various degrees of loyalty on a five-point scale? Not only is it difficult to get agreement as to what these factors mean, but their use in evaluations is particularly subject to personal or racial bias. When appraisals are used to determine who gets salary increases or promotions, they become "selection devices" and thus subject to the equal employment guidelines.[3] Courts have been particularly suspicious of appraisal systems that use such vague and subjective factors as "loyalty" and "capacity for growth."

Trait-rating shares with some of personality testing the assumption that there is one psychological conformation that makes the best executive. Yet jobs differ in their psychological requirements: Sales managers may require more aggressiveness than do laboratory managers.[4] And even where jobs are alike, people with vastly different personalities may perform equally well. Frequently, the emphasis on traits gives the advantage to the conformist who never rubs anyone the wrong way but also never has original ideas. One large company offered the following choices for the single trait, "cooperation."

1. Concedes nothing. Obstructive, antagonistic.

2. Poor mixer. Tries to run with the ball. Occasionally indulges in obstructive argument.

3. Generally adapts self to person and situations. Responsive to leadership and reasonably tactful.

4. Willing and eager to please. Works in complete harmony with group. Adaptable and courteous.

5. Adapts self very well without sacrificing standards. Goes out of his way to promote common end.

Note by favoring the manager who is "willing and able to please" over the one who "tries to run with the ball," this company is giving first priority to good human relations as opposed to decisive decision making. Yet those at the very top are often 100 percent rugged individualists. Howard Hughes would never have gotten passing marks for outgoing personality and Henry Ford, Sr., got along pretty well without too much sense of humor. Most executives are strange combinations of strengths and weaknesses.

Alternate rating methods

Because of these criticisms of traditional rating scales, personnel researchers have tried to develop new rating procedures that are less affected by raters' personal biases and less concerned with such imponderables as traits. Among the best known of these new forms of rating are *forced distribution,* the *critical incidents* technique, and *behaviorally anchored rating scales.*[5]

Forced distribution. Forced distribution is familiar to students as the old principle of "grading on the curve." The manager who uses this system

---

[3] Subjective factors are also suspect when they are used as criteria, for validating tests. See Chapter 11.

[4] One study found that an intense sense of honesty almost guaranteed failure on a particular type of sales job. John C. Miner, "Management Appraisal," in W. Clay Hamner and Frank L. Schmidt, eds., *Contemporary Problems in Personnel,* rev. ed. (Chicago: St. Clair, 1977), p. 233.

[5] For a discussion of a variety of other techniques, including the forced choice or paired comparisons technique, see Lawrence Cummings and Donald Schwab, *Performance in Organizations: Determinants and Appraisals* (Glenview, Ill.: Scott, Foresman, 1973).

of rating is expected to rank subordinates by group, instead of ascribing a set of rating points to each individual. In a typical system, the top 10 percent of the managers are placed in the highest class, 20 percent in the next, 40 percent in the middle bracket, 20 percent in the next-to-lowest, and 10 percent at the very bottom.

This system obviously eliminates the danger that the manager will be overly lenient. Moreover, it is easy to explain and administer. Yet this scheme has distinct drawbacks: In effect, it assumes that all groups have the same proportion of average, poor, and outstanding managers. But this is not likely to be true, particularly when there are only a few managers in a given group. Forced distribution is greatly resented by both bosses and subordinates. That is why the armed forces, which had experimented with this approach after World War II, later abandoned it.

Critical incidents. The critical incident technique of rating is also known as the "critical requirement system" and the "performance-record program."

The first step is to draw up for each job a list of *critical job requirements.* For a foreman, for instance, these requirements might include "improving equipment," "getting along with staff," "meeting schedules," and so forth. Typical job requirements for a sales manager might be "developing new customers" and "avoiding losses."

Once the critical job requirements have been determined, the next step is to train managers to be on the lookout for *critical incidents* or outstanding examples of the subordinate's success or failure in meeting the requirements. The manager lists the incidents as he or she observes them and gradually builds up a record for each subordinate, with the "debits" on one side and the "credits" on the other:

Dealing with Unions

9/21 Failed to consult with steward before making transfer.	8/6 Persuaded steward to withdraw grievance in regard to employee discharged for excessive absenteeism.
11/7 Made transfer in violation of sect. 39 (c) of contract.	12/3 Gave excellent answer to union grievance.

Normally, no attempt is made to balance the "debits" and the "credits." And yet the critical incident method does provide the raw materials for other forms of appraisal.

The great advantage of this approach is that all ratings are based on objective evidence rather than on a subjective evaluation of traits. It is no longer enough for the boss to say, "Joe has trouble dealing with people." The boss can cite specific incidents to prove this contention. To ensure objectivity, the manager is requested to record each incident immediately instead of trying to think back over, say, the last six months before making a rating.

On the other hand, care must be taken to ensure that the manager's recordkeeping does not degenerate into supervision in detail. He should emphasize *what* is accomplished, not *how* it is accomplished. Further, keeping a "little black book" in which mistakes are recorded conflicts with the philosophy that management should not overemphasize blame-finding.

Behaviorally anchored rating scales. This technique involves the development of rating scales, which are custom made for each job. In somewhat simplified form the main steps are:

1. Meetings are held with the managers who will rate the people holding the job in question. These managers are asked to list several key dimensions of proficiency on the job. (For example, a rating scale developed for college professors included such dimensions as Depth of Knowledge, Interpersonal Relations with Students, and Ability to Motivate.)[6]

2. The same or a different group provides examples of good, average, and poor performance for each dimension. (For a professor's Interpersonal Relations with Students, an example of good performance might be "When a class doesn't understand a concept, this professor could be expected to sense it and act to correct the situation," while an example of average performance might be "During lectures this professor could be expected to tell students with questions to see him during his office hours.")

3. A number of such *behaviors* are generated and each is given a value ranging from 1 (very poor behavior) to 7 (outstanding behavior).

4. Once the scale is completed, raters use it to evaluate the *expected* behaviors of each person being rated. Individual rating scores are computed on the basis of each person's typical or expected behavior on each scale.

Behavioral scales have three main advantages. In the first place, those who do the rating can participate in developing the scale and are therefore more likely to understand and use it. Second, since the items are highly specific there is less chance of such errors as ambiguity, excessive leniency, or halo effect. Finally, this technique focuses on behavior (*how* the managers work) rather than traits (their personalities) or performance (how *much* they can put out). Normally, behavior is easier for the manager to change than either personality or performance (particularly since performance may be affected by factors not under the individual manager's control). Thus, behavioral ratings may be particularly useful for coaching or training.

A major disadvantage is the time and cost of developing rating scales for each separate job (although families of jobs may sometimes be combined). Further, since *expected* rather than actually observed behavior is rated, ratees can always deny that in fact they ever behave as the raters say they would. Finally, since this technique emphasizes methods rather than results, it may encourage the manager to overemphasize the specific behaviors rated. (To return to our previous example: to get a high rating a professor in a large class may feel compelled to answer all questions at length, thus leaving little time for the main lecture.)

[6] The example is from Oren Harari and Sheldon Zedeck, "Development of Behaviorally Anchored Scales for the Evaluation of Faculty Teaching," *Journal of Applied Psychology,* 58 (1973), 261–65. See also James G. Goodale, "Behaviorally-based Rating Scales," in Hamner and Schmidt, eds., *Contemporary Problems in Personnel.*

Evaluating these techniques. Each of these techniques has supporters, as do other techniques not discussed here. But no technique has been shown to be uniformly superior to traditional rating scales. Indeed, some argue that training managers to improve their effectiveness in using traditional scales may result in much greater payoff than would equal time spent in developing special techniques.[7] It can be argued that it makes little difference what appraisal system is used, provided the managers involved can understand it.

The evaluation interview

Many organizations require each manager to discuss subordinates' progress with them periodically. Evaluation interviews serve two purposes: (1) they serve as a form of feedback, which helps subordinates evaluate their progress and where they stand in the eyes of their boss, and (2) they provide an opportunity for managers to counsel subordinates on how to improve their performance.

Superiors frequently recoil at the thought of having to tell their subordinates how they stand or what they need to do to improve themselves. Too often managers fool themselves into thinking that their subordinates really know their weaknesses already, and they are often shocked when a subordinate tells them "Since you never complained, I thought I was doing OK." Well-conducted evaluation interviews can reduce such misunderstanding. As one junior executive commented, "Before this evaluation system was installed, the only time the boss would tell you how you were doing was when you were in trouble. If he'd say, 'I'd like to talk about your future,' that meant you were really going to get chewed out."

But evaluation interviews are not easy. Poorly handled they may lead to hostility and even greater misunderstanding. Consequently, many organizations spend considerable effort on training their managers to handle evaluation interviews, giving particular emphasis to listening techniques. To ensure that no essential part of the interview is left out, managers are often encouraged to follow a standardized outline. For example:

1. The superior tells the subordinate the purpose of the interview, that it is designed to help him or her do a better job.

2. The superior presents the evaluation, giving the strong points first, then the weak points, and ending on a positive note. (Sometimes this is called a "sandwich," since the meat—the criticism—is surrounded by blander material.)

3. Next the superior asks for comments. He (or she) anticipates that the subordinate may show some hostility to negative evaluations and allows him to blow off steam. The superior accepts any criticism or aggression on the part of the subordinate and does not expose unjustified excuses.

4. The superior then encourages the subordinate to give his own version of his progress and problems.

5. The interview closes with a discussion of what the subordinate can do to improve his performance in the future and what the superior can do to help.

[7] John Miner, "Management Appraisal."

Some managers start the interview by asking the subordinate, "Tell me, how do *you* think you are doing?" Then they show the subordinate the evaluation. This has the advantage of letting the subordinate tell his or her side of the story first; it is often easier for a person to criticize himself than to accept criticism from others.

Difficulties in conducting evaluation interviews

In recent years many organizations have become discouraged with appraisal programs. The rating period often turns out to be a time of apprehension and discomfort for managers and subordinates alike. Despite the publicity with which appraisal programs are typically introduced, many managers merely go through the motions of conducting interviews; others "forget" about them altogether. It is not uncommon for managers to hand subordinates their ratings without comment or to explain the rating in a rather embarrassed fashion without giving the subordinate a chance to comment or reply.

Why are managers generally so unenthusiastic about the evaluation program? Many have little skill in listening techniques; others, feeling that their primary function is "to get work out," have little interest in taking time from their "main job" to develop subordinates.

Yet even managers who are sympathetic to the principles of management development feel uncomfortable when they have to criticize people they work with on a daily basis. As one manager said, "I dread the time when I have to give ratings. Nobody appreciates them, and I get into an endless series of arguments, which makes it that much tougher to get the work out. People hold a grudge every time I tell the truth."

Subordinates tend to react to performance evaluation with defensiveness, suspicion, and hostility. They hope the boss will recognize their merits but fear that he or she will criticize them unfairly. Since many are primarily concerned with defending themselves, they resist the boss's criticisms and suggestions. In fact, evidence suggests that subordinates tend to rate their own performance higher than do their bosses (and few view themselves as below average); consequently the interview turns out to be a deflating, ego-damaging experience. Criticism may result in lower, not higher performance, particularly in the areas most criticized. Even praise may have an uncertain effect.[8]

Another explanation for the widespread resistance to conventional forms of evaluation interviews lies in two assumptions: (1) people want to be told where they stand, and (2) if they are told their weaknesses, they can change for the better. Neither assumption is universally valid, as the examples at the top of the next page suggest.

Perhaps the trouble here is that interviews serve two purposes. First, they relay the superior's judgments as to the subordinate's performance (judgments with important implications for salary increases and possible promotions), and second, they are designed to help subordinates improve their performances. Some authorities contend that these two objectives—*judgmental* and *developmental*—are so inconsistent that the details of the performance ratings should be kept secret and that performance rating and

[8] For a review of the evidence, see Miner, "Management Appraisal."

A liberal arts college decided to rate faculty members on a scale from 1 (drop from faculty) to 5 (deserves substantial pay increase) and to reveal the results to each faculty member. The rating program was conducted by a joint faculty-student committee. A 65-year-old professor was given a rating of 2 on the grounds that her teaching was getting dull. The professor's grade for a lifetime of devoted service was a D! She was too old to change her ways, and in any case the college had no intention of dropping her a few years before retirement.

Consider a laboratory division head who is technically brilliant but suffers from shyness and insecurity in dealing with people. Would telling him of his failure improve his dealings with people? Of course not. Certainly it wouldn't help him gain self-confidence.

evaluation interviews should be treated as separate processes. Secrecy is desirable, these authorities argue, because except in the hands of an exceptionally skilled interviewer, evaluation interviews focused on actual rating scores are likely to foster more antagonism than understanding. Furthermore, unless ratings are kept confidential they are unlikely to be candid. The evidence suggests that nonsecret ratings tend to be higher than secret ones, and there is reason to fear that managers are unwilling to give low ratings to aggressive employees who are likely to challenge them.

When to use evaluation interviews

There are no simple answers to the questions of whether an evaluation interview will be useful and what sort of interview should be used in a given situation. The choice depends on the subordinate's needs and the superior's skills.[9] The manager should use the form of interview that he or she finds most comfortable. For instance, the superior who tries to use the nondirective interview with no understanding of the approach will simply give the subordinate the impression that he is two-faced, particularly if the nondirective approach is totally inconsistent with his normal pattern of supervision. In any event, the manager should recognize that the objectives of the interview vary from one person to another. For example:

- If the fault is difficult or impossible to correct, there is no point in discussing it at all (unless the subordinate demands to know why he or she hasn't been promoted).

- If managers have faults that are correctable, it may be better to let them bring them up themselves when they see fit. Since evaluation interviews are held periodically, there is no need for supervisors to be disappointed if subordinates don't give a perfect self-analysis during the first session. The important thing is that the subordinates make gradual progress in correcting their limitations if they can and in accepting limitations if they cannot overcome them.

- In some cases individuals' performances may be so poor as to raise the possibility of their being discharged. Under such circumstances it is only fair that they be given warning, even though there is little chance of changing their behavior.

[9] Lawrence Cummings and Donald Schwab, "Designing Appraisal Systems for Information Yield," *California Management Review,* 20, No. 4 (Summer 1978), 18–25.

The appraisal interview is actually a form of coaching. So why formalize the process? After all, good managers recognize that coaching should occur more frequently than once every six months; they hold the equivalent of an evaluation interview whenever they think a subordinate will profit from it. On the other hand, poor managers will probably only go through the motions of a proper evaluation interview (which may do more harm than good) or perhaps ignore it altogether.

Thus, a companywide policy requiring periodic evaluation interviews is most useful for the *average* supervisor, for it forces him to take time off from his duties, to think through how each of his subordinates has been progressing, and then to sit down with each subordinate to talk over their long-range relationships.

Management by objectives

Designed to overcome the limitations of traditional systems, Management by Objectives (MBO), sometimes called results-oriented appraisal or Work Planning and Review, has been widely adopted by many organizations. MBO is based on concrete objectives, which are set jointly by superior and subordinate.[10] Together they establish short-term performance goals, ways the subordinate can improve his efficiency and that of his department (for example, cut idle machine time by 5 percent, reduce scrap by 3 percent, or install a new production line by January 30). At the end of a set period (six months or a year), they meet again to evaluate how well these goals have been met, to discuss what can be done better, and to set new goals for the next year.[11] Thus the subordinate is judged by standards he helped determine.

MBO consists of three important elements: goal setting, participation, and appraisal.

Goal setting. MBO goals should be objective and measurable if possible (reduce scrap by 3 percent); if not, they should at least be specific ("develop understanding of computer techniques among subordinates"). In either case, goals should be realistic but tough—tough enough to make the managers stretch a bit.

Individual goals should be consistent with organizational objectives. If top management plans to increase sales by 15 percent, it is not sufficient for manufacturing to set a goal of increasing production by only 5 percent (on the other hand, MBO may provide the mechanism by which manufacturing may signal top management that the 15 percent goal is unrealistic). Similarly, the goals of various departments should dovetail: it makes little sense for sales to commit to a new computerized credit system by March 1 if systems won't

[10] The concept of MBO was originally proposed by Peter Drucker in *The Practice of Management* (New York: Harper, 1954), and suggested as a performance appraisal technique by Douglas McGregor in "An Easy Look at Performance Appraisal," *Harvard Business Review*, 35, No. 3 (May 1957), 90–94. More recent studies and reviews include Stephen Carroll and Henry Tossi, *Management by Objectives,* (New York: Macmillan, 1973); Miner, "Management Appraisal"; and F. E. Schuster and Alvin Kindall, "Management by Objectives—Where We Stand," *Human Resources Management,* 13, No. 1 (September 1974), 8–11.

[11] Sometimes the subordinate writes a self-appraisal before this meeting.

have a program ready until late July. To help resolve these problems of coordination, some companies give managers overlapping responsibilities to set joint or team goals.[12]

Joint goal setting is not enough, however. An effective MBO program requires that managers anticipate snags and barriers and that they work out an *action plan* showing in detail how the goals are to be reached. Regardless of the date the new computerized credit system is to be introduced, sales personnel must be trained to use it. This means the sales manager must plan a training program, not just for his staff but perhaps for himself as well. In addition to performance objectives, subordinates may set *personal development* objectives, which will help them reach their performance objectives (and perhaps prepare them for promotion). For a sales manager, such a personnel development objective might be to spend more time with the marketing research staff so as to anticipate changes in customer preferences, or to attend a leadership program to improve relations with subordinates. Properly used, an MBO program sets the direction for both individual careers and the organization as a whole; but it requires intensive participation on the part of managers at all levels, from top to bottom.

MBO goal setting has two main advantages. In the first place, as we have seen in Chapter 3, the mere process of goal setting is highly motivating. People like to know what they are expected to do. Those with high need achievement, in particular, gain satisfaction from meeting goals, particularly tough ones. Since MBO goals are custom-made for the special characteristics of each manager's job, they are especially motivating.

Second, MBO emphasizes the future, which can be changed, rather than the past, which cannot. Applied throughout the organization, MBO becomes more than a method of appraisal: it becomes a style of management that emphasizes forward planning rather than aimless fire fighting.[13] Thus it develops into a powerful technique for nonfinancial budgeting and for communicating management's priorities. It requires management to define exactly what it wants to accomplish and to specify all important objectives, especially those commonly ignored in traditional financial budgets (such as equipment maintenance, employee and product development, and customer relations). It helps clarify responsibilities, organize the job, and iron out problems in advance. As a result it makes decision making more rational for both boss and subordinate. It facilitates interdepartmental communications and coordination. Since MBO forces management to think about improving interpersonal effectiveness, it is also a program of organization development.

Participation. In principle, MBO programs permit subordinates to set goals either by themselves or jointly with their superiors, thus facilitating inter-

[12] Wendell French and Robert Hollmann, "Management by Objectives: The Team Approach," *California Management Review*, 17, No. 3 (Spring 1975), 13–22.

[13] In some organizations, MBO has gone through three stages. At first it was chiefly a means of performance appraisal. Next it became a planning technique used to decide *how* the organization should reach its objectives. Finally, it began to be viewed as a strategic planning tool to help management reevaluate its objectives and determine *where* it should be going. Sometimes these objectives conflict. George Strauss, "MBO: A Critical View," *Training and Development Journal*, 26, No. 4 (April 1972), 10–15.

nalized motivation. Frequently, too, managers help set not only their own goals but also those of the larger organization. The fact that these goals are accepted voluntarily and put in writing increases the sense that a contract has been struck and helps hold individual managers to their commitment.[14]

Further, in contrast to the "closed system" implied by traditional ratings, MBO gives subordinates an active role, increases their sense of control over their environment, and reduces their dependence on the boss. Finally, by emphasizing specific performance rather than character traits, MBO permits recognition of the innovative manager who gets results by unconventional means.

Appraisal. In principle, with MBO, subordinates are evaluated against standards they helped set themselves. Usually the atmosphere is less punitive and arouses less anxiety than with conventional appraisals. The boss becomes less a judge and more a coach. The concern is not with what went wrong last period, but how can errors made last period be corrected in the next.

At its best, the MBO process is a two-way street. Both the subordinate's performance and the relationship between the boss and the subordinate are reviewed. The boss may ask the subordinate what he, as the superior, can do, refrain from doing, or do differently to help the subordinate do an even better job. This approach gives a better balance to the interview, since each party is evaluating the other and both recognize that the subordinate's efficiency is greatly affected by what the superior does.

Limitations

Despite the initial enthusiasm with which many organizations greeted this new approach, experience suggests that MBO has a number of limitations. In the first place, the theory that subordinates set goals by themselves (or jointly with their bosses) may turn out to be illusory. It all depends on whether the participative approach, which is required for goal setting by the subordinate, is consistent with the boss's ordinary management style. The boss who regularly consults with subordinates finds this new approach quite easy. Not so the boss who is decisive and directive and never takes time to listen. With such a boss, MBO, by setting highly specific goals (and usually goals that get tougher each year) merely makes the subordinate feel less secure.

In any case, knowing that his boss is the one who hands out rewards, the typical subordinate may look anxiously for some indication as to what this boss thinks are proper goals. Once these become clear, he will quickly adopt them with "enthusiasm." Indeed, some subordinates might prefer their boss to indicate a preference from the start, instead of making them go through guessing games. Further, with organization-wide goal setting, the individual's freedom to set a personal goal is sharply reduced. If top management sets a goal to increase production by 15 percent, a foreman can suggest only means of reaching that goal. At the most, individual subordinates have the freedom to *negotiate* goals, not to set them independently. At times this negotiation

[14] Gerald Salancik, "Commitment and Control of Organizational Behavior and Belief," in Gerald M. Salancik and Barry Staw, eds., *New Directions in Organizational Behavior* (Chicago: St. Clair, 1977).

process turns into a game. After all, a manager's apparent "performance" is a function of his initial goal. If his goals are set low, it is easy to look good. And so the trick, in some situations, is to set a low initial goal and sell one's boss that this goal is really hard to reach.

Because MBO places heavy stress on measurable standards, it may cause problems in dealing with intangible, unmeasurable aspects of the job. Production, which is measurable, is emphasized over employee development, which is not. Because of this difficulty, quality may be sacrificed for sheer quantity; trivial items may assume undue importance because they can be counted.

A laboratory director set as her goal the enhancement of her laboratory's professional prestige. Since prestige is difficult to measure, she set as her performance target a certain number of papers to be read at professional meetings. To fill this quota she "encouraged" individual subordinates to accept the writing of papers as goals for themselves. The result, as might be expected, was that the required number of papers were read, but they were of such poor quality that they lowered rather than raised the laboratory's prestige. (The story might have been less tragic if the director's subordinates had felt really free to reject their assignments.)

As our example illustrates, creative work, such as research, personnel, or advertising, is often difficult to measure, as indeed is most staff work (since it must achieve its results through others).

Overemphasizing measurable data also encourages covering up poor performance or actually falsifying data. A subordinate may slight long-run improvement to look good during the current evaluation period. Since each individual is encouraged to make himself look good, cooperation is discouraged. In addition, to the extent that a manager's overall performance is evaluated on the basis of a relatively few measures, there is a danger that accidental factors outside his control may distort the picture. During a period of rapid change, goals may become outmoded long before the next review period comes around. Perhaps the real test of a manager is the ability to handle the unexpected. Yet in times of crisis MBO is often ignored.

Unless an endless number of factors are considered, some significant items may be ignored or fall into chinks between measured goals. When one goal must be achieved at the expense of another, the manager has only imperfect standards for choice. He or she may easily emphasize side goals over the main show. ("I could meet all my goals in developing new accounts, but in so doing I would lose $1,000,000 in bread-and-butter sales.")

Making MBO work

MBO has been introduced into many companies, but according to one study, in fewer than 10 percent of these was the system really successful.[15] Organizations must commit a great deal of time and effort if MBO is to become a new way of organizational life. It is simply too easy to go through the motions of setting goals and then to ignore them. Frequently there is a boomerang effect: the high hopes that some managers set when MBO is first announced

[15] Schuster and Kindall, "Management by Objectives—Where We Stand."

lead to sad disillusionment when the promised participation turns out to be a sham. Successful introduction of MBO may require a full-scale Organization Development effort (see our next chapter). Further, unless management constantly reemphasizes its commitment to MBO (especially by practicing MBO at its own level), the entire process will gradually atrophy.[16]

The main problem is that in many cases a participative system is grafted on an autocratic organization. In practice, MBO can be used for different purposes. Autocratic managers can use MBO to impose specific goals on subordinates. Manipulative managers may listen to subordinates' gripes as part of the MBO process and then induce these subordinates to accept (presumably voluntarily) the goals that higher management had intended from the start. But only the managers who are convinced of the value of internalized motivation are likely to permit their subordinates to participate on an equal basis in setting goals not just for themselves but for the wider organization.

The research suggests that of the two main aspects of MBO, goal setting and participation, it is the setting of clear, concrete goals, not the sense of participation, that is important for increased performance. Concrete goals direct performance, reduce uncertainty, and serve as an instrument of communications—and they do so whether goals are introduced directly or participatively. So traditional and human relations-oriented managers may find MBO useful, particularly if they do not engender unrealistic expectations about participation. Joint goal setting is more effective than goal setting by the boss, but only if the boss uses participation on a day-to-day basis.

On the other hand, as we have seen, excessive emphasis on a few measurable goals may lead to other elements of the manager's performance being ignored. Nevertheless, used with discretion, goal setting provides a framework within which subordinates are motivated and receive specific cues about how they stand and what they should do to improve.

Promotions and salary increases

Should MBO be used for determining who should get promotions or salary increases? Here there are many uncertainties. A manager's past performance on his present job may provide only an imperfect indicator of his potential for a new job, especially if one job requires the day-to-day supervision of a work team and the higher job involves long-term planning and coordination with staff groups. Other factors besides past performance must be taken into account in making promotion decisions, including the manager's success in special broadening assignments. In addition, personality traits, as disclosed by good selection tests or in assessment centers, may be relevant.

Some organizations separate evaluation of managerial *potential* from evaluation of present *performance* (with judgments as to potential kept confidential). The evaluations occur at different times, and different forms are used for each purpose. Often the evaluation of potential is not even shown to the subordinate.

[16] John M. Ivancevich, "Changes in Performance in a Management by Objectives Program," *Administrative Science Quarterly*, 19, No. 4 (December 1974), 563–74.

MBO may not be appropriate for determining who should get a salary increase either, since it provides little basis to compare one manager against another. Yet any salary program that bases salary on performance must make such comparisons. Therefore, a separate procedure may have to be established for salary purposes. Thus an organization may have as many as three appraisal programs, each for differing purposes: for promotions, for salary increases, and for coaching.

Separating coaching appraisal from the other two has another advantage. It separates the boss's developmental function from his judgmental one. But having three different procedures may lead to chaos (as well as much paper work), particularly if the ratings are inconsistent with each other. A manager who regularly meets MBO goals yet is never promoted may become terribly frustrated.

Certainly salary increases should be consistent with appraisals, whether or not appraisals are based on subordinate-set goals. Salary appraisal should be a fairly explicit procedure in which individuals are (in most cases) told the basis for pay decisions. Although MBO results should perhaps be a major factor in this process, the reward system should take into account a broader set of variables than does MBO. Unmeasurable aspects of performance (for example, whether the manager is improving his relations with other departments) as well as such factors as seniority, the organization's salary position, and salaries paid by competitors should all be considered.

Perhaps in organizations with "closed" personnel systems, promotion prospects will be kept secret. It is possible, however, for a manager in an "open" system to conduct an appraisal interview that combines the three forms of appraisal:

"Joe, you've met every one of your MBO targets. Congratulations. There will be a good salary increase for you. It might have been even more if you'd had greater success in handling some of the troublesome problems not listed in the MBO plan, such as. . . . You may wish to concentrate on these next year. We ought to think about the future, too. As we mentioned last time, the XYZ job requires certain skills. What kind of progress are you making in acquiring these?"

Conclusion

Performance appraisal serves two important but conflicting purposes in the management development program: (1) It provides a systematic, objective means for selecting those who should be promoted or receive salary increases, and (2) it is a tool to help a manager train subordinates (as well as to help subordinates improve themselves). In theory, selection, salary administration, and training can be combined in one attractive management-development package. Higher management can use ratings for promotional and salary administration purposes and as a form of feedback (through the evaluation interview) to inform subordinates where they stand and to suggest ways in which they can do better.

Unfortunately, the information the organization obtains from an evaluation program designed primarily to permit an objective evaluation of a large number of managers is seldom useful for coaching individuals. Further, since evaluation interviews combine judgmental and developmental aspects, superiors *and* subordinates have come to dread the time when these interviews must be held. Even if the interview is supposed to permit the subordinate to express himself freely, the subordinate can never forget that the boss is not just a coach but also the one who hands out rewards and punishments. Thus, the subordinate wants above all to look good in the eyes of the boss and is particularly afraid of being unjustly criticized. The superior, meanwhile, is apprehensive about provoking the subordinate's antagonism.

Because of the general inadequacy of traditional appraisals, many organizations have switched to MBO. MBO's emphasis on measurable goals makes evaluation more objective, and subordinate involvement in goal setting tends to make goals more realistic and acceptable to the individual. Nevertheless MBO is hardly the perfect solution to the organizational problem. There is considerable conflict among its various functions: appraisal, goal setting, participation, and organizationwide planning. Often goals are set just as autocratically with MBO as without it. In addition, MBO is only of slight use in determining who should be promoted.

Different appraisal systems rate different factors: rating scales focus primarily on traits; the critical incident and behaviorally anchored systems are concerned chiefly with specific behavioral incidents, and MBO deals with results. Yet in a perhaps misplaced (and fruitless) effort to become objective, all these have become complex, and none adequately measures the manager's full contribution to the organization. The wise organization will proceed flexibly, without becoming wed to any one method. The method itself, however, may be less important than the commitment to make it work. Without such commitment almost any program is likely to fail.

As far as development itself is concerned, appraisals are only part of the picture. We now turn to management training and organization development.

problems

1 • *Robert Jackson*

Robert Jackson, 25, has been an advertising copywriter in your department for three years. He designs advertisements to be placed in newspapers and magazines. He must work closely with the art and sales departments, as well as with the vice-president in charge of the whole division.

Bob is an extremely enthusiastic worker with good ideas. When you, the manager of the department, hired him, you hoped that he would advance rapidly. He still can, but he has considerable trouble in dealing with people. He is too impatient with the artists in the art department, seems to fidget whenever he notices one of them taking a break, and is constantly pushing them to finish his work.

In dealing with the people in the sales department, he makes it perfectly clear that his ideas are always best. During a recent conference, when the Vice President was thinking out loud, Bob shouted out his own answer, and cut the VP off. It was a good answer, and the VP didn't mind, but some of the other people thought Bob had behaved badly. You are quite concerned about the animosity he is creating in your department.

A new company policy requires that each employee have an evaluation interview every six months. There are no performance-rating forms. This is Jackson's first evaluation under the new policy.

1. What should your strategy be in handling the evaluation interview with Jackson?
2. Role-play this interview. Jackson is quite sure that his ideas are good and will press for a substantial pay increase.

2 • *MBO for a Professor*

Assume you are the head of a university teaching department. Pick a professor you know. Set a series of concrete objectives which you, as department head, would like this professor to meet. How would you present these objectives to this professor?

3 • *Problems with Ratings*

"Management tells me that I shouldn't give everybody top rating, but instead I should spread my ratings out and give some people Improvement Needed or Unsatisfactory. (You know we have five ratings: Unsatisfactory, Improvement Needed, Good, Excellent, and Outstanding.) Well, as soon as I started giving out ratings I got complaints. I gave half the group Outstanding, but still the entire office is in turmoil. Instead of keeping their ratings secret, they all tell their friends.

"Take Jane. She just goes through the motions of doing her job. She is slow, unimaginative, and never shows any initiative except in stretching her break time. I thought I was being generous in giving her an Excellent, but she was furious. She wanted to know exactly what she was doing wrong—and she let me know I don't do my job too well, either, so how could I judge? Then there's Mike. He has an awful absenteeism record and his work is full of mistakes. He doesn't argue with me about that, but still thinks the Good I gave him shows little consideration for someone who has given 30 years of his life to this organization. He screamed so loud that two old-time employees who do have good records (and did get Outstanding) came to intervene on his behalf.

"Management says these are supposed to be objective evaluations. I'm supposed to rank people on the basis of their *relative* contribution to the organization. But instead I got to have an iron-clad court case if I give anyone a rating less than Outstanding. But if I do that, Personnel screams at me too. What should I do?"

1. What likely mistakes did this supervisor make?
2. Advise her as to what she should do.

organization development and management training

Although organization development is concerned primarily with the organization as a whole, and management training deals with individual managers, the two subjects overlap, and they can conveniently be considered together. Organization development (OD) is in a sense the broader topic and the one that has received the greatest recent attention. Nevertheless, OD grew out of management training, so it is appropriate to consider management training first.

Management training

Forms of management training. To begin with, it must be made clear that management training takes many forms and deals with many subjects. Coaching by one's boss, job rotation schemes, performance evaluation—all are, in a sense, forms of training. The manager also learns important lessons with every word of praise, every reprimand, every promotion. The subjects dealt with by management training may range from public speaking to the impact of recent tax legislation. This section, however, will focus on just one form of management training: formal programs designed to improve managerial skills, chiefly in human relations areas—how to get along with one's boss, subordinates, or peers.

Historical development. Management training became significant first in World War II, when crash programs were instituted to train new foremen. After the war, the spread of human relations and foremen's unions led companies to engage more extensively in foreman training as a means both of persuading foremen that they were indeed part of management and of reducing the petty tyrannies that earlier had contributed to the growth of blue-collar unions. At about the same time, selected groups of managers began to attend university-run executive programs, typically from two to six weeks' full time. From these humble beginnings, management training spread until it now covers all levels of the organization.

Over the years, a number of ingenious training techniques have been developed. Although useful for disseminating facts or sharpening skills, few of these techniques were effective in inducing behavioral change. During the 1960s a number of organizations experimented with a new and seemingly still more powerful technique: T-group training (to be discussed later). Powerful as this technique proved, when applied to management it, too, had shortcomings, among which was the problem of transferring abilities learned in the T-group to the job. It was largely because of the limitations of both traditional and T-group training that training specialists began turning to the broader forms of planned organizational change, which have come to be known as OD. But before considering these developments in greater detail we need to look at the requirements for effective training.

Requirements for effective training

Through trial and error, those concerned with training programs have begun to learn some of the conditions that are required for successful interpersonal training. These conditions relate both to the nature of the training program and to the organizational environment in which it occurs.

Problems as the trainees see them. The training program should start with the felt needs of the trainees themselves, and they should see it as a means of solving their *own* problems. Training in some companies is on the level of the charm school or the booster talk. Or it may be presented in theoretical, abstract terms that participants are unable to translate into practice. One way to ensure that a training program is built around problems as the trainees see them is to invite them to participate in setting up the program (or at least to survey their felt needs before launching the program). With "open" personnel systems, managers can select the courses they want to take, rather than being sent to courses whether they wish them or not.

Nature of the program

Unfreezing. The people who take part in the program must be dissatisfied with their old ways and willing to "unfreeze" their attitudes. A wise personnel director once told us that he never starts a training program until the people to be trained (as well as their superiors) are anxious for the program. If people are forced into a training program against their will, they may resent and sabotage it.

Evidence suggests that training is more valuable for managers who have just been promoted or are about to be promoted, since these are the ones most in need of an expanded viewpoint. Confronted by a new job, they are anxious to develop new skills and willing to discard old points of view. This enthusiasm for learning is especially strong among staff specialists, such as accountants or engineers, who are being promoted into line positions where they will be faced with an entirely new set of problems.

Involvement. Trainees must be encouraged to work through to their own conclusions. The only way they can understand a problem is to think it out for themselves. They suspect the fast talker who tries to trick them into accepting ready-made solutions.

A trainee can memorize what the instructor thinks is right, but this does not make it his own. Particularly in the area of emotional (as distinct from conceptual) learning, people learn primarily through experience, not through passive listening. Real learning is "gut" learning. If there is to be a carry-over from the classroom to the office or shop, it is essential that the trainee *feel* through the problem, experiencing and overcoming its difficulties while working toward a solution. We emphasize the word *feel* because many of the problems in this area are emotional, involving the ways managers see, and feel about, the people and events that affect them deeply.

Without emotional involvement, trainees are likely to develop intellectually satisfying answers that they fail to implement in practice. For example, they may do a beautiful job of analyzing a case that focuses on inability to listen to the other person's point of view—and ten minutes later totally fail to listen to another trainee's comments.

Group influence. Human-relations training is often more effective when it is conducted in groups, for most attitudes in this area are group-conditioned. For instance, a foreman will be less likely to consult with a steward if fellow foremen feel that to do so is being soft.

We have already discovered that group discussion at times provides an effective means of changing attitudes. When group norms are involved, it is easier to change members as a group than it is to change individuals. When a group of managers with common problems decides to change together, no individual has the unsettling feeling of being a pioneer, of being different. The group provides its members with emotional support, and they learn from each other.

Typically, attitudes and behaviors begin to change only when the trainees recognize that they all have problems in common which they have not been able to handle satisfactorily (for instance, handling an unreasonable steward and living under a tight budget). It helps if they can work off their resentment— let off steam—a bit before moving on to the next step. The opportunity to share one another's burdens reduces frustration and makes them more willing to consider new approaches.

Experiments with change. A training program is more effective if it makes allowances for the difficulties of giving up old ways of doing things.

Understandably, people feel more secure with old patterns of behavior that have proven reasonably satisfactory in the past. And they resent suggestions that their performance is unsatisfactory. Similarly, they object to outsiders telling them what to do; they feel that their long experience makes them more qualified than any trainer.

One approach to handling this problem is to encourage trainees to consider new practices without attacking the old ways directly; that is, to ask them to consider a range of alternatives without committing themselves to any particular one. They should be encouraged to try new ways tentatively. Only after they have tested the new procedures on an experimental basis can they be expected to change their behavior permanently. This process of experimentation with change in a "safe environment" is central both to T-groups and OD, as we shall see below.

Carry-over.   For training to mean anything, it must move from the intellectual to the practical level. It must provide skills that are useful to the managers in solving problems on the job—skills that higher management will permit them to practice.

To summarize much of the above: effective training that changes attitudes should run through the three stages. In the *unfreezing* stage, trainees learn to be dissatisfied with their old patterns of behavior. In the *change* stage, they experiment with new patterns in a safe environment away from everyday pressures. In the *refreezing* stage, they adopt these forms for practical use and carry them to the job.

Of the various points listed above, the last one, carry-over, may be the most critical. Training rarely results in lasting behavioral change unless there is a supportive organizational atmosphere.

Organizational climate

Training is difficult to evaluate, for reasons we shall discover. By and large, the results of training have been somewhat disappointing. Managers may report enthusiastically about a course, and their behavior may change a bit in the first few days after leaving class; but long-range improvements resulting from training—at least from conventional training—are rarely observed.

How can we explain these negative results? Except for boredom, some programs have little impact on trainees, even while they are in class. More important, what is learned in class is too often not useful on the job, especially when it conflicts with the behavior expected of the trainees by their bosses and even by their subordinates. If training is to be worthwhile, trainees must feel free to apply what they learn. When the organizational climate denies this freedom, subordinates are more likely to imitate their boss than to follow what they have learned in class.

The influence of the organization—in particular, the attitude of top management—is crucial to the success of a training program. In many companies management regards training as of only marginal importance and consequently gives it only token support. Many managers feel that training is purely a staff function for which line has no responsibility, or they institute training programs merely because it is the fashionable thing to do. Yet attitudes of this sort are quickly discerned by the trainees themselves, who may begin to feel that training is a waste of time and resent being held as a captive audience in a training class. As long as management thinks of the training process as something apart from everyday activities on the job, the chances that training will affect behavior are slim indeed.

Where higher management does not *in practice* support the objectives of training, managers feel uncertain about whether to follow the theory of the course or the example of their boss. As a result, they appear vacillating and inconsistent. Subordinates can become confused if their hard-as-nails supervisor begins to listen to them before bawling them out. Uncertain of whether their boss is going to be "tough" or practice "human relations," subordinates find this unpredictability highly frustrating. Under the circumstances, it may be a blessing that so many supervisors leave their training in the classroom and never let it interfere with their daily behavior.

In the establishment of a training course, there is often little effort to find out why managers behave as they do or to consider whether company policy or top management behavior may be the cause of whatever seems wrong; instead training is viewed as a magic cure for all ills. Managers often talk as if only their subordinates' behavior needed changing, not their own. Trainees often say, "I wish my boss would take this course. He's the one who needs it."

Too often, training programs stress dealing with only subordinates, yet the trainee's biggest problem may be dealing with the boss. Only frustration results if training teaches managers to adopt new approaches, and these managers then find that the organization won't let them do so.

Only limited results can be obtained by training lower management alone, particularly if the training is of the typical classroom variety. Possibly the best way to train foremen is to train the general foreman first; but it is difficult to train the general foreman until the superintendent has been trained, or at least induced, to behave in a manner that permits those on lower levels to try out new techniques.

Does this mean that the only way to start is with the board of directors? Perhaps. The board of directors of one of the nation's largest companies established a human relations committee, whose job, in effect, is to train top management. Top management then trained the next lower level of management and so on down the line in a carefully planned program, until finally the general foreman trained the foremen.

As we shall see, there are very definite advantages in having bosses train the people they supervise. Yet there are managers, otherwise competent, who are just poor trainers. Further, if all training is done by the boss, there is a real danger that the organization will perpetuate its past mistakes and allow little room for new ideas. Training conducted by line personnel is not the complete solution to the problem.

More important than the person who conducts the training is the organizational atmosphere in which it occurs. For training to be effective, this atmosphere must permit the manager to experiment with new patterns of behavior and to learn through making mistakes. But even changes in atmosphere must come from the top (or at least be approved by the top). Organizations are social systems, and it is difficult to change one part without changing the rest. Growing recognition of this interdependency has led many companies to establish integrated programs of organization development and to place less stress on individualized management training.

Conventional training techniques

Now let us examine some of the more common conventional training techniques. These techniques are designed for many purposes, but few, if any, completely satisfy the criteria listed above. Yet all of them have some value either as part of a comprehensive program or in organizations that are unable to mount such a comprehensive program.

Lecturing, the traditional form of teaching, gives the trainer the greatest degree of control over the training situation. Material can be presented exactly as the lecturer wishes, with little danger that anyone will talk back.

Lectures

Instructors who can keep their classes constantly stimulated through the sheer force of their ideas—and who are powerful enough to effect changes in the behavior of those who listen to them—are rare indeed. A lecture is unlikely to change fixed attitudes and certainly is of little help in developing skills. It is useful chiefly in presenting background facts—for example, the meaning of a new union contract.

The cases that we present at the ends of chapters are typical of those used in this common form of training.

The case method

The success of the case method depends directly on the ability of the instructor. Under an unskilled instructor, the trainees tend to look upon the case as a puzzle that can be solved by finding the right answer. They make value judgments about each character and try to identify the "villain." Often, too, a poorly conducted discussion will degenerate into a rambling session from which the participants derive no learning. Skillful instructors, on the other hand, emphasize useful ways of thinking about human relations rather than ways of reaching specific conclusions. They put stress on:

- Increasing the trainee's power of observation, helping that person to ask better questions and to look for a broader range of problems (for instance, not "Who is to blame?" but "Why did it happen?").
- Encouraging the group to look for more and more implications in each solution, keeping them away from pat analyses and oversimplified solutions.
- Helping students to discard vague principles, such as "Be tactful" or "Apply the golden rule," and urging them to consider not only *what* to do but *how* to do it.
- Encouraging the trainees to test their solutions against reality.

In the university classroom the case method introduces a note of realism that is absent from abstract, theoretical discussions. For management trainees in business or government, however, cases are always less realistic than the actual problems that arise on the job. Even though practicing managers may discuss cases with enthusiasm, they tend to look upon the discussion as a game in which they solve the *other* company's problems, not their own. This lack of *emotional* involvement may make it difficult to effect any basic change in the behavior and attitudes of the trainees.

Simulation

By *simulation* is meant a broad range of techniques in which trainees act out samples of real organizational behavior, to practice in making decisions or working together as a group, or both. It involves learning through doing, rather than through memorizing principles. In effect, it is a form of vestibule training. Since it is more realistic than the case method, it may lead to greater involvement.

The *management game* is one form of simulation that involves several teams, each of which is given a "firm" to operate for a number of "periods." In each period each team must decide what prices to set, how much to produce, how much to spend on advertising and on research, how much of an inventory to maintain, and so forth. Since the teams are competing with each other, each firm's decisions will affect the results of all the other firms. Typically, these decisions are fed into a computer which is programed to behave somewhat like a real market. At the end of each period the computer reports back how well each firm has done. This report provides the data needed for the next period of play. The winner, of course, is the firm that has accumulated the largest profit by the end of the game. Often the game ends in a post mortem in which the participants analyze their mistakes and attempt to generalize from their experience.

What do participants learn from such games? Primarily, how to make better decisions, to select and analyze relevant data, and to choose from among alternatives. Most management games are concerned with the external environment of business, particularly marketing, and its quantifiable aspects. Though participants gain some experience in working together, their chief concern is with making decisions, not implementing them. They provide little insight into the problems connected with organizational structure or personnel management. Only rarely is the game enlarged to afford each team an opportunity to analyze its own interpersonal problems. Management games often generate much enthusiasm among players. There is still a good deal of doubt, however, about the extent of carry-over from game to job. (Management games are also used in assessment centers, see p. 192.)

The *in-basket* technique is a form of simulation that permits emphasis on internal as well as external problems. A typical in-basket exercise might be as follows:

An "executive" (the trainee) is catapulted into a new job on the sudden death of a predecessor, whose in-basket contained a number of letters, memos, and notes of phone conversations—all accumulated over the last few days. A host of urgent problems must be faced: a union grievance (as well as a poorly written proposed reply drafted by a subordinate line manager), a complaint from an important customer, and a sudden supervisory vacancy for which there are three obvious candidates.

The trainee is given a short period of time to deal with these problems, either by drafting a reply at once or getting further information. After all trainees handle their own identical in-baskets, they meet to discuss the logic behind how they handled them.

This technique provides experience both in making decisions and in implementing them. It differs from the business game in that there is no feedback on how well the decision "worked."

Role-playing is a form of simulation emphasizing human-relations problems. Parts are assigned to students to act out as they would in real life. It differs from ordinary drama in that the actors are given no lines to memorize; rather, they must improvise as they go along. (For examples of cases susceptible to role-playing, see Chap. 15.) Among the advantages of role-playing are these:

- It helps participants to appreciate other points of view (a foreman may play the role of a union steward).
- It helps trainees to experience a situation emotionally.
- It makes trainees more self-conscious and analytical of their behavior than they would be in real life.

Even the trainees who merely observe a role-playing session profit from observing the mistakes of others. Certainly this is a highly dramatic technique for arousing interest and stimulating class participation.

Nevertheless, role-playing has some disadvantages. It deals with problems formulated by the instructor, not with those bothering the trainee. Thus many are viewed as unrealistic. Further, the cases must of necessity be oversimplified, since they focus on the players' interactions and tend to ignore the environment in which the problem arises.

Other forms of simulation may also be utilized. Participants may be given roles—such as plant manager, sales manager, purchasing agent, and comptroller—and information about the jobs which these individuals might normally have. Then several emergencies are assumed to occur—for instance, a large rush order and a major equipment breakdown—and the trainees are required to solve the problems. Such simulation provides training in both decision making and human relations, and after each "period" the participants can profitably hold a post mortem about how they handled their problems.

The main techniques discussed share one common characteristic: the problems they consider are presented by the trainer rather than the group and are therefore looked upon as somewhat artificial or not pertinent. Thus, participants tend not to become emotionally involved or to develop insights relating to their own values or behavior. In order to obtain greater participation, a number of organizations turned to T-groups.

T-group training

T-group training (the "T" stands for training) is also known as *sensitivity training* and *laboratory training,* and is akin to *encounter groups.* Regardless of the name, the technique has strong supporters and strong detractors.

Though T-group training dates back to the 1940s, only around 1960 did interest spill out into private industry. Yet by the mid-1960s, the list of firms that had at least experimented with this radically new form of training read like a blue book of American industry.

T-group training differs from the kinds of training previously discussed in that it is concerned with real, not simulated, problems existing within the training group itself—not in the organization outside or in some hypothetical case. Rather than just teach skills and intellectual understanding, it seeks to change underlying attitudes and thus behavior on the job.

Although individual trainers may differ in emphasis, T-group training can be used to help participants:

- Learn more about themselves, especially their emotions.
- Develop insights into how they react to others and how others react to them.
- Discover how groups work and how to diagnose human-relations problems.
- Find out how to behave more effectively in interpersonal relations, and in particular, how to manage people through means other than power.
- Develop honest relations in which feelings are expressed openly.
- Confront interpersonal problems directly, so that they can be solved, rather than trying to avoid them, smooth them over, or seek a compromise that is not really a solution.

T-group training is often called *laboratory training* because T-groups are, in effect, laboratories in which people experiment on themselves and generate data for their own discussions. T-groups are really small discussion groups with no set leader. (The trainer merely raises questions and provides occasional comments.) Frequently the groups are totally unstructured; they have no set task or agenda except for a strong focus on the feelings and mutual impact of the participants. Learning takes place through analyzing one's emotions rather than intellectually through logic. The group talks about what seems important at the moment. It is felt that the lack of structure will motivate people to bring their feelings out in the open where they can be analyzed and dealt with in a more rational fashion. The OD director of a large company provided us with an example of how T-groups work in practice.

"Last week we had a session with a lot of executives at various levels, including the vice-president of one of our major divisions. After three days most people were feeling pretty open with their comments. Even the VP was talking quite freely, though it was obvious the junior people were deferring to him. Then he made a very pompous comment. A junior engineer, not in his division, snapped, 'What a bunch of malarkey!' The VP reddened a bit. I asked, 'Does that bother you?' 'Nope,' he said, 'I can take it.'

"The discussion went on to other things, but I noticed the VP wasn't saying anything. So when we had an evaluation session, I commented, 'Bob [the VP], you haven't said anything the last 30 minutes. Is your mind on other things?'

"His reply came slowly. 'If you thought I ignored Bill's comments, you're wrong. I've spent the last half-hour thinking how this is the first time anybody disagreed with me since I became VP five years ago. I wondered how I must react when something big comes up? How do I come over to those who work with me? I've always thought the people under me didn't have any ideas of their own. How much am I responsible for this?' "

In a well-conducted T-group, the trainees, in effect, train one another, though the trainer helps by asking skillful questions, as the above example illustrates. At times, too, the trainer provides feedback as to the interpersonal processes developing within the group.

Effective T-groups go through the three stages discussed in the early part of this chapter: unfreezing, in which participants develop, often through shock, a sense of dissatisfaction with their present behavior; change, in which they experiment with new behavior; and refreezing, in which they develop an internalized commitment to a new approach.

Though all T-group training generally takes the same over-all form, T-group trainers differ somewhat in their emphasis. One school focuses upon *individual* emotions (and the training this school offers is often called *sensitivity* training); the other is more concerned with relations *among* members of the group. Sensitivity training is in a sense the deeper form of training, and the line between it and psychotherapy sometimes becomes vague. Sensitivity training is also akin to such movements as transactional analysis, Synanon and Esalen groups, and Alcoholics Anonymous.

Both forms of T-groups have been subject to much debate. Two main arguments have been made against their use as a form of management training.

Controversies regarding T-groups

Excessive stress. Critics argue, first, that T-group trainers create stress situations for their own sake. There is a danger that training of this sort may do a better job of tearing people apart than of bringing them together. At worst, T-groups may trigger hidden psychological instabilities, leading to mental breakdown or, at best, to a frustrating experience that interferes with real learning. (In addition, it is argued that such training interferes with personal privacy, particularly in firms that make attendance at such programs almost compulsory.) [1]

Defenders counter that one of the hallmarks of skilled trainers is that they keep tensions within bounds and that they make sure that critical comments are "caring" rather than destructive. Further, the tensions generated in T-groups are no greater than those endemic to any large organization. To these arguments, critics reply that many organizations send to T-group training only those who "need" it most—frequently the most unstable. And, too often,

---

[1] Recently a federal appeals court ruled that a "race relations seminar" (designed to foster racial tolerance) might violate a federal employee's First Amendment rights if it permitted "inquiries into personal beliefs and association choices," especially if "the seminar compelled her to disclose facts about her home life, her beliefs, and her associations which had nothing to do with Air Force duties." Presumably, the same principles would apply to a requirement that an employee attend a T-group involuntarily.

groups are started by unqualified trainers who lack the skill to keep pressures at tolerable levels.

The impartial observer must note that there have been cases in which T-group training has led to personal damage. But this may be an argument chiefly for better care in selecting trainers and the restriction of organizationally sponsored T-groups to forms that stress group learning rather than sheer expression of emotion.

Carry-over difficult. It is charged that whatever changes occur in the T-group tend to fade out once the trainee returns to an unsympathetic environment where company policy and the boss's attitude may inhibit the exercise of newly-learned skills. T-group members learn chiefly to get along with other T-group members. Managers who have learned to express their emotions openly may find their honesty misunderstood by those who have not shared the managers' experiences. "Laboratory values are so different from the values of most organizations that if individuals learned well at the laboratory they would probably tend to conclude that they should not use their new learning back home except where they have power and influence." [2]

Because of this problem, acknowledged by all, there has been a trend toward "family" T-groups consisting of all those who work together. Thus, all the top people in a department are trained at once. But such grouping raises serious ethical questions, since attendance is scarcely voluntary. Further, as long as only part of the total organization has been trained, difficulties in communications may arise among those who have adopted the new values and those who adhere to the old ones. The answer may be to provide T-group training for everyone, but this may be prohibitively expensive. Even if it were possible to send everyone through T-groups, the kind of "dirt" aired in such sessions and the intense feelings often engendered by them may in fact make it harder for managers to work together after the session is over. T-group training may improve the interpersonal relations for some managers, but may be harmful for others.

Organization development

Since the mid-Sixties, in part because of the problems discussed above, many organizations have switched from T-groups to a broader, more eclectic approach to management change, now generally known as organization development.[3] As the name implies, OD seeks to change not only individuals but also the values and behavior patterns of the organizations within which they work.

As the field has grown, OD has taken on a wide variety of forms, ranging from attempts to improve relations within single departments through changes in the structure of the organization as a whole and even relations among

[2] Chris Argyris, "On the Future of Laboratory Training," *Journal of Applied Behavioral Sciences,* Vol. 3, No 2 (April 1967), p. 163.

[3] See Wendell French and Cecil Bell, Jr., *Organization Development,* 2nd. ed. (Englewood Cliffs, N.J.: Prentice-Hall, 1978); Robert Golembiewski, *Renewing Organizations* (Itasca, Ill.: Peacock, 1972).

organizations as a whole—for example, between unions and managements, between community leaders and representatives of minority groups, and even between countries. Among the possible outcomes of an OD program are increased individual trust, redesigned jobs, participative work groups, new approaches to reducing conflict, higher productivity, and greater organizational flexibility. Six common denominators of most OD programs are:

1. They are heavily concerned with changing attitudes and improving interpersonal relations.

2. Solutions to organizational problems are generated by organizational members, rather than imposed from above.

3. There is heavy emphasis on a self-diagnosis process, often called *action research*.

4. Problems are typically attacked at the group or work-team level first, before problems at other levels are considered.

5. Heavy use is made of the three-stage attitude change model (unfreezing, change, refreezing).

6. The change process is initiated and monitored by a *consultant.*

OD and T-groups

Compared to T-groups, OD is characterized by less deep intervention (therefore less danger of engendering excess psychological stress) and greater emphasis on carry-over and on organizational (as opposed to group or individual) factors. Some approaches to OD still make use of T-groups in a modified form, but they do this as only one step in an integrated program.

T-groups seek to increase their participants' ability to be good group members in *any* situation; OD seeks actual improvement in interpersonal relations in specific organizations. T-groups are essentially artificial groups, and they deal with tensions that arise in their own little world—tensions that in a sense are artificially created. OD, by contrast, is concerned with tensions that arise on real jobs. It takes as its bailiwick not just relations within groups, but also relations among groups and even among organizations.

Despite this major difference, the two forms of development have much in common. Their shared point of departure is the individual, rather than the constraints within which he or she works. Although OD's ultimate goal is increased organizational effectiveness—a behavioral rather than an attitudinal measure—OD programs typically start with individual attitudes and utilize confrontations and experiences within groups as their primary learning techniques (as opposed, say, to lectures, individual coaching, or structural changes introduced from the top). Both T-groups and OD share a common faith in "interpersonal trust," in facing interpersonal problems directly, so they can be solved, rather than trying to avoid, smooth over, or compromise them in a way that is not a lasting solution.

Step-by-step progression

As suggested earlier, an effective OD program typically consists of a number of parts, each designed with the needs of the particular organization in mind. Many programs move by steps, as their focus shifts from the individual to the organization and from emotions toward structure. For convenience of exposition, let us describe one *possible* sequence of techniques, with the warning that OD rarely proceeds this smoothly and that no two consultants utilize exactly the same approaches.

Step one might be a T-group. In terms of overall OD design, the intent is to open people up and to develop problem-solving and analytic skills that will be useful at later stages.

Step two could involve a problem-solving exercise such as running a mock company or even constructing a building out of Tinkertoy pieces, followed often by some kind of feedback, then a discussion of the interpersonal dynamics at work during the exercise. The purpose of step two is to permit the application of the skills developed in step one and also to permit their testing in a different kind of reality.

Step three could then deal directly with the on-the-job problems faced by the work team. It would permit application of the generalized skills developed in step one and the specific insights acquired in step two. Here the purpose is to make actual changes in on-the-job relations and to monitor their effectiveness.

Step four might be like step three, except that it would deal with relations among work teams, departments, or groups of supervisors and subordinates or staff and line personnel. In general, the purpose here is to help groups understand one another, with the hope that improved understanding will lead to better cooperation.

Step five could involve going beyond strictly interpersonal relations to deal with structural changes affecting the organization as a whole—changes not only in tables of organization and reporting relationships, but in job descriptions, evaluation programs, communications systems, and the like. Presumably, the interpersonal trust developed in earlier stages now permits problems at this level to be confronted more realistically. Among the solutions that might evolve from such a program are MBO and matrix organization.

Very few OD programs cover all five steps. Indeed, a major criticism is that step five, organizationwide structural change, is often ignored altogether. Some programs stop at step two, without an institutional effort to obtain carry-over or application to the job.

Though the example above imperfectly reflects reality, it stresses the critical point that OD must solve three problems: confrontation (information-getting or unfreezing), change, and carry-over (action or refreezing). Let us consider these in turn.

Confrontation

Perhaps the thing that distinguishes OD from other forms of consultancy is its imaginative use of confrontation. Broadly defined, *confrontation* is a diagnostic or information-getting process in which organizational members obtain feedback on their behavior in a form that will provide insights useful for improving their performance. Thus confrontation is change-oriented feedback.

The object of this feedback normally is to induce participants to compare their (or the system's) *actual* behavior with their *idealized* concept of that behavior. The resultant "perceptual gap" may serve a combination of purposes:

1. The comparison may reveal such a discrepancy between intended (or desired) and actual behavior that it will disturb the previously stable psychological equilibrium and introduce "unfreezing"; i.e., a desire for change or a "conviction of sin."

2. By bringing problems to the surface, confrontation can define (and even dramatize) their nature.

3. It can help the organization make informed and realistic choices as to possible behavioral change.

Thus confrontation should occur not just once, but it can be repeated at every stage of the OD process. Indeed, some observers say that a major purpose of OD is to make confrontation an organizational way of life.

Feedback must be in a form that is believable and that leads to action. Note that confrontation in itself does not automatically guarantee unfreezing. For feedback to be accepted, it should be dramatic enough to induce disequilibrium but not so threatening that it leads to greater defensiveness. It should be in a form that increases rather than decreases interpersonal trust, otherwise participants are unlikely to trust or learn from each other. Neither will they feel as free to experiment with new forms of behavior.

Forms of confrontation vary greatly. T-groups, of course, provide a great deal of feedback to their members, but even so simple a device as the feedback of videotapes made in ordinary management meetings can be extremely effective in illustrating weaknesses. (In observing the video feedback of his performance at a product planning meeting, a manager learned to his dismay that he constantly interrupted his colleagues.) Simulations, such as the management game, can generate data on how a group performs. After the simulation is over, the group evaluates the effectiveness of its internal processes.

The best-known OD technique, the *management grid,* uses a series of questionnaires (as well as simulations) to force managers to confront the gap between their idealized and their present behavior. "You have to build a model," says Robert Blake, the grid's originator, "as if you had no past tradition, no past practices, cult, or ritual. Then you see how lousy you really are in comparison with where you should be. So the ideal is a searchlight for seeing the actual. You have to close the gaps once you see them. You can't live with contradictions." [4]

Other OD programs begin with an employee attitude survey or with a series of interviews with subordinates and peers. The findings of these studies are then reported to the management group with identification of source removed. If the studies are well conducted, they identify problems that require management's attention; often, these problems are ones that management had been unaware of or had ignored.

A fairly typical OD effort involved a hotel chain. Here the president was concerned with the relations between headquarters staff (such as accounting and sales) and their counterparts in individual hotels.

---

[4] *Business Week,* October 18, 1969, p. 159.

The consultant intensively interviewed a sample of people from all levels and then reported back to a meeting consisting of the president, the heads of the headquarters' staff groups, and the general managers of the various hotels. Sample items from his report:

Headquarters staff people: The president expects us to introduce change and upgrade quality, but the general managers won't let us into the hotels to do it.

General managers: The corporation talks decentralization but we have little voice in setting our own advertising policy.

Hotel staff people: Our rewards come entirely from the hotel managers. We have no chance of being promoted into headquarters, and no one in headquarters is interested in our future.[5]

The *survey feedback* approach makes use of employee attitude questionnaires.[6] Typically, top management is closely involved in selecting the types of questions to be asked. Usually they relate to subjects such as organizational climate, pay and benefits, supervisor/employee benefits, or opportunities for personal growth. The consultant then collects questionnaire responses from employees at all levels. Next, the overall questionnaire findings are reported back to a meeting of the top management group with the consultant present. Members of the group are asked to help interpret the data, to consider plans to deal with the problems the data reveal, and then to consider how this data may be introduced at the next lower level. Similar meetings are held at successively lower levels. Each division, department, or section meets in turn to discuss the implications of survey findings pertaining to its own unit. Thus, change starts at the top but eventually involves the entire organization.

Intergroup exercises may involve two groups that have had difficulty working together in the past. Each group is instructed to meet by itself and to write down answers to questions like the following:

How do you view the other group?

How do you think the other group views you?

What's your best guess as to how the other group thinks you view it?

The two groups meet together, and each divulges its list. Each group is permitted to ask the other to enlarge upon its answers, but argument is not permitted. Exercises such as this often reveal misunderstandings, which sometimes can be easily cleared up. In any case, the parties have obtained considerably greater insight into the sources of their difficulties.

Change

Only a fuzzy line separates the confrontation and change stages. Once confrontation has identified the key problems and persuaded the parties that

---

[5] Adapted, with slight modification, from Richrd Beckhard, "An Organization Improvement Program in a Decentralized Company," *Journal of Applied Behavioral Science,* Vol. 2, No. 1 (January 1966).

[6] D. A. Nadler, P. H. Mirvis, and C. Cammann, "The Ongoing Feedback System," *Organization Dynamics,* Spring 1976, pp. 63–80.

change is necessary, the next step is to analyze the problems in greater detail, to generate alternative solutions, and then to evaluate their relative advantages and disadvantages.

Put another way, presumably the initial confrontation unfreezes *attitudes;* the change stage requires participants to unfreeze their *behaviors* and to develop and test new skills. If the confrontation periods have generated a supportive atmosphere in which resistance to change has been reduced, participants will feel free to experiment with new behaviors. They will try these on for size before adding them as permanent parts of their repertoire.

Change is handled in a variety of ways, depending on the nature of the program. Sometimes change is quite straightforward. Using data disclosed by feedback as a springboard for discussion, the OD consultant seeks to induce managers to suggest solutions to their problems. The group is challenged to develop new ways of relating to each other and to test out their choices in terms of their impact on the larger social systems. In the hotel case (discussed above), a list of recommendations was developed, many of which were implemented. For example, one of the hotel staff people was appointed to provide needed liaison between headquarters and the hotels.

The solution of other types of problems requires learning new attitudes and skills. To facilitate the learning process, OD programs utilize three main approaches. *Didactic instruction* involves lectures, exercises, readings and the like, all of which are designed to suggest new ways of handling problems identified during the confrontation period. If subordinates complain about inadequate guidance, the consultant may give a short lecture on the strengths and weaknesses of MBO as a goal-setting technique. In *modeling* (or identification) participants learn to copy the behavior of their consultant or other respected members of their group.[7] For example, the frank, open discussion in the T-group described earlier provided a model for the VP when he "opened up" himself to analyze his own reactions to criticism. Finally, there is *internalization.* Here, instead of directly copying the behavior of others, the participant experiments with new patterns of behavior on his own. Once having decided that he should change, our VP, for example, must now "try out" a variety of new approaches to encourage subordinates to express their opinions more honestly.

Refreezing

Refreezing involves both making a *commitment* to try new behavioral patterns and then some form of *maintenance activity* to prevent slipping back into earlier behavior patterns.

Recent research suggests that a formal commitment to try out new behavior patterns, particularly if made in a public setting, helps refreeze both behaviors and the attitudes associated with them. But pledges to change job-related behavior, made in an OD setting, are often forgotten back on the job; and even if the new behaviors are tried on the job, they often fade out

[7] For a discussion of the difference between modeling and internalization, see Edgar Schein, "Organizational Socialization and the Practice of Management," in Barry Staw, ed., *Psychological Foundations of Organizational Behavior* (Santa Monica, Ca.: Goodyear, 1977).

as participants become discouraged. To avoid fade-out, it often helps to establish formal mechanisms providing continual feedback as to whether the new behaviors or procedures are being implemented. Managers in one company hold "sensing sessions" to diagnose interpersonal problems that may be impeding their operations. Periodic attitude surveys may also serve this feedback function.

Feedback alone, of course, is not enough. The new behaviors must be rewarded by the participants' peers and superiors, for in an unsympathetic atmosphere the new skills will soon be forgotten.

OD: a continuous process

Refreezing should not be the last step, because OD involves not just solving specific problems, but learning an entire process of action research or problem-solving.[8] While maintenance activities help ensure that participants are doing what they have committed themselves to do, yesterday's commitments may not be appropriate in today's circumstances. So, at its best, OD teaches groups to diagnose and evaluate their ever-changing problems on a continuous basis. The process as a whole may run as follows:

Problem → Research on → Evaluation → Commitment → Maintenance → Reevaluation
identification nature of of alternate to one
               problem   solutions   solution

Controversies regarding OD

OD has been highly controversial. For some it is almost a religion. Others see it as a form of charlatanism. There is a continuing debate among OD's critics and supporters and among proponents of alternative OD techniques. The following are some of the points at issue:

Loss of managerial decisiveness. One charge against OD is that it makes managers so sensitive to the feelings of others that they are unwilling to make hard decisions. OD-trained managers sometimes talk for talk's sake and luxuriate in the expression of feelings rather than take action. Furthermore, they may be so "open" and honest in the expression of their feelings that their behavior approaches downright rudeness. Questions have been raised as to the value of complete openness under every circumstance. Excess honesty can often hurt a relationship, even in marriage.

OD supporters reject these arguments. They insist that OD is designed to help managers face problems, not run away from them. OD values "have within them a very real toughness: In dealing with each other, we will be open, direct, explicit. Our feelings will be available to one another, and we will problem-solve rather than be defensive."[9] OD does not "value all openness. It values openness which helps the individuals involved to learn."[10] Open-

---

[8] In other words, OD should be concerned not only with whether policies are being carried out, but also with whether they are appropriate. It should emphasize what Argyris calls double-loop learning. See Chris Argyris, "Double-Loop Learning in Organizations," *Harvard Business Review* (September 1977), 115–25.

[9] Sheldon A. Davis, "An Organic Problem-Solving Method of Organizational Change," *Journal of Applied Behavioral Science,* Vol. 3 (January 1967), p. 4.

[10] Argyris, "On the Future of Laboratory Training," p. 162.

ness, it is argued, is a relationship of trust between people, permitting them to understand each other. It is neither "diplomacy," which hides problems, nor irresponsible "honesty," which requires individuals to express their feelings without regard to their impacts on others. And it is suggested that by providing managers with a broader range of facts (including facts about how other participants feel) OD helps them to make better decisions.

Perhaps the real question is whether participants in OD can pass through the stage of concern about feelings and interpersonal relations to the stage of realistic examination of organizational problems. Nevertheless it is relevant that many organizations now offer their managers courses dealing in such topics as rational decision making, assertiveness, and bargaining—all of which are designed to increase managerial decisiveness.[11]

Attitudes vs. structure. A related objection to OD is that it places excessive emphasis on feelings and informal relationships rather than on structural elements such as job descriptions, formal responsibilities, promotion and compensation schemes, work flows, and the like. Opponents argue that OD approaches the problem of change from the most difficult end, the human personality, when changes in structure can achieve results more economically and with less pain. Lasting value changes are extraordinarily hard to induce when they are not supported by preceding or simultaneous changes in structure. By contrast, structural changes can change attitudes quite quickly and relatively permanently. "Indeed, it is now well established that one's attitudes are *determined* by the behaviors one engages in—rather than vice versa, as traditionally had been thought. This is especially true when individuals perceive that they have substantial personal freedom or autonomy in choosing how they will behave."[12]

OD supporters argue that attitudinal or value changes are necessary preconditions for either behavioral or structural change. OD not only helps managers make better decisions, but it makes decisions easier to implement. Change of any sort will be resisted if introduced by autocratic methods, and this is especially true with regard to changes in managerial skills. Participative supervision is unlikely to work as long as managers are "interpersonally incompetent." Job enrichment or MBO programs have little chance of success unless line managers are emotionally in tune with these programs' objectives.

Thus the basic question is whether one should change from within or from without. These two approaches have been called by their critics "conversionist" and "engineering." In its early days, most OD stressed attitude change. More recently, greater emphasis has been given to structural considerations. Among the forms of change introduced through OD have been a reduction in the number of organizational levels, matrix organization, job redesign, MBO,

---

[11] An implicit assumption behind much conventional OD is that the typical manager is too assertive or domineering. Conventional OD places great stress on consideration and listening. Arguably, assertiveness training implies just the opposite. Actually, consideration and assertiveness are not so much opposites as equally important aspects of the communications process.

[12] J. Richard Hackman, "Work Design," in J. Richard Hackman and J. Lloyd Suttle, *Improving Life at Work* (Santa Monica, Ca.: Goodyear, 1977), p. 102.

the installation of a Scanlon Plan (see Chapter 20), the establishment of task force work teams, and even changes in office architecture to facilitate communications. It is increasingly recognized that the attitudinal and structural approaches complement rather than contradict each other. Thus, new skills are often required to make structural change work, while structural changes help reinforce behavioral skills.

Treatment of conflict. Opponents have charged that OD programs tend to ignore the realities of power and conflict. Indeed, some early OD literature seemed to suggest that conflict was due entirely to lack of understanding and could be eliminated merely by improving interpersonal skills. Even today some versions of OD imply that once the parties are imbued with sufficient "trust" and "openness," they will renounce the use of power. Opponents of OD argue that this is highly unrealistic, that there are real differences of interest (as between subordinates and superiors or between unions and management), that these differences will persist and might increase, even after the parties get to know each other better, and that often they are resolved only on the basis of relative power advantages.

In recent years, OD consultants have begun to recognize that power is indeed one lever to effect organizational change, and some have begun to incorporate training in bargaining skills as part of their programs. There is increasing recognition that although OD may not finally resolve all conflict, it does help to bring conflict out in the open and to equip managers with skills to channel conflict in constructive directions.

**Motivation for
entering OD**

Too often OD has been introduced for the wrong reasons. OD for a while was a fad, and many organizations experimented with it just because it was the thing to do, without understanding what OD was really trying to accomplish. Other organizations viewed it as a form of fun and games, which might boost employee morale. If OD leads to better understanding, they argued, so much the better. Better understanding never did anyone any harm; and besides, OD shows the employees that the organization cares for them.

In other instances OD has been used by top management as a means of straightening out subordinates or as a means of selling an unpopular set of changes. Under these conditions, so-called participation is merely a sham.

Many organizations have entered OD with unrealistic expectations, viewing it as a magic cure-all. When early progess proved slow, these organizations became discouraged—and thus concluded that OD would never work. Such organizations become "inoculated" against resuming OD later on.

Thus, organizational motivation is critical. It makes a big difference whether the consultant is being called in to deal with specific problems or just to provide "some OD training." It also makes a difference whether the management representative who brings the consultant in is seeking to improve his personal pattern of behavior—or (as is more common) wants to change the behavior of others. Managers should feel free to opt out of the program if they wish, and there should be clear understanding both of the process involved and the goals OD is seeking to achieve. Finally, the organization should recognize that gains through OD are slow and that it sometimes requires several years before meaningful progress materializes.

Evaluating training and OD effectiveness

Management training and OD are still in their infancy, and much of the activity in this area is done on faith, with little hard evidence of its effectiveness. Organizations seem to be following a "policy that is best characterized as spending millions for training, but not a penny for training evaluation." [13]

Evaluation of any training program is difficult. Student evaluations are somewhat suspect, since real learning is often frustrating, and the inspiration peddler may win the popularity contest over the trainer who poses difficult questions.

It is possible, perhaps with before-and-after tests, to measure changes in attitudes during training; but as we have seen, attitudes developed in class may fade away rapidly in an unsympathetic back-home environment. A more important consideration is whether training changes on-the-job behavior. The trainee's performance can be evaluated by the boss, subordinates, and fellow workers, and this evaluation may be made just before training, immediately after training, and well after training (the last series to see whether change has persisted). Unfortunately, the fact that the evaluators know that the trainee has gone through training may influence their judgments.

To many members of management, the crucial test is whether training increases efficiency and profits. In practice, it is extremely difficult to isolate the impact of training on organizational effectiveness, because so many other factors may be responsible, such as changes in technology or market conditions. Ideally, one should take a number of identical groups doing the same work under identical conditions and then train the managers of some of these groups and leave the others as controls. Yet, in real organizations (as opposed to those created in the research lab) it is difficult to find groups that will remain identical (except for the characteristics being studied) throughout the research.

Persistent current research into the lasting impact of training, particularly T-group training, is demonstrating that T-groups do change attitudes and even behavior. Whether trainees benefit seems to be related to (1) how well they react during training and their willingness to accept feedback reports (and these, in turn, seem to be related to basic personality variables such as ego strength, and flexibility) and (2) the trainee's security, power, and autonomy on the job.

Evaluating OD is even harder than evaluating individual training. In the first place, OD involves changes in an entire organization, thus making it even more difficult to select appropriate control groups. Second, most OD programs involve a variety of separate techniques. Even if we can determine that the program as a whole has been a success, we may find it difficult to isolate which portions of the program made the greatest difference.

Despite these problems it now seems clear that OD can lead to improved

---

[13] John R. Campbell, *et al., Managerial Behavior, Performance, and Effectiveness* (New York: McGraw-Hill, 1970), p. 49.

organizational performance if introduced under the right circumstances, but it is also clear that a poorly planned program may do more harm than good. For OD to be successful, at least the following conditions must prevail:

- Top management must support it strongly.
- Changes must be made in structures and policies and must be consistent with any changes in attitudes which the program produces.
- All portions of the organization must change in a synchronized manner.
- Sufficient time must be allowed for all those involved to work out their problems. In practice, this appears to mean at least seven days of participation in any one program.[14]

Beyond this, the limited evidence suggests that no form of OD is uniformly best; however, OD programs using several forms of intervention (e.g., survey feedback, the Grid, and intergroup exercises) are more effective than those using one technique only. Finally, OD seems more likely to be successful in high-technology, constantly-changing organizations in which a great deal of coordination is required among work groups and rapid communication is needed up and down all organizational levels. OD may be particularly useful in countering the kinds of devisiveness that appears to be inherent in increasing specialization and professionalization. It is also appropriate if a matrix organization is to work. On the other hand, in industries with stable environments and easily routinized jobs, OD appears to be less worthwhile.

Conclusion

We have looked at both management training and organization development. Management training supplements other developmental techniques such as job rotation and performance evaluation. Such training is necessary to help promotable managers prepare for advancement, to assist managers in keeping up with technological developments, to build morale in lower-level managers by demonstrating top management's interest in them, and above all, to help improve interpersonal relations.

Technical training is fairly straightforward. But if training in interpersonal relations is to result in behavioral change on the job, two difficult conditions must be met. First, it must lead to attitudinal change, and this means that the training must be focused on feelings as well as on intellectual principles. Usually this also requires some kind of confrontation and unfreezing. Second, the organizational environment must permit the trainee to practice on the job the skills learned in the training session.

Conventional training techniques, such as lectures, case discussion, and even role-playing meet these two conditions only to a very small degree. For a while, a number of companies looked to T-groups as the sure-fire answer. But in the hands of some trainers, T-groups were excessively stressful, and there was the problem of fade-out in an unsympathetic home environment.

[14] Jerry Porras and P. O. Berg, "The Impact of Organization Development," *Academy of Management Review*, Vol. 3, No. 2 (April 1978), 249–66.

Faced with either restricting training to a rather superficial level or seeking to change the organizational environment, a number of companies have selected the second course. OD represents our most ambitious effort to make training realistic and sustaining, and to eliminate the barrier between the classroom and the job.

OD goes beyond traditional training in that it seeks to introduce change in the organization as a whole, not just in the individual. It seeks alterations in reward systems and structures, not just in attitudes. It utilizes all the principles discussed at the beginning of the chapter; i.e., it deals with problems as trainees see them; it seeks to involve them in proposing their own solutions to these problems; it makes use of the principles of unfreezing and carry-over; and it makes heavy use of group influence. Of course, many more companies must experiment with the use of OD before we will be able to judge its effectiveness objectively, but its initial results have been promising.

OD has on occasion been viewed as a panacea. There have been totally unrealistic expectations as to what it might accomplish—expectations that could not possibly be met. OD is not a solution in itself. It is only a means of assisting the parties in *working* through their problems, and the work involved may be hard. Furthermore, it should be viewed as a continuing process in which the organization continually reexamines its processes to keep them consistent with a changing environment.

Finally, we should mention that OD is increasingly being combined with more conventional training in topics such as decision making, assertiveness, bargaining, and TA. A second noteworthy new development is that OD is being offered in conjunction with structural changes such as job redesign and MBO. Thus OD is being viewed more and more not as an isolated process, which stands on its own, but as a critical part of a systems approach to organizational change.

problems

1 · *Old Line Engineering*

The Old Line Engineering Corporation, which has an enviable reputation for well-crafted products, has recently branched out into high process technology. It has won a defense contract for a state-of-the-art product that is to be produced with very tight deadlines. The work is very complex, involving specialist groups: physicists, chemists, materials engineers, and others. The new product consists of separate parts, each of which must be integrated with the others, and each of which must work with very high reliability. The entire package can weigh no more than one kilogram. Each group is anxious to get as much of this limited space for its own gadgets as possible. To make the project work, a great deal of communications between specialists will be required.

Since this is a completely new line of work for the company, at least one thousand new professionals must be hired. Although the production workers are skilled craftsmen, many must have new training. Given the time pressure, production and design may occur simultaneously, meaning that the engineers will have to spend a good deal of time on the shop floor. Further, since the product is difficult to make, the workers on the job may be able to make useful suggestions to the engineers.

Top management is known as being tough. It has always had tight controls as well as rigid rules and standards. The company pays well, but it expects its employees to do things the company way.

1. What kinds of problems will this company face as it develops and produces this new product?
2. What kind of OD program does it need?
3. What kind of structural changes may be necessary?

2 • Hotel Corporation

Hotel Corporation has grown rapidly through the purchase of locally owned hotels. The company president hopes to project a consistent corporate "with-it" image and to enjoy economies of scale through centralizing some operations. Headquarters staff departments include: marketing, reservations, finance, interior decoration, culinary, and methods standardization. For the most part, these departments are staffed by whiz kids straight from college.

Each hotel is managed by an experienced general manager, usually retained from the previous ownership and familiar with local conditions.

Frictions have been developing among staff departments. Finance, for example, objects to Interior Decoration's insistence that each hotel feature original works of contemporary sculpture. The president's spouse intervenes on Interior Decoration's side and purchases much of the sculpture personally.

Staff people report considerable unrest at the local level. Many of the local hotel managers are petty autocrats, uncooperative, and "too busy" to see visiting staff members. Lower-level functionaries resist change: several chefs insist that nationally prescribed menus violate local tastes. A Dallas head bartender insists that Texas customers want more than one ounce of gin in their gin fizzes.

The company president has just returned from a T-group. Full of enthusiasm, she would like all her managers to have the benefit of T-groups. She also wants to introduce internalized motivation throughout the organization. You are an OD expert, and she asks your advice.

1. What are this company's problems?
2. What advice would you give the president?

part 5

compensation

wage and salary administration

Ask people why they work, and chances are they will say to make money. True, men and women want more from their jobs than just a wage or salary—yet this is a basic need. Even teachers and ministers, who may willingly accept less take-home pay for more on-the-job satisfaction, regard *relative* pay as highly important. A professor may be fairly unconcerned about the fact that he earns less than a bricklayer, but still he may become enraged if Professor *X* across the hall, with six publications fewer than his, gets a salary increase while he does not. Pay provides more than a means of satisfying physical needs—it provides recognition and a sense of accomplishment. Alleged wage and salary inequities are among the most dangerous sources of friction and low morale in an organization.

Without a sound policy of *wage administration*, wages are often determined on the basis of "personalized," arbitrary decisions without regard for the overall wage structure.[1] (For the sake of brevity, we will talk about "wage administration" rather than "wage and salary administration," since roughly the same problems are in-

---

[1] For further description of wage and salary administration techniques, see Thomas H. Patten, *Pay: Employee Compensation and Incentive Plans* (New York: Free Press, 1977); David Belcher, *Compensation Administration* (Englewood Cliffs, N.J.: Prentice-Hall, 1974); and Richard I. Henderson, *Compensation Management* (Reston, Va.: Reston, 1976).

volved.) Wage administration is a *systematic procedure* for establishing a sound compensation structure. By reducing inequities among employees' earnings, a good wage-administration program raises individual morale and reduces inter-group friction. It also sets wages high enough to permit the organization to recruit satisfactory employees (but not so high as to cause unnecessary expense), motivates people to work for pay increases and promotions, reduced union and employee grievances, and enables management to exercise centralized control over the largest single item of cost: wages and salaries. But, as we shall see, some of these objectives are in conflict.

Aspects of wage and salary administration

There are four closely related aspects of wage administration: wage and salary surveys, job evaluation, merit rating, and incentives. *Wage and salary surveys* are designed to determine the general pay level in the community and industry, thus giving a company a base for setting its own rates. *Job evalatuion* establishes the relationships between wages on various jobs within the organization. Together, wage surveys and job evaluation set the "base" or minimum rates for each job.

Instead of setting one rate for each job, many companies establish a series of rates or *steps*. New employees normally start at the *base rate* for the job; then, as they gain proficiency and seniority, they advance through *merit rating* to higher steps. (Merit rating on one job should not be confused with *promotion* from one job to another.)

Companies with *incentive* plans pay the base rate only for a "normal" amount of production, as determined by time study. If a worker produces more than normal, he receives an extra incentive bonus. Similarly, salaried personnel may qualify for bonus earnings of one kind or another.

The personnel department is normally responsible for the administration of the wage and salary program and often has a special division that concentrates on this function. Top management, however, has a continuing responsibility to review wage and salary policies, and every level of management may become involved in merit rating and in introducing a new job-evaluation program.

In this chapter we shall review the factors that must be taken into account in setting the over-all wage level through wage and salary surveys. Then we shall look at job evaluation and merit rating, and finally we shall consider some of the special problems involved in salary administration for executives and engineers. (Incentives will be considered in Chap. 19.)

Determining the overall wage and salary level

Determining the overall wage and salary policy—whether to pay wages and salaries that are high, average, or below-average as compared with standards elsewhere—is one of management's most difficult decisions. What factors must management take into account in making this decision?

- Wage policy is related to recruitment and selection policy, for high wages attract more job applicants and permit management to choose employees from a wider reservoir of talents.[2] Moreover, they help maintain morale and make employees more reluctant to quit their jobs. Yet high wages in themselves do not guarantee motivation for high productivity unless the employee somehow perceives that harder work will in fact be rewarded by higher pay. (A sound merit-rating and promotional policy may provide such motivation.)

- Employment conditions naturally affect wage policy. When there is a great deal of unemployment, a nonunionized company may be able to hire all the people it needs at the legal minimum wage. When the labor market is tight, an employer may have to pay more than the going rate if it is to recruit qualified new employees.

- If a company is anxious to gain a retputation in the community as a good employer and a good citizen—as are many public utilities—it may decide to pay high wages to insure good public relations. Small organizations not in the public spotlight are not under compulsion to follow suit.

- Unionized companies may be forced to pay high wages as a result of union pressure. Nonunionized companies may pay equally high wages to keep the union out. Yet if wages are too high, other employers may object that the company is "unstabilizing the market" and may exert subtle pressures to bring the company into line.

- A company's profitability sets limits on its wage policy. The company that is losing money cannot afford to pay more than the minimum; the company that is known to be profitable is expected by the community and its employees to pay liberally.

- Wage policies may be influenced by other factors too. Companies known for their stability of employment need not pay wages as high as those in which layoffs are frequent. Substantial fringe benefits may also reduce the need for high wages.

Once the organization has decided on its overall wage policy, the next question it must answer is this: What are other companies paying on *comparable* jobs? This information is useful in determining whether the company is meeting community standards and also in bargaining with the union. The U.S. Bureau of Labor Statistics collects data for many jobs in large cities, and employers' and trade associations often make available more detailed data. There are times, however, when a company is obliged to conduct a *wage survey* itself.

This is not an easy task. What are "comparable" jobs in other companies? It is simple enough to call another company and ask, "What are you paying your machine operators?" The other company answers $9.10 an hour; that makes you feel good, since you pay $9.20. But the other company failed to mention that their operators also earn incentive bonuses and do easier work than yours. To ensure getting data that are really comparable, the organization should collect much data.

Rarely are two jobs performed in exactly the same way in different firms. Consideration must also be given to fringe benefits and continuity of employment. It is traditional, for instance, for maintenance people in factories to get lower pay than maintenance people who work for construction firms, because the latter are less assured of steady employment.

---

[2] If an organization pays high wages, it must pay more attention to selection; if it pays low wages, it must stress training.

What companies should you use as the basis of your comparison—companies in the same community regardless of industry or companies throughout the country in your industry? The management of nationwide firms faces the problem of whether to pay uniform wages throughout all its plants or to adjust to community wage patterns. At times it is far from clear in what industry a firm should be classified. For instance, is a firm that makes rubber soles in the shoe industry or the rubber industry? Unionized firms are under pressure to pay the wages equivalent to those paid by other firms that have contracts with the same unions, even though these firms may be in other industries.

After the wage-survey figures have been gathered, the organization must exercise great caution in interpreting them, particularly if, as often happens, there is no central tendency or clear "going rate." The survey itself, however, does provide a series of bench marks against which the company can compare its present wage rates and decide whether adjustments are necessary to make them consistent with its overall wage policy. Surveys are meaningful chiefly for "key" jobs common to many firms. Wages for jobs that are unique to a given firm cannot be set by wage surveys alone.

The company should keep its rates under constant review—if the workers are unionized, of course, management will have little chance to forget this need. New surveys should be made periodically to determine whether the company's rates are getting out of line.

Once the overall wage level has been set, the company can turn to a consideration of individual rates. Here job evaluation is widely used.

Job evaluation

Strictly speaking, job evaluation is a method of determining the *relationships among* wage and salary rates, not the rates themselves. In practice it is hard to consider these two questions separately. In theory, for instance, the completion of a job-evaluation program need not lead to any increase in the total wage bill: some people will get increases others decreases. In practice, however, some increase in the wage bill is necessary if the program is to be accepted by the employees; normally no one gets his wage cut. Furthermore, if the rates that are finally set for any job are out of line with prevailing rates for that job in the community, the job-evaluation program may have to be adjusted.

Job evaluation is a systematic way of applying judgment, but it does not eliminate the need for exercising judgment. It is not an automatic process, for it is administered by people and is subject to all the human frailties.

There are many methods of job evaluation, some of which are quite simple but many of which are extremely complicated. In essence, however, all forms of job evaluation are designed to enable management to determine how much one job should pay relative to others. The *point system* is the most common system of job evaluation, though the *ranking, job-classification,* and *factor-comparison methods* are also widely used.[3]

[3] The *ranking* method, as its name implies, involves listing a given set of jobs in order of importance, from highest to lowest, taking into account the characteristics of each job as a whole (though sometimes specific factors, such as job difficulty, are given special attention). The *job classification* system, used by many government agencies, is also somewhat self-descriptive. First, a set of job

The point system   The point system involves four steps, which we will first describe briefly and then discuss at some length:

Step 1: A manual or yardstick is drawn up (for an example, look at pp. 399–400), which provides a set of standards against which each job can be compared. Notice that the manual lists a number of *factors* on which each job is to be rated and then breaks each factor down into a number of *degrees.* Each degree is worth a certain number of *points.*

Step 2: The requirements of each job are described and listed in a standardized fashion in what is called a *job description* or *job specification.* (See p. 375 for an example.)

Step 3: Each job—as described in the job specification— is rated, one factor at a time, in accordance with the manual. A point value is assigned to each factor. Then the points are added up.

Step 4: Each job is slotted into a *job classification* in accordance with its evaluated point total. A wage rate is then assigned to the job.

Step 1: setting up the manual

It is difficult to draw up a job-evaluation manual that is consistent and free from ambiguity. Because of this difficulty, many companies adopt standardized, ready-to-use plans prepared by such organizations as the National Metal Trades Association. Other companies, particularly those that have jobs with unique characteristics, prefer to draft their own custom-made manual. In either case, management should be aware of some of the problems involved in preparing job-evaluation manuals.

Selecting factors.   What are the factors or dimensions on which the jobs are to be evaluated? Each factor represents a certain characteristic of the job that management feels is worth compensating. Two of the best-known plans, those of the National Metal Trades Association and the National Electrical Manufacturers Association, use the following factors, with the weights indicated:

Skill (total 50%)

Education 14%
Experience 22%
Initiative and ingenuity 14%

Responsibility (total 20%)

Equipment, process 5%
Material or product 5%
Safety of others 5%
Work of others 5%

Effort (total 15%)

Physical demand 10%
Mental or visual 5%

Job Conditions (total 15%)

Working conditions 10%
Hazards 5%

---

classifications or grades is established (say from Grade 1 to Grade 12); then the level of difficulty of each classification is carefully described; and finally individual jobs are fitted into what seems their most appropriate classification. All this is done without the elaborate analysis that occurs in the point system. The *factor comparison* system is too complex to describe here; see Patten, *Pay,* pp. 230 ff.

Naturally, different factors are used in evaluating supervisory jobs than in evaluating, say, production or clerical jobs. A job-evaluation manual for supervisory jobs might list such factors as public contacts, staff contacts, complexity of duties, responsibility for money, and number of employees supervised—factors that would be largely irrelevant on hourly-paid jobs.

Some plans have used as many as 40 factors, but the trend has been to use considerably fewer. A plan with fewer factors is simpler and easier to understand, and statistical studies have shown that almost the same results are obtained when only two or three factors are used. Thus, increasing the number of factors may not result in a more "accurate" job evaluation. Still, it may be desirable to have a reasonably large number of factors to help reduce employee complaints that important factors are ignored.

Selecting degrees. Just as inches are a basic unit in determining length, so degrees are the basic unit in measuring the importance of any one factor in a given job. There is no set rule governing the number of degrees into which a factor should be broken down. If the scope of the jobs to be evaluated covers a wide range, from unskilled through highly skilled, there will be a large number of degrees. However, if there are too many degrees it may be hard to distinguish one from another.

It is helpful to define the degrees as closely as possible (for example, see problem 1, end of chapter). "Lifts weights in excess of 50 lb" is more specific than "Lifts heavy weights." But there is a danger in being *too* specific. Physical effort is more than a matter of pure weight-lifting; constantly carrying a number of small bulky objects may be more tiring than infrequently lifting an easily grasped heavy object.

Assigning weights to factors and degrees. Next, point values must be assigned to each degree of each factor. The table summarizes the point values that have been assigned by the manual in problem 1.

			Degrees					Points assigned to factors
Factors	1	2	3	4	5	6	7	
Education	20	40	60	80	100	120	140	
Training	20	40	60	80	100	120	140	
Physical effort	25	50	75	100				
Dexterity	60	120	180	240				
Mental effort	20	40	60	80				
Responsibility	25	50	75	100				
Working conditions	20	40	60	80	100			
Safety	20	40	60	80	100			

At best, this process must be completely arbitrary. One must, for example, decide whether a requirement of "two years of college or equivalent" is worth more or fewer points than "hard work with constant physical strain."

The number of points may total 500 or 1,000 or even more. The reason is purely psychological: it is easier to justify not putting a person into a higher rate range if he is 10 points off out of 1,000 than if he is 1 point off of 100. Note that since the relative standing of the jobs is the thing that counts, it makes no difference if point values are added or multiplied, provided each factor is treated in the same way.

Step 2: drawing up job specifications

Although many knotty problems of judgment are involved in drawing up the job-evaluation manual, in practice the really difficult disputes start when job evaluation moves from the general to the specific—when specific individuals first become involved in drawing up job specifications.

Job titles.   The first question is one that is discussed in an earlier context: what does a particular job consist of? How should one draw the boundaries around a specific job title?

The common union insistence that an employee should not work outside his classification has important ramifications here. Questions of status are also involved. A highly skilled programmer might object to the same job title as someone with no skill at all. A man who is proud of being called the "executive assistant to the division manager" may be very unhappy to have his title changed to "clerk II."

Job description.   Next, each job must be described—that is, a list must be compiled of its duties and responsibilities (see the inadequate example on pp. 400–401). Particularly in unionized plants, the job description must be prepared with great care, since many union members refuse to perform duties not specifically listed in their job descriptions.

Management faces a dilemma here. If it includes only a few of a person's duties in a job description, he or she may well refuse to perform others. Yet every additional requirement in the description tends to inflate the number of points given to the job and therefore improves the union's case for getting more pay. Further, a job's real nature is misrepresented when the job description gives equal weight to main functions and to those performed rarely. On the other hand, there is the danger that jobs will be defined so narrowly and rigidly that job enrichment will be almost impossible.

Furthermore, job description cannot be performed in a vacuum, for it impinges on many areas of status and informal organization. An impressive job description builds up one's prestige. Purely as a matter of pride, workers want their job description to sound difficult. Companies that have tried to base their job descriptions on questionnaires filled out by the employees themselves have discovered that there is a strong tendency to puff up one's job beyond recognition.

Job specification.   The next procedure is to formulate the job specification itself. This means breaking the general job description down into specific categories, one for each factor. Here, for each job, one must decide such questions as how many years of schooling are required, how much noise is involved,

| | | | Code 369 |
| | | | Date Jan. 30, 19-- |

Job title Maintenance Mechanic **Department** Main Assembly

Factor	Rating	Points	Rating basis
Knowledge	C	84	Requires ability to interpret drawings and execute complex instructions; must be able to set up and operate high-speed manufacturing equipment as well as to diagnose and repair equipment breakdowns.
Experience	E	132	Two years on-the-job training required plus at least one year's experience as an operator.
Initiative and ingenuity	D	112	Equipment can break down frequently and unpredictably. Analysis of causes of breakdown difficult. Search procedure to determine cause of breakdown often follows standard sequence, but considerable initiative is required.
Physical effort	B	20	Intermittent physical activity required to adjust and replace equipment. Some physical effort when nuts are frozen, etc.
Mental and visual effort	D	40	Nature of work varies. Considerable concentration required during periods of machine breakdown. Alertness is required to avoid mistakes.
Responsibility	D	80	Probable loss from errors $500-$1,000.
Working conditions	D	60	Almost continuous noise. Occasionally must work in cramped quarters or in unusual positions.
Safety	C	50	Danger that equipment will be inadvertently started while being worked on. Possibility that equipment may break under stress. Low possibility of burns.

Total points 578 **Evaluated by** CB **Checked by** BW

Job specification with points assigned.

and so forth. (An example of a job specification is illustrated on p. 375.) A careful job specification is useful in selection and training as well as in actual job evaluation.

Now we come to the critical point: rating each job by assigning a certain number of degrees to each factor. The points are then computed and added together. The total is the *evaluated point score* for the given job (in the example on p. 375, it is 578 total points).

Though job specifications and the job-evaluation manual may make rating easier and more systematic, rating is still entirely a matter of judgment. As such, it is subject to all sorts of human bias, including:

The halo effect. (See our discussion, p. 329.)

Leniency. Raters tend to be overly generous in handing out points There is no harm in this provided they are equally generous with all jobs, since job evaluation is a matter of *relative* standing.

Consistency. Regardless of how carefully the manual has been written, there will be countless questions of interpretation. The problem is to achieve consistency in interpretation. Seemingly irrational decisions that are consistent with each other may be better than more rational decisions that are inconsistent.

One plan assigned 100 points for constant noise and 80 points for intermittent noise. A machine on which many of the employees worked made a great deal of noise 300 times a minute, but this job was classified as having intermittent noise. When a new job was established in this shop, the union insisted that it should be evaluated as being subject to "constant noise." Management objected on the ground that this noise had been rated as intermittent for years and that if 20 points were added to this new job for constant noise, 20 points should be added to all other jobs in the shop. Doing this would amount to giving a general wage increase to 30 percent of the employees. The company argued that the union should wait until the contract expired to demand a change.

Eventually the matter went to arbitration. Though the arbitrator agreed that the noise sounded pretty constant to him, he still ruled for the company. He pointed out that the purpose of job evaluation was to establish *relative* wage rates and that to give this job an additional 20 points would disturb the traditional relationship among jobs.

From this point on, evaluation schemes vary a great deal. We will describe one common variety.

Once the point scores for each job have been calculated, they are plotted on a graph with point scores on one axis and present wage rates on the other. Notice that in the graph, the utility assembler is evaluated at 300 points and now makes $5.40 an hour.

Next a trend line is drawn through the data, either freehand or in accordance with some mathematical formula. Jobs that lie above the trend line are presumably overpaid; those that lie below are underpaid. In the example given, the assembler is overpaid by 20 cents an hour, the tool and die maker underpaid by 20 cents.

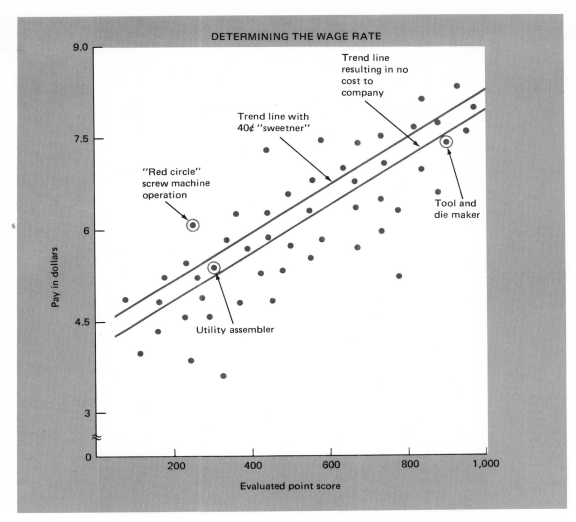

DETERMINING THE WAGE RATE

If the trend line has been properly drawn, the cost of bringing the under-paid jobs *up* to the trend line is just balanced by the savings achieved by bringing those that are overpaid *down* to the line. If the rates are adjusted in this way, roughly half the employees will get wage increases and half will get wage cuts. However, such widespread wage cuts will make it extremely difficult to win acceptance of the plan (since the worker who is about to get a cut will normally react much more violently than the one who is about to get a raise). Management can adopt two approaches to make the change more palatable:

1. "Sweeteners." Management may decide to offer a "sweetener"—a wage adjustment that will make the plan more acceptable. For example, it may draw the trend line 40 cents above the present mid-point, causing fewer workers to suffer wage cuts. The utility assembler, for instance, would get a

20 cent raise instead of a 20 cent cut, while the tool and die maker would get a 60 cent raise. This sweetener is sometimes called an "adjustment for inequities." Note that it costs the company as much as an across-the-board wage increase. (Normally management determines the size of the "sweetener" by referring to collective bargaining or wage surveys.)

2. "Red-circle rates." Management may also guarantee the employees who are now overpaid that as long as they *personally* are on this job the rate will not be cut. However, anyone who takes their place will receive only the rate set by job evaluation. This is traditionally called "red-circling" the job. (Note that in the figure the screw-machine operator has been red-circled.)

Often, too, when there is a general wage increase, the employees on red-circle jobs get no increase or only a partial increase until the evaluated rate catches up with the red-circle rate.

Job classifications. Actually, instead of separate wage rates for each job, it is common under job evaluation to bracket jobs with roughly similar

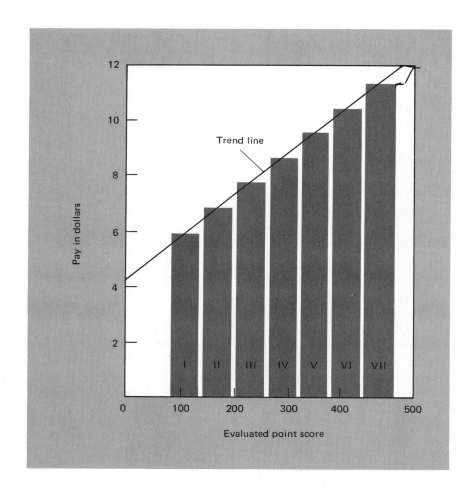

point totals into *job classifications* (sometimes called labor grades). Each of these receives the same rate of pay (see chart on p. 378).

Since moving from one job classification to another constitutes a promotion, management should give careful thought to the number of job classifications it establishes (see page 157). If there are too few classifications, it will be hard to promote employees and give them the feeling that they are moving ahead. On the other hand, if there are too many grades, every time a worker changes his work slightly, he or she may move into a different classification with a different rate of pay. Too many changes create expense and confusion.

Policy problems

There is far more to job evaluation than merely going through the mechanical procedures we have just described. True, by following these procedures management can tentatively slot each job into a classification, and for each classification it can set a wage or salary rate. However, job evaluation cannot provide scientifically determined or objectively fair rates. As we have seen, it is a highly subjective process and there is much room for judgment and human error.

But it is not enough to strive for complete objectivity. The crucial question is not whether management has followed the job-evaluation procedures with scrupulous care but whether the resulting wage and salary structure meets the objectives of sound wage administration. In particular, does the structure provide rates that seem fair to those concerned? Will it attract and retain competent employees?

In short, an effective program of job evaluation should be concerned with employee values on the one hand and going market rates on the other. These criteria are sometimes called "internal" and "external" standards. A technically sound job-evaluation plan that ignores either of these standards is bound to lead to friction and to fail in achieving its objectives. To complicate matters even further, these standards themselves are often in conflict.

Who gets compared. Usually there are separate job-evaluation programs for production, technical, supervisory, and clerical personnel. Perhaps from a theoretical point of view it would be fairer to compare jobs in all these categories against each other, but the practical difficulties would be enormous. The less jobs have in common, the more difficult it is to compare them.

Internal standards

The job requirements of nurse, sales engineer, and riveter, for example, have so little in common that it would be almost impossible to get agreement on which factors are the relevant ones to compare. Fortunately, there is little need to do so. People tend to compare their jobs only with those "close by" them. A clerical worker is unlikely to compare her wage with that paid for any specific production job (though she may feel that all production workers earn too much). Consequently, as long as it doesn't lead to discrimination on the basis of age, sex, or race, it is possible to establish separate programs for each group and to exercise a separate set of criteria for each program.

It has even been suggested that there should be separate job-evaluation programs for automated and nonautomated jobs. On automated jobs, responsibility is the most important factor; on nonautomated jobs, skills are most important. A program that gives equal weight to both factors might not be fair to either kind of job. Recent research suggests that once other factors (such as the training time required for the job) are held constant, people on routine jobs tend to receive higher pay than do people on nonroutine jobs.[4]

Rates should seem fair. A major cause of employee discontent is the *status inconsistency* that develops when various measures of status, such as job title and size of office, get out of line. Two of the major determinants of status are the nature of a person's work and the size of the paycheck. Great dissatisfaction arises when the *people concerned* decide that these determinants are out of line. One purpose of job evaluation, therefore, is to realign the status ladder so as to reduce the perceived inconsistencies between pay and job requirements. Here, it is the view of the people affected that is important, not the so-called objective measurements of some staff person or outsider.

Employees in most situations have a pretty good idea of what various jobs are worth. In part this is a matter of tradition. Job *A* has always paid more than job *B*. Yet the "accepted" wage structure varies widely from one situation to another.

In many cities police officers and fire fighters enjoy "pay parity"; i.e., they receive the same pay. In others, police officers are paid more.

In plant *X*, maintenance plumbers are paid more than electricians. In plant *Y*, the reverse is true. In plant *Z*, all maintenance classifications receive the same pay. These relations have existed for a long time in each plant, and all parties regard them as fair.

Job evaluation may be most readily accepted (and most acutely needed) in new plants and offices, where there are no traditional rates, and in old plants where technological change has thrown all the old job responsibilities and wage relationships into a state of flux.

In any case, care must be taken not to disturb established status hierarchies. If employees are generally satisfied with current pay relationships, why upset the applecart to achieve the theoretical equity afforded by job evaluation? If job *A* has always paid more than job *B*, in the eyes of the employees job *A* is a better job. An "*A*" person has always had a tendency to look down on a "*B*" person. Now suppose job evaluation leads to higher pay for job *B* than for job *A*. The pay on job *A* has not been cut, but status is a relative thing and job *A* now has lower status than job *B*. The "*A*" people consider themselves demoted; they are frustrated, lose interest in their work, and may even quit or take a militant antimanagement position in the union.

Job evaluation can also unwittingly upset promotional sequences. Let us assume that jobs *A* and *B* are in the same "seniority district"—that is, when there is a vacancy in either job, employees from the entire "district" may bid for it. Naturally if job *A* originally paid more than job *B*, the senior person would tend to move to job *A* and turn down job *B*. Moving to job *A* would be considered a promotion. Now job evaluation reverses this relationship: job

[4] Robert B. Lucas, "Hedonic Wage Equations and Psychic Wages," *American Economic Review* 67, No. 4 (September 1977), 549–58.

B becomes the better job. People who had previously chosen job *A* over job *B* are understandably bitter. Then senior people on job *A* will be getting less than junior people on job *B*. Of course, management may permit the senior individuals on job *A* to "bump" the junior people from job *B*, but the bumping period will be one of confusion and expense to management and of great ill-feeling on the part of employees.

Another problem arises in evaluating hard, dirty jobs. According to worker logic, clean jobs are better than dirty ones. New people should start at the bottom, at the hardest, dirtiest, least desirable jobs. Then, as they acquire seniority, they should move up to better, easier, higher-paying jobs. But this is contradictory to the logic of job evaluation, which says that more points should be given for hard work and dirty conditions. Yet people will resist being "promoted" into a higher-paying job that has lower status. In practice, this problem is solved by giving very low point values to the factors of physical effort and job conditions—or by socially separating the two kinds of jobs so that there will be little invidious comparison. At times management disregards the logic of job evaluation almost completely; dirty jobs are paid less than clean jobs. But the dirty job is a starting job through which all employees must move. As an employee get promoted, he or she moves by the ordinary process of seniority from a dirty, low-paid, low-status job to a cleaner, higher-paid, higher-status job.

Similarly, people in dead-end jobs, which offer little opportunity for promotion, feel that they should be somehow recompensed for this disadvantage. So do employees whose jobs have been automated. Perhaps their work requires less skill and effort than before. Nevertheless, their output has been greatly increased, and they feel that some of the benefits should go to them. Strict job evaluation would say that since less skill and effort are required, the wage for the job should be cut.

Another question concerns the differentials between skilled and unskilled work (in effect, the slope of the trend line mentioned on p. 377). Often the sequence runs something like this: the union asks that wage increases be given on a cents-per-hour basis (say 40 cents an hour for all employees). Management concedes this demand, and differentials are reduced. Predictably, the skilled tradespeople object. Next time around they are given "special adjustments" that tend to restore the previous relationship. Thus the relative size of the differentials varies from time to time, depending in part on internal union pressures.

Thus, there are many factors that wage administration must take into account other than the abstract requirements of the job as determined by job evaluation. We should emphasize again that the objective is to obtain wage standards that *seem fair* to the people involved. The outsider should not substitute his frame of reference for that of the people involved (except on moral and legal grounds to prevent sex or ethnic discrimination).

External factors

It is not enough for wage administration to achieve internal consistency, however, for employees and their unions compare their wages with those paid on comparable jobs in other organizations. If wages lag behind those paid for similar work elsewhere, some employees may quit, the rest may grow dissatisfied, and it will be harder to hire replacements. External comparisons are more likely to be made in some situations than in others.

- Skilled maintenance personnel and unskilled common laborers are more likely to make such comparisons than are workers who hold jobs in the middle range of the spectrum. Maintenance jobs are pretty much alike throughout the community; the carpenter, for instance, knows what he can earn elsewhere. To a lesser extent the same is true of unskilled laborers' jobs, the starting jobs at which new employees are hired.

  In some recent years, wages in the unionized building trades have risen faster than they have in manufacturing. As a consequence, manufacturing firms have been placed under pressure to give special increases to their skilled maintenance personnel (such as plumbers or electricians)—increases not justified by job evaluation (and of course, when one group receives a special increase, other groups insist on them too).

  There is less market pressure on semiskilled jobs. These are not hiring jobs; one must have considerable seniority to earn them. Although semiskilled employees may become dissatisfied with low pay, they are less willing to quit because they will lose their seniority, pension rights, and so forth. In any case, most semiskilled jobs are relatively specialized; there are fewer comparable jobs, so fewer comparisons are made.

- Comparisons are more likely to be made in times of full employment when a new worker can choose among employers and when older employees can transfer to jobs elsewhere.

- Workers are less likely to make comparisons if the plant is geographically isolated or if the type of work is so highly specialized that there are few comparable jobs.

- Research suggests that there are considerable differences among employees in terms of the "reference groups" with which they make wage and salary comparisons. These differences relate to background, personality, and occupation.[5] For example, blue-collar workers, generally, and lower-level managers tend to compare their earnings with co-workers and relatives; upwardly mobile employees and those with higher education tend to make comparisons outside their own companies. Among staff personnel (such as engineers) the higher their professional orientation, the more likely that their comparisons will be with jobs in other organizations.

Thus, the pressure to meet comparable rates is higher in times of full employment and in certain job ranges. Many companies use wage surveys to keep their wages from getting inadvertently out of line, in terms of either overall wage levels or of specific jobs that are common to many enterprises.

Reconciling internal and external standards

What should an organization do when internal and external standards conflict, when the rates set by job evaluation are lower than those set by the market? High-wage companies need not worry too much about this problem, since most of their evaluated rates are well above those of the market.

---

[5] Paul S. Goodman, "An Examination of Referents Used in the Evaluation of Pay," *Organizational Behavior and Human Performance* Vol. 12 (1974), 170–95; Martin Patchen, *The Choice of Wage Comparisons* (Englewood Cliffs, N.J.: Prentice-Hall, 1961).

However, the lower the organization's average pay, the more likely wage rates set by job evaluation will be below those determined by the market.

Job evaluation frequently favors groups different from those favored by the market. According to one of the earliest discussions of this topic:

The jobs which tend to rate high as compared with the market are those of janitor, nurse, and typist, while craft rates are comparatively low. Weaker groups are better served by an evaluation plan than by the market; the former places the emphasis not on force but on equity. Ideally, for a system of factors to accurately reflect the market, it should give heavy weight to those considerations to which the market most responds: skill, job conditions and bargaining power.[6]

Some sort of adjustment is required when the market rate on a specific job is higher than the evaluated rate. Many companies pay an "out-of-line" rate. Other companies engage in trial-and-error adjustments to make their job-evaluation scheme conform more closely to market forces. For instance, if some rates are well above the market and others below, the job-evaluation manual may be giving the wrong weights to the various factors, and these weights should be corrected.

The greater the difference between evaluated rates and market rates and the lower the company's average pay, the more point-juggling and factor-balancing will be required to devise an acceptable wage structure. Finally, there comes a point where job evaluation simply isn't worth the trouble. A really low-wage employer in a highly competitive industry, for instance, will have little use for job evaluation. It will pay the lowest rate it can to recruit or retain employees for each job.

Many companies follow market rates exclusively for skilled jobs and use job evaluation only for semiskilled jobs on which it is difficult to make comparisons with other companies. Or a company may pay prevailing rates on jobs for which such rates exist and then use job evaluation to interpolate other job rates between those set by the market.

Thus, if job evaluation is flexible enough, there need be little conflict between the rates it establishes and the external standards set by the market. But this very flexibility may lead to conflict with internal standards. According to job evaluation, jobs Q and R are equally difficult, and for years they have been paid the same rate. Then a tremendous demand arises in the community for workers to do job R. On the principle of adjusting to market rates, R's pay is raised while Q's remains the same. Q protests, "My job is as hard as his. Why shouldn't I get an increase too?" Whether satisfactory adjustments can be made, however, depends at least as much on how the plan is administered as on the rates that are set.

Avoiding sex discrimination

As we have seen, there is a long tradition that "women's jobs" pay less than those normally held by men, even when women (for example, nurses)

[6] Clark Kerr and Lloyd H. Fisher, "Effect of Environment and Administration on Job Evaluation," in Paul Pigors and Charles A. Myers, eds., *Readings in Personnel Administration* (New York: McGraw-Hill, 1952), p. 392.

go through longer periods of education and training than do men (for example, truck drivers). Since this was a traditional relationship, most people also tended to accept it as "fair." The sex differential met the standards of both internal and external equity.

Today these traditional relationships are being challenged. The Equal Pay Act of 1963 requires that men and women receive equal pay for "equal work requiring equal skill, effort, and responsibilities that are performed under similar working conditions." Though this wording seems to apply only to jobs that are exactly equal, attempts are being made to require that jobs of "comparable worth" be paid the same. If successful, these efforts may force organizations to drop the common practice of separately evaluating clerical and manufacturing jobs. Indeed, the future may bring much closer government scrutiny of all company wage administration practices and undermine the old principle that jobs be paid in accordance with supply and demand.

Administration

Any system of job evaluation is doomed to failure unless it is accepted as fair by all parties concerned. Introducing a job-evaluation plan sets loose a host of fears. Employees fear that job evaluation will upset the old structure of social relations; supervisors fear that it will deprive them of their traditional prerogative to set the wages of those who work for them; the union fears that it will reduce the scope of collective bargaining. All may look on job evaluation as an impersonal, impossible-to-understand system that threatens their old established ways of doing things.

One way of reducing these fears is to make the plan easier to understand; indeed, there is a trend toward greater simplicity. Another is to involve the maximum number of people in administering the plan. In general, the larger the number of people who take part, the more likely the plan is to be accepted—though there is always danger that if too many people are involved in the early stages, they will spend so much time in discussion that the plan will never be put into effect.

In a nonunionized organization, the job-evaluation program is sometimes administered by a committee representing a broad range of departments. The line supervisors involved are consulted, and their approval is required before a job specification is made final. Moreover, the individual workers are consulted when the job specifications are drawn up. Usually the personnel department acts as general coordinator for the program, though a few companies assign this task to the industrial engineering department.

One of the problems of administration is deciding on the proper degree of centralization. Should job evaluation be conducted on an officewide, a plantwide, or a companywide basis? To what extent should the individual supervisor be permitted to make exceptions in special cases (for example, to grant a salary increase to avoid losing an exceptionally good worker)? Too much centralization severely limits the freedom of the individual manager; too little makes it possible for a manager to be exceptionally liberal, thus adding unnecessary expense and raising the danger that others will feel discriminated against.

The trend is toward allowing managers to make exceptions but only with the approval of the personnel department.

Once a plan has been set up, constant "maintenance" is needed to keep inequities from arising. Changes may occur either in wage rates elsewhere or in the job requirements of particular jobs. New jobs are created and must be evaluated. Suppose, after a plan has been put into effect, that one group is still very much upset over the wage rate it has received. Neither wage rates elsewhere nor job requirements within the company have changed. Should the job-evaluation administrator give this group another hearing and perhaps yield to its pressure? Many authorities suggest that the administrator should be quite willing to make adjustments *before* the plan is finally adopted, but should strongly resist pressure for change *after* the plan has been adopted. If the administrator does not stand fast, every discontented group will make trouble, and unrest will persist indefinitely.

Regardless of the care shown by job evaluators, average ratings tend to drift upward. Jobs are constantly changing over time. The employee whose job has become harder will almost certainly ask that the job be evaluated upward, and the boss will be hard-pressed not to recommend that this request be granted. But the individuals whose job has become easier and less challenging are likely to keep very quiet about this fact (psychologically they may not even accept that it has occurred). If their boss is aware of the change, he will doubtless feel that to initiate a pay cut will be a sure way to antagonize his employees.

Wage drift

Similarly, if a job is filled by an exceptionally competent person, there will be pressure to rate the job higher, and it will be difficult to downgrade the job when the person leaves. Finally, even on jobs on which there have been no changes at all, as the job holders get older and see their colleagues on other jobs get raises, they begin to lobby both union and management to get their own jobs upgraded too (often calling for a "long-overdue increase" if there is no recent change to justify it).

Thus job rates are flexible only one way—upward—and the drift may be substantial. If it leads to a great feeling of inequity among employees or if the resultant wage rates are unrealistic in terms of the labor market, then a totally new job evaluation may be required.

Union attitudes toward job evaluation vary greatly, more in response to the overall quality of union-management relations than to union policy toward job evaluation as such. Union objections center around the charge that job evaluation is a management tool used to restrict or eliminate collective bargaining. By its very nature, some union leaders argue, job evaluation prevents a realistic consideration of market forces or bargaining strength, and it makes it impossible to work out adjustments suited to individual needs.

*The role of
the union*

Nevertheless, job evaluation is often introduced in the first place in response to the union's insistence that something be done to eliminate wage inequities. Union proponents of job evaluation argue that job evaluation is merely a systematic framework for negotiation.

In practice, the role of the union varies from outright opposition to complete participation. The UAW, for instance, is firmly opposed to evaluation. As a consequence, some automobile manufacturers engage in informal evaluation for their own purposes but make no use of it in negotiations. The Steelworkers' Union, on the other hand, participated actively in an industrywide job evaluation program covering most of the basic steel industry.

Some of the unions that believe in complete participation appoint specially trained representatives to assist in the process. Local unions often select members who are then trained by management to sit on joint union-management evaluation committees. These committee members participate equally with management in writing job descriptions, rating jobs, and setting rates. A different approach is for the company to conduct the entire evaluation but to secure union approval at every stage, or to guarantee the union the right to object only to the end product.

One reason for the union's reluctance to take an active part in the evaluation procedure is its realization that job evaluation is a thankless job. Many of the questions that arise concern disputes between union members over who should have higher status. Regardless of how impartial the union officers try to be, some members will accuse them of favoritism. Rather than make themselves the butt of complaints, many officers would prefer to let management take the responsibility and reserve for themselves the freedom to criticize from the sideline. For this same reason, management is often glad to pass the buck to the union, if it will accept it.

Management has good reason to encourage the union to take an active role in job evaluation. To repeat the theme of this chapter, one of the primary objectives of job evaluation is to devise a wage structure that workers regard as fair. The union is in an ideal position to sample worker opinions.

Whether job evaluation is desirable depends directly on the state of union-management relations. Certainly a joint committee will turn into a battleground if a cold war is in progress between the parties. On the other hand, if management is flexible in its attitude toward job evaluation and if the union is favorable to it, there may be very little distinction between bargained and evaluated rates.

When should management engage in job evaluation?

Job evaluation has been adopted in many organizations just because it is the "proper" thing to do. Those responsible for its administration are often more concerned with developing a technically perfect product than with measuring its impact on people or finding out whether it is accomplishing what it is designed to do.

Job evaluation is always expensive to administer and to keep up to date. It almost invariably leads to headaches for management and to friction with workers and unions. By altering relative wage rates, job evaluation disrupts established social and psychological relationships and opens a Pandora's box of troubles. Even though management institutes evaluation in response to the union's demands for fairer wage rates, friction with the union over the administration of the program is almost inevitable. Therefore, many personnel directors feel that job evaluation should be avoided as long as problems are not too serious. The real question is whether evaluation will improve matters enough to be worth the trouble—or whether it will actually make matters worse.

Job evaluation has the best chance of success when:

- It does not cause undue disruption of either traditional wage patterns or established promotional ladders.
- The overall wage level is relatively high, so that not too many adjustments or exceptions must be made to meet market pressures *or* when the company is so isolated from other firms (in terms of either geography or job requirements) that comparisons with wages elsewhere are difficult to make.
- Relations with the union are generally good, the union accepts an active role in administering the program, and there is little internal conflict within the union.
- There is broad participation in administering the program throughout all levels of management.
- The company is willing to pay a "sweetener" to encourage acceptance.

Merit rating

Many organizations use merit rating to determine which employees should receive *merit increases* that lift their wages or salaries above the minimum set by job evaluation. Occasionally, merit rating is also used to determine who will be promoted from one job to another. As such, it is similar to performance evaluation at the management level (See Chap. 15). Organizations that make use of merit rating hope to reward outstanding performance and motivate all employees to work harder. Instead of a single wage or salary rate for each job, organizations that practice merit rating normally have a *rate range*. For example, the rate range of Job Class III might be from $7.80 to $9.40 (see chart, next page). Each range is divided into a series of intervals, or *steps* (the steps are 40¢ apart in the chart). A new employee starts at the bottom step and is subject to periodic *merit reviews,* which are usually conducted by the supervisor. These reviews determine whether the employee should receive a raise that will carry him or her up one or more steps. They are made at regular intervals, possibly every six or twelve months. In conducting the review, the supervisor often makes use of a *merit-rating form* (see p. 389), which provides a convenient means of summarizing the employee's weaknesses and strong points. After the review has been completed, the supervisor often sits down with the employee to communicate the results in a *merit-rating interview,* which is analogous to the appraisal interview at the management level.

Merit rating gives rise to several special problems, each of which we will discuss in turn.

Rate ranges

Rate ranges normally overlap—that is, the highest step in one job classification may pay more than the lowest step in the next job classification. In the chart on p. 388, for example, the top step of job class III pays $.60 more than the lowest step of job class IV. What happens if an employee is at the top step of one job classification—must he take a cut in pay to move into a

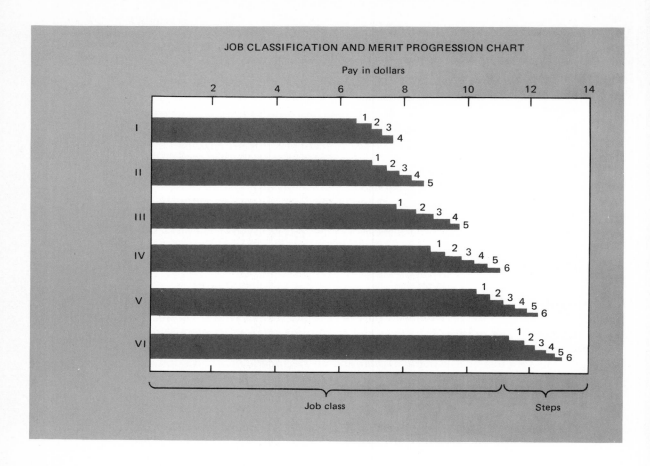

JOB CLASSIFICATION AND MERIT PROGRESSION CHART

Pay in dollars

higher job classification? Normally he does not; he carries his old rate of pay with him and starts from the equivalent step in his new classification.

Not uncommonly, the rate ranges for higher job classifications are wider than those for lower job classifications. In our example, job class I has a range of only $1.20, whereas job class VI has a range of $2.00. Wider ranges are customary on higher-paid jobs to provide employees with more opportunity to display unusual skills on more difficult work.

Merit reviews and merit interviews   Merit rating of hourly-paid and lower-ranking salaried employees involves many of the problems of performance rating that we discussed in Chapter 15. There are many types of rating forms, though the check-the-box type is the most typical. As in performance rating, such sources of bias as the halo effect and over-leniency reduce the effectiveness of the rating process.

In theory, the merit-rating interview gives the supervisor a chance to discuss each subordinate's problems with him and to coach him to do a better job. In practice, supervisors show little sympathy for the interview process and tend to conduct their interviews in a mechanical and insensitive manner; it is possible, of course, to improve their proficiency through training.

Unions in general oppose merit rating, insisting that it opens the door to rivalry and bad feeling among employees and to favoritism on the part of supervisors. They would prefer that all employees receive the same rate, and they feel that if there is to be a rate range, employees should move up from step to step purely by seniority.

Union attitudes toward merit reviews

When merit-rating systems are established in unionized plants, the union tends to pressure management into giving each employee an increase every time a rating period comes around. If an employee is skipped over, the union files a grievance and requires management to explain why he or she did not receive an increase. Understandably, grievances of this sort often lead to recriminations and bad feelings. Yet where management yields to such pressures, wage increases from one step to another depend exclusively on seniority rather

NAME *Howard Bowman*		JOB *Tool crib attendant*
DATE *7/16/80*		FOREMAN *David Thatcher*

If on job less than six months, state time_____

Supervision required	4	Attendance	4
Job knowledge	2	Adaptability	2
Attitude, conduct, cooperation	4	Judgment	1
Safety	3	Quantity	4
Housekeeping	2	Quality	2
		Rating	28

Remarks *An able employee who shows a tendency to be lazy. He knows his job well but is frequently late to work and uncooperative with other employees*

Reviewed by Board ☑

Rating Code
1. Top
2. Above average
3. Average
4. Below average
5. Unsatisfactory

Merit rating form.

than performance. Sometimes a compromise is worked out whereby employees automatically move up one step each review period until they reach the "mid-step" halfway between the top and bottom of the range. Pay increases above the mid-step are given purely at the discretion of management. (In government service, however, it is quite common for increases to be based entirely on seniority.).

When should merit rating be used?

In theory, merit rating should relax the rigidity of job evaluation (which emphasizes the job, not the person who performs it) and should provide recognition for performance. It should also raise both productivity and morale, since employees who do a good job are rewarded. In practice, however, employees often come to expect that raises will be given automatically, instead of as a reward for good work. Indeed, for an employee to be denied an increase is sometimes regarded as a form of discipline and is sharply resented unless it is clearly justified. Moreover, as we saw earlier (Chap. 15), it is difficult to evaluate managerial performance. Evaluation of rank-and-file blue-collar and clerical employees is almost equally hard. Yet a poorly administered merit-rating program may lead to constant tension and ill feeling between supervisors and subordinates (and between management and union). Employees may become demoralized when they reach the top of their range, particularly if there is little realistic chance of their being promoted to a higher ranking job. Understandably, they become upset when they see younger (and presumably less competent) employees getting raises, which are denied to them. Under these circumstances there is often great pressure to raise the top of the range.

In general, merit rating should not be introduced unless the employees themselves accept the principle that there may be a legitimate difference in compensation among employees who hold the same job title. If employees think such distinctions are unfair, they are bound to resist any attempt to create them. Such distinctions are most likely to be accepted by highly skilled workers and by white-collar workers. On highly skilled production jobs there is a significant difference between outstanding performance and merely adequate performance, and white-collar workers are particularly anxious to advance in their work. For this reason, and because of blue-collar union opposition, rate ranges are considerably more common among white-collar than among blue-collar employees.

Finally, subordinates are not likely to accept merit rating as fair unless they trust their supervisors as individuals and have confidence in the merit rating process as a whole. To the extent possible, ratings should be based on objective rather than subjective factors. Above all, supervisors should be prepared to explain to subordinates the precise grounds for the evaluation they were given.[7]

Salary administration for executives

Salary administration for executives involves most of the problems that apply to clerical and production employees, but it also includes certain peculiar problems of its own. Indeed, some argue that principles of wage administration, developed at the factory level, are just not applicable to management.

Generalized vs. individualized increases

In this inflationary period, employees generally—both blue-collar and managerial—have come to expect regular pay increases. For blue-collar workers, these increases normally take the form of across-the-board pay hikes given simultaneously to all employees (supplemented at times by promotions and merit raises). In unionized companies, the size of the increases is naturally determined by collective bargaining.

Some companies give their white-collar and managerial employees increases identical to those given blue-collar employees, the logic being that to treat one group differently would result in great antagonism. But other unionized companies feel such uniformity is unwise because it makes nonunion employees dependent on the union for the size of their increase and perhaps leads these employees to identify with the union. Furthermore, if increases

---

[7] W. Clay Hamner, "How to Ruin Motivation with Pay," in W. Clay Hamner and Frank L. Schmidt, *Contemporary Problems in Personnel,* rev. ed. (Chicago: St. Clair Press, 1977).

are given across the board, individual differences are not taken into account, and such differences are especially important at the managerial level. For these reasons, across-the-board increases, given all employees at the same time, are less frequent at the white-collar than at the blue-collar level and are utilized less frequently still for managers.

The typical practice is a periodic review of each manager's salary, perhaps every year, often on the anniversary date of his or her entrance into the company. This is the equivalent of merit rating at lower levels. In such a salary review, the size of an increase is largely determined on the basis of an evaluation by his direct superior. Under such circumstances, most executives will receive an increase at least approximating the change in cost of living since the previous review (zero increases are rarely given except to the downright incompetent), but really large increases go only to those whose performance has been truly outstanding.

A modification of this approach is to require the salaries of all managers to be reviewed at fixed, fairly infrequent intervals (say, every two years). The boss of an outstanding manager may also initiate an earlier review of the manager's salary. Thus the up-and-coming managers tend not only to receive increases more frequently than do run-of-the-mill managers, but they also get larger increases each time around.

To determine managerial salaries, many companies use a modified version of the standard job-evaluation procedure—that is, they go through the normal steps of job description, point rating, and establishing salary grades and salary ranges. And yet executive jobs are particularly hard to describe. They are more complex than lower-level jobs, and, particularly at higher levels, no two jobs are alike. The manager of plant *A,* which concentrates on experimental work, has a different set of responsibilities from those of the manager of plant *B,* which specializes in routine, mass-production work. Yet both executives have the same title: "plant manager."

Managerial job evaluation

Obviously most of the factors used to evaluate subordinates' jobs (such as skill or working conditions) are not appropriate to an evaluation of executive responsibility. Executive jobs, after all, require a great deal of decision making, planning, and supervising others. Yet these special executive skills are often difficult to define, measure, or reduce to the "degrees" that are required by most forms of job evaluation.

Moreover, since there is usually a great difference between the efficiency with which two executives perform the same job, executive jobs are usually assigned salary ranges (say, $30,000 to $45,000) rather than a specific salary ($38,150). Obviously, for jobs on which there is a broad range between merely satisfactory and outstanding performance, the salary ranges will also be broad.

Since individual differences are so significant at the executive level, performance appraisal may be more important than job evaluation. The two programs must be closely coordinated, however, to prevent inequities from arising (for instance, to prevent executives of equal merit from being paid more in division *A,* which has a generous division manager, than they are in division

Keeping costs in line

B, whose manager is more cost-conscious). Many companies permit a certain amount of flexibility in their evaluation system to provide for individual bargaining—that is, to make it possible to grant a special raise to keep a good manager who has had a better offer from another organization.

Excessive flexibility can cause trouble. In being overgenerous in granting salary increases to his or her subordinates, the executive can both jeopardize his company's profit position and create inequities between departments. Expectations arise in some departments that all employees will receive merit increases annually. When this happens, the "merit" increase becomes the equivalent of an across-the-board increase, and those who fail to get increases feel discriminated against. To keep costs down, prevent inequities, and preserve merit rating as a means of rewarding good performance, some guidelines are necessary. Departments can be given quotas that they cannot exceed without special authorization. For example, the average increase may not exceed 10 percent, or not more than half the employees may receive increases in any one year.

Regardless of how the quota is set, problems are likely to occur. Often each department is given an equal merit-increase budget (say, 10 percent of present salaries), which can be allocated among deserving managers as the department head feels appropriate. But an equal budget for each department is equitable only if, on the average, the managers in each department are equally deserving of salary increases. Suppose we have two adjoining departments. Department *A* has many long-service managers, most of whom are already at the top of their salary ranges. Department *B* has a number of younger managers, many of whom are growing quite rapidly on the job. Clearly, it would be inequitable to give the same quota to each department. Furthermore, regardless of how the overall size of the quota is determined, having a fixed quota at all may foster dangerous competition among executives, since the only way one executive can get a large salary increase is at the cost of his or her colleagues, who get a smaller one.

Obviously, no one guideline is sufficient. Nevertheless, even in companies that do not follow rigid programs, higher management, the personnal department, and the accounting department all police the salary structure. An executive whose structure gets out of proportion may well have to give some careful explanations to the boss.

Communicating salary positions

The details of the executive salary program are often kept secret—either by design or because of poor communications. Top management fears that all sorts of rivalry and bad feeling will develop if each executive knows what his or her colleagues are getting. But there is little justification for keeping an executive from knowing how he stands himself, relative to the average. At times, for example, in companies with managerial rate ranges, an executive who receives $45,000 a year has no idea whether he is already at the top of his salary grade, or whether he can reasonably expect to receive additional salary increases without having to go to a higher-ranking job. Uncertainty of this sort leads to the suspicion that raises are distributed purely on the basis of favoritism.

Research suggests that company managers have generally inaccurate pictures of how their pay stacks up against others.[8] They tend to *over*estimate the pay received by their subordinates and peers and to *under*estimate the pay received by their superiors. Thus they undervalue both their own present position and the worth of a possible promotion. Doing better than the other person serves as an effective form of motivation for many, but how can such motivation operate if the executive doesn't know what the other person is getting?

A final argument in favor of eliminating secrecy relates to pay's function as a form of feedback concerning performance. Feedback tends to raise productivity, but secrecy about relative pay eliminates one important form of feedback. Thus a strong case can be made for letting each executive know where he stands relative to the *average* earned by his colleagues (even if he is not told precisely what everyone makes). Once secrecy is reduced, however, it becomes extremely important that the method by which compensation is determined seem fair and defensible. Indeed it has been argued that the main reasons for keeping compensation confidential are managerial laziness and unwillingness to devise rational, equitable compensation schemes.

The question of salary secrecy is still quite controversial. Perhaps it is more important that the method of salary determination be understood and trusted than that specific salary figures be disseminated. Salary openness would seem more appropriate in fields such as sales, where performance can be fairly objectively measured, than in fields where performance measurement is subjective at best.

Extra compensation

As one goes higher in the management hierarchy, one finds that base salaries are supplemented more and more heavily with bonuses and fringe benefits. These range from free life insurance and liberal retirement benefits to company-paid membership in the country club and even (for top executives) free use of a limousine and chauffeur.[9] It is estimated that the value of all forms of extra compensation averages from 30 to 40 percent of base salaries for middle management to over 100 percent at the top.

Companies have two main purposes in designing managerial compensation packages. First, they wish to motivate their executives by rewarding them for top performance. Secondly, in a period when top-notch executives are increasingly likely to move from job to job, companies view their compensation schemes both as golden handcuffs, which may discourage present executives from leaving, and as a means of recruiting executives from other organizations.

Tax advantages are perhaps the chief reason why executives themselves are interested in supplemental compensation. Deferred income, such as retire-

[8] Edward E. Lawler III, "Reward Systems," in J. Richard Hackman and J. Lloyd Suttle, eds., *Improving Life at Work* (Santa Monica: Goodyear, 1977).

[9] Benefits of this sort play an even greater role in compensating executives in many European countries than they do in the U.S. Even in this country there are some interesting differences in the form of compensation stressed as a means of motivating management. Banks emphasize pensions, manufacturing firms stock options and appreciation rights, and retail stores bonuses. John P. Campbell and others, *Managerial Behavior, Performance and Effectiveness* (New York: McGraw-Hill, 1970), pp. 55–57.

ment benefits, is subject to tax only when it is received (when presumably the recipient will be in a lower tax bracket), and such benefits as country-club memberships and liberal expense accounts do not count as income at all (provided some showing can be made that these have a relationship to company business). Recent laws have reduced tax advantages of extra-salary forms of compensation. Nevertheless they are still substantial.

Tax advantages are an attraction chiefly for the older, higher-paid executives, and this same group places greatest importance on pensions. Junior executives with growing families and large mortgages seem to be interested primarily in take-home income. Indeed, one study indicates that executives as a whole want only a small proportion of their income in the form of benefits.[10] By in effect imposing a ceiling on their own income, top executives have squeezed salary levels below them and have imposed their own scale of compensation preferences upon those who have different needs and interests. Some companies have begun to experiment by permitting each executive to decide for himself how he will divide his compensation among take-home pay and various fringe benefits. This kind of flexibility has tax disadvantages, however, unless it is extended to non-managerial employees as well.

Bonuses. Bonuses relate rewards to performance. These are generally allocated according to a predetermined formula. Some formulae are based on overall company performance. The annual bonus fund may consist of 5 percent of any company profit in excess of 10 percent of net worth. Alternatively the amount of the bonus may depend on meeting specific performance standards (say, reducing inventory by 5 percent). The Bell System's Long Term Incentive Plan combines these approaches. Half of the awards are based on the company's overall return on capital, the other half on the individual's achievement of thirteen technical service measurements.

In 1977 the Bell System awards totaled a modest $4 million, divided among 320 top managers nationwide. DuPont's more generous approach reaches down into middle management. In 1978, DuPont distributed $80 million among 11,000 managers. Bonuses may take the form of cash or stock. Often actual payout is deferred for five years or more, with the understanding that executives who leave before that time forfeit their rights to collect.

Stock options and appreciation rights. Stock options were once an important form of compensation for top management. Stock options permitted participating executives to purchase a specified number of shares of company stock at some future date but at a price close to that prevailing when the options were issued. Thus, if the price of the stock went up, the executive could buy below market and so stand to make a profit (taxed at the low rate for capital gains), whereas if the price fell he or she did not have to pick up the option.

The advantages of stock options were twofold: they were a means of increasing the manager's after-tax income, and they were designed to increase

[10] Thomas A. Mahoney, "Compensation Preferences of Managers," *Industrial Relations*, 3, No. 3 (May 1964), 135–44.

motivation by giving the manager a stake in the enterprise's financial success. In this way, large companies might compete with small, aggressive competitive firms that offered their managers a sense of direct ownership and the possibility of winning a big jackpot if their firm were successful.

Despite these advantages, the use of stock options has declined considerably in recent years. There are three main reasons for this. In the first place, the stock market stopped rising, so options often had little value. Secondly, to qualify for tax advantages the manager had to hold the stock for at least three years, during which time its price might decline considerably. Thus the executive's apparent gain became a heavy loss. Finally, Congress greatly reduced and eventually almost eliminated options' tax advantages.

In their place, many companies have provided so-called Stock Appreciation Rights (although these go by a variety of names). An SAR gives an executive the right to collect the value of the increase in the company's stock price between the date the SAR is issued and the date it is "exercised." Suppose an executive receives a bonus of 1,000 SARs for outstanding performance this year. Currently the company's stock sells at $60. Three years from now, when the price has climbed to $80, the executive exercises his rights. The executive receives a cash payment from the company of $20,000 (the $20 increase in the stock's price multiplied by 1,000 SARs).

The executive's profit on the SARs is taxable as ordinary income. Nevertheless, the SAR plan allows the executive to avoid the risk of actually taking a loss. Further, it provides a strong incentive to manage the company so that its stock appreciates in value. (Indeed, some authorities are concerned that SARs may lead executives to concentrate their attention on day-to-day fluctuations in the stock market and thus neglect long-term reforms that might have an immediate adverse effect on the market but a beneficial effect over the long run.)

The range of alternative reward systems is bewilderingly complex. Some companies offer bonuses, stock options, and SARs simultaneously. To intensify the motivational effect, some companies pay bonuses not in cash but in SARs. Thus the motivation effect of bonuses is combined with the retention effect of SARs.

Deferred compensation. Deferred compensation takes a variety of forms. It is common for companies to offer contracts to key executives which provide that upon retirement these executives will be rehired as "consultants" for as long as 15 years at, say, $50,000 a year. The phantom nature of this consultancy is demonstrated by the provision in many contracts that the sum be paid to the executive's spouse if the executive dies first. An advantage of deferred plans, at least to the executives concerned, is that they allow early retirement with little loss of income.

Executive perquisites. Executives often enjoy many perquisites: country club membership, use of the company airplane (and sometimes its use by the executive's spouse), low interest loans, life insurance, a free annual physical checkup, personal financial counseling, an attractive executive dining room, a company car, and sometimes even a chauffeur. Though critics claimed that such "perks" are merely a form of tax avoidance, companies defend them on a variety of grounds. A clothing company may justify selling suits to its managers at half of wholesale price by claiming that these managers model the company's styles. Similarly, free medical examinations are commonly justified on the grounds that healthy managers function more effectively. A country club is useful for making contacts with executives from other organizations. A chauffeur can double as a bodyguard, an increasingly important need as kidnap threats grow. Despite these claims the U.S. Internal Revenue Service has become less and less sympathetic to such perks (they are considerably more important in Europe because of higher taxes there).

Salaries and bonuses as motivators

Now that we have examined various forms of management compensation, it may be useful to look at their motivational impacts. Some critics argue that the traditional concept of salary administration (salaries and fringe benefits alone) is more appropriate for the factory than for management. They argue that money can be an effective motivator for higher performance only if managers perceive that increased efforts will lead to increased monetary rewards. The trouble with most compensation plans, the critics suggest, is that managers do not believe such a relationship exists. They have little confidence in performance appraisal procedures, believing instead that both salaries and fringe benefits are primarily a function of seniority, education, performance in *past* years, and even more irrelevant criteria such as favoritism or sheer luck.[11] To put it another way; pay is important to managers, not just for the material goods it buys, but because it is concrete feedback as to how well they are doing. When pay is not seen as a measurement of performance, it does not motivate performance.

Generous fringe benefits and various forms of deferred compensation of course serve as golden handcuffs which reduce managerial turnover. But low turnover is not an undiluted advantage to either the organization or the individual manager. Both parties often gain when a stalemated executive quits to begin a second career somewhere else.

The practical implications of these arguments are that there should be greater emphasis on bonuses for individual productivity and less emphasis on straight salaries, standardized fringe benefits (which are received regardless of individual effort), deferred compensation, and group incentives. The amount of the bonus should be permitted to fluctuate from period to period and should be tied in closely with measures of *individual* performance.

Logical as this approach may seem, a number of problems have inhibited its widespread implementation. Though managers feel that compensation should reflect performance, thay also feel that factors such as past service

---

[11] For most managers, "getting ahead" means promotion to a higher-ranking job, rather than salary increases in a particular job. Promotions, however, are based on factors other than performance in the recent past—factors such as apparent qualifications for the job to which the manager is being promoted, special training, and being in the right place at the right time. None of these is necessarily or directly related to the manager's recent performance; and to the extent that these factors determine who is promoted, the motivating impact of promotion is reduced.

should be taken into account. Managers want stable, reasonably predictable income. Thus considerations of motivation and equity may conflict. Further, as we have seen in Chapter 15, appraisal of individual performance was never easy; but with technological change requiring more teamwork, it is becoming increasingly difficult to isolate individual performance. If nothing else, the administrative cost is substantial. Trying to measure exactly the contributions of each manager is time consuming and may be too threatening to the boss's relationships with his subordinates. The gains in increased motivation may be more than offset by various costs involved.

These considerations explain why many companies base their bonuses on overall company profits or provide stock options or SARs. All these are based on organization-wide rather than individual performance.

Salary administration for engineers and scientists

Applying standard job-evaluation techniques is even more difficult for engineers and scientists than it is for executives. Job classification means relatively little in professional work. Although an engineer's salary may increase year by year, through merit rating, in many companies, when he reaches the top step of one job classification, he is almost automatically advanced to the next higher classification. But this promotion may mean relatively little change in work.

Furthermore, there is ambiguity about when an employee has moved from one job to another, for job definitions are quite elastic. An engineer may be required to work on a more difficult assignment for several months before the change in his or her job status is officially recognized by a formal promotion. And the distinction between an engineer doing "more responsible" work and an engineer doing "less responsible" work is often vague. The jobs of both may change over time as new projects come in and old ones are completed.

As a consequence, the emphasis in salary administration for engineers is usually on the individual worth of the particular engineer rather than on the job he or she is doing at the present. Yet engineering supervisors often claim that it is hard to measure individual professional ability. Since engineers normally work on projects that have never been attempted before, it is difficult to predict in advance how long a given project should take. Two engineers may be assigned to what seem to be equally time-consuming projects. Yet engineer A finishes long before engineer B. Is this because engineer A is better? Or because A's solution is slipshod? Or because the two projects were not really of equal difficulty?

Engineering supervisors may tend to exaggerate the difficulty of making judgments on professional output. The evaluation of professionals may be no more difficult that the evaluation of managers, with intangibles playing a major role in both cases. In any case, engineering and scientific salaries are often set largely on the basis of the individual's education and years of experience. Thus, two engineers, both with a master's degree and ten years of experience, will get roughly the same salary unless one is clearly outstanding. A number of organizations publish statistics on the salaries received by engineers with various degrees and various years of experience. Depending on the company's overall salary policy, it can decide to base its salaries on the median, above the median, or below the median shown by these *maturity* curves.[12]

Unfortunately, the rigid use of maturity curves leaves little opportunity to reward individual excellence. Some companies use not one maturity curve but several: one, for example, for the top performing 25 percent of each experience-education group, a second for the middle 50 percent, and a third for the bottom 25 percent. Such a plan requires some fairly arbitrary decisions about who falls into the various performance categories. To avoid arbitrariness, many companies use maturity curves merely as guidelines. Regardless of what plan is used, however, the central dilemma remains: basing salary on experience reduces motivation for effective performance, but performance is difficult to measure. Further, to recruit engineers with scarce skills during periods of high demand, companies have to pay the market rate, which may be well above that set by the maturity curve. When this happens a newcomer may earn more than an oldtimer, even though they may both have the same education and experience. No wonder discontent with salaries is a primary cause of dissatisfaction among engineers and a major reason for their high mobility among firms.

Conclusion

Monetary reward is the primary motivation for most employees. It helps satisfy economic needs and needs for recognition and accomplishment. Yet, *relative* earnings—how employees' earnings compare with one another's—are more important to many employees than is their actual take-home pay. Without a sound wage and salary administration program, it is difficult for management to recruit or maintain a motivated work force.

Wage administration is a particularly delicate activity, since it deals with one of our most sensitive areas, our pocketbook. And because it results in the comparison of one employee with another, it cannot help but lead to emotionally fraught rivalries and resentments. The struggle for a salary increase often shows human behavior at its very worst.

Some managers feel that the way to avoid all these problems is to retreat to the Olympian heights of "scientific objectivity." But as we have seen, such aloofness requires that they ignore many of the most troublesome economic and human relationships in our society.

At best, wage and salary administration can only channel conflict and provide for a systematic review of difficult problems.

---

[12] Similar salary curves based on age and experience are often used to determine pay for public school teachers.

problems

1 • *Job Evaluation Manual*

The following is a simplified example of a *poorly designed* job-evaluation manual. Read it carefully and try to find the bugs, the areas of inconsistency, and the areas of ambiguity.

Degrees	*Points*

Education

1. None required.	20
2. Ability to speak English.	40
3. Four years school or equivalent.	60
4. Grade school or equivalent.	80
5. Graduate of high school or equivalent.	100
6. Two years college or equivalent.	120
7. College degree or equivalent.	140

Training required

1. Less than one week.	20
2. One week to four weeks.	40
3. Four weeks to six months.	60
4. Six months to a year.	80
5. A year to two years.	100
6. Two years to four years.	120
7. More than four years.	140

Physical effort

1. No significant amount required.	25
2. Frequent handling of lightweight material. Must lift or handle objects of less than five pounds.	50
3. Repetitive or sustained physical effort. Usually handling average weight material or occasionally working with heavyweight material. Lifting not over 30 pounds.	75
4. Hard work with constant physical strain or immediate severe strain. Lifting over 75 pounds required.	100

Dexterity

1. None required.	60
2. Low degree of dexterity required.	120
3. Considerable skill and craftsmanship required.	180
4. Very high order of skill.	240

Mental effort

1. Flow of work is intermittent. No pressure of work. Attention required only at intervals.	20
2. Operation requires frequent but not continuous attention. Inspection work where flaw is easily detected.	40

3. Close attention is required at all times. Eye-hand coordination needed.   60
4. High degree of concentration. Very close, exacting use of eyes.   80

Responsibility

1. Little possibility for mistakes.   25
2. Small losses might occur but mistakes are easily caught. Errors might go up to $25 a week.   50
3. Substantial loss possible before errors are discovered. Losses might be very great but normally shall not exceed $200 a week.   75
4. Responsible for an important operation. Errors could cause substantial damage.   100

Working conditions

1. Works regularly under desirable working conditions.   20
2. Works regularly under poor working conditions; illumination and ventilation are considered only adequate.   40
3. Works under conditions which entail some sacrifice of personal comfort: heat, noise, dirt, and cold.   60
4. Works under difficult conditions such as high, though not continuous noise, heat, cold (such as work in refrigerator), and so forth.   80
5. Works under highly hazardous or difficult conditions, such as continual high noise, constant movement from refrigerator or hot room, constant dust.   100

Safety

1. Almost no hazards.   20
2. Some chance of personal injury such as scratches and bruises.   40
3. May be subject to moderately serious injury if proper precautions are not taken.   60
4. Exposure to health hazard which might result in incapacitation if proper precautions are not observed. Minor accidents are common.   80
5. Must be constantly on guard against serious accidents which often occur in spite of precautions.   100

2 • *Job Description*

Using the preceding job-evaluation manual and the following job description, evaluate the job of a press and liner operator. Notice that this job description is also inadequate. Observe the areas of ambiguity that develop as you try to apply the manual.

Job Description of Press and Liner Operator

This operator works in a can-making factory, stamping out ends for the cans on a machine which makes 200 ends a minute.

An operator works in front of the machine. Sheets of metal are put into the rear. Circular ends are punched out by a metal punch which resembles a cookie cutter. These ends pass through several complicated operations and drop onto a rack.

Operators take piles of ends and put them in crates. Each pile includes about 40 ends and weighs about 3 lbs. A good deal of dexterity is required, otherwise the ends will slither all over the floor. Lift-truck operators take filled crates to storage until needed.

Operators also watch the machine closely, stop it when something goes wrong and make minor repairs. Major repairs are made by mechanics.

Usually, operators can tell if something is wrong by changes in the noise. The punch makes a very loud staccato sound.

When ends are coming through poorly, each one must be inspected separately. Otherwise one operator can talk to the next one. Operators must stand all day except for short rest periods.

Operators can and do cut their fingers on ends, although they are encouraged to wear gloves. Also, if they don't shut the machine down when making repairs (they are instructed to do so), they can seriously injure their fingers.

If they fail to pay attention to their work, a lot of bad ends can go past them. These must be reinspected by inspectors and discarded. Such inattention rarely lasts more than 20 minutes. Ends are worth perhaps one cent each.

About three weeks are required to train an operator. There are no education requirements other than the ability to speak English. However, the company believes that people with low intelligence are not aware when the machine is operating improperly.

3 • *Foundry Wages*

The foundry has always been regarded as one of the worst places to work in the Pushem Manufacturing Company. The work is hot, dirty, and heavy. Brawn rather than brains is considered the chief requirement to get the job done.

Yet according to the job evaluation plan, "physical ability" and "working conditions" are weighted relatively lower than "responsibility," "training," and "skill." As a consequence, most of the foundry jobs are rated at the bottom of the wage scale.

In recent years it has been increasingly difficult to get foundry help. Management has had to take workers who could not get jobs elsewhere—thus further lowering the already low social status of the foundry in the eyes of the other employees. The whole matter has now reached a crisis. There are seventeen vacancies in the foundry, and it is impossible to hire new workers at the evaluated rate.

1. How should this problem be handled? Should management completely revise its job-evaluation program? Should it make foundry jobs an exception to job evaluation?
2. How should management deal with the reactions of other workers if it decides to increase foundry wages but not other wages?

4 • *Bank Wages at Bemus Bay*

The Busti National Bank has just decided to open a branch in Bemus Bay, an exclusive resort located about 20 miles from Arkwright, a large city. There is no bank there at present.

Busti is anxious to determine the appropriate wage for the clerical staff it expects to hire. Clerks in the bank's offices in Arkwright receive a starting wage of $160 a week, but through promotions they can work up to $210. As a matter of company policy, these wage rates have been set at the midpoint of the range for other banks in Arkwright.

A survey of the local businesses at Bemus Bay,

primarily realty and insurance offices and offices for local stores, indicates that the "going rate" for qualified clerical personnel is $225–$250 a week. The higher rates in Bemus Bay may be attributed in part to the substantially higher cost of living in this resort town, the limited number of young women seeking employment, and the fact that there are no other banks in Bemus Bay. Banks in Arkwright have traditionally paid lower wages than other businesses, on the grounds that banks offer better working conditions and higher prestige.

1. What should the Busti Bank establish as its hiring rate for clerical personnel? What factors should be considered in making the decision?
2. Could the bank justify to its Arkwright employees the fact that it was paying higher wages in Bemus Bay?

Employee benefit programs

Employee benefits, sometimes called fringe benefits, are compensation other than wages or salaries. Today, such benefits comprise more than 30 percent of the compensation of the typical U.S. employee, and the proportion is increasing annually. In recent years, fringes have grown twice as fast as wages and salaries.

To be more precise, a national sample of business firms disclosed that the typical company was paying $90 per week per employee for benefits in 1977.[1] During the early 1930s, in contrast, benefits comprised less than 4 percent of typical payroll costs. In the decade 1967–1977, benefit costs almost tripled!

Certainly today, the term *fringe* is a misnomer. Fringes are no longer "extras"; a vast majority of Americans rely on them as their first line of defense against illness, unemployment, and old age, as well as the source of their vacations and holidays. Today, fringes provide protection from the contingencies of life from day of employment to retirement and beyond (many programs provide protection for the employee's widow as well).[2]

18

---

[1] Benefit levels, in part related to profitability and tradition, vary by industry. One survey suggests that petroleum companies are likely to pay 50 percent more than textile manufacturers for employee benefits. (Chamber of Commerce of the United States, *U.S. Employee Benefits, 1977*), p. 5, 9.

[2] This chapter emphasizes generous programs of large, profitable firms. Many small organizations offer little more than the legally required social security benefits. For example, 22 percent of the under-65 population has no hospital insurance (Social Security Bulletin, Feb. 1975).

*Why fringe benefits
have expanded*
Why this growing emphasis on benefits? Why should they be preferred to their dollar value in actual pay, which employees presumably can spend as they wish? Several factors seem to be involved.

*Employee
demands*

Paradoxically, as our country has become richer and more self-assured, the desire to eliminate risk and increase personal security has grown stronger. The prevalence of fringe benefits reflects a strong urge to eliminate insecurity of every conceivable kind. It also represents a demand for more leisure— paid holidays and vacations—with money to enjoy it.

Employees could buy most of these benefits directly, but in general they find it more convenient to have their contributions for benefits deducted from their paychecks. If the money never appears in their paychecks and is never available for them to spend, the whole process becomes less painful. In most instances, too, fringes provide important income tax savings. When they are paid for by the company, the employee does not have to pay tax on them. The employer handles almost all the administrative problems, from selecting the insurance carrier and the coverage to accumulating premium funds and filing claims. In addition, employees recognize that the mass purchasing power provided by an organization can buy various insurance and benefit plans more cheaply. And employers are in a better position to know whether they are getting their money's worth in negotiating with banks, insurance companies, and the like.

Unions

Collective bargaining has also contributed to the growth of fringes. Unions compete with one another, and there is a considerable amount of prestige attached to being the first union to win a "new model" fringe, such as dental insurance. Union members may give their leaders more credit for a new benefit than for an equally costly increase in pay. And if one union wins such a benefit, other unions feel pressured to follow suit. Non-union firms feel compelled to join the parade if they are to maintain their status and continue attracting good new employees.

Employers

Employers provide fringes partly to raise employee morale, to meet their social responsibility, and to make more effective use of their work force. The next box is an example of these three factors working simultaneously.

A pension plan would have reduced the employee's sense of inequity, satisfied management's need to feel socially responsible, and permitted it to make more effective and flexible use of its work force.

With the possible exception of profit-sharing plans, however, it would not be realistic to expect benefit plans to motivate higher productivity. Historically, many managements had this illusion: employees would be grateful for the organization's beneficence and, in turn, would express their appreciation by harder work. Such paternalism has lost its appeal in our modern world.

Joe, who is 64, has worked for a small company for more than forty years. During this time he has won a host of friends and has earned a reputation as a hard worker. In recent years he and his wife have suffered several spells of illness that have almost wiped out his savings. Now his eyesight is failing, and the quality of his work is lower.

Without a pension plan, Joe's company has two choices. It can leave Joe's personal problems to Joe and discharge him, hoping that he can survive on his social security benefits. But discharging Joe would undoubtedly result in deep resentment among his fellow employees, who would feel that the company's action was unjust. Many would wonder if the company will treat them as callously when they get old. Management itself might feel uncertain about whether it has met its social responsibilities.

Alternatively, management might keep Joe on indefinitely and provide him with whatever work he could do. But this would mean that Joe's department would be burdened with a largely unproductive employee, and it would make everyone's work much more difficult. Eventually, the day might come when Joe would be able to do no work at all, and the company would still be faced with the necessity of terminating his employment.

Scope of major benefit programs

The typical benefits package is made up of four main components:[3]

- Pay for time not worked: vacations, holidays, overtime pay
- Insurance: health, life, disability, injury
- Retirement: public and private pension plans
- Services and perquisites: subsidized employee activities and use of company products and facilities

An approximate measure of the costs involved (including legally required contributions) is given in the accompanying table[4]

	Percent added for each payroll dollar
Supplementary pay	11%
Insurance	5
Pensions	12
Services	1

Thus, if average wages are $200 per week, the employer pays $10 for insurance and $24 for the retirement program of each employee (perhaps

[3] The term *package* is often used in labor relations to refer to the total economic settlement agreed to by management. Since the costs of many insurance and other employee benefits cannot be precisely determined in advance of actual company experience, such "package" settlements (e.g., "And the company agreed to 45¢ in fringe benefits") allow both parties to exaggerate, if they wish, the magnitude of the costs or benefits involved in the contract. Normally they are stated in terms of cents per hour.

[4] Statistics derived from the authors' own estimates and data compiled by John Sullivan, "Indirect Compensation: The Years Ahead," *California Management Review,* Vol. XV, No. 2 (Winter 1972), p. 73.

$2500 per year per employee). But such data may not connote the magnitude of these costs. In 1975, General Motors paid out $2.7 billion for benefits, or $5,500 per hourly worker.

While larger companies were paying out nearly 40 percent of their wage and salary costs in benefit plans, government was even more generous. New York City in 1976 paid benefits that added 66 percent to its employment costs!

Types of benefits

Pay for time not worked	*During workweek*	*Not at work*
	Paid lunch periods	Annual vacations
	Rest periods	Holidays
	Wash-up and get-ready time	Pay for jury duty
	Premium pay	Unemployment benefits
Insurance	*Private plans*	*Public plans*
Family income in case of death	Group life insurance	Survivor's benefits under social security
Disability	Payouts from profit sharing or pension funds	Workmen's compensation
	Accident insurance	Social security disability benefits
	Disability insurance	State disability insurance benefits
Illness	*Private plans*	*Public plans*
	Hospital/surgical plans	Workmen's compensation (where job related)
	Medical/dental/drug reimbursement plans	Medicare (after age 65)
	Preventive medical programs—clinics and health maintenance organizations	
	Major medical insurance (prolonged illness)	
Retirement	*Private plans*	*Public plans*
	Pensions	Social security
	Deferred profit sharing	
	Thrift plans	
Services and perquisites	*All employees*	*Management or top management*
	Paid meals	Company autos
	Subsidized loans	Club memberships
	Tuition rebates	Annual physical checkup
	Discounts on company products	Financial counseling
	Recreational programs	

In early years, benefit plans were available chiefly in large, more profitable organizations and in government. Now, because of the pressures and incentives we have previously described—from employees, unions, and employers themselves—an increasingly high proportion of employees have some elements of a benefits program. Of those under 65, however, 22 percent still have no hospital insurance, and many small companies do not provide pension plans or paid vacations. In 1970, only half of the workers in the private sector had pensions.

Pay for time not worked

The demand for leisure is being met with more holidays, longer vacations, and shorter workweeks. Employees have received more and more paid holidays in recent years, with the typical organization now providing 8 to 12 days per year. The number of holidays celebrated keeps increasing, with half the union contracts specifying 10 or more paid holidays per year.[5] If the holiday falls on Sunday, it is often observed on Monday. Less frequently, Friday is the day off if the holiday falls on Saturday. Some companies treat an employee's birthday as a holiday; and days off before or after Christmas, Thanksgiving, and New Year's Day are becoming increasingly common.

The typical unionized worker given holidays and vacations may now work about forty-seven weeks per year.[6] And paid vacations keep getting longer. Normally, the length of an employee's vacation depends on the length of service. In a few industries, such as steel and the California canning industries, sabbatical leave programs permit long-service employees to take extended paid vacations at lengthy intervals. Employees with 8 or more years of service may take 13 weeks' vacation every 5 years.[7]

Many of these leisure fringes involve administrative problems. Scheduling vacations is complicated. Do senior workers get choice vacation times, even though they have three weeks, leaving junior employees to take their one week at undesirable times? Petty jealousies and coercive comparisons flourish. Similarly, there can be many ambiguities surrounding pay for holidays. If an employee entitled to sick leave is ill on a holiday, should another day off be given? Is an employee who is absent from work the day before a holiday entitled to holiday pay? (Management fears that employees will seek to stretch their holidays.) Can an employee with 4 weeks' vacation take 10 mini vacations of 2 days each? Conversely, can employees save up unused vacation time? For how many years?

At one time, the 6-day, 48-hour (even 54- or 60-hour) workweek was the rule in this country. The 40-hour workweek (usually 5 days) became standard only during the New Deal days of the 1930s. Ever since then, unions

---

[5] Only 6 percent provided that many in 1965 (*Daily Labor Report,* December 26, 1974).

[6] John Zaulsky, "Shorter Work Years—Early Retirement," AFL-CIO *Federationist* (August 1977), p. 4.

[7] When these plans were first established, it was hoped that employees would use this time to go back to school or to take extensive trips, thus widening their horizons, but there is little evidence that much of this has occurred.

have passed resolutions asking a further reduction to 30 hours.[8] For the most part, such demands have relatively low priority, for the average worker seems to prefer increased pay to shorter hours. Indeed, most workers want to work overtime (at time-and-a-half or double-time pay), and companies that have scheduled such overtime for a lengthy period of time often find it difficult to eliminate. A considerable number of workers use their free time to "moonlight" on other jobs, thus also demonstrating that increased income is favored over leisure.

*Overtime and
similar penalty
provisions*

Overtime pay penalizes the employer who violates the normal workweek, but it compensates employees for working extra hours. It protects the employee's leisure time, helps to spread work and reduce unemployment.

The Fair Labor Standards Act requires that hours worked in excess of 40 per week be paid at the rate of one-and-a-half times the regularly hourly rate, but company policies and union-management contracts often go beyond this requirement. Overtime may be paid for hours in excess of 8 in a single day. In some industries, especially the building trades, overtime is paid at twice the regular pay (double time) rather than just time-and-a-half. Interestingly, even with these extra costs, in 1973 at the peak of a recession, 17 million workers were still earning overtime pay.

Numerous other provisions penalize the company for disturbing the normal workweek. Shift differentials, perhaps 40 cents an hour, are often paid to those working the evening (4 P.M. to midnight), night (midnight to 8 A.M.), or split shift (bus drivers, for example, working 7 A.M. to 10 A.M., 3 P.M. to 6 P.M.). "Call in" pay is often given to those who are called in but not given work. Similar provisions apply when workers are called in on short notice.

*Unemployment
and
job protection*

The imposed leisure of layoffs can have catastrophic effects on an employee's living standards. To reduce the impact of unemployment, the government has established an unemployment insurance program, largely financed by employer contributions. Benefits paid by such programs vary greatly from state to state but generally amount to less than 50 percent of prior earnings. (The net loss of income is reduced because unemployment benefits are not taxable, and unemployed workers save the cost of going to work.)

Because of the relative inadequacy of these benefits, a number of unions (especially those in industries with cyclical employment patterns, such as steel, autos, rubber, and cement) have obtained contract provisions for *supplementary unemployment benefits*. These SUBs, when combined with ordinary employment insurance, can bring the employee's income very close to prelayoff earnings. (Indeed, some older, senior employees feel discriminated against in having to work while their unemployed junior workmates receive substantial weekly checks. Thus, some labor contracts now allow senior workers to elect to be laid off—instead of their junior colleagues—when management wants

---

[8] A few unions, especially in the building trades, have won workweeks considerably shorter than 40 hours. A notable example is the New York City construction electricians, who negotiated a 25-hour week plus 5 hours guaranteed overtime.

a temporary reduction in the size of the work force.) Of course, during periods of extended, substantial layoffs, these funds can become exhausted.

To receive governmental unemployment insurance, the employee must be willing to take another suitable job. But this requires an administrative determination of what jobs are suitable. May a machinist turn down a job offer as tool crib attendant and still retain his benefits?

Since the cost of SUB and (in most states) unemployment insurance is closely related to the company's unemployment record, the existence of these benefits provides an incentive for companies to keep their employment stable. Indeed, the programs were designed with this objective in mind. SUB is a direct outgrowth of union demands for a guaranteed annual wage. In a few instances, *guaranteed employment plans* are in effect. Management may guarantee all employees with at least two years seniority at least 2,000 hours of work per year and pay a worker regular wages even if there is no work available. In return for these guarantees, management often obtains greater flexibility in transferring employees to different jobs or—as in the case of longshoremen—the right to introduce labor-saving techniques.

Work guarantees reduce fluctuations in employment; unemployment insurance and SUB benefits lessen the impact of short-term unemployment; but what happens when plants are shut down forever or technological change forces a permanent reduction in size of the work force? To meet these problems, a number of plans have been developed, again largely as a result of union pressure. Perhaps the simplest of these plans provides *severance pay*, usually lump-sum payments related to length of service, which helps tide the workers over until they find other jobs. Such payments can be as high as two years' income.

More complicated plans involve the establishment of special funds under which displaced workers can receive a variety of benefits including weekly payments, job training (to make them qualified for new careers), and vocational guidance. Sometimes union-management-administered, these plans are an imaginative effort to recognize management's responsibilities to employees whose skills and experience have been devalued through no fault of their own.[9] Another form of job protection that has been written into union-management agreements guarantees the same pay for an employee who is transferred from a discontinued job to a lower-rated one in the same company.[10]

Health protection and insurance

Most organizations now provide several forms of protection against the loss of income and extra expense caused by sickness.

Workmen's compensation (see Chap. 13) covers only injuries that arise

---

[9] One of the best known examples was the Armour Company's program to aid displaced packinghouse workers. See George Shultz and Arnold R. Weber, *Strategies for the Displaced Worker* (Westport, Conn.: Greenwood Press, 1976). The program combined relocation expenses, retraining allowances, severance pay, early retirement and aid in finding new jobs.

[10] Some idea of the magnitude of costs involved here can be gleaned from the experience of the New York Central and Pennsylvania railroads, whose wage protection and severance pay costs totaled nearly $65 million in the first two years after their merger. (*The Wall Street Journal*, August 25, 1970, p. 30). In addition, the federal government allocated several hundred million dollars to compensate rail workers who lost their Penn Central jobs because of route abandonment.

out of employment. Since most medical bills arise from other causes, many organizations pay all or a major share of the cost of health insurance programs such as Blue Cross (chiefly hospital bills), Blue Shield (chiefly doctors' bills), or the equivalent sold by private insurance companies.

An insurance program rarely, if ever, covers all medical costs, although there has been some tendency to increase the comprehensiveness of such programs. To understand the nature of the restrictions on medical protection, two sets of distinctions must be made. The first relates to the differences between *indemnity* and *service* plans. Indemnity plans are usually cheaper because they provide an upper limit to the costs per unit of service, such as $50 per day for a semi-private hospital room or $25 to have a cyst removed. Because of inflationary increases in medical costs, indemnity plans often do not cover a substantial proportion of the bill. Service plans such as Blue Cross (in most states) provide full coverage regardless of cost, but even Blue Cross plans normally place a limit on the number of days of hospital care (say 60 days) that they provide.

The other distinction relates to *first-dollar* and *last-dollar* protection. First-dollar protection sets an upper limit to the amount of benefits: it may pay the first $500 of doctors' costs or the first 60 days in the hospital. Last-dollar protection is a form of deductible insurance. Usually the last-dollar benefits involve coinsurance; that is, the employee must pay a certain percentage (perhaps 20 percent) of the costs. Major medical insurance is a good example of last-dollar benefits combined with coinsurance. Typically such a program might pay 80 percent of the medical costs in excess of $100 in any 2-months' period. Thus, major medical insurance helps reduce the cost of catastrophic, extended illness, which may involve expenditures of $50,000 to $100,000.

Insurance experts often argue that last-dollar protection is socially more desirable than first-dollar, since most families can afford to pay first dollars. What really destroys a family's financial independence is the last-dollar expense of a major illness. Yet, if forced to make a choice, unions frequently prefer first-dollar insurance because a higher percentage of their members will receive benefits from it (even if catastrophic illness is not covered).[11]

Companies and unions both are worried that the increasing availability of health insurance will (1) further inflate the costs of scarce medical resources and (2) encourage physicians to hospitalize patients and too frequently prescribe complex procedures. On the other side, unions and employees fear that the rise in medical costs will make the benefits too low.[12]

Some employees and their unions, dissatisfied with the sum total of medi-

[11] Among the disadvantages of first-dollar benefits is that it is quite expensive to process numerous small claims. The cost of administration of health insurance plans is well over 10 percent of benefits, and this does not include the extra costs to doctors and hospitals of filling out forms, costs which in one way or another are passed on to the employer. The best and most expensive plans combine first- and last-dollar insurance. An example of this might include Blue Cross, Blue Shield, and major medical. But even a program such as this may provide limited, if any, protection against mental illness or tuberculosis.

[12] At Ford Motor Company, for example the cost of health insurance was the equivalent of $120 per car in 1977 ($2,000 per worker per year) up from $22 per car 12 years earlier. (*Daily Labor Report*, March 23, 1978.)

cal insurance provided by employers, are demanding that coverage include items such as eyeglasses, dental bills, orthodonture, and psychiatric services. (The last two are particularly expensive, and they raise management control problems: when is psychotherapy a matter of employee preference and when is it a critical medical need?) In 1978, dental plans already covered 44 million people, up from only 13 million in the U.S. in 1970.

The result is conflicting pressure: management wants costs controlled, while employees and their unions are seeking improved benefits.

Some unions have sought to establish union-operated clinics that can set cost standards, which will help in evaluating what the membership is receiving in benefits. Management may seek to establish programs that require a fixed level of contributions (costs), rather than promise workers a fixed level of benefits. Thus management contributes so many dollars per employee into its various health insurance programs; depending on usage, the level of benefits will vary. Employees typically prefer guaranteed benefit levels.

Sick leave. Medical plans provide for the costs of doctors and hospital services, but what about the loss of income when an employee is unable to work? To meet this need, organizations often allow a certain number of days as paid *sick leave,* particularly for salaried employees.[13] Sick leave can be easily abused. Employees who are not sick may take advantage of it, whereas those who do not use it sometimes feel cheated. Comments like this are common: "I've still got 11 days of unused sick leave this year. I don't see why I haven't got that time coming to me." To deter the use of sick leave as an extra holiday, thus vastly increasing its cost, companies may require a doctor's certificate to prove illness. They may refuse to pay sick leave for the first day or two of illness but pay a bonus to employees who do not use their entire leave (possibly an extra day's pay for every three days of unused leave).[14]

Health maintenance organizations.[15] Employers are now required to offer their employees an alternative to traditional hospital/medical insurance coverage that will provide broader prepaid family medical care.[16] The HMO is a medical organization with a broad range of specialties. It receives a fixed annual fee per employee (or family), regardless of illness or procedures. These HMO's stress preventative medicine, group practice, and clinics (in contrast

---

[13] Disability benefits under the federal social security program are also paid to employees who are totally disabled, and various state programs (notably in California and New York) provide short-term benefits for employees who cannot work because of sickness or accident.

[14] Companies may begin to consider "sick leave banks." Some of the employees' allotted sick leave days is pooled, to be drawn on if they exhaust their own sick leave. Presumably there is group pressure to restrain depleting this common fund, and the employer can grant a certain amount of extra sick leave without additional cost.

[15] Usually referred to as HMO's.

[16] Under a federal law passed in 1973, the government is committed to encouraging the development of health maintenance organizations. Employers need not pay the full cost of such coverage. Many choose to reimburse employees for only the traditional coverage leaving the employee to pay the difference for this comprehensive medical program. Some very large companies are establishing their own HMO's instead of joining local medical plans.

to personal physicians). Their purpose is to discourage doctors and patients from using expensive procedures and hospitalization. Thus, employees are encouraged to have early checkups (before serious illness), and the amount of reimbursement does not depend on whether or not they are hospitalized.[17] It is expected that better and less costly medical care will result.[18]

Retirement

Since employees do not expect to work all their lives, pension demands tend to be strong, although younger employees—particularly when they are unmarried—may not be as interested as older employees. Traditionally, management gave little thought to retirement plans. When employees were too old to work, they were either unceremoniously dropped from the payroll or given a lump-sum payment as a reward for their years of service. People were expected to save for their old age, or their children were expected to take care of them—and then there was always the county old folks home.

By the 1920s a few responsible companies pioneered formal retirement programs, which typically included a fixed retirement age (often 65) coupled with a guarantee of a regular, often very modest monthly income thereafter. The Social Security Act of 1935 established a federal program of retirement benefits that now provides a base level of protection for a majority of American families. But the federal program provides little more than the bare minimum necessary for survival, and today most large organizations supplement this with private programs of their own. (In recent years, however, Congress has increased benefit rates faster than the cost of living has risen.) Like any form of insurance or annuity, pension programs can be legally and financially complicated. Here are some of the major issues.

Size of benefits

Most pension plans relate benefits to past earnings, but there is a trend to weight more heavily the income received in the last years of employment. Unions also press for higher minimums, which tend to reduce the relationship to actual earnings. Today, in the more liberal companies, pensions and federal social security benefits together may total as much as 80 percent of an employee's preretirement income (after tax), whereas 25 percent was much more common a decade ago.[19]

[17] These plans are patterned after the highly successful program pioneered by the Kaiser Company in California.

[18] An in-between approach is the individual physicians association. Employees still have their own private doctor, but they must choose one who agrees to be monitored by a specially created medical association that can enforce predetermined cost standards, cost of service, and decide whether or not expensive procedures were justified. See Peter Drucker, "The Future Shape of Health Care," *The Wall Street Journal,* July 19, 1978.

[19] In many cities, police, firefighters, and even sanitation and subway workers are permitted to retire at half pay after 20 years of service, and in New York City, in some cases, with almost full pay after 40 years. These extremely liberal pension provisions—far more liberal than in the private sector—have contributed to the financial crises affecting many cities. In New York, pension costs came to 40 percent of payroll in 1976! Many pension plans are integrated with social security. Benefits are stated in terms of combined private pension and government social security payments. The latter, of course, involves contributions shared between employer and employee.

Who pays?   Early pension plans typically provided for a significant employee contribution, perhaps half. Now the trend is clearly toward having the employer pay the full cost. Nevertheless, many managers believe that if employees pay at least part of the cost, they will be more reasonable in their demands for greater benefits. (In 1972, employee contributions came to only 6 percent of the costs of pension plans.)

Age of retirement   Trends in retirement age are confusing. The 1978 amendments to the Age Discrimination in Employment Act protect most employees from being forced to retire before they reach 70 (see Chap. 8).[20] Yet many employees choose to retire even before they reach 65, the previous most common mandatory age in most companies. More employees apparently desire increased leisure or a less pressureful life. In General Motors, for example, the average age of retirement for production and office workers is 56. At General Foods, only one employee in three retires as late as age 65; and at IBM, only one in six does.[21] In the steel industry, if management decides to eliminate a department, all employees over 45 years old with 20 years of service get full retirement benefits.[22] A recent survey of major U.S. companies disclosed that 70 percent of all retirees apply for social security before age 65, the most typical age being 62.[23] Some of the retirement before 65, of course, is for serious health reasons. During recessions, it occurs as the result of discouragement over layoffs.

Several years ago in the auto and farm equipment industries, employees on arduous assembly lines demanded that the UAW negotiate a contract allowing them to retire with full pension rights after 30 years of service (25 years for foundry workers).[24] To the dismay of management, many critical off-the-line workers (e.g., tool and die makers) took advantage of this new contract and left their jobs.

A few companies insist on their highest level of executives retiring before age 65, presumably to ensure that top management will be most vigorous and innovative. The military permits retirement at half pay after only 20 years of service, but most of those who take advantage of this attractive option then start a second career. Our societal values affect the retirement decision. Insofar as we stress leisure more than accomplishment, greater numbers will

[20] Private firms employing 20 or more employees are covered by this legislation. It excludes "bona fide" executives or those in high policymaking positions who are eligible for pensions of $27,000 or more a year.

[21] *The Economist* (Aug. 5, 1978), p. 57. This U.K. publication also notes that European governments are encouraging early voluntary retirement, to reduce unemployment among young people. Belgium permits workers within 5 years of the statutory retirement age to retire early if they are replaced by young, unemployed workers either directly or indirectly, and France provides greater pensions for those who retire when they reach 60, rather than staying until 65.

[22] Arnold Weber, "Conflict and Compression: The Labor Market Environment of the 1980s" in Clark Kerr and Jerome Rosow, eds., *Work in America: The Decade Ahead* (New York: Van Nostrand, 1979).

[23] A study of The Conference Board reported in Bureau of National Affairs, *Daily Labor Report* (Dec. 12, 1978), A-1.

[24] This was the 1973 Ford-UAW contract. See also James Walker, "The New Appeal of Early Retirement," *Business Horizons* (June 1975), 43–48.

opt for a relaxed mode of life. In the past, observance of the work ethic made it embarrassing not to hold a conventional job.

Aside from the exceptions we have indicated, private pension plans and social security normally provide sharply reduced benefits for early retirement; however, there are usually special provisions for disabled employees who retire early.[25] Some observers, particularly in the government, are concerned because the numbers claiming disability appear to be rising at a suspiciously high rate.

Management may encourage early retirement to solve a problem of obsolete skills or an overage work force. During a period of diminishing employment, the average age of the work force tends to increase, and it becomes more difficult to hire young employees with critical technical skills. Encouraging early retirement may open up additional opportunities for promotion and hiring. Early retirement may also be used as an alternative to severance pay when layoffs are necessary, owing to a plant being shut down permanently or its work force cut back severely. Depending on how many employees are involved and the economic position of the organization, such early retirements may provide either sharply reduced benefits or the *same* benefit levels that would have obtained had retirement taken place at age 65. The reduced benefits would reflect the smaller investment in the plan, over fewer years, for a younger worker. Management may encourage retirements by offering a "no-benefit-level-difference," but employees have begun successfully to challenge such forced retirement as representing discrimination on the grounds of age, forbidden by federal statute.

Mandatory retirement inevitably creates problems. People age at different rates; some are physiologically and mentally ready to retire at 60, others at 75 or 80. With a fixed retirement age, some are retired too soon, some too late; but making a ruling for each person involves potential discrimination and bad feelings. To resolve this problem, many universities traditionally permit early retirement at the professor's option, set a mandatory retirement age, and then permit a limited number of people to continue employment on a year-to-year basis by mutual agreement. Some companies have similar rules.

Related to this is the practice of adapting the individual to retirement by stages. Over several years the workweek may gradually be reduced, and the employee eventually has the status of a part-time worker. In Scandinavia, workers "glide" between the ages of 60 and 70. In Japan, official retirement is at 55. Most employees stay on in less secure jobs after that time, but not as a part of the regular work force. Although we probably want people to be free to make choices consistent with their own needs, there can be economic problems associated with a society in which an increasing number of people are not working. As both birth and death rates decline, the percentage of people who are not working is bound to increase, since the proportion of older people will be increasing.

---

[25] Costs of financing the plans are based largely on average years of life past the normal retirement age, and each year of early retirement can represent a significant increment of cost.

Defined contribution vs. defined benefit. As with all fringes, pension commitments can be made in terms of a guaranteed level of employer contribution or a guaranteed level of benefits. Each involves some risks for both parties. Employers know their costs if they specify fixed contributions. Of course, if pension plans have better than predicted earnings (because of higher prevailing interest rates or stock prices), employers must still make the same contribution, so they do not gain the advantage of lower costs. Similarly, although employees may appear to gain an advantage with defined benefits, those whose pension plans have been tied to successful companys' profit-sharing plans have gained substantially. (For a fuller discussion of profit sharing, see Chap. 20.) On balance, employers appear to favor defined contributions; employees prefer defined benefits.

Profit sharing and employee stock ownership

As discussed in Chapter 20 profit-sharing plans can be an incentive to motivate greater identification and improved performance. Some organizations with unstable year-to-year earnings seek to substitute profit sharing for pensions. (If there is a substantial number of older employees, the substitution would not be popular.) Benefits to the employee are still tax deferred and can begin after retirement, when tax rates are likely to be lower. There is no employer's commitment for a fixed contribution each year; it depends on profitability.

Thrift plans are designed to encourage employees to save for emergencies and retirement. The typical plan permits an employee to set aside some percentage of total earnings, and this amount is then supplemented by a matching company contribution.[26] The proceeds for each employee are then invested in company stock or some combination of stock and government bonds. The bonds may be preferable if there is concern that volatility in stock prices may depress morale in a falling market.

Some corporations such as IBM also subsidize the purchase of their own stock as a means of allowing employees to share in the capital growth enjoyed by shareholders. Some years ago, the United Auto Workers turned down Ford's offer to contribute to employee stock ownership, but the union has had some second thoughts on the matter—another indication, perhaps, of the long-run trend toward obliterating class differences in the United States. Just as an increasing number of employees receive salaries instead of hourly wages, more of them are interested in stock ownership.

Companies hope that stock ownership will encourage employees to identify with their firms, understand the need for, and benefits of, increased productivity, and accept the role of profits in a free enterprise system.[27]

Employee Stock Ownership Plan (ESOP)

Another employee benefit also helps companies improve their financial position. Federal legislation encourages companies to create employee stock-ownership plans, which can typically become part of a pension plan or be

---

[26] In 1974, Du Pont spent $152 million on such a plan—well over $1,000 per employee.

[27] Unresolved question: can workers vote the shares they own directly through these funds? Also note that with worker share ownership, workers double their insecurity when the company fails.

drawn upon after termination.[28] Here is a typical example of how these new ESOP plans work.

> Company X needs capital to expand production, but new stock would be difficult to issue because of market conditions. Instead it borrows $1 million from a bank through its newly created ESOP trust and the company also guarantees the loan. The $1 million is then used to buy 100,000 new shares of company stock at $10 per share. Each year the company will pay 10 percent of its payroll to the trust, which covers principal amortization and interest on the bank loan to the trust. The payment to the trust is tax deductible as long as the trust uses each year's payment to release a comparable proportion of the stock it holds to employee accounts. Employees, in turn, get an extra benefit—stock with perhaps increasing value if the company is growing. Stock ownership may develop a greater commitment to the organization. The cost to the company may be less than the cost of a direct bank loan, and in some cases ESOP may help a company which otherwise would be closed out of the equities market "go public." Thus the plan can be used by companies that are publicly owned or those contemplating "going public."

This legislation (often called ERISA) was passed to correct a number of problems and abuses experienced by workers with their company pension plans, largely relating to absence of vesting and inadequate funding provisions.[29] The law places very rigid standards on the financial terms of company pension plans, and has many complexities that provide enormous administrative problems for management. The new law also specifies that all pension plans must cover all employees who are at least 25 years old and who have one year or more of service.

Employee Retirement Income Security Act of 1974

Vesting. In the past, many employees lost their pensions because they quit or were fired before retirement or their company disappeared. The law now requires companies to adopt vesting; that is, to provide employees with a guaranteed right to some proportion of accrued pension benefits, depending on length of service. Basically, an employer must choose one of several vesting formulas:

1. All pensions become 100 percent vested after 10 years of service; that is, employee is entitled to accrued benefits to date.

2. Employee is entitled to 25 percent of accrued benefits after 5 years of service, 50 percent of benefits after 10 years, and 100 percent of accrued benefits after 15 years of employment.

3. Employee is entitled to 50 percent of benefits when age plus length of service equals the number 45, if there is a minimum of 5 years of service.[30]

[28] The stock is usually vested in 10 years. Large, financially well-established companies also have an incentive to establish ESOP plans. Exxon and AT&T, for example, obtain an extra 1 percent investment tax credit for comparable sums set aside for employees in an ESOP.

[29] In 1972, for example, 1,227 pension plans were terminated and 20,000 workers lost some $50 million in pension benefits. (*The Wall Street Journal*, August 28, 1974, p. 1.)

[30] Note that vesting does not mean that after these minimum service periods, 5 to 15 years, an employee will receive the same pension that would have been received with work to normal retirement at 65. Rather, vesting is a guarantee of receiving the pension benefits accumulated up to the date of leaving.

Obviously, vesting increases employers' costs. Formerly, employees who left before retirement lost their accrued benefits. The funds they left behind could then be used for other pensions. Vesting also weakens the grip of the so-called golden handcuffs that bind employees to employers because of pensions.

Prior to ERISA, many firms did have some vesting. Unions that organized a number of small companies in a geographic area would negotiate master pension plans. These plans would cover all employees and permit them to move freely among firms in the group, without sacrificing their pensions.

Portability. Closely related to vesting is portability. The law makes some provisions for an employee to carry accrued pension benefits and deposit them with a new employer (with no taxes due). This procedure is designed to reduce the employer's resistance to hiring older workers and having to make up for their rather costly pensions (since there will not be many years of service over which to spread the cost of that pension). If an employer does not have an established plan, accrued pension funds can be invested in an Individual Retirement Account in the employee's name, to accumulate interest, tax-free, until the normal age of retirement.

On balance, although vesting and portability increase costs, employers and employees have something to gain by allowing for mobility. Employees who stay on a job or with an organization merely to keep their pensions are probably not going to be very effective. On the other side, employers who may have been reluctant to terminate an unsatisfactory employee, particularly one who was moving close to retirement, now have more flexibility. And employers who want to hire an older worker now are less inhibited by the high costs of maintaining a pension for an employee who will not work many years.

Funding. Before ERISA, employers had two choices. They could fund employee pension benefits by (1) yearly putting aside money to pay the cost of "one year's pension credit" or (2) starting to pay for the pension only after an employee retired. The employer who made the first choice gradually built up a fund; the one who made the second only promised to pay.

Promises were sometimes unfulfilled. Companies went bankrupt or funded plans with their own speculative common stock.[31] Occasionally, pension plans controlled by unions utilized the large accumulations of money to finance risky real estate ventures and to reward speculators who had been good to them. More conservative companies funded their pensions by buying annuities from recognized insurance companies that guaranteed a certain level of benefits would be paid to employees when they retired. Now, each year, employers must put aside enough to cover accrued pension benefits for all new employees. They must also begin paying off (by funding) the accrued pension benefits

---

[31] Of course, a profitable growth company found that its stock made an excellent pension plan investment, since the value of the stock—and thus the value of future pensions—increased more rapidly than that of a fund made up of more diversified investments.

of their other employees.[32] ERISA also introduced a new government pension termination insurance that guarantees payments to those who had pensions in funds that became insolvent.

ERISA allows common stock plans but sets high standards of fiduciary responsibility for pension funds. A single company's stock or other company asset may not be more than 10 percent of the assets of a pension fund. Conflict of interest is prohibited (fund trustees may not derive personal gain from the investment policies of the fund), and trustees are personally liable for "imprudent" investments.

It is by no means clear what effect this is having on pension fund portfolios. In the past, employers benefited from a booming stock market that lowered the cost of pension funds. (Increasing stock prices raised the value of the assets in the fund and lowered the required company contributions.) This provided a major support for the stock market as well. More recently, when market prices sagged and bond interest rates soared, fund administrators placed an increasing proportion of portfolios into bonds and mortgages. The latter policy, of course, will hurt the funds if inflation becomes rampant.

Such decisions are of major consequence to the economy as well as to the worker. The total value of private and public pension plans in 1978 was $500 billion. At that time, 20 to 25 percent of New York Stock Exchange stocks and 40 percent of corporate bonds were held by pension funds! Many companies spend more on pension funds annually than on new plant and equipment. It is not uncommon for the value of a company's retirement fund to exceed half the value of its new worth. Thus, pension funds are more than protection for retired workers: they are one of the primary sources of capital in our society.

Perquisites, services, and amenities

Companies provide a wide variety of goods and services that contribute to employee standards of living. Employee cafeterias frequently offer subsidized meals, and some companies sell their own products at a substantial discount to employees. Where work is arduous, clothing may be provided. In remote locations, employees often receive free transportation, generous travel allowances, and even free or subsidized housing. It is common to pay moving expenses when an employee is required to move from one location to another. At times, moving expenses are construed broadly to include trips back and forth from the old location to the new one until a new house is found, payment of a realtor's fee, mortgage financing, and guarantees that a former home will not be sold at a loss.

The list grows: day-care centers for children of working mothers, on-the-job personal counseling, recreation centers (camps, country clubs, lakes, athletic fields) and sports equipment to allow employees and their families to enjoy modestly priced weekend or holiday vacations. The companies hope

---

[32] These so-called past service credits, which were unfunded, must be paid off in a 30- to 40-year period under the new law; the employer can no longer start paying pension costs after retirement takes place.

to develop *esprit de corps* and loyalty as employees from various departments and levels interact.

As self-realization becomes a more sought-after goal, employees want their jobs to be fulfilling. Since few jobs provide an exact match between company needs and employee desires, employees want released time (at their regular salaries) to pursue personal professional interests, not leisure. Thus law firms get requests from their younger, community-conscious attorneys to have some time to take civil rights cases that provide no fees. Research scientists want time to pursue their own experiments, apart from their normal assignments. Many employees expect the organization to allow them to go to professional meetings (on company time and expense account) and to take company-paid college courses or other self-development programs.

Amenities

Attractive working conditions can also be considered an employee benefit: air conditioning, modern furnishings, comfortable and spacious lounges, parking, even gardens and art displays. Obviously, the facility's age and location are critical factors here. New office buildings in the suburbs can provide more of these benefits than older factories can, especially those in the inner city. What is interesting, however, is the increasing attention to esthetics, often manifested in construction that is costly to build and to maintain. Although few industrial psychologists now attribute greater productivity to working conditions, employees *are* attracted by pleasant surroundings.

Companies having large white-collar staffs find it particularly expensive to provide private offices, but prospective employees turn away from huge, unbroken spaces in which dozens or even hundreds work in close proximity. A number of innovative efforts are being made to use growing plants and new types of partitioning to break up such areas and give employees some sense of "territory" and privacy. The energy drain of high noise levels also encourages such arrangements.

Although these amenities never appear in fringe benefit budgets, they can represent significant outlays and require careful planning to make sure that the benefits are worth the expenditure.

Benefit program administration

Management, struggling to keep administrative costs under control, finds that fringes are usually more expensive than estimated and more difficult to budget than salaries.[33] The pension law (ERISA) is extraordinarily complicated, and many of the record-keeping paperwork costs are not apparent when management first seeks to adjust to the law. In fact, many smaller companies have dropped their pension plans entirely, to avoid the costs of living up to the complex requirements of ERISA. Others have opted for the establishment of Individual Retirement Accounts (IRA's) in the name of each eligible employee, contributing up to 15 percent of the employees' earnings to those

---

[33] Changes in interest rates (affecting funded plans), in tax laws, in employee turnover, in the average age of employees, in the incidence of illness and accidents, and many other difficult-to-predict items all affect costs.

separate accounts. Health and retirement programs can be administered by insurance companies, but costs are passed on to the insured company.

Benefit programs also require constant decisions about seemingly petty details that are of considerable importance to employees (and may set precedents for expensive action by the company).

Suppose the plant closes down for a national day of mourning on the death of an ex-President. Should employees be paid for the day's work lost? Including or excluding lost opportunities for piecework? Should those (such as watchmen) who are required to work, anyway, receive double pay? (Or even double-and-a-half, on the assumption that this is the equivalent of over-time?) Should an employee who is on vacation at the time get an extra day of vacation? How about those who regularly work Saturday and Sunday, and the day in question is one of their regular days off?

Or suppose the company's medical coverage excludes routine medical examinations. Where does one draw the line between these and genuine medical emergencies? How does one deal with a doctor's bill that seems to be completely out of line (and is submitted by the employee's cousin)?

Inept handling of service programs injures employee morale as easily as inept supervision does. Thus, *fringe* benefits, a marginal aspect of the personnel program, become a sensitive area requiring considerable managerial planning and skill.

Services designed to build employee morale may backfire with disastrous results, as some companies that operate plants overseas or in company towns have discovered. Service programs that provide housing, food, schools, and the like often develop into rich sources of employee grievances. Who gets the company cars or club memberships? When is it fair for the company to raise house rentals or the price of food in the company restaurant? How often should hash be served?

Most companies seek to get out of the housing business, even in so-called company towns, and out of the food business by bringing in food-service concessionaires. (But even when concessionaires are brought in, the average employee will blame the company for poor food or high prices.)

Allowing employee choice

Usually, employers institute programs because they think they are good for their employees or, more commonly, because other organizations have done so. Likewise, unions are more likely to follow patterns set by other unions, instead of asking the members what they want. In both cases, employee preferences are important.

Employers have two choices in seeking to make benefit plans more responsive to employees' preferences. They can utilize attitude surveys and polling techniques to ascertain what employees want, or they can develop procedures that allow employees to tailor their benefit programs to their own needs.

A modest number of studies have measured employee preferences among alternative forms of compensation; for example, between straight pay and various forms of fringe benefits. Much of this research has confirmed the obvious—such as older managers being more interested in pensions than are younger managers—but some of these studies have had unexpected findings. In a 1963 study, workers in one company indicated preference for a dental insurance program over a four times more costly life insurance program.[34]

These surveys need to be designed by experts to ensure that employees are able to understand what their choices and trade-offs really are. Such surveys must clarify the relevant costs and also give a realistic picture of the various benefit choices. A medical plan will not typically cover all health costs: there is usually a deductible, numerous ailments may be excluded, and only a percentage of the patient's expenses are recoverable. Of course, polling will also reveal that employees have strong differences both in needs and preferences. This has encouraged a small number of companies to experiment with *cafeteria plans,* often after surveying employee desires.

Cafeteria benefit plans. The purpose of these plans is to tailor benefits to individual preferences, within limits.

Under these plans, employers provide minimal "core" coverage in life and health insurance, vacations and pensions. The employee buys additional benefits to suit his own needs, using credits based on salary, service and age. . . . A new benefit will cost less under a cafeteria plan . . . because it is highly unlikely that every employee will choose it. Moreover, at least part of its cost may be offset by making it an option that the employee buys in place of another benefit or by paying part of the bill through payroll deductions."[35]

Additional costs may result, however. Cafeteria plans are more expensive to administer, and there is always the danger of an adverse selection factor increasing the costs. If more medical insurance is taken by employees who tend to be most often ill, in contrast to all employees being required to have the same coverage, insurance premiums for medical coverage will rise.

ERISA requires employers to provide employees with adequate explanations of their benefit programs. Even without cafeteria choices, employees need current information to understand what is being offered. Cafeteria plans, however, may require even more information about the relevant costs of benefits. In making the trade-offs between one type of benefit and another, the employee compares real cost data. For the first time, employees may become aware of how much their employer has been paying for benefits they took for granted. As new or improved benefits are requested, employees might also bear in mind that salary goes up more slowly when benefits increase more rapidly.

Contributory vs.
noncontributory

From one point of view, employees always contribute to the benefit plans they receive, since the employer's cost is an alternative to higher salaries. With cafeteria plans and the growing practice of unions announcing new agree-

[34] Stanley Nealey, "Pay and Benefit Preferences," *Industrial Relations,* Vol. 3, No. 1 (October 1963), 17–28.
[35] "Companies Offer Benefits Cafeteria-Style," *Business Week* (November 13, 1978), 116 ff.

ments—perhaps a package consisting of 50 cents per hour in increased wages and 15 cents per hour in improved benefits—this elementary point of economics becomes clear.

Employers have tried to retain the principle of employee contributions in the face of mounting pressure for all noncontributory benefits. Employee contributions reduce the company's costs, and people may place a higher value on something they have paid for than on something received free. Management also hopes that if employees' contributions mount as benefits expand, the expense may stem demands for more and more fringes.

Conclusion

By 1985, benefits may comprise more than 50 percent of total compensation costs, and their rate of growth may accelerate in the years to come, as new ones become popular and old ones continue to increase in size. Employee counseling programs (regarding preretirement, personal finances, and career interests) are on the increase, as are demands for dental and legal insurance. Chrysler Corporation now has a company-paid program that provides legal help for 150,000 UAW members. It covers personal problems ranging from traffic cases to divorce, child custody, and tax disputes.

There is greater interest in postretirement benefits (medical insurance and improved pensions to reflect continued increases in the cost of living). As more people work on salaries (instead of commission or an hourly wage), it is reasonable to assume that income protection plans, longer paid vacations, and medical plans will all become more expensive for companies.

Although many benefit programs began as aspects of paternalism, employees now take them very seriously and consider them one of the most important elements of their compensation for working. Indeed, many employees believe that they have the equivalent of a property right in their perpetuation. A personnel executive observed tartly that in the 1950s employees resisted and resented any intrusion on their lives by the company, but now they want extensive services: [36]

Then, it was "stay out of my life!" Now, with the sad state of society, with family, churches, and the schools often disqualified, the job and the employer become central.

In the face of these pressures, management must constantly decide on (1) the *total* expenditure on benefits—would the money be better spent on increasing wages and salaries, or must it be spent at all? and (2) the division of funds among alternative programs—will an extra 10 cents an hour for holidays have an impact on morale and motivation that is different from the impact of the same money spent on retirement benefits? But it should be emphasized that management is not completely free to give employees only the benefits it thinks desirable. Employees (and their unions) expect that employers will keep up with their neighbors. As new programs are introduced in other organizations, management comes under pressure to go along. And as changes are

[36] Robert Feagles, senior vice-president for personnel, First National City Bank (New York), quoted in *Fortune* (December 1970), 80.

made in tax laws and in the social security program, management must undertake compensating adjustments.

Controversy will continue over the dividing line that separates public and private concerns; that is, where should the line be drawn between services that ought to be provided by the employer and services that ought to be offered by the family, the community, and church and social organizations? The simple criterion, "satisfying employee needs," is not adequate. Human needs are multitudinous, and dissatisfaction that will affect job performance may come from many sources beyond the reach of management. Insofar as a greater share of pension benefits and accident and health insurance is provided by government administered programs (even though the costs may be borne directly by the firm or shared with employees), the individual's tie to a single organization is reduced. Also, government programs result in uniform benefits, regardless of where one works, and reduce concern about management *paternalism.*

Above all, management must consider the motivational aspect of fringes. What sorts of behavior do fringes motivate, and are these reactions and attitudes desirable? Do employees take fringes for granted, since they do not know the cost of what they are getting? Or do they mentally add the cost to their paychecks? Some managers are disappointed because they are not compensated by at least a recognition of the expense involved, but those who are looking for credit are often accused of taking a paternalistic attitude.

Other managers do not ask for gratitude from their employees, but for a sense of loyalty to the organization. Lavish recreational, health, and educational benefits, however, may foster a sense of overdependence among some employees; among others, a destructive resentment against paternalism. But neither employees nor employers may want to loosen the tie, since both find satisfactions in the sense of loyalty and identification that can be the byproduct of a well-administered, generous benefit program.

Pensions, stock purchase plans, and vacation benefits may be instituted to reduce employee turnover, but many dynamic organizations question the value of having employees place strong emphasis on seniority. Fringe benefits make it difficult for employees to leave their jobs and for employers to discharge them. Because employees have more to lose with their jobs, arbitrators in grievance cases require more conclusive evidence of wrongdoing before they will sustain a discharge. Early retirement programs create opportunities for promotion and for new talent and energy, but they may also remove valued, experienced people who are still needed.

In general, fringes benefit all employees equally, or they reward tenure rather than performance. A management primarily concerned with motivation might be better advised to consider incentive plans, which seek to relate earnings directly to performance. We turn to these programs in our next chapter.

1 • *Creeping Costs*

The Faraday Insurance Company undertook a blood-bank program in response to what seemed to be an important employee need. When company employees or members of their families were ill and required a transfusion, one or more other employees who had voluntarily signed up would be called by the company personnel office to report to one of the local hospitals. Recently, the personnel department noted that the costs of this program are greater than originally anticipated. Often a great many telephone calls have to be made before a donor can be located. This task requires almost full-time services of one clerk. Moreover, some donors do not return to work until the next day, even though the transfusion has been given in the morning, and overtime replacements have to be brought in.

1. How would you weigh the cost of this program against the benefits it provides?
2. Is there any way of cutting costs without nullifying the advantages of the program and without damaging the company's reputation?

2 • *Day Care for Working Mothers*

Crittenden Electronics in Los Angeles has received a petition signed by three-quarters of its women employees requesting that the company sponsor a day-care center for children of working mothers. The union has not been enthusiastic, although it has not taken a stand against the proposal. The work force of 2,800 has 1,500 women, of whom 500 have children below school age. Such programs are expensive (estimates vary widely, but $1,000 per child per year would probably be conservative). The issue has attracted a great deal of attention in the plant, and it has become a focal issue for women's rights groups, blacks, and other cause-oriented younger employees. Management expects to keep increasing its proportion of women workers, but the union and the company are concerned about the possibility that heavy expenditures in this area may limit wage increases.

1. Consider the criteria you would use in evaluating the proposal for his new benefit.
2. What studies would you undertake in the evaluation process?
3. How would you handle the problem of this benefit, which has special appeal to what is now only 18 percent of the work force?

3 • *Answering Union Demands*

You are the industrial relations director. In negotiations, your union makes the following demands:
- Full orthodontic costs for all employees and their children.
- Two weeks paid paternal leave for new fathers (married and otherwise).
- Three days' bereavement pay for deaths of grandparents, uncles, and aunts.
- Company to make up difference between regular pay and pay received while serving on juries, National Guard, or Army Reserve, or time spent working for antiwar organizations.
- Three days off per year for "personal activities."
- A provision that all employees be allowed at least two of their vacation weeks during the summer months, plus $100 vacation expense bonus.
- Triple time for work on holidays.
- Fifty percent extra pay for working on the midnight shift.

1. How would you evaluate each of these demands? What information would you need? How would you cost out each demand? What information would you need in addition to costs? How would you obtain it?
2. What demands do you think are most justified, from the point of view of employees? from the point of view of the company? from the point of view of society as a whole?
3. What safeguards would you insist on to prevent abuses of the benefits, provided they were granted?

incentives and performance standards

Management often supplements wages and salaries with increments commensurate with employee performance. These are variously called incentives, commissions, bonuses, and piecework plans; all are designed to motivate employees to improve their performance.

Such incentive compensation plans must have a base line, or normal work standard, so that performance over and above this standard can be rewarded. The base must be high enough so that employees are not given extra rewards for what is merely an average day's work; but it should not be so high that additional amounts are almost impossible to earn, and the level of difficulty should be the same for all. Management may also set workload or output standards (often called *measured day work*) even when no financial incentives are provided.

In this chapter we shall look first at the contribution of such standards of measurement, then at the use of workload standards and incentives in white-collar jobs, and then for blue-collar, production jobs.

Why measured performance is important

Productivity is increased when an employee has a specific, easily viewed target, rather than a vague job description or a supervisor's exhortations. Compare the motivational impact of telling a salesperson to "work harder" or say-

ing, "Your quota is 100 gross per month." The growing emphasis on "management by objectives" reflects the need for these targets at managerial levels, as well. Such objectives are sources of feedback *(How close am I getting? How good am I?)* and they can provide the ego satisfactions associated with a sense of accomplishment *(THIS is how much I've done).*

Workload standards make it easier to set work assignments equitably. Can Jones operate two machines? Can a receptionist announce visitors, answer the telephone, and also type correspondence? Management must be able to measure the quantity of work that can reasonably be expected of each employee. In turn, such measurements should result in a fairer distribution of work.

A manager may need an operational definition of a job to be able to judge whether an employee is performing adequately. Whether the subordinate is busy or idle is often a poor measure of effectiveness. The bustling employee may be doing unnecessary things or spending too much time on some tasks, to the detriment of others. Also, if an equitable workload can be specified, an employee can be provided with a means of earning more than the base salary for the job. Such *incentive plans* have many problems, as we shall describe later, but their appeal is great. Let us examine this appeal.

Incentive systems allow an employee to earn more by working more, without a potentially arbitrary supervisor awarding a merit increase or recommending a promotion. Salaries and fringe benefits are often the same for mediocre and outstanding performers; but with financial incentives, the superior employee can receive substantially more and know that there is a direct relationship between effort and reward. A pay plan that provides immediate, as distinct from delayed, rewards for performance can be a powerful stimulus.

Built-in economic motivation

Clear, unambiguous targets can add job interest. They provide a catalyst, a focal point, and an inner direction that helps organize the working day.

Greater autonomy and job interest

"It gives you a good feeling to know that you can knock off 30 percent of your quota right away. You have to be good to do that. And then there's that nice feeling of knowing you can coast anytime you want, because that big chunk is under your belt already."

"I want a job where I can see my run output, know I'm fully responsible for it, and I'll get credit for it."

Thus the employee can periodically change the trade off between an easier pace and more income. The supervisor is less likely to be pushing for higher output, and employees feel they can vary their pace to suit their moods and needs. Moreover, the opportunity to set goals, improve one's "score," and race the clock may add interest to tedious jobs.

By ensuring that employees will be paid on the basis of production, rather than on the number of hours they work, incentive systems enable the firm to predict its labor costs. Particularly in highly competitive industries like

Increased control over labor costs

textiles and clothing, this ability to look ahead is highly important. Incentives . also make it possible for management to develop more accurate cost-accounting estimates in establishing budgets and in preparing bids on new contracts.

Peformance standards have been established for both white- and blue-collar jobs, but the approaches to these two areas involve elements of commonality and difference. We will look at performance standards in both white- and blue-collar settings in turn, and then compare the two.

White-collar and managerial workload standards

How hard is an executive working, and what motivation will produce harder work? Upper management jobs are not easy to define explicitly, and how they are performed depends a great deal on the style and personality of the manager. Output may not be seen for some period of time: a manager may spend months, even years consummating a merger or assessing the worthwhileness of a large capital appropriation. Most companies, therefore, devote little effort to calculating work loads. Instead, top managers receive broad overall targets that, it is hoped, will both motivate high performance and provide a yardstick for measuring the executive's worth. The measurements may be

Growth in earnings per share of the company's stock

Penetration of new markets or number of new, successful products

Success of diversification or integration programs

Many companies (as described in Chap. 14) build executive bonus plans and deferred compensation schemes around these kinds of broad targets or goals.

As one moves down the organization hierarchy, jobs can be defined more clearly, and short-run goals and tagets can be established. Well-managed companies give middle managers specific objectives in sales, costs, and profits. Managers are not told *how* to achieve these objectives, but their progress is monitored monthly or quarterly. Accomplishment is reinforced by bonuses, merit increases, and promotions.

Still further down the line, employees may be paid according to how well they meet the company's standards. Stockbrokers, department store clerks, and most field salespersons receive commissions based on the business they generate. Many salespersons also receive valuable gifts and trips to exotic resorts as extra stimulus to energetic performance.

Since the standard established for each job is critical in determining employee income, it becomes important to understand how these standards are established.

Historical records

For many jobs, historical records provide the basis for setting performance standards. When examining back records, Company X notes that in Ohio it has sold an average of $162,000 worth of tools per month. When a new salesperson is hired, this sum becomes the quota. If economic conditions change in Ohio or if new competition develops, the quota might easily become outdated.

Such standards tend to overreward employees when business conditions are good and penalize them in bad years.

There are other obvious defects here. An employee following an enormously energetic predecessor may receive a more difficult standard or quota than one succeeding a poor performer. In some instances sales personnel actually retard their performance for fear that an extremely successful month or year will set an unbeatable standard for the upcoming accounting period.

When setting quotas, it is helpful to have a substantial number of records to examine. More credible performance standards are likely to be set in a department store chain with many similar stores and many similar people selling identical merchandise than in an organization with a number of dissimilar employees performing unique functions. Even in the chain, however, there can be doubts concerning the equity of standards. Salespeople at stores located in a growing city will have more opportunities for sales than will their counterparts in a town characterized by declining population, economic dislocations, or bitter competition among stores. Adjustment is usually a highly subjective process.

Diversified jobs

Quota systems are based on the assumption that employees will be more motivated to perform if they are compensated in proportion to their diligence. Many jobs, however, are really more complex than they first appear, and a single standard or quota may not be a fair measure of how well the *total* job is performed. Two examples:

1. A company markets small pumps to machinery manufacturers. It is naive to think that the salesperson's job involves only selling. Observing salespeople in action, one quickly learns that effective representatives spend considerable time
   a) analyzing and reporting back to the company on changing customer requirements and the impact of competition
   b) helping customers with their service problems involving the merchandise, delivery, and quality
   c) investigating potential new customers and new applications of the company's product (often called missionary work)
2. Egbert asks her secretary to arrange full travel plans and itinerary, to set up conferences, and to compose more routine correspondence. Grimshaw, in contrast, requires his secretary to do only routine tasks: filing, typing, and making phone calls. At the end of the day, Egbert's secretary may be behind in her *observable* workload—typing and filing—and may appear less productive than Grimshaw's secretary, who has completed all routine tasks.

Under a simple quota system, a sales representative might receive high earnings and encouragement for ignoring all but the easiest-to-sell customers, for high-pressuring people into buying the wrong equipment, for failing to ensure proper installation and service, and for ignoring new trends in competitor equipment. To avoid this, many sophisticated companies seek ways of measuring more than gross sales.

The salesperson described above might be asked to keep track of the number of visits to prospective as well as established customers, to write field reports on customers' needs and intentions, to detail service work and handling of complaints. Conceivably, the representative might receive bonus credits for winning a new customer from a competitor or for selling a product that the company was most anxious to put on the market.

Even with such elaborations, management must recognize that its standards (and the financial incentives that bolster them) are at best subjective and perhaps not totally equitable. To provide real equity in earnings opportunities, management must study each job to determine the amount of work accomplished by a typical employee working at an average pace. This would then become the baseline for a bonus system to reward above-average performance.

Most nonproduction jobs have an important unmeasurable quality; they cannot be precisely programmed. The best employees will use discretion and will add or subtract tasks to meet job problems. A good file clerk, for example, will assign priorities, decide when to ask for help on a problem, and develop new files if they are needed. Such discretionary components, while not quantifiable, may make the difference between a good and a mediocre employee.

Distortions in bonus plans. A number of factors that the employee cannot control may also distort bonus earnings and injure motivational effectiveness. New competitors, a slump in the market, or technological changes could limit the sales potential of a particular product and thus reduce sales commissions. Company policies can limit the opportunity to earn bonuses.

Differences in taxes in various countries often motivate multinational companies to let their profits rise in countries where taxes are low. Heavier cost allocations are assigned to work done in countries where taxes are high, thereby reducing the paper profits of managers in those countries.

Other distortions are created by managers who find ways of shifting costs from their departments to others, damaging the other departments' chances for bonuses.

Ideal standards. Ideally management should adjust quotas and standards to the situation and give special credits for work required by unanticipated problems (spending extra time with customers because of a product's imperfection, for example). In general, management has been reluctant to set objective or scientific performance standards for white-collar jobs. We will better understand this reluctance after seeing how difficult the process is for even routine production jobs.

Workload standards and incentives for production work

Factory production jobs are easily adaptable to objective workload standards and opportunities for incentive earnings. Typically, they are highly repetitive, have a short job cycle, and produce a clear, measurable output.

Before explicit workload standards can be set, however, management must

1. Describe the job (see discussion in Chapter 8).
2. Decide how the job is to be performed by the employee (motion study).
3. Decide how fast the job can be performed (time study).

Motion study

Essentially, motion study involves: (1) analyzing how the job is currently performed, (2) questioning whether steps can be eliminated or combined, and (3) setting up a quicker, easier way of doing the job. To do this, the engineer looks at the flow of work to, and from, the employee and at the employee's movements, including walking and finger motions. The main purpose of such a job study is to question existing procedures and to suggest ways of saving time and employee effort. Which motions can be eliminated? Can simple movements be substituted for more complicated movements that require greater dexterity? Can the sequence of operations be rearranged so that both hands will be kept busy instead of one remaining idle? Can symmetrical, rhythmic, or circular motions be substituted for straight-line, jerky, or uncoordinated motions?

Limitations of "the best way." The industrial engineer uses these motion-study techniques to determine *the best way* for a worker to do a particular job. Behind this effort is the assumption that there actually is a best way. What are the limitations of this assumption?

First, everybody is forced to work in the same way; the fact that people are different is ignored. The best method for a right-hander may not be the best method for a leftie. Moreover, always doing something the same way—even the best way—may be more fatiguing than varying the method.

Motion study often pays little attention to the sequence of motions or the value of pauses. Carried to its logical extreme, insistence on the "one best way" would eliminate the windup from the baseball pitch. The tendency in motion study is to consider each motion separately, rather than to determine whether it contributes to *overall* efficiency. Considered by itself, the windup is clearly an unnecessary motion.

More important, behind this assumption lurks the implication that the seasoned worker's years of experience on the job are useless and that an engineer with a few hours' observation can determine the best method. To be sure, the engineer with a trained and questioning mind can spot mistakes that the worker has always overlooked. Yet it is not safe to ignore the worker's experience altogether.

Further, even if the method that the engineer finally devises is clearly better than the existing method, it may not be accepted by the workers. Certainly if they are skeptical of the engineer's method and enthusiastic about their own, chances are that the output will be greater if they maintain the established, less efficient method.

Time study

Once the proper way of doing a job has been determined by motion study, it is possible to begin time study. Time study is a procedure for determining the *standard time* required to do a job. Usually it consists of four steps:

429

1. Selecting the employee
2. Determining the *observed* time
3. Applying a correction factor
4. Introducing *allowances* for fatigue, personal time, and contingencies

Selecting the employee. A typical union contract includes the following provision:

The time standards shall be based on the time required by a qualified normal employee working at a normal pace under normal conditions, using the proper method with normal material at normal machine speeds.

Notice how often the word *normal* is used: what are the normal machine speed, normal material, and normal conditions? Usually these are prescribed by the industrial engineer, and all the details are listed on the time-study form. It is essential that these details be listed accurately; for if, some months later, workers feel that the sheet of metal they are working with is thicker than that used in the original time study, they can always claim higher piece-rate earnings than were originally allowed.

What is the *proper method?* That is the one best way, of course, which we have already mentioned.

What is meant by *normal* worker, *normal* work pace? These questions constitute a major area of contention between management and union. Few technicians try to find *normal* employees. Instead, they time the work rates of typical employees. If these workers seem to work at a pace slower or faster than the technician's preconception of *normal,* they apply certain corrections (which we will discuss later) to reconcile the observed speed with their own notions.

Timing the job. After workers have been selected and the job conditions have been described, the timers are almost ready to start. But they must first divide the job into elements. An *element* is a clearly distinguishable motion, such as placing a piece in a jig. Each element is usually timed separately. The technician is interested not only in the total time for the entire *cycle,* but also in the time needed to perform each element. Close examination of *elemental* times enables the observer to determine which delays—with materials, machines, or operators—can be eliminated.

How should the length of the study be determined? Practice varies, but it is usual to time enough job cycles to ensure that an adequate sample is obtained. Unless the whole operation is unusually long, at least 10 or 20 cycles are observed.

Timing is usually done with a stopwatch and recorded on a form. Once the timing has been completed and the necessary calculations have been made, the observer has a number of readings for each element. Doubtless, the readings will vary. The usual practice is to throw out all abnormal values—those that are too high or too low—before taking an average; a subjective process.[1]

[1] An increasing use of videotape eliminates the pressure of timing employees while they are working. Element times can then be derived from the tape, and tapes can be preserved, should questions arise about the validity of the standard.

Applying a correction factor. The next step is to apply a correction factor to adjust for the fact that the worker observed may be working at a pace slower or faster than normal. Correction factors are applied frequently through *effort-rating. Effort-rating* means that the time-study specialist estimates at what percentage of normal the operator is working. If the specialist estimates that the operator is working at only 90 percent of normal pace, then the observed time is obviously too long. The normal time can be obtained by multiplying the observed time by .90.

Effort-rating assumes that the observer has in the back of his head some standard of what constitutes normal pace. Time-study engineers once felt that normal pace could be determined objectively and *scientifically*, but today it is generally conceded to be a matter of judgment. What one person considers normal performance, another may consider slow.

How is the standard to be determined? Basically, this is the age-old question of what constitutes a "fair day's work," the subject of frequent union-management negotiation. According to one union contract, "A normal pace is equivalent to a man walking without load on smooth, level ground at a rate of three miles per hour." Nonunion plants (and many unionized plants as well) normally follow benchmark standards set by leading industrial engineers. One such standard calls for typing 50 words a minute or dealing a deck of cards in 30 seconds (but one engineer insists that only 27 seconds are required).

Often, movies are taken of employees working at standard pace. When run at the speed that has been negotiated as "normal," they provide criteria for judging the pace of people on new jobs. These films are also used in training time-study specialists to judge "normal" pace.

In spite of its seeming simplicity, effort-rating, with some justification, has been attacked as being arbitrary and imprecise.

Predetermined time systems. Because of the obvious disadvantages of traditional forms of time study, many industrial engineers utilize predetermined time systems (sometimes called synthetic data). The use of standard data completely eliminates the need for timing each job. How does this work?

First, the best method for each job is determined, as discussed above, and waste motions are eliminated. Then the basic motions for each hand are carefully listed. Once this is done, reference is made to the "standard times" developed by engineering firms for each basic motion.[2] The standard times allowed for each motion are merely added together to get the equivalent of "corrected time."

There are a number of advantages to this technique. By sidestepping time study and the rating problem, it eliminates endless union-management wrangles (if the union accepts the standard data and, what is more unlikely, if its members accept the results). A worker can no longer fool the time-study person by pretending to work fast, nor does the time-study person (now better called an industrial engineer) have to worry about being outsmarted. There

---

[2] For example, a typical standard data table gives the following times for a drill press operator: Moving part to be processed from skid to machine—.08 minutes; blowing jig element of press clear of chips—.06 minutes.

is no longer a problem of consistency. Predetermined data make the rate-setting process quicker, cheaper, more mechanical, and less subject to personal discretion. Indeed, computers can be used to calculate piece rates.

If the predetermined time method is advantageous, why is it not used universally? There are many objections to it.

In this method it is assumed that the time for each motion can be determined without considering its position in the complete sequence. But this would be true only if each movement started at rest and ended at rest. Efficient workers develop a rhythm in their work, and their speed in any one part of the job depends in part on what they have just done and what they intend to do next.[3]

In spite of these criticisms, standard-data systems do provide a rough check on the times obtained through direct observation. When a standard-data system is applied to a number of roughly similar jobs, such as using a drill press in a standardized fashion, it may result in considerably greater consistency between standards than does time study. Indeed, one union, the International Ladies Garment Workers', has developed its own standard data for use in setting piece rates for dresses.

Allowances

Once the time for a particular job has been determined, either by corrected time study or on the basis of standard data, the industrial engineer adds a certain percentage *allowance* to this time to account for what the worker may lose in personal time (going to the washroom, getting a drink of water) or because of fatigue or unexpected contingencies.

The *fatigue* allowance is designed to compensate for the worker's increasing weariness. Fatigue allowances are often set uniformly for all jobs, although larger allowances are sometimes made for heavier jobs. *Allowance for contingency* is a general catch-all category that may include setup time, delay for materials, time for oiling, and other stoppages beyond the operator's control. Sometimes an arbitrary allowance is made to cover all such contingencies. More often, a contingency allowance is computed on the basis of a rough time study made over a period of several days.

Establishing standards

After these time and motion study procedures are completed, management is in a position to establish workload standards specifying the quantity of work that can be expected from an average employee in a particular job. The standards are based on too many subjective calculations to be the "scientifically determined rates" envisioned by early "scientific management" advocates, but they do provide measured day work.

The process of measurement can stop here, and it will provide what is typically called *measured day work.* Now the supervisor has quantitative performance standards to give the employee and to judge him by. Many companies, however, prefer to go one step farther and develop an incentive payment

---

[3] The speed at which a baseball player can run from home plate to first base depends on whether the player (a) has just bunted or driven a line drive, and (b) intends to stop at first or go on to second. It might also depend on whether the player is first one up and still slightly tired from running in from center field at the end of the previous inning.

plan for workers who *exceed* these standards. The additional pay is usually proportionate to the amount by which they exceed the standards. Such incentive or piecework systems are designed to allow most employees to earn 20 to 25 percent more than they would under daywork conditions.

Surely it seems that incentive systems should eliminate many sources of industrial conflict and employee-relations problems—after all, they encourage delegation of responsibility, increase worker motivation, and strengthen management's control. Unfortunately, incentive plans have been the source of serious friction between labor and management. Why should a program that is theoretically sound prove so deficient in practice?

Employee responses that challenge incentive systems

To understand why incentive plans tend to generate conflict, we must first assess employees' reactions to incentives.

The work group imposes a ceiling

Employees rarely produce as much as they can in response to incentives. Initially, members of inexperienced groups may work to capacity, but most employees are quick to learn that such behavior is *dangerous*. Employees fear that if they begin to pull down earnings that are too high under a particular piece rate, management will decide that the rate is too generous.

Management usually promises that rates will not be cut unless there are changes in working conditions or procedures. Employees, however, believe that management will always find an excuse to restudy a job if incentive earnings are very high.

Further, many workers fear that if they increase their production markedly, they will work themselves out of a job—that is, that management will not be able to sell the increased output, and some workers will be expendable.

Moreover, incentive plans may threaten the status hierarchy within the group. Older workers, who customarily have the highest status, may be unable to match the pace of their younger colleagues and thus find that their relative earnings have declined. Naturally, to protect their social position the older workers put pressure on the younger ones to underproduce.

In response to all these factors, the work group establishes ceilings (bogies) for the proper or safe level of output. The employee who overproduces is belittled as a "rate-buster." New employees are indoctrinated into the group's standard almost as soon as they enter the department:

This was my first job. The foreman told me I was on piecework and to make just as much as I could. I was scared and anxious to make a good impression, so I tried pretty hard.

About an hour had passed when several guys told me, "Take it easy—don't knock yourself out." I thought they were showing kindness, so I thanked them and kept plugging ahead.

Then an older man came to me and said, "Let me give you a piece of advice. The most we ever make on that piece is sixty an hour, and a new man doesn't make that much. If you want to make any friends here, I'd watch your count pretty closely."

"How come?" I asked.

"Because if we put out more than that, they'll cut our rates. We'll have to work that much harder for the same amount of money."

As a result of pressures, most workers will try to maintain and report approximately the same safe output. If the group inadvertently overproduces, this excess is concealed and reported on a day when the group falls short of its normal output.

Rate busters are workers who ignore the group's norms and produce at a level substantially above the ceiling agreed upon. They trade away social acceptability for higher income. The friction that develops between rate-busters and the other group members may cause severe supervisory problems. To force rate-busters to conform, the group may attempt sabotage or ostracism, neither being conducive to harmonious working relationships.

Struggling for "better" rates

Employees under an incentive plan often struggle to obtain more desirable or looser rates. They believe that the time-study engineer cannot evaluate precisely how many pieces per day or per hour each worker should be able to complete. They know that certain subjective judgments are involved. Consequently, they suspect that management will try to make them work harder than they should to obtain a reasonable bonus.

This distrust shows itself most dramatically when the time-study engineer appears in the shop, for example:

(Starkey is advising Tennessee, a relatively inexperienced worker, how to deal with time-study men.)

"If you expect to get any kind of a price, you got to outwit that——You got to use your noodle while you're working, and think your work out ahead as you go along! You got to add in movements you know you ain't going to make when you're running the job! Remember, if you don't——them, they're going to——you! . . . Every movement counts!

". . . You were running that job too damn fast before they timed you on it! I was watching you yesterday. If you don't run a job slow before you get timed, you won't get a good price. They'll look at the record of what you do before they come around and compare it with the timing speed. Those time-study men are sharp! . . ." [4]

Both sides may legitimately disagree over the frequency and importance of equipment failures, material shortages, or imperfections that delay production. Obviously, the employees want to ensure that allowances are ample; management wants to ensure that wages are kept within reasonable limits.

Time-study engineers may see the employees as tricksters who feign difficulties and are always pressuring for looser standards, whether legitimate or not. The engineers may even overcompensate for the expected bluffs and shenanigans of employees. Fearing the embarrassment of being tricked into setting a rate that is too loose, they initially take extra pains to set a tight rate. Employees recognize this tendency and restrict their efforts as a counterbalance.

[4] William F. Whyte, *et al.*, *Money and Motivation* (New York: Harper, 1955), p. 32.

Thus, the introduction of new jobs often marks the outbreak of a cold war. Employees learn by experience that if they object vigorously to the rates and repeatedly fail to meet the standard output, eventually they may be able to win a slight loosening of the rates. Management recognizes that by giving in to such pressures it only encourages further slowdowns and grievances. The war rages until the employees are convinced that they can do no better and management is satisfied that it has won something approximating a reasonable standard. The ultimate result is a negotiated rate that may depart significantly from the time-study data. Management is tempted to concede rather than suffer a prolonged loss of output when the situation involves a small group of workers who control a potential bottleneck in the work flow.

Here is a classic description of this cold war at a time when $1.33 per hour was a satisfactory wage rate:

The setting of rates and the reaction by the operators is a routine you have to go over again and again, forever and ever apparently, as long as there shall be garment rates, and broken needles. You study carefully and set the rate, say 49½ cents a dozen for hemming. You post the rate and then the operator has a fit. She says she "can't make nothing on that rate." She says she's been here on the line for 23 years and no young squirt time-study man is going to push her around. You tell her there's a lot of factors involved (what would we do without those involved factors?), and that management wants to meet the operators half way and continue to enjoy mutual confidence for the highest production, Sleep Tite quality, and high earnings based on output and ability. The operator says she "can't buy no groceries on mutual confidence" and is going to go to work at the Packing Plant unless something is done about the rate. The other girls in the unit glare at management and exchange significant looks and talk so much about it all day that production goes off 12 dozen. You promise to analyze the situation and make an "eight-hour study" to check for any factors that might have been overlooked (or involved). . . .

You agree to raise the rate from 49½ cents per dozen to 50¼ cents. Two weeks later the operator is running away with the rate and making $1.33 an hour, within 17 cents of the machinist, who is the best machinist in the area and knows more about a Singer machine than the Singer people.[5]

While they are being observed in a time-study, employees try to prove that they have to work very slowly indeed. Then, after the rate has been set, they do just the opposite. They try to find short cuts: devising ways to run the machine faster, using special jigs or fixtures, leaving out some of the required operations. To avoid punishment for using unapproved short cuts and to avoid retiming of the job, all deviations from the standard procedure must be kept secret.

Thus employees may earn large incentive bonuses, but productivity may not increase proportionately. Sometimes management is deceived into thinking its rates are in line because the incentive earnings do not appear abnormally high. In part this merely reflects the adroitness of the work group in establishing output ceilings. Loose rates are hidden by carefully controlled output restriction, and the benefits from these rates are taken in the form of increased leisure on the job rather than increased earnings.

[5] Richard Bissell, *7½ Cents* (Boston: Little, Brown, 1953), pp. 132–34.

In their efforts to earn high bonuses, employees may pressure management for higher-quality materials and better maintenance. Employees are also likely to neglect work that does not help them increase their earnings—for example, keeping their work area clean, oiling equipment, and caring for tools. As a result, management is confronted with higher overhead costs.

Frequently, too, these plans provide employees with "average earnings" during delays that are beyond their control. This provision, in turn, motivates employees on occasion to seek delays and to fail to take adequate care of their own equipment. They may pressure job-setters, maintenance and tool-room personnel, and even supervisors to "adjust" the time records by incorrectly reporting the time when a breakdown occurs. In this way, employees can inflate "machine time" idle that is due to factors beyond their control and can understate the time they were actually able to devote to their job. Further, the emphasis on quantity may induce employees to pay only perfunctory attention to quality. As a result, inspection costs rise significantly.

In administering incentive plans, it is assumed that as improvements are made in the process, new work rates will be established, calling for lower wage rates. In practice, however, management is often reluctant to renew the long tedious struggle over rate-setting, and therefore does not insist that a new rate be set every time a minor change is made on the job.

Thus, these minor job changes have a cumulative effect. Just as job evaluation rates tend to drift upward, so incentive rates tend to become "looser" over time. Earnings will become unjustifiably high in relation to employee effort, and the company will not benefit from investments it makes to improve technology, scheduling, and supervision.

Coercive intergroup comparisons

Because incentive plans may affect relative earnings, they have the potential to upset long-established status relationships between groups. Certain work has traditionally been considered as relatively low-paying and undesirable. Under a loose incentive rate, groups performing these jobs may begin to earn substantially more than do workers on higher-status jobs. Almost invariably, intergroup bickering and dissatisfaction will arise, and management will be pressured to reestablish the traditional relationship between rates. A slight concession made by management in order to avoid serious disagreement on one job may mushroom into substantially higher labor costs throughout the organization.

When one group of workers begins to earn bonuses so large that their relative position in the earnings hierarchy is altered, the unstablizing effect on other groups may force management to take action—sometimes in the form of a contrived engineering change that will justify retiming. Thus, management cannot really live by the maxim, "We never cut a rate." But reducing a rate is a painful process for all concerned. The lesson it teaches employees with high earnings is to exercise greater restraint—that is, greater control over output—next time.

Union attitudes

Because incentives can create unfavorable intergroup comparisons (between those with incentive pay, or loose rates, and those without incentives, or tight rates), because they can pit worker against worker (more energetic against lazy), and because incentives can affect employment, many unions have policies discouraging their use. To craft unions, they are an anathema, since they encourage "rushing the work."

Once installed, however, incentives are tenaciously kept because of the extra earnings. In the late 1960s, the Steelworkers' Union insisted that steel company management extend incentives to nearly all workers, including maintenance employees and technicians, whose work was in any way related to production. Similarly, when Western Electric and General Electric sought to abolish incentives, the Electrical Workers' Union fought to keep them. Thus, many unions find themselves in the position of opposing incentive systems in principle but fighting for them in practice!

The supervisor's contribution

The supervisor-employee relationship is the place to begin working out incentive problems. Supervisors must be trained in the administration of the incentive plan, and they must feel that it is part of their job. When the rate-setting process is in the hands of industrial engineers, the supervisor is tempted to respond to employees' questions by claiming, "I don't understand them either. Those engineers in time-study work these things out, not me."

If the supervisors complain to management, their criticisms are often discounted as outgrowths of employee pressure, and management prefers to avoid a concession to one department that will be demanded by other departments.

Yet, these attitudes undermine the whole system. When employees realize that their supervisor is isolated from the rate-setting process, they fear that management will take advantage of them. When employees find that the supervisor is informed, willing to go to bat for them when they are right and unwilling to collude with them when they are wrong, the whole tenor of the system is likely to improve.

Improving the supervisor/ time-study relationship

Supervisors often have a strong incentive to support their work groups in the struggle with management. Since employees on loose rates are satisfied, there are few "cold war" grievances or slowdowns. Employees working under loose rates have energy left over to pitch in during an emergency. In addition, the supervisor's own production record is likely to look better when employees regularly produce more than the norm. Time-study staff people deplore such supervisory attitudes, for they know that even slight concessions quickly grow to major proportions as other groups demand rates that are equally loose. Intraplant pay distortions spring up when easy rates make it possible for some employees to make disproportionately high earnings, and the time-study people are embarrassed. As a result, they feel that the supervisor is too weak, too willing to concede to employee and union pressure.

It is important for the employees that the supervisor play an active role in rate setting. Time-study personnel must accept this role. After approving the time of the study and the selection of employees to be studied, the supervisor may then get in touch with the union steward. These two, with the time-study technician, can discuss the upcoming study before it is explained to the employees involved. This training should enable supervisors to participate intelligently in their dialogue with the employees and help them to understand employee complaints as well as industrial engineering procedures and requirements.

For some jobs, leisure is a more important incentive than potentially greater earnings. Using leisure as an incentive may improve performance on unpleasant jobs that are difficult to supervise and that require only a fixed quantity of work. When employees finish a predetermined quantity of work they are free to go home. "Cities using this incentive for garbage collection crews have found overall productivity increasing substantially." [6]

Incentives for auxiliary employees

In addition to the immediate supervisors, employees who transport materials, maintain equipment, distribute tools, and perform inspections are in a position to influence the pace and efficiency of incentive employees' work. These service workers become resentful when they do not receive extra compensation although their efforts are essential to the incentive employees' earnings. Whenever the incentive employees work harder, they must work harder, too.

In many companies, auxiliary employees receive extra compensation in proportion to the piecework earnings of the incentive workers. It is assumed that auxiliary work increases in roughly the same ratio as the size of the bonus earnings. For a toolroom worker, the formula might be based on total plant production; for material handlers, the bonus might be based on the production of the department or departments they service.

The manager must be careful, however, not to let auxiliary bonuses encourage undesirable practices. For example, an inspector who is paid a bonus in proportion to the incentive earnings of the group as a whole may be less diligent in looking for rejects. Supervisors who are rewarded in proportion to the incentive earnings of their subordinates may be similarly motivated to agitate for looser rates for their people.

The challenge of incentives for management

Incentive payment plans are most popular where individual effort has a major influence on the rate of production. They are least popular in continuous-process production (chemicals) or assembly lines, since in these operations it is more difficult for the individual to affect the work pace. Although technological change may decrease the use of incentives, approximately 25 percent of manufacturing employees in the U.S. have been working under incentive plans over a number of years. Of course, the growing importance of service occupations relative to manufacturing will decrease the relative importance of incentives.

[6] E. S. Savas, "An Empirical Study of Competition in Municipal Service Delivery," *Public Administration Review* (November–December 1977), 723.

Automation highlights a flaw in most traditional incentive systems. With automated equipment, continuity and regularity become more important to productivity than sporadic bursts of speed or effort. The employees' real job is to keep the equipment going. As might be expected, their job becomes easier if they can spot minor troubles early enough to make proper adjustments. That kind of alertness can sometimes be encouraged by a bonus, calculated on the percentage of the eight-hour day that the equipment is operating.

Rewarding continuity vs. effort

Typical incentives reward employees for extra effort rather than for productivity. Management therefore must determine the amount of effort that should be expended by each employee. Although industrial engineers assume that there is a direct connection between effort and reward, this is not always the case. Employees may be rewarded for complicating their jobs and causing more breakdowns, and they may be penalized for finding shortcuts! Technological changes that increase productivity are often accompanied by retiming and rate cuts. In the next chapter, we shall discuss incentive plans that give employees financial rewards for increased productivity even when their effort expenditure has not increased.

Incentive plans may generate healthy pressures within the work group: employees concerned about raw material shortages, equipment problems, and scheduling can urge management to expedite the flow of work. After all, they now have a stake in conditions that foster high productivity.

On the other hand, some naive managements regard the financial incentive plan as a cure-all. Faced with weak and ineffective supervision, difficulties and delays in work flow, low morale, and unsatisfactory output levels, management decides that all these problems can be solved by incentives. Also, shortsighted managements may neglect nonmonetary incentives, which can be powerful motivators.

Incentives do not replace supervision

Companies that expect enormous labor cost savings from installing incentive plans often become disillusioned. Workers can restrict output, and there are heavy costs associated with the special engineering, accounting, work inspection, and grievance negotiations.

Incentives can also discourage management from making technological changes, because employees will resist retiming and new rates. But if the jobs are not retimed, management may not be able to recoup the capital costs of what was designed to be labor-saving equipment.

Actually, an incentive plan neither eliminates nor reduces the need for good supervision. It requires alert, skilled supervisors to facilitate the rate-setting process and to handle the difficulties inherent in any plan. Worker confidence and good relationships with employees and union are essential if the plan is not to become bogged down by constant bickering.

If management institutes an incentive plan, it must be willing to pay the price of administering it. Management must be willing to struggle with grievances and to correct inequities resulting from differences in the relative tightness or looseness of incentive rates for different jobs. It must also avoid the temptation to establish a looser rate when critical production is at stake or to offer incentive pay as "extra remuneration" to gain acceptance of technological changes. Concessions made during good times will cause trouble when profit levels decline. There is also the strong tendency for rates to become increasingly loose over time, for more money to be paid for less productivity. Incentives are wasteful when they are used to bring production levels *up* to reasonable standards; they should be used only to compensate employees for performance *above* such standards.

Blue-collar vs. white-collar incentives

Some of the problems management faces in deriving adequate returns from the *potential* of incentive payment plans may be summarized when we contrast sales representatives' commissions with production workers' piecework plans.

Group restrictions. Salespeople typically work alone and are less bound by group norms of what constitutes suitable output. Inclined to be more individualistic and more achievement oriented, they are more responsive to the opportunity to earn more, and less concerned with establishing a "bogey."

Flexibility. When management wants to push a particular item, it is easier to offer an especially high temporary commission rate than to change a piecerate. The latter involves invidious comparisons among large numbers of employees. Their surveillance is usually aided by the union's insistence that no one be given the opportunity for greater earnings unless all receive it, and that once established, such changes cannot be rescinded without additional study and negotiation. Thus, factory piecerates and work study may make the introduction of change more difficult because of the implications these changes have for employee pay and workload. But commission structures can be quickly changed.

Validity. Considering the larger group and its demands for equity and comparability, management has had to develop somewhat scientific methods for measuring workload or relative performance in blue-collar work. Such methods have not been widely applied to white-collar work, largely because of greater variability among jobs and the possibility of variability within jobs. Most commission plans assume comparable territories, but the measurements are subjective at best. Sales representatives (who are generally nonunion) accept the likelihood that inequities will be ironed out when they eventually move to more lucrative territories. The factory worker demands equal opportunity now!

Unmeasured work. Since most white-collar jobs are more complex, they are likely to contain unmeasured aspects. Salespeople may neglect "missionary work" or other sales services if they are too responsive to target activities that help them to derive extra income. The factory worker is more constrained, more tightly supervised, and more likely to be performing a job in which the incentive can take into account almost the total task. All incentives, however, run the risk of biasing job performance, of encouraging employees to ignore the more subjective parts of their jobs.

Cost of administration.   Sales incentive plans are relatively inexpensive to administer, since they are less precise and involve fewer coercive comparisons than production incentive plans. There is real danger, however, that the cost of production worker piecework plans can begin to approximate the benefits received. A great deal of managerial effort must be devoted to handling grievances, retiming jobs, and evaluating downtime and changes in quality of materials.

Conclusion

There is little question that objective measures of work performance can be used to increase productivity. They provide employees and their supervisors with comparable data indicating the quality of job performance and where rewards are due. When these measures are combined with immediate financial returns, the motivational effects may be even stronger.

Unfortunately, these advantages cannot be secured without costs. One important cost involves the redirection of effort. The responsibilities that are difficult to measure (quality of work, cooperation with fellow employees) are bypassed, in favor of job elements that are easy to measure. Also the rate-setting process itself can become a source of controversy. Employees are sensitive about even slight inequities in standards. Production workers become enraged when they must perform a heavier proportion of tight-rated jobs than their neighbors. Management must be aware of changing job content and working conditions, since such alterations affect the workload. Introducing changes also becomes more difficult when their impact on workload and earnings must be calculated precisely and explained to employees. These problems are reduced somewhat by organizationwide incentives, which we will discuss in the next chapter.

problems

1 • *Leisure As an Incentive*

Berea is a supervisor in a parts clean-up department. When the laboratory finds that some piece of equipment has failed or has a serious quality problem and repair is too costly, the equipment is sent to Berea's group. They, in turn, dismantle the equipment, clean up the components, and place them in stock as spare parts.

Berea has noticed that her subordinates will work very hard for several hours to win an ex-

tended work break. Last week when they finished an especially large group of motors, she told them they could leave early. It was about an hour before quitting time. They returned the next day with enormous vitality, worked at a similar pace, and finished what Berea considered to be a good day's work in about five hours. She allowed them to leave early again, and for about two weeks the same pattern was followed with unflagging effort and great esprit. When Berea's manager heard about the practice, however, he said it had to stop, since the working hours for all employees had been established by the laboratory, and favoritism should not be practiced.

1. What do you think of offering free time rather than money as an incentive?
2. Would the fact that these employees worked in isolation affect your judgment of Berea's action?
3. How relevant is the fact that the employees responded very favorably to this type of incentive and appeared likely to continue to do so? Are there other hidden costs?

2 · *When Can Incentives Be Ignored?*

A group of production employees refuses to work faster than "base rate" as a protest against the elimination of a soft-drink machine near their work area. Top management is pressuring supervisors "to do something" quickly, for scheduling throughout the plant is affected by the decreased output. The foreman is reluctant to succumb to employee pressure, because of the bad precedent that would be set and because the machine itself was a nuisance—cups, bottle caps, and bottles were strewn about the area, and the dispenser encouraged loitering. Disciplinary measures are being considered against the ringleaders for organizing a slowdown. Some members of management are urging caution, claiming, as the workers themselves do, that the employees do not have to work at an *incentive pace*. The company provides the opportunity for workers to earn a bonus if they wish to work more intensively than a *daywork pace*, but this decision is up to the employees. Other members of management take the opposite point of view: in accepting work at an incentive rate, workers are obligated to try for such additional earnings. As a protest, these workers are making concerted effort to hold back production.

1. Comment on the merits of the divergent opinions within management on the employees' obligation to seek incentive earnings.
2. Discuss the approach management should take to arrest the workers' protest action. (There is no union in the organization.)

3 · *Sales Quotas*

The Superior Floor Covering Company has an incentive program for its salespeople. Incentive earnings are based on the amount of sales in relation to an assigned quota. The quota is computed each year by management, taking into account the number and type of customers in each salesperson's territory and the previous year's sales records for the company and for its competitors. In the administration of this incentive program, the following problems have arisen. Suggest the type of analysis you would undertake to provide data that might lead to a solution and the alternative plans you would consider in eliminating these difficulties. Note also the parallels between the problems here and those involving blue-collar, manufacturing incentive plans.

1. The top-earning salespeople also complain that their base quotas increase each year, reflecting their previous success. This, too, they feel is discrimination against success.
2. Management believes that the company is not acquiring as many new accounts as it should. So-called missionary work, trying to induce a store that has not previously purchased Superior products to become a customer, takes more time and energy than selling old customers. Also, the results of this missionary work may not show up for several years. The present incentive plan gives no credit for this type of work. Should extra allowances be given for new accounts? How will this affect the overall sales effort of the company?

4 · *Keeping a Good Thing Secret*

Ames Hardware manufactures and distributes small hand tools to local hardware stores. This is a highly competitive field, and its salespeople work on straight commission based on the sales potential of the area. The company calculates the sales potential of each area. Somewhat surprisingly, the sales staff in Alaska has consistently outperformed every other area. Recently, a new accountant who was sent to work in the company's distribution center in Fairbanks learned their secret.

At dinner one night, one of the staff told the accountant how a unique small tool the company makes for carpentry can be adapted quite simply to help start autos with defective batteries or starter motors—of great importance in Alaskan winters. The accountant was sworn to secrecy: "If they ever find this out in the head office, they will raise the base line so high on our commission plan that we will lose all the benefits we're getting from this product that we really invented."

1. How can management cope with this kind of problem; that is, employees making job breakthroughs but hiding them or failing to share them because disclosure will penalize their incentive earnings? (It is to the company's advantage to encourage innovation, but the incentive plan discourages open use of innovations that would require a reconsideration of what is a fair quota.)
2. More specifically, is there anything the accountant can do to get this information out of Alaska without hurting his new friend or their relationship? What are the accountant's responsibilities here?

5 · *Who Gets Tight or Loose Jobs?*

Work assignments cause constant wrangling among machine-shop employees and with their supervisor. Several senior employees have filed grievances claiming that their foreman discriminated against them.

Waljack says his incentive earnings were cut 4 percent because he was assigned several jobs with very tight rates. Most of the other employees, nearly all with less seniority, were assigned highly desirable jobs with looser rates. Waljack says the supervisor dislikes him and was punishing him.

The department foreman told the superintendent who reviewed the grievance that it was not serious. "Another of the older people's effort to get the good jobs and leave the dregs for the younger ones. They want me to spend hours analyzing every job, figure out each bonus, then give only high-paying jobs to senior workers. I'd spend all my time on earnings schedules instead of on efficient production schedules."

The superintendent also spoke to the union chief steward. The union feels that the company's incentive system provides easy means for foremen to reward friends and punish those they don't like (possibly union supporters). The union wants management to take this power away from foremen.

The department itself is divided on the issue. Some fear the union will set up a system distributing good work according to seniority, and newer employees might take wage cuts. But they do not like the supervisor holding assignments like a club over their heads.

The personnel department cautions about far-reaching implications of any management decision. The supervisor's right to make work assignments is crucial to management's ability to operate efficiently. The union could limit this ability if it got a foot in the door in this case.

1. As the superintendent, how would you evaluate the case? Assuming that Waljack has some grounds for complaint, how would you deal with it in a way that would avoid other problems?
2. Can the right to make work assignments be separated from other aspects of incentive-plan administration?

part 6

new approaches to incentives and motivation

organizationwide incentives and participation

20

In this chapter we shall discuss some of the approaches that attempt to provide broader employee motivation than do individual incentive plans. These approaches serve a dual purpose: (1) to increase productivity and (2) to improve morale by giving employees a feeling of participation in and identification with their company.

As we discussed in the preceding chapter, individual incentive plans often do not provide adequate motivation. Even when they are successful in inducing employees to work harder, their value as an incentive is reduced by output restriction, conflicts over rate-setting, and intergroup conflict. Nor are high wages, fringe benefits, and good working conditions in themselves a complete answer to the problem of motivation. These inducements may be effective aids in recruiting and retaining good employees, but they provide little help in motivating them to work harder.

We will examine five techniques that are being used by management to provide greater motivation and sense of identification: (1) group incentives, (2) profit sharing, (3) suggestion systems, (4) employee-management and union-management consultative committees, and (5) the Scanlon Plan. Finally, we will compare these techniques with "workers' participation in management" schemes that exist in many countries in Europe and Asia.

Group incentives

With group incentives each member of the group receives a bonus based on the output of the group as a whole, unlike individual piecework, in which each employee receives a bonus based on his or her individual output. The "group" may include the entire plant or company. More frequently it consists of a single department that works on a single process or product. In these smaller groups, output standards are usually set by time study, just as they are in individual piecework.

Group incentives are particularly useful when the job assignments of members of the group are so interrelated that it is difficult to measure the contribution of any single employee to total production. Group incentives make it possible to reward workers who provide essential services to production workers, yet who under individual piecework are usually paid only the regular day rates. Moreover, in theory at least, since everyone's earnings are dependent on everyone's efforts, the group may put pressure on the laggard individual to work harder. Certainly, as the spread of automation makes individual piecework less appropriate, companies that wish to retain some form of incentive may turn increasingly to group incentives.

Group incentives encourage cooperation among employees, whereas individual piecework militates against cooperation. Since all the members of the group share in the same bonus, conflict is reduced between workers on "tight" rates and workers on "loose" rates. Rather than struggling with one another over choice work locations, materials, and job assignments—the sources of much friction under individual piecework—the employees work out their own allocation problems, knowing that everyone will share in the final result. For example, waitresses who pool tips are often eager to help each other out of jams.

On the other hand, group incentives share many of the disadvantages of individual-incentive plans. The workers still fear that if they produce too much management will cut the rates. Many of the intergroup differences that we discussed in the previous chapter remain. Also, since each individual may feel that his own efforts have very little effect on the over-all output of the group, he or she may be less motivated to work harder than under individual piecework.

Group incentive systems that include an entire company or plant are less common than those that include only a single department. These broader systems are usually based not on time study but on some general measure of production, such as pounds produced or value of goods produced. For example, it was proposed in one union-management negotiation session in the automobile industry that the company put aside $10 for every car produced and that the whole fund be divided among all the employees. Company-wide systems often call for less than 100 percent gain-sharing—that is, a 10 percent increase in production results in a less than 10 percent increase in earnings.

Company-wide plans naturally eliminate the intergroup incentive problems and fights over time study that we have discussed. Most important, they make employees less fearful of the introduction of new equipment, since all gains in productivity are usually shared by all employees (in contrast to individual piecework, where the gains can be taken away through a new time study).

In 1977, Xerox distributed $105 million to its employees (11.2 percent of their salaries). Of this, 60 percent went into retirement accounts. The remainder was distributed according to employee choice, including cash, Xerox stock, or one of three special savings plans.

Until 1978, Sears contributed 11 percent of its pretax earnings to its profit sharing fund, but Sears expected this fund to provide a substantial portion of employees' retirement benefits. In 1978 Sears reduced its contributions to 6 percent of earnings and liberalized its separate pension plan. As of that date the fund's assets totaled $2.6 billion (averaging $8,400 per eligible employee), of which $1.9 billion was in Sears stock. The fund owned 21 percent of Sears' shares outstanding.

In smaller plants, company-wide incentive systems may provide some incentive for the average employee to work harder. However, in larger plants, where hundreds or even thousands of employees share in the bonus, the employee may feel there is little relationship between his own effort and the ultimate reward, and consequently may feel little motivation to increase production. Moreover, the union may oppose the scheme unless the amount of the bonus and the method of computing it are determined through collective bargaining.

Profit sharing   In profit-sharing plans, employees receive a bonus that is normally based on some percentage (often 10 to 30 percent) of the company's profits beyond some fixed minimum.[1] For example, employees might receive 25 percent of all profits in excess of 6 percent of the company's net worth.

In some profit-sharing plans, the bonus is paid directly to employees, usually at the end of the year. However, *deferred* plans, as they are called, are more common. In deferred plans, the bonus is deposited in a fund to provide retirement or death benefits for employees (and perhaps made available for use in time of emergency). With such deferred plans, the company hopes to obtain the advantages of both profit-sharing and fringe benefit programs. (A third, fairly rare form of profit sharing allows the employee to choose between deferring his benefits or taking advantage of them at once.)

Profit sharing has a long history, but only in recent years has it gained widespread popularity. One of the best-known plans is that of the Lincoln Electric Company, which in some years has paid a bonus that doubles employees' pay. Sears Roebuck, Prentice-Hall, Procter and Gamble, and Eastman Kodak also have profit-sharing plans of one type or another.

The advocates of profit sharing claim that it strengthens employees' sense of involvement with the company: It makes them feel like partners in the enterprise, it motivates them to work harder, cut waste, push sales, and so forth. And under the deferred plans, profit sharing makes it possible for the

---

[1] As we have discussed elsewhere, many companies have instituted a form of profit sharing through providing stock options for their top executives and encouraging their employees generally to buy the company's stock.

company to provide pensions and fringe benefits without increasing fixed costs, for the company makes contributions only in profitable years.

Yet profit sharing has severe limitations, which may explain its failure to be more widely adopted. For one thing, it provides even less relationship between individual effort and ultimate reward than do group incentive plans. After all, profits depend on a great many factors other than individual performance: the state of the market, sales efficiency, technological development, and so forth. Moreover, the fact that the payoff occurs years after it is earned means that there is a long delay between effort and reward, and this delay tends to impair the worker's feeling of working toward a goal. To complicate matters even further, many workers find it hard to understand how profits are computed, and particularly where labor-management relations are bad, they may suspect that a good deal of sleight of hand is involved in the calculations.[2] If employees are to feel any relationship at all between their own efforts and their share of profits, management must divulge considerably more information about its financial condition than is commonly done in most companies. Further, this information should be shared on a continuing basis, not just annually.

What often happens is that employees tend to regard profit sharing as just another fringe benefit ("added gravy"). Naturally they are happy to get a bonus once a year, but they recognize little concrete relationship between how hard they work and how much they get. With direct distribution plans, employees begin to count on their annual profit-sharing checks as part of their regular income. Thus, profit sharing may add relatively little to satisfaction during good years but make employees angry with their seeming pay cut in bad years. Under deferred profit-sharing plans, pensions and welfare benefits are put on a rather insecure basis, for they depend not on how long an employee has been with the company but on whether the company has made a profit during that time. Still, in companies that can afford no other form of pension plan, even this is probably better than nothing.

Although profit sharing has been extremely successful in some companies, many have tried it for a few years and then abandoned it. Its success seems to depend to a large extent on the company's overall personnel policy and on the state of union-management relations. Although it may provide motivation for employees to work harder, particularly in smaller companies, its chief merits would seem to lie in raising morale, in keeping the union out (if this is indeed a merit), and perhaps in reducing pressure for wage increases.

Suggestion systems

Suggestion systems are quite common in American industry. Their purposes are to:

1. Give management the benefit of employee suggestions on how to improve company efficiency. The average worker may have countless ideas on how to

---

[2] The president of one company with a "profit-sharing" plan once told us, "I don't think my profit figures are any of my employees' business. I give them a bonus each year which is fair. They trust me." But do they? And do they really feel that they are *involved* in a profit-sharing plan?

cut waste, eliminate unnecessary motions, prevent safety hazards, and so forth. Unless there is some systematic way of bringing these ideas to management's attention, a reservoir of ingenuity and experience may be overlooked.

2. Raise employee morale by giving them a chance to express their ideas on how the job should be done, to display their creative talents, and to take pride in seeing their ideas accepted—in other words, to reduce the employee's feeling that "as far as the company is concerned I'm just a machine. Nobody wants my ideas."

In the typical suggestion system, a worker writes an idea on a special form and drops the form into a special box. All suggestions go directly to the suggestion director or to a suggestion committee. The practicability of each suggestion is then explored and evaluated, usually in consultation with the supervisors who might be affected. If the suggestion is accepted, the employee receives a reward, often 10 to 25 percent of the savings produced by the suggestion during the first year. For suggestions whose savings cannot be measured, token awards of from $5 to $25 are paid. If the suggestion is rejected, most companies insist that the employee be given a detailed explanation of why it was turned down, along with encouragement to make more suggestions in the future. It is customary to promote suggestion plans by means of active publicity programs, posters, articles in plant newspapers, award presentations, and so forth.

A reasonably successful plan may elicit fifty or more suggestions from every hundred employees each year, 25 to 35 percent of which will be acceptable. Frequently, however, results are a good bit less impressive than that. Employee response to a given suggestion plan may be poor because it is ineptly administered, with inadequate publicity or explanation of how the program is run. Moreover, delay in evaluating suggestions may give employees the impression that their ideas are not being given serious consideration. If the suggestion needs considerable time to be evaluated, progress reports should be issued to the employee to let him know that his idea has not been forgotten. If it is turned down, a careful explanation of why it has been rejected is important.

Even with good administration, suggestion plans often have only limited success. Employees may feel that the rewards are too meager, particularly when they amount to only 10 percent of the first year's savings. This means that management keeps the remaining 90 percent the first year and 100 percent of the savings in future years. Of course, even when awards are small on a percentage basis, it is not unusual for an employee to earn several thousand dollars for an especially good suggestion.[3]

Employees may fear that their suggestions will backfire—that in effect they may be suggesting themselves out of a job. The employee who makes a labor-saving suggestion is not likely to be very popular with his fellow employees, even though no one loses his job right away. The reward for the suggestion goes to the individual, but the suggestion may have disastrous effects on the

[3] IBM, United Airlines, and General Dynamics have paid out awards of more than $40,000 for a single suggestion.

entire group. Understandably, a group attitude may develop that discourages employees from making suggestions.

The very fact that suggestions are submitted and rewarded on an individual basis may generate serious resentment within the group. On the worker level especially, many of the best ideas grow out of long-term group discussions. If one person turns in an idea as his own suggestion, the rest may accuse him of larceny. In a sense, the suggestion system discourages teamwork in working out ideas and encourages individual workers to keep their ideas to themselves.

In addition, all suggestions must be submitted in writing, even though the average worker can do a much better job explaining himself orally, particularly if he can demonstrate his idea and answer questions directly.

In most instances the suggestion system bypasses the supervisor. Yet many suggestions point up areas where the supervisor has fallen down on the job or suggest ideas that the supervisor should have thought of. Understandably, employees fear that the supervisor may retaliate if his failures are exposed, and they hesitate to make suggestions at all. Some companies try to get around this problem by giving the supervisor credit for all suggestions made in his department. The employees submit their suggestions directly to the supervisor instead of to the suggestion committee, and the supervisor helps in evaluating suggestions and handing out rewards. In Russia, foremen are given bonuses when their subordinates submit award-winning suggestions.

Other problems arise when employees become dissatisfied because they think their award is too low or when the company implements a suggestion but refuses to pay an award on the grounds that the idea was already under consideration at the time the suggestion was made. The company runs the risk of being sued unless it handles cases like this with great care. To protect itself against charges of violating its own rules, the company must keep extensive records, and the cost of doing so may exceed the value of the suggestions themselves.

Suggestion systems sometimes arouse union opposition because, as a form of upward communication, they usurp what the union regards as one of its rightful functions. Many companies permit union representatives to sit in on the suggestion committee, in an effort to win union cooperation in implementing the plan and to alleviate workers' fears that their ideas are not being fairly evaluated.

In general, the success of the suggestion system depends largely on the quality of the overall personnel and labor-relations atmosphere. If the union suspects management's every move, and if supervisors discourage subordinates from doing things on their own—then employees will keep new ideas to themselves.

To sum up: a well-run suggestion system may yield a never-ending stream of ideas that cut costs and increase the employees' feeling of accomplishment and participation. However, many plans are often poorly administered. Even when well administered, they often bypass both supervisor and union and place primary emphasis on the individual, though most problems involve the entire group.

Consultative committees

In an attempt to avoid the suggestion system's exclusive emphasis on individual workers, many companies have tried to elicit broader group participation by setting up consultative committees. The purpose of these committees is to improve two-way communication with lower levels of the organization. They give lower-ranking supervisors or employees a chance to express their points of view directly to top management, thus bypassing intermediate levels. For example, the first-line supervisors may elect representatives to meet weekly or monthly with the general manager to present and discuss current problems, ask about rumors, pose questions, and ventilate gripes.

Management may institute similar committees for consultations with hourly-paid employees or their union. Joint worker-management or union-management consultative committees are involved in many activities: solving production problems, cutting waste, reducing accidents, planning recreational programs, and soliciting for the Community Chest.

Union-management committees normally work in three areas:

1. *Collective bargaining.* Consultative committees have proved extremely useful in facilitating collective bargaining on such matters as job evaluation, incentive rates, and job transfers. These committees permit the orderly, systematic consideration of problems that would otherwise be handled piecemeal through the grievance procedure.

2. *Welfare activities.* Often joint committees assist in running athletic programs, handling welfare funds (perhaps derived from the profit from coffee machines), and so forth. These are areas in which the company has no special interest so long as workers are satisfied, and it is glad to let employees share responsibility.

3. *Production problems.* In some industries consultative committees have been established to explore such persistent production problems as scrap, productivity, and safety. Committees of this sort are common only in companies that enjoy good labor-management relations, however, since production decisions are traditionally conceded to be management prerogatives. They are an essential part of the quality of work life programs discussed in Chapter 21.

In unionized companies, consultative committees give the union leadership an opportunity to make a positive contribution toward running the company rather than merely sitting on the sidelines or filing grievances. Often they provide management with a valuable source of information on worker and union problems, and they provide union officials with a better understanding of management's problems. Thus, they have a potential ability to improve the general tenor of labor-management relations. Management may also use these committees as a sounding board by releasing information on sales trends, safety problems, and so forth, in the hope that it will be passed along to workers at lower levels.

Nevertheless, joint committees labor under several disadvantages, which sometimes limit their effectiveness:

- Committee members may not communicate effectively with the workers back in the shop. Indeed, as they learn more and more about management's point of view, they may become more and more removed from the other workers. They may become extremely aware of production or safety problems, but they may fail to pass their enthusiasm on to the rest of the shop. Production committees, for example, are rarely successful unless the committee members energetically canvass their constituents for ideas.

The now-defunct Human Relations Committee in the basic steel industry suffered from the disadvantages of isolation from the rank-and-file membership. Consisting of top-level representatives of union and management, it operated largely without verbal fireworks and in secrecy—thus giving the average member little feeling of participation in collective bargaining and even leading some to suspect that their officers were in collusion with management against their best interests. This suspicion may have contributed to the defeat of union president David McDonald by I. W. Abel, a man committed to more conventional collective bargaining techniques.

- Consultative committees run the risk of impairing the morale and status of the middle managers whom they bypass.

- The success of these committees depends pretty much on the over-all quality of labor-management relations. If committee meetings are looked upon primarily as battlefields in a continuous war between union and management, little will be accomplished.

- Finally, consultation in itself does not provide a specific incentive for individual employees to work harder. True, employees do gain personal satisfaction from influencing company policy and seeing their ideas adopted, but in our society we require a more specific goal toward which we can work, most often in the form of an economic reward. Thus the consultative committees that have proved most fruitful have been those with some highly specific incentive for cooperation: to win the war, to save the company from going out of business, to earn more pay, or to remove accident hazards.

For consultative committees to be successful in solving production problems, there must be participation throughout all levels of the organization as well as a definite incentive or goal to unite everyone's efforts. On the other hand, such complete participation is not required if the committee's efforts are restricted to handling collective-bargaining problems or fringe areas. Probably this explains why consultative committees have been most useful in solving specific, limited problems. They do not, in themselves, provide motivation for higher production or a general sense of participation.

The Scanlon Plan

The Scanlon Plan is one of the most interesting approaches to securing widespread employee participation and obtaining industrial peace and higher productivity.[4] Although

---

[4] The late Joseph Scanlon, author of this plan, rose from an ordinary worker in a steel plant to be a top officer of the United Steelworkers of America and later a Lecturer at the Massachusetts Institute of Technology. For fuller discussion of the plan see Frederick G. Lesieur, ed., *The Scanlon Plan: A Frontier in Labor-Management Cooperation* (New York and Cambridge: Wiley and The Technology Press, 1958); George Strauss and Leonard R. Sayles, "The Scanlon Plan: Some Organizational Problems," *Human Organization* 16, No. 3 (Fall 1957), pp. 15–22; Frederick G. Lesieur and Elbridge Pluckett, "The Scanlon Plan Has Proved Itself," *Harvard Business Review* 47, No. 5 (October 1969), pp. 100–118; R. A. Ruh, R. L. Wallace, and C. F. Frost, "Management Attitudes and the Scanlon Plan," *Industrial Relations* 12, No. 1 (October 1973), 282–88; and Paul S. Goodman and B. Moore, "Factors Affecting the Acquisition of Beliefs about a New Reward System," *Human Relations* 29, No. 6 (November 1976).

the plan is not widely accepted, we shall discuss it in some detail because it seems to avoid many of the problems raised by other plans. The plan consists of two basic parts: a wage formula or incentive and a new form of suggestion system.

The *wage formula* is designed to distribute the gains of increased productivity proportionally among all employees involved. Although each formula is tailor-made to the needs of the particular company, wages are typically tied to the sales value of goods produced, so that, for example, for every 1 percent increase in productivity there is a 1 percent increase in wages and salaries. In contrast to usual incentive plans, bonuses are paid to the clerical force, salespeople, supervisors, and sometimes even to top management.

Notice that this is really a form of group incentive covering the entire plant. As we have seen, a bonus of this sort is valuable not only as an incentive to productivity, but also as a yardstick by which the participants can measure the plant's success.

The mechanics of the *suggestion system* are simple: In each department a union *production committeemember* is elected or appointed by union officers. The production committeemember and the foreman constitute a departmental *production committee*, which meets periodically to discuss suggestions from individual employees and to formulate general plans for the improvement of productivity. Rejected suggestions or suggestions that affect the plant as a whole are referred to a plant-wide *screening committee*, which includes top management as well as the union leadership.

Note how the Scanlon Plan differs from the typical suggestion system: Instead of individual rewards for accepted suggestions, the group gains as a whole through a higher bonus whenever productivity is increased. The union takes an active part instead of worrying whether suggestions will result in a speedup. Individuals cooperate with each other in developing suggestions instead of keeping their ideas to themselves. Further, under a suggestion system management normally waits passively for workers to submit suggestions; frequently under the Scanlon Plan management itself suggests problems for mutual discussion.

Before the Scanlon Plan was put into operation in a particular printing plant, management had tried to introduce a conveyor system. The plans had been developed exclusively by the engineers, without consulting the employees. The system immediately ran into trouble and the employees showed little interest in making it work.

After the Scanlon Plan was accepted management decided to try another conveyor system, but to introduce it in a different manner. Employees were shown a small scale model of the proposed layout and encouraged to make criticisms and suggestions for improvements. On the basis of these comments the joint production committee made modifications to eliminate "bugs" that the engineers had not foreseen. The new system was enthusiastically accepted by the employees.[5]

Both the quantity and quality of suggestions seem to be higher under the Scanlon Plan than under the typical suggestion system.

[5] Adopted from George Shultz, "Worker Participation in Production Problems," *Personnel*, 28, No. 3 (November 1951), 201–11.

As a means of increasing productivity, the Scanlon Plan has met with varied success. In the Athens, Tennessee plant of the Midlands-Ross Corporation, the monthly bonus averaged nearly 15 percent. But in 6 of the first 27 months the plan was in operation, productivity was too low to warrant a payment.[6]

In summary, there are gains for everybody under a successful Scanlon Plan: (1) more and better suggestions, (2) higher productivity and profits, (3) decreased resistance to change, (4) better union-management relations, (5) greater cooperation among work groups and between individuals and supervisors, and (6) increased motivation to work. And yet the Scanlon Plan, promising though it seems, is not a cure-all for every industrial ill.

1. If the plan is to be successful, management must be willing to make substantial changes in its attitudes. Traditional company prerogatives must be forgotten. Foremen, superintendents, and even the company president must learn to consult with subordinates and be willing to listen to sharp criticism. In companies that already practice general supervision and enjoy a good system of upward and downward communication, the transition to the Scanlon Plan may be relatively easy. Others may find that the plan requires adjustments that they are unwilling to make.[7]

2. The Scanlon Plan presents the union with a real dilemma. In fact, the plan is bound to fail unless the union officers give up the militant view that the "member is always right." But there is also a danger that the officers may become too concerned with jacking up production. Indeed, as the officers become more and more closely identified with management's point of view, they tend to become alienated from the average member. This dilemma may be partly resolved if the officers are careful to explain new developments to the rank-and-file and to listen carefully to their reactions. Still, the plan blurs the union's primary function of providing representation for its members.

3. As we have seen, one of the disadvantages of traditional incentive plans is that they engender ill-feeling among groups—both where technology makes one group's earnings dependent on the production of another group, and where groups suspect each other of having "loose" rates. The Scanlon Plan presumably eliminates this problem by establishing plant-wide incentives. But a plant-wide incentive means that each individual's earnings are dependent on the effort of the entire plant. Harder work by any one individual will bring him only negligibly higher monetary return. Ideally, self-satisfaction, the desire for praise from fellow workers, and interest in the group as a whole will be sufficient to elicit high productivity. But for this to happen there must be a high degree of cohesion and employee identification with the plant as a whole.

How likely is this to occur? The answer depends on a number of factors,

---

[6] *The Wall Street Journal,* December 9, 1976, p. 1.

[7] Introduction of the Scanlon Plan may require a major Organization Development program. See Carl F. Frost, "The Scanlon Plan: Anyone for Free Enterprise?" *MSU Business Topics* (Winter 1976), 25–33.

including the size, homogeneity, and history of the work group. One thing is certain: There are bound to be some rivalries among groups, and all parties will need skill in human relations to prevent these rivalries from reaching serious proportions. There always is the danger that one department will ask, "Why should we work so hard when Department Y has fallen so far behind?" The larger the plant, the greater are the possibilities for dissension, and the more difficult it becomes to maintain support for plantwide production goals.

4. The Scanlon Plan has been successful both in very depressed companies, where the employees have cooperated to save their jobs, and in prosperous companies, where the employees realized that there were big bonuses to be won. The plan may be less successful in industries where the market conditions make it difficult to sell increased output and where greater productivity may in fact mean fewer jobs (in economic terms, where demand is inelastic). Nor do we know what happens when a successful plan goes through a long period of poor earnings (some have weathered short periods).

In short, the Scanlon Plan seems to be most successful where both union and management are able to make substantial changes in their patterns of behavior, where good internal communications exist within and between both groups, and probably only in smaller organizations.

Workers' participation in other countries

The Scanlon Plan and other forms of workers' formal participation in management have received relatively little attention in the United States and Canada, where (aside from a few cases of employee-owned businesses) "participation" generally refers to a style of leadership involving delegation and group decision making. Elsewhere in the world, however, formal schemes for workers' participation have been the subject of much discussion and experimentation. Israeli *kibbutzim* are self-governing communal farms, often with factories attached, in which leadership is rotated and major decisions are made by majority vote. Yugoslav plants, in theory, are run by the workers themselves through elected work councils, which make general policy and have the right to hire and fire the plant manager. Larger German companies operate under *codetermination*, in which seats on the "supervisory boards" (roughly equivalent to boards of directors in North America) are filled half by employee representatives and half by management representatives (however, since—except in the iron and steel industries—the chairman is normally a management representative and has a double vote, management keeps control of the board). Worker representation is also required on company boards in Sweden and Norway and is being vigorously proposed in Britain. Joint consultation committees (often called work councils) have been established in many countries.

Most of these participation schemes differ from the Scanlon Plan in three important ways. First, they provide no direct incentives for productivity. Second, the various committees operate at the plant or company instead of at the work force level. Third, in practice they deal chiefly with personnel rather than production problems.

Supporters of participation schemes argue that not only is participation morally and politically sound but that it reduces alienation and class conflict, raises morale and productivity, and improves union-management relations. It is difficult to generalize about how these schemes work in practice. Management's fears that it would lose its ability to manage have proved largely groundless, although the need to consult worker representatives may have slowed down the decision-making process. By and large, the main impact seems to be in the area of labor-management relations.

In most European countries, collective bargaining has traditionally been restricted to establishing nationwide wage levels. Participation has, in effect, introduced plant-level collective bargaining of the United States variety, with its emphasis on such subjects as promotions, layoffs, training, work conditions, and individual grievances.[8] Yet consultative committees here and overseas seem to suffer from many of the same problems: their discussions are focused on company or plant-level problems rather than problems affecting the shop and the individual employee. Little effort is made to involve individual employees in solving work problems or providing positive internalized motivation for work.

Conclusion

We have looked at six plans designed to raise employee morale and promote a sense of identification with the entire organization. All six plans seem to reach these goals through changing human relationships. Group incentives and profit sharing aim for greater cooperation among individuals. Suggestion systems and consultative committees seek to improve communications between individual employees and higher management. Both objectives are sought by the Scanlon Plan and by the "workers' participation" schemes that exist overseas.

Each of these plans has been adopted by management as a panacea for a whole range of industrial-relations ills. Yet none of them will work well except in an atmosphere of good labor-management relations and sound managerial, organizational, and personnel practices.

[8] In some ways European participation goes beyond U.S. collective bargaining. In some countries, management is required to consult with (and even obtain the consent of) workers' representatives regarding such subjects as new plant location, ecological practices, and investment decisions. Further, management is required to share considerably more information about future plans than is common in the U.S.

quality of work life

Recent years have seen a great deal of concern with the quality of work life, occasioned in part by reports of a revolt against work and a sharp decline in productivity growth in both the United States and Canada. It is widely believed that job satisfaction and motivation have declined, and to counteract these trends managements are trying a variety of new approaches. Two of the most notable are job redesign and goal setting. Each of these is designed to increase motivation and to restore challenge and meaning to work. The thrust of these techniques is to change the job itself.

Another movement proposes to give employees greater freedom to choose the hours they work. This movement for new work schedules is supported strongly by those women who view it as a means of combining work careers with raising a family. Men who wish to share more fully in family raising also endorse it, as do workers regardless of sex who prefer not to be tied down to the conventional 9 to 5 Monday-Friday schedule.

At first glance the two approaches' solutions to workplace discontent appear radically different. The first approach seeks to make jobs more challenging. The second approach ignores the job itself but makes it easier for workers to leave it. Nevertheless, the two approaches share a common interest in increasing workers' discretion and self-control.

The discussion which follows outlines one of the most exciting recent developments in the personnel field: the growing concern with the quality of work life.

**The extent
of workplace
dissatisfaction**

Many observers have noted that workers are becoming increasingly dissatisfied with their jobs. Although not all scholars agree, some believe our cultural values are undergoing a massive change, particularly among younger workers. They argue that the generation brought up during the campus revolts of the 1960s is particularly resistant to authority. Well educated, relatively secure in their jobs, and interested in doing their own things, these workers resist accepting the boring, challengeless jobs that their elders saw as inevitable.

Evidence as to whether there is, in fact, a growing dissatisfaction with work is somewhat mixed. Some 80 or 90 percent of employed workers regularly report themselves either satisfied or very satisfied with their jobs. As the following table indicates, these figures have changed very little in recent years. On the other hand, satisfaction with particular aspects of the job has lessened considerably.

Question: All in all, how satisfied would you say you are with your job?

Response category	Percent responding:		
	1969	1973	1977
Very satisfied	46	52	47
Somewhat satisfied	39	38	42
Not too satisfied	11	8	9
Not at all satisfied	3	2	3

Question: "How true . . . is this of your job?"

	Percent answering "very true"		
	1969	1973	1977
The pay is good.	40	41	27
The job security is good.	55	53	42
My fringe benefits are good.	42	44	33
The hours are good.	57	51	43
The work is interesting.	63	61	53
I am given a chance to do the things I can do best.	45	41	31
I am not asked to do excessive amounts of work.	43	34	28
My supervisor is very concerned about the welfare of those under (him/her).	45	41	34

Source: Robert P. Quinn and Graham Staines, *1977 Quality of Employment Survey* (Ann Arbor, Michigan: Institute of Social Research, University of Michigan, 1978), Table 13.1. Percentages rounded.

Why has one measure of satisfaction remained stable while the other has dropped? Psychologists are far from certain. Perhaps it means merely that despite declining satisfaction with specific aspects of the job, the decline has not proceeded far enough so that workers are willing to protest actively. (Saying that one is satisfied with one's job may be like responding, "Fine, thanks," to the question "how are you today?" Unless one wants to complain actively, one gives the conventional, expected answer.) In any case the evidence does not suggest a revolt against *work* itself. Far more workers think their work is interesting than think their pay is good.

Perhaps the question of whether dissatisfaction has *increased* is irrelevant. What may be more relevant is the number of jobs that provide little challenge and are insufficiently motivating. Even if workers are resigned to these jobs, their abilities are inefficiently utilized.

The nature of mass production work

New approaches to motivation in mass production work have been concerned chiefly with semi-skilled work in manufacturing, especially machine tending and assembly line jobs. Such jobs are not unique, however, in their lack of obvious challenge. Many offices today can best be described as white-collar factories, with acres of desks and work tables stretching as far as the eye can see. Minutely described, mechanized short-cycle jobs, requiring such tools as card punchers or typewriters, are performed by clerical personnel, few of whom receive much sense of achievement from their work. Many service workers, telephone operators and dishwashers, for example, have equally routine jobs.

The way mass production jobs have traditionally been designed has been heavily influenced by the scientific management movement, whose founder was Frederick W. Taylor.[1] Taylor believed in (1) high specialization (breaking down jobs into very small parts) and (2) in specifying exactly how each part should be done (separating the physical work from thinking). In analyzing mass production work scholars have concentrated on eight main characteristics. We shall call these autonomy, skill, significance, identity, feedback, variety, attention, and social relations.[2]

Task characteristics

Autonomy. Mass production jobs are designed to eliminate all employee discretion. As Taylor put it:

[1] Taylor (1856–1915) was the world's first well-known industrial engineer. His studies of work place and job design influenced the development of mass production work throughout the world, even in Russia. Taylor believed that the best way to motivate people was through payment by result or piecework.

[2] The term *task characteristic* refers to the intrinsic characteristics of the task *itself*, as opposed to the wider environment in which the job is performed. Our list of characteristics is adopted from the work of J. Richard Hackman and Edward E. Lawler III. See Hackman's "Work Design," in J. Richard Hackman and J. Lloyd Suttle, eds., *Improving Life at Work* (Santa Monica, Cal.: Goodyear, 1977).

Each man must learn to give up his particular way of doing things, adapt his methods to the many new standards, and grow accustomed to receiving and obeying directions covering details, large and small, which in the past have been left to individual judgment.[3]

Following Taylor's principles, management engages in engineering studies, which carefully predetermine the exact motions and pace for each employee. Workers are confined to a fixed work position and are permitted to leave it only with permission. In principle, this procedure ensures that the work will be done quickly in a uniform, predictable fashion, and that it will be precisely coordinated with other jobs.

Skill. It goes almost without saying that such highly specialized and programmed jobs deprive the worker of any real sense of skill. Workers who exercise skill take pride in their achievement, but the person who has learned his job in a few hours knows that he can be replaced by almost anyone who happens along. This is one reason why mass-production workers tend to exaggerate the complexity of their jobs: It is too humiliating to admit how simple their work actually is. They may use their ignored skills to process grievances or to sabotage.

Task significance. It is equally obvious that the individual mass production worker's job lacks task significance.[4] Even if the final product is as newsworthy as a space probe to Mars, the individual's contribution may seem trivial (and few products have the significance of a space probe). The meaninglessness of work is accentuated when organizations seem to emphasize quantity over quality. "Why should I do a good job," the typical worker says, "when no one else cares?"

In a largely fruitless effort to instill pride of craftsmenship, some companies have engaged in such public relations activities as a "My Job Contest" in which employees are given rewards for letters describing the meaning of their work. Many companies take new employees on a trip through the plant to show them how their particular jobs fit into the larger picture. In indoctrinating new employees, the telephone company stresses the importance of their jobs in saving lives and helping people in trouble.

The evidence suggests that the impact of such efforts to change job attitudes is likely to wear off quickly. On the other hand, task significance may be increased if workers are permitted direct contact with the people they serve or if the employee is a member of a small work team (provided, of course, that the team as a whole is motivated toward high productivity).

Task identity. Task significance is closely related to task identity, the ability to complete an identifiable task. We all feel that we are accomplishing something when we can break our work down into identifiable units and

---

[3] Frederick W. Taylor, *Shop Management* (New York: Harper, 1919), p. 113.

[4] Task significance has been defined as "the degree to which the job has a substantial impact on the lives and work of other people, whether in the immediate organization or the external environment." Hackman, "Work Design," p. 130.

complete them successfully. If we have two assignments to complete, we breathe a sigh of relief as soon as we finish one. When we are driving a long distance, we break the trip down into sections and feel great satisfaction as we pass by each check point.

Mass-production work characteristically fails to provide this sense of completion, or even a feeling of progress toward a goal. Since each employee does only a small, specialized part of the total job, he rarely has a chance to look at the final product and say, "Mine, all mine." It is more common, instead, to hear, "This job is endless. It just goes on and on. You don't feel that you are getting anywhere."

Even professionals often lack task identity. Physicians in large clinics may complain that they rarely see the same patient twice and so rarely finish what they started. Radiologists who examine hundreds of X-ray films daily, may have little contact with live patients. In some hospitals, nursing duties are so fragmented that twenty or more nurses, nurses' aides, and orderlies deal with the same patient, but none see him or her as a whole person.

Social work suffers from similar problems. Five or six specialists (probation officers, school psychologists, family counselors) may all deal with parts of a single family's problems, but no one is responsible for pulling the pieces together. Engineering work may be similarly specialized. College-trained draftsmen in an engineering construction company may work on numerous projects but feel that they make an insignificant contribution to each.

Feedback. If we are to have a feeling of accomplishment, we must have some way of measuring progress. We want to know "how we are doing." Only by setting up some goal and knowing that we have reached it can we feel a sense of achievement. Many routine jobs are considered monotonous precisely because they provide no means of checking progress.

Variety. Mass production jobs tend to be tedious and repetitive. An important determinant of job satisfaction is the length of the job cycle: how long it takes to perform a job operation before having to start it all over again. For a college professor, the work cycle may be a semester; for the skilled craftsman, it may be several days or weeks. But for the worker on a machine or assembly line, the work cycle may last less than a minute. If a worker simply tightens one or two bolts over and over again there is deadening lack of variety. As one worker put it:

"The job gets so sickening. Day in and day out I pick two bolts, one with each hand, fasten them in place, and then tighten each in turn. Over and over. Seventy-two times an hour. God knows how many million times a year. I keep doing it in my sleep, only then it is a nightmare."

Furthermore, work pace is rigidly prescribed. Most people like to vary their work rhythms; they may work fast for a while and then gradually slow down as the day wears on. This variety of pace helps to reduce both fatigue and boredom. The typical assembly line, however, makes no provision for the preference of individual workers. More autocratic than any foreman, the assembly line sets a relentless rhythm to which all must adjust.

Fortunately, on most mass-production jobs workers do have a slight opportunity to vary their pace through "building a bank" or "getting into a hole." On some jobs a worker can hurry up a bit and build up a reserve, or "bank," of completed work and then take a break for a few seconds while the work slides by. By pushing 15 seconds ahead and then falling 15 seconds "in a hole," an energetic worker can earn a 30-second break, a small victory at best.

Attention.   Another factor affecting workers' satisfaction with their jobs is the amount of attention it requires. Research scientists enjoy their work because it is constantly new and challenging and absorbs all their attention. Jobs like this are said to require *depth attention.* At the other extreme are so-called *no attention* jobs, which are so routine that one's conscious mind is free to wander at will. Dishwashing is an example of such work; so is driving over a straight highway with little traffic.

The least satisfying jobs are those that require *surface attention.* Here one is obliged to perform a routine, unchallenging chore, but at the same time to remain relatively alert. Watching control gauges, inspecting parts, grading exam papers, and adding up columns of figures all require surface attention. They neither provide challenge, interest, or autonomy (as do depth-attention jobs) nor permit daydreaming (as do no-attention jobs).

These classifications, of course, are simply points on a continuum, for there are relatively few purely no-attention jobs. Further, the attention required by a particular job depends largely on the ability of the individual employee. A bright person may find that a job requires only surface attention, while someone who is less able (or less well trained) may find the same job requires depth attention.

Social relations.   The physical confinement of many factory jobs reduces the opportunity for social relations. Often employees socialize on the basis of proximity rather than occupational status. Congenial on-the-job relationships reduce boredom and permit workers to express their total personality, especially when the job requires only a small segment of their abilities. Yet, feeling little identification with their occupation, workers on mass production jobs are relatively unlikely to make friendships that carry over after work.

Assembly-line workers are restricted to a very small area and can talk only with those directly on either side or, occasionally, across the line. Machine operators have somewhat more flexibility in making social contacts although a high noise level may make ingenious facial expressions and hand signs necessary as a substitute for words. Of course, work breaks provide an opportunity for social contacts.

Adjusting to mass-production work

How do employees adjust to mass-production work? Many learn to ignore the job by daydreaming, to modify the job, or to play various games at work. Others take more decisive action, either leaving or sabotaging the work.

Daydreaming.   Almost all workers regard surface attention jobs as boring, mentally exhausting, and undesirable. (This is true even if the same work might require depth attention from someone else.) But some workers can adjust moderately well to monotonous no-attention jobs. These workers seem to have little need to derive satisfaction from the job itself; they spend their working days daydreaming. One employee told us, "If I thought about the job all the time I'd go nuts. I think about vacation and going hunting. I don't even know I'm working."

Games and high jinks.   In spite of its obvious inefficiency, some people like to mow their lawns in fancy figure eights. Making a game out of work provides variety, gives the worker a chance to show creativity, and supplies goals to work toward. Here is a self-description provided by an office worker in a large insurance company.

"As operator I had to complete 720 units in 4 hours with no more than 11 errors. The job was extremely boring. Each pack usually contained 180 account cards. These came in two kinds of forms, a #1 form and a #4 form. Usually each pack had the same number of each type, and I played basketball with #1's vs. the #4's. Punching in the 7 digits of the policyholder account number was my way of dribbling the ball down the floor, and pushing the button that rang up the total was the ball going through the basket. Usually the scores were close, and on a couple of occasions the game went into overtime— that is, it was continued into the next pack."

On jobs that are not tightly machine-paced, the worker may experiment with various speeds. Workers on piecework are particularly likely to set goals for themselves (sometimes called "bogies") and to engage in elaborate calculations to make sure that they produce neither more nor less than the bogey. Although the primary purpose of these calculations is to avoid overproduction (which might lead to a cut in the piece rate), they also provide a diversion from the monotony of work.

Social games also provide a form of diversion. Gambling is common in many workplaces: flipping coins to see who pays for coffee, World Series pools, bookmaking, and numbers games. Horseplay, lunch-time card games, and gossip around the watercooler can provide satisfaction, particularly for those with high social needs. In the context of humdrum routine, human ingenuity is able to extract pleasure from seemingly trivial events.

One guy opens a window, another slams it shut; or someone turns on a ventilating fan, someone snaps it off. They argue, yell, come to blows, and everybody gets excited. "Man this is neat! The best thing that happened all day. Wow, what a fight!". . . In a desparate need for variety, conflict can break up routine.[5]

Modifying the job.   Workers can sometimes reduce the monotony of their jobs by introducing variations in their work that are unplanned by management. They may exchange work, modify parts of the job, or avoid some parts altogether. They drag out set-ups, find excuses to pick up parts more

[5] Robert Schrank, *Ten Thousand Working Days* (Cambridge, Mass.: MIT Press, 1977), p. 229.

frequently than necessary, and perhaps let the machine break down for a slight change of pace.

Antimanagement activities. In a sense, antimanagement activities are an overt reaction to the frustration of mass-production work. Active union participation, for example, provides an opportunity to release aggression and to enjoy a sense of skill and accomplishment that is denied on the job. Similarly, sabotage and wildcat strikes enable a demoralized work group to let off steam. In Detroit, after long periods of overtime work on boring assembly-line jobs, employees often enjoy the prospect of a strike!

Job redesign

Job redesign is a term describing efforts to restructure jobs to reduce dissatisfaction and increase productivity, especially in mass-production industry. Particularly advanced in some European countries, especially in Sweden, job redesign is viewed as a means of reducing high turnover and absenteeism rates (turnover once averaged 70 percent annually in some Swedish automobile assembly plants and absenteeism was close to 20 percent). There have also been some important experiments with job redesign in North America. Among the approaches tried, in roughly increasing order of complexity, are the following: job rotation, job enlargement, establishment of natural work units, improving feedback, job enrichment, and natural work teams. As we shall see, these techniques overlap considerably and rarely is one technique used alone.

Job rotation. This most simple of workplace reforms permits workers to switch jobs either in terms of a fixed schedule or on an ad hoc basis (to cope with absenteeism or emergencies) without changing the characteristics of the jobs themselves. Thus, workers gain more variety in their work and perhaps in their social relations. It gives them a chance to learn additional skills. Further since jobs are continually exchanged, no one gets stuck with a dirty task permanently. Management also benefits, since workers become able to perform a number of different jobs in the event of an emergency.

Some workers object to being rotated from job to job and jolted out of their routine. Being an "expert" on one particular type of work gives them a feeling of status and importance that they lose when they move around. Our studies suggest that in general, those who oppose job rotation work on no-attention jobs and enjoy daydreaming. On the other hand, workers whose regular job already prevents daydreaming endorse rotation as a relief from monotony.

Job enlargement. This approach combines tasks "horizontally," typically lengthening the work cycle. At times the worker may be permitted to follow a job from beginning to end. At Saab some workers, whose job cycle averaged 1.8 minutes, were given the task of assembling an entire engine, a 30-minute undertaking. Longer job cycles require additional skills and provide a greater sense of variety, task identity, and accomplishment. Job enlargement often allows workers to control the speed of the machines they run and even to turn these off for short breaks.

Some forms of job enlargement merely add together a large number of similar unchallenging tasks: for example, an electronic assembler no longer fastens one tube to a chasis over and over again, now he fastens five. For some people, the additional complications are not intrinsically challenging. For them, job enlargement converts a no-attention job into one requiring surface attention.

Establishing natural work units. Jobs can be rearranged into natural units or batches, so that the employee can gain a feeling of accomplishment every time a batch is finished. The desire to finish a unit has a strong pulling power, thus enhancing motivation. Furthermore, establishing units helps pinpoint job responsibility and measure performance.

The following quotation describes one of the earliest examples of how boring work, telephone central office maintenance, was broken down into natural units:[6]

There is no challenge to diagnosing trouble, and the job is very confining since a man can work for hours within the space of a few feet. There is never a real experience of progress. When the job is finished the worker starts all over again.

In one office the frames on which the men worked were subdivided by means of chalk lines. . . . Each block required between one and a half and two hours to complete. The worker made his choice of . . . unit. . . . The benefits of this pattern of work were immediately apparent. . . . Once a man selected a block he worked until it was finished.

Every time a man completed a unit he took a smoke or a stretch. Even lunch and quitting time found no untagged units. The men liked the plan and the supervisors reported that complaining decreased and the trouble with meeting work schedules was eliminated.

For work that cannot be divided into beginnings and ends, natural units can be created in other ways. Each member of an office typing pool can be made responsible for the work of a given professor, or a telephone installer can provide service in a specific section of town. One caution: assignments of this sort must be made carefully to ensure that the workload is divided fairly.

Feedback. As we stressed earlier, employees like to know how well they are doing. To provide feedback some companies post bar graphs that compare the length of time actually taken to complete jobs as compared to the time planned. A telephone company circulates monthly indices of efficiency, particularly among its white-collar employees.

Research suggests that the more objective and more frequent the feedback, the more motivating it becomes. It is advantageous for the worker to learn about his progress directly, as he does his job, rather than from a supervisor on an occasional basis. Workers may suspect the supervisor's message; on

[6] Norman Maier, *Psychology in Industry* (Boston: Houghton Mifflin, 1955), p. 489.

the other hand, they are likely to believe data they have helped gather themselves.

Computers and other automated machines sometimes can be used to provide individuals with data now blocked from them. Many clerical operations, for example, are now programmed on computer consoles. These consoles often can be programmed to provide the clerk with immediate feedback in the form of a CRT display or a printout indicating that an error has been made. Some systems even have been programmed to provide the operator with a positive feedback message when a period of error-free performance has been sustained.[7]

Job enrichment. This approach goes beyond job enlargement in that it adds "vertical" or quasi-managerial elements, especially planning, supply, and inspection. Thus it contributes to workers' sense of autonomy and control over their work. Job enrichment was applied to the work of clerks who assembled telephone directories.

Before the change, directories were assembled on a production line basis. Work was passed from clerk to clerk for a total of 21 steps, many of which were merely for verification. After the change, each clerk was given complete responsibility for assembling either an entire directory or an alphebetical part of one, thus combining 21 jobs into one. Follow up checkers were eliminated because employees were now expected to check their own work for accuracy. The clerks were permitted to talk directly to advertising sales representatives to clear up ambiguity in the ad copy these representatives submitted, thus bypassing their bosses. Finally, they themselves set the deadline dates after which new copy would not be accepted for the next directory issue.[8]

As a result turnover dropped, fewer errors were made, and more work was done with fewer people.

Job enrichment frequently includes the following elements:

- Giving workers whole tasks.
- Introducing new and more difficult tasks not previously handled. *Example:* Operators maintain their own equipment.
- Increasing the accountability of individual workers for their own work. *Examples:* Lab technicians sign their own reports rather than have bosses check them. Production workers inspect their own work and initial the inspection tags.
- Introduce elements of planning and coordination. *Examples:* Maintenance people decide priorities of repair jobs. Operators decide when to order supplies.
- Giving workers additional authority and freedom on their own jobs. *Examples:* Correspondents are allowed to use their own language in answering letters rather than following standard forms. Employees decide when to take their own coffee breaks. Telephone service representatives grant customers credit without consulting their bosses.

[7] Richard Hackman, "Job Design," p. 140.

[8] Robert Ford, "Job Enrichment Lesson from AT&T," *Harvard Business Review* (January 1973), 96–106.

- Dealing directly with clients or suppliers. *Example:* Workers "expedite" their own supplies from material control, bypassing their supervisors.

Self-managing work teams. This most advanced form of job redesign involves a group form of job enrichment. Typically, such teams (sometimes called "autonomous work groups") meet periodically to determine job assignments, schedule work breaks, and even decide the rate of production.

At a Philips TV plant in the Netherlands, groups of seven or eight are given total responsibility for assembling sets. The group "not only performs the entire assembly task but also deals directly with staff groups such as procurement, quality, and stores, with no supervisor or foreman to act as intermediary or expediter. If something is needed from another department or something goes wrong that requires the services of another department, it's the group's responsibility to deal with that department." [9]

At Volvo truck assembly plant, "the production team, a group of 5 to 12 men with a common work assignment, elects its own chargehand, schedules its own output within standards set by higher management, distributes work among its members and is responsible for its own quality control." [10]

The Topeka plant of General Foods, which makes Gaines Dog Food, was set up with work teams of 7 to 14 members. Activities usually handled by separate groups, such as quality control, maintenance, janitorial work, industrial engineering, and even personnel became the responsibility of the group as a whole. Individual jobs were often rotated, but key decisions were made on a group basis. Initially each worker was paid the same rate, with pay increases being given when the group decided that one of its members had picked up additional skills. The group screened new applicants for jobs and apparently even "expelled" (discharged) poor performers. [11]

Work teams have been given responsibility for developing relations with vendors, determining which operations can be handled individually and which by the group as a whole, setting work pace (sometimes fast in the morning, slow in the afternoon), training new employees, and, at one company, even keeping financial records. Sometimes work team members serve in roles normally reserved for staff personnel or supervisors: chairing the plant safety committee, redesigning equipment, or troubleshooting customers' problems. [12] Self-managing work teams are especially appropriate when the nature of the task makes it difficult for an individual to do a whole job alone.

As we shall discuss in greater detail, job redesign frequently leads to greater satisfaction, higher quality, lower turnover, and (less often) higher productivity. It achieves these objectives, in part, through altering the task

Underlying motivational mechanisms

[9] William F. Dowling, "Job Redesign on the Assembly Line: Farewell to Blue-Collar Blues?" *Organizational Dynamics* (Autumn 1973), 54.

[10] *Ibid.,* p. 59.

[11] The program apparently no longer works as well as it did at first. See Richard Walton, "Work Innovation at Topeka: After Six Years," *Journal of Applied Behavioral Science,* Vol. 17 (July 1977), 422–33.

[12] The equivalent of self-managing work teams at the managerial level is organization by product or matrix organization.

dimensions. The psychological process at work may be explained by what has been called the expectancy theory, a shortened version of which is illustrated below: [13]

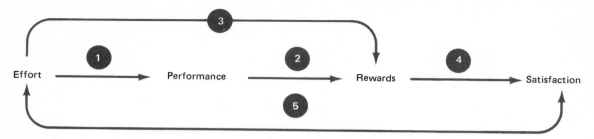

Following the numbered relationships indicated in the diagram, let us analyze what happens when job redesign is successfully introduced (often, of course, it is not).

① Since workers have greater freedom to determine how they do their work, they work more effectively.[14]

② The altered task characteristics provide greater psychological rewards from performance. For example, finishing a natural unit provides a greater sense of completion (or task identity) than does working on an endless task. Similarly, if workers decide *how* a job should be done, actually successfully completing it demonstrates their decision-making and technical skills (both to themselves and to the outside world). Thus workers may be rewarded by both a sense of self-achievement and praise (and higher status) from one's peers.

③ Just working on an enriched job may be psychologically rewarding (perhaps because there is greater variety), regardless of whether one actually finishes it.[15]

④ The sense of skill and accomplishment gained from doing a job helps satisfy ego needs.[16] Praise from one's peers may satisfy social needs.

⑤ Finally, the feedback provided by many forms of job redesign completes the loop.

Yet job redesign will not be equally motivating for everyone. Not everyone wants more responsibility. Some people already obtain all the challenge and stimulation they want, either at home or at work (overstimulation can be even more frustrating than understimulation). The evidence is somewhat mixed, but it suggests that when jobs provide increased opportunity for learning and discretion, people with strong ego needs respond more positively to

---

[13] For a fuller discussion, see Donald Schwab and Lawrence Cummings, "A Theoretical Analysis of the Impact of Scope on Employee Performance," *Academy of Management Review*, Vol. 1 (April 1976).

[14] If the redesigned job is beyond the worker's ability to handle, however, performance may drop.

[15] There is psychological evidence that moderate variety is stimulating and satisfying, regardless of the activity performed.

[16] A much debated question is whether job redesign can change the pattern of needs themselves. According to some researchers, the challenge of redesigned jobs may be so great that workers who have previously centered their lives on satisfying social needs off the job will now find satisfaction in doing the job itself.

work than do those with weak ego needs.[17] This doesn't mean that the more challenge the better. Jobs can be made more challenging than even workers with high ego needs *want* or are *able* (two separate points) to handle. The difficult trick is to find the right amount of work stimulation for every worker.

Ego needs are not the only relevant factor. Employees who are satisfied with their pay, supervision, and working conditions are more likely to react favorably to redesigned work than are those who are dissatisfied.[18] Expectations also play a role: college-trained draftsmen expect more challenging work than do their high-school trained counterparts. Finally, it is reasonable to assume that strength of social needs will influence how people respond to forms of job redesign, such as self-managing work teams, which involve much social interaction.

Sociotechnical change. Job redesign does more than satisfy egoistic needs. New and more effective social and workflow relations are introduced (hence the term *social-technical systems* applied to redesigned jobs by some scholars).[19] Particularly in self-managing work teams the following developments occur:

- Small work groups are established: typically, these groups are considerably smaller (only four to eighteen members) than the large departments they partially replace. Being smaller, they are more cohesive. Not only do members participate in group decision-making processes, but group pressures force individuals to adhere to these decisions. Opportunities to satisfy social needs are substantially increased.

- Among the drawbacks of the conventional method of having each worker do part of the job is the high cost of maintaining a smooth workflow. Employee *A* must work just as fast as employee *B*, or employee *B* will be slowed down. Each extra person in the work flow increases the number of *interfaces* and makes coordination more difficult. Job enlargement and enrichment reduce the number of such interfaces, and self-managing work groups relieve management of the task of coordinating.[20]

- There are substantial changes in worker-management relations. The work group takes on many of the foreman's responsibilities.

The best-publicized job redesign experiments have also been accompanied by improvement in the work environment. Indeed, some have argued that these improvements have a more significant impact on job attitudes than

---

[17] J. Richard Hackman, "Work Design," pp. 118–120. Hackman asks, "What percentage of the workforce actually desires higher order need satisfactions at work and so are likely to respond positively to enriched jobs? Some observers estimate that only 15 percent of rank-and-file employees are so motivated. Others are more optimistic."

[18] Greg Oldham, J. Richard Hackman, and John Pearce, "Conditions Under Which Employees Respond Positively to Enriched Work," *Journal of Applied Psychology*, Vol. 61 (1976), 395–403.

[19] Louis Davis and James Taylor, *Design of Jobs* (Middlesex, England: Penguin, 1972).

[20] *Buffering* is a job redesign technique in itself. *Buffer stocks* are placed between workers at adjacent stages in the work flow. Thus, instead of passing his finished work directly over to employee *B*, employee *A* produces for stock and employee *B* draws from stock as needed. Since the workers are *uncoupled,* each is free to work at his or her own pace; further if employee *A*'s machine breaks down, employee *B* is not likely to be immediately affected.

do any changes in job design themselves. These have begun to reduce what a prominent union leader calls

the double standard that exists between workers and management. . . . Workers challenge the symbols of elitism typically taken for granted, such as salary payment versus hourly payment; time clocks for blue-collar workers; well-decorated dining rooms for white-collar workers versus plain, Spartan-like cafeterias for blue-collar workers; privileged parking for the elite but catch as you can for workers.[21]

At General Foods' Topeka dog food plant, for instance, there are no reserved parking lots, no time clocks, and no differentiation in decor between management offices and worker lounges. Workers are free to make phone calls on company time (just like management). A number of companies have begun to pay blue-collar workers on a salary basis. Such reductions in status differentials not only tend to reduce dissatisfaction; they also help an atmosphere of trust and confidence to develop between workers and management and thus help improve communications generally.

Wider organizational changes

Organizations are systems, and no one part alone can be changed. Job redesign is unlikely to be effective unless it is accompanied by complementary changes in other aspects of organizational life.

Introducing job redesign. In some companies, higher management or some special staff group draws up the job redesign plan, and the improved jobs are imposed on workers whether they (or their unions) like them or not. In a sense, management uses autocratic techniques to reach participatory objectives. The autocratic approach is consistent with the human relations approach of the Forties and Fifties which gives workers freedom on the assumption that it will make workers happier. Allowing workers to design their jobs permits a greater sense of participation. The limited evidence suggests that job restructuring will be more successful if those involved help plan it and retain the freedom to opt out, either individually or as a group. (In some situations, the conventional assembly line has been continued alongside enriched jobs, and workers are permitted to choose between the two kinds of work.)

Impact on other departments. It is difficult to introduce a radically new job redesign program in one department without affecting others. In one coal mine, the freedom granted to a self-managing work team led to much jealousy and friction with other miners; the less favored miners derisively called their colleagues "super-miners." [22] A self-managing work team in a toy factory worked so well that it disrupted the work flow of the factory as a

---

[21] Vice-president Irving Bluestone of the United Automobile Workers, "Comments on Job Enrichment," *Organizational Dynamics* (Winter 1974), 47.

[22] Eric Trist, Gerald Susman, and Grant Brown, "An Experiment in Autonomous Working in an American Underground Coal Mine," *Human Relations,* 30, No. 3 (1977), 201–36.

whole and earned incentives so high that they disrupted the entire plant's social structure. In short, while strengthening relations *within* a work group, job redesign may threaten those *between* groups.

Pay.   When workers take on more responsibility, they want more pay. Management argues that increased satisfaction and more interesting work should be reward enough. Often management fears that if it pays one group of workers more, other groups will want similar pay increases, even if their work has not changed. There may be constant disputes as to how the financial gain (if any) from job redesign is to be distributed, and effective resolution of this problem may require some sort of group incentive such as the Scanlon Plan.

Changes in management.   For workers one of the main advantages of job redesign is greater freedom to make decisions on their own, rather than having supervisors hover over them. Understandably, this freedom is threatening to supervisors. Sometimes job redesign results in fewer supervisors being needed; in any case those who remain must learn to let subordinates make decisions by themselves.[23]

Equally difficult adjustments must be made by higher management. Among the problems associated with the General Foods' Topeka dog food factory was that

Economically it was a success, but it became a power struggle. It was too threatening to too many people. . . . The problem has not been so much that the workers could not manage their own affairs as that some management and staff personnel saw their own positions threatened because the workers performed too well.[24]

Some of the most successful job redesign programs have been introduced in small, new, plants which are removed from the contaminating influences of the larger and more traditional parent organization. The problems involved in introducing major work structure changes in large organizations are immense. It is equally difficult to extend successful experiments from the small departments in which they started to the larger organization.

In sharp contrast to the situation in Europe, most of the best publicized job redesign changes in North America have taken place in nonunion plants. Unions in the United States and Canada find the issue of job redesign fuzzy and hard to deal with. Despite their dissatisfaction with work, the *expressed* demands of most union members are for higher wages, better fringe benefits, and more job security. Especially during stagflation, such attitudes are understandable, particularly since few workers can imagine alternatives to the traditional ways of doing mass production work.

The role of the union

[23] One reason self-managing work teams were not being used more widely in the TV plant discussed on p. 467 is that foremen in the Netherlands are unionized. Management feared a foremen's strike were the plan extended. Robert Schrank, *Ten Thousand Working Days*, p. 221.
[24] "Stonewalling Plant Democracy," *Business Week*, March 28, 1977, p. 78.

Many union leaders are suspicious of the entire job redesign movement, viewing it as a form of manipulation and speedup as well as an attempt to divert workers' attention from their economic problems. Furthermore, the problem of worker dissatisfaction is difficult to handle through the traditional adversary techniques of collective bargaining. "A union demand is a negotiable demand which, if not satisfied, can be met by a strike," said an AFL-CIO leader. "How do you talk about [job redesign] questions in terms of a negotiable demand and a possible strike?" [25]

Unionists object chiefly to job redesign programs that management introduces unilaterally, without consulting the union. But any such programs, regardless of how introduced, are likely to affect pay, promotional ladders, and job descriptions. (Typically, unions seek to ensure that employees work only within a narrowly defined "job description"; job redesign blurs the boundaries between jobs and even blends worker and supervisory functions.) Unions resist changes in any of these areas unless management makes compensating concessions.

Despite these suspicions, unions and managements have joined together in several instances (notably the United Auto Workers and the major automobile manufacturing firms) to sponsor joint research and experimentation on new ways of doing work. Such a program has been credited with saving General Motors' Tarrytown, New York plant from being closed. Three carefully studied, joint union-management programs came to quite different results.

A joint program among unionized professional engineers at the Tennessee Valley Authority led to substantial changes in design procedures as well as the introduction of more flexible work hours for some employees.

An experiment with self-managing work teams at a unionized coal mine was quite successful for a while but was then partially abandoned in the face of growing union-management hostility in the coal industry generally and the previously mentioned jealousies between "superminers" and those who apparently preferred to work under more conventional arrangements.

An experiment at an auto mirror plant introduced an Earned Idle Time Program, which permitted workers to knock off the job (with full pay) once they had finished their daily work quota. Further gains were not achieved, however, in part because the plan, imposed by top management and top union, gained little grass roots support.

*Evaluating
job redesign*

How successful have job redesign projects been to date? Reports are mixed, and evaluation is difficult. It is hard to separate the results of job redesign from the impact of other developments occurring at the same time. Furthermore, even if one can demonstrate success in one situation, comparisons between situations are difficult to make. "Experimental sites" differ greatly in their technologies, the nature of the work force, and the kinds of changes introduced.

Nevertheless, what do available reports tell us? Turnover, absenteeism, and grievances have generally gone down. Quality has improved, sometimes dramatically, and satisfaction, to the extent it has been measured, has increased.

[25] Nat Goldfinger quoted in David Jenkins, *Job Power* (Baltimore: Penguin 1974), p. 317.

About productivity there is more question. Productivity at the automated and job-restructured Topeka dog food plant is much higher than at its traditional counterpart in Kankakee, but Topeka has a much higher capital investment per employee. The European experience suggests that the greatest productivity gains accrue from reducing the rigidity of the assembly line. Since the work force is more flexible (and work flow relations are less complex) a single bottleneck is less likely to disrupt the entire production process. Employees are more likely to handle unexpected problems on their own, technological change is easier to introduce, and costs are saved because fewer first-line supervisors and staff personnel are required. On the other hand, special purpose equipment is used less effectively.

Ironically, although job redesign has been presented as a motivator, in practice it may work like a hygiene. Turnover, absenteeism, and satisfaction improve. But as far as productivity is concerned, the clearest gain seems to be that the workforce is more flexible, not that it is more highly motivated.

A high percentage of job redesign efforts have been abandoned as unsuccessful. The trouble in most cases has been not the particular form of job redesign proposed, but the way the change has been implemented. A new plan may be announced with a blaze of fanfare but quietly dropped because of unanticipated resistance from such interest groups as foremen.

When should job redesign be introduced? The limited research suggests that job redesign is more likely to be successful if the following conditions are met:

- the workers involved should have relatively high ego needs, and, if self-managing work teams are to be introduced, they should also have high social needs.
- management philosophy generally should be sympathetic to participation;
- lower and middle level managers must be willing to permit their subordinates greater autonomy (perhaps there should be job redesign for management itself);
- the technology should be appropriate for the kind of redesign proposed. When heavy equipment investments have already been made (as in many existing plants) only limited job redesign is possible, except at prohibitive costs.
- management must be willing to share with its workers any financial gains resulting from the redesign program.
- when workers are unionized, the union should be consulted and participate on a fully equal basis.

Finally, management must give careful attention to the way job redesign is implemented. Because of the social tensions it engenders, piecemeal changes may be difficult. Job redesign may work best as part of a wider Organization Development effort.

Goal-setting

Job redesign changes, as we have seen, are more likely to lead to improved satisfaction, quality, and turnover than to productivity. Sales managers have known for years that one

Much of the research has been done in logging. A typical experiment involved an attempt to increase the productivity of logging crews. Supervisors were trained to set goals, based on average tree-size and other factors. Hard, but not impossible goals were given to ten experimental logging crews but no goals to ten equivalent control crews. The experimental groups were told that the goals represented minimum standards of acceptable performance but that no one would be penalized for not meeting them. Both experimental and control groups were given forms to record their output. The result? The experimental crews' productivity increased significantly, while that of the control crews showed almost no change.

These loggers were on piecework. Other experiments have involved workers paid on an hourly basis, so that increased effort did not lead to increased compensation. In one such experiment, truck drivers met a goal of loading their logging trucks to 92 percent of the legal weight; previously they had averaged 60 percent. In this case, after the goals were set, the truckers began to keep records of their performance and to compete with each other.

of the most effective ways to raise productivity is to set tough, clear-cut goals, but behavioral scientists have begun to study this phenomenon only recently.

By now there is considerable research on goal-setting.[26] This research suggests, first, that people produce more if they are set specific goals rather than merely asked to "work as hard as you can," and, secondly, that the harder the goals, the harder people work. But there is a proviso. For goal setting to be effective, the goals must be *accepted* by the people involved. Goals which are not accepted are not motivating.

What determines whether goals are accepted? Obviously they should be seen as reasonable and not impossible to reach. But other factors are relevant too. People with high need for achievement will accept tougher goals than will those who are low in this trait. People are more likely to accept a goal if they have reached it in the past (or even come moderately close to reaching it), if they trust the person who set the goal, and if they compare themselves with others who have reached it.

Feedback. As we have seen earlier, feedback often contributes to satisfaction. Yet the research suggests that feedback is motivating only if there is a goal involved. Although the control logging crews kept production records, they had no impact. The truckers had always had access to their load weights, but they paid little attention to this information until goals were set. Once a goal is set, some knowledge of results is required so that workers can determine where they stand at any given time.

Participative goal setting. One way to ensure that goals are accepted is to allow those involved to set them themselves, either individually or in a group. Particularly when goals are set by one's fellow workers, one feels under

[26] The research has been conducted both in experimental laboratories (often with psychology students as subjects) and in industry. See, for example, Gary Latham and Gary Yukl, "A Review of Research on the Application of Goal Setting in Industry," *Academy of Management Journal,* Vol. 18 (December 1975), 824–45.

considerable social pressure not to be a shirker. However, the experiments that have contrasted *own* and *imposed* goals suggest that own (participative) goals are not necessarily more motivating than imposed goals, particularly if the latter are set by competitors or trusted supervisors.

Money. Monetary rewards are not essential for successful goal setting (as the truck-loading case illustrates). But earning more money is often a goal in itself, and in our society considerations of equity suggest that people should earn more if they work harder on paid jobs (in sports, of course, it is a different matter). An unfair goal, one not sufficiently rewarded, is not likely to be accepted.

Commitment. Goals are more likely to be motivating if people commit themselves to goals voluntarily, publicly, and then recommit themselves.[27] Goals set by others are less likely to be accepted truly voluntarily than are goals one sets for oneself.

All this suggests that job redesign and goal setting are complementary rather than competitive approaches to improving organizational effectiveness. Without natural work units it may be difficult to set goals at all. Workers assigned to enriched jobs or self-managing work teams are more likely to set tough goals for themselves than are those who work on traditional, routine tasks.

Goals provide more than generalized motivation. They give subordinates a clearer picture of what they are supposed to accomplish. Furthermore, goals set standards against which higher management can evaluate subordinate performance. Indeed, when there are clear goals and feedback is provided, the subordinate can tell for himself whether he is performing adequately. Thus, the need for detailed supervision is reduced, and employee satisfaction is enhanced.[28]

Goals may take many forms. Budgets and sales quotas are two examples. Management-by-objectives is a process by which both financial and nonfinancial goals are set on a systematic basis.

Use of goals

On jobs that provide little satisfaction, leisure may be a strong reward. Some organizations allow employees who have finished their day's work to go home and still collect eight hours' pay. In England this practice is known as "job and finish." In North America, electric-meter readers, letter carriers, garbage collectors often work on this basis. In these occupations close supervision is impossible. (Of course, if an employee finishes much too soon, the supervisor has an indication that the work has been assigned inequitably. Still management must be careful not to kill incentive by using a few free minutes as an excuse to give to raise an employee's workload.)

[27] Gerald Salancik, "Commitment and Control," in Barry Staw and Gerald Salancik, eds., *New Directions in Organizational Behavior* (Chicago: St. Clair Press, 1977).
[28] Tough goals, as long as they are felt to be fair, contribute to both productivity and satisfaction. Reaching a difficult goal provides a real sense of accomplishment.

Some problems.   Goals are not without drawbacks. They work best when they are specific and easily measurable, but not every important goal (for example, employee development) can be made highly specific. Emphasis on any specific goal may result in other goals being ignored that are almost equally important. Individual goals discourage teamwork; group goals discourage individual responsibility. Goals must be frequently reemphasized, or they begin to be ignored; on the other hand, overemphasis on goals which employees have not accepted truly voluntarily may lead to frustration and revolt. Indeed, goal-setting is one of the most critical of leadership activities.

New work schedules

The basic assumption behind job redesign is that changes in work content will result in increased satisfaction and productivity. By contrast, many organizations are acting as if they believed that employees' primary demands were not for improvements in the nature of work but for greater freedom to leave it. The last few years have seen the growing acceptance of new approaches to work scheduling: the ten-hour-day-four-day week, flextime, and job sharing, as well as the expansion of an older arrangement, part-time work.

What these plans have in common is that they are designed to provide greater opportunities for employees to enjoy their life *off*, as opposed to *on*, the job. The 4-day week provides longer weekends. Flextime permits workers to choose a work schedule that fits into their off-the-job activities. Work sharing and part-time work permit employees to spend fewer hours on the job. For some workers these new work schedules represent a changing life style, which downgrades work as a source of satisfaction. But for many women it represents just the opposite: an opportunity to combine work with family life. Indeed work schedules have become a major issue for some women's groups.

The 4-day week

The 10-hour day, 4-day week (sometimes called concentrated workweek or the 4–40 plan) was the first of the recent innovative approaches to work scheduling which have been tried widely in this country. The advantages of the plan are clear. By concentrating the work week into four days, the plan provides an extra day to run errands, to take trips to the country, to engage in recreation at home, and (for some) even to hold a second job. Further commuting time is reduced. This is an attractive package and, according to polls, a high percentage of workers now on conventional work schedules would prefer to shift to the new plan.

In practice experience with the 4–40 plan has been mixed. Some organizations report decreased absenteeism, reduced turnover, and higher productivity. In some tight labor markets, the plan provides the organization a valuable competitive edge in recruiting new employees. Unmarried and childless younger workers find the new schedule particularly attractive, especially if they participate actively in weekend recreation (in fact, it seems as if attitude towards recreation determines attitude toward the plan).

On the other hand, many companies have participated in 4–40 and then dropped it. The workers were enthusiastic at first but then found that the gain of the three-day weekend was more than offset by the fatigue of the 10-hour day and the loss of free evening time. Working mothers in particular find it difficult to raise children under these conditions. Organizations that must operate five days a week find it hard to schedule the fifth day (half crews on Monday and Friday are a common but rarely satisfactory solution). Further, unless supervisors put in a 50-hour week, they must leave part of the workforce unsupervised. Finally, under many union and government contract rules, work in excess of 8 hours per day must be paid on an overtime basis.

Not untypical was the experience of the Chyrsler Corporation Tappan, New York, parts depot. Started in early summer, the program was terminated in October. "The biggest complaint was caused by the need to rotate jobs Monday and Friday." a union spokesman said. "We found that workers wanted to stay on their own jobs." Enthusiasm for 3-day weekends was seasonal, waning when employees' children returned to school. Further, the 10-hour day gave them little time at home.

In some situations, concentrated workweeks make greater sense. It is greeted with enthusiasm by salesmen and work crews who travel a great deal and can return home only over weekends. Workers in out of the way posts have even more unusual schedules.

A uranium mine in northern Canada flies its personnel up to 500 miles to their work at the beginning of the week. They work 11 hours a day for 7 days and then are flown home for a full week layover. Meanwhile a second crew takes over.

Similar schedules are common for oil rigs, while firemen in some communities work a 24-hour day followed by two or more days off. But these are special situations. Under more normal conditions, 4–40 has created more problems than it solves. Most unions oppose the 10-hour day unless overtime premiums are paid for the last 2 hours.

Unlike the 4–40 plan, the main virtue of flextime is lack of rigidity. First *Flextime* introduced into Europe, this new work scheduling procedure is now widely enjoyed (for example by some 40 percent of Swiss workers) as an alternative to the age-old and until now presumed inviolate tradition of fixed working hours. The plan spread to the U.S. in the early 1970s, and by 1978 covered an estimated 3.5 million workers.

The principle behind flextime is that each employee should have some freedom to choose his or her work schedule. Flextime presumes a required *core* period in which all employees are expected to be at work. Typically, the core might be from 9 to 11 A.M. and from 2 to 4 P.M. In addition to this 4-hour core there is a *band* of other hours in which employees can work, perhaps 7 to 9 A.M. and 4 to 6 P.M. plus part of the lunch period. Some organizations allow employees to work less than 8 hours on some days in exchange for more than 8 hours on other days, as long as their weekly or monthly total equals a "normal" number of hours. Often workers keep track of their own hours, or a mechanical device may be activated by each workers' special key. Thus, aside from the core period, employees—depending on their personal elections—will have different work schedules. Now, what are the advantages of flextime?

- Flextime is especially advantageous to working parents, since it permits them to adjust their hours to their childrens' school schedules. Beyond this, employees can adjust their work schedules to allow time to visit dentists, to run errands, or to avoid traffic jams.[29] Since employees set their own hours of work, they are less likely to be late or absent. There is less reason to take a full day off just because of an unavoidable midday appointment.

- In turn, flextime can have an impact on supervisory-employee relations. Supervisors have less need to act as policemen. Further, the plan greatly reduces demeaning requests for "personal time off" and irritating investigations over whether tardiness or absence is legitimate.

- Individuals differ in their physiological rhythms. Flextime permits them to adjust working hours to when they are likely to perform best and to enjoy leisure when they want it most.

- Even more critically, through flextime management says to employees: "You're adults, you're responsible. We're substituting your self-control for externally imposed supervisory control." Since individuals know their needs and values better than any outsider, they are in a better position to undertake tradeoffs (is it better to take off two hours today and work longer tomorrow?). The resulting boost in morale should be reflected in better feelings about the organization and also improved performance.

- Finally, flextime reduces the double standard that exists when managers are permitted to schedule their own work hours and employees are not.

Many organizations report substantial benefits from flextime: increased productivity, greater satisfaction, reduced tardiness, absenteeism, and turnover, and less time spent on coffee breaks (people who set their own schedules are less likely to be fatigued than are people who work schedules set by others). By contrast with the 4–40 plan, few organizations that have embraced flextime have abandoned it.

Nevertheless introducing flextime is never easy; further there are a variety of situations for which it is not suited. In the first place, flextime creates many problems where teamwork is required, such as on an assembly line, or in activities such as nursing or police work, where one person cannot leave his post until relieved by another.[30]

Complex scheduling arrangements are often required, especially when minimum-size work crews are needed at all times. From management's point of view, it is far easier to let employees work out these scheduling details by themselves. Once employees become accustomed to taking responsibility on a group basis for scheduling, they may also take responsibility for other

[29] On the other hand, flextime may disrupt carpools.

[30] Individuals can trade their assignments so that the requisite number of people are always present, but arranging these trades may be difficult. Sometimes even assembly-line work may be modified to permit flextime. The early bird who works on one end of the line may produce a bank which the next person on the line, who reports to work later, may handle later on. Adjustments of this sort, however, are always complex.

aspects of work, thus facilitating the kind of participative atmosphere in which self-managing work teams may develop. Running an operation with some people absent may require those on duty to learn unfamiliar jobs. All in all, flextime is consistent with job redesign.

Another problem relates to supervision. If 12 hours elapse between the time the first employee reports for work and the last one leaves the office— but the supervisor is on duty for only 8 hours—then the office will be unsupervised for 4 hours. Possibly this is actually an advantage. The supervisor will be forced to delegate authority during this 4-hour period and to engage in planning rather than detailed supervision, something that may be good for both worker and supervisor.

In practice, flextime is most common in professional and clerical work. This kind of work usually requires less teamwork than does manufacturing. Further, clerical activities tend to be heavily female, and at this stage in society's development working mothers feel the greatest need for the flexibile hours.

Flextime plans differ in the degree of flexibility they allow. Some plans require workers to pick a schedule and then stick to it; others allow schedule shifts on a daily basis, sometimes even without advance notice. Some permit workers to pick the length of their lunch hour and to take breaks of various lengths during the day; others allow flexibility only with regard to the starting and quitting time. Although some jobs permit greater flexibility than do others, employers frequently feel they need uniform policies to prevent cries of favoritism.

Some organizations permit employees to vary the number of hours they work per day or even per week, usually with the provision that time lost in one period be made up later on. In the Swiss countryside, for example, the 1800 hour work year is the norm. Workers put in long hours in the winter and then spend much of the summer on vacation or tending their farms. In the U.S., flexibility of this sort would create financial complications. The Fair Labor Standards Act requires overtime premiums for work in excess of 40 hours per week. Government contracts and many unionized firms are required to pay similar premiums for those working in excess of eight hours per day.

Almost the ultimate form of flexibility allows the worker to decide on a day-to-day basis whether he wants to work or not. West Coast longshoremen, for example, report to the union hiring hall when they feel like it, and senior (class A) longshoremen are pretty well guaranteed work (or at least show up pay). As one man put it: "A real San Francisco longshoreman is an independent cuss. He's not a slave to the calendar. He figures out what he needs and he works to meet his needs, but when the day is nice, and the steelhead are running, why work?"

Perhaps some day a large proportion of our society will enjoy such freedom. So far, the number is small.

Part-time work

Part-time work represents another form of flexibility. Demand for part-time work is increasing rapidly, particularly among mothers, students, and older workers. By the late 1970s, over one-third of female employees and one-eighth of male employees worked on a part-time basis, and demand for part-time jobs was even greater than its supply. Part-time work was once also temporary work, but a growing number of employees now have permanent part-time positions.

It is understandable why part-time work is attractive for many workers. Organizations are also learning that many qualified employees are available only on a part-time basis. Very often part-time workers have better productivity records and lower absenteeism and turnover than full-time workers. Professionals may produce almost as much work in a six-hour day as they would in eight hours. Further, there are many jobs that don't require full-time coverage.

Nevertheless, many of the disadvantages of flextime also apply to part-time work. Scheduling and supervision are often difficult. Usually it is just as expensive to train a part-time employee as a full-time one. The social security tax structure acts to make part-time employees more expensive than full-time ones. On the other hand, many employers provide part-time employees relatively fewer fringe benefits, even though the trend is rapidly changing toward treating both groups equally.

Part-time work is concentrated in sales and service activities, such as fast foods. However, Control Data runs a factory in St. Paul, Minnesota, that is staffed completely by part-timers. So far, there are few part-time managers, but part-time work is attractive to talented professionals who might otherwise be unavailable:

I am an assistant vice-president and economist at the Federal Bank of Boston. I am the head of the National Business Conditions Section at the Bank, and for two years I have been a part-time worker. How can a supervisor work part-time? The Director of Research certainly entertained some doubts when I told him that after my daughter was born, I wanted to work only 20 hours a week. In large part, it has worked because while I am the official head of the section, I share my supervisory work with the other economist in it. Like team teaching, we have team management, with one member of the team being slightly more equal. I also have bright, well-motivated workers in my section who are happy to take responsibility for their work. I do about the same job I used to do, but for less pay. I also work harder while at the bank. And of course, I take a lot of work home, which I also did when I worked full-time.[31]

Job sharing. This is a form of part-time work that has attracted considerable attention. Here a single job is divided between two people, each of whom works part time (say 20 hours a week or 6 months a year). In some cases a husband and wife may share a single professional position (with complications if their marriage falls apart). Although there are some philosophical attractions to this form of work schedule, particularly for those who view it as a step towards eliminating the differences in sex roles, the main advantage is that the job in question is staffed on a full-time basis. Nevertheless, job sharing has the disadvantage that it will work only if two individuals can be found, each of whom is willing to work an unusual schedule that directly complements his partner's. When one partner quits or becomes unhappy with the arrange-

---

[31] Francine Gordon and Myra Strober, *Bringing Women into Management* (New York: McGraw-Hill, 1975), p. 88.

ment, a replacement may be difficult to find. Other forms of part-time work are more flexible and therefore more popular.

Union attitudes

The bulk of the experiments with unconventional work schedules have occurred with non-union white-collar workers. Unions are rather suspicious of these new developments, and this is almost as true in Europe as it is in the U.S. One reason for this suspicion is that management sometimes introduces new schedules in union plants without consulting the union; the union insists this is a matter for joint negotiation. From the union point of view, the solution to work schedule problems is shorter hours without lower pay. Eight hours a day is the most anyone should ever work, many unionists say, and every effort should be made to reduce this figure. Part-time work is opposed unless part-time workers receive fringe benefits equal to those of full-time workers. Flextime is feared because it may blur job jurisdictional lines. Further, since flextime supposedly leads to higher productivity, management should pay higher wages for workers who partake of it. Some unions look upon flextime chiefly as a means for management to reduce its overtime payment.

Recently, however, as their members have shown greater interest in flextime and part-time work, white-collar unions in particular have begun to drop their opposition.

Shift work

Flextime increases employees' freedom to pick their own work hours. By contrast there is another trend—the growth of shift work—which forces employees to work at times most workers find undesirable.

Shift work is not a new phenomenon. It has existed for years in police and fire protection, newspapers, hospitals, transportation, public utilities, and the like. But in recent years it has become more common in manufacturing as well. Of course, many steel and chemical plants have always operated day and night because their processes can't be turned off except at great expense. However, as other factories have grown more capital intensive, it has become more and more costly to keep them idle during the evening and night. Further, changes in pricing of electricity now make it financially advantageous to schedule production during off-peak hours, when utilities often charge lower rates than during the day. The percentage of manufacturing employees on shift work has increased from 21 percent in the early 1960s to almost 30 percent today, of which some 21 percent are on the second or evening shift (ending at midnight) while 8 percent are on the night or "lobster" shift (beginning at midnight).

Traditionally, office work was done almost entirely during the day, but this is changing, too. Computers are too costly to lie idle; therefore, many banks, public utilities, and similar institutions keep their data processing operations working around the clock. As a consequence of all these developments, the total number of shift workers in the United States in all industries (not just manufacturing) has been estimated at 10 million, with the number in Canada being proportionally almost as high.

Some employees prefer being assigned to shift work because it allows them to make alternative use of the daytime hours. But most find that late hours interfere with normal family and social life. (However, bowling leagues and other recreations formed especially for shift workers have become common.)

A variety of schedule patterns are available, and any organization contemplating multiple shifts should consider the alternatives. Sometimes a special shift handles weekends; in other cases, employees exchange weekends off.

Many organizations practice shift rotation. Here employees work day shift for one week or month, evening shift the next period, and finally night shift. This procedure avoids charges of discrimination, tends to equalize overtime, and prevents jockeying for favorable work schedules. But it requires employees to get used to constantly changing sleeping and working hours, not an easy thing to do as anyone knows who has flown across a number of time zones. A large variety of physical and psychological illnesses—digestive problems, chest pains, poor sleep, and fatigue—have been associated with shift work.[32]

Some slight overlap on shift hours (say 15 minutes) often permits needed exchange of information on problems that have occurred and helps avoid frictions between shifts.

"Those day shift slobs leave the messy work for us."

"We fix them; you should see what we leave for them."

On the other hand, shift overlap can make 24-hours coverage difficult.

Unions have traditionally opposed shift work and have insisted that those required to work it be compensated by "shift differentials." Double payments for nontraditional hours are common in the construction industry. In other industries these differentials are considerably less.

Conclusion

Job redesign and new work schedules are designed to counteract the growing work discontent that many (but not all) observers have noted in recent years. Beyond this it is hoped that they (as well as goal setting) will contribute to higher productivity.

According to its advocates, job redesign harnesses workers' unused abilities and fosters teamwork. Through enlarging workers' discretion, job redesign also makes work more challenging and as a consequence raises both productivity and satisfaction. In terms of expectancy theory, job redesign and goal setting techniques both make it easier for workers to convert effort into performance. Further, they make performance itself more rewarding, particularly if performance permits workers to demonstrate valued skills and to attain fair, accepted goals. Finally, job redesign smooths work flow and reduces the need for close supervision.

However, job redesign is not as universally appropriate as some of its advocates make it sound. Challenge is motivating particularly for those with high need for achievement; for less ambitious employees, greater challenge

---

[32] Decisions about whether or not to rotate shifts and how often rotation should occur represent a good arena for employee participation.

may be oppressive. For many workers, the best part of job redesign is that it permits them greater opportunity to socialize on the job.

Furthermore, the opportunities to redesign work are relatively limited. Conceivably, automobiles could be made on a completely craft basis and the assembly line eliminated. But to do so would be prohibitively expensive. In many situations, the range of feasible changes may not be broad enough to make a major difference. Workers are not likely to find much challenge on an assembly line or even in a reorganized dog food factory. Job enrichment may give rise to unrealistic expectations that workers will be given ever-increasing freedom to make essential work decisions. Few managements are prepared to permit this.

Efforts to introduce job redesign are not always successful. Job redesign may require changes in pay rates, promotional policies, and supervisory methods. All this may engender resistance from unions, middle and lower management, and even from other workers who may be jealous of the seemingly special privileges being given to the workers whose jobs are being changed.

On the other hand, job redesign's novelty should not be exaggerated. Craftsmen, for example, enjoyed enriched jobs long before the term *job enrichment* was invented. Indeed, some observers believe that as the more routine jobs are taken over by machines, the average level of challenge will increase in the jobs that remain—without an explicit job redesign effort.

Despite these cautions, most people would like a little more control over their work lives, and job redesign may help provide this. Further, job redesign permits more efficient use of manpower in many cases (apart and beyond any questions of satisfaction or motivation).

A number of organizations have concentrated, however, not on changing the nature of the job but the hours one works. New work schedules are often thought of as alternatives to job redesign. The demand for new work schedules has been largely associated with the growing number of women in the work force. Flextime permits greater flexibility in planning leisure activities and in coordinating work and family relations. It gives workers considerably more control over their work lives.

Despite other differences, workplace reforms share the common denominator of allowing workers greater freedom: to decide *how* to do the job, in the case of job redesign; to decide *when* to do it, in the case of flextime. Furthermore, new work schedules are difficult to introduce without changes in the way work is organized. Flextime may require job rotation, job enlargement, or group decisions as to how tasks are to be handled when some workers and even the supervisor are absent.

Neither job redesign nor new work schedules exhaust the possibilities of workplace reforms. Many workers are more concerned with hygienes than motivators; for them higher wages, better job security, and the various amenities enjoyed by management (for example, a more comfortable workplace environment) may be more important than either a slight increase in job discretion or greater freedom to choose when to do one's essentially boring work. Other workers want opportunities to get ahead, particularly greater opportunity to participate in key decisions affecting their own careers.

1 · *Money Transfers*

International money transfers at Hometown Bank are handled by two departments—Remittances and Inquiries—in separate buildings.

Remittances consists of 120 employees, divided into three groups: markers, keyers, and releasers. Cables from customers throughout the world requesting fund transfers are sent first to *markers.* Upon receipt of a cable, a marker must decide how the money is to be routed. This process is complicated by lack of standardization of international messages and by translation problems. To determine the routing, the marker uses a variety of resource materials, including account and code listings, bank directories, and maps. Routing information is then written in red pencil over the text of the cable. Finally, the marker initials the cable and sends it to a keyer in a separate room.

The *keyer* enters the coded information into a computer program and passes it to a *releaser* who checks all the pertinent information and then, if all seems correct, presses a button initiating the transfer.

The workload in the department fluctuates considerably, but the typical day's load involves several thousand cables and as much as $100 million. On a large order, a day's delay may cost a customer several thousand dollars interest. The department strives for one-hour service. Mistakes—often big mistakes—are common.

The inquiries department (60 employees) handles customer complaints when mistakes are made. It is divided geographically (South America, Africa, etc.). Each inquiry clerk is responsible for complaints and adjustments involving a small group of customers in one geographical area.

This department handles a large volume of work but is less production oriented than Remittances. Inquiry clerks are often frustrated by repeated errors made in Remittances, but their complaints have not reduced the mistakes. They must deal with complicated and tedious adjustments as well as irate customers.

Suggest how this work operation might be reorganized. Note that much of it is routine but requires a high degree of accuracy. Note, too, that without careful security checks, millions of dollars might be diverted illegally.

2 · *Dirty Bottles*

The Milwaukee Brewing Company has been plagued with trouble among its *bottle inspectors,* whose job is to check each bottle carefully, to make sure that it is absolutely clean as it leaves the bottle-washing machine. Though there have been many attempts to develop mechanical inspecting devices, none has worked with 100 percent accuracy. Consequently, each bottle must be visually inspected as it passes by the inspector on a conveyor belt. Although this job is highly paid, it is hard to find people to take it, and many quit after working on it a few months.

1. What seems to be the basic problem here?
2. What suggestions can you make for solving it?

3 · *Candy Wrappers*

All candy made by the Quality Candy Company is wrapped by hand. Candy is brought by chute to each wrapper, who wraps each piece, then drops it into another chute, which leads to packers in another room.

Each wrapper handles a different kind of candy, and work locations are isolated from one another.

1. How will the wrappers react to this sort of work?
2. What can be done to increase their morale and output?

part 7

conclusion

personnel challenges and the future

This last chapter allows authors some leeway to seek broad generalizations and to speculate about the future. Speculation is dangerous, of course, because it makes one sound glib and falsely prophetic. Further, ours is a dynamic society, and the future is rarely an extrapolation of the past. Nevertheless, many of the trends that will shape ensuing decades have already begun to show themselves. We shall seek to identify these and their impact on management's personnel policies. Since many represent extensions of the issues we have been explaining in preceding chapters, this discussion will also summarize our major conclusions.

New pressures and constraints

More regulations

The past decade has witnessed an avalanche of new legislation and new government rulings affecting the management of people. Hiring, promotional policies, pension rights, working conditions—all have been regulated, and this trend of more government involvement is likely to intensify.

Previous chapters reviewed the government regulations that seek to eliminate discrimination on the basis of race, religion, sex, age, and physical condition. Many

managements have been surprised at how many of their practices potentially discriminate. Height or strength requirements not absolutely required by the job may deter the hiring of women or Orientals. A poorly designed workplace may cause difficulty for handicapped employees. Benefit plans often provide benefits more favorable to one sex than the other. Although the practice is not illegal, employers have been criticized for locating facilities in areas with inadequate low-priced housing or public transportation, which results in fewer jobs for low-income minorities.

Management must critically review its customary practices in every business area that affects the physical and economic welfare of both potential recruits and current employees. Personnel departments will play increasingly active roles as advisors, auditors, and stabilization coordinators.

Given the pressures on a democratic government from various organized interest groups, it should come as no surprise to management that many regulations and pressures will not be mutually compatible.

Early in 1979, Sears filed a lawsuit against the federal government, charging that its requirements to increase employment of women and blacks contradicted other policies that encourage the employment of males: preference to veterans, negotiated seniority preferences, and new restraints on mandatory retirement before age seventy.[1]

Because of these competing demands and the continual need to make trade-offs, personnel policy making will be inherently frustrating: every improvement for one group will come at the expense of another's interests.

Employee demands for civil rights

Management must be prepared to justify many personnel decisions that in the past could be made unilaterally, even arbitrarily. More personnel matters will end up in courtrooms instead of conference rooms. Employees increasingly demand civil rights at work comparable to those they enjoy in the community—to contradict the hierarchy, to have free speech at work, to obtain a fair hearing and due process every time promotion is denied or disciplinary action applied.

The manager must always assume the possibility of an adversary proceeding. Therefore, the organization must develop and consistently administer uniform, objective criteria for every personnel decision: who gets recruited, hired, or promoted; who receives a bonus, sick pay, leaves of absence, and so on.

At the same time, it will be more difficult to reward (or punish) employees differentially. Employees are more alert to potential as well as actual discrimination; the grounds for charging discrimination are continuing to expand. Almost any management that provides a differential advantage, even on merit, is likely to be challenged. Of course, this will make it more difficult to devise compensation and promotion plans that encourage excellence.

Increased recordkeeping

As external institutions play a more important role in determining personnel policies, management will need ever more voluminous and detailed

---

[1] The case is reviewed in *Newsweek*, February 5, 1979, p. 86.

records. In part, this results from the requirements of federal agencies for records that enable them to assess whether or not the organization is discriminating or acting illegally. Even more important, insofar as these increasingly pervasive regulations encourage employees to seek redress in the courts for real or imagined discrimination, management must depend on its personnel records to defend its actions. (If Bill doesn't get promoted or is discharged, what evidence can be presented that the decision was objectively justified?)

This will require management to have even better records than it maintained in the past—and these same employee personnel records will be even more open to inspection and challenge by affected personnel.[2]

More emphasis on performance measures

Most organizations have done a poor job of measuring the performance of nonproduction workers. This will have to change, not only because a greater proportion of jobs are at the professional/technical/managerial levels, but because employees are more likely to challenge promotions and discharges that they consider discriminatory. As we noted in our discussion of testing and appraisal, many measures of job performance are either too subjective or not clearly valid. Society, too, is demanding more objective measures of professional performance—of doctors and teachers, for example.

In the past, management could "retire" its problems. Now growing competitive pressure on labor costs combined with the extended minimum age for mandatory retirement will force organizations to find ways of identifying who is not effective. It will be increasingly difficult to transfer people and to decide who is no longer competent without solidly defensible measures of job performance that go beyond subjective supervisory evaluations. But, as we have noted, ineffectiveness in one job or career path should not bar the employee from other career opportunities. With better performance measures should come greater willingness to make major shifts in responsibility. The unsuccessful project manager may do very well supervising a more routine function; staff executives who can't develop fruitful advisory relationships may do better in line operations. At the same time, organizations must continue to improve their "outplacement" capabilities, facilitating the movement of people to new jobs in other settings when the organization no longer has jobs for which they are suited.

Social accounting

The community as a whole expects more from the business community than it ever has before. Society expects cleaner air and water effluents, less traffic congestion, better jobs. It is hardly surprising that some experts have begun to speak of "social accounting." A few organizations have begun to draw up a balance sheet showing the organization's commitment to being a good corporate citizen and a good employer. At times a "quality of work life" report is included in the corporation's annual report. It reviews accident

---

[2] The right to inspect and challenge records affect students as well, of course. Further, potential employers cannot obtain these records without student authorization.

rates, female and minority employment and promotion, and comparative measures of job satisfaction.[3]

Escalating employee expectations and demands

At the turn of the century, almost 40 percent of employees were recently arrived immigrants with limited education and modest expectations. They were docile and dependent and thus easy to supervise. Today less than 5 percent of our nonagricultural work force is foreign born. Now and for the foreseeable future, employees will be ever more demanding.

American workers have had more years of schooling and have grown up in a more affluent society than their parents.[4] There have also been cultural changes. Society is stressing individual fulfillment. The growing popularity of what is called "humanistic psychology," which emphasizes fulfillment and self-actualization, and the growing cultural emphasis on personal satisfaction have contributed to this "revolution of rising expectations."[5]

And as one demand is satisfied, new ones take its place—from more meaningful work to day care centers and prepaid dental plans. Only naive managers expect a new benefit or favorable policy to provide an extended period of placidity and satisfaction. And there is really no way for benefits to grow as rapidly as aspirations. The manager should not expect gratitude or harmony.

Earlier personnel theories assumed that there were just two kinds of workers: loyal family retainers and strong-backed "economic men." Both were motivated to hold their jobs and incomes at almost any personal cost. Now it is much more difficult to generalize. An ever-widening range of motivation extends from the worker who dislikes any on-the-job constraints and who finds work repellent to the overmotivated professional who wants to do so much that he or she may begin to interfere with the work of others. For some employees, money is all-important; for others, interesting, absorbing work is critical. The extremes can be extraordinary. A recent news story contrasted the effort put forth by top government officials who enjoyed enormous intrinsic satisfaction, with the lackadaisical performance of large numbers of lower-ranked government employees. The top officials often worked 80 to 100 hour, 6½ to 7 day weeks![6] This growing disparity is likely to continue as the average

Greater differences among employees

[3] In Europe what are called "social balance sheets" are apparently becoming common. One Swiss food company issued an extensive report, which included admissions that the "company paid women less than men, that many of its jobs were 'extremely boring,' and that its emissions of nitrous dioxide has risen over a four-year period by 2 percent." *Business Week*, November 6, 1978, p. 175.

[4] Between 1947 and 1977, the number of people who had completed twelve or more years of schooling almost doubled!

[5] Some psychiatrists speak of the growing inward-looking personality and the reluctance to assume responsibility as part of our "narcissistic" age. Cf. Christopher Lasch, *The Culture of Narcissism* (New York: Norton, 1978).

[6] *The Wall Street Journal*, January 30, 1979, p. 1.

work week gradually declines for nonmanagers to around 35 hours (counting breaks), and the complexities and demands of managerial jobs continue to grow.

Who bears the risks?

In earlier periods, the employee bore the risks of life's uncertainties. Declining company business or personal illness would result in lost wages, even discharge. Management had almost complete flexibility to adjust work locations, schedules, workloads, and even discharges as it saw fit. With the introduction of strong unions and written contracts, a balance of power and mutual obligations emerged. Fixed hours, seniority for layoffs, predictable promotion ladders, and formal disciplinary procedures involving due process all limit management's flexibility.

The balance may now be shifting even more towards employees. Management must seek to find some way of coping with changing economic conditions in the context of relatively inflexible government policies and employee expectations.

Employees want management to assume most of the burden of adjusting to economic uncertainties. Employees want the organization to provide long-term job security while they decide when they would like extended leaves of absence and where they will work.

Ebasco, a well-known company specializing in the design of power plants and consulting, recently developed a new policy to cater to employee living preferences. Many technical employees are given the choice of working in New York City or in several "satellite" offices in the suburbs. An executive vice-president commented, ". . . the company is going to try to bring projects to offices situated where the majority of people working on them live." [7]

Need for security

Although there has been concern that work may become less important than leisure, it seems to us that the job and the workplace will occupy an even more critical place in the lives of most people. As we have seen, work can provide satisfactions ranging from a sense of personal accomplishment for being able to handle challenging tasks to the reassuring social life of the work group. It may appear paradoxical that the same employees who demand more options and flexibility also want their organizations to keep and protect them. As both communities and families become less stable, it is likely that organization membership will become a valued source of psychological support. Fortunately, there may be some economic return to employers. Perhaps increasing dependence on the workplace will lead to more loyalty and commitment, as it has in Japan.

More flexible careers

Traditionally employees have had a simple, three-stage work life:

Schooling → Career → Retirement

The rapidity with which organizational needs change and the acceptability of individual changes in career expectations leads to more complex patterns:

[7] *Business Week*, January 15, 1979, p. 61.

Schooling → Career 1 → Advanced Training for Career 1 → Promotion → Training for New
Career 2 → Career 2 → Partial Retirement → Career 3 → Full Retirement

With longer, healthier lives and a greater sense that one can shape one's own destiny, employees are reluctant to commit themselves to fifty years on the same job or a narrow range of jobs. We will hear more about midcareer changes in personal goals, just as we hear about technological shifts causing organizations to retrain their engineers to become managers or their production people to become field service personnel. Employees feel freer to reject promotions that involve geographic changes or unattractive new responsibilities. Even management job enrichment efforts can no longer assume that all employees want the same increased responsibility and challenge. Some may want simpler jobs. Some employees want to trade off leisure or autonomy for pay and status. Many seek flexible work hours or part-time work; others want partial early retirement. The organization that can adapt to a heterogeneous work force will find eager, useful employees.

The organization will lose potentially valuable employees if it insists that they all be the same. Business executives may take pay cuts to work as part- or full-time managers for the arts and social service organizations. More professionals will set up small service organizations and work for their former employers as contractors and consultants. It will become commonplace for organizations to grant extended leaves to women to have children and to men and women to retool themselves for new careers and specializations.

With this increase in choice and career complexity will come a decrease in fixed retirement. Legislation already extends to seventy the minimum age for mandatory retirement. Since people age differently, some will have to leave earlier, and many will continue to be vigorous contributors until age 70 or beyond. Inevitably there will have to be more flexibility in retirement and more use of partial retirements, what the Scandinavians call the "glide."

Government will surely encourage this. In the past about three employed persons have supported every one on Social Security. With lower birth rates, early retirements, and other social factors, it is anticipated that this ratio will drop to two to one after the year 2000. Our society cannot be adequately productive given that projected ratio unless organizations provide part-time and extended employment plans for those with family responsibilities, handicaps, and for the aging.

Managements may gain from employee demands for more flexibility. When decisions are made *for* employees rather than *by* them, the results can be both lower motivation and lower productivity. Often, employees are promoted when they would prefer to stay on their present jobs or even to switch career lines. Sometimes companies make training programs so attractive that employees who have no interest in learning attend the sessions simply to avoid the daily routine.

More self-selection

Should management rely more on self-selection—seeing who volunteers for new job assignments and even requiring some modest sacrifice from those who receive certain types of advanced training—candidates would be more highly motivated. Certainly employees will be more committed to goals they have set themselves. Furthermore, they know their own capabilities and interests better than do their supervisors.

Organizations in the future

Compared with the past, fewer people are employed in basic manufacturing and relatively more in such service activities as insurance, education, research, selling, finance, and personal care. This trend will continue. There will be more white-collar and less blue-collar work. But it is difficult to extrapolate this trend into predictions about management style and human relations. To be sure, some new organizations will engage in highly professionalized, high-technology research and consulting services. But there will also be large numbers of routine tasks in white-collar factories.

How much bureaucracy?

Although a growing proportion of the labor force will work in large organizations, small organizations will also persist. The conglomerate trend shows no signs of abating, and there are many financial incentives for managers to integrate many formerly independent operations. But there will also be room for small business: consumers like individualized boutiques, and companies buy technical and consulting services from small contractors who specialize in programming or office design.

Americans have always feared aggregations of power. Critics have frequently portrayed large organizations as bureaucratic destroyers of individual differences and initiative. Many observers tend to idealize the small organization. Still, one cannot accurately predict the quality of work life or work relations from organizational size alone. Large organizations usually are more flexible and less bureaucratic than they appear on paper. The great quantity of functional specialists and professionals they employ make lateral relations as important as hierarchical ones. Thus, the very structure of large organizations may counter any tendency to overroutinize or overconstrain the individual.

Research suggests that large organizations often provide more job satisfaction than do smaller ones. Unchallenged authoritarianism is much easier to maintain in a family-owned small business than in a large, impersonal organization with its checks and balances in personnel procedures, its appeal channels, and its multiple levels for review and approval. Similarly, larger, more heterogeneous organizations can tolerate a broad range of individual differences. Small organizations, like small groups, sometimes develop clear-cut norms and prejudices. They often distrust outsiders or individuals with different ideas.

Management as a work force

Recent interest in OD and MBO reflects the recognition that management is the organization's most important work force.[8] In an earlier age,

---

[8] Professionals and managers now hold one out of four jobs in the U.S work force! (Eli Ginzberg, "The Professionalization of the U.S. Labor Force," *Scientific American*, Vol. 240, No. 3, March 1979, pp. 48–53.)

organizations simply assumed that although workers had to be supervised and motivated, all managers enthusiastically sought the same goal: organizational success. Now we recognize that management also has informal groups, its divergent goals, and productivity problems. Personnel challenges exist as much, if not more, at managerial levels than at the level of operating work. We can expect increasing emphasis on such motivational and control techniques as MBO. Similarly, OD and other management development programs that seek to reintegrate the organization, minimize intergroup conflicts, and develop organizationwide commitment will flourish.

Today organizations are adopting matrix forms and admitting the legitimacy of competing—even conflicting—sources of authority and goals. And individuals feel freer to challenge authority and rules.

There is one troublesome trend in the growing professionalization of the work force. Too much emphasis may be placed on such credentials as formal college degrees. This tendency will work against the effort to be more flexible in career lines, to consider employees for a wider range of job opportunities, and to promote on the basis of demonstrated ability alone.

The personnel challenge: a systems approach

The tensions, changes, and pressures we have been discussing constantly tempt management to look for sure-fire solutions. Given the difficulty of managing people and organizations, this search for pat answers is hardly surprising. But the search will be in vain. As we have noted, human problems keep going through mutations; solve one and another appears. Human wants are not finite; there is no perfect organization. But perhaps the most important reason to avoid one-formula answers is that even formulas have no simple application. The implementation of new personnel and organizational behavior technology will require dealing with the organization as a system, not mechanically applying a set of guidelines.

Too often organizations fall into the trap of believing that a new incentive plan will put an end to wrangling over compensation or that MBO will settle all boss-subordinate problems. This rarely happens. Every program, regardless of how wisely chosen it may be, brings with it a series of problems.

Company X decided to introduce a short training program for minority workers. Those who completed the course were guaranteed promotions to journeymen status. Within three weeks, a number of unanticipated problems arose:

1. Older journeymen complained that the new program involved reverse discrimination, since they had been promoted only after a long apprenticeship. "It's unfair to promote these newcomers automatically without extra compensation for those of us who came up the hard way," they said.

2. Trainees, too, became anxious; it was rumored that those who failed would be fired and that the course would be very tough.

3. The company had originally planned to conduct the training course for two and a half hours: last two working hours of the day and a half-hour of the employees' own time. Employees complained bitterly that they were too tired to train after the normal

work day and that it was unfair to make them "work" on company premises without compensation, when they should be getting premium overtime.

4. Some employees were so poorly prepared that remedial sessions in math had to be scheduled, but these conflicted with the production schedule. Eventually, additional part-time workers had to be hired.

What was originally perceived as a simple training program involved difficult communications, union-management, and production problems. As each problem was solved, another took its place. The manager who had placed his faith in carefully drawn up plans was inevitably frustrated. Our conclusion is not that new programs should not be started but that management should not expect them to be foolproof. It's always going to be necessary to modify and negotiate, and the personnel department will have to contribute advisory and audit skills.

Human problems are difficult to compartmentalize. No training program will deal only with training problems and methods; it will have ramifications throughout the organization. Administering these ramifications almost inevitably involves delicate give-and-take with employees, informal group leaders, often the union, and various levels of the management hierarchy. And many of these discussions will have to be repeated and reviewed.

Thus personnel specialists should not think of themselves as technicians who are expert in procedures and program design. Rather, they must develop their relationship skills and knowledge of organizations as complex human systems.

No right answer   Few of the questions at issue have absolute answers. What the speaker perceives as correct will depend on vantage point and self-interest:

- Which is fairer, layoffs on the basis of seniority or layoff procedures that consider whether seniority was affected by previous discriminatory procedures?
- If one-half of 1 percent of employees *may* have their hearing damaged by exposure to certain noisy equipment and if it will cost $3 million to reduce the noise level further, is it worth that amount to guarantee no hearing loss?
- Is it discrimination in air transport to allow male stewards a higher maximum weight than women stewardesses because men have a heavier bone structure?

Managing human resources is inherently frustrating. Most problems do not get solved forever; at best, management improves the situation. Problems that are solved are succeeded by countless new ones. It is no wonder that management may be tempted to seek panaceas. The temptation, however, must be avoided.

The claims for new programs are usually exaggerated. Even more important, no new program—whether it is called MBO, job enrichment, or OD—can be successful unless it is carefully integrated with the other practices and structures of the organization. Organizations are *systems*.

Conclusion

Only the naive manager expects human problems to stay solved; they recur to baffle and challenge administrative skill. But understanding the underlying trends and forces at work can help managers to develop more ethical, effective policies and a basic understanding of the dimensions of the problems with which they must cope.

We hope we haven't discouraged you by forswearing formula answers and constantly stressing complexity, interdependence, and the difficulty of changing one element without impinging on something else—which will then need adjustment, too. But management is difficult and therefore deservedly well rewarded. The manager who can deal effectively with contradictory employee wants and demands, with inconsistent and ever-changing governmental constraints, and with the inevitable politics of any human organization is much sought after by both the private and the not-for-profit sector. These are among the demanding jobs in our society, but they can also be exciting, fulfilling, and challenging. You need never fear that people problems will dull your senses or your spirits; be assured: you will never have a dull moment.

problems

1 • *Discrimination or Litigiousness?*

Philipo Arnes was discharged for poor productivity. Over a six-month period, his machine output was 15 percent lower than the minimum management had established on that particular job. Arnes had been employed for two years, and his output had always been at the minimum. During the last six months, it had slipped to an unsatisfactory level.

Arnes filed a discrimination case, charging:

"About six months ago management appointed a new supervisor in my department. From the first I knew he didn't like me, and whenever he could he made unpleasant remarks to me. The minute I did anything he didn't like he threatened me with some penalty. I knew he was just looking for an excuse to get rid of me, and that dagger hanging over my head made me nervous. I just couldn't work well with all my fears. Until that company gets supervisors who don't discriminate, they can't expect good work."

Arnes' supervisor told a very different story:

"Arnes is a very cocky guy who from the first minute I came into the department was always daring me to do something. No matter what I asked him to do, he would complain and swear. He said there was nothing I could do to get him to work harder because he was a protected minority group member. After repeated warnings and two written penalties, I felt I had no choice but to fire him."

1. How can management avoid this type of case?
2. How would you go about assessing the relative merits of the case?

2 • *An Elite Corps of New Consultants*

Southern Consulting was a very large management consulting firm with hundreds of professional employees. It specialized in a wide range of marketing, financial, and personnel management services. One of the senior partners conceived of an elite corps of junior consultants who would be very selectively hired from the best graduate schools and trained to rapidly assume major responsibilities.

About a dozen such recent graduates were hired in 1980. Each knew that he or she had been hired in preference to hundreds of others, and they soon became a closely knit group. They all received temporary assignments as part of a rotation plan that would enable them to work in most of the company's key areas in three years.

At least five of the trainees felt their assignments were unworthy of their capabilities. Several others liked their work but felt they were reporting to inept supervisors. They frequently discussed their various complaints and devised a number of ways to let top management know that they were critical of some of the company's personnel decisions. Top management met several times with the group to explain the logic of their assignments, but their dissatisfactions continued.

1. What role did the trainees' level of expectation play in this group's expression of dissatisfaction? How might small group factors have affected the group?
2. What significance would you give to this constant grousing?
3. What options are open to management now?

3 · *Civil Rights for Employees*

The following are actual incidents. Consider what action, if any, management should take with regard to the employee's off-the-job activities.

1. A manager of a public utility was arrested for interfering with a policeman seeking to quell a riot. The employee was part of the group causing the disturbance, and the incident was widely reported in the press.

2. An airline flight attendant, nude, was pictured in a well-known magazine featuring sexy photos. Her name, that of her employer, and certain company insignia accompanied the photograph.

3. The public relations director of a large company has published a novel. His company has high visibility and a public image problem. The novel, widely cited as depicting corporation and corporate executives in a demeaning light, suggests that senior executives are avaricious, immoral, and untrustworthy.

name index

subject index

b

c

d